Longman Dictionary of
Language Teaching and Applied Linguistics

Longman Dictionary of

LANGUAGE TEACHING AND APPLIED LINGUISTICS

Jack C. Richards and Richard Schmidt

Fourth edition

**Longman
is an imprint of**

Harlow, England • London • New York • Boston • San Francisco • Toronto • Sydney • Singapore • Hong Kong
Tokyo • Seoul • Taipei • New Delhi • Cape Town • Madrid • Mexico City • Amsterdam • Munich • Paris • Milan

PEARSON EDUCATION LIMITED

Edinburgh Gate
Harlow CM20 2JE
Tel: +44 (0)1279 623623
Fax: +44 (0)1279 431059

Website: www.pearson.co.uk

First edition published 1985
Second edition published 1992
Third edition published 2002
Fourth edition published in Great Britain in 2010

© Pearson Education Limited 1985, 1992, 2002, 2010

The rights of Jack C. Richards and Richard Schmidt to be identified
as authors of this Work have been asserted by them in accordance
with the Copyright, Designs and Patents Act 1988.

Pearson Education is not responsible for the content of third party internet sites.

ISBN 978-1-4082-0460-3

British Library Cataloguing in Publication Data
A CIP catalogue record for this book can be obtained from the British Library

Library of Congress Cataloging in Publication Data
A CIP catalog record for this book can be obtained from the Library of Congress

10 9 8 7 6 5 4 3 2 1
14 13 12 11 10

Typeset in 9.5/12pt Sabon by 35
Printed in Malaysia (CTP-VVP)

GUIDE TO THE DICTIONARY

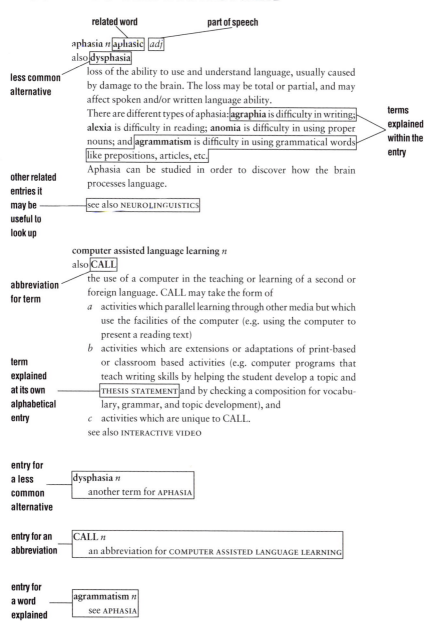

related word   part of speech

aphasia *n* aphasic *adj*
also dysphasia

less common alternative

loss of the ability to use and understand language, usually caused by damage to the brain. The loss may be total or partial, and may affect spoken and/or written language ability.
There are different types of aphasia: **agraphia** is difficulty in writing; **alexia** is difficulty in reading; **anomia** is difficulty in using proper nouns; and **agrammatism** is difficulty in using grammatical words like prepositions, articles, etc.

terms explained within the entry

Aphasia can be studied in order to discover how the brain processes language.

other related entries it may be useful to look up

see also NEUROLINGUISTICS

computer assisted language learning *n*
also CALL

abbreviation for term

the use of a computer in the teaching or learning of a second or foreign language. CALL may take the form of

a activities which parallel learning through other media but which use the facilities of the computer (e.g. using the computer to present a reading text)

b activities which are extensions or adaptations of print-based or classroom based activities (e.g. computer programs that teach writing skills by helping the student develop a topic and

term explained at its own alphabetical entry

THESIS STATEMENT and by checking a composition for vocabulary, grammar, and topic development), and

c activities which are unique to CALL.

see also INTERACTIVE VIDEO

entry for a less common alternative

dysphasia *n*
another term for APHASIA

entry for an abbreviation

CALL *n*
an abbreviation for COMPUTER ASSISTED LANGUAGE LEARNING

entry for a word explained elsewhere

agrammatism *n*
see APHASIA

INTRODUCTION

Who is this dictionary for?

This dictionary is intended for:

- students taking undergraduate or graduate courses in language teaching or applied linguistics, particularly those planning to take up a career in the teaching of English as a Second or Foreign Language or in foreign language teaching
- language teachers doing in-service or pre-service courses, such as the UCLES Diploma in Teaching English to Adults
- students doing introductory courses in linguistics and related areas
- teachers and others interested in the practical applications of language study

Why this dictionary?

Language teaching and applied linguistics are fields which have their own core subject matter and which also draw on a number of complementary fields of study. Among the core subject matter disciplines are second language acquisition, methodology, testing, and syllabus design. The complementary fields of study include both the language based disciplines such as linguistics, sociolinguistics, and psycholinguistics, as well as the education based disciplines such as curriculum development, teacher education, and evaluation. The result is that students taking courses in language teaching and applied linguistics encounter a large number of specialized terms which frequently occur in articles, books and lectures. This dictionary attempts to clarify the meanings and uses of these terms.

The scope of the dictionary

The dictionary was written for those with little or no background in language teaching or applied linguistics.

We have given special attention to English, and the majority of the examples in the dictionary are from English, but the dictionary will also be helpful to those interested in other languages. Although the dictionary is not intended primarily for those who already have a specialized training in language teaching or applied linguistics, it will serve as a reference book in areas with which they are less familiar. It should also be useful to general readers who need further information about the terms which occur in the fields of language teaching and applied linguistics.

Language teaching and applied linguistics

This dictionary includes the core vocabulary of both language teaching and applied linguistics. The field of language teaching is concerned with the development of language programmes and courses, teaching methodology, materials development, second language acquisition theory, testing, teacher training and related areas. The dictionary includes terms from the following areas of study in the field of language teaching:

- teaching methods and approaches in language teaching
- curriculum development and syllabus design
- second language acquisition
- the teaching of listening, speaking, reading and writing
- computer assisted language learning
- teacher education in language teaching
- English grammar and pronunciation
- language testing, research methods, and basic statistics

The dictionary also includes terms from the field of applied linguistics. For the purposes of this book, "applied linguistics" refers to the practical applications of linguistics and language theory and includes terms from the following areas of study:

- introductory linguistics, including phonology, phonetics, syntax, semantics and morphology
- discourse analysis
- sociolinguistics, including the sociology of language and communicative competence
- psycholinguistics, including learning theories

What the dictionary contains

This dictionary contains some 3500 entries, which define in as simple and precise a way as possible, the most frequently occurring terms found in the areas listed above. Each term has been selected on the basis of its importance within an area and reflects the fact that the term has a particular meaning when used within that area, a meaning unlikely to be listed in other dictionaries. Many of these terms were included in the third edition of this dictionary, but in preparing the fourth edition, a number of items no longer in common use were delated, revisions were made to a number of entries, and some 360 new entries have been added to reflect current usage in language teaching and applied linguistics.

Our aim has been to produce clear and simple definitions which communicate the basic and essential meanings of a term in non-technical language.

Definitions are self-contained as far as possible, but cross references show links to other terms and concepts.

Acknowledgements

This edition of the dictionary has been prepared by Jack C. Richards and Richard Schmidt.

We would like to thank those who contributed to earlier editions of this dictionary, particularly Heidi Kendricks, who contributed to the first and second editions, the late John Platt, who contributed to the first and second editions, and the following who gave valuable suggestions to earlier editions: Christopher Candlin, John W. Oller (Jr), Lyle Bachman, Graham Crookes, Ken Hylands, Stephen Jacques; and Youngkyu Kim for assistance in the area of testing, research design, and statistics.

We are grateful to Ms Media Shojaee for suggestions for new items to be included in the fourth edition.

A

AAAL *n*

an abbreviation for **American Association for Applied Linguistics**

AAE *n*

an abbreviation for African American English

AAVE *n*

an abbreviation for African American vernacular English
see African American English

ability grouping *n*

in teaching, the placement of students in groups or classes according to their ability in a skill or subject, e.g. based on their language proficiency. Groups containing students of different ability levels are known as *mixed ability groups* or *heterogeneous groups*, while groups composed of students with similar abilities, achievement, etc., are known as *homogeneous groups*.
see GROUPING

ablaut *n*

a process by which an inflected form of a word is formed by changes in the vowel of the stem. For example, the past tense of *sing* is *sang* and the plural of *goose* is *geese*.

aboriginal language *n*

see INDIGENOUS LANGUAGE

absolute *n*

an adjective or adverb that cannot have a comparative or superlative form. For example *perfectly* and *unique* already express the idea of "to a maximum degree" and cannot therefore be used with comparative forms as in *most *perfectly*, or *more *unique*.

absolute clause (phrase, construction) *n*

a non-finite adverbial clause or other adverbial construction that is not linked syntactically to the main clause, e.g.
As far as I can tell, she is not having any problems with the course.

abstract noun *n*

see CONCRETE NOUN

ABX discrimination *n*

in PSYCHOLINGUISTICS, a task in which three stimuli are presented in
a trial. A and B are different (for example, the words *ramp* and *lamp*)
and the subject's task is to choose which of them is matched by the final
stimulus.

academic discourse *n*

the language and discourse of academic genres. The study of academic
discourse focuses on the nature, contexts, production and interpretation of
discourse and texts that occur in academic settings.
see also ENGLISH FOR ACADEMIC PURPOSES, GENRE, REGISTER

academic language *n*

the special registers and genres of language used in the learning of academic
subject matter in formal schooling contexts. Learning academic language is
essential for MAINSTREAMING second language learners and for students
studying ENGLISH FOR ACADEMIC PURPOSES.

academic literacy *n*

the ability to understand and participate in the academic discourse of
academic genres, e.g. in fields such as science, law and literature, including
the ability to produce and understand written and spoken texts as well as
recognizing the social norms and discursive practices of academic communities. The field of ENGLISH FOR ACADEMIC PURPOSES seeks to develop
the skills of academic literacy.

academic vocabulary *n*

the most frequently occurring vocabulary in academic texts. In English a
core academic vocabulary of some 600 words (e.g. words such as *evidence,
estimate, feature, impact, method, release*) is common to a wide range of
academic fields and accounts for around 10% of the words in any academic
text. Students need to be familiar with this vocabulary if they are to complete academic courses successfully. The teaching of academic vocabulary
is an aspect of ENGLISH FOR ACADEMIC PURPOSES. Academic vocabulary is
determined from analysis of a corpus of academic English. Academic
Vocabulary may be compared with Technical Vocabulary, which refers to
words specific to a particular topic, field or discipline.

Academic Word List *n*

a list of 570 word families which is said to make up the core vocabulary of
much academic writing, based on an analysis of a large corpus of academic

texts but excluding the 2000 most frequent word in English. The list has been widely used in the teaching of ENGLISH FOR ACADEMIC PURPOSES.

see ENGLISH FOR SPECIAL PURPOSES

accent[1] *n*

greater emphasis on a syllable so that it stands out from the other syllables in a word. For example, in English the noun '*import* has the accent on the first syllable *im-* while the verb *im'port* has the accent on the second syllable -*port*:

This car is a foreign imp̲o̲r̲t̲.
We imp̲o̲r̲t̲ all our coffee.

see also PROMINENCE, STRESS

accent[2] *n*

in the written form of some languages, particularly in French, a mark which is placed over a vowel. An accent may show:

a a difference in pronunciation (see DIACRITIC)
For example, in the French word *prés* "meadows", the **acute accent** on the *e* indicates a different vowel sound from that in *près* "near" with a **grave accent**.

b a difference in meaning without any change in pronunciation, e.g. French *ou* "or" and *où* "where".

accent[3] *n*

a particular way of speaking which tells the listener something about the speaker's background.

A person's pronunciation may show:

a the region or country they come from, e.g.
a northern accent
an American accent

b what social class they belong to, e.g.
a lower middle class accent

c whether or not the speaker is a native speaker of the language, e.g.
She speaks English with an accent/with a German accent.

see also DIALECT, SOCIOLECT

accent[4] *n*

another term for STRESS

accent discrimination *n*

discrimination or bias against speakers with foreign, regional, or social class ACCENTS[3], for example in employment or in legal proceedings.

see also FORENSIC LINGUISTICS

accent reduction *n*

programmes designed to help second language speakers speak a second or foreign language without showing evidence of a foreign accent. Such programmes reflect the fact that many second language speakers experience discrimination based on their accent. There is no evidence however that reduction in a foreign accent necessarily entails an increase in intelligibility. Hence many educators argue for a greater tolerance of foreign accents.

see also ENGLISH AS AN INTERNATIONAL LANGUAGE

acceptability judgement task *n*

one of several types of tasks (or tests) that require subjects to judge whether particular sentences are possible or not in either their native language or a language they are learning. If the task instructions specify that subjects are to judge whether or not a sentence is acceptable, the task is called an **acceptability judgement task**; if they are asked to judge whether a particular sentence is grammatical, the task is usually called a **grammaticality judgement task** (or test).

acceptable *adj*, **acceptability** *n*

a term referring to a linguistic utterance (for example, a word, a particular pronunciation, a phrase or a sentence) that is judged by NATIVE SPEAKERS to be grammatical, correct, or socially appropriate, either in general or in a particular community or context.

acceptable alternative method *n*

see CLOZE TEST

acceptable word method *n*

see CLOZE TEST

access *n*, *v*

in COMPUTER ASSISTED LANGUAGE LEARNING, locating or obtaining information or data. **Sequential access** means locating information in sequence, for example by fast forwarding an audio cassette. **Direct access** or **random access** means locating information directly, in such a way that access time is not dependent on its location.

accidental gap *n*

in WORD FORMATION, a non-occurring but possible form, for example *unsad* as an ANTONYM of *sad*. When learners produce such forms, these are considered to be examples of OVER-GENERALIZATION.

accommodation[1] *n*

shifts in the style of speaking people make such as when a person changes their way of speaking to make it sound more like or less like the speech of the person they are talking to. For example, a teacher may use simpler words and sentence structures when he/she is talking to a class of young children. This is called **convergence**. Alternatively a person may exaggerate their rural accent because they are annoyed by the attitude of someone from the city. This is called **divergence**. Convergence is a strategy in which people adapt to each other's speech by adjusting such things as speech rate, pauses, length of utterance, and pronunciation.

see also ACCENT[3]

accommodation[2] *n*

see ADAPTATION[2]

accomplishments *n*

see ASPECT

accountability *n*

the answerability of all those involved in applied linguistics for the quality of their work. For example, test developers need to be able to explain the rationale behind the assessment techniques they use and their results to test takers and test users; language programme administrators are accountable to clients who pay for special courses, as well as to students for the quality of instruction; and public school programme administrators are account-able to parents and other members of the public. Accountability includes the documentation and reporting of procedures used to develop curriculum and courses and of practices used in the hiring of teachers, selection of materials, evaluation of teachers and courses and the assessment of learners and learning outcomes.

accredited interpreter *n*

see INTERPRETATION

accredited translator *n*

see TRANSLATION

acculturation *n*

a process in which changes in the language, culture, and system of values of a group happen through interaction with another group with a different language, culture, and system of values. For example, in second language learning, acculturation may affect how well one group (e.g. a group of

5

immigrants in a country) learn the language of another (e.g. the dominant group).

see also ACCULTURATION MODEL, ASSIMILATION^2, SOCIAL DISTANCE

acculturation model *n*
in second language acquisition, the theory that the rate and level of ultimate success of second language acquisition in naturalistic settings (without instruction) is a function of the degree to which learners acculturate to the target language community. Acculturation may involve a large number of social and psychological variables, but is generally considered to be the process through which an individual takes on the beliefs, values and culture of a new group.

accuracy *n*
see FLUENCY

accuracy order *n*
also **difficulty order**
some linguistic items, forms, and rules seem to be consistently produced with higher accuracy than others by language learners, permitting such items to be ordered with respect to their relative difficulty. Accuracy orders based on CROSS-SECTIONAL RESEARCH are sometimes taken as evidence for an order of acquisition, although such claims need to be reinforced through LONGITUDINAL METHOD.

accusative case *n*
the form of a noun or noun phrase which shows that it functions as the direct object of the verb in a sentence. For example, in the German sentence:
Ursula kaufte einen neuen Tisch.
Ursula bought a   new   table.
in the noun phrase *einen neuen Tisch*, the article *ein* and the adjective *neu* have the inflectional ending *-en* to show that the noun phrase is in the accusative case because it is the direct object of the verb.
see also CASE^1

achievements *n*
see ASPECT

achievement test *n*
a test designed to measure how much of a language learners have success-fully learned with specific reference to a particular course, textbook, or programme of instruction, thus a type of CRITERION-REFERENCED TEST. An

achievement test is typically given at the end of a course, whereas when administered periodically throughout a course of instruction to measure language learning up to that point, it is alternatively called a PROGRESS TEST. Its results are often used to make advancement or graduation decisions regarding learners or judge the effectiveness of a programme, which may lead to curricular changes.

The difference between this and a more general type of test called a PROFICIENCY TEST is that the latter is not linked to any particular course of instruction and is thus a type of NORM-REFERENCED TEST. For example, an achievement test might be a listening comprehension test if all of its items are based on a particular set of dialogues in a textbook. In contrast, a proficiency test might use similar test items but would not be linked to any particular textbook or language SYLLABUS.

acoustic cue *n*

an aspect of the acoustic signal in speech which is used to distinguish between phonetic features. For example VOICE ONSET TIME is an acoustic cue which is used to distinguish between the sounds /t/ and /d/

acoustic filtering *n*

(in listening comprehension) the ability to hear and identify only some of the sounds that are being spoken. For example, when someone is learning a foreign language, the speech sounds of their native language may act as a filter, making it difficult for them to hear and identify new or unfamiliar sounds in the foreign language.

acoustic phonetics *n*

see PHONETICS

acquisition *n*

see FIRST LANGUAGE ACQUISITION, LANGUAGE ACQUISITION, SECOND LANGUAGE ACQUISITION

acquisition order *n*

another term for ORDER OF ACQUISITION

acrolect *n*

see POST-CREOLE CONTINUUM, SPEECH CONTINUUM

acronym *n*

a word made from the initials of the phrase it stands for, for example "IPA" for International Phonetics Association or International Phonetics Alphabet.

ACT (pronounced "act-star") *n*
   see ADAPTIVE CONTROL OF THOUGHT

ACTFL *n*
   an abbreviation for **American Council on the Teaching of Foreign Languages**

ACTFL Oral Proficiency Interview *n*
   also **OPI**
   a structured interview carried out to assess a learner's ability to use the
   target language in terms of the levels described by the ACTFL PROFICIENCY
   GUIDELINES, used as an assessment of speaking proficiency.

ACTFL Proficiency Guidelines *n*
   proficiency descriptions developed under the auspices of the American
   Council on the Teaching of Foreign Languages (ACTFL). Since their latest
   revision in 1996, the guidelines consist of descriptions of ten proficiency
   levels: Novice Low, Novice Mid, Novice High, Intermediate Low, Intermediate Mid, Intermediate High, Advanced Low, Advanced Mid, Advanced
   High, and Superior.

action research *n*
   1 research that has the primary goal of finding ways of solving problems,
      bringing about social change or practical action, in comparison with
      research that seeks to discover scientific principles or develop general
      laws and theories.
   2 (in teacher education) teacher-initiated classroom research that seeks to
      increase the teacher's understanding of classroom teaching and learning
      and to bring about improvements in classroom practices. Action research
      typically involves small-scale investigative projects in the teacher's own
      classroom, and consists of the following cycle of activities. The teacher
      (or a group of teachers)
      a selects an aspect of classroom behaviour to examine in more detail (e.g.
         the teacher's use of questions)
      b selects a suitable research technique (e.g. recording classroom lessons)
      c collects data and analyzes them
      d develops an action plan to help bring about a change in classroom
         behaviour (e.g. to reduce the frequency of questions that the teacher
         answers himself or herself)
      e acts to implement the plan
      f observes the effects of the action plan on behaviour.

action zone *n*

in teaching, the pattern of teacher-student interaction in a class as reflected by the students with whom the teacher regularly enters into eye contact, those students to whom the teacher addresses questions, and those students who are nominated to take an active part in the lesson.

active listening *n*

in language teaching, a procedure for teaching listening in which students show their understanding of what a speaker says by repeating (often in other words) what the speaker has said or by responding in other ways to show comprehension.

active/passive language knowledge *n*

see PRODUCTIVE/RECEPTIVE LANGUAGE KNOWLEDGE

active teaching *n*

another term for DIRECT TEACHING

active vocabulary *n*

see PRODUCTIVE/RECEPTIVE LANGUAGE KNOWLEDGE

active voice *n*

see VOICE[1]

activities *n*

see ASPECT

activity *n*

in language teaching, a general term for any classroom procedure that requires students to use and practise their available language resources.

see also DRILL, TASK, TECHNIQUE

activity theory *n*

a learning framework associated with SOCIOCULTURAL THEORY in which individuals are said to act on objects (employing social and cultural resources including language and patterns of behaviour) in order to achieve specific learning outcomes.

acute accent *n*

the accent', e.g. on French *prés* "meadows".

see also ACCENT[2]

adaptation[1] *n*

changes made in the use of published teaching materials in order to make them more suitable for particular groups of learners, e.g. by supplementing, modifying or deleting parts of a textbook.

adaptation[2] *n*

also **equilibration**

in Piagetian theory, a cover term for two ways in which a child adapts to his or her environment: **assimilation**[3], interpreting new information in terms of the child's current knowledge, and **accommodation**[2], changing the child's cognitive structure to understand new information.

adaptive control of thought *n*

also **ACT***

a model of skill learning, involving a progression from a controlled stage based on DECLARATIVE KNOWLEDGE to an autonomous stage based on PROCEDURAL KNOWLEDGE. Processes involved in this development include **proceduralization** (the translation of propositional knowledge into behavioural sequences, **chunking** (the binding together of commonly occurring units, which allows more information to be maintained in WORKING MEMORY), GENERALIZATION, **rule narrowing**, and **rule strengthening**. Language acquisition is seen in this model as a type of skill learning.

adaptive testing *n*

a form of individually tailored testing in which test items are selected from an ITEM BANK where test items are stored in rank order with respect to their ITEM DIFFICULTY and presented to test takers during the test on the basis of their responses to previous test items, until it is determined that sufficient information regarding test takers' abilities has been collected. For example, when a multiple-choice adaptive vocabulary test is administered, a test taker is initially presented with an item of medium difficulty. If he or she answers it correctly, then a slightly more difficult item is presented, whereas if the item is answered incorrectly, then a slightly easier item is presented. An ORAL PROFICIENCY INTERVIEW can be viewed as a type of adaptive testing in the sense that an interviewer (i.e. tester) adjusts the difficulty level of language on the basis of an evolving assessment of the interviewee's (i.e. test taker's) language ability. Adaptive testing finds its most promising application in COMPUTER ADAPTIVE TESTING.

additive bilingual education *n*

also **additive bilingualism**

a form of BILINGUAL EDUCATION in which the language of instruction is not the mother tongue or home language of the children, and is not intended to replace it. In an additive bilingual education programme the first language is maintained and supported.

For example, the bilingual programmes in French for English-speaking Canadians are intended to give the children a second language, not to replace English with French.

When the language of instruction is likely to replace the children's first language, this is called **subtractive bilingualism**.

see also IMMERSION PROGRAMME

address form *n*
also **address term, form/term of address**
the word or words used to address somebody in speech or writing. The way in which people address one another usually depends on their age, sex, social group, and personal relationship.

For example, many languages have different second person pronoun forms which are used according to whether the speaker wants to address someone politely or more informally, e.g. in German *Sie – du*, in French *vous – tu*, in Spanish *usted – tu* and in Mandarin Chinese *nín – nǐ* (you).

If a language has only one second person pronoun form, e.g. English *you*, other address forms are used to show formality or informality, e.g. *Sir*, *Mr Brown*, *Brown*, *Bill*. In some languages, such as Chinese dialects and Japanese, words expressing relationship, e.g. father, mother, aunt, or position, e.g. teacher, lecturer, are used as address forms to show respect and/or signal the formality of the situation, for example:

Mandarin Chinese:	*bàba*	*qǐng*	*chǐ*
	father	please	eat!
Japanese:	*sensei*	*dozo!*	(a polite request)
	teacher/sir	please!	

The address forms of a language are arranged into a complex **address system** with its own rules which need to be acquired if a person wants to communicate appropriately.

see also COMMUNICATIVE COMPETENCE

address system *n*
see ADDRESS FORM

address term *n*
see ADDRESS FORM

ad hoc interpreting *n*
informal translation of spoken interaction, for example during social events or business meetings.

see also INTERPRETATION

adjacency pair *n*

a sequence of two related utterances by two different speakers. The second utterance is always a response to the first.

In the following example, speaker A makes a complaint, and speaker B replies with a denial:

A: *You left the light on.*

B: *It wasn't me!*

The sequence of *complaint – denial* is an adjacency pair. Other examples of adjacency pairs are *greeting – greeting, question – answer, invitation – acceptance/non-acceptance, offer – acceptance/non-acceptance, complaint – apology.*

Adjacency pairs are part of the structure of conversation and are studied in CONVERSATION ANALYSIS.

adjacency parameter *n*

(in GOVERNMENT/BINDING THEORY) the parameter by which a language does or does not exhibit the ADJACENCY PRINCIPLE.

adjacency principle *n*

(in GOVERNMENT/BINDING THEORY) the principle that a complement that can be assigned case (see CASE ASSIGNER) must occur adjacent to the head of its phrase and cannot be separated from it by other material. For example, a transitive verb in English must not be separated from its direct object: *She liked very much him. The principle does not apply to such languages as French, in which *J'aime beaucoup la France* (literally 'I love very much France') is the unmarked word order.

adjectival noun *n*

an adjective used as a noun, e.g. *the poor, the rich, the sick, the old.*

see also SUBSTANTIVE

adjective *n*

a word that describes the thing, quality, state, or action which a noun refers to. For example *black* in *a black hat* is an adjective. In English, adjectives usually have the following properties:

a they can be used before a noun, e.g. a <u>heavy</u> bag

b they can be used after be, become, seem, etc. as complements, e.g. the bag <u>is heavy</u>

c they can be used after a noun as a complement, e.g. these books make the bag <u>heavy</u>

d they can be modified by an adverb, e.g. a <u>very heavy</u> bag

e they can be used in a comparative or superlative form, e.g. *the bag seems
heavier now.*

see also COMPLEMENT, COMPARATIVE, ATTRIBUTIVE ADJECTIVE

adjective complement *n*
see COMPLEMENT

adjective phrase *n*
a phrase that functions as an adjective. For example,
The woman in the corner is from Italy.

adjunct *n*
ADVERBIALS may be classified as adjuncts, conjuncts, or disjuncts. An
adjunct is part of the basic structure of the clause or sentence in which it
occurs, and modifies the verb. Adverbs of time, place, frequency, degree,
and manner, are examples of adjuncts.
He died in England.
I have almost finished.
Conjuncts are not part of the basic structure of a clause or sentence. They
show how what is said in the sentence containing the conjunct connects
with what is said in another sentence or sentences.
Altogether it was a happy week.
However the weather was not good.
Disjuncts (also called **sentential adverbs**) are adverbs which show the
speaker's attitude to or evaluation of what is said in the rest of the sentence.
Naturally, I paid for my own meal.
I had to pay for my own meal, unfortunately.
see also ADVERB

adjunct course *n*
in teaching language for academic purposes, an approach to Content Based
Instruction in which a language course is linked with a content course in
an academic area, such as an English course that is linked to a course in
economics. The adjunct course is designed to give students the language
skills necessary for success in the content course.

adjunction *n*
(in GENERATIVE GRAMMAR) a process by which one CONSTITUENT, such as
a word or phrase is adjoined or attached to another to form an extended
constituent.

For example, in the sentence *He shouldn't do that*, we can say that the negative *not* (in contracted form) has been adjoined to the auxiliary *should* to form the extended auxiliary *shouldn't*.
Adjunction is governed by rules that may vary from language to language.

admissions test *n*
also **screening test**
a test designed to provide information about a test taker's likely success in a particular programme before entry into the programme in order to decide whether to admit the applicant or not, thus also called a screening test.

adnominal *n, adj*
a word or phrase which occurs next to a noun and which gives further information about it.
For example, an adnominal may be:
a an adjective,
    e.g. *blue* in *the blue sea*
b another noun,
    e.g. *jade* in *the jade statue*
c a phrase,
    e.g. *at the corner* in *the shop at the corner*.
An adnominal is a type of MODIFIER.

adolescent learner *n*
see YOUNG LEARNER

adposition *n*
a cover term for PREPOSITION and postposition.

adult learner *n*
see YOUNG LEARNER

advance organizer *n*
(in teaching) an activity which helps students organize their thoughts and ideas as a preparation for learning or studying something. For example, a discussion which takes place before students listen to a lecture and which is intended to help them follow the lecture more easily, or a preview of the main ideas covered in a reading passage before reading it.

adverb *n*
a word that describes or adds to the meaning of a verb, an adjective, another adverb, or a sentence, and which answers such questions as *how?*, *where?*, or *when?*. In English many adverbs have an -ly ending.

For example, **adverbs of manner** e.g. *carefully, slowly,* **adverbs of place** e.g. *here, there, locally,* and **adverbs of time** e.g. *now, hourly, yesterday.* A phrase or clause which functions as an adverb is called an **adverb phrase/adverb clause.**

see also ADVERBIAL, ADVERB PARTICLE, ADVERBIAL CLAUSE, ADJUNCT

adverbial *n, adj*
any word, phrase, or clause that functions like an ADVERB. An adverb is a single-word adverbial.

adverbial clause *n*
a clause which functions as an adverb.
For example:
When I arrived I went straight to my room. (adverbial clause of time)
Wherever we looked there was dust. (adverbial clause of place)
We painted the walls yellow to brighten the room. (adverbial clause of purpose)
see also ADVERB, PREPOSITION

adverbial phrase *n*
a phrase that functions as an adverb. For example,
After dinner we went to the movies.

adverb particle *n*
also **prepositional adverb**
a word such as *in, on, back,* when it modifies a verb rather than a noun. Words like *in, out, up, down, on,* may belong grammatically with both nouns (e.g. *in the box, on the wall*) and verbs (e.g. *come in, eat up, wake up, die away*). When they are linked with nouns they are known as PREPOSITIONS and when they are linked with verbs they are known as adverb particles. The combination of verb+adverb particle is known as a PHRASAL VERB.

advocacy *n*
in education, the process of promoting change through demonstrating to others that proposed changes are desirable, feasible, affordable, and appropriate. In planning or implementing curriculum and other kinds of educational changes it is often necessary to gain the support of influential people or groups who have resources, power, or authority to facilitate proposed changes. Advocacy may include political action and lobbying but also involves understanding the attitudes and positions of key decision-makers and STAKEHOLDERS and informing them of information and arguments to

persuade them of the educational, social, economic and other benefits of proposed changes. See also SITUATIONAL ANALYSIS.

affect *n*

a term referring to a number of emotional factors that may influence language learning and use. These include basic personality traits such as shyness, long-term but changeable factors such as positive and negative LANGUAGE ATTITUDES, and constantly fluctuating states such as enthusiasm, ANXIETY, boredom, apathy, or elation. One theory suggests that affective states are largely determined by the balance between the subjectively assessed level of challenge in an activity and the subjectively assessed level of skill that one brings to that activity. For example, when faced with classroom tasks that are much higher than their level of skill, language learners feel anxious and frustrated; when given tasks that are well below their ability level, they feel bored; giving learners interesting tasks that are challenging but within their ability is most likely to elicit a positive affective response.

affected object *n*

see OBJECT OF RESULT

affective domain *n*

see DOMAIN³

affective filter hypothesis *n*

a hypothesis proposed by Krashen and associated with his monitor model of second language development (see MONITOR HYPOTHESIS). The hypothesis is based on the theory of an **affective filter,** which states that successful second language acquisition depends on the learner's feelings. Negative attitudes (including a lack of motivation or self-confidence and anxiety) are said to act as a filter, preventing the learner from making use of INPUT, and thus hindering success in language learning.

affective filtering *n*

the selection of one variety of speech as a model for learning the language in preference to other possible models because of affective factors. For example, second language learners might hear English spoken by many different groups (e.g. parents, teachers, different social and ethnic groups) but model their own speech on only one of these, such as the speech of their friends of the same group (= their PEER GROUP).

affective meaning *n*

another term for CONNOTATION

affective variable *n*
see COGNITIVE VARIABLE

affirmative *adj*
a grammatical construction that expresses a positive meaning, in contrast to a negative construction.
The plane has arrived. (affirmative)
The plane has not arrived. (negative)

affix *n*
a letter or sound, or group of letters or sounds (= a MORPHEME), which is added to a word, and which changes the meaning or function of the word.
Affixes are BOUND FORMS that can be added:
a to the beginning of a word (= a **prefix**), e.g. English *un-* which usually changes the meaning of a word to its opposite: *kind – unkind*
b to the end of a word (= a **suffix**), e.g. English-*ness* which usually changes an adjective into a noun: *kind – kindness*
c within a word (= an **infix**), e.g. Tagalog -*um-* which shows that a verb is in the past tense: *sulat* "to write" – *sumulat* "wrote"
see also COMBINING FORM

African American English *n*
also **AAE, African American Vernacular English (AAVE), Black English (BE), Black English Vernacular (BEV), Ebonics**
a variety of English spoken by some African Americans, particularly those living in concentrated urban areas. There are conflicting views on the origin of African American English. Some claim that is similar to varieties of English spoken by whites in the southern states (therefore, clearly a dialect of English), while others consider it to be a CREOLE, independently developed from Standard English and more deserving of the word LANGUAGE than that of DIALECT.
African American English has been the focus of national attention in the US beginning with the onset of the civil rights movement in the 1960s. AAE has sometimes been erroneously linked with inferior genetic intelligence, cultural deprivation, or laziness and viewed as an educational problem. However, researchers have shown that AAE has a structure and system of its own, no less complex than other language varieties. Some of the differences between AAE and Standard American English (SAE) are:
In phonology, AAE makes use of an l-deletion rule, creating identical pairs such as *toll* and *toe*, and a consonant cluster simplification rule that creates identical pairs such as *pass* and *passed*.

African American Vernacular English (AAVE)

In syntax, AAE speakers can delete the verb *to be* in the same environments in which SAE permits *to be* contracted, for example the verb *is* in *He is nice* can be contracted to *He's nice* in SAE and deleted (*He nice*) in AAE. In semantics, AAE speakers can make distinctions that are not easily made in SAE. For example, the invariant form *be* in *John be happy* conveys the idea that John is always happy (a different meaning from *John is happy* or *John happy*), and the sentence *John* BEEN *married* (with stress on *been*) conveys the idea that John has been married for a long time (not that he has been married but perhaps is not now).

African American Vernacular English (AAVE) *n*
    another term for AFRICAN AMERICAN ENGLISH

affricate *n* **affricated** *adj*
    a speech sound (a CONSONANT) which is produced by stopping the airstream from the lungs, and then slowly releasing it with friction. The first part of an affricate is similar to a STOP, the second part is similar to a FRICATIVE.
    For example, in English the /tʃ/ in /tʃaɪld/ *child*, and the /dʒ/ in /dʒæm/ *jam* are affricates.
    see also MANNER OF ARTICULATION, PLACE OF ARTICULATION

agency *n*
    a philosophical term referring to the capacity for human beings to make choices and take responsibility for their decisions and actions. Agency, together with its connections to IDENTITY and societal context, is an important construct in SOCIOCULTURAL THEORY and CRITICAL PEDAGOGY.

agent *n*
    (in some grammars) the noun or noun phrase which refers to the person or animal which performs the action of the verb.
    For example, in the English sentences:
    Anthea cut the grass.
    The grass was cut by Anthea.
    Anthea is the agent.
    The term agent is sometimes used only for the noun or noun phrase which follows *by* in passive sentences, even if it does not refer to the performer of an action, e.g. *everyone* in *She was admired by everyone.*
    see also SUBJECT, AGENTIVE CASE, AGENTIVE OBJECT

agentive case *n*
    (in CASE GRAMMAR) the noun or noun phrase that refers to the person or animal who performs or initiates the action of the verb is in the agentive case.

For example, in:
Tom pruned the roses.
Tom is in the agentive case.
But the subject of the verb is not necessarily always in the agentive case. In the sentence:
Tom loves roses.
Tom does not perform an action, but his attitude to roses is mentioned. *Tom* in this sentence is therefore not agentive but dative (see DATIVE CASE[2]).
see also CASE GRAMMAR

agentive object *n*
the object of a verb which itself performs the action of the verb.
For example, in the sentence:
Fred galloped the horse.
Fred initiates the action, but it is *the horse* which actually gallops.
see also AGENT, AGENTIVE CASE

agent θ-role *n*
see under θ-THEORY/THETA THEORY

agglutinating language *n*
also **agglutinative language**
a language in which various AFFIXES may be added to the stem of a word to add to its meaning or to show its grammatical function.
For example, in Swahili *wametulipa* "they have paid us" consists of:
wa   me   tu   lipa
they + perfective marker + us + pay
Languages which are highly agglutinating include Finnish, Hungarian, Swahili, and Turkish, although there is no clear-cut distinction between agglutinating languages, INFLECTING LANGUAGES, and ISOLATING LANGUAGES.
Sometimes agglutinating languages and inflecting languages are called *synthetic languages.*

AGR *n*
see AGREEMENT

agrammatism *n*
see APHASIA

agraphia *n*
see APHASIA

agreement[1] *n*

in general, two elements agree if they have at least one feature in common. For example, in English the third person singular subject *John* in the sentence *John goes to work early* must be followed by the form of the verb *go* that is also marked for third person singular. In some languages, such as Spanish and Arabic, adjectives must agree in both gender and number with the nouns they modify. A traditional term for agreement is CONCORD.

In GOVERNMENT/BINDING THEORY, agreement is considered to be the relation between a specifier head (**AGR**) and its specifier. Agreement in this sense includes both subject-verb agreement and assignment of structural case.

agreement[2] *n*

another term for CONCORD

AI *n*

an abbreviation for ARTIFICIAL INTELLIGENCE

AILA *n*

an abbreviation for **Association Internationale de Linguistique Appliquée/ International Association of Applied Linguistics**

aim *n*

see OBJECTIVE

alertness *n*

see ATTENTION

alexia *n*

see APHASIA

algorithm *n*

an explicit set of instructions that specify in detail the steps to go through in order to perform some operation. For example, changing a declarative sentence such as *She went to the store* into an interrogative sentence *Where did she go?* according to a series of steps as a classroom exercise is an example of applying an algorithm.

alienable possession *n*

see INALIENABLE POSSESSION

alliteration *n*
the repetition of an initial sound, usually a consonant, in two or more words that occur close together. For example:
D̲own the d̲rive d̲ashed d̲ashing D̲an.

allomorph *n*
any of the different forms of a MORPHEME.
For example, in English the plural morpheme is often shown in writing by adding -*s* to the end of a word, e.g. *cat* /kæt/ – cats /kæts/. Sometimes this plural morpheme is pronounced /z/, e.g. dog /dɒg/ – *dogs* /dɒgz/, and sometimes it is pronounced /ɪz/, e.g. *class* /klɑːs/ – classes /'klɑːsɪz/.
/s/, /z/, and /ɪz/ all have the same grammatical function in these examples, they all show plural; they are all allomorphs of the plural morpheme.

allophone *n* **allophonic** *adj*
any of the different variants of a phoneme. The different allophones of a phoneme are perceptibly different but similar to each other, do not change the meaning of a word, and occur in different phonetic environments that can be stated in terms of phonological rules. For example, the English phoneme /p/ is **aspirated** (see ASPIRATION) when it occurs at the beginning of a syllable (as in *pot*) but **unaspirated** when it is preceded by /s/ (as in *spot*) and may be **unreleased** when it occurs at the end of an utterance (as in "he's not her *type*"). These aspirated, unaspirated, and unreleased sounds are all heard and identified as the phoneme /p/ and not as /b/; they are all allophones of /p/.

alpha (α) *n*
another term for SIGNIFICANCE LEVEL

alphabet *n* **alphabetic** *adj*
a set of letters which are used to write a language.
The English alphabet uses roman script and consists of 26 letters – a, b, c, etc.
The Russian alphabet uses cyrillic script and consists of 31 letters – *а*, б, в, etc.
The Arabic alphabet uses arabic script and consists of 29 letters – ا, ب, ت, etc.
see also ALPHABETIC WRITING

alphabetic method *n*
a method of teaching children to read. It is used in teaching reading in the mother tongue.

21

Children are taught the names of the letters of the alphabet – *a* "ay", *b* "bee", *c* "see", etc. – and when they see a new or unfamiliar word, e.g. *bag*, they repeat the letter names – "bee ay gee". It is thought that this "spelling" of the word helps the child to recognize it.

see also PHONICS

alphabetic writing *n*
a writing system made up of separate letters which represent sounds (see ALPHABET).

Some examples of alphabetic writing systems are:

a Roman (or Latin) script, used for many European languages including English. It has also been adopted for many non-European languages, e.g. Swahili, Indonesian and Turkish.

b Arabic script, used for Arabic and languages such as Persian, Urdu and Malay, which also uses roman script.

c Cyrillic script, used for Russian and languages such as Ukrainian and Bulgarian.

see also IDIOGRAPHIC WRITING, SYLLABIC WRITING

alpha (α) error *n*
see TYPE I ERROR

ALTE *n*
an abbreviation for **Association of Language Testers in Europe**

alternate form reliability *n*
also **equivalent form reliability, parallel form reliability**
one approach to estimate the RELIABILITY of a test. In this approach, two or more forms of a test that are different but equivalent in content and difficulty are administered to the same group of test takers. Then a COR-RELATION COEFFICIENT between the total scores of the alternate forms of the test is calculated. The resulting correlation coefficient is interpreted as a numerical index of the extent to which the alternate forms are equivalent to each other or consistent in measuring test takers' abilities. For practical reasons, however, this method of assessing test reliability is used less frequently than an INTERNAL CONSISTENCY RELIABILITY approach.

alternate forms *n*
also **equivalent forms, parallel forms**
two or more different forms of a test designed to measure exactly the same skills or abilities, which use the same methods of testing, and which are of equal length and difficulty.

In general, if test takers receive similar scores on alternate forms of a test, this suggests that the test is reliable (see RELIABILITY).

alternate response item *n*
see TEST ITEM

alternation *n* **alternant** *n*
the relationship between the different forms of a linguistic unit is called alternation. The term is used especially in MORPHOLOGY and in PHONOLOGY. For example, the related vowels /iː/ and /e/ in:
deceive /dɪˈsiːv/ *deception* /dɪˈsepʃən/
receive /rɪˈsiːv/ *reception* /rɪˈsepʃən/
are in alternation.
The ALLOPHONES of a PHONEME and the ALLOMORPHS of a MORPHEME are also in alternation, or alternants.

alternation rules *n*
see SPEECH STYLES

alternative *n*
see MULTIPLE-CHOICE ITEM

alternative assessment *n*
various types of assessment procedures that are seen as alternatives or complements to traditional standardized testing. Traditional modes of assessment are thought not to capture important information about test takers' abilities in a L2 and are also not thought to reflect real-life conditions. Procedures used in alternative assessment include self-assessment, peer assessment, portfolios, learner diaries or journals, student–teacher conferences, interviews, and observation.
see AUTHENTIC ASSESSMENT, PERFORMANCE ASSESSMENT

alternative hypothesis *n*
see HYPOTHESIS

alveolar *adj*
describes a speech sound (a CONSONANT) which is produced by the front of the tongue touching or nearly touching the gum ridge behind the upper teeth (the **alveolar ridge**).
For example, in English the /t/ in /tɪn/ *tin*, and the /d/ in /dɪn/ *din* are alveolar STOPS.

In English alveolar stops are made with the tip of the tongue, but alveolar FRICATIVES – the /s/ in /sɪp/ *sip*, and the /z/ in /zuː/ *zoo* – are made with the part of the tongue which is just behind the tip, the blade.

see also LAMINAL, PLACE OF ARTICULATION, MANNER OF ARTICULATION

alveolar ridge *n*
also **alveolum**
see PLACE OF ARTICULATION

ambi-bilingualism *n*
the ability to function equally well in two or more languages across a wide range of domains.

ambiguous *adj* ambiguity *n*
a word, phrase, or sentence which has more than one meaning is said to be ambiguous.

An example of **grammatical ambiguity** is the sentence:
The lamb is too hot to eat.
which can mean either:
a the lamb is so hot that it cannot eat anything
or:
b the cooked lamb is too hot for someone to eat it
There are several types of **lexical ambiguity**:
a a word can have several meanings, e.g. *face* meaning "human face", "face of a clock", "cliff face" (see also POLYSEMY)
b two or more words can sound the same but have different meanings, e.g. *bank* in *to put money in a bank, the bank of a river* (see also HOMONYMS[3])
Usually, additional information either from the speaker or writer or from the situation indicates which meaning is intended.
Ambiguity is used extensively in creative writing, especially in poetry.
see also DISAMBIGUATION

Ameslan *n*
an acronym for American Sign Language
see SIGN LANGUAGE

amygdala *n*
a part of the brain believed to be important in directing ATTENTION and attaching emotional value to stimuli.

analogy *n*
also OVERGENERALIZATION

in language learning, a process by which unknown forms are constructed according to the pattern of other forms that the learner knows. For example, knowing that the past tense of *sing* is *sang*, a learner might guess by analogy that the past tense of *fling* is *flang*.

analysis of covariance *n*
a statistical procedure (similar to ANALYSIS OF VARIANCE) used to statistically equate groups in order to control the effects of one or more variables, called COVARIATES in this type of analysis. For example, if we were comparing the effect of a teaching method on three groups of participants, and one group had a higher MEAN IQ than the others, analysis of covariance could be used to make the groups equivalent by adjusting the effects of IQ.
see also ANALYSIS OF VARIANCE

analysis of variance *n*
a statistical procedure for testing whether the difference among the MEANS of two or more groups is significant, for example, to compare the effectiveness of a teaching method on three different age groups.
see also ANALYSIS OF COVARIANCE

analytic approach *n*
see SYNTHETIC APPROACH

analytic induction *n*
(in QUALITATIVE RESEARCH), the process of taking one case of data, developing a working hypothesis to explain it, examining additional cases to see if the hypothesis explains them, revising the hypothesis as appropriate, and searching for negative cases to disprove the hypothesis. Although not all qualitative research follows this approach, this inductive cyclical approach to data analysis and theory building has been highly influential.

analytic language *n*
another term for ISOLATING LANGUAGE

analytic scoring *n*
in testing, a method of scoring that separates and weights different features of the test taker's performance on a writing or speaking task and assigns separate scores to each feature. The commonly analyzed features in writing tasks include content, organization, cohesion, style, register, vocabulary, grammar, spelling, and mechanics, whereas those in speaking tasks include pronunciation, fluency, accuracy, and appropriateness.
see also HOLISTIC SCORING

analytic style *n*

see GLOBAL LEARNING

anaphora *n* **anaphor** *n* **anaphoric** *adj*

a process where a word or phrase (**anaphor**) refers back to another word or phrase which was used earlier in a text or conversation.

For example, in:

Tom likes ice cream but Bill can't eat it.

the word *it* refers back to *ice cream*: it is a substitute for *ice cream*, which is called the ANTECEDENT of *it*.

Some verbs may be anaphoric, for example the verb *do* in:

Mary works hard and so does Doris.

does is anaphoric and is a substitute for *works*.

In BINDING THEORY the term *anaphor* refers to a somewhat different concept and is subject to certain restrictions (see under BINDING PRINCIPLE).

ANCOVA *n*

an abbreviation for ANALYSIS OF COVARIANCE

animate noun *n*

a noun which refers to a living being, for example persons, animals, fish, etc. For example, the English nouns *woman* and *fish* are animate nouns.

Nouns like *stone* and *water* are called inanimate nouns.

see also SEMANTIC FEATURES

anomia *n*

see APHASIA

anomie *n*

also **anomy**

feelings of social uncertainty or dissatisfaction which people who do not have strong attachments to a particular social group may have. Anomie has been studied as an affective variable (see COGNITIVE VARIABLE) in second/foreign language learning. In learning a new language people may begin to move away from their own language and culture, and have feelings of insecurity. At the same time they may not be sure about their feelings towards the new language group. Feelings of anomie may be highest when a high level of language ability is reached. This may lead a person to look for chances to speak their own language as a relief.

ANOVA *n*

an abbreviation for ANALYSIS OF VARIANCE

antecedent *n*
> see ANAPHORA

anthropological linguistics *n*
> a branch of linguistics which studies the relationship between language and culture in a community, e.g. its traditions, beliefs, and family structure. For example, anthropological linguists have studied the ways in which relationships within the family are expressed in different cultures (kinship terminology), and they have studied how people communicate with one another at certain social and cultural events, e.g. ceremonies, rituals, and meetings, and then related this to the overall structure of the particular community.
> Some areas of anthropological linguistics are closely related to areas of SOCIOLINGUISTICS and the ETHNOGRAPHY OF COMMUNICATION.

anticipation error *n*
> see SPEECH ERRORS

anticipatory coarticulation *n*
> see ASSIMILATION

anticipatory structure *n*
> a structure that refers forward to information contained later in a sentence.
> *It surprised me* to learn that she was only 21.
> *It's not until next week* that we will be able to meet.

anticipatory subject *n*
> see EXTRAPOSITION

anti-cognitive theory *n*
> see COGNITIVE THEORY

anti-essentialism *n*
> see ESSENTIALISM

antonym *n* **antonymy** *n*
> a word which is opposite in meaning to another word. For example, in English *dead* and *alive*, and *big* and *small* are antonyms.
> A distinction is sometimes made between pairs like *dead* and *alive*, and pairs like *big* and *small*, according to whether or not the words are gradable (see GRADABLE).

27

A person who is not *dead* must be *alive*, but something which is not *big* is not necessarily *small*, it may be somewhere between the two sizes. *Dead* and *alive* are called **complementaries** (or ungradable antonyms); *big* and *small* are called gradable antonyms or a **gradable pair**.
Some linguists use the term antonym to mean only gradable pairs.
see also SYNONYM

anxiety *n*
    see LANGUAGE ANXIETY

a-parameter *n*
    see ITEM RESPONSE THEORY

apex *n*
    the tip of the tongue
    see also APICAL, PLACE OF ARTICULATION

aphasia *n* **aphasic** *adj*
    also **dysphasia**
    loss of the ability to use and understand language, usually caused by damage to the brain. The loss may be total or partial, and may affect spoken and/or written language ability.
    There are different types of aphasia: **agraphia** is difficulty in writing; **alexia** is difficulty in reading; **anomia** is difficulty in using proper nouns; and **agrammatism** is difficulty in using grammatical words like prepositions, articles, etc.
    Aphasia can be studied in order to discover how the brain processes language.
    see also NEUROLINGUISTICS

apical *adj*
    describes a speech sound (a CONSONANT) which is produced by the tip of the tongue (the apex) touching some part of the mouth.
    For example, in English the /t/ in /tɪn/ *tin is* an apical STOP.
    If the tongue touches the upper teeth, the sounds are sometimes called apico-dental, e.g. French and German /t/ and /d/. If the tongue touches the gum ridge behind the upper teeth (the alveolar ridge), the sounds are sometimes called apico-alveolar, e.g. English /t/ and /d/.
    see also PLACE OF ARTICULATION, MANNER OF ARTICULATION

a posteriori syllabus *n*
    see A PRIORI SYLLABUS

apostrophe s *n*
the ending '*s* which is added to nouns in English to indicate possession. For example:
Michael's son
The director's car.

applied linguistics *n*
1 the study of second and foreign language learning and teaching.
2 the study of language and linguistics in relation to practical problems, such as LEXICOGRAPHY, TRANSLATION, SPEECH PATHOLOGY, etc. Applied linguistics uses information from sociology, psychology, anthropology, and INFORMATION THEORY as well as from linguistics in order to develop its own theoretical models of language and language use, and then uses this information and theory in practical areas such as syllabus design, SPEECH THERAPY, LANGUAGE PLANNING, STYLISTICS, etc.

applied research *n*
research designed to produce practical applications, contrasted with basic research, i.e. research that is designed to generate knowledge or validate theories that may not have any direct application. ACTION RESEARCH is a form of applied research. Second language acquisition is considered a type of applied research by some and basic research by others.

apposition *n* **appositive** *n, adj*
When two words, phrases, or clauses in a sentence have the same REFERENCE, they are said to be in apposition. For example, in the sentence:
My sister, Helen Wilson, will travel with me.
My sister and *Helen Wilson* refer to the same person, and are called appositives.
The sentence can be rewritten with either of the two appositives missing, and still make sense:
My sister will travel with me.
Helen Wilson will travel with me.

appraisal system *n*
1 in language teaching, procedures that an institution, school or organization has in place to provide for regular review and assessment of teachers' performance. Appraisal may include appraisal by a supervisor, by a colleague, by students, or self-appraisal.
2 in NEUROLINGUISTICS, a brain-system that evaluates stimuli (such as a target language) in terms of such criteria as novelty, relevance, coping ability, and self- and social-image.

appraisal theory *n*
a developing area within discourse analysis and conversation analysis and associated with Halliday's Systemic Functional Linguistics. Appraisal theory is concerned with the way speakers convey attitudinal meaning during conversation. It deals with the way speakers communicate such attitudes as certainty, emotional response, social evaluation, and intensity. Appraisal is mainly realized lexically, although it can also be realized by whole clauses.

appreciative comprehension *n*
see READING

apprenticeship of observation *n*
the understanding of teaching that student teachers bring with them to a teacher training course based on the thousands of hours they have spent observing and experiencing different forms of teaching as school children. A focus of teacher education programmes is therefore to explore ideas and beliefs about teaching and learning that pre-service teachers bring with them, and the extent to which these ideas affect their willingness or ability to acquire new understandings of teaching.

approach *n*
in language teaching, the theory, philosophy and principles underlying a particular set of teaching practices.
Language teaching is sometimes discussed in terms of three related aspects: approach, METHOD, and **technique**.
Different theories about the nature of language and how languages are learned (the approach) imply different ways of teaching language (the method), and different methods make use of different kinds of classroom activity (the technique).
Examples of different approaches are the aural–oral approach (see AUDIO-LINGUAL METHOD), the COGNITIVE CODE APPROACH, the COMMUNICATIVE APPROACH, etc. Examples of different methods which are based on a particular approach are the AUDIOLINGUAL METHOD, the DIRECT METHOD, etc. Examples of techniques used in particular methods are DRILLS, DIALOGUES, ROLE-PLAYS, sentence completion, etc.

appropriateness *n* **appropriate** *adj*
the extent to which a use of language matches the linguistic and sociolinguistic expectations and practices of native speakers of the language. When producing an utterance, a speaker needs to know that it is grammatical, and also that it is suitable (appropriate) for the particular situation.
For example:

Give me a glass of water!
is grammatical, but it would not be appropriate if the speaker wanted to be polite. A request such as:
May I have a glass of water, please?
would be more appropriate.

see also GRAMMATICAL[1,2], CORRECT, COMMUNICATIVE COMPETENCE

appropriate word method *n*
see CLOZE TEST

appropriation *n*
in second language learning, the processes by which language learners make the characteristics of one language and culture their own by adapting it to their own needs and interests. For example the ways in which speakers of Singapore and Malaysian English have made this variety of English distinctive and unique through incorporating features from Chinese, as with the use of a final sentence particle "lah" in informal speech, as in " My turn to pay for lunch today lah!".

approximant *n*
a sound produced by the approach of one articulator towards another but without the vocal tract being narrowed so much that a turbulent airstream is produced. English /r, l, y, w/ are approximants and can be further subdivided into SEMIVOWELS or GLIDES (/y/ and /w/) and LIQUIDS (/l/ and /r/).

approximative system *n*
see INTERLANGUAGE

a priori syllabus *n*
in language teaching, a distinction is sometimes made between two kinds of syllabuses. A syllabus prepared in advance of a course, and used as a basis for developing classroom activities, may be referred to as an a priori syllabus. This may be contrasted with a syllabus which is not developed in advance but which is prepared after a course is taught, as a "record" of the language and activities used in the course (an **a posteriori syllabus**). And an a posteriori syllabus is sometimes called **a retrospective syllabus**.
see also SYLLABUS

aptitude *n*
see LANGUAGE APTITUDE

aptitude test *n*
see LANGUAGE APTITUDE TEST

aptitude-treatment interaction *n*

the relationship between a learner's personal strengths and weaknesses in learning and the learning situation, including the type of programme one is enrolled in. The study of such interactions is motivated by the idea that learners will learn best in a situation in which the demands of the classroom or other learning context match their areas of aptitude. For example, a learner with high ORAL MIMICRY ABILITY may learn better in one type of language programme, while one high in GRAMMATICAL SENSITIVITY may learn better in another.

archaism *n*

a word or phrase that is no longer used, such as the second person singular pronoun *thou*, or whose usage is limited to specific contexts, such as *thereof*, *hereto*, in legal documents.

areal linguistics *n*

the study of the languages or dialects which are spoken in a particular area. An example is a study of two neighbouring languages to see how they influence each other in terms of grammar, vocabulary, pronunciation, etc.

see also DIALECTOLOGY

argument *n*

in LOGIC, the thing talked about (see PROPOSITION).

in GENERATIVE GRAMMAR, the thematic role of a noun in relation to a verb (see CASE THEORY, THETA THEORY).

argumentation *n*

see ESSAY

argumentative writing *n*

see MODES OF WRITING

article *n*

a word which is used with a noun, and which shows whether the noun refers to something definite or something indefinite.

For example, English has two articles: the **definite article** *the*, and the **indefinite article** *a* or *an*.

The main use of the definite article in English is to show that the noun refers to a particular example of something, e.g.:

a by referring to something which is known to both the speaker and the hearer:

She is in the garden.

He is at the post office.

b by referring backwards to something already mentioned:
There is a man waiting outside. Who, the man in the brown coat?
c by referring forward to something:
The chair in the living room is broken.
d by referring to something as a group or class:
The lion is a dangerous animal.
The main use of the indefinite article in English is to show that the noun refers to something general or to something which has not been identified by the speaker, e.g.:
a by referring to one example of a group or class:
Pass me a pencil, please.
b by referring to something as an example of a group or class:
A dog is a friendly animal.
When nouns are used without an article in English, this is sometimes called zero article. For example:
Cats like sleeping.
Silver is a precious metal,
see also DETERMINER

articulation *n* **articulate** *v*
the production of speech sounds in the mouth and throat (see VOCAL TRACT). In describing and analyzing speech sounds a distinction is made between the MANNER OF ARTICULATION and the PLACE OF ARTICULATION.

articulator *n*
a part of the mouth, nose, or throat which is used in producing speech, e.g. the tongue, lips, alveolar ridge, etc.
see also PLACE OF ARTICULATION

articulatory loop *n*
see WORKING MEMORY

articulatory phonetics *n*
see PHONETICS

articulatory setting *n*
the overall posture, position or characteristic movements of the organs of speech typical of a particular language or dialect. For example, speakers of English make much more active use of both lip and tongue movements than speakers of some languages (Japanese, for example), while Arabic has

many consonants formed towards the back of the oral cavity, producing an overall "heavier" velarized or pharyngealized sound (see VELARIZATION, PHARYNGEALIZATION).

artificial intelligence *n*
also **AI**
the ability of machines to carry out functions that are normally associated with human intelligence, such as reasoning, correcting, making self-improvements and learning through experience. Computer programmers try to create programs which have this capacity.

artificial language[1] *n*
also **auxiliary language**
a language which has been invented for a particular purpose, and which has no NATIVE SPEAKERS.
For example, Esperanto was invented by L. L. Zamenhof and was intended to be learned as a second language and used for international communication.
Artificial languages are also invented for experiments on aspects of natural language use.
see also NATURAL LANGUAGE

artificial language[2] *n*
in computer programming, a code system made up of symbols, numbers or signs, such as the programming language COBOL.

ASCII *n*
An abbreviation for **American Standard Code for Information Interchange**

aspect *n*
a term used to denote the activity, event, or state described by a verb, for example whether the activity is ongoing or completed. Two types of aspect are commonly recognized:
lexical aspect (or **inherent lexical aspect**) refers to the internal semantics of verbs, which can be grouped into a number of categories:
1 **states**, verbs that refer to unchanging conditions (see STATIVE VERB), for example *be, have, want*
2 **activities**, verbs referring to processes with no inherent beginning or end point, for example *play, walk, breathe*
3 **accomplishments**, which are **durative** (last for a period of time) but have an inherent end point, for example *read a book, write a novel*

34

4 **achievements**, which are nondurative and have an inherent end point, for example *finish, realize, arrive*.

grammatical aspect, on the other hand, refers to the resources provided by a language (such as verbal auxiliaries, prefixes and suffixes) to encode different perspectives taken by a speaker towards activities, events, and states. Languages make available different options for realizing aspect grammatically. English has two grammatical aspects: PROGRESSIVE and PERFECT.

see also TENSE[1]

aspect hypothesis
see LEXICAL ASPECT HYPOTHESIS

Aspects Model *n*
see GENERATIVE THEORY

aspirate *v* **aspirated** *adj*
the very small puff of air that sometimes follows a speech sound.
For example, in English the /p/ is aspirated at the beginning of the word /pæn/ *pan*, but when it is preceded by an /s/, e.g. in /spæn/ *span* there is no puff of air. The /p/ in *span is* **unaspirated**.
In phonetic notation, aspiration is shown by the symbol [ʰ] or ['], e.g. [pʰɪn] or [p'ɪn] *pin*.
Aspiration increases when a word or syllable is stressed, e.g.:
Ouch! I stepped on a PIN.

aspiration *n*
a puff of air (acoustically, a period of voicelessness) after the release of an articulation. For example, in English the stop consonants /p, t, k/ are **aspirated** when they are syllable initial, as in initial sounds of *pie, tie, kite*. When these phonemes are preceded by /s/, e.g. in *span, stairs*, and *skate*, there is no puff of air and these sounds are **unaspirated**.
Aspiration increases when a word or syllable is stressed. For example, in the phrase *a piece of pie*, aspiration is more noticeable in the word *pie* than in the word *piece*.

assessment *n*
a systematic approach to collecting information and making inferences about the ability of a student or the quality or success of a teaching course on the basis of various sources of evidence. Assessment may be done by test, interview, questionnaire, observation, etc. For example, assessment of the comprehension ability of an immigrant student may be necessary to

discover if the student is able to follow a course of study in a school, or whether extra language teaching is needed. Students may be tested at the beginning and again at the end of a course to assess the quality of the teaching on the course. The term "testing" is often associated with large-scale standardized tests, whereas the term "assessment" is used in a much wider sense to mean a variety of approaches in testing and assessment.

see also TESTING

assessment criteria *n*
the features of a student's performance on an activity which will be used as the basis for judging a student's performance. For example in assessing a student's writing, assessment criteria might include grammatical accuracy, punctuation, and organization of ideas.

assimilated word *n*
a word which was originally a *borrowing* from another language but which is now regarded as part of the native vocabulary of a language, such as *coffee*, which was originally a borrowed word from Arabic.

assimilation[1] *n*
a phonological process in which a speech sound changes and becomes more like or identical to another sound that precedes or follows it. For example, in English the negative PREFIX appears as *im-* before words beginning with a bilabial stop (e.g. *possible:impossible*) but as *in-* before words beginning with an alveolar stop (e.g. *tolerant:intolerant*).
Assimilation in which a following sound brings about a change in a preceding one is called **regressive assimilation** or **anticipatory coarticulation**. For example, the rounding of the lips during /s/ in *swim* is due to the anticipation of the lip action required for /w/.
Assimilation in which a preceding sound brings about a change in a following one is called **progressive** or **perseverative assimilation**. For example, the difference between the /s/ in words like *cats* and the /z/ in *dogs* and the difference between the final /t/ in *dropped* and the final /d/ in *praised* are examples of progressive assimilation because the final sound (/s/ or /z/, /t/ or /d/) depends on whether the preceding consonant is voiced or not.
A third type of assimilation, coalescent assimilation takes place when two sounds in a sequence come together to produce a sound with features from both original sounds. For example, the final alveolar stop /d/ of *could* and the initial palatal /y/ of *you* may coalesce to become a palatal AFFRICATE [dʒ] in a phrase like *could you?* This process is commonly referred to as **palatalization**.

assimilation[2] *n*

a process in which a group gradually gives up its own language, culture, and system of values and takes on those of another group with a different language, culture, and system of values, through a period of interaction.

see also ACCULTURATION, SOCIAL DISTANCE

assimilation[3] *n*

see ADAPTATION[2]

associative learning *n*

learning which happens when a connection or association is made, usually between two things.

For example:

a When someone hears the word *table*, they may think of the word *food*, because this word is often used with or near *table*. This is called **association by contiguity**.

b When someone hears the word *delicate*, they may think of the word *fragile*, because it has a similar meaning. This is called **association by similarity**.

c When someone hears the word *happy*, they may think of the word *sad*, because it has the opposite meaning. This is called association **by contrast**.

Associative learning theory has been used in studies of memory, learning, and verbal learning.

see also VERBAL LEARNING, WORD ASSOCIATION, PAIRED-ASSOCIATE LEARNING

associative meaning *n*

the associative meaning of a word is the total of all the meanings a person thinks of when they hear the word.

For example, in a word association test a person might be given a word (a **stimulus**) and then asked to list all the things they think of (the **response**).

For example:

stimulus	response
Puppy	*warm*
	young
	furry
	lively
	kitten

warm, young, furry, lively, kitten make up the associative meaning of puppy for that person.

Associative meaning has been used in studies of memory and thought.

see also WORD ASSOCIATION, STIMULUS-RESPONSE THEORY

associative memory *n*

a memory system that stores mappings of specific representations to inputs, outputs, and other representations. In CONNECTIONISM, a memory system that learns to reproduce input patterns as output patterns is called **autoassociative.**

asyllabic *adj*

see SYLLABLE

asynchronous communication *n*

in COMPUTER ASSISTED LANGUAGE LEARNING, communication that is not instantaneous and can be accessed and read by the recipient at a later time. Language classes often use this type of communication in the form of bulletin boards or discussion lists.

see also SYNCHRONOUS COMMUNICATION

attention *n*

the ability a person has to concentrate on some things while ignoring others. Subsystems of attention that have been identified include **alertness** (an overall readiness to deal with incoming stimuli), **orientation** (the direction of attentional resources to certain types of stimuli), **detection** (cognitive registration of a particular stimulus), and **inhibition** (deliberately ignoring some stimuli). In SLA theory, it has been proposed that nothing can be learned from input without it being the object of some level of attention and detected; whether such detection must be conscious is controversial. **Sustained attention,** the ability to direct and focus cognitive activity on specific stimuli for a period of time, is necessary for such language tasks as reading a newspaper article or any complex sequenced action.

attitude *n*

see LANGUAGE ATTITUDES

attitude scale *n*

a technique for measuring a person's reaction to something. A common scale is the **Likert scale.** With this a statement of belief or attitude is shown to someone, and he or she is asked to show how strongly he or she agrees or disagrees with the statement by marking a scale like the one shown below:
Foreign languages are important for all educated adults.

1	2	3	4	5	6	7
strongly disagree		disagree		agree		strongly agree

attribution theory *n*

the theory that the causes people attribute to perceived successes and failures in their lives play a significant role in their subsequent level of MOTIVATION and behaviour. For example, learners may attribute their relative success or failure in language learning to such factors as ability, the classroom environment, good or poor teaching, interest, strategy use, support from others, etc. Attributions can be classified on the basis of **locus of control** (internal factors such as effort vs. external factors such as the textbook or teaching method), **stability** (stable factors such as personality vs. unstable factors such as mood), and **controllability** (controllable factors such as effort vs. uncontrollable factors such as language aptitude). Although there may be a **self-serving bias** that leads to ascribing success to internal factors and failures to external ones, it is generally believed that learners who attribute both success and failure to internal factors such as effort are most likely to maintain their motivation at a high level.

attributive adjective *n*

an adjective which is used before a noun.

For example, *good* in *a good book* is an attributive adjective.

An adjective which is used after a verb, especially after the verbs *be*, *become*, *seem*, etc. is called a **predicative adjective**. For example, *good* in *The book was very good.*

Many adjectives in English are like *good*, and can be used both attributively and predicatively, but some, like *main* and *utter*, can only be used attributively, e.g. *a busy main road, an utter fool*, and some, like *afraid* and *asleep*, can only be used predicatively e.g. *The boy was asleep, The dog seems afraid.* Many nouns in English can also be used attributively, e.g. *paper* in *a paper cup.* Languages differ in the extent to which they use adjectives attributively, predicatively, or in both positions.

see also ADJECTIVE

attriters *n*

see LANGUAGE ATTRITION

attriting language *n*

see LANGUAGE ATTRITION

attrition *n*

see LANGUAGE ATTRITION

audience *n*

when writing any type of text, the writer's understanding of the readers for whom the text is intended. The writer's understanding of the readers' beliefs, values and understandings can have an influence on how the writer structures the text and the features the writer includes in it. Good writing is said to reflect the writer's consideration of the audience.

audio journal *n*
    also **tape journal** *n*
    a technique for giving feedback on a student's spoken language in which the student receives personalized feedback on his or her performance based on short student recordings, done individually at home or out of class. Audio journals may be regarded as the spoken equivalent of a writing journal.

audiolingual method *n*
    also **audiolingualism, aural–oral method, mim–mem method**
    a method of foreign or second language teaching which (a) emphasizes the teaching of speaking and listening before reading and writing (b) uses DIALOGUES and DRILLS (c) discourages use of the mother tongue in the classroom (d) often makes use of CONTRASTIVE ANALYSIS. The audiolingual method was prominent in the 1950s and 1960s, especially in the United States, and has been widely used in many other parts of the world.
    The theory behind the audiolingual method is the **aural–oral approach** to language teaching, which contains the following beliefs about language and language learning: (a) speaking and listening are the most basic language skills (b) each language has its own unique structure and rule system (c) a language is learned through forming habits. These ideas were based partly on the theory of STRUCTURAL LINGUISTICS and partly on BEHAVIOURISM. Criticism of the audiolingual method is based on criticism of its theory and its techniques (see COGNITIVE CODE APPROACH, COMMUNICATIVE APPROACH).
    see also APPROACH, MIM–MEM METHOD

audiology *n*
    the study of hearing and hearing disorders, particularly the nature of hearing loss and the treatment of people suffering from hearing disorders.

audio-script *n*
    also **tape script**
    In language teaching course books and materials, a printed text containing a transcript of spoken dialogues and other spoken texts occurring in the course-book's audio or video components.

audio-visual aid *n*
    an audio or visual device used by a teacher to help learning. For example, pictures, charts, and flashcards are visual aids; radio, records, and tape-recorders are auditory aids. Film, television, and video are audio-visual aids.

audio-visual method *n*
also **structural global method**
a method of foreign language teaching which was developed in France in the 1950s and which
a teaches speaking and listening before reading and writing
b does not use the mother tongue in the classroom
c uses recorded dialogues with film-strip picture sequences to present language items
d uses drills to teach basic grammar and vocabulary.
The audio-visual method is based on the belief that
a language is learned through communication
b translation can be avoided if new language items are taught in situations
c choice of items for teaching should be based on a careful analysis of the language being taught.
see also AUDIOLINGUAL METHOD

auditing *n*
see DEPENDABILITY

auditory *adj*
of or related to hearing.

auditory discrimination *n*
the ability to hear and recognize the different sounds in a language. In particular the ability to recognize the different PHONEMES, and the different STRESS and INTONATION patterns.
see also PERCEPTION

auditory feedback *n*
when a person speaks, they can hear what they are saying, and can use this information to monitor their speech and to correct any mistakes. This is called auditory feedback.
For example, in the following utterance the speaker uses auditory feedback to correct his/her pronunciation:
Would you like a cup of cea or toffee – I mean tea or coffee?
see also FEEDBACK, DELAYED AUDITORY FEEDBACK, KINESTHETIC FEEDBACK

auditory learner *n*
a learner whose preferred learning style is to learn by listening, rather than learning in some other way, such as by reading.
See also COGNITIVE STYLE/LEARNING STYLE, KINAESTHETIC LEARNER, VISUAL LEARNER

auditory/oral method *n*
a method for educating deaf or HEARING-IMPAIRED children which relies on using their remaining or **residual hearing** and hearing aids. Best results are achieved through early diagnosis of the hearing loss and the use of normal language input. This is said to allow children to acquire normal language rules, and to maximize the opportunity for the learning of PROSODIC and SUPRASEGMENTAL FEATURES of speech.

auditory perception *n*
see PERCEPTION

auditory phonetics *n*
see PHONETICS

auditory processing *n*
the mental processing of auditory information or input particularly speech sounds, as compared to those processes involved in processing visible messages (VISUAL PROCESSING).

aural language *n*
also **oral language**
language that has been spoken, as compared to written language.

aural-oral approach *n*
see AUDIOLINGUAL METHOD

aural-oral method *n*
another term for AUDIOLINGUAL METHOD

Australian Second Language Proficiency Ratings *n*
see INTERNATIONAL SECOND LANGUAGE PROFICIENCY RATINGS

authentic assessment *n*
various types of assessment procedures for evaluating test takers' achievement or performance using test tasks that resemble real-life language use as closely as possible.
see ALTERNATIVE ASSESSMENT, PERFORMANCE ASSESSMENT

authenticity *n* **authentic** *adj*
(in teaching) the degree to which language teaching materials have the qualities of natural speech or writing. In language teaching a distinction is made

between materials that have been specially prepared to illustrate or practise specific teaching points (such as reading passages, listening texts, or model conversations) and those that have been taken from real-world sources. Texts which are taken from newspapers, magazines, etc., and tapes of natural speech taken from ordinary radio or television programmes, etc., are called authentic materials.

It is argued that these are preferred classroom resources since they illustrate authentic language use.

(in testing) the extent to which test tasks correspond to language use in a non-test (i.e. target language use) situation.

authentic materials *n*
in language teaching, the use of materials that were not originally developed for pedagogical purposes, such as the use of magazines, newspapers, advertisements, news reports, or songs. Such materials are often thought to contain more realistic and natural examples of language use than those found in textbooks and other specially developed teaching materials.

authoring system *n*
(in COMPUTER ASSISTED LEARNING) a computer program which is designed to allow teachers and materials designers to write a computer lesson without requiring them to learn how to write a PROGRAM. The teacher concentrates on creating the lesson material, while the authoring system handles such things as the exercise format and the processing of answers.

autism *n*
a brain disorder characterized by impaired social interaction and communication and restricted and repetitive behaviour. Differences in communication are often present from an early age, and may include delayed onset of babbling and unusual gestures. Some individuals with autism do not develop enough natural speech to meet daily communication needs, and many have difficulties with complex language, FIGURES OF SPEECH and INFERENCING.

autoassociative *adj*
see ASSOCIATIVE MEMORY

automaticity *n*
the ability to carry out an activity or to process information without effort or attention.
see AUTOMATIC PROCESSING

automatic processing *n*
the performance of a task without conscious or deliberate processing. In cognitive psychology, two different kinds of processing employed in carrying out tasks are distinguished. **Controlled processing** is involved when conscious effort and attention is required to perform a task. This places demands on short-term memory (see MEMORY). For example a learner driver may operate a car using controlled processing, consciously thinking about many of the decisions and operations involved while driving. **Automatic processing** is involved when the learner carries out the task without awareness or attention, making more use of information in long-term memory (see MEMORY). Many skills are considered to be "learned" when they can be performed with automatic processing.

In language learning, the distinction between controlled and automatic processing has been used to explain why learners sometimes perform differently under different conditions. For example, a learner may speak a foreign language with relatively few grammatical errors in situations where automatic processing is being used (e.g. when talking in relaxed situations among friends). The same learner may speak less fluently and make more grammatical errors when controlled processing is being used (e.g. when speaking in public before an audience). The presence of the audience distracts the speaker, who uses more controlled processing and this interferes with his or her accuracy and fluency.

automatic translation *n*
see under COMPUTATIONAL LINGUISTICS

autonomous learning *n*
see LEARNER AUTONOMY

autonomy *n*
in language learning, the ability to take charge of one's own learning and to be responsible for decisions concerning the goals, learning processes, and implementation of one's language learning needs. The result is an **autonomous learner,** as compared to one who depends on others to make such decisions. In SELF DETERMINATION THEORY, autonomy refers to the human need to actively participate in determining one's own behaviour. This is not necessarily the same as independence, however, since we can freely choose to do what others want us to do.
see also LEARNER AUTONOMY

autonomy principle *n*
the idea that grammatical notions cannot be reduced to nonlinguistic concepts.

autosegmental phonology *n*

a theory of phonology that does not view representations as merely a linear string of segments but in terms of tiers, each of which is autonomous. Autosegmental phonology has been shown to be especially relevant for the treatment of phonological TONE[1].

auxiliary *n*

another term for AUXILIARY VERB

auxiliary language *n*

another term for LINGUA FRANCA and ARTIFICIAL LANGUAGE

auxiliary verb *n*

also **auxiliary**

a verb which is used with another verb in a sentence, and which shows grammatical functions such as ASPECT, VOICE[1], MOOD, TENSE[1], and PERSON. In English *be*, *do*, and *have* and the MODAL verbs like *may*, *can*, and *will* are all auxiliaries. For example:

She is working.

He didn't come.

They have finished.

You may go now.

Can you manage?

They will arrive tomorrow.

The verbs *working*, *come*, *finished*, *go*, *manage*, and *arrive* in these sentences are called **lexical verbs**, or **full verbs**. Lexical verbs can be used as the only verb in a sentence, e.g. *She works at the factory*. *Be*, *do*, and *have* can also be used as lexical verbs, e.g. *He is happy*, *She does computer studies at university*, and *They have three children.*

availability *n* **available** *adj*

when people are asked to think of the words that can be used to talk about a particular topic, they will be able to think of some words immediately. Those words which they remember first and most easily are said to have a high availability.

For example, when a group of secondary school children were asked to list words for *parts of the body*, they included *leg*, *hand*, *eye*, *nose*, and *ears*. These were the five most available words.

Available words are not always the most frequently occurring words in a language. Availability has been used as a criterion for selecting vocabulary for language teaching.

see SYLLABUS DESIGN

avoidance strategy *n*

when speaking or writing a second/foreign language, a speaker will often try to avoid using a difficult word or structure, and will use a simpler word or structure instead. This is called an avoidance strategy. For example, a student who is not sure of the use of the relative clause in English may avoid using it and use two simpler sentences instead:

That's my building. I live there.

instead of

That's the building where I live.

B

BAAL *n*

an abbreviation for **British Association for Applied Linguistics**

babbling *n*

speech-like sounds produced by very young children. Babies begin to produce babbling sounds like /dæ/, /mæ/, /næ/, /bæ/, at the age of about three or four months. At around 9–12 months, real words begin to be produced.

baby talk *n*

another term for CARETAKER SPEECH

backchaining *n*

another term for BACKWARD BUILD-UP

back channel cue *n* **back channelling** *n*

see FEEDBACK

back formation *n*

in MORPHOLOGY, a type of WORD FORMATION through the removal of an AFFIX from an existing word. For example, speakers of English have formed the verbs *televise*, *peddle*, and *babysit* from *television*, *peddler*, and *babysitter*, respectively.

New words are more commonly formed by adding affixes to existing words.

background *n*

see FUNCTIONAL SENTENCE PERSPECTIVE

background information[1] *n*

see GROUNDING

background information[2] *n*

in TRANSLATION and INTERPRETATION, information about the content of the source text that facilitates the translator's or interpreter's task by providing definitions of terms and contextual information.

backgrounding *n*

a grammatical device for shifting the information focus of a sentence (see FUNCTIONAL SENTENCE PERSPECTIVE), such as the use of NOMINALIZATION to lesson the focus on a cause or agent.

The destruction of the crops was the result of severe winds.
Foregrounding allows important information in a sentence to be highlighted.
Severe winds destroyed the crops.

background knowledge *n*
in reading, PRIOR KNOWLEDGE that readers make use of in understanding a text. This can include topic-related knowledge, as well as cultural, linguistic and world-knowledge. Background knowledge enables the reader to make greater use of TOP-DOWN PROCESSING.

back propagation *n*
see LEARNING RULE

back-shift *n*
see DIRECT SPEECH

backsliding *n*
(in *second language acquisition*) the regular reappearance of features of a learner's INTERLANGUAGE which were thought to have disappeared. Sometimes a learner who appears to have control of an area of grammar or phonology will have difficulty with particular linguistic features in situations which are stressful or which present the learner with some kind of communicative difficulty. Errors may then temporarily reappear.
Research into backsliding suggests that such errors are not random but reflect the linguistic system the learner had learned at an earlier stage of his or her language development.

back vowel *n*
see VOWEL

backward build-up drill *n*
also **backchaining**
a language teaching technique associated with AUDIOLINGUALISM in which a sentence pattern or pronunciation feature is practised by getting students to repeat successively longer portions of it, starting with the last part and extending backwards to the beginning. For example to practise the unstressed "to" in "Give it to him" the teacher may have students repeat "him", "to him", "it to him", "Give it to him".

backwash effect *n*
see WASHBACK

balanced bilingual *n*
a person who is equally proficient in two languages.

band *n*
(in testing) a level of performance in a rating scale that describes what a test taker has achieved in a test.
see also LEVEL

bandscales *n*
see STANDARDS

bare infinitive *n*
see INFINITIVE

bar notation *n*
(in some linguistic theories) a device used to give a more detailed and consistent analysis of constituents.
For example, the noun phrase:
the mayor of Casterbridge
can be shown as:
N – mayor
N' (called **N-bar**) – mayor of Casterbridge
N" (called **N-double-bar**) – the mayor of Casterbridge
In a diagrammatic representation it would be:

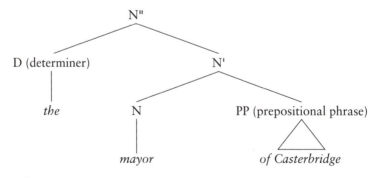

see also X-BAR THEORY

basal *adj*
when a course to teach reading has a number of graded parts, the first or most basic part is called the **basal reading programme**, and uses basic reading textbooks called **basal readers**.

base component *n*

see GENERATIVE THEORY

base form *n*

another term for ROOT or STEM[1].
For example, the English word *helpful* has the base form *help*.

baseline data *n*

in research, data to which other data can be compared.
For example, when examining the performance of non native speakers on a particular task, it is often important to have baseline data from native speakers for comparison, not simply to assume that native speakers would perform perfectly according to the researcher's idea of what is correct or normal. Such data would come from a **baseline study**.

Basic English *n*

a simplified type of English developed by C. K. Ogden and I. A. Richards in 1929. It was intended to be used as a second language for international communication. Basic English used only 850 words and fewer grammatical rules than normal English, but it was claimed that anything that could be said in ordinary English can also be said in Basic English.

see also LINGUA FRANCA

basic interpersonal communication skills *n*

also **BICS**

the type of language proficiency needed to perform tasks such as interpersonal and social communication rather than academic language tasks.

see also COGNITIVE ACADEMIC LANGUAGE PROFICIENCY

basic research *n*

see APPLIED RESEARCH

basic skills *n*

(in education) skills which are considered to be an essential basis for further learning and for learning other school subjects. Reading, writing and arithmetic are often considered the basic skills in mother tongue education.

basic vocabulary *n*

also **core vocabulary**

In language teaching, a set of words based on frequency of usage as well as other criteria, which are considered to provide the basis for everyday communication.

Estimates of the size of a basic vocabulary for language learners range from 800 to 4000 words.

basic writing *n*

a subfield of composition studies in the US that deals with the teaching of writing to students at college or university level who have not mastered the genre of academic writing. Basic writing courses are often directed to assist students who have been traditionally excluded from higher education, such as urban immigrant and refugee adults in college and pre-college settings.

basilect *n*

see POST-CREOLE CONTINUUM, SPEECH CONTINUUM

battery of tests *n*

also **test battery**

a group of tests that are given together to a test taker or group of test takers.

behavioural objective *n*

also **performance objective, instructional objective**

(in developing a CURRICULUM) a statement of what a learner is expected to know or be able to do after completing all or part of an educational programme. A behavioural objective has three characteristics:

a it clearly describes the goals of learning in terms of observable behaviour

b it describes the conditions under which the behaviour will be expected to occur

c it states an acceptable standard of performance (the criterion).

For example one of the behavioural objectives for a conversation course might be:

"Given an oral request, the learner will say his/her name, address and telephone number to a native speaker of English and spell his/her name, street, city, so that an interviewer can write down the data with 100 per cent accuracy."

"Given an oral request" and "to a native speaker" describe the conditions, and "with 100 per cent accuracy" describes the criterion, in this objective.

see also OBJECTIVE

behaviourism *n*

a theory of psychology which states that human and animal behaviour can and should be studied only in terms of physical processes, without reference to mind. It led to theories of learning which explained how an external event (a **stimulus**) caused a change in the behaviour of an individual (a **response**), based on a history of reinforcement. Behaviourism was used by

psychologists like Skinner, Osgood, and Staats to explain first language learning, but these explanations were rejected by adherents of GENERATIVE GRAMMAR and many others.
see also STIMULUS-RESPONSE THEORY, COGNITIVE PSYCHOLOGY

behaviourist psychology *n*
another term for BEHAVIOURISM

behaviourist theory *n*
another term for BEHAVIOURISM

belief systems *n*
in language teaching, ideas and theories that teachers and learners hold about themselves, teaching, language, learning and their students.
see TEACHER BELIEF SYSTEMS, LEARNER BELIEF SYSTEMS, LEARNER BELIEFS

benchmark *n*
a detailed description of a specific level of performance expected of a second learner in a particular area at a certain proficiency level in the language. The purpose of establishing the benchmark is to have a point of reference that can be used to compare the learner's performance at a later point in time.
Benchmarks are often defined by samples of L2 learner performance. For example, in L2 writing assessment, a benchmark L2 learner's paper is used in representing exemplary performance on a specific level of a SCORING RUBRIC.
see STANDARDS, STANDARDS MOVEMENT

benefactive case *n*
(in CASE GRAMMAR) the noun or noun phrase that refers to the person or animal who benefits, or is meant to benefit, from the action of the verb is in the benefactive case. For example, in the sentences:
Joan baked a cake for Louise.
Joan baked Louise a cake.
Louise is in the benefactive case.

best practice *n*
a term used particularly in the UK and Australia to describe an example of practice in a particular area that is regarded as exemplary and a standard against which others may be compared. It suggests thoughtful, principled behaviour informed by research or by a concern to maintain quality. E.g. "best practice in teacher education programmes", "Best practice in on-arrival programmes for immigrants".

beta (ß) error *n*
see TYPE II ERROR

betwccn-groups design *n*
another term for BETWEEN-SUBJECTS DESIGN

between-subjects design *n*
or **between-groups design**
an experimental design where each participant serves in only one experimental condition.

bias *n*
also **test bias**
a test or a single test item is biased if its scores are consistently too high or too low for an individual test taker or a group of test takers, which is a systematic error in the measurement process of the test. Test bias can be minimized through sensitivity review where reviewers review every test item to identify offensive language or biased content or through DIFFERENTIAL ITEM FUNCTIONING analysis.

BICS *n*
an abbreviation for BASIC INTERPERSONAL COMMUNICATION SKILLS

bicultural *adj* **biculturalism** *n*
a person who knows the social habits, beliefs, customs, etc. of two different social groups can be described as bicultural.
A distinction is made between biculturalism and BILINGUALISM. For example, a person may be able to speak two languages, but may not know how to act according to the social patterns of the second or foreign language community. This person can be described as bilingual, but not as bicultural.

bidialectal *adj* **bidialectalism** *n*
a person who knows and can use two different DIALECTS can be described as bidialectal. The two dialects are often a prestige dialect, which may be used at school or at work and is often the STANDARD VARIETY, and a non-**prestige** dialect, which may be used only at home or with friends.
see also BILINGUAL, BILINGUAL EDUCATION, DIGLOSSIA

bidialectal education *n*
see BILINGUAL EDUCATION

Big Books *n*

in teaching reading, an enlarged reading text used in early literacy programmes. The enlarged format allows children to be able to see the print while it is being pointed to and read by the teacher so that they can begin to make the association between oral and written language and note the process of reading right to left across the page. Typically they contain short stories of high interest to learners, rhyme patterns that children can notice and learn, extensive large pictures, and have repetitive phrases and controlled vocabulary.

bilabial *adj*

a sound articulated by bringing together the upper and lower lips, for example English /m/, /p/ and /b/ in the words *my, pet, bird.*
see PLACE OF ARTICULATION

bilingual *adj*

a person who uses at least two languages with some degree of proficiency. In everyday use bilingual usually means a person who speaks, reads or understands two languages equally well (a **balanced bilingual**), but a bilingual person usually has a better knowledge of one language than another.
For example, he/she may:
a be able to read and write in only one language
b use one language in different types of situation or DOMAINS, e.g. one language at home and another at work
c use one language for talking about school life and the other for talking about personal feelings
The ability to read and write a second or foreign language does not necessarily imply a degree of bilingualism.
see also COMPOUND BILINGUALISM, DIGLOSSIA, MULTILINGUALISM

bilingual dictionary *n*

a dictionary in which definitions are given in full or in part in another language.

bilingual education *n*

the use of a second or foreign language in school for the teaching of content subjects. Bilingual education programmes may be of different types and include:
a the use of a single school language which is not the child's home language. This is sometimes called an IMMERSION PROGRAMME.
b the use of the child's home language when the child enters school but later a gradual change to the use of the school language for teaching some

subjects and the home language for teaching others. This is sometimes called **maintenance bilingual education.**

   c the partial or total use of the child's home language when the child enters school, and a later change to the use of the school language only. This is sometimes called **transitional bilingual education** or **early exit bilingual education.**

When the school language is a STANDARD DIALECT and the child's home language a different dialect (e.g. Hawaiian Creole, Black English) this is sometimes called **bidialectal or biloquial education.**

see also BILINGUALISM, ADDITIVE BILINGUAL EDUCATION

bilingualism *n*

the use of at least two languages either by an individual (see BILINGUAL) or by a group of speakers, such as the inhabitants of a particular region or nation. The use of two languages by an individual is known as *individual bilingualism,* and the knowledge of two languages by members of a whole community or the presence of two languages within a society is called *societal bilingualism.* When two languages or language varieties occur in a society, each having very different communicative functions in different social domains it is known as *diglossia.*

see also COMPOUND BILINGUALISM, MULTILINGUALISM

biliterate *adj*

see LITERACY

bimodal distribution *n*

see MODE

bi-modal input *n*

see SUBTITLES

binary feature *n*

a property of a phoneme or a word which can be used to describe the phoneme or word.

A binary feature is either present or absent.

For example, in English a /t/ sounds different from a /d/ because a /d/ is pronounced with the vocal cords vibrating (is voiced), and a /t/ is pronounced with the vocal cords not vibrating (is voiceless). VOICE is therefore one of the features which describe /d/ and /t/. This is usually shown like this:

/d/ [+voice] (= voice present)

/t/ [–voice] (= voice absent)

binary opposition

When a binary feature can be used to distinguish between two phonemes, like voice with /d/ and /t/, the phonemes are in **binary opposition** (see also DISTINCTIVE FEATURE).
Binary features are also used to describe the semantic properties of words (see also SEMANTIC FEATURES).

binary opposition *n*
    see BINARY FEATURE

binding principle *n*
    (in Government/Binding Theory) a principle which states whether or not expressions in a sentence refer to someone or something outside their clause or sentence or whether they are "bound" within it.
    For example, in:
        Ann hurt herself.
    Ann is a REFERRING EXPRESSION referring to someone in the real world and *herself* is an ANAPHOR referring to *Ann*. It is said to be "bound" to *Ann*.
    In the sentence:
        Ann hurt her.
    the *her* is a pronominal (see PRONOUN) which refers to another person in the real world who may or may not have been mentioned in a previous sentence or utterance. It is not "bound" to *Ann*.
    In second language research, investigations have been made into the Binding Principle in languages other than English, e.g. Korean, and how this may affect the acquisition of English.
    see also BOUNDING THEORY

binding theory *n*
    part of the GOVERNMENT/BINDING THEORY. It examines connections between noun phrases in sentences and explores the way they relate and refer to each other (see BINDING PRINCIPLE)

biolinguistics *n*
    a branch of linguistics that studies language in relation to the biological characteristics of humans, particularly features of anatomy and physiology.

bioprogram hypothesis *n*
    the hypothesis that children are born with inborn abilities to make basic semantic distinctions that lead to particular types of grammar. According to the bioprogram hypothesis, some creole languages show the underlying structures of the bioprogram, as do some of the early features used by children when they acquire their first language.

56

bi-polar adjective *n*
  see SEMANTIC DIFFERENTIAL

biscriptualism *n*
  competence in reading and writing two scripts of the same language such as
  the ability of a speaker of standard Chinese to be able to read romanized
  Chinese as well as Chinese written in Chinese characters.

biserial correlation (r$_b$) *n*
  see CORRELATION

bi-uniqueness *n*
  see NATURAL MORPHOLOGY

Blackboard *n*
  see LEARNING MANAGEMENT SYSTEM

black box model *n*
  a term derived from physics and used to refer to a system that can be
  represented in terms of observable inputs to the system and observable
  outputs from it, although precisely what the system is and how it works
  cannot be observed. The system is thus contained in a "black box".
  Language learning is sometimes described as a black box problem because
  although we can observe the language which learners hear and see and the
  sentences they produce, we cannot observe what goes on inside the black
  box, i.e. how they actually learn language.

Black English (BE) *n*
  another term for AFRICAN AMERICAN ENGLISH

Black English Vernacular (BEV) *n*
  another term for AFRICAN AMERICAN ENGLISH

blank slate *n*
  see INITIAL STATE

bleeding order *n*
  in PHONOLOGY, when rules are ordered so that the application of one
  rule destroys the input of another rule, this is called a bleeding order. For
  example, in French there is a rule that nasalizes a vowel before a nasal-
  consonant and another rule that deletes a syllable final nasal consonant,
  producing words like [bõ] from underlying /bon/. If the nasal deletion rule
  were applied before the vowel nasalization rule, this would destroy the

blend

input to the second rule and [bō] could not be derived. Bleeding order is contrasted with a **feeding order**, in which the output from one rule becomes the input to another. For example, English has both a plural formation rule that produce consonant clusters in words like *tests* and *dogs*, and consonant cluster simplification rules that apply somewhat differently in different varieties. If a speaker pronounces a word such as *tests* as if it were "tess", this suggests that plural formation has applied first and has fed (created the environment for) the consonant simplification rule. However, if a speaker pronounces *tests* as if it were "tesses", this suggests that consonant cluster simplification applied first and fed (created the environment for) the plural formation rule.

blend *n*
    another term for PORTMANTEAU WORD
    see also BLENDING.

blended learning *n*
    the provision of learning opportunities though a combination of several different forms of learning, typically through a combination of technology-based resources and conventional teacher or book-based learning. Parts of a foreign language course might be provided through a textbook, for example, and the rest delivered online.

blending *n*
    also **portmanteau word**
    in MORPHOLOGY, a relatively unproductive process of WORD FORMATION by which new words are formed from the beginning (usually the first phoneme or syllable) of one word and the ending (often the RHYME) of another. Examples of **blends** formed this way are English *smog* (formed from *smoke* and *fog*), *vog* (*volcano* and *fog*), *brunch* (*breakfast* and *lunch*), and *Singlish*, *Taglish*, and *Japlish* from *Singapore English*, *Tagalog English*, and *Japanese English*, respectively.
    Blending is usually not considered part of I-LANGUAGE.

blocking *n*
    in MORPHOLOGY, a process that blocks the application of an unproductive word formation rule, if it would produce a word with the same semantics as an already existing word. For example, the English suffixes –ness (productive) and –ity (unproductive) are very similar (compare *curious/curiosity* and *furious/furiousness*). Since words such as *graciousness* and *gloriousness* exist, new words *graciocity* and *gloriocity* cannot be created.
    see also ACCIDENTAL GAP

blog *n*

also **web blog**

an electronic journal kept by a **blogger,** who regularly updates the journal (known as **blogging**). Blogs normally function either as personal diaries or as news journals, and typically contain a title, a text, and links. The language used is generally informal. Although blogs are usually kept and maintained by a single individual they can also serve to facilitate interaction between the writer and reader. Blogs are used in many ways including for personal use, in business and in education. They also have potential in second and foreign language learning, encouraging both reading and writing, promoting discussion and providing feedback.

Bloom's taxonomy *n*

a taxonomy of OBJECTIVES for the cognitive domain (see DOMAIN) developed by the American educationalist, B. S. Bloom, and widely referred to in education and educational planning. Bloom's taxonomy consists of 6 levels, ranging from **knowledge** (which focuses on reproduction of facts) to **evaluation** (which represents higher level thinking). The six levels in Bloom's taxonomy are:

Level	*Characteristic Student Behaviours*
Knowledge	Remembering, memorizing, recognizing, recalling
Comprehension	Interpreting, translating from one medium to another, describing in one's own words
Application	Problem-solving, applying information to produce some result
Analysis	Subdividing something to show how it is put together, finding the underlying structure of a communication, identifying motives
Synthesis	Creating a unique, original product that may be in verbal form or may be a physical object
Evaluation	Making value decisions about issues, resolving controversies or differences of opinion

body *n*

(in composition) those sections of an ESSAY which come between the introduction and the conclusion and which support and develop the THESIS STATEMENT.

body language *n*

the use of facial expressions, body movements, etc. to communicate meaning from one person to another.

In linguistics, this type of meaning is studied in PARALINGUISTICS.

see also PROXEMICS

book flood *n*

an approach to the development of reading skills particularly in settings where English is a SECOND LANGUAGE, in which students are exposed to a large number (i.e. a "flood") of high-interest reading materials, i.e. a type of EXTENSIVE READING programme.

book report *n*

in teaching, a student's oral or written account of a book he or she has read, used to stimulate careful reading of a book and thoughtful discussion of it.

borrowing *n* **borrow** *v*

a word or phrase which has been taken from one language and used in another language.

For example, English has taken *coup d'état* (the sudden seizure of government power) from French, *al fresco* (in the open air) from Italian and *moccasin* (a type of shoe) from an American Indian language.

When a borrowing is a single word, it is called a **loan word**.

Sometimes, speakers try to pronounce borrowings as they are pronounced in the original language. However, if a borrowed word or phrase is widely used, most speakers will pronounce it according to the sound system of their own language.

For example, French /garaʒ/ *garage* has become in British English /ˈgærɑːʒ/ or /ˈgærɪdʒ/, though American English keeps something like the French pronunciation.

borrowing transfer *n*

see SUBSTRATUM TRANSFER

bottom-up processing *n*

see TOP-DOWN PROCESSING, INTERACTIVE PROCESSING, COMPREHENSION

boundaries *n*

divisions between linguistic units. There are different types of boundaries.
For example, boundaries may be
a between words, e.g. *the##child*
b between the parts of a word such as STEM[1] and AFFIX, e.g. *kind#ness*
c between SYLLABLES, e.g. /beɪ + bi/ *baby*
see also JUNCTURE

boundary effect *n*

the effect of a test being too easy or too difficult for a particular group of test takers, resulting in their scores tending to be clustered toward or at either end or boundary of the test score distribution. A boundary effect that results from a test being easy so that their scores are clustered toward or at the top of the distribution is called a **ceiling effect**, whereas a boundary effect that results from a test being too difficult so that their scores are clustered toward or at the bottom of the distribution is called a **floor effect**.

bound form *n*

also **bound morpheme**

a linguistic form (a MORPHEME) which is never used alone but must be used with another morpheme, e.g. as an AFFIX or COMBINING FORM. For example, the English suffix -*ing* must be used with a verb stem, e.g. *writing, loving, driving*.

A form which can be used on its own is called a free form, e.g. *Betty, horse, red, write, love, drive*.

bounding node *n*

see BOUNDING THEORY

bounding theory *n*

in GOVERNMENT/BINDING THEORY, a theory that is concerned with how far a constituent can move within a sentence. The main principle of bounding theory is the **subjacency** condition, which forbids movement across more than one **bounding node**. Bounding nodes in English include S, NP, and CP. For example, the sentence * *Who did you hear the rumour that Mary kissed?* is ungrammatical, because it is derived from the structure in (a) which would require moving who over two bounding nodes, NP and CP.

(a) Who did you hear [NP the rumour [CP that Mary kissed t]]

In (a) the NP stands for Noun Phrase; the CP stands for Complement Phrase, and the t stands for "trace" and shows the place from which the wh-word was extracted.

bound morpheme *n*

another term for BOUND FORM

b-parameter *n*

see ITEM RESPONSE THEORY

brainstorming *n* **brainstorm** *v*

1 (in language teaching) a group activity in which learners have a free and relatively unstructured discussion on an assigned topic as a way of

generating ideas. Brainstorming often serves as preparation for another activity.

2 (in teaching writing) a form of prewriting (see COMPOSING PROCESSES) in which a student or group of students write down as many thoughts as possible on a topic without paying attention to organization, sentence structure or spelling. Brainstorming serves to gather ideas, viewpoints, or ideas related to a writing topic and is said to help the writer produce ideas.

Other writing activities sometimes included under brainstorming are:

clustering: the student writes a topic or concept in the middle of a page and gathers ideas into clusters around the topic.

word bank: the student lists words that come to mind about a topic and then arranges them into categories.

mapping: the student prepares a graphic representation of key words to be used in a composition.

branching *n*

(in COMPUTER ASSISTED LEARNING) moving from one place to another within a lesson, usually on the basis of how well a student has performed on a task. The process of deciding which of several alternative paths through lesson material is best suited to the student using the programme, based on previous performance, is known as **selective branching**.

branching direction *n*

the tendency for relative clauses to follow a particular order in relation to the noun they modify. In some languages, such as English, relative clauses usually precede the noun they modify. For example:

The cheese <u>that the rat ate</u> was rotten.

English is thus said to favour a **right branching direction**. Japanese, however, primarily makes use of a **left branching direction**, because the modifying clause typically appears to the left of the head noun. For example:

Nezumi ga tabeta chizu wa kusatte ita.

rat   ate   cheese   rotten   was

In second language learning the difficulty of learning relative clauses may be influenced by whether the learner's first language and the TARGET LANGUAGE have the same branching direction.

branching programme *n*

see PROGRAMMED LEARNING

breath group *n*

a stretch of speech which is uttered during one period of breathing out.

see also SPEECH RHYTHM

bridge course *n*

in teaching ENGLISH FOR ACADEMIC PURPOSES, this is an academic content course (e.g. in history or economics) taught specially for students of limited English proficiency. A bridge course aims to help the students make the transition from a language course to regular academic courses in their field of study. Bridge courses may be taught by a second language teacher who is familiar with the content area, or by a content teacher with some familiarity in second language teaching. Bridge courses differ from SHELTERED COURSES in that they usually follow closely a language-based course for second language learners, and because they do not usually correspond directly to a content course in the same area for native speakers.

British National Corpus *n*

a very large collection of samples of written and spoken language, designed to represent a wide cross-section of current British English.

broad notation *n*

see TRANSCRIPTION

broad transcription *n*

see TRANSCRIPTION

Broca's area *n*

an area in the left frontal lobe of the brain that is associated primarily with motor control of speech production.

Brown Corpus *n*

a pioneering corpus compiled in the 1960s, totaling about a million words drawn from a wide variety of sources representing current American English.

burnout *n*

see TEACHER BURNOUT

business English *n*

a branch of English for Special Purposes or EAP that focuses on the language skills needed to function in a business setting. These skills include presentation skills and other skills needed in sales, marketing, management and other positions beyond the entry level in a business.

buzz groups *n*

(in teaching) a group activity in which groups of students have a brief discussion (for example, five minutes) to generate ideas or answer specific questions. Buzz groups may be used as preparation for a lecture, or as an activity during a lecture.

by-phrase *n*

in SYNTAX, an optional constituent of a passive sentence headed by *by* and containing the logical subject, for example in the sentence *The law was passed by the legislature in 1999, the legislature* is the logical subject or agent, though not the surface subject. Some languages (Arabic, for example) do not permit passive by-phrases. Some prepositional phrases headed by *by* are not by-phrases in this sense, for example *by the river* in *John went for a walk by the river.*

C

CA *n*

an abbreviation for CONTRASTIVE ANALYSIS. Also an abbreviation for CONVERSATION ANALYSIS

CACD *n*

an abbreviation for **computer-assisted classroom discussion**

CAH *n*

an abbreviation for the **contrastive analysis hypothesis**

CAI *n*

an abbreviation for COMPUTER-ASSISTED INSTRUCTION

CAL *n*

an abbreviation for COMPUTER-ASSISTED LEARNING

CAL *n*

also an abbreviation for the Center for Applied Linguistics, located in Washington, DC.

CALICO *n*

an abbreviation for **Computer Assisted Language Instruction Consortium**

CALL *n*

an abbreviation for COMPUTER-ASSISTED LANGUAGE LEARNING

CALP *n*

an abbreviation for COGNITIVE ACADEMIC LANGUAGE PROFICIENCY.

calque *n*

see LOAN TRANSLATION

call-word *n*

see DRILL

Cambridge Exams

a set of examinations developed by Cambridge ESOL (also known as UCLES) which place students according to 5 levels of proficiency from basic (1) to advanced (5):

1 Key English Test (KET)(1)
2 Preliminary English Test (PET)
3 First Certificate in English (FCE)
4 Certificate of Advanced English (CAE)
5 Certificate of Proficiency in English (CPE).

candidate *n*
another term for TEST TAKER

can-do statements *n*
an approach to describing learning outcomes associated with the COMMON
EUROPEAN FRAMEWORK, which describes the learner's performance or some
aspect of it in terms of what the learner is able to do. For example:
*The learner can express simple opinions on familiar topics in a familiar
context.*
The "can-do" statements of learning outcomes are linked to different levels
on a proficiency band or scale.

canonical *n*
typical or usual. For example, the canonical word order of English is SVO
(subject-verb-object), although other orders are possible.

canonical form *n*
the form of a linguistic item which is usually shown as the standard form.
For example, the plural morpheme in English is usually shown as -*s*, even
though it may appear as -*s*, -*es*, -*en*, etc., -*s* is the canonical form.

canonical order *n*
also **canonical word order**
the basic order of the constituents subject (S), object (O) and verb (V) in a
particular language. For example, the canonical order of English is SVO,
while in Japanese the canonical order is SOV.

captioned video *n*
see SUBTITLES

captioning *n*
see SUBTITLES

cardinal vowel *n*
any of the VOWELS in the cardinal vowel system. The cardinal vowel system
was invented by Daniel Jones as a means of describing the vowels in any

language. The cardinal vowels themselves do not belong to any particular language, but are possible vowels to be used as reference points.

The cardinal vowel [i] is made with the front of the tongue as high as possible in the mouth without touching the roof of the mouth. It is a **front vowel**. By gradually lowering the tongue, three more front vowels were established: [e], [ɛ] and [a]. The difference in tongue position for [i] and [e], for [e] and [ɛ] and for [ɛ] and [a] is approximately equal and the difference in sound between each vowel and the next one is also similar. All these front vowels are made with fairly spread lips.

Cardinal vowel [ɑ] is made with the back of the tongue as low as possible in the mouth. It is a **back vowel**. By gradually raising the back of the tongue from the [ɑ] position, three other cardinal vowels were established: [ɔ], [o] and [u]. These three are made with the lips gradually more rounded.

These eight vowels are known as the **primary cardinal vowels**. The five vowels: [i], [e], [ɛ], [a] and [ɑ] are **unrounded vowels** and [ɔ], [o] and [u] are **rounded vowels**.

With the tongue in these eight positions, a secondary series of cardinal vowels was established. Where the primary cardinal vowels are unrounded, the **secondary cardinal vowels** are rounded. Where the primary cardinal vowels are rounded, the secondary cardinal vowels are unrounded.

primary	unrounded i e ɛ a ɑ	rounded ɔ o u
secondary	rounded y ɸ œ Œ ɒ	unrounded ʌ ɣ ɯ

The primary cardinal vowels	The secondary cardinal vowels

caretaker speech *n*

also **motherese, mother talk, baby talk**

the simple speech used by mothers, fathers, babysitters, etc., when they talk to young children who are learning to talk.

Caretaker speech usually has:

a shorter utterances than speech to other adults

h grammatically simple utterances

c few abstract or difficult words, with a lot of repetition

d clearer pronunciation, sometimes with exaggerated INTONATION patterns

Caretaker speech is easier for children to understand, and many people believe that it helps children to learn language.

see also FOREIGNER TALK

carrel *n*

in a LANGUAGE LABORATORY or multimedia centre, an installation containing individual recording decks and headphones, or a computer, video and TV monitor for student use. Carrels may be arranged in rows or other layouts. In a language laboratory, a carrel is also known as an **audio booth**.

cascade model *n*

an approach to teacher training and curriculum innovation in which one group receives training in the innovation (e.g. a new teaching method) and goes on to train other groups, who continue the process. In this way the innovation is said to "cascade" downwards. This model of dissemination allows new ideas and practices to reach large numbers of teachers relatively quickly.

see MULTIPLIER EFFECT

case[1] *n*

(in some languages) a grammatical category that shows the function of the noun or noun phrase in a sentence. The form of the noun or noun phrase changes (by INFLECTION) to show the different functions or cases. For example, German has four cases, NOMINATIVE, ACCUSATIVE, DATIVE, GENITIVE. Endings on the article change to show the case (the function) of the noun, e.g.:

Nominative case (table is the subject of the sentence)

Der Tisch ist gross.

The table is big.

Accusative case (table is the object of the sentence)

Karin kaufte den Tisch.

Karin bought the table.

Some languages, e.g. Russian, have more than four cases, others have fewer, and some have none at all. In these languages the functions shown by case marking may be shown by WORD ORDER or by PREPOSITIONS.

English marks case only on pronouns. Three cases are recognized:
Nominative: I, we, you, he, she, it, they, who
Objective: me, us, you, him, her, it, them, who(m)
Genitive: my, our, your, his, her, its, their, whose.

case²

see CASE GRAMMAR

case assigner *n*

(in CASE THEORY) an element that assigns a particular function, a case (see CASE¹), to a noun phrase in a sentence. Case assigners are often verbs or prepositions.

case grammar *n*

an approach to grammar developed in the 1970s which stresses the semantic relationships in a sentence. Parts of case grammar have been incorporated into more recent versions of GENERATIVE GRAMMAR.
see also AGENTIVE CASE, BENEFACTIVE CASE, DATIVE CASE², FACTITIVE CASE, INSTRUMENTAL CASE, LOCATIVE CASE, OBJECTIVE CASE

case methods *n*

in language teaching and teacher education, the use of cases as a form of pedagogy. A case consists of a report of (usually successful) practice prepared by a practitioner. It attempts to explore what experienced practitioners in a particular field (law, business, industry, teaching) know and do and presents an account of "craft knowledge" as compared to the "theoretical know-ledge" that is often the focus of traditional academic courses. Case methods are often used in the preparation of professionals in law and business and are also thought to be useful in teaching and teacher education. In teacher education, students may study and react to accounts of how teachers developed courses, conducted classes, and responded to particular teaching issues and problems. In business English courses, case accounts presenting the circumstances of a particular company, office, or individual, may form the basis of a variety of language development activities. Case methods should not be confused with a CASE STUDY.

case study *n*

the intensive study of an aspect of behaviour, either at one period in time or over a long period of time, e.g. the language development of a child over one year. The case study method provides an opportunity to collect detailed information that may not be observable using other research techniques (compare CROSS-SECTION(AL) METHOD), and may or may not be based on the assumption that the information gathered on a particular individual, group, community, etc., will also be true of the other individuals, groups or communities.

case theory *n*

this theory, which is part of Chomsky's UNIVERSAL GRAMMAR, stipulates that each noun phrase in a sentence is assigned a case which shows its function in the sentence.
These cases (see CASE[1]) may be shown by morphological endings; for example, in:
Monica's dress
Monica is in the GENITIVE CASE. She is the possessor of the dress. But in many instances the case of a noun phrase is an abstract concept which is not evident in the surface sentence. For example, in:
You should ask Paul.
Paul is in the ACCUSATIVE CASE because he is the OBJECT of *asked* but this fact is not shown by any ending. However, it becomes obvious when a pronoun is used instead of *Paul*:
You should ask him. (object pronoun)
not **You* should *ask he.*
see also θ – THEORY/THETA THEORY

CASLA *n*

an abbreviation for computer application in second language acquisition

casual speech *n*, **casual style** *n*

see COLLOQUIAL SPEECH

CAT *n*

an abbreviation for COMPUTER ADAPTIVE TESTING
an abbreviation for COMPUTER ASSISTED TRANSLATION

cataphora *n* **cataphoric** *adj*

the use of a word or phrase which refers forward to another word or phrase which will be used later in the text or conversation is called cataphora.
For example, in the sentence:
When I met her, Mary looked ill.
the word *her* refers forward to *Mary*.
Examples of cataphoric sentences are:
My reasons are as follows: One, I don't . . .
Here is the news. The Prime Minister . . .
see also ANAPHORA

categorial grammar *n*
see MONTAGUE GRAMMAR

categorical perception *n*
the ability of humans to focus on distinctive acoustic features of speech and to ignore irrelevant differences such as differences between two speakers. Categorical perception develops very early in FIRST LANGUAGE ACQUISITION as children become sensitive to differences between phonemic categories of the language they are hearing and less sensitive to differences within those categories. In SECOND LANGUAGE ACQUISITION, establishing categorical perception in accordance with the phonemic categories of the target language is much slower, and in some cases it appears not to happen at all.

categorical scale *n*
see SCALE

categorize *v* **categorization** *n*
to put items into **groups** (**categories**) according to their nature or use. For example:
a nouns may be categorized into ANIMATE and inanimate nouns.
b verbs may be categorized into TRANSITIVE and intransitive verbs.

category *n*
see GRAMMATICAL CATEGORY[2]

category symbol *n*
see GRAMMATICAL CATEGORY[2]

category system *n*
an observation system used to code, classify or analyze different classroom behaviours. Many different category systems have been used for observing and describing language classes, including COLT (the Communicative Orientation of Language Teaching), and FOCUS (Foci on Communication Used in Settings). These systems attempt to provide a set of categories which can be used to describe objectively different dimensions of classroom behaviour, such as the purpose of a communicative event, the media used for communicating content, the manner in which the media are used, and the areas of content that are communicated. Other approaches allow researchers to develop separate category systems for different research sites and research questions.
see also INTERACTION ANALYSIS, HIGH INFERENCE CATEGORY

catenation *n* **catenate** *v*

the linking of sounds together in speech, such as the grouping of phonemes into SYLLABLES, and the grouping of syllables and words through ASSIMILATION[1], ELISION, and JUNCTURE. Languages differ in the way they combine sounds. Two languages may share many sounds, but combine them in different ways. Spanish learners of English for example may pronounce *steak* as /esteɪk/, because although Spanish has the combination /-st/ after a stressed vowel it does not have it before one.

causative verb *n*

a class of transitive verbs that show that someone or something makes something happen. There are several types of causative verbs and constructions:

a One set consists of the verb *cause* itself and synonyms such as *bring about, lead to, result in,* or *give rise to.*

b In English, there are also some constructions that give causative meaning to a small number of verbs (*let, have, make*) that do not always have causative meaning outside the construction, for example in the sentence *She let* (or *had* or *made*) *him paint the house.*

c some verbs can be used both transitively with causative meaning and intransitively with inchoative meaning, for example *break* (compare *He broke the vase* and *The vase broke*), *grow* (compare *She is growing vegetables in the garden* and *The vegetables are growing rapidly*), and *melt* (compare *Climate change is melting the world's glaciers* and *The glaciers are melting*).

see also INCHOATIVE VERB, ERGATIVE VERB

cause-effect method *n*

see METHODS OF DEVELOPMENT

CBI *n*

an abbreviation for CONTENT-BASED INSTRUCTION

CBT *n*

an abbreviation for COMPUTER-BASED TEST(ING)

c-command *n*

in SYNTAX, a relationship between NODES of a tree in which neither node is dominated by the other but both are dominated by the same higher nodes, similar to the idea of siblings and all their descendants in a family tree.

CCR *n*

see CLASSROOM-CENTRED RESEARCH

CEELT *n*
>an abbreviation for **Cambridge Examination in English for Language Teachers**

CEIBT *n*
>an abbreviation for **Certificate in English for International Business and Trade**

ceiling effect *n*
>see BOUNDARY EFFECT

CELIA *n*
>an abbreviation for COMPUTER-ENHANCED LANGUAGE INSTRUCTION ARCHIVE

CELT *n*
>an abbreviation for **continuing education for language teachers**
>see PRESERVICE EDUCATION

CELTA *n*
>an abbreviation for **Certificate in English Language Teaching to Adults**, an introductory qualification for people who have little or no language teaching experience.

CELTYL *n*
>an abbreviation for **Certificate in English Language Teaching to Young Learners**

central executive *n*
>see WORKING MEMORY

central nervous system *n*
>the part of the nervous system which consists of the brain and the spinal cord.

central tendency *n*
>(in statistics) any estimate of the central point around which scores tend to cluster. The most common measures of central tendency are the MEAN, the MEDIAN, and the MODE.

central vowel *n*
>see VOWEL

cerebral dominance *n*

also **lateralization**

the development of control over different functions in different parts of the brain. As the brain develops, it is thought that different bodily functions (e.g. speech, hearing, sensations, actions) are gradually brought under the control of different areas of the brain. Those parts of the brain which control language are usually in the left hemisphere. One area in the left hemisphere is known as **Broca's area**, or the speech centre, because it is an important area involved in speech. Another area called **Wernicke's area** is thought to be involved in understanding language. Damage to these areas of the brain leads to different types of APHASIA. Whether or not there is a relationship between lateralization and a CRITICAL PERIOD for language acquisition has been much debated.

certification *n*

a designation awarded by a professional society to assure that a person is qualified to perform a job or task. Certification seeks to apply professional standards in training programmes, to increase the quality of practice, and to provide a form of accountability. In language teaching there is no international governing body for the certification of language teachers and certification, if it exists at all, is normally done through the state teacher education system. Some private organizations however such as Cambridge University and Trinity College in the UK offer initial and advanced teacher training qualifications such as the CELTA and DELTA programmes as an attempt to provide recognized qualifications for English language teachers.

certified interpreter *n*

see INTERPRETER

certified translator *n*

see TRANSLATOR

change agent *n*

a person who acts as a link between different participants involved in change in a system. For example if a new curriculum was being implemented in a school, the teacher is a link between the curriculum planners and the learners, and is therefore a change agent.

change from above *n*

in historical linguistics and sociolinguistics, language change that reflects mostly conscious social factors, such as the importation of a French-like pronunciation of /r/ into German in emulation of French prestige norms, or the conscious adoption of features of African American Vernacular English that have covert prestige. This may be contrasted with **change from below**, which does not reflect prestige norms or rules but is more likely the product of unconscious, long-term language drift. An example is the recent vowel shift in several varieties of American English in which low tense vowels rise and other vowels move into the vacated space. Change from above has been compared to MONITORING in second language learning and use.

change from below *n*
see CHANGE FROM ABOVE

channel *n*
1 (in SOCIOLINGUISTICS) the way in which a MESSAGE is conveyed from one person to another.
The two most common channels of communication are speech and writing. Other examples are the use of drum beats, smoke signals, or flags.
2 (in INFORMATION THEORY) the path along which information is sent. In telephone communication, for example, the message is changed into electrical signals by the telephone and the channel of communication is the telephone wire.

charged words *n*
also **loaded words**
words which have a degree of CONNOTATION (i.e. which carry either positive or negative as opposed to neutral meaning). For example:

charged word	neutral word
crazy	eccentric
jock	athlete
fag	homosexual

checklist *n*
in assessing or measuring behaviour, the use of a list of skills or behaviours that an observer checks off while observing someone doing something, such as while observing a student-teacher teach a lesson.

child centred *adj*
in teaching or curriculum development, approaches in which teaching and learning are organized around the child's needs, interests, learning styles, etc.
see LEARNER-CENTRED

child directed speech *n*
another term for CARETAKER SPEECH

CHILDES *n*

a database of longitudinal language acquisition data maintained at Carnegie Mellon University.

child language *n*

the type of language spoken by young children who are still learning their mother tongue.

Child language is different from adult language in many ways. For example:

a different sentence structures, e.g. *Why not you coming?* instead of *Why aren't you coming?*

b different word forms, e.g. *goed* instead of *went*, *mouses* instead of *mice*. Differences like these show that children have their own set of rules, and do not learn language by simply imitating adults.

see also FIRST LANGUAGE ACQUISITION

chi-square *n*

also **chi-squared, χ^2**

(in statistics) a procedure used to determine whether the relationship between two or more different variables is independent. For example, if we wanted to find out if there is a relationship between ability to write and belonging to a particular social or economic group, a chi-square(d) test could be used. It measures whether a particular distribution of observed values is sufficiently different from an expected distribution to indicate that it cannot be explained as a chance occurrence.

see also CONTINGENCY TABLE

choral practice *n*

also **choral repetition, chorus repetition**

in teaching, practice by a whole group or class of students, such as when a group of students reads aloud from a passage or repeats a dialogue. Choral practice is sometimes used as a preparation for individual practice or to develop fluency.

chronological order *n*

(in composition) a paragraph in which the information is arranged according to a sequence in time. For example:

First . . . after that . . . later . . .

see also SPATIAL ORDER

chunk *n*

a unit of language that forms a syntactic or semantic unit but also has internal structure, for example:

1 a unit of text that is longer than a sentence and shorter than a paragraph
2 a unit of language longer than a word but shorter than a sentence and which plays a role in comprehension and production.
see FORMULAIC LANGUAGE
also known as LEXICAL PHRASE, ROUTINE, GAMBIT

chunk analysis *n*
   see CHUNKING

chunk building *n*
   see CHUNKING

chunking *n*
   a term used in several different ways:
   1 referring to the process of combining smaller, frequently co-occurring units (e.g. morphemes, words, etc.) into larger ones (see CHUNK) that can be stored or processed together as a unit. For example, utterances such as:
   in the final analysis
   I told you so
   Y'know what your problem is?
   can each be produced word by word according to productive rules of grammar, but if a speaker (or writer) uses some of them repeatedly, they are likely to be stored in memory as chunks. This process can also be called **chunk building** or **fusion**.
   see also ADAPTIVE CONTROL OF THOUGHT
   2 referring to the processes of dividing larger units into smaller parts. For example, a long text can be broken into chunks that a learner works on separately. This process can also be called **chunk analysis**.
   3 referring to the process of organizing linguistic materials into **hierarchical chunks** as an aid to memory. For example, a telephone number such as 8089569238 would be difficult to remember as an undifferentiated string. However, if it is broken into chunks such as 808 (area code) + 956 (exchange) + 9238 (number), it is much easier to remember. Telephone companies around the world differ in the ways in which they chunk these numbers, but each of them has a system that does this in some fashion.

CI *n*
   an abbreviation for CONFIDENCE INTERVAL

citation form *n*
   the form a word has when it is cited or pronounced in isolation, which may be different from the form it has when it occurs in context. For example, the

word *the* is usually pronounced with a tense vowel in its citation form, while it has a lax vowel when it is followed in context by a word beginning with a consonant.

clarification request *n*

in conversation, a request by a listener for clarification of a previous utterance by a speaker. For example:
Could you say that again?
Did you say. . . . ?

class *n* classify *v*

(in linguistics) a group of linguistic items which have something in common. For example, in all languages words can be grouped (classified) into WORD CLASSES according to how they combine with other words to form phrases and sentences, how they change their form, etc. So *horse*, *child*, *tree* belong to the English word class noun, and *beautiful*, *noisy*, *hard* belong to the English word class adjective.
see also FORM CLASS, OPEN CLASS, TAXONOMIC

classical test theory *n*

also **true score model**
a test theory that assumes that a test taker's **observed score**, a score that this person actually received on a test, has two additive components as follows:

X =	T	+	E
Observed Score	True Score		Error Score

where **true score** is defined as a hypothetical score of a test taker's true ability, which is thought of as the average of the scores a test taker would be expected to obtain if this person took the same test an infinite number of times. According to this theory, the true score remains constant and any non-systematic variation in the observed score is due to the error score.
see also ITEM RESPONSE THEORY

classification methods *n*

see METHODS OF DEVELOPMENT

classifier[1] *n*

a word or affix used with a noun, which shows the sub-class to which the noun belongs.
For example, in Malay *ekor* "tail" is a classifier for animals and is used with numerals:
lima ekor lembu "five oxen"
five   ox

Some languages such as Malay, Chinese, and various African languages have an extensive system of classifiers. In English, a few classifiers are still used, e.g. *head of* in:
five head of cattle
In languages such as Swahili, the affix classifying a noun is also added to its MODIFIERS, PREDICATE, etc.

classifier² n
(in SYSTEMIC LINGUISTICS) a word in a NOUN PHRASE which shows the sub-class to which a person or thing belongs.
For example, nouns and adjectives can function as classifiers:

classifier	noun classified
electric	*trains*
steam	*trains*

see also MODIFIER, HEAD

classroom-based evaluation/classroom based assessment n
the collection of information about learners, teachers, and teaching in the classroom in a normal school learning situation to assess the quality of teaching and learning. Classroom-based evaluation is often an approach to FORMATIVE EVALUATION.

classroom-centred research n
also **CCR, classroom-process research, language classroom research**
second language orientated research carried out in formal instructional settings (rather than in naturalistic, untutored settings), especially in relation to the effects of classroom practices of teachers and students on learners' achievement, performance in class and attitudes. Classroom-centred research has focused on such things as the linguistic features of classroom language (see CLASSROOM DISCOURSE), observation of the structure of oral communication between teachers and learners, error treatment, communication strategies, turn-taking patterns, code-switching, and other factors that are believed to influence second language acquisition. Classroom-centred research uses both quantitative and qualitative methods, including research techniques derived from INTERACTION ANALYSIS and ETHNOGRAPHY, as well as quasi-experimental methods of comparison examining the effects of specific teaching methods and experimental studies of the effects of aspects of interaction and processing that are associated with classroom instructional processes.

classroom discourse n
the type of language used in classroom situations. Classroom discourse is often different in form and function from language used in other situations

because of the particular social roles students and teachers have in classrooms and the kinds of activities they usually carry out there. For example, teachers tend to rely on a discourse structure with the following pattern:

initiation – response – evaluation

In this typical three-part structure, the teacher initiates a question in order to check a student's knowledge, a student responds, and the student's response is evaluated with FEEDBACK from the teacher.

The restricted kind of discourse students encounter in classrooms is thought to influence their rate of language development.

see also QUESTIONING TECHNIQUES

classroom dynamics *n*

the patterns of interaction among members of a class, as seen in the verbal and non-verbal communication among class members and the communication networks that are established. Positive interaction among students leads to group cohesiveness within a class, providing a more receptive environment for teaching and learning.

see GROUP DYNAMICS

classroom ethos *n*

also **classroom climate** *n*

the affective dimensions of a classroom such as the atmosphere and feelings of the classroom that can promote or detract from effective classroom teaching and learning.

see CLIMATE

classroom interaction *n*

the patterns of verbal and non-verbal communication and the types of social relationships which occur within classrooms. The study of classroom interaction may be a part of studies of classroom DISCOURSE, TEACHER TALK, and SECOND LANGUAGE ACQUISITION.

see also INTERACTION ANALYSIS

classroom language *n*

see CLASSROOM DISCOURSE

classroom layout *n*

the arrangement of desks and other items of furniture in a classroom. In language teaching, classroom layout is believed to have an influence on both teaching and learning and has an influence on the teacher's ACTION ZONE. Typical layouts include the horseshoe (desks in a three-sided square), chairs in a circle, traditional rows, or nested tables in groups.

classroom management *n*

(in language teaching) the ways in which student behaviour, movement, interaction, etc., during a class is organized and controlled by the teacher (or sometimes by the learners themselves) to enable teaching to take place most effectively. Classroom management includes procedures for grouping students for different types of classroom activities, use of LESSON PLANS, handling of equipment, aids, etc., and the direction and management of student behaviour and activity.

classroom observation scheme *n*

in CLASSROOM RESEARCH, an observational form (often in the form of a grid) that consists of a set of categories that can be used to record and describe teaching and learning behaviours in the classroom such as the frequency of question types and interactional moves.

classroom-process research *n*

see CLASSROOM-CENTRED RESEARCH

classroom research *n*

research that seeks to obtain information or explore hypotheses about the nature of teaching and learning in classrooms. It includes a variety of different research techniques which have in common: a question, problem, or hypothesis, collection of data, and analysis and interpretation of data. Such research may be quantitative or qualitative and may be conducted by the teacher, a researcher, or the teacher in some form of collaboration with others.

see also ACTION RESEARCH, OBSERVATION

clause *n*

a group of words which form a grammatical unit and which contain a subject and a FINITE VERB. A clause forms a sentence or part of a sentence and often functions as a noun, adjective, or adverb.

For example:

I hurried home.

Because I was late, they went without me.

Clauses are classified as **dependent or independent**, e.g.:

I hurried	because I was late.
independent	dependent
clause	clause

A clause is different from a **phrase**.

A phrase is a group of words which form a grammatical unit. A phrase does not contain a finite verb and does not have a subject-predicate structure:

For example:

> I liked _her expensive new car_.
> George hates _working in the garden_.

Phrases are usually classified according to their central word or HEAD, e.g. NOUN PHRASE[1], VERB PHRASE, etc.

see also DEPENDENT CLAUSE, RELATIVE CLAUSE

cleft sentence *n*

a sentence which has been divided into two parts, each with its own verb, to emphasize a particular piece of information. Cleft sentences usually begin with *It* plus a form of the verb *be*, followed by the element which is being emphasized.

For example, the sentence *Mrs Smith gave Mary a dress* can be turned into the following cleft sentences:

> _It was Mrs Smith_ who gave Mary a dress.
> _It was Mary_ that Mrs Smith gave the dress to.
> _It was a dress_ that Mrs Smith gave to Mary.

In English a sentence with a *wh-clause* (e.g. *what I want*) as subject or complement is known as a **pseudo-cleft sentence**. For example:

> A good holiday is what I need.
> What I need is a good holiday.

cliché *n*

a word or expression which has lost its originality or effectiveness because it has been used too often. For example:

> It's a crying shame.

click *n*

a stop made with an ingressive velaric airstream, found in a number of African languages.

CLIL *n*

an abbreviation for CONTENT AND LANGUAGE INTEGRATED LEARNING

climate *n*

(in teaching) the affective aspects of the classroom, such as the feelings generated by and about the teacher, the students or the subject matter, along with aspects of the classroom itself that contribute positively or negatively to the learning atmosphere. An effective teacher is said to create a suitable climate for learning by influencing students' attitudes and perceptions in a positive way. This may be achieved through:

1 establishing an atmosphere in which academic goals are emphasized
2 promoting high standards and monitoring and rewarding achievement
3 maintaining an orderly environment
4 building expectations for success.

clinical linguistics *n*

a branch of linguistics that involves the application of linguistic description and analysis to the field of SPEECH PATHOLOGY. Clinical linguists are concerned with various types of communicative impairment, including developmental speech and language disorders and AUTISM.

clinical supervision *n*

(in teacher education) an approach to teacher supervision which focuses upon the improvement of teaching by means of systematic observation of teaching performance and focused feedback by the supervisor. Clinical supervision involves:
1 a close face-to-face relationship between a teacher and a supervisor
2 a focus on the teacher's actual behaviour in the classroom, with the goal of improving the teacher's skill as a teacher
3 a three-stage strategy consisting of:
   a a planning conference, in which the teacher discusses his or her goals, methodology, problems, etc., with the supervisor and they decide on what the supervisor should observe and what kind of information about the lesson he or she should collect
   b classroom observation, in which the supervisor observes the teacher in his or her classroom
   c feedback conference, in which the teacher and the supervisor review the data the supervisor has collected, discuss the effectiveness of the lesson, and decide on strategies for improvement, if necessary.

clipping *n*

the shortening of a word by dropping or "clipping" one or more syllables. E.g. *doc* – doctor, *lab* – laboratory, *math* – mathematics.

clitic *n*

a grammatical form which cannot stand on its own in an utterance. It needs to co-occur with another form which either precedes or follows it. Some languages have clitic pronoun forms which are attached to the verb. In English, *n't* the contracted form of *not* in *couldn't*, *isn't*, and *don't* can be considered a clitic.

CLL *n*

an abbreviation for COMMUNITY LANGUAGE LEARNING

closed captioned films
see SUBTITLES

closed-captions *n*
see SUBTITLES

closed-choice questions *n*
also **closed question**
see QUESTION

closed class *n*
see OPEN CLASS

closed-ended response *n*
see TEST ITEM

close description *n*
also **thick description**
in qualitative research, detailed description that seeks to describe an event, situation or phenomenon with as much information as possible.

closed pairs *n*
in pair work, pairs of students working independently from other students in the class. This can be compared with **open pairs,** in which a pair of students carry out an activity in front of others, as a way of modelling an activity or in order to focus on accuracy.

closed question
see QUESTION

closed set *n*
see OPEN CLASS

closed syllable *n*
see SYLLABLE

close vowel *n*
also **high vowel**
see VOWEL

closings *n*
strategies speakers use to bring a conversation to a close and which serve to indicate that neither speaker will initiate further turns or topics. Closings

are often achieved through an exchange of three or more **moves**, they are often preceded by **pre-closings**, such as *anyway, I have to go now*, or *Look at the time* and often involve standard formulaic expressions.
see also CONVERSATIONAL OPENINGS

closure *n*

(in teaching) that part of the lesson which brings it to an end. An effective lesson closure is said to reinforce the key teaching points of the lesson and help students transfer learning to the next lesson.
see also ENTRY

clozentropy *n*

a method of scoring cloze tests, based on the acceptable word method. A cloze test is first given to a group of native speakers, and their responses are listed in frequency order. When the test is given to non-native test takers, someone who responds with a high frequency word scores more than someone who responds with a low frequency word.
see also CLOZE TEST

cloze passage *n*

see CLOZE TEST

cloze test *n*

a technique for measuring reading comprehension as well as overall language proficiency. In a cloze test, words are deleted from a reading passage at regular intervals, leaving blanks. There are two widely used ways to create the blanks. The first is known as **rational deletion**, where words are deleted on the basis of some rational decision (e.g. PARTS OF SPEECH), which results in **rational cloze**. For example, prepositions may be deleted to assess test takers' knowledge of English prepositions. The second is known as **fixed ratio deletion** or **nth word deletion**, where every nth word is deleted. For example, every fifth word may be deleted. The test taker must then read the passage and try to guess the missing words.
For example, a **cloze passage** looks like this:
A passage used in _____ cloze test is a _____ of written material in _____ words have been regularly _____. The subjects must then _____ to reconstruct the passage _____ filling in the missing _____.

Here, the test taker has to guess *a, passage, which, removed, try, by, words*. The cloze procedure can also be used to judge the difficulty of reading materials (i.e. READABILITY).
If the cloze procedure is being used for language testing, the test taker is given a score according to how well the words guessed matched the original

cluster

words, or whether or not they made sense. Two types of scoring procedure are used:

a the test taker must guess the exact word that was used in the original passage (as in the above example). This is called the **exact word method**.

b the test taker can guess any word that is appropriate or acceptable in the context. This is called the **acceptable word method** (also the **appropriate word method**, the **acceptable alternative method**, and the **contextually appropriate method**).

cluster *n*
see CONSONANT CLUSTER

clustering *n*
see BRAINSTORMING

cluster reduction *n*
see CONSONANT CLUSTER REDUCTION

CMC *n*
an abbreviation for COMPUTER-MEDIATED COMMUNICATION

CMS *n*
see LEARNING MANAGEMENT SYSTEM

coaching *n*
an approach to teacher development in which teachers work together in mutual, collaborative professional development. Unlike **mentoring**, with coaching the relationship is usually reciprocal. Both teachers are working to improve their teaching and involved in on-going peer observation.

coarticulation *n*
in PHONETICS, the overlapping of adjacent articulations.
In PHONOLOGY, the spreading of phonetic features to neighbouring segments.
see ASSIMILATION

cocktail party phenomenon *n*
the ability that humans have in social gatherings to listen selectively to speech coming from one source (for example, a conversation some distance away) while ignoring other sources (for example, the speech of other guests, even those who are closer). REDUNDANCY in conversation helps make this possible, but the phenomenon is a specific example of the more general

human ability to pay ATTENTION selectively to some stimuli while ignoring others.

see also DICHOTIC LISTENING

coda *n*

see SYLLABLE

codability *n*

the degree to which an aspect of experience can be described by the vocabulary of a language.

Languages differ in the degree to which they provide words for the description or naming of particular things, events, experiences, and states. For example, English makes a distinction between *blue* and *green* whereas some languages have a single word for this colour range.

code¹ *n*

a term which is used instead of LANGUAGE, SPEECH VARIETY, or DIALECT. It is sometimes considered to be a more neutral term than the others. People also use "code" when they want to stress the uses of a language or language variety in a particular community. For example, a Puerto Rican in New York City may have two codes: English and Spanish. He or she may use one code (English) at work and the other code (Spanish) at home or when talking to neighbours.

see also CODE SELECTION, CODE SWITCHING

code² *n*

a term used by the British educational sociologist Bernstein for different ways of conveying meaning in a social context. Bernstein distinguished between **elaborated code** and **restricted code**. The restricted code is said to have a more reduced vocabulary range, to use more question tags, to use PRONOUNS like *he* and *she* instead of nouns and to use gestures such as hand movements to help give meaning to what is said. It is claimed that speakers using a restricted code assume that their addressees share a great many of their attitudes and expectations.

On the other hand, persons using an elaborated code are said to make greater use of adjectives, more complicated sentence structures and the pronoun *I*. The elaborated code is claimed to be more explicit and speakers using it do not assume the same degree of shared attitudes and expectations on the part of the addressee. It has been claimed that while middle-class children have access to both codes, working-class children have access only to the restricted code.

There has been a great deal of controversy over Bernstein's codes as they have been linked to theories which relate language learning to social class and educational policies.

see also DEFICIT HYPOTHESIS

code³ *n*

any system of signals which can be used for sending a MESSAGE. A natural language is an example of a code, as are Morse code, braille, and SIGN LANGUAGE.
The medium through which the signals are sent (e.g. by telephone, in writing) is called the CHANNEL (b).

code mixing *n*

a mixing of two codes (see CODE¹) or languages, usually without a change of topic. This is quite common in bilingual or multilingual communities and is often a mark of solidarity, e.g. between bilingual friends or colleagues in an informal situation. Code mixing can involve various levels of language, e.g. phonology, morphology, grammatical structures or lexical items.
Bilingual or multilingual speakers, for example, may think that one of their languages, e.g. English, has more appropriate lexical items for something they want to express in a particular situation and they incorporate these into the grammatical structure of the other language, in this case Mandarin Chinese:

A: Zuótiān de party zěnmeyàng?
  Yesterday's party how
  How was yesterday's party?
B: Bié tí party bù party le!
  Don't mention party no party no longer
  Don't talk to me about the party!

Sometimes a type of code mixing even acquires a special name, e.g. *Ugewa* (the mixing of English and Cantonese by Hong Kong university students).

see also CODE SELECTION, CODE SWITCHING

code selection *n*

the selection of a particular language or language variety for a given situation. If someone uses more than one code when communicating with others, they usually select one code for certain purposes (in certain places and with certain people) and use another code for other purposes (in other places and with other people). This code selection is often quite regular and its patterns can be investigated.

For example, an older Chinese person in Singapore may use Hokkien (a Southern Chinese dialect) at home, Singapore English at work, and Bazaar Malay to Indian or Malay stallholders at the market. The code a person selects may often depend on the ethnic background, sex, age, and level of education of the speaker and of the person with whom he/she is speaking.
see also CODE SWITCHING, DIGLOSS, DOMAIN[1]

code switching *n*
a change by a speaker (or writer) from one language or language variety to another one. Code switching can take place in a conversation when one speaker uses one language and the other speaker answers in a different language. A person may start speaking one language and then change to another one in the middle of their speech, or sometimes even in the middle of a sentence. For example, from the speech of a German immigrant in Australia:
Das handelt von einem secondhand dealer and his son.
"That is about a . . ."
Code switching can be a sign of cultural solidarity or distance or serve as an act of identity.
see also CODE SELECTION

coding *n*
a research technique in which data that have been collected are turned into classes or categories (i.e. **codes**) for the purpose of counting or tabulation. For example in conducting a NEEDS ANALYSIS, students' responses to questions on a questionnaire may be classified into different classes or codes, or when coding classroom data into such categories as initiation, response or evaluation.
see also IRE

coefficient alpha *n*
another term for CRONBACH'S ALPHA

coefficient of correlation *n*
see CORRELATION COEFFICIENT

coefficient of determination *n*
also r^2
a measure of the amount of variability shared or predicted by two VARIABLES[2]. It is equal to the square of r (*r* = coefficient of CORRELATION). For example, a correlation coefficient of +.70 indicates that 49% of the variability is

shared by the two variables, i.e. 51% of the variability is not shared or predicted by the variables.

cognate *n, adj*

a word in one language which is similar in form and meaning to a word in another language because both languages are related. For example English *brother* and German *Bruder*.

Sometimes words in two languages are similar in form and meaning but are BORROWINGS and not cognate forms.

For example, *kampuni* in the African language Swahili is a borrowing from English *company*.

see also FALSE COGNATE

cognition *n* cognitive *adj*

the various mental processes used in thinking, remembering, perceiving, recognizing, classifying, etc.

see also COGNITIVE PSYCHOLOGY

cognitive academic language proficiency *n*

also CALP

a hypothesis proposed by Cummins which describes the special kind of second language proficiency which students need in order to perform school learning tasks. Cummins suggests that many classroom tasks are cognitively demanding and often have to be solved independently by the learner without support from the context. The ability to carry out such tasks in a second language is known as CALP. Cummins contrasts this kind of language proficiency with **Basic Interpersonal Communication Skills (BICS)**. This refers to the language proficiency needed to perform other kinds of tasks which are not directly related to learning academic content, such as interpersonal communication. Interpersonal and social communication is relatively undemanding cognitively and relies on context to clarify meaning. According to Cummins, different kinds of tests are needed to measure CALP and BICS, and a learner's skill in BICS does not predict performance on CALP.

cognitive code approach *n*

an approach to second and foreign language teaching which was proposed in the 1960s and which is based on the belief that language learning is a process which involves active mental processes and not simply the forming of habits. It gives importance to the learner's active part in the process of using and learning language, particularly in the learning of grammatical rules. Although it has not led to any particular method of language teaching, the COMMUNICATIVE APPROACH makes some use of cognitive code principles.

cognitive demand of instruction *n*
also **cognitive load**
the cognitive demands of instruction in academic subject matter in formal schooling contexts. The cognitive difficulty of different subjects in the curriculum (e.g. math, science) will depend on various factors, such as the extent of student's prior knowledge, the cognitive complexity inherent in the instructional task, student interest in the topic, the effectiveness of the teacher and the materials, and the mode and pace of presentation.

cognitive development *n*
also **stage theory of development**
developmental changes in cognitive abilities, processes, and structures. The best known theory of childhood cognitive development is that of Piaget, who proposed that such development consists of four major stages, labeled: **sensorimotor stage** (birth to 2 years). The child's cognitive system is limited to motor reflexes at birth.
preoperational stage (2 to 6 or 7 years). Children acquire representational skills and especially language.
concrete operational stage (6/7 to 11/12). Children are able to understand concrete problems and take multiple perspectives into account.
formal operational stage (11/12 to adult). At this stage children are capable of logical, theoretical, and abstract cognitive operations.

cognitive domain *n*
see DOMAIN

cognitive grammar *n*
a theory that views language as consisting solely of conventional pairings of phonological and semantic units.
see also COGNITIVE LINGUISTICS, CONSTRUCTION GRAMMAR

cognitive linguistics *n*
an approach to LINGUISTICS which stresses the interaction between language and cognition, focusing on language as an instrument for organizing, processing, and conveying information. Issues addressed within cognitive linguistics include structural characteristics of language such as prototypicality (see PROTOTYPE), METAPHOR, and IMAGERY; functional principles of language organization such as **iconicity** (nonarbitrary relationships between meanings and expressions); the interface between SYNTAX and SEMANTICS; and the relationship between language and thought.
see also LINGUISTIC RELATIVITY

cognitive load *n*

the idea that the more a person has to learn or process in a short amount of time, the more difficult it is to process that information in WORKING MEMORY. For example, the cognitive load of studying a subject in a second language is much higher than studying the same subject in one's native language, because the brain must work to decode the language while simultaneously trying to understand the new information. In L2 reading, the cognitive load of a text is one factor that influences the difficulty of a text for the reader.

cognitive meaning *n*

another term for DENOTATION

cognitive overload *n*

also **information overload**

in language teaching, a situation when a learner has too much information to process in real time or in order to make a decision. For example if the language processing demands of an activity go beyond the processing limits of the learner, it may result in anxiety and stress as well as inability to carry out the activity.

cognitive process *n*

also COGNITIVE STRATEGIES

any mental process which learners make use of in language learning, such as INFERENCING, GENERALIZATION, DEDUCTIVE LEARNING, MONITORING, and MEMORIZING.

cognitive psychology *n*

a branch of psychology that deals with such processes as ATTENTION, PERCEPTION, COMPREHENSION, MEMORY, and LEARNING. In contrast with BEHAVIOURISM, cognitive psychology is concerned with mental processes and the representation of knowledge in the mind. Many cognitive psychologists work within an INFORMATION PROCESSING paradigm, which assumes that the mind is a symbol-processing system and that these symbols are transformed into other symbols when acted on by different processes, while others have adopted models proposed by CONNECTIONISM.

cognitive science *n*

a discipline which draws on research in LINGUISTICS, MATHEMATICS, neuroscience, philosophy, PSYCHOLINGUISTICS, COGNITIVE PSYCHOLOGY, ARTIFICIAL INTELLIGENCE and other fields. Cognitive science deals with the scientific study of thinking, reasoning and the intellectual processes of the mind; it is concerned with how knowledge is represented in the mind, how language is understood, how images are understood, and which mental processes underlie INFERENCING, learning, problem solving and planning.

cognitive strategies *n*
learning strategies that operate directly on incoming information in ways that enhance learning. Examples include **rehearsal** (repeating key words or phrases silently or aloud, organizing (e.g. summarizing what has been read or heard), using memory heuristics e.g. a KEYWORD or visual image), and INFERENCING.

cognitive style *n*
see LEARNING STYLE

cognitive theory *n*
a theory that describes phenomena in terms of mental constructs in the mind of individuals. Most contemporary theories of linguistics view language and grammar as properties of the human mind. Cognitive theories of second language learning include such concepts as HYPOTHESIS FORMATION, INTAKE, INTERLANGUAGE, and so on, all mental (cognitive) phenomena. Some other theories, including both BEHAVIOURISM and ETHNOMETHODOLGY, are **anti-cognitive**, insisting on behavioural explanations of phenomena and rejecting speculation about the mind.

cognitive variable *n*
variables associated with cognitive functioning that may affect learning, including language learning. These may include general intelligence, LANGUAGE APTITUDE, MEMORY, and the ability to analyze and evaluate. Cognitive variables are sometimes contrasted with **affective variables** that may also influence learning. Affective variables are more emotional in nature and include such factors as EMPATHY, LANGUAGE ATTITUDES, LANGUAGE ANXIETY, and MOTIVATION.

coherence *n* **coherent** *adj*
the relationships which link the meanings of UTTERANCES in a DISCOURSE or of the sentences in a text.
These links may be based on the speakers' shared knowledge. For example:
A: *Could you give me a lift home?*
B: *Sorry, I'm visiting my sister.*
There is no grammatical or lexical link between A's question and B's reply (see COHESION) but the exchange has coherence because both A and B know that B's sister lives in the opposite direction to A's home.

In written texts coherence refers to the way a text makes sense to the readers through the organization of its content, and the relevance and clarity of its concepts and ideas. Generally a PARAGRAPH has coherence if it is a series of sentences that develop a main idea (i.e. with a TOPIC SENTENCE and supporting sentences which relate to it).

see also SCHEME, TEXT LINGUISTICS, CONVERSATIONAL MAXIM

cohesion *n*

the grammatical and/or lexical relationships between the different elements of a text. This may be the relationship between different sentences or between different parts of a sentence. For example:

a A: *Is Jenny coming to the party?*
B: *Yes, she is.*
There is a link between *Jenny* and *she* and also between *is . . . coming* and *is.*

b In the sentence:
If you are going to London, I can give you the address of a good hotel there.
the link is between *London* and *there* (see ANAPHORA).

see also COHERENCE

cohort *n*

(in research) a group of people who have some feature in common, such as age, IQ, or number of months they have studied a foreign language.

collaborative assessment *n*

a type of assessment that arrives at a consensus collaboratively among different teachers teaching the same course regarding which common features to assess in a learner's response, product, or performance and how consistently to use assessment criteria for this purpose.

collaborative evaluation *n*

(in language programme evaluation) the assessment and evaluation of a curriculum or programme that is carried out jointly by classroom teachers, researchers, or other trained educational experts.

collaborative learning *n*

a general term for an approach to teaching and learning which makes use of learners working together in small groups. A form of collaborative learning which involves specific roles and responsibilities for group members and for the use of group-based activities is known as COOPERATIVE LEARNING.

collaborative research *n*

(in teacher development programmes) research that is carried out by a teacher in collaboration with others, such as another teacher or teachers, a school consultant, a university researcher, or between a teacher and learners. Collaborative research is an essential component of some models of ACTION RESEARCH.

collaborative teacher development *n*

forms of teacher development that involve systematic investigation of teaching and learning over time and which involve a teacher in a usually voluntary collaboration with others involved in the teaching process (e.g. mentors, researchers, teacher educators, other teachers, learners) and in which professional development is the prime purpose. Examples of collaborative teacher development are TEAM TEACHING, teacher study groups, and ACTION RESEARCH.

collective noun *n*

a noun which refers to a collection of people, animals, or things as a group. For example *school, family, government* are collective nouns. When collective nouns are used in the singular, they may be used with either a singular verb or a plural verb. For example:

The government is going to look into this matter.

The government are looking into this matter.

The use of the plural verb suggests that the noun refers to something which is seen as a group of individuals, whereas the use of the singular verb suggests something seen as a single whole.

see also NOUN

collocation *n* **collocate** *v*

the way in which words are used together regularly.

Collocation refers to the restrictions on how words can be used together, for example which prepositions are used with particular verbs, or which verbs and nouns are used together.

For example, in English the verb *perform* is used with *operation*, but not with *discussion*:

The doctor performed the operation.

* *The committee performed a discussion.* Instead we say:

The committee held/had a discussion.

perform is used with (collocates with) *operation*, and *hold* and *have* collocate with *discussion*.

high collocates with *probability*, but not with *chance*:

a high probability but *a good chance*

do collocates with *damage*, *duty*, and *wrong*, but not with *trouble*, *noise*, and *excuse*:

> *do a lot of damage, do one's duty, do wrong*
> *make trouble, make a lot of noise, make an excuse*

see also IDIOM

colloquialism *n*

a word or phrase that is more commonly used in informal speech and writing. For example *boss* is a colloquialism for *employer*.

see also COLLOQUIAL SPEECH

colloquial speech *n*

also CASUAL SPEECH, CASUAL STYLE, INFORMAL SPEECH

an informal type of speech used among friends and others in situations where empathy, rapport or lack of social barriers are important. Colloquial speech is often marked by the use of slang or idioms and by other linguistic characteristics such as deletion of subject or auxiliaries (e.g. as in "Got the time?" instead of "Do you have the time?"). Colloquial speech is not necessarily non-prestige speech and should not be considered as SUBSTANDARD. Educated native speakers of a language normally use colloquial speech in informal situations with friends, fellow workers, and members of the family.

see also STYLE

combining form *n*

a BOUND FORM that can form a new word by combining with another combining form, a word, or sometimes an AFFIX. For example, the combining form *astr(o)-*, 'star', can form the word *astrology* with the combining form *-(o)logy*, the word *astrophysics* with the word *physics*, and the word *astral* with the suffix *-al*. Groups of MORPHEMES like the *-blooded* of *warm-blooded* or the *-making* of *trouble-making* are also sometimes regarded as combining forms.

see also WORD FORMATION

comment *n*

see TOPIC[2]

comment clause *n*

a clause which comments on another clause in a sentence. For example:

> *She is, I believe, a New Zealander.*
> *Coming from you, that sounds surprising.*

Comment clauses function as ADJUNCTS or disjuncts, and are optional in the sentence structure.

commissive *n*
see SPEECH ACT CLASSIFICATION

common core *n*
(in language teaching) those basic aspects of a language (e.g. vocabulary and grammar) which a learner needs to know whatever his or her purpose is in learning the language. When designing a language SYLLABUS a teacher must decide how much of the language content of the course must be common core and how much must be directed to the learner's particular needs, e.g. for science or business.
see also ENGLISH FOR SPECIAL PURPOSES

Common European Framework (CEF) *n*
also **Common European Framework of References for Languages (CEFR)**
a guideline for describing levels of achievement in language learning for foreign languages across Europe, including English, developed by the European organization the Council of Europe. It describes six levels of achievement divided into three broad divisions, which describe what a learner should be able to do in reading, listening, speaking and writing at each level:

A	Basic User
A1	Breakthrough
A2	Waystage
B	Independent User
B1	Threshold
B2	Vantage
C	Proficient User
C1	Effective Operational Proficiency
C2	Mastery

The Common European Framework is intended to provide a common basis for describing communicative performance and to serve as a basis for developing language syllabuses, curriculum guidelines, examinations, and textbooks, regardless of the target language.

common noun *n*
see PROPER NOUN

communication *n* **communicate** *v*
the exchange of ideas, information, etc., between two or more persons. In an act of communication there is usually at least one speaker or **sender**, a

MESSAGE which is transmitted, and a person or persons for whom this message is intended (the **receiver**). Communication is studied from many disciplinary perspectives, is often viewed as a discipline in its own right, and is central to SOCIOLINGUISTICS, PSYCHOLINGUISTICS, and INFORMATION THEORY.

see also COMMUNICATIVE COMPETENCE, SPEECH EVENT

communication arts *n*

in a mainstream curriculum, those aspects of the curriculum that deal with verbal, non-verbal, and visual forms of communication, such as radio, TV, dance and drama.

communication disorder *n*

a disability or impairment that affects a person's ability to communicate, either verbally or non-verbally.

communication network *n*

the range of **persons** that members of a group communicate with. In any group (e.g. students in a class or members of a school staff), some members communicate more frequently with one another than with others, depending on their relationships, frequency of contact, etc. Communication networks may be studied as part of the study of BILINGUALISM and DIGLOSSIA as well as in studies of second language acquisition, since language learning and language use may depend upon both the frequency of use of a language as well as on whom one uses it to communicate with.

communication strategy *n*

a way used to express a meaning in a second or foreign language, by a learner who has a limited command of the language. In trying to communicate, a learner may have to make up for a lack of knowledge of grammar or vocabulary. For example the learner may not be able to say *It's against the law to park here* and so he/she may say *This place, cannot park*. For *handkerchief* a learner could say *a cloth for my nose*, and for *apartment complex* the learner could say *building*. The use of PARAPHRASE and other communication strategies (e.g. gesture and mime) characterize the INTER-LANGUAGE of some language learners.

see also ACCOMMODATION, FOREIGNER TALK

communication theory *n*

another term for INFORMATION THEORY

communicative approach *n*

also **communicative language teaching**

an APPROACH to foreign or second language teaching which emphasizes that the goal of language learning is COMMUNICATIVE COMPETENCE and which seeks to make meaningful communication and language use a focus of all classroom activities. The communicative approach was developed particularly by British applied linguists in the 1980s as a reaction away from grammar-based approaches such as SITUATIONAL LANGUAGE TEACHING and the AUDIOLINGUAL METHOD. The major principles of Communicative Language Teaching are:

1 learners use a language through using it to communicate
2 authentic and meaningful communication should be the goal of class-room activities
3 fluency and accuracy are both important goals in language learning
4 communication involves the integration of different language skills
5 learning is a process of creative construction and involves trial and error

Communicative language teaching led to a re-examination of language teaching goals, syllabuses, materials, and classroom activities and has had a major impact on changes in language teaching world wide. Some of its principles have been incorporated into other communicative approaches, such as TASK-BASED LANGUAGE TEACHING, **cooperative language learning**, and CONTENT-BASED INSTRUCTION.

communicative competence *n*

knowledge of not only if something is formally possible in a language, but also whether it is feasible, appropriate, or done in a particular SPEECH COMMUNITY.

Communicative competence includes:

a **grammatical competence** (also **formal competence**), that is, knowledge of the grammar, vocabulary, phonology, and semantics of a language (also see COMPETENCE)

b **sociolinguistic competence** (also **sociocultural competence**), that is, knowledge of the relationship between language and its nonlinguistic context, knowing how to use and respond appropriately to different types of SPEECH ACTS, such as requests, apologies, thanks, and invitations, knowing which ADDRESS FORMS should be used with different persons one speaks to and in different situations, and so forth (see also APPROPRIATENESS, PRAGMATICS, ROLE RELATIONSHIP)

c **discourse competence** (sometimes considered part of sociolinguistic competence), that is, knowing how to begin and end conversations (see also SPEECH EVENTS, COHESION, COHERENCE)

d **strategic competence**, that is, knowledge of COMMUNICATION STRATEGIES that can compensate for weakness in other areas.

communicative drill *n*
see MEANINGFUL DRILL

communicative function *n*
the extent to which a language is used in a community. Some languages may be used for very specific purposes, such as the language called *Pali*, which is used only for religious purposes in Buddhism. Other languages are used for almost all the communicative needs of a community, e.g. Japanese in Japan.

communicative interference *n*
interference (see LANGUAGE TRANSFER) which is caused by the use of rules of speaking (e.g. greetings, ways of opening or closing conversations, address systems – see ADDRESS FORM) from one language when speaking another. For example, conversations in English often open with a health question (*How are you?*) but in other languages, such as Malay, open with a food question (*Have you eaten yet?*). A Malay-speaking student learning English who opened a conversation in English with *Have you eaten yet?* would be speaking with communicative interference from Malay to English.

communicative language teaching *n*
another term for COMMUNICATIVE APPROACH

community language *n*
also **heritage language**
a language used within a particular community, including languages spoken by ethnic minority groups.
For example, in Australia, apart from English, languages such as Italian, Greek, Polish, Arabic, and Australian Aboriginal languages are community languages.

Community Language Learning *n*
also **CLL**
a METHOD of second and foreign language teaching developed by Charles Curran. Community Language Learning is an application of **counselling learning** to second and foreign language teaching and learning. It uses techniques developed in group counselling to help people with psychological and emotional problems. The method makes use of group learning in small or large groups. These groups are the "community". The method places emphasis on the learners' personal feelings and their reactions to language learning. Learners say things which they want to talk about, in their native language. The teacher (known as "Counselor") translates the learner's sentences into the foreign language, and the learner then repeats this to other members of the group.

community literacy *n*

Reading skills associated with non-school-related reading, such as those required to participate in neighbourhood or community activities and the reading of signs, advertisements and documents.

community of practice *n*

A term used to refer to a group of individuals (e.g. language teachers in a school) participating in communal activities that involve collaboration to achieve shared goals. Central to the concept of community of practice is the idea of learning through social participation, particularly in an organizational setting. Through such participation participants negotiate roles and identities, share knowledge, and find solutions to problems. The concept identifies a social grouping by reference to shared practice rather than abstract characteristics such as class, gender, or language, and provides a context for the study of language use and language learning. In sociolinguistics and linguistic anthropology it is often preferred over the older concept of a SPEECH COMMUNITY.

comparative *n*

also **comparative degree**

the form of an adjective or adverb which is used to show comparison between two things. In English, the comparative is formed with the suffix *-er*, or with *more*:

$$\text{This is} \begin{cases} \textit{better} \\ \textit{more useful} \end{cases} \textit{than that.}$$

The **superlative** is the form of an adjective or adverb which shows the most or the least in quality, quantity, or intensity. In English, the superlative is formed with the suffix *-est* or with *most*:

$$\text{She is} \begin{cases} \textit{the tallest} \\ \textit{the most beautiful} \end{cases} \textit{in the class.}$$

comparative clause *n*

also **comparative sentence**

a clause which contains a standard with which someone or something referred to in an INDEPENDENT CLAUSE is compared. In English, comparative clauses are often introduced with *than* or *as*:

Tom is much taller <u>than John is</u>.
Jane doesn't write <u>as neatly as Fiona does</u>.

comparative degree *n*

another term for COMPARATIVE

comparative historical linguistics *n*

also **comparative philology, philology, historical linguistics**

a branch of linguistics which studies language change and language relation-ships. By comparing earlier and later forms of a language and by comparing different languages, it has been possible to show that certain languages are related, e.g. the INDO-EUROPEAN LANGUAGE. It has also been possible to reconstruct forms which are believed to have occurred in a particular language before written records were available. For example *$*p$* in an ancestor language to all the Indo-European languages is said to be related to /p/ in Sanskrit as in *pita* "father" and /f/ in English as in *father*.

see also DIACHRONIC LINGUISTICS

comparative linguistics *n*

a branch of linguistics which studies two or more languages in order to compare their structures and to show whether they are similar or different. Comparative linguistics is used in the study of language types (see TYPOLOGY) and in COMPARATIVE HISTORICAL LINGUISTICS. It is also used by some applied linguists for establishing differences between the learner's native language and the TARGET LANGUAGE[1] in the areas of syntax, vocabulary, and sound systems.

see also CONTRASTIVE ANALYSIS

comparative philology *n*

another term for COMPARATIVE HISTORICAL LINGUISTICS

comparative relative clause *n*

also **object of comparative relative clause, OCOMP**

see NOUN PHRASE ACCESSIBILITY HIERARCHY

comparative sentence *n*

another term for COMPARATIVE CLAUSE

comparison and contrast method *n*

see METHODS OF DEVELOPMENT

compensatory instruction *n*

also **compensatory education**

a special education programme for children whose home background is said to lack certain kinds of language experience. For example, children who are not read to at home or who do not have story books at home.

see also CULTURAL DEPRIVATION

compensatory strategy *n*

A communication strategy in which a learner compensates for the fact that a task may be beyond his or her communicative ability; e.g., by avoiding saying something that he or she would find hard to express, or by restating something because the interlocutor is having difficulty understanding the speaker.

competence *n*

(in GENERATIVE GRAMMAR) the implicit system of rules that constitutes a person's knowledge of a language. This includes a person's ability to create and understand sentences, including sentences they have never heard before, knowledge of what are and what are not sentences of a particular language, and the ability to recognize ambiguous and deviant sentences. For example, a speaker of English would recognize *I want to go home* as an English sentence but would not accept a sentence such as *I want going home* even though all the words in it are English words. Competence often refers to an ideal speaker/hearer, that is an idealized but not a real person who would have a complete knowledge of the whole language. A distinction is made between competence and PERFORMANCE, which is the actual use of the language by individuals in speech and writing.

see also COMMUNICATIVE COMPETENCE, SELF DETERMINATION THEORY

competencies *n*

in COMPETENCY BASED TEACHING, descriptions of the essential skills, knowledge and behaviours required for the effective performance of a real world task or activity. Activities such as "A job Interview" or "Taking telephone messages" are regarded as collections of competencies or units of competency. For example the activity "Working on a factory floor" includes the following competencies:

follow instructions to carry out a simple task

respond appropriately to supervisor's comments

request supplies

state amount of work already completed

state problem and ask for help if necessary

Such written descriptions of what a student is able to do with the language, usually in terms of target language performance, are known as Competency Statements.

competency based teacher education *n*

an approach to teacher education which focuses on the skills and competencies which are thought to constitute effective teaching.

competency based teaching *n*

also **competency based education/instruction**

an approach to teaching that focuses on teaching the skills and behaviours needed to perform COMPETENCIES. Competencies refer to the student's ability to apply different kinds of basic skills in situations that are commonly encountered in everyday life. Competency Based Education is based on a set of outcomes that are derived from an analysis of tasks learners are typically required to perform in real-life situations. Competency Based Language Teaching is an application of the principles of CBE to language teaching and has been widely used for the development and teaching of work-related and survival-orientated language teaching programmes for adults. CBE is believed to improve the quality of teaching and learning because of its focus on learning outcomes.

complement *n* **complementation** *n*

(in grammar) that part of the sentence which follows the verb and which thus *completes* the sentence. The commonest complements are:

a subject complement: the complement linked to a subject by be or a linking verb:
She is a doctor.

b object complement: the complement linked to an object:
We made her the chairperson.

c adjective complement: the complement linked to an adjective:
I am glad that you can come.

d prepositional complement: the complement linked to a preposition:
They argued about what to do.

While ADJUNCTS are optional parts of sentences, complements are often obligatory parts of the sentences in which they occur. A clause which functions as a complement is called a **complement(ary) clause**. For example:
The question is why you did it.

In GENERATIVE GRAMMAR, the term complement has a broader meaning, referring to an expression that combines with a HEAD to become a larger constituent of essentially the same kind. For example, in *read a book*, *a book* is the complement of the verb *read*; in *at the end*, *the end* is the complement of the preposition *at*; in *bags of groceries*, *of groceries* is the complement of the noun *bags*. In English complements usually follow their heads.

see also PARAMETER

complementaries *n*

see ANTONYM

complement(ary) clause *n*
    see COMPLEMENT

complementizer *n*
    any of a set of clause-introducing words, such as *that* in *He thought that Gore had won*, *if* in *I wonder if this is the right road*, and *for* in *They are keen for you to come*.
    see also COMPLEMENT

complementizer deletion *n*
    the process of deleting a complementizer, for example, *I know you'll be happy* (from *I know that you'll be happy*).

complexity *n*
    a composite measure of language use, normally reflecting the length of utterances and the amount of subordination used. In studying a second language learner's discourse or interlanguage complexity is one measure of L2 development.

complex NP constraint *n*
    a condition on transformations in early generative syntax that stated that no element contained in an S dominated by an NP with a lexical head may be moved out of that NP. More recently, this has been reinterpreted as an example of SUBJACENCY.

complex sentence *n*
    a sentence which contains one or more DEPENDENT CLAUSES, in addition to its independent, or main, clause. For example:
    When it rained, we went inside.
    (dep cl)   (ind cl)
    A sentence which contains two or more independent clauses which are jointed by co-ordination is called a compound sentence. For example:
    He is a small boy but he is very strong
    (ind cl)   (ind cl)
    I'll either phone you or I will send you a note.
    (ind cl)   (ind cl)
    A sentence which contains only one PREDICATE is called a **simple sentence**. For example:
    I like milk.
    (pred)

complex transitive verb *n*
see TRANSITIVE VERB

componential analysis *n*

1 (in semantics) an approach to the study of meaning which analyzes a word into a set of meaning **components** or semantic features. For example, the meaning of the English word *boy* may be shown as:
<+human> <+male> <– adult>
Usually, componential analysis is applied to a group of related words which may differ from one another only by one or two components. This approach was developed in ANTHROPOLOGICAL LINGUISTICS for the study of kinship and other terms in various languages.

2 any approach to linguistics which analyses linguistic units, usually words or sounds, into smaller parts or components. This approach has been used in phonology and semantics.
see also DISTINCTIVE FEATURE, SEMANTIC FEATURES

components *n*
see COMPONENTIAL ANALYSIS

composing processes *n*

in composition and writing, the different stages employed by writers.
Three stages are often recognized in the writing process:

1 **rehearsing** (also known as **prewriting**): activities in which writers look for a topic or for ideas and language related to a topic before beginning writing.

2 **writing** (also known as **planning, drafting, composing**): activities in which writers note down ideas in rough form.

3 **revising** (also known as **editing, postwriting**): activities in which writers check, revise and rewrite what they have written.

These stages in writing do not necessarily occur in sequence but may recur throughout the composing process. A PROCESS APPROACH to the teaching of writing focuses on encouraging the development of these composing processes.

composition *n*

1 writing as an activity which is intended to increase a person's skills or effectiveness as writer.

2 the name for such an activity or subject in school.

3 a piece of written work produced to practise the skills and techniques of writing or to demonstrate a person's skill as a writer. In language teaching, two types of writing activities are sometimes distinguished:

   a free composition, in which the student's writing is not controlled or limited in any way, such as essay questions, or writing about a particular topic.

   b controlled composition, in which the student's writing is controlled by various means, such as by providing questions to be answered, sentences to be completed, or words or pictures to describe.

see also MODES OF WRITING, METHODS OF DEVELOPMENT

compositionality principle *n*
also **Frege's principle**

the principle that the meaning of a composite expression is built up from the meanings of its basic expressions.

compound adjective *n*
see COMPOUND WORD

compound bilingualism *n*

the theory that a bilingual person relates words to their meanings in one of two ways.

Compound bilingualism means that the bilingual has one system of word meanings, which is used for both the first and the second language. For a French/English bilingual, the French word *pain* ("bread") and the English word *bread* have the same meaning.

Co-ordinate bilingualism means that the bilingual has two systems of meanings for words; one system is for the words the person knows in the first language and the other is for the words he or she knows in the second language.

For a French/English bilingual the French word *pain* and the English word *bread* would not have exactly the same meanings. This theory was an attempt to show how the different conditions under which people become bilingual could lead to different systems of meaning. The distinction between compound and co-ordinate bilingualism has been used in studies of vocabulary learning, but has not been found useful as a general model of bilingualism.

compound noun *n*
see COMPOUND WORD

compound predicate *n*

a PREDICATE containing two or more verbs sharing a single SUBJECT. For example:

   Spring came and went too quickly.

compound sentence *n*
see COMPLEX SENTENCE

compound subject *n*
a subject which consists of two or more elements joined by *and* and normally taking a plural verb. For example:
Beer and wine do not mix.

compound word *n*
a combination of two or more words which functions as a single word. For example *self-made* (a **compound adjective**) as in *He was a self-made man* and *flower shop* (a **compound noun**) as in *They went to the flower shop.* Compound words are written either as a single word (e.g. *headache*), as hyphenated words (e.g. *self-government*), or as two words (e.g. *police station*).
see also PHRASAL VERB

comprehensible input¹ *n*
INPUT language which contains linguistic items that are slightly beyond the learner's present linguistic COMPETENCE
see also INPUT HYPOTHESIS

comprehensible input² *n*
spoken language that can be understood by the listener even though some structures and vocabulary may not be known. According to Krashen's theory of language acquisition, comprehensible input is a necessary condition for second language acquisition.

comprehensible output hypothesis *n*
another term for OUTPUT HYPOTHESIS

comprehension *n*
the identification of the intended meaning of written or spoken communication. Contemporary theories of comprehension emphasize that it is an active process drawing both on information contained in the message (BOTTOM-UP PROCESSING) as well as background knowledge, information from the context and from the listener's and speaker's purposes or intentions (TOP-DOWN PROCESSING).
see also LISTENING COMPREHENSION, READING COMPREHENSION

comprehension approach *n*
(in language teaching) an APPROACH to second and foreign language teaching which emphasizes that:

a before learners are taught speaking, there should be a period of training in listening comprehension

b comprehension should be taught by teaching learners to understand meaning in the TARGET LANGUAGE[1]

c the learners' level of comprehension should always exceed their ability to produce language

d productive language skills will emerge more naturally when learners have well developed comprehension skills

e such an approach reflects how children learn their first language.

Although this approach has not led to a specific METHOD of language teaching, similar principles are found in the TOTAL PHYSICAL RESPONSE METHOD and the NATURAL APPROACH (2).

computational linguistics *n*

the scientific study of language from a computational perspective. Computational linguists are interested in providing computational models of natural language processing (both production and comprehension) and various kinds of linguistic phenomena. The work of computational linguists is incorporated into such practical applications as speech recognition systems, SPEECH SYNTHESIS, automated voice response systems, web search engines, text editors, and language instruction materials.

computer adaptive test(ing) *n*

also **computerized adaptive test(ing)**

a test administered by computer in which the difficulty level of the next item to be presented to test takers is estimated on the basis of their responses to previous items and adapted to match their abilities.

see ADAPTIVE TESTING, ITEM RESPONSE THEORY

computer-administered test(ing) *n*

see COMPUTER-BASED TEST(ING)

computer aided translation *n*

see COMPUTER ASSISTED TRANSLATION

computer assisted conversation *n*

written discussion that takes place via computer networks.

computer assisted instruction *n*

also **CAI, computer assisted language learning (CALL), computer based instruction** the use of a computer in a teaching programme. This may include:

a a teaching programme which is presented by a computer in a sequence. The student responds on the computer, and the computer indicates whether the responses are correct or incorrect (see PROGRAMMED LEARNING).

b the use of computers to monitor student progress, to direct students into appropriate lessons, material, etc. This is also called **computer-managed instruction**.

see also INTERACTIVE

computer assisted language learning *n*
   also **CALL**
   the use of a computer in the teaching or learning of a second or foreign language. CALL may take the form of

a activities which parallel learning through other media but which use the facilities of the computer (e.g. using the computer to present a reading text)

b activities which are extensions or adaptations of print-based or classroom based activities (e.g. computer programs that teach writing skills by helping the student develop a topic and THESIS STATEMENT and by checking a composition for vocabulary, grammar, and topic development), and

c activities which are unique to CALL.

see also INTERACTIVE VIDEO

computer assisted learning (CAL) *n*
   also **computer assisted instruction (CAI), computer aided learning**
   the use of a computer in teaching and learning and in order to help achieve educational *objectives*. The first kinds of CAL programs which were developed reflected principles similar to programmed instruction (see PROGRAMMED LEARNING). The computer leads the student through a learning task step-by-step, asking questions to check comprehension.
   Depending on the student's response, the computer gives the student further practice or progresses to new material (see BRANCHING). In more recent CAL courseware students are able to interact with the computer and perform higher level tasks while exploring a subject or problem.
   see also INTERACTIVE VIDEO

computer-assisted test(ing) *n*
   see COMPUTER-BASED TEST(ING)

computer assisted translation *n*
   also **CAT, computer aided translation**

translation with the aid of a computer program, usually a database containing examples of previously translated sentences, phrases and other stretches of speech, which the translator can consult before accepting, rejecting, or modifying the translation. Computer assisted translation should not be confused with MACHINE TRANSLATION.

computer-based test(ing) *n*
also **computer-administered test(ing), computer-assisted test(ing)**
a test in which items are presented to test takers on a computer. COMPUTER ADAPTIVE TESTING is a special case of more general computer-based testing.

computer conferencing *n*
a form of computer-mediated communication. Computer conferencing programs rely on the filing and organizing powers of a host computer and boost up the participation and management of group discussions through an electronic network. The discussions can be in real time, in which case the discussants are logged on to a computer simultaneously, or they can be in non-real time. Computer conferencing has many applications in language teaching, such as its use as a forum for classroom discussions and as a means of introducing process writing to students.

Computer-Enhanced Language Instruction Archive *n*
also **CELIA**
a computer-assisted language learning software archive accessed via gopher and FTP.

computer language *n*
a system used to write computer programs, consisting of elements such as symbols, commands and functions which are combined according to specific rules to perform operations on specific types of data. Dozens of computer languages have been designed for different purposes. Computer "languages" have many interesting formal properties, but do not have the functional properties associated with natural languages.

computer literacy *n* **computer literate** *adj*
the ability to communicate and analyze information working online or using a computer in other ways.

computer-mediated communication *n*
also **CMC**
using one or more computers to facilitate communication between two or more people. INTERNET RELAY CHAT (IRC) is one popular form of this.

concept *n*

the general idea or meaning which is associated with a word or symbol in a person's mind. Concepts are the abstract meanings which words and other linguistic items represent. Linguists believe all languages can express the same concepts, although some languages may have fewer names for some concepts than are found in other languages, or may distinguish between concepts differently. The forming of concepts is closely related to language ACQUISITION, and the use of concepts to form PROPOSITIONS is basic to human thought and communication.

concept checking *n*

in teaching the meaning of a new item, a term that is sometimes used to refer to techniques for checking that students have understood its meaning. For example after presenting the difference between the past perfect and the perfect, the teacher may use questions or other techniques to see if students have identified the correct time reference of a sentence in the past perfect.

concept formation *n*

(in child development) the process of forming CONCEPTS, and an important part of the development of thought.

concept load *n*

see LEXICAL DENSITY

concept question *n*

in teaching, a question that is used to find out if a learner has understood a new item. The question is designed to check the key concepts of the item and normally requires a yes/no or short answer.

see CONCEPT CHECKING

conceptual framework *n*

also **theoretical framework**

in research, a THEORY or set of theories linked to particular research purposes that gives coherence to an empirical inquiry. For example, GEN-ERATIVE GRAMMAR constitutes a conceptual framework that is appropriate for certain kinds of research and is linked to preferred types of research methods.

conceptualization *n*

see CONSTRUAL

conceptual meaning *n*

another term for DENOTATION

conceptual metaphor *n*

see METAPHOR

concessive clause *n*

a dependent clause giving information which contrasts with information contained in an independent clause, and which is usually introduced by *although* or *while*. For example,

Although she is only 13, Tina is an excellent pianist.

conclusion *n*

see ESSAY

concord *n*

also **agreement**

a type of grammatical relationship between two or more elements in a sentence, in which both or all elements show a particular feature. For example, in English a third person singular subject occurs with a singular verb, and a plural subject occurs with a plural verb (**number concord**):

He walks They walk

Concord may affect CASE, GENDER, NUMBER, and PERSON.

see also GOVERNMENT

concordance *n* **concordancing** *v*

a list of all the words which are used in a particular text or in the works of a particular author, together with a list of the contexts in which each word occurs (usually not including highly frequent grammatical words such as articles and prepositions). Concordances have been used in the study of word frequencies, grammar, discourse and stylistics. In recent years the preparation of concordances by computers has been used to analyze individual texts, large samples of writing by a particular author, or different genres and registers. A collection of texts for such purposes is called a CORPUS. Computer concordances are now often used in the preparation of dictionaries, since they enable lexicographers to study how words are used in a wide range of contexts.

concordancer *n*

software that searches for words of phrases in a corpus and displays the selected item or items in a list together with their surrounding context. Concordancers enable the uses of words to be displayed together with contexts of use (see below) and are used in discourse analysis and other forms of language analysis. They are also sometimes used by teachers to provide students with examples of authentic language use. The following are examples of some contexts for the word *forecast* in a written corpus:

... calculations a second. The centre makes *forecasts* 10 days ahead for 18 national meteorological . . .

. . . any action whose success hinges on a *forecast* being right. They might end up doing a lot . . .

. . . stands up in the House of Commons to *forecast* Britain's economic performance for the next . . .

. . . labour of its people. This gloomy *forecast* can be better understood by looking closely . . .

. . . but three months earlier the secret *forecast* carried out by Treasury economists suggested . . .

concrete noun *n*

a noun which refers to a physical thing, rather than a quality, state, or action. For **example** *book*, *house*, and *machine* are concrete nouns. A noun which refers to a quality, state, or action is called an **abstract noun**. For example *happiness*, *idea*, and *punishment* are abstract nouns.

see also NOUN

concrete operational stage *n*

see COGNITIVE DEVELOPMENT

concurrent validity *n*

(in testing) a type of VALIDITY that is based on the extent to which a test correlates with some other test that is aimed at measuring the same skill, or with some other comparable measure of the skill being tested. For example, to determine the concurrent validity of a new L2 listening comprehension test, one could calculate the correlation between scores of a group of test takers on this test with their scores on an existing valid and reliable test of L2 listening comprehension at about the same time. The resulting CORRELATION COEFFICIENT would provide a measure of the concurrent validity of the test.

conditional *n*

a grammatical MOOD which describes an imaginary or hypothetical situation or event. In some languages it is expressed by adding an AFFIX to the verb, e.g. *je donnerais* ("I would give") in French, where *ais* is the conditional affix added to the verb infinitive *donner* ("to give"). In English, *should* and *would* are also sometimes described as the conditional in sentences such as:

We should like to meet her. I would go if I could.

conditional clause *n*

(in English) ADVERBIAL CLAUSES beginning with *if*, *unless* or conjunctions with similar meanings, where a state or situation in one clause is dependent on something that may or will happen, and which is described in another clause. For example:

If it rains, we will go home.
If you worked harder, you would succeed.
You won't be able to drive unless you have a licence.

conditional forms *n*

the different grammatical forms used in conditional clauses. Four kinds of conditionals are often referred to in language teaching:

First conditional: if + present simple tense + modal verb with future reference (e.g. *will/shall/may*): *If it rains we will stay home.*

Second conditional: if + simple past tense + modal verb with future-in-the-past reference (e.g. *would, could, might*): *I would buy a car if I could afford it.*

Third conditional: if + past perfect tense + modal verb with future-in-the-past reference (e.g. *would/could/might*) + have +*ed* participle: *If I had known you were sick I would have sent you flowers.*

conditioned response *n*

(in behaviourist psychology (see BEHAVIOURISM)) a response which is not a normal or automatic response to a STIMULUS but which has been learned through the formation of a chain of associations (see STIMULUS-RESPONSE THEORY). Behavioural psychologists believe that people are conditioned to learn many forms of behaviour, including language, through the process of training or **conditioning**, and that learning consists of stimulus-response connections.

conditioning *n*

see CONDITIONED RESPONSE

conference *n* **conferencing** *v*

in teaching, a semi-structured face-to-face conversation between a teacher and a student or a small group of students in which work being undertaken is discussed. For example in a writing class a student may present a collection of his or her writing in a portfolio and discuss the selection in the portfolio, difficulties encountered, and strengths and weaknesses. The teacher gives feedback on progress, suggested improvements, etc.

conference interpretation *n*

see INTERPRETER

confidence interval *n*

also CI

a range of values with a lower and an upper limit between which an unknown population parameter value is expected to lie with a certain degree of probability. For example, a 95% confidence interval indicates that we are 95% confident (or there is a 95% probability) that an unknown population parameter value will fall within that interval. The wider the CI, the more confident we are that it is likely to contain the population parameter value.

confirmatory factor analysis *n*

see FACTOR ANALYSIS

conjoining *n* **conjoin** *v*

(in GENERATIVE GRAMMAR), a term used for the linking together of words, phrases, or clauses, etc., which are of equal status. For example:

John likes <u>apples</u> and <u>pears</u>.

Betty went <u>to the butcher's</u> and <u>to the supermarket</u>.

see also CONJUNCTION, EMBEDDING

conjugation[1] *n*

a class of verbs which follow the same pattern for changes in TENSE, PERSON, or NUMBER. For example, in French there are four regular conjugations as well as irregular verbs. The verbs *donner* "to give", *parler* "to speak", *chercher* "to look for", etc., are described as belonging to the *-er* (or 1st) conjugation.

conjugation[2] *n* **conjugate** *v*

the way in which a particular verb changes (conjugates) for TENSE, PERSON, or NUMBER. For example, the French verb *donner* "to give": *je donne* "I give", *nous donnons* "we give", *je donnerai* "I shall give", *j' ai donné* "I have given, I gave".

conjunct *n*

see ADJUNCT

conjunction *n*

also **connective**

1 a word which joins words, phrases, or clauses together, such as *but, and, when*:

John <u>and</u> Mary went.

She sings <u>but</u> I don't.

Units larger than single words which function as conjunctions are sometimes known as **conjunctives**, for example *so that, as long as, as if*

She ran fast <u>so that</u> she could catch the bus.

Adverbs which are used to introduce or connect clauses are sometimes known as conjunctive adverbs, for example *however, nevertheless*:
> She is 86, <u>*nevertheless*</u> *she enjoys good health.*

2 the process by which such joining takes place.
There are two types of conjunction:

a **Co-ordination**, through the use of **co-ordinating conjunctions** (also known as **co-ordinators**) such as *and, or, but*. These join linguistic units which are equivalent or of the same rank.
For example:
> *It rained,* <u>*but*</u> *I went for a walk anyway.*
> *Shall we go home* <u>*or*</u> *go to a movie?*

The two clauses are **co-ordinate clauses.**

b **Subordination**, through the use of **subordinating conjunctions** (also known as **subordinators**) such as *because, when, unless, that*. These join an INDEPENDENT CLAUSE and a DEPENDENT CLAUSE
For example:
> *I knew* <u>*that*</u> *he was lying.*
> <u>*Unless*</u> *it rains, we'll play tennis at 4.*

conjunctive *n*
> see CONJUNCTION

conjunctive adverb *n*
> see CONJUNCTION

connected speech *n*
> spoken language when analyzed as a continuous sequence as opposed to the analysis of individual sounds or words in isolation.

connectionism *n*
> a theory in COGNITIVE SCIENCE that assumes that the individual components of human cognition are highly interactive and that knowledge of events, concepts and language is represented diffusely in the cognitive system. The theory has been applied to models of speech processing, lexical organization, and first and second language learning. Connectionism provides mathematical models and computer simulations that try to capture both the essence of INFORMATION PROCESSING and thought processes. The basic assumptions of the theory are:
>
> 1 Information processing takes place through the interactions of a large number of simple units, organized into networks and operating in parallel.
> 2 Learning takes place through the strengthening and weakening of the interconnections in a particular network in response to examples encountered in the INPUT.

3 The result of learning is often a network of simple units that acts as though it "knows" abstract rules, although the rules themselves exist only in the form of association strengths distributed across the entire network.

Connectionism is sometimes referred to as **parallel distributed processing (PDP)** or **neural networks**. There are slight differences among these terms, and over time connectionism has come to be viewed as the most general term.

see also LEARNING RULE

connective *n*

another term for CONJUNCTION

connotation *n* **connotative** *adj*

the additional meanings that a word or phrase has beyond its central meaning (see DENOTATION). These meanings show people's emotions and attitudes towards what the word or phrase refers to. For example, *child* could be defined as a *young human being* but there are many other character-istics which different people associate with *child*, e.g. *affectionate, amusing, lovable, sweet, mischievous, noisy, irritating, grubby*.

Some connotations may be shared by a group of people of the same cultural or social background, sex, or age; others may be restricted to one or several individuals and depend on their personal experience.

In a meaning system, that part of the meaning which is covered by connota-tion is sometimes referred to as **affective meaning, connotative meaning,** or **emotive meaning.**

connotative meaning *n*

another term for CONNOTATION

consciousness *n*

in general, subjective experience, especially awareness both of stimuli in the INPUT and of one's own mental processes. Consciousness is also closely associated with intentionality, and for this reason it is often unclear whether a claim that some aspect of language learning is unconscious should be taken to mean that the learning takes place without intention, without the learner's paying attention, or without the learner's being aware of the result of learning or the fact that learning took place. There has also been controversy for centuries concerning the role of consciousness in scientific explanation. Many researchers accept INTROSPECTION as a valid tool for assessing consciousness, if proper safeguards are observed. Others subscribe to the theory of EPIPHENOMENALISM and argue that conscious experience can be neither a valid explanation of behaviour nor a proper object of science. For these reasons, many second language researchers prefer to frame their questions in terms of relatively better defined and tractable issues such as IMPLICIT (versus explicit) learning or INCIDENTAL (vs. intentional) learning.

consciousness raising *n*

in teaching, techniques that encourage learners to pay attention to language form in the belief that an awareness of form will contribute indirectly to language acquisition. Techniques include having students infer grammatical rules from examples, compare differences between two or more different ways of saying something, observe differences between a learner's use of a grammar item and its use by native speakers. A consciousness-raising approach is contrasted with traditional approaches to the teaching of grammar (e.g. drilling, sentence practice, sentence combining), in which the goal is to establish a rule or instil a grammatical pattern directly.

consecutive clause *n*

an adverbial clause that expresses consequence or result, e.g. The bus took so long *that we were late*.

consecutive interpretation *n*

see INTERPRETATION

consensus task *n*

a task that requires pairs or groups of learners to come to agreement.
see also CONVERGENT QUESTION

consent *n*

see INFORMED CONSENT

consequential validity *n*

a type of validity that is based on the extent to which the uses and interpretations of a test that may have an impact on society will result in fair and positive social consequences for all STAKEHOLDERs including test takers.

conservatism thesis *n*

see LEARNABILITY THEORY

consolidation *n*

in language teaching, that stage in the lesson when the teacher reviews new material or provides additional practice to reinforce what has been taught.

119

Consolidation normally occurs at the end of a lesson. It can be compared with **revision**, which takes place at a later time and serves to remind students of previously presented material.

consonant *n*

a speech sound where the airstream from the lungs is either completely blocked (STOP), partially blocked (LATERAL) or where the opening is so narrow that the air escapes with audible friction (FRICATIVE). With some consonants (NASALS) the airstream is blocked in the mouth but allowed to escape through the nose.

With the other group of speech sounds, the VOWELS, the air from the lungs is not blocked.

There are a number of cases where the distinction is not clear-cut, such as the /j/ at the beginning of the English word *yes* where there is only very slight friction, and linguists have sometimes called these **semi-vowels** or **semi-consonants**.

see also MANNER OF ARTICULATION, PLACE OF ARTICULATION

consonant cluster *n*

a sequence of two or more consonants at the beginning of a syllable (e.g. /spl/ in *splash*) or the end of a syllable (e.g. /sts/ in *tests*). In English, with clusters of two, either the first sound is /s/ or the second one is an APPROXIMANT (l, r, w, or y); in initial clusters of three, the first sound is always /s/, the second is a voiceless stop (/p,t,k/), and the third is an approximant. In final position, many more clusters are possible, but most final clusters of three or more consonants are formed as the result of adding a plural or past tense inflection to a STEM and therefore end in /t/, /d/, /s/ or /z/.

Languages differ greatly in the ways in which consonants can form clusters and in which positions in a word clusters can occur. Spanish, for example, permits fewer clusters than English, and the Polynesian languages do not permit any clusters.

consonant cluster reduction *n*

also **consonant cluster simplification**

a process of simplifying CONSONANT CLUSTERS by omission of one or more consonants, especially common in casual speech. For example, English final clusters of three or four consonants are often simplified by dropping a middle consonant, e.g. when pronouncing *facts* (which ends in /kts/) as if it were *facks* (ending in /ks/). Consonant cluster reduction is also common in language learning when the target language permits sequences of consonants that do not occur in the learner's native language.

see also EPENTHESIS

consonant cluster simplification *n*

see CONSONANT CLUSTER REDUCTION

consonant harmony *n*

consonant articulation agreement within a word. In first language acquisition, children may pronounce a word like *doggy* as *doddy* or *goggy*. In second language learning, a learner may find it difficult to pronounce a word like *synthesis*, tending to say *synsesis*, *synthethis* or *synthethith* because of consonant harmony.

see also MANNER OF ARTICULATION, PLACE OF ARTICULATION

consonant system *n*

the CONSONANTS of a language form systems. For example, English has, among other consonants, two parallel series of STOPS:

	bilabial	alveolar	velar
voiceless	p	t	k
voiced	b	d	g

Maori, a Polynesian language, has only one series: /p/, /t/, /k/ with no voiceless/voiced contrast (see VOICE^2).

constant comparison method *n*

(in QUALITATIVE RESEARCH) a method meant to generate GROUNDED THEORY within the logic of ANALYTIC INDUCTION. The basic processes of the constant comparison method are the coding and grouping of data and the formation of hypotheses in parallel with data collection. This contrasts sharply with most methods of QUANTITATIVE RESEARCH, in which hypotheses are stated at the outset, then tested.

constative *n*

see PERFORMATIVE

constituent *n*

a linguistic unit (usually in sentence analysis) which is part of a larger construction (see CONSTITUENT STRUCTURE).

see also DISCONTINUOUS CONSTITUENT, CHUNKING

constituent analysis *n*

also **immediate constituent analysis**

a technique sometimes used in teaching and in grammatical analysis in which a sentence is analyzed into its main parts or constituents, hierarchically arranged to show their relationship to each other. It results in a description of a phrase, clause or sentence as one of a hierarchy of grammatical categories assigned to the linguistic units.

see CONSTITUENT STRUCTURE

constituent identification *n*

see CHUNKING

constituent structure *n*

another term for PHRASE STRUCTURE

constraint *n*

a principle of UNIVERSAL GRAMMAR that prohibits certain types of grammatical operations from applying to certain types of structures.

constraints *n*

see OPTIMALITY THEORY

constriction *n* **constricted** *adj*

(in the production of speech sounds) the narrowing of any part of the mouth or the throat (the VOCAL TRACT) to restrict the passage of the airstream from the lungs.

see also MANNER OF ARTICULATION

construal *n*

also **conceptualization**

the way in which people perceive, comprehend, and interpret the world around them. In COGNITIVE GRAMMAR, expressions differ in meaning depending not only on the entities they designate but also the construals employed to structure their conceived scenes. For example, a speaker may choose to say *my dad* or *my father*, *Mary lives in Chicago* or *Mary is living in Chicago*, based not on objective facts about the situation described but the perspective from which a speaker chooses to view a scene.

construct *n*

a concept that is not observed directly but is inferred on the basis of observable phenomena and that can help in the analysis and understanding of events and phenomena. Examples of constructs used in the study of language are ROLE and STATUS.

constructed-response item *n*

a type of test item or test task that requires test takers to respond to a series of open-ended questions by writing, speaking, or doing something rather than choose answers from a ready-made list. The most commonly used types of constructed-response items include fill-in, short-answer, and performance assessment.

see also SELECTED-RESPONSE ITEM

construction *n*

an ordered arrangement of words that forms a larger unit, for example, a determiner plus a noun forms a noun phrase.

see also CONSTRUCTION GRAMMAR

construction grammar *n*

a linguistic theory that assumes that form-meaning correspondences are the basic units of language. These units include **construction**s, each of which has a specific syntactic configuration that is associated with a specific set of semantic relations. Constructions exist independently of the particular words that appear in them, but the semantics of the words that appear in a construction fuse with the semantics of the construction itself. For example, in sentence (b) the verb "sneeze" (normally an INTRANSITIVE VERB) takes on the meaning of "cause to move" that is part of the **resultative construction** that is common to both (a) and (b):

(a) *John pushed the book off the shelf.*
(b) *John sneezed the tissue off the table.*

In contrast with many linguistic theories that treat abstract principles and formal operations as the essence of language and consider constructions to be epiphenomenal (a by-product of deeper realities, uninteresting in themselves), the notion of construction described by construction grammar is much closer to the notions of "structure" and SENTENCE PATTERN that are found in language teaching.

constructionism *n*

see SOCIAL CONSTRUCTIONISM

constructivism *n*

a social and educational philosophy based on the beliefs that:

1 knowledge is actively constructed by learners and not passively received

2 cognition is an adaptive process that organizes the learner's experiential world.

3 all knowledge is socially constructed

Constructivists believe that there are no enduring, context-free truths, that researcher BIAS cannot be eliminated, that multiple, socially constructed realities can only be studied holistically rather than in pieces, and that the possibility of generalizing from one research site to another is limited. Learning is seen as involving reorganization and reconstruction and it is through these processes that people internalize knowledge and perceive the world. In language teaching, constructivism has led to a focus on learning strategies, learner beliefs, teacher thinking and other aspects of learning which stress the individual and personal contributions of learners to learning. A constructivist view of teaching involves teachers in making their own sense of their classrooms and taking on the role of a reflective practitioner.

construct validity *n*

(in testing) a type of VALIDITY that is based on the extent to which the items in a test reflect the essential aspects of the theory on which the test is based (i.e., the CONSTRUCT). For example, the greater the relationship that can be demonstrated between a test of COMMUNICATIVE COMPETENCE in a language and the theory of communicative competence, the greater the construct validity of the test.

contact language *n*

see PIDGIN

content analysis *n*

1 (in research) a method used for analyzing and tabulating the frequency of occurrence of topics, ideas, opinions and other aspects of the content of written and spoken communication. For example, content analysis could be used to determine the frequency of occurrence of references to males, females, adults, children, Caucasians, non-Caucasians, etc., in a set of language teaching materials, in order to discover if any particular attitudes or themes were unintentionally being communicated in the material.

2 (in testing) a method in which a panel of experts are called upon to analyze the content of a test to judge the degree to which the test content actually represents what the test is designed to measure. A systematic comparison of the test content with the TEST or ITEM SPECIFICATIONs to which the test is constructed is often made for this purpose. It is used in establishing CONTENT VALIDITY and CONSTRUCT VALIDITY.

Content and Language Integrated Learning *n*

also **CLIL**

a term used mostly in Europe for **content-based instruction.**

124

content areas *n*

also **content fields**

the subjects other than language which are taught in a school curriculum. In countries with immigrant populations, particularly in the United States, a contrast is made between the teaching of English to non-native speakers of English and teaching in the regular school programme for other students where the focus is on the content areas, i.e. maths, science, social studies, geography, etc. A course which teaches immigrant students the writing skills they need in the content areas may be known as writing in the content areas.

see also CONTENT BASED INSTRUCTION

content-based ESL *n*

see CONTENT-BASED INSTRUCTION, SHELTERED ENGLISH

content-based instruction *n*

also **CBI, content-based learning, content and language integrated learning, CLIL**

a method that integrates language instruction with subject matter instruction in the target language, for example, studying science, social studies or mathematics through the medium of English in a **content-based ESL** program. Examples of content-based instruction include IMMERSION, LANGUAGE ACROSS THE CURRICULUM, AND SHELTERED ENGLISH.

content-based learning *n*

see CONTENT-BASED INSTRUCTION

content course *n*

a course in any area apart from language. In EAP programmes a distinction is often made between content courses (i.e. regular courses in different fields) and language courses (courses developed for ESL students).

content knowledge *n*

in teaching, teachers' knowledge of their subject matter. For example, a language teacher's content knowledge includes his or her knowledge of grammar, learning theories, phonetics, etc. Teachers' knowledge of their subject matter is assumed to affect how well they understand items they are asked or choose to teach, how well they are able to provide explanations, and how they construct learning activities for learners.

see PEDAGOGICAL CONTENT KNOWLEDGE

content reading *n*

the reading of books and other printed materials that contain information needed for learning in the CONTENT AREAS, such as textbooks or other study materials, in contrast with reading which is for pleasure or relaxation.

content schema *n*

in theories of reading comprehension, a distiction is sometimes made between two kinds of **schema** that people make use of in understanding texts. **Content schema** refers to background knowledge about the content of a text, i.e. depending on whether it is a text about an earthquake, the economy, French art or cooking. This type of schematic knowedge is contrasted with **formal schema**, i.e. knowledge about the formal, rhetorical, organizational structure of diferent kinds of texts, such as whether the text is a simple story, a scientific text, a news report, etc. Knowledge of both types of schemata influence how a reader understands a text.

see SCHEMA THEORY

content validity *n*

(in testing) a type of VALIDITY that is based on the extent to which a test adequately and sufficiently measures the particular skills or behaviour it sets out to measure. For example, a test of pronunciation skills in a language would have low content validity if it tested only some of the skills that are required for accurate pronunciation, such as a test that tested the ability to pronounce isolated sounds, but not STRESS, INTONATION, or the pronunciation of sounds within words. Content validity is of particular importance in CRITERION-REFERENCED TESTS, where the test content must represent the content of what has been taught in a course.

content word *n*

words can be divided into two classes: **content words** and **function words**. Content words are words which refer to a thing, quality, state, or action and which have meaning (**lexical meaning**) when the words are used alone. Content words are mainly nouns, verbs, adjectives, and adverbs, e.g. *book, run, musical, quickly.*

Function words are words which have little meaning on their own, but which show grammatical relationships in and between sentences (**grammatical meaning**). Conjunctions, prepositions, articles, e.g. *and, to, the,* are function words.

Function words are also called **form words, empty words, functors, grammatical words, structural words, structure words.** Content words are also called **full words, lexical words.**

see also WORD CLASS

context *n* **contextual** *adj*

that which occurs before and/or after a word, a phrase or even a longer UTTERANCE or a TEXT. The context often helps in understanding the particular meaning of the word, phrase, etc. For example, the word *loud* in *loud music is* usually understood as meaning "noisy" whereas in *a tie with a loud pattern* it is understood as "unpleasantly colourful". The context may also be the broader social situation in which a linguistic item is used. For example, in ordinary usage, *spinster* refers to an older unmarried woman but in a legal context it refers to *any* unmarried woman.

see also CONTEXTUAL MEANING

context clue *n*

also **contextualization clue**

in comprehension, information from the immediate setting surrounding an item in a text and which provides information that can be used to understand the meaning of an item. Such clues may be lexical or grammatical. In speech context clues include the verbal, paralinguistic and non-verbal signs that help speakers understand the full meaning of a speaker's utterances in context.

context-embedded language *n*

communication occurring in a context that offers help to comprehension through such things as the situation and setting, visual clues, gestures and actions. In such a situation the learner can make more use of TOP-DOWN PROCESSING to infer meanings. At the same time the speaker may communicate less explicitly since much of the meaning is known from the context. This can be compared with **context-reduced language**, in which there are few contextual clues to support comprehension and which relies therefore on linguistic elaboration. The distinction between context-reduced and context-embedded language has been used in explaining the nature of instruction in academic subjects in formal school contexts and the role of background knowledge in communication.

context of situation *n*

the linguistic and situational context in which a word, utterance or text occurs. The meaning of utterances, etc., is determined not only by the literal meaning of the words used but by the context or situation in which they occur.

context-reduced language *n*

see CONTEXT-EMBEDDED LANGUAGE

contextualization *n* **contextualize** *v*

in language teaching, the provision of examples of how a new learning item is used in a meaningful or real context in order to reinforce the communicative use of the new item and to help students better understand and remember it. For example after teaching the use of imperatives in giving instructions, the teacher might give out copies of recipes and ask students to identify examples of imperatives.

contextually appropriate method *n*
see CLOZE PROCEDURE

contextual meaning *n*

the meaning a linguistic item has in context, for example the meaning a word has within a particular sentence, or a sentence has in a particular paragraph. The question *Do you know the meaning of war?* For example, may have two different contextual meanings:

a it may mean *Do you know the meaning of the word war?*, when said by a language teacher to a class of students.

b it may mean *War produces death, injury, and suffering*, when said by an injured soldier to a politician who favours war.

contingency table *n*

a table that displays data concerning two VARIABLES[2]. For example, if we wanted to determine the relationship between the scores students obtained on a grammar test and the number of hours spent in preparation for the test, a contingency table could be used to show the number of students obtaining different test scores according to the amount of time they spent in preparation. The CHI-SQUARE test can be used to test the STATISTICAL SIGNIFICANCE of the relationship between the two variables (i.e., between the scores and the preparation time).

Test scores				
Hours spent in preparation	$0 \to 10$	$0 \to 20$	$21 \to 40$	Total
	10	6	4	20
	2	5	9	16
Total	12	11	13	36

A contingency table

continuant *n*

a CONSONANT that is produced when the primary constriction in the vocal tract is not narrowed to the point where the air flow through the mouth is blocked. These sounds can be maintained as long as there is air in the lungs. Continuants include FRICATIVES (e.g. /s, z, f, v/), LIQUIDS (/l, r/, and GLIDES (/w, y/). NASALS are usually considered non-continuants, because although they can be maintained, the vocal tract is stopped.

continuing education *n*

in the US, educational programs provided for adults, apart from the K-12 school system, which often include basic skills, recreational, advanced and technical studies.

continuous *n*

another term for PROGRESSIVE

continuous assessment *n*

an approach to assessment in which students are assessed regularly throughout the programme rather than being given a single assessment at the end. This is thought to give a more accurate picture of student achievement.

continuum *n*

see SPEECH CONTINUUM

contour tone *n*

tones that are specified as gliding movements within a pitch range. Languages that have contour tones, such as Chinese, are **contour tone languages**. see TONE[1]

contraction *n*

the reduction of a linguistic form and often its combination with another form. For example:

I shall   into   *I'll*
they are   into   *they're*
did not   into   *didn't*

contrastive analysis *n*

also **CA**

the comparison of the linguistic systems of two languages, for example the sound system or the grammatical system. Contrastive analysis was developed and practised in the 1950s and 1960s, as an application of

STRUCTURAL LINGUISTICS to language teaching, and is based on the following assumptions:

a the main difficulties in learning a new language are caused by interference from the first language (see LANGUAGE TRANSFER)

b these difficulties can be predicted by contrastive analysis

c teaching materials can make use of contrastive analysis to reduce the efects of interference.

Contrastive analysis was more successful in PHONOLOGY than in other areas of language, and declined in the 1970s as interference was replaced by other explanations of learning difficulties (see ERROR ANALYSIS, INTERLANGUAGE). In recent years contrastive analysis has been applied to other areas of language, for example the discourse systems (see DISCOURSE ANALYSIS). This is called **contrastive discourse analysis**.

see also COMPARATIVE LINGUISTICS

contrastive discourse analysis *n*

see CONTRASTIVE ANALYSIS

contrastive pragmatics *n*

the study of cultural differences in the way speech acts and other aspects of speaking are realized, such as by comparing differences between the ways people from two different cultures realize the speech act of "apologizing".

contrastive rhetoric *n*

the study of similarities and differences between writing in a first and second language or between two languages, in order to understand how writing conventions in one language influence how a person writes in another. Writing in a second language is thought to be influenced to some extent by the linguistic and cultural conventions of the writer's first language, and this may influence how the writer organizes written discourse (DISCOURSE STRUCTURE), the kind of SCRIPT or SCHEME the writer uses, as well as such factors as TOPIC[1], audience, paragraph organization, and choice of VOCABULARY or REGISTER.

see also CONTRASTIVE ANALYSIS

contrastive stress *n*

see STRESS

consultative speech/style *n*

sometimes used to refer to a style of speaking used with others who do not share the speaker's background knowledge or experience and hence need more background knowledge than is normally used in COLLOQUIAL SPEECH.

control group *n*

(in research) one of two groups used in certain kinds of experimental research, the other being the **experimental group**. For example, if we wanted to study the effectiveness of a new teaching method, one group (i.e. the experimental group) may be taught using the new method, and another group (i.e. the control group), by using the usual teaching method. The control group is chosen because of its equivalence to the experimental group (e.g. by assigning participants to the two groups at random). In studying the effects of the new method, the experimental group is compared with the control group.

controllability *n*

see LOCUS OF CONTROL

controlled composition *n*

see COMPOSITION

controlled languag*e* *n*

the language of a classroom activity, task, text or exercise which has been modified in order to reduce the linguistic complexity of the activity, to highlight specific features of language, or to focus on grammatical accuracy. For example an activity might be prepared that limits the tenses practised to the present and past tense. This can be compared with an activity in which the language is not controlled or limited in any way, i.e. which seeks to practise AUTHENTIC language.

controlled practice

see PRACTICE ACTIVITIES

controlled processing *n*

see AUTOMATIC PROCESSING

convenience sample *n*

see SAMPLE

conventionalized speech *n*

another term for ROUTINE

convergence[1] *n*

the process of two or more languages or language varieties becoming more similar to one another. For example:

a if one language variety gains status, then the speakers of another variety may change their pronunciation to be more like it, and use words and grammatical structures from it

b if speakers of two language varieties mix together, by moving to the same area for example, both varieties may change to become more like each other.

see also DIVERGENCE[1]

convergence[2] *n*

see ACCOMMODATION

convergent question *n*

a question that encourages student responses to converge or focus on a central theme. Convergent questions typically require a single correct answer and elicit short responses from students. Convergent questions may be useful when the teacher wants to focus on specific skills or information or requires short responses, such as when attempting to find out whether students can locate a specific piece of information in a reading passage.

see also CLASSROOM DISCOURSE, DIVERGENT QUESTION, EVALUATIVE QUESTION, QUESTIONING TECHNIQUES

convergent thinking *n*

discussion, analysis, etc., of ideas, topics, etc., that result in a common conclusion, as compared with that which produces a variety of different interpretations or conclusions. The latter is known as DIVERGENT THINKING. The differences between these two kinds of thinking is a factor in the design of instructional tasks.

convergent validity *n*

(in testing) a type of VALIDITY that is based on the extent to which two or more tests that are claimed to measure the same underlying CONSTRUCT are in fact doing so. For example, to establish convergent validity of two tests that are claimed to measure the same construct (e.g. L2 listening comprehension), they are administered to the same group of test takers and the test scores are correlated. If a high correlation is obtained, this is an indication that they are measuring the same construct. If not, one of the tests is considered to be measuring something else (e.g. L2 reading comprehension).

see CONSTRUCT VALIDITY, DISCRIMINANT VALIDITY

conversational analysis *n*

see CONVERSATION ANALYSIS

conversation analysis *n*
also **conversational analysis**
a research tradition evolving from ETHNOMETHODOLOGY which studies the social organization of natural conversation (also referred to as **talk-in-interaction**) by a detailed inspection of tape recordings and transcriptions. Concerned with how meanings and pragmatic functions are communicated in both mundane conversation and such institutional varieties of talk as interviews and court hearings, conversation analysts have investigated such topics as the sequential organization of talk, turn-taking, and the ways that people identify and repair communicative problems.
see also ADJACENCY PAIR, CONVERSATIONAL MAXIM, DISCOURSE ANALYSIS, ROLE, SPEECH ACT, TURN-TAKING

conversational implicature *n*
see CONVERSATIONAL MAXIM

conversational maxim *n*
an unwritten rule about conversation which people know and which influences the form of conversational exchanges. For example in the following exchange
    a: Let's go to the movies.
    b: I have an examination in the morning.
B's reply might appear not to be connected to A's remark. However, since A has made an invitation and since a reply to an invitation is usually either an acceptance or a refusal, B's reply is here understood as an excuse for not accepting the invitation (i.e. a refusal). B has used the "maxim" that speakers normally give replies which are relevant to the question that has been asked. The philosopher Grice has suggested that there are four conversational maxims:
a The maxim of quantity: give as much information as is needed.
b The maxim of quality: speak truthfully.
c The maxim of relevance: say things that are relevant.
d The maxim of manner: say things clearly and briefly.
The use of conversational maxims to imply meaning during conversation is called **conversational implicature**, and the "co-operation" between speakers in using the maxims is sometimes called the co-operative principle.
see also ADJACENCY PAIR, COHERENCE, REALITY PRINCIPLE

conversational openings *n*
(in conversational interaction) the strategies a person uses to begin a conversation. These include clearing the throat, body movement, eye movement, and repeating a previous part of the conversation.
see also TURN TAKING

conversational routine *n*
see FORMULAIC LANGUAGE

conversational rules *n*
also **rules of speaking**
rules shared by a group of people which govern their spoken conversational behaviour. Conversational rules may, for instance, regulate when to speak or not to speak in a conversation, what to say in a particular situation, and how to start and end a conversation. These rules vary not only between different languages (LANGUAGE[1]) but also between different social groups speaking the same language.
see also CONVERSATIONAL ANALYSIS, CONVERSATIONAL MAXIM

conversational style *n*
a particular way of participating in conversation. People differ in the way they take part in normal conversation. Some people participate very actively in conversation, speaking fairly quickly and with little or no pausing between turns. This is called a **high involvement style**. Other people may use a slower rate of speaking, longer pauses between turns and avoid interruption or completion of another speaker's turn. This is called a **high considerateness style**.

conversion *n*
a change in the grammatical category of a word from one word class to another without adding an affix.
Formal clothes are a *must* at a wedding. (conversion of verb to noun)
It *pains* me to think of it. (conversion of noun to verb)

co-occurrence restriction *n*
in some models of syntactic analysis, restrictions on the elements in the sentence so that they can only occur with certain elements and not with others. For example, the sentence:
*Anita laughed the baby
would be ungrammatical as the verb *laugh* cannot co-occur with an OBJECT; it is **intransitive**.

co-occurrence rule *n*
see SPEECH STYLES

co-operating teacher *n*
also **master teacher**

(in teacher education) an experienced teacher in whose class a student teacher does his or her practice teaching. The role of the co-operating teacher is to help the student teacher acquire teaching skills and to give feedback on his or her teaching.

co-operation *n*

(in learning) working together with one or more peer(s) to solve a problem, complete a learning task, share information or get FEEDBACK on performance.

co-operative learning *n*

also **collaborative learning**

an approach to teaching and learning in which classrooms are organized so that students work together in small co-operative teams. Such an approach to learning is said to increase students' learning since (a) it is less threatening for many students, (b) it increases the amount of student participation in the classroom, (c) it reduces the need for competitiveness, and (d) it reduces the teacher's dominance in the classroom.

Five distinct types of co-operative learning activities are often distinguished:

1 **Peer Tutoring**: students help each other learn, taking turns tutoring or drilling each other.
2 **Jigsaw**: each member of a group has a piece of information needed to complete a group task.
3 **Co-operative Projects**: students work together to produce a product, such as a written paper or group presentation.
4 **Co-operative/Individualized**: students progress at their own rate through individualized learning materials but their progress contributes to a team grade so that each pupil is rewarded by the achievements of his or her teammates.
5 **Co-operative Interaction**: students work together as a team to complete a learning unit, such as a laboratory experiment.

Co-operative-learning activities are often used in COMMUNICATIVE LANGUAGE TEACHING.

The use of Co-operative Learning principles in language teaching is known as **Cooperative Language Learning**.

co-operative principle *n*

see CONVERSATIONAL MAXIM

co-ordinate bilingualism *n*

see COMPOUND BILINGUALISM

co-ordinate clause *n*
see CONJUNCTION

co-ordinating conjunction *n*
see CONJUNCTION

co-ordination *n*
see CONJUNCTION

co-ordinator *n*
see CONJUNCTION

copula *n* **copulative** *adj*
also **linking verb**
a verb that links a SUBJECT to a COMPLEMENT. For example:
  He is sick. She looked afraid.
The verb *be* is sometimes known as the copula since this is its main function in English. The following are copulative verbs, i.e. they can be used copulatively: *feel, look, prove, remain, resemble, sound, stay, become, grow, turn, smell, taste.*
see also TRANSITIVE VERB

copula absence *n*
see COPULA DELETION

copula deletion *n*
also **copula absence**
in many languages, including Russian, Arabic, Thai, and all English-based creole languages, the copula (e.g. English *be*) is absent in the present tense, so that sentences such as *She working* and *He real nice* are fully grammatical.
see also AFRICAN AMERICAN ENGLISH

core curriculum *n*
a curriculum organized around subject matter that is considered essential for all students in a programme. English is part of the core curriculum in most schools around the world.

coreferential *adj*
expressions are coreferential if they refer to the same person, event, or thing. For example, in the sentence *Susan told me an interesting story about herself,* *Susan* and *herself* are coreferential because they refer to the same person.

core grammar *n*

> within the framework of Chomsky's UNIVERSAL GRAMMAR, a grammar which contains all the universal principles of language as well as special conditions or rules (PARAMETERS) which can be "set" for particular languages. Parameters may vary from one language to another. For example, in some languages, e.g. English, the HEAD of a phrase is first, in Japanese the head is last. Aspects of a language which are not predictable from the Universal Grammar are considered not to belong to the core grammar but to the **periphery or peripheral grammar.**
>
> It is claimed that, in first language acquisition, the initial universal grammar of a child consists of fixed principles and open (that is "unset") parameters. As the child receives input from his or her first language, the open parameters are fixed for a particular language and the child's L1 core grammar results. Researchers have investigated the role of core grammars in second language acquisition.

core vocabulary *n*

> in language teaching, the essential words together with their meanings that are needed in order to be able to communicate and understand at a basic level.

coronals *n*

> the class of sounds that includes LABIALS, ALVEOLARS, and PALATALS.

corpus *n*

> a collection of naturally occurring samples of language which have been collected and collated for easy access by researchers and materials developers who want to know how words and other linguistic items are actually used. A corpus may vary from a few sentences to a set of written texts or recordings. In language analysis corpuses usually consist of a relatively large, planned collection of texts or parts of texts, stored and accessed by computer. A corpus is designed to represent different types of language use, e.g. casual conversation, business letters, ESP texts. A number of different types of corpuses may be distinguished, for example:
>
> 1 **specialized corpus**: a corpus of texts of a particular type, such as academic articles, student writing, etc.
> 2 **general corpus or reference corpus**: a large collection of many different types of texts, often used to produce reference materials for language learning (e.g. dictionaries) or used as a base-line for comparison with specialized corpora

3 **comparable corpora:** two or more corpora in different languages or language varieties containing the same kinds and amounts of texts, to enable differences or equivalences to be compared

4 **learner corpus:** a collection of texts or language samples produced by language learners

corpus linguistics *n*

an approach to investigating language structure and use through the analysis of large databases of real language examples stored on computer. Issues amenable to corpus linguistics include the meanings of words across registers, the distribution and function of grammatical forms and categories, the investigation of **lexico-grammatical associations** (associations of specific words with particular grammatical constructions), the study of discourse characteristics, register variation, and (when learner corpora are available) issues in language acquisition and development.

Corpus of Contemporary American English *n*

a large corpus of American English, with entries distributed across genres of fiction, popular magazines, newspapers, and academic journals, as well as spoken language.

corpus planning *n*

a type of LANGUAGE PLANNING

a deliberate restructuring of a language, often by government authorities. This may be done by giving it, for example, an increased range of vocabulary, new grammatical structures, sometimes even a new or more standardized writing system.

For example, in Malaysia, where Bahasa Malaysia (Malay) has become the national language, attempts have been made to construct new vocabulary in areas such as business, education and research. Similar efforts have been made for Swahili in East Africa.

correct *adj* correctness *n*

a term which is used to state that particular language usage, e.g. the pronunciation of a word, is *right* as opposed to *wrong*. For example:

This is the correct pronunciation.

The term often expresses a particular attitude to language usage (see PRESCRIPTIVE GRAMMAR). It has become more common to abandon absolute judgements of *right* and *wrong* and to consider a usage as being more or less appropriate (APPROPRIATENESS) in a particular social setting.

see also ERROR

correction for guessing *n*

a mathematical adjustment to correct for the effects of random guessing by test takers. It is not generally recommended in scoring a teacher-constructed test, but when it is used, test takers should be informed that their scores will be corrected for guessing or penalized.

corrective recast *n*

see RECAST

correlation *n*

a measure of the strength of the relationship or association between two or more sets of data. For example, we may wish to determine the relationship between the scores of a group of students on a mathematics test and on a language test. Different types of correlation are reported in the applied linguistics literature, whose use is determined by the types of variables that are correlated. The **Pearson product-moment correlation** (r) is a measure of association between two continuous variables. The **point-biserial correlation** (r_{pbi}) is a measure of association between a continuous variable and a dichotomous or binary variable (e.g., gender – male versus female). The **biserial correlation** (r_b) is a measure of association between a continuous variable and an artificially dichotomized variable (i.e. a variable that is continuously measurable has been reduced to two categories (e.g. age – old versus young or test score – pass versus fail)) but is rarely used nowadays. The **tetrachoric correlation** is a measure of association between two artificially dichotomized variables (i.e. both variables that are continuously measurable have been reduced to two categories each). The **phi correlation** (ϕ) is a measure of association between two genuinely dichotomous variables. The **Spearman rank-order correlation** or **Spearman's rho** (ρ) is a measure of association between two ordinal variables. The **Kendall rank-order correlation** or **Kendall's tau** (τ) is another measure of association between two ordinal variables but better deals with tied ranks (i.e. when two or more test takers have the same score and thus occupy the same rank) than the Spearman's rho does.

correlational research *n*

research carried out to examine the nature of the relationship between two naturally occurring variables.

correlation coefficient *n*

also **coefficient of correlation**

a numerical index of the degree of relationship between two variables that ranges in value from –1.00 (i.e. a perfect negative relationship) through

0.00 (i.e. total absence of a relationship) to +1.00 (i.e. a perfect positive relationship). A correlation coefficient indicates both the direction (i.e. positive or negative) and the strength (i.e. the size or magnitude) of the relationship. For example, if students received quite similar scores on two tests, their scores would have a high positive correlation. If their scores on one test were the reverse of their scores on the other, their scores would have a high negative correlation. If their scores on the two tests were not related in any predictable way, their scores would have a zero correlation. The closer an absolute value of the correlation coefficient is to 1.00, the stronger the relationship between two variables is regardless of the direction of its correlation coefficient.

correlative conjunction *n*

co-ordinating CONJUNCTIONS used in pairs in a parallel construction. For example:

both . . . and
either . . . or
neither . . . nor

COTE *n*

an abbreviation for **Certificate for Overseas Teachers of English**

co-text *n*

those texts that occur together with or prior to a text and that influence the meaning of a text. The notion of co-text suggests that in order to understand a text, assumptions are made about preceding texts that provide a context for understanding the text. For example the phrase "To See or Not to See" occurring in an advertisement for a movie assumes that the reader is familiar with the famous line from Hamlet "To be or not to be", which is a co-text for the advertisement.

counselling learning *n*

see COMMUNITY LANGUAGE LEARNING

countable noun *n*

also **count noun**

a noun which has both singular and plural forms. For example:

word – words, machine – machines, bridge – bridges

A noun which does not usually occur in the plural is called an **uncountable noun** or a **mass noun**. For example:

education, homework, harm.

see also NOUN

counter-example *n*

an example that falsifies a hypothesis or claim. For instance, an utterance such as *He goed* in learner speech is a counter-example to the claim that people learn simply by imitating what they hear in input.

coursebook *n*

in language teaching, a book (usually as part of a series of books) that contains all the materials necessary for a particular type of language learner at a particular level (e.g. intermediate level adults). Such a book is typically based on an integrated or multi-skills syllabus i.e. one that contains sections on grammar functions, vocabulary, listening, speaking, reading and writing.

course density *n*

(in course design and syllabus design (see COURSE DESIGN)) the rate at which new teaching points are introduced and reintroduced in a course or syllabus in order to achieve a satisfactory rate of learning. In language courses where the main emphasis is on grammar and vocabulary, learners can generally learn four or five items per hour for active use and another four or five for passive use. Targets of 2000 items for active use and a further 2000 for passive recognition are commonly set for a 400 hour course of instruction.

course design *n*

also **language programme design, curriculum design, programme design**
(in language teaching) the development of a language programme or set of teaching materials. Whereas **syllabus design** generally refers to procedures for deciding what will be taught in a language programme, course design includes how a syllabus will be carried out. For example:

a what teaching METHOD and materials will be needed to achieve the OBJECTIVES
b how much time will be required
c how classroom activities will be sequenced and organized
d what sort of PLACEMENT TESTS, ACHIEVEMENT TESTS and other sorts of tests will be used
e how the programme will be evaluated (see EVALUATION)

Course design is part of the broader process of CURRICULUM DEVELOPMENT.
see also COURSE DENSITY

course management system *n*
also **CMS**
see LEARNING MANAGEMENT SYSTEM

courseware *n*

computer programs used in COMPUTER ASSISTED LEARNING.

court interpreter *n*

an interpreter with the specialized knowledge necessary to provide INTERPRETATION during judicial proceedings. The requirements for court interpretation regarding training, experience, and certification varies from country to country.

see also INTERPRETER

covariance *n*

a measure of the degree to which two variables vary together.

see also ANALYSIS OF COVARIANCE

covariate *n*

a variable whose effect is statistically controlled in the ANALYSIS OF COVARIANCE

coverage *n*

the degree to which words and structures can be used to replace other words and structures, because they have a similar meaning. For example *seat* includes the meanings of *chair*, *bench*, and *stool*, and *What time is it please?* can replace *Could you kindly tell me the time?* Coverage is a principle used to help select language items for language teaching, since items with a high degree of coverage are likely to be most useful to language learners.

see also SELECTION

covert language policy *n*

see LANGUAGE POLICY

covert prestige *n*

positive attitudes towards a LANGUAGE or VARIETY that are not often overtly expressed. For example, in many SPEECH COMMUNITIES, there is a standard variety that has obvious prestige and is associated with education and status, while a non-standard variety in the same area may not be overtly valued. The prestige of the standard variety can be shown in many ways, including a tendency of speakers to report that they use standard forms more often than they do. However, sometimes speakers report using non-standard forms more frequently than they do in fact, indicating that there is a kind of covert prestige associated with this variety as well.

c-parameter *n*

see ITEM RESPONSE THEORY

CPE *n*

an abbreviation for **Certificate of Proficiency in English**

CPH *n*

an abbreviation for CRITICAL PERIOD HYPOTHESIS

creative construction hypothesis *n*

a theory about how second and foreign language learners work out language rules. The theory was proposed by Dulay and Burt, who claim that learners work out the rules of their TARGET LANGUAGE[1] by:

a using natural mental processes, such as GENERALIZATION

b using similar processes to first language learners

c not relying very much on the rules of the first language

d using processes which lead to the creation of new forms and structures which are not found in the target language. For example:
*She goed to school. (instead of *She went to school*)
*What you are doing? (instead of *What are you doing?*)

creative thinking *n*

in education, innovative and adaptive thinking based on the ability to identify problems, form hypotheses, and apply novel and appropriate solutions to unfamiliar and open-ended tasks. An important goal of many educational programmes is to develop students' creative thinking skills.

creative writing *n*

types of writing such as fiction, drama and poetry that reflect the writer's originality, imagination, feelings and which do not describe factual events.

creole *n*

a PIDGIN language which has become the native language of a group of speakers, being used for all or many of their daily communicative needs. Usually, the sentence structures and vocabulary range of a creole are far more complex than those of a pidgin language. Creoles are usually classified according to the language from which most of their vocabulary comes, e.g. English-based, French-based, Portuguese-based, and Swahili-based creoles. Examples of English-based creoles are Jamaican Creole, Hawaiian Creole and Krio in Sierra Leone, West Africa.

see also CREOLIZATION, POST-CREOLE CONTINUUM

creolization *n*

the process by which a PIDGIN becomes a CREOLE.
Creolization involves the expansion of the vocabulary and the grammatical system.

criterion[1] *n*

an acceptable standard with which a test taker's response, product, or performance is compared or against which it is evaluated.

criterion[2] *n*

see BEHAVIOURAL OBJECTIVE

criterion measure *n*

(in testing) a standard against which a newly developed test (i.e. a **predictor**) can be compared as a measure of its VALIDITY. A criterion measure may be another test that is well known to be a valid measure of the same ability or another valid indicator of performance.

see also CRITERION-RELATED VALIDITY

criterion-referenced test(ing) *n*

a test that measures a test taker's performance according to a particular standard or criterion that has been agreed upon. The test taker must reach this level of performance to pass the test, and a test taker's score is interpreted with reference to the criterion score, rather than to the scores of other test takers, which is the case with a NORM-REFERENCED TEST.

criterion referencing *n*

in testing, the use of descriptions of what students should be able to do with language in order to determine the pass score in a test or informal assessment.

criterion-related validity *n*

(in testing) a type of VALIDITY that is based on the extent to which a new test is compared or correlated with an established external CRITERION MEASURE. For example, a new test of L2 vocabulary can be validated by correlating the test score of the new test with that of some other criterion measure representing an identified CONSTRUCT (i.e. L2 vocabulary knowledge).

Two kinds of criterion-related validity are identified: CONCURRENT -VALIDITY and PREDICTIVE VALIDITY.

criterion variable *n*

another term for DEPENDENT VARIABLE

critical age *n*

see CRITICAL PERIOD

critical applied linguistics *n*

an approach that applies the theories and methods of CRITICAL THEORY to problems in language education, literacy, discourse analysis, language in the workplace, translation, and other language related domains.

critical comprehension *n*

see READING

critical discourse analysis *n*

a form of DISCOURSE ANALYSIS that takes a critical stance towards how language is used and analyzes texts and other discourse types in order to identify the ideology and values underlying them. It seeks to reveal the interests and power relations in any institutional and socio-historical context through analyzing the ways that people use language.

critical incident analysis *n*

a procedure used in teacher education and other fields in which an incident from a teacher's experience that triggered significant new awareness or change, is examined for its meaning and significance. For example a student may question the value of a teaching technique the teacher is using and has always believed in. The incident may later be written about or discussed with others and through systematic questioning about such events, teachers are challenged to reflect on their beliefs and practices, allowing their understanding of teaching and themselves as teachers, to develop.

critical linguistics *n*

an approach to the analysis of language and of language use that focuses on the role that language plays in assigning power to particular groups within society. Critical linguistics is based on the study of texts and the way texts are interpreted and used. The assumption is the relation between form and function in discourse is not arbitrary or conventional but is determined by cultural, social, and political factors, i.e. that texts are inherently ideological in nature.

critical literacy *n*

an approach to the teaching of literacy which seeks to show how social identities and power relations become primary goals of analysis, critique, and study. Critical reading in such an approach seeks not only to develop the ability to interpret texts but also the ability to perceive the connections between social conditions and the reading and writing practices of a culture, to be able to analyze those practices, and to develop the critical and political awareness to take action within and against them.

critical pedagogy *n*

an approach to teaching that seeks to examine critically the conditions under which language is used and the social and cultural purposes of its use, rather than transmitting the dominant view of linguistic, cultural and other kinds of information. Both the process of teaching and learning and its study are viewed as inherently evaluative or ideological in character.

critical period *n*

also **critical age**

the period during which a child can acquire language easily, rapidly, perfectly, and without instruction. In Lenneberg's original formulation of the **critical period hypothesis**, this period was identified as ranging from age two to puberty. Lenneberg believed that brain LATERALIZATION is complete at puberty, making post-adolescent language acquisition difficult, with complete learning of a second language a goal unlikely to be realized. Some researchers now hold that the critical age for the acquisition of phonology may be as early as five or six, while there is perhaps no age limit for the acquisition of vocabulary. Some theorize that there is no critical period at all, that it is possible to learn a second language perfectly after puberty, while others argue that there is a steady decline in language learning ability with age, with no sharp breaks identifying a critical period. For this reason the term **sensitive period** is sometimes preferred. Whether critical period related learning deficits are biologically, socially, cognitively, or affectively based has also been the subject of much dispute.

critical period hypothesis *n*

see CRITICAL PERIOD

critical reading *n*

1 reading in which the reader reacts critically to what he or she is reading, through relating the content of the reading material to personal standards, values, attitudes or beliefs, i.e. going beyond what is given in the text and critically evaluating the relevancy and value of what is read.

2 a level of reading in which the reader seeks to identify the underlying ideology of a text, which is realized not so much by what the writer writes about but by how people, events and places are talked about. Critical reading focuses on the analysis of textual ideologies and cultural messages, and an understanding of the linguistic and discourse techniques with which texts represent social reality. Critical reading is one dimension of critical pedagogy.

critical theory *n*

originally a form of social theory, now also used to refer to an educational philosophy and movement that emphasizes the importance of critical examination of topics and practices where issues of social justice are at stake. The goal of critical theory is to identify, confront, and resolve problems of injustice through the processes of awareness, reflection, and argumentation. Language and language use is an important focus of critical theory since language is believed to play a key role in creating or maintaining power and in expressing ideological positions because it represents participants' values either directly or indirectly. Empowerment and emancipation from the constraints of social institutions and structures are key themes in most critical approaches.

critical thinking *n*

a level of reading comprehension or discussion skills when the learner is able to question and evaluate what is read or heard. In language teaching this is said to engage students more actively with materials in the target language, encourage a deeper processing of it, and show respect for students as independent thinkers.

Cronbach's alpha *n*

also **coefficient alpha**

a measure of internal consistency based on information about (a) the number of items on the test, (b) the VARIANCE of the scores of each item, and (c) the VARIANCE of the total test scores. Mathematically speaking, it is equivalent to the average of the reliability estimates for all possible splits. When items are dichotomously scored, Cronbach's alpha results are equal to those of KR20, which is why KR20 is considered a special case of Cronbach's alpha.

see also INTERNAL CONSISTENCY RELIABILITY, SPLIT-HALF RELIABILITY

cross-cultural analysis *n*

analysis of data from two or more different cultural groups, in order to determine if generalizations made about members of one culture are also true of the members of other cultures. Cross-cultural research is an important part of sociolinguistics, since it is often important to know if generalizations made about one language group reflect the culture of that group or are universal.

cross-cultural communication *n*

an exchange of ideas, information, etc., between persons from different cultural backgrounds. There are often more problems in cross-cultural communication than in communication between people of the same cultural background. Each participant may interpret the other's speech according to his or her own cultural conventions and expectations (see CONVERSATIONAL RULES). If the cultural conventions of the speakers are widely different, misinterpretations and misunderstandings can easily arise, even resulting in a total breakdown of communication. This has been shown by research into real-life situations, such as job interviews, doctor-patient encounters and legal communication.

see also CONVERSATIONAL MAXIM

cross-cultural pragmatics *n*
the study of similarities and differences in cultural norms for expressing and understanding messages, such as differences in the conventions for the realization of SPEECH ACTS.

cross-linguistic influence *n*
a cover-term used to refer to phenomena such as BORROWING, INTERFERENCE, and LANGUAGE TRANSFER in which one language shows the influence of another. It is sometimes preferred to the more widely used term "transfer" and especially "interference", because "cross-linguistic influence" avoids associations with BEHAVIOURISM.

cross-over groups *n*
(in teaching) a group activity in which the class is initially divided into groups for discussion. After a period of time, one or more member(s) of each group move to join other groups, and the discussion continues. This allows for ideas to be shared without the need for a whole-class feedback session.

cross-section(al) method *n*
also **cross-section(al) study**
a study of a group of different individuals or subjects at a single point in time, in order to measure or study a particular topic or aspect of language (for example use of the tense system of a language). This can be contrasted with a **longitudinal method** or **longitudinal study**, in which an individual or group is studied over a period of time (for example, to study how the use of the tense system changes and develops with age).

CRT *n*
an abbreviation for CRITERION-REFERENCED TEST(ING)

CTEFLA
an abbreviation for **Certificate in Teaching English as a Foreign Language to Adults** (now replaced by CELTA).

C-Test *n*

a variation of the cloze test where beginning with the second word in the second sentence the second half of every second word in a reading passage is deleted with the first sentence intact. Only the exact word method is used.

cue *n*

(in language teaching) a signal given by the teacher in order to produce a response by the students. For example in practising questions:

cue	response
time	*What time is it?*
day	*What day is it?*

Cues may be words, signals, actions, etc.
see also DRILL

cued recall *n*

see RECALL

Cuisenaire rods *n*

a set of 10 small blocks of wood with a uniform cross-section but with different lengths, each rod having its own colour. The rods were developed to teach arithmetic but were introduced into language teaching by Caleb Gattegno and his teaching method called SILENT WAY in which they were used to teach and practise sounds, words and sentence formation.

cultural capital *n*

the resources needed to be a successful member of a society. These may include one's knowledge, skills, and experiences. **Linguistic capital** includes any dimension of language knowledge or proficiency that is valued in a community or COMMUNITY OF PRACTICE, such as knowing a prestige language, speaking with a particular ACCENT, or being skilled at the use of professional JARGON.

cultural disadvantage *n*

also **cultural deprivation**

the theory that some children, particularly those from lower social and economic backgrounds, lack certain home experiences and that this may lead to learning difficulties in school. For example, children from homes which lack books or educational games and activities to stimulate thought and language development may not perform well in school. Since many other factors could explain why some children do not perform well in school, this theory is an insufficient explanation for differences in children's learning abilities.
see also COMPENSATORY INSTRUCTION, CULTURAL RELATIVISM

cultural imperialism *n*

in language teaching, the transmission of ideas about a dominant culture during the course of teaching (i.e. via textbooks, the choice of content, etc.) in which certain cultural sterotypes and values are presented as universal and superior while others (either by omission or by direct presentation) are viewed as inferior.

cultural literacy *n*

familiarity with cultural and other types of knowledge (e.g. literary, historical, political, artistic) regarded as necessary for informed participation in a nation or culture. Cultural literacy may or may not be something possessed by a person who is bilingual.

culturally relevant curriculum/instruction *n*

curriculum and instructional practices that acknowledge the beliefs, norms and values of learners in relation to content and concepts being taught. This may influence the choice of content, examples, modes of presentation, grouping structures, learning strategies, etc., in order to promote better understanding and learning.

cultural pluralism *n*

a situation in which an individual or group has more than one set of cultural beliefs, values, and attitudes. The teaching of a foreign language or programmes in BILINGUAL EDUCATION are sometimes said to encourage cultural pluralism. An educational programme which aims to develop cultural pluralism is sometimes referred to as **multicultural education,** for example a programme designed to teach about different ethnic groups in a country.

cultural relativism *n*

the theory that a culture can only be understood on its own terms. This means that standards, attitudes, and beliefs from one culture should not be used in the study or description of another culture. According to this theory there are no universal cultural beliefs or values, or these are not regarded as important. Cultural relativism has been part of the discussions of LINGUISTIC RELATIVITY and CULTURAL DEPRIVATION.

cultural studies *n*

an academic field that studies the conditions under which individuals acquire or lose social and historical identities (their "culture") through the use of various symbolic systems, including language.

culture *n*

the set of practices, codes and values that mark a particular nation or group: the sum of a nation or group's most highly thought of works of literature, art, music, etc. A difference is sometimes made between "High" culture of literature and the arts, and small "c" culture of attitudes, values, beliefs, and everyday lifestyles. Culture and Language combine to form what is sometimes called "Discourses", i.e. ways of talking, thinking, and behaving that reflect one's social identity.

The cultural dimension of language learning is an important dimension of second language studies. Education is seen as a process of socialization with the dominant culture. In foreign language teaching the culture of the language may be taught as an integral part of the curriculum.

culture fair *adj*

also **culture free** *adj*

(in language testing) a test which does not favour members of a particular cultural group, because it is based on assumptions, beliefs, and knowledge which are common to all the groups being tested, is called culture fair. For example, the following test item is not culture fair:

Bananas are — (a) brown, (b) green, (c) yellow.

The item is culturally biased because for some people bananas are thought of as yellow, but for others green bananas are eaten, and cooked bananas are brown. If only one of these answers is marked as correct, the test favours a particular cultural group.

culture shock *n*

strong feelings of discomfort, fear, or insecurity which a person may have when they enter another culture. For example, when a person moves to live in a foreign country, they may have a period of culture shock until they become familiar with the new culture.

curriculum[1] *n*

1 an overall plan for a course or programme, as in *the freshman composition curriculum*. Such a programme usually states:

    a the educational purpose of the programme, in terms of aims or goals

    b the content of the programme and the sequence in which it will be taught (also known as the *syllabus*)

    c the teaching procedures and learning activities that will be employed (i.e. *methodology*)

    d the means used to assess student learning (i.e. *assessment* and testing)

    e the means used to assess whether the programme has achieved its goals (i.e. *evaluation*)

2 the total programme of formal studies offered by a school or institution, as in the *secondary school curriculum.*

curriculum² *n*

another term for SYLLABUS

curriculum alignment *n*

the extent to which the different elements of the curriculum (goals, syllabus, teaching, assessment) match. For example if a curriculum is organized communicatively, but assessment procedures are based on grammatical criteria or if teaching materials in a course do not reflect the objectives there will be a lack of curriculum alignment.

curriculum development *n*

also **curriculum design**

the study and development of the goals, content, implementation, and evaluation of an educational system. In language teaching, curriculum development (also called syllabus design) includes:

a the study of the purposes for which a learner needs a language (NEEDS ANALYSIS)

b the setting of OBJECTIVES, and the development of a SYLLABUS, teaching METHODS and materials

c the EVALUATION of the effects of these procedures on the learner's language ability.

curriculum frameworks *n*

see STANDARDS

curriculum guide *n*

a written document describing the academic curriculum of a school and usually containing a description of its teaching philosophy, its goals and objectives, and its methods of teaching and assessment.

curriculum ideology *n*

the beliefs and values which provide the philosophical justification for educational programmes and the kinds of aims they contain. An ideology represents a particular point of view concerning the most important knowledge and value from the culture. Common curriculum ideologies in language teaching are:

1 *academic rationalism*: the view that the curriculum should stress the intrinsic value of the subject matter and its role in developing the learner's intellect, humanistic values and rationality. This justification is often used for justifying the teaching of classical languages.

2 *social and economic efficiency*: the view that the curriculum should focus on the practical needs of learners and society and the role of an educational programme in producing learners who are economically productive. This is the commonest aim associated with the teaching of English.

3 *learner-centredness*: the view that the curriculum should address the individual needs of learners, the role of individual experience, and the need to develop awareness, self-reflection, critical thinking, learner strategies and other qualities and skills believed to be important for learners to develop.

4 *social-reconstructionism*: the view that schools and teaching should play a role in addressing social injustices and inequality. Education is not seen as a neutral process, and schools should engage teachers and learners in an examination of important social issues and seek ways of resolving them. This is the ideology of critical pedagogy.

5 *cultural pluralism*: the view that schools should prepare students to participate in several different cultures and not merely the culture of the dominant social and economic group.

cursive writing *n*

also **longhand**

handwriting in which the letters within a word are joined, as compared with MANUSCRIPT WRITING in which letter forms look like ordinary type and are unconnected within each word.

examples:

cursive writing   manuscript writing

cutoff score *n*

a score on a CRITERION above or below which test takers are classified as either masters or non-masters of the criterion concerned. For example, if the cutoff score is set at 80 out of 100 (i.e. 80%), then only those who score at or above 80 are considered to have successfully mastered material covered in a course and are eligible for graduation or advancement to the next higher level.

see STANDARD SETTING

cyclical approach *n*

another term for SPIRAL APPROACH

D

Daedalus Integrated Writing Environment *n*

a package of computer tools to help students develop their skills in writing and critical thinking, designed to run on a local area network (LAN).

Daedalus Interchange *n*

in COMPUTER ASSISTED LANGUAGE LEARNING, a software program used in language courses that allows synchronous communication, peer editing, and citation instruction, among other features.

dangling modifier *n*

(in composition) a phrase or clause that does not modify anything in a sentence or which refers to the wrong word in a sentence.

For example, in the sentence:

Walking home from school, the fire engine came screeching around the corner.

the phrase *walking home from school* modifies *fire engine*, making an inappropriate sentence. This could be corrected to:

Walking home from school, <u>I saw</u> the fire engine come screeching around the corner.

The phrase *walking home from school*, now modifies *I* in the main clause, and the sentence is no longer inappropriate

data *n* (singular **datum**)

(in research) information, evidence or facts gathered through experiments or studies which can be analyzed in order to better the understanding of a phenomenon or to support a theory.

data bank *n*

see DATABASE

database *n*

also **data bank** *n*

a large body of information or data which is intended to be used for a specific purpose. In a language programme, a database which contains information about students' tests scores on all tests taken in the institution may be established. Later, this database may be used to determine students' rates of learning or the effectiveness of tests for particular purposes. In first or second language acquisition research, a database may contain examples of sentences produced by learners at different stages of learning, which could later be analyzed for a variety of purposes.

data driven teaching *n*, **data driven learning** *n*
> in language teaching, teaching that is informed by authentic real-life language use based on information derived from a corpus.

dative alternation *n*
> in English, sentences containing a logical direct and indirect (DATIVE[1]) object can be realized in two alternative ways:
> V NP to/for NP, for example, *he threw the ball to his son* or *he cut a piece of cake for her*, the **prepositional dative construction**
> V NP NP, for example, *he threw his son the ball*, *he cut her a piece of cake*, the **double object construction**
> Not all verbs permit both versions of the alternation.

dative case[1] *n*
> the form of a noun or noun phrase which usually shows that the noun or noun phrase functions as the INDIRECT OBJECT of a verb.
> For example, in the German sentence:
> > *Sie gab der Katze eine Schale Milch.*
> > She gave the cat a dish (of) milk
> in the noun phrase *der Katze*, the article has the inflectional ending –er to show that the noun phrase is in the dative case because it is the indirect object of the verb.
> see also CASE[1]

dative case[2] *n*
> (in CASE GRAMMAR) the noun or noun phrase which refers to the person or animal affected by the state or action of the verb is in the dative case.
> For example, in the sentences:
> > *Gregory was frightened by the storm.*
> > *I persuaded Tom to go.*
> *Gregory* and *Tom* are in the dative case. Both Gregory and Tom are affected by something: Gregory is frightened and Tom experiences persuasion.
> The dative case is sometimes called the **experiencer case**.

daughter (dependency) *n*
> see SISTER (DEPENDENCY)

DCT *n*
> see DISCOURSE COMPLETION TEST

dead language *n*

also **extinct language**

a language that no longer has any native speakers.

decision-making *n*

in teaching, thinking processes employed by teachers in planning, conducting and evaluating lessons or aspects of lessons, particularly when different instructional choices are involved. Two kinds of decision-making are often referred to:

1 **pre-active decision-making**: decisions that are made prior to teaching, such as determining the content of a lesson

2 **interactive decision-making**: unplanned decisions made during a lesson, such as a decision to drop a planned activity

Decision-making has been viewed as a central component of teacher thinking. Teachers' classroom actions are characterized by judgements and decisions that shape and determine the effectiveness of teaching. However, not all teacher action can be explained in terms of decision-making. Teachers' actions are also guided by routines and by tacit or intuitive plans of action.

declarative *n*

see SPEECH ACT CLASSIFICATION

declarative knowledge *n*

also **factual knowledge** (in cognitive psychology and learning theory), one of two ways information is stored in LONG TERM MEMORY.

Declarative knowledge is information that consists of consciously known facts, concepts or ideas that can be stored as PROPOSITIONS. For example, an account of the tense system in English can be presented as a set of statements, rules, or facts, i.e. it can be learned as declarative knowledge. This can be contrasted with **procedural knowledge**, that is knowledge concerning things we know how to do but which are not consciously known, such as "how to ride a bicycle", or "how to speak German". Procedural knowledge is acquired gradually through practice, and underlies the learning of skills. Many aspects of second language learning consist of procedural rather than declarative knowledge.

see also ADAPTIVE CONTROL OF THOUGHT

declarative sentence *n*

a sentence which is in the form of a STATEMENT. For example:

I'm leaving now.

Declarative sentences may or may not have the function of a statement.

For example:

I suppose you're coming this evening.
often functions as a question.
I'd like you to leave immediately.
often functions as an order or request.

declension *n* **decline** *v*

a list of the case forms (see CASE[1]) of a noun phrase in a particular language.
For example, in German:

nominative case:	*der Mann*	"the man"
accusative case:	*den Mann*	"the man"
dative case:	*dem Mann*	"to the man"
genitive case:	*des Mannes*	"of the man"

decoding *n* **decode** *v*

the process of trying to understand the meaning of a word, phrase, or sentence. When decoding a speech UTTERANCE, the listener must:

a hold the utterance in short term memory (see MEMORY)

b analyze the utterance into segments (see CHUNKING) and identify clauses, phrases, and other linguistic units

c identify the underlying propositions and illocutionary meaning (see SPEECH ACT).

Decoding is also used to mean the interpretation of any set of symbols which carry a meaning, for example a secret code or a Morse signal.
see also ENCODING, MESSAGE, INFORMATION PROCESSING, INFORMATION THEORY

deconstruct *v*

also **problematize**

to undermine (or problematize) an established way of thinking about things by analyzing a concept or IDEOLOGY which was previously taken for granted. For example, one might question taken-for-granted ways of thinking about learning and teaching, learners and teachers, and so forth.
see also HEGEMONY

decontextualized *adj*

examples of language use (e.g. in a textbook lesson) that are presented without information concerning how they were used in a real context and which consequently fail to represent fully the meaning of a sentence or utterance. Many language teaching approaches (e.g. WHOLE LANGUAGE, COMMUNICATIVE LANGUAGE TEACHING), argue that language should always be presented in context.

decreolization *n*

the process by which a CREOLE becomes more like the standard language from which most of its vocabulary comes. For example, an English-based creole may become more like Standard English. If educational opportunities increase in a region where a creole is spoken and the standard language is taught, then there will be a range from the creole spoken by those with little or no education to the standard language spoken by those with high levels of education. This has been happening in countries like Jamaica and Guyana where there is a range from an English-based creole to a variety close to standard educated English.

see also POST-CREOLE CONTINUUM

deduction *n*

in composition, two ways of presenting an argument are sometimes contrasted: reasoning by deduction and by **induction**. Reasoning by deduction proceeds from a generalization to particular facts which support it, whereas reasoning by **induction** involves moving from particular facts to generalizations about them.

see also ESSAY

deductive learning *n*

also **learning by deduction**

an approach to language teaching in which learners are taught rules and given specific information about a language. They then apply these rules when they use the language. Language teaching methods which emphasize the study of the grammatical rules of a language (for example the GRAMMAR TRANSLATION METHOD) make use of the principle of deductive learning.

This may be contrasted with inductive learning or learning by induction, in which learners are not taught grammatical or other types of rules directly but are left to discover or induce rules from their experience of using the language. Language teaching methods which emphasize use of the language rather than presentation of information about the language (for example the DIRECT METHOD, COMMUNICATIVE APPROACH, and COUNSELLING LEARNING) make use of the principle of inductive learning.

deep structure *n*

see GENERATIVE THEORY

deficit hypothesis *n*

also **verbal deficit hypothesis**

the theory that the language of some children may be lacking in vocabulary, grammar, or the means of expressing complex ideas, and may therefore be inadequate as a basis for success in school. Applied linguists have criticized this hypothesis and contrasted it with the **difference hypothesis**. This states that although the language of some children (e.g. children from certain social and ethnic groups) may be different from that of middle-class children, all DIALECTS are equally complex and children can use them to express complex ideas and to form a basis for school learning.

see also CULTURAL DEPRIVATION

defining relative clause *n*
    also **restrictive relative clause**
    a CLAUSE which gives additional information about a noun or noun phrase in a sentence. A defining relative clause restricts or helps to define the meaning of the noun. It usually begins with *who*, *which*, *whom*, *whose*, or *that*, and in written English is not separated from the noun by a comma:
    The man whom you met is my uncle.
    The woman that you want to speak to has left.
    This may be contrasted with a **non-defining relative clause** (also called a **non-restrictive relative clause**), which gives additional information but which does not restrict or define the noun or noun phrase. In writing, it is separated by a comma:
    My uncle, who is 64, still plays football.

defining vocabulary *n*
    a basic list of words with which other words can be explained or defined. Defining vocabularies are used to write definitions in dictionaries for children and for people studying foreign languages. They are based on research into WORD FREQUENCY. In the *Longman Dictionary of Contemporary English*, all definitions are written using a 2000 word defining vocabulary, so that anyone who knows the meaning of those 2000 words will be able to understand all the definitions in the dictionary.

definite article *n*
    see ARTICLE

definition method *n*
    see METHODS OF DEVELOPMENT

degenerate *adj*
    (in GENERATIVE THEORY) the claim that the input to language learners is degenerate, that is, imperfect or containing performance errors. Because learners have no principled way to distinguish between degenerate and

properly formed utterances, it is believed that exposure to input alone is insufficient to explain how language is learned.

deictic *adj* deixis *n*

a term for a word or phrase which directly relates an utterance to a time, place, or person(s).

Examples of deictic expressions in English are:

a   *here* and *there*, which refer to a place in relation to the speaker:
  The letter is here. (near the speaker)
  The letter is over there. (further away from the speaker)

b   *I* which refers to the speaker or writer.
  you which refers to the person or persons addressed.
  he/she/they which refer to some other person or persons.

delayed correction *n*

in language teaching, an error correction technique in which the teacher corrects a learner's error some time after an error has been made, rather than immediately, in order to avoid interrupting fluency practice. For example the teacher may put a list of tense errors on the board after students have carried out a role-play activity.

delayed recall *n*

see IMMEDIATE RECALL

deletion *n* delete *v*

when a speaker leaves out a sound, morpheme, or word from what he/she is saying, this is called deletion. For example, in casual or rapid speech, speakers of English often delete the final consonant in some unstressed words, so *a friend of mine* becomes *a friend o'mine*.

delexical verbs *n*

high-frequency verbs such as *do*, *make*, *take*, and *get* in their collocations with other words, which have little lexical content on their own but which take their meaning from the words with which they co-occur, as is seen in the different meanings of *make* in *make a mistake*, *make progress*, or *make it through*.

DELTA *n*

an abbreviation for **Diploma in English Language Teaching to Adults** (UCLES)

DELTYL *n*

an abbreviation for **Diploma in English Language Teaching to Young Learners** (UCLES)

demonstrative *n*

a word (a PRONOUN or a DETERMINER) which refers to something in terms of whether it is near to or distant from the speaker. The demonstratives in English are: *this*, *that*, *these*, *those*.

For example:

You take these books (here) and *I'll take those* (there).

In Indonesian they are *ini* and *itu*.

buku ini (book this)

buku itu (book that)

denotation *n* **denotative** *adj*

that part of the meaning of a word or phrase that relates it to phenomena in the real world or in a fictional or possible world.

For example, the denotation of the English word *bird is* a two-legged, winged, egg-laying, warm-blooded creature with a beak. In a meaning system, **denotative meaning** may be regarded as the "central" meaning or "core" meaning of a lexical item. It is often equated with referential meaning (see REFERENCE) and with **cognitive meaning** and **conceptual meaning** although some linguists and philosophers make a distinction between these concepts.

see also CONNOTATION

denotative meaning *n*

see DENOTATION

dental *adj*

describes a speech sound (a CONSONANT) produced by the front of the tongue touching the back of the upper front teeth.

For example, in French the /t/ in /tɛr/ *terre* "earth" and the /d/ in /du/ *doux* "sweet" are dental STOPS.

In English, /t/ and /d/ are usually ALVEOLAR stops. The use of dental in place of alveolar sounds by non-native speakers of English helps to create a "foreign accent".

see also PLACE OF ARTICULATION, MANNER OF ARTICULATION

dependability *n*

also **replicability**

(in QUALITATIVE RESEARCH) the issue of whether the same study using the same methods in a similar context would produce the same results (similar to the concept of RELIABILITY in QUANTITATIVE RESEARCH). However, since qualitative researchers believe that the prospects for true replicability are rare, dependability is often approached in other ways, for example by having another person systematically review the data and procedures used by the researcher (a technique sometimes called **auditing**).

dependency grammar *n*

a grammatical theory in which the verb is considered to be the central and most important unit. Verbs are classified according to the number of noun phrases they require to complete a sentence. This number is called the **valency** of the verb. The English verb *blush*, for instance, would have a valency of one:

The verb *give*, as in *The salesgirl gave Jane the parcel* would have a valency of three:

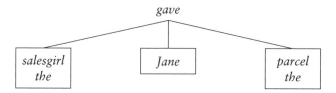

This type of grammar has been developed mainly in France and Germany and is different from many other grammars because of its verb-centred approach.

see also CASE GRAMMAR

dependent clause *n*

also **subordinate clause**

a clause which must be used with another clause to form a complete grammatical construction. It depends on the other clause and is subordinate to it. A clause which can be used on its own is called an independent clause. For example:

> <u>*When it rains*</u>, *please bring in the washing.*
> dependent   independent
> clause   clause
> *She told me*   <u>*that she was going abroad*</u>
> independent dependent
> clause   clause

Dependent or subordinate clauses are often linked to independent clauses by a subordinating CONJUNCTION like *when*, *that*, etc., or by a relative pronoun like *who*, *whose*, etc.

An independent clause (also called a **main clause** or a **principal clause**) does not depend on another clause, although it may be linked to another independent clause, or to a dependent clause. For example:

I will put the money in the bank or *I will spend it.*
independent   independent
clause   clause
I am going straight home after *I've seen the movie.*
independent   dependent
clause   clause

dependent preposition *n*

a preposition that always occurs with a particular noun, verb or adjective or before another word. For example the prepositions in:
interested in, depend on, bored with

dependent variable *n*

also **criterion variable**

(in research) a VARIABLE[1] that changes or is influenced according to changes in one or more **independent variables**. In empirical studies, one or more variables (the independent variable) may be studied as a cause or **predictor** that is hypothesized to have an effect on another variable (the dependent variable). For example, we may wish to study the effects of attitudes and motivation on language proficiency. Attitudes and motivation would be the independent variables, while language proficiency would be the dependent variable.

depth interview *n*

a detailed and extended INTERVIEW covering a wide range of topics in order to obtain as much information as possible and to explore unknown variables that are introduced during the interview.
see also FOCUSED INTERVIEW, GUIDED INTERVIEW

derivation *n*

in PHONOLOGY, the process of applying a set of phonological rules to an underlying form. For example, in French one can derive a form such as [bõ] *bon* ("good") from an underlying form /bon/ by means of two rules, one of which nasalizes a vowel before a nasal consonant, the second of which deletes a syllable-final nasal consonant.

in MORPHOLOGY and WORD FORMATION, the formation of new words by adding AFFIXES to other words or morphemes. For example, the noun *insanity* is derived from the adjective *sane* by the addition of the negative prefix *in-* and the noun-forming suffix *–ity*. Derivation typically results in changes of PARTS OF SPEECH. It can be contrasted with INFLECTION, which never changes the lexical category.

in SYNTAX, the process of applying grammatical rules to underlying forms, for example, in deriving S-STRUCTURE from D-STRUCTURE.

derived score *n*

(in statistics) any type of score other than a RAW SCORE. A derived score is calculated by converting a raw score or scores into units of another scale. For example, the number of correct responses in a text (the raw score) may be converted into grades from A to F (a derived score).

see also STANDARD SCORE

DES *n*

an abbreviation for Diploma in English Studies (UCLES)

description *n*

see ESSAY

descriptive adequacy *n*

see GENERATIVE THEORY

descriptive function *n*

see FUNCTIONS OF LANGUAGE[1]

descriptive grammar *n*

a grammar which describes how a language is actually spoken and/or written, and does not state or prescribe how it ought to be spoken or written.

If a descriptive grammar of a non-prestige variety of English were written, it might show, for example, that speakers of this variety sometimes said:

I seen 'im. instead of *I saw him.*

'im 'n' me done it. instead of *He and I did it.*

see also PRESCRIPTIVE GRAMMAR

descriptive research *n*

an investigation that attempts to describe accurately and factually a phenomenon, subject or area. Surveys and case studies are examples of descriptive research. The study of language teaching methodology has sometimes been criticized because of the lack of descriptive research describing how teachers actually use methods in the classroom.

see also BASIC RESEARCH, APPLIED RESEARCH, ACTION RESEARCH, CLASSROOM-CENTRED RESEARCH

descriptive statistics *n*

statistical procedures that are used to describe, organize and summarize the important general characteristics of a set of data. A descriptive statistic is a number that represents some feature of the data, such as measures of CENTRAL TENDENCY and DISPERSION.

descriptive writing *n*

see MODES OF WRITING

descriptor *n*

a description of the level of performance required of a test taker for a specific level or BAND on a rating scale. A descriptor can be general, consisting of a short sentence, or fairly detailed, consisting of a paragraph with several sentences.

see also SCORING RUBRIC

deskilling *n*

the loss of skills which a person once had through lack of use. In teaching, deskilling refers to the removal of a teacher's responsibility and participation in certain important aspects of teaching, leaving the teacher to deal with lower-level aspects of instruction. Some educators argue that the over-dependence on textbooks deskills teachers, since textbooks do much of the thinking and planning that teachers themselves should be allowed to do.

detection *n*

see ATTENTION

determiner *n*

a word which is used with a noun, and which limits the meaning of the noun in some way. For example, in English the following words can be used as determiners:

a ARTICLES, e.g. *a* pencil, *the* garden
b DEMONSTRATIVES, e.g. *this* box, *that* car
c POSSESSIVES, e.g. *her* house, *my* bicycle
d QUANTIFIERS, e.g. *some* milk, *many* people
e NUMERALS, e.g. the *first* day, *three* chairs

developmental bilingual education *n*
also **late-exit bilingual education**

bilingual education programmes for language minority students who enter school with limited or no proficiency in English but who are proficient in other languages. Such programmes are intended to maintain the students' proficiency in home languages while promoting effective development of English.

developmental error *n*

an ERROR in the language use of a first or second language learner which is the result of a normal pattern of development, and which is common among language learners. For example, in learning English, first and second language learners often produce verb forms such as *comed*, *goed*, and *breaked* instead of *came*, *went*, and *broke*. This is thought to be because they have learned the rule for regular past tense formation and then apply it to all verbs. Later such errors disappear as the learners' language ability increases. These OVER-GENERALIZATIONS are a natural or developmental stage in language learning.
see also INTERLANGUAGE, ERROR ANALYSIS

developmental feature *n*

see MULTIDIMENSIONAL MODEL

developmental functions of language *n*

according to Halliday, a young child in the early stages of language development is able to master a number of elementary functions of language. Each of these functions has a choice of meanings attached to it. He distinguishes seven initial functions:

a **Instrumental** ("I want"): used for satisfying material needs
b **Regulatory** ("do as I tell you"): used for controlling the behaviour of others
c **Interactional** ("me and you"): used for getting along with other people
d **Personal** ("here I come"): used for identifying and expressing the self
e **Heuristic** ("tell me why"): used for exploring the world around and inside one
f **Imaginative** ("let's pretend"): used for creating a world of one's own
g **Informative** ("I've got something to tell you"): used for communicating new information.

At about 18 months, the child is beginning to master the adult's system of communicationn, including grammar, vocabulary and meaning components (see FUNCTIONS OF LANGUAGE²)

developmental interdependence hypothesis *n*

see THRESHOLD HYPOTHESIS

developmental psychology *n*

a branch of psychology which deals with the development of mental, emotional, psychological, and social processes and behaviour in individuals, particularly from birth to early childhood.
see also GENETIC EPISTEMOLOGY

developmental sequence *n*

(in second and foreign language learning) a succession of phases in acquiring new linguistic forms. An important issue in theories of SECOND LANGUAGE ACQUISITION is whether learners' errors result from LANGUAGE TRANSFER or are sometimes DEVELOPMENTAL ERRORS. It has been suggested that a developmental sequence may explain how many learners acquire the rules for NEGATION in English. Learners may first produce forms such as *I no like that* (instead of *I don't like that*) and *No drink some milk* (instead of *I don't want to drink any milk*), even when the learner's mother tongue has similar negation rules to English. As language learning progresses, a succession of phases in the development of negation is observed, as *no* gives way to other negative forms such as *not* and *don't*. A developmental sequence is thus said to occur with the development of negation in English.

developmental testing *n*

see FIELD TESTING

devoicing *n*

see VOICE[2]

diachronic linguistics *n*

an approach to linguistics which studies how languages change over time, for example the change in the sound systems of the Romance languages from their roots in Latin (and other languages) to modern times or the study of changes between Early English to Modern British English. The need for diachronic and synchronic descriptions to be kept apart was emphasized by the Swiss linguist Saussure. Not all approaches to linguistic analysis make this distinction (see GENERATIVE PHONOLOGY).

see also COMPARATIVE HISTORICAL LINGUISTICS

diacritics *n*

small added marks placed over, under, or through a letter that can be used to distinguish different values of a sound. For example, the addition of ~ distinguishes the velarized lateral /ɫ/ in *feel* from the non-velarized /l/ in *leaf*.

diagnostic questionnaire *n*

a learner questionnaire used to find out what problems students report they have when using a second language. It is usually given at the beginning of a course as part of a NEEDS ANALYSIS.

diagnostic test *n*

a test that is designed to provide information about L2 learners' strengths and weaknesses. For example, a diagnostic pronunciation test may be used to measure the L2 learners' pronunciation of English sounds. It would show which sounds L2 learners are and are not able to pronounce or whether their pronunciation is intelligible or not. Diagnostic tests may be used to find out how much L2 learners know before beginning a language course to better provide an efficient and effective course of instruction.

diagramming *n*

(in teaching composition) a technique which is sometimes used to show how the parts of a sentence are related. For example:

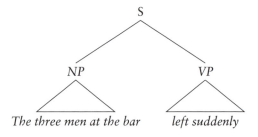

see also BASE COMPONENT

dialect *n* **dialectal** *adj*

a variety of a language, spoken in one part of a country (regional dialect), or by people belonging to a particular social class (social dialect or SOCIO-LECT), which is different in some words, grammar, and/or pronunciation from other forms of the same language.
A dialect is often associated with a particular ACCENT[3]. Sometimes a dialect gains status and becomes the STANDARD VARIETY of a country.
see also SPEECH VARIETY

dialect levelling *n*

also **koinéization**

a process through which dialect differences become reduced, for example when people speaking different dialects move to a new area and the variety spoken in that place after a time becomes a more common variety with fewer features associated with the specific dialects of those who migrated there. Dialect levelling has been a major process in the formation of both American and other varieties of English such as New Zealand English.

dialectology *n*

the study of the regional variations of a language (see DIALECT).

Usually, studies in dialectology have concentrated on different words used in various dialects for the same object or on different pronunciations of the same word in different dialects.

see also AREAL LINGUISTICS

dialogic teaching *n*

in teacher education, teaching which centres around planned and focused conversation among teachers and addresses teaching and learning issues. During such conversations teachers examine their own beliefs and practices and engage in collaborative planning, problem-solving and decision-making.

dialogue *n*

(in language teaching) a model conversation, used to practise speaking and to provide examples of language usage. Dialogues are often specially written to practise language items, contain simplified grammar and vocabulary, and so may be rather different from real-life conversation.

dialogue journals *n*

written (electronically or by hand) or orally recorded discussions between student and teachers in a writing programme, about school-related or other topics of interest to student.

Dialogue journals may be used to develop writing skills, to enable teachers to assess the value of a course or get student feedback and to develop fluency in writing.

see LEARNING LOG

diary study *n*

(in second language acquisition) a regularly kept journal or written record of a learner's language development, often kept as part of a longitudinal study (see LONGITUDINAL METHOD) of language learning. In many diary studies, the researcher and the diarist are the same person, and the diarist records examples of his or her own linguistic productions, hypotheses about the target language, information about the communicative setting involved (i.e. the participants, the purpose, etc.), and information concerning affect. In other studies, a researcher analyzes diaries kept by one or more learners who may or may not have been given guidance about what to include. Diary studies are often used to supplement other ways of collecting data, such as through the use of experimental techniques.

dichotic listening *n*

a technique which has been used to study how the brain controls hearing and language. Subjects wear earphones and receive different sounds in the right and left ear. They are then asked to repeat what they hear. Subjects find it easier to repeat what they heard in one ear than in the other, and this is thought to indicate which brain hemisphere controls language for them (see BRAIN). The ability to perceive language better in the right ear than the left ear is called a **right-ear advantage,** and the ability to perceive language better in the left ear is called **left-ear advantage.**

dichotomous scoring *n*

a scoring method where items are scored either right or wrong, mostly used in tests adopting a TRUE/FALSE ITEM or MULTIPLE-CHOICE ITEM format.

dictation *n*

a technique used in both language teaching and language testing in which a passage is read aloud to students or test takers, with pauses during which they must try to write down what they have heard as accurately as possible.

diction *n*

1 a term sometimes used to describe the way in which a person pronounces words, particularly the degree of clarity with which he or she speaks.
2 (in composition) the choice of words employed by the writer, particularly the extent to which the words the writer uses are thought suitable and effective for different kinds of writing.

dicto-comp *n*

a technique for practising composition in language classes. A passage is read to a class, and then the students must write out what they understand and remember from the passage, keeping as closely to the original as possible but using their own words where necessary.

see also DICTATION

dictogloss *n*

a technique for teaching grammatical structures in context. The teacher reads a short passage at normal speed containing specific grammatical structures. Students take notes then work in small groups and attempt to reconstruct the passage using the correct grammatical structures.

see also DICTO-COMP

DIF *n*

an abbreviation for DIFFERENTIAL ITEM FUNCTIONING

170

difference hypothesis *n*

see DEFICIT HYPOTHESIS

differential item functioning *n*

a test item that functions differently either for or against a particular group of test takers (e.g. those with Korean as their L1 or those with French as their L1). A DIF item may be considered biased when a score difference between two or more groups is due to a factor (e.g. test takers' L1) that is not the construct being tested (e.g. L2 listening comprehension).

difficulty index *n*

see ITEM FACILITY

difficulty order *n*

see ACCURACY ORDER

difficulty parameter *n*

see B-PARAMETER

digital divide *n*

the fact that those with access to technology have an unfair advantage over those who do not.

diglossia *n*

when two languages or language varieties exist side by side in a community and each one is used for different purposes, this is called diglossia. Usually, one is a more standard variety called the **High variety** or **H-variety**, which is used in government, the media, education, and for religious services. The other one is usually a non-prestige variety called the **Low-variety** or **L-variety**, which is used in the family, with friends, when shopping, etc.

An example of diglossia can be found in the German speaking part of Switzerland, where the H(igh) variety is a form of standard German (Hochdeutsch) and the L(ow) variety is called Schwyzertüütsch, which is a range of regional Swiss dialects. Other countries where diglossia exists are, for example, Haiti and the Arab nations.

see also BILINGUALISM, MULTILINGUALISM, CODE SELECTION

diminutive *n*

(in MORPHOLOGY) a form which has an AFFIX with the meaning of "little", "small", etc. For example, in Spanish –*ito/-ita* in *besito* ("a little kiss") and *mesita* ("a little table") or English, -*let* as in *piglet* and *starlet*, and -*ling* as in *duckling*.

d-index *n*
see ITEM DISCRIMINATION

diphthong *n* **diphthongal** *adj* **diphthongize** *v*
a vowel in which there is a change in quality during a single syllable, as in the English words *boy, buy, bow*. Diphthongs can be analyzed as a sequence of two vowels or as VOWEL + GLIDE.

direct access *n*
see ACCESS

directional hypothesis *n*
see ONE-TAILED TEST

directive *n*
see SPEECH ACT CLASSIFICATION

direct method *n*
a method of foreign or second language teaching which has the following features:
a only the target language should be used in class
b meanings should be communicated "directly" (hence the name of the method) by associating speech forms with actions, objects, mime, gestures, and situations
c reading and writing should be taught only after speaking
d grammar should only be taught inductively (see DEDUCTIVE LEARNING); i.e. grammar rules should not be taught to the learners
The direct method was developed in the late nineteenth century as a reaction against the GRAMMAR TRANSLATION METHOD and was the first oral-based method to become widely adopted. Some of its features were retained in later methods such as SITUATIONAL LANGUAGE TEACHING.

direct negative evidence *n*
see EVIDENCE

direct object *n*
see OBJECT[1]

direct object relative clause *n*
another term for OBJECT RELATIVE CLAUSE

direct speech *n*

a style used to report what a speaker actually said, without introducing any grammatical changes. In English, the speaker's words may be written between quotation marks, for example, *"You are a thief", he said*. This may be contrasted with **indirect speech** (also **reported speech**), for example, *He said I was a thief*.

direct teaching *n*

also **active teaching**

sometimes used to describe an approach to teaching which seeks to increase achievement by focusing the teacher's attention on specific, analytical and academic objectives, by coverage of objectives to be tested, by engagement of students in tasks, and by giving feedback which focuses on the degree to which objectives have been achieved. Attention is given to promoting student success in learning through a teacher-directed style of teaching in which the teacher provides a favourable CLIMATE for learning.

see also TIME ON TASK

direct test *n*

a test that measures ability directly by requiring test takers to perform tasks designed to approximate an authentic target language use situation as closely as possible. An example of a direct test of writing includes a test that asks test takers to write an essay; an ORAL PROFICIENCY INTERVIEW (OPI) is an example of a direct test of speaking, which is conducted face to face between an interviewer and an interviewee.

see also INDIRECT TEST, SEMI-DIRECT

disambiguation *n* **disambiguate** *v*

the use of linguistic analysis to show the different structures of an ambiguous sentence. For example:

The lamb is too hot to eat.

can be analyzed as:

a The lamb is so hot that it cannot eat anything

or:

b The cooked lamb is too hot for someone to eat it.

see also AMBIGUOUS

discontinuous constituent *n*

parts of a sentence which belong to the same CONSTITUENT but which are separated by other constituents are called a discontinuous constituent. For example:

    a in French, the negative of the verb is formed with the discontinuous
       constituent ne . . . pas as in:
       Paul ne mange pas beaucoup.
       "Paul doesn't eat much."
    b in English, the phrasal verb *pick up* in
       The player picked the ball up.
       is a discontinuous constituent.

discourse *n*

a general term for examples of language use, i.e. language which has been
produced as the result of an act of communication.

Whereas grammar refers to the rules a language uses to form grammatical
units such as CLAUSE, PHRASE, and SENTENCE, discourse normally refers to
larger units of language such as paragraphs, conversations, and interviews.
Sometimes the study of both written and spoken discourse is known as
DISCOURSE ANALYSIS; some researchers however use discourse analysis to
refer to the study of spoken discourse and TEXT LINGUISTICS to refer to the
study of written discourse.

In POSTMODERNISM and CRITICAL DISCOURSE ANALYSIS, discourse is used
to indicate not only any kind of talk but also the meanings and values
embedded in talk. In this sense, a **dominant discourse** refers to an institutionalized way of thinking and talking about things.

discourse accent *n*

(in writing) those characteristics of writing produced by **non-native writers**
which make it different from the writing of **native writers**. For example,
non-native patterns of rhetorical organization in an essay or non-native use
of cohesive devices, topics, and paragraph organization may contribute to
a writer's discourse accent.

see also CONTRASTIVE RHETORIC

discourse analysis *n*

the study of how sentences in spoken and written language form larger
meaningful units such as paragraphs, conversations, interviews, etc. (see
DISCOURSE).

For example, discourse analysis deals with:

    a how the choice of articles, pronouns, and tenses affects the structure of
       the discourse (see ADDRESS FORMS, COHESION)
    b the relationship between utterances in a discourse (see ADJACENCY PAIRS,
       COHERENCE)
    c the MOVES made by speakers to introduce a new topic, change the topic,
       or assert a higher ROLE RELATIONSHIP to the other participants

Analysis of spoken discourse is sometimes called CONVERSATIONAL ANALYSIS. Some linguists use the term TEXT LINGUISTICS for the study of written discourse.

Another focus of discourse analysis is the discourse used in the classroom. Such analyses can be useful in finding out about the effectiveness of teaching methods and the types of teacher-student interactions.

see also SPEECH EVENT

discourse community *n*

a group of people involved in a particular disciplinary or professional area (e.g. teachers, linguists, doctors, engineers) who have therefore developed means and conventions for doing so. The type of discourse used by a discourse community is known as a GENRE. The concept of discourse community thus seeks to explain how particular rhetorical features of texts express the values, purposes, and understandings of particular groups and mark membership of such groups.

discourse competence *n*

see COMMUNICATIVE COMPETENCE

discourse completion test *n*

also **DCT**

a type of questionnaire that presents a sociolinguistic description of a situation followed by part of a discourse designed to elicit a specific SPEECH ACT. The responses elicited can then be analyzed as speech act realizations of the desired type. For example, a discourse completion test designed to elicit some kind of apology, might produce responses such as:

I'm sorry.
I won't do that again.
What can I do to fix the situation?

discourse marker *n*

a class of expressions consisting of words (*however*, *still*), phrases (*as a matter of fact*) or clauses (*to make myself clear*) that serve to monitor and organize ongoing discourse. Discourse markers serve a variety of functions in spoken discourse, including indicating topic boundaries (*so*, *right*), openings (*well then*), closure or pre-closure (*so*) as well as reflecting the ongoing interaction between speaker and hearer (*you know*, *you see*, *I mean*).

discourse structure *n*

another term for SCHEME

discovery learning *n*

also **inquiring-based learning**

(in education) an approach to teaching and learning which is based on the following principles:

a Learners develop processes associated with discovery and inquiry by observing, inferring, formulating hypotheses, predicting and communicating.

b Teachers use a teaching style which supports the processes of discovery and inquiry.

c Textbooks are not the sole resources for learning.

d Conclusions are considered tentative and not final.

e Learners are involved in planning, conducting, and evaluating their own learning with the teacher playing a supporting role.

A number of language teaching approaches make use of discovery based approaches to learning, particularly communicative language teaching (see COMMUNICATIVE APPROACH) and the SILENT WAY.

discrete *adj* **discreteness** *n*

(of a linguistic unit) having clearly defined boundaries.

In PHONOLOGY, the distinctive sound units of a language (the PHONEMES) are considered to be discrete units. For example, the English word *pin* would consist of three such units: /p/, /ɪ/, and /n/.

discrete item *n*

in language teaching, a learning item such as a sound , word, or sentence pattern, that is isolated and practised out of context in order to give particular attention to the item itself. Later it may be practised in context. For example the teacher may drill a specific sound contrast using MINIMAL PAIRS, and later practise the sound contrast in a dialogue.

discrete-point test *n*

a language test that measures knowledge of individual language items, such as a grammar test with different sections on tenses, adverbs, and prepositions. Discrete-point tests are based on the theory that language consists of different parts (e.g. grammar, pronunciation, and vocabulary) and different skills (e.g. listening, speaking, reading, and writing) and these are made up of elements that can be tested separately. Tests consisting of MULTIPLE-CHOICE ITEMS are usually discrete-point tests. Discrete-point tests can be contrasted with INTEGRATIVE TESTS.

discriminant validity *n*

also **divergent validity**

(in testing) a type of CONSTRUCT VALIDITY that is based on the extent to which two or more tests that are claimed to measure different underlying CONSTRUCTs are in fact doing so. For example, to establish discriminant validity of two tests that are claimed to measure the different constructs (e.g. L2 listening and L2 vocabulary), both tests are administered to the same group of test takers using the same method (e.g. MULTIPLE-CHOICE ITEMs for both tests) and the test scores are correlated. If a weak or no correlation is obtained, this is an indication that they are indeed measuring different constructs.

see CONSTRUCT VALIDITY, CONVERGENT VALIDITY, MULTI-TRAIT MULTI-METHOD METHOD

discrimination[1] *n*

see STIMULUS-RESPONSE THEORY

discrimination[2]

also **discrimination power**

(in testing) the degree to which a test or an item in a test distinguishes among stronger and weaker test takers. For example, if test takers are known to have different degrees of ability but all score around 85% on a test, the test fails to discriminate. A measure of the discrimination of a test is known as a **discrimination index**.

see also ITEM DISCRIMINATION

discrimination index *n*

see DISCRIMINATION

discrimination power *n*

another term for DISCRIMINATION

discursive practices *n*

a term used in CRITICAL DISCOURSE ANALYSIS to refer to the processes of production, distribution and interpretation that surround a text and which must be taken into account in text analysis. These practices are themselves viewed as embedded in wider social practices of power and authority.

discussion method *n*

an approach to teaching which consists of a goal-focused group conversation involving either groups of students or the whole class, and which usually involves interaction about subject matter between a teacher and students. Four common types of discussion procedures are used, which differ according to the degree of teacher control.

1 **recitation:** a teacher directed and highly structured discussion in which the teacher checks to see if students have learned certain facts
2 **guided discussion:** a less structured discussion in which the teacher seeks to promote understanding of important concepts
3 **reflective discussion:** the least structured form of discussion in which students engage in critical and creative thinking, solve problems, explore issues, etc.
4 **small group discussion:** the class is divided into small groups, with students assuming responsibility for the discussion.

disjunct *n*
> also **sentential adverb**
> see ADJUNCT

dispersion *n*
> (in statistics and testing) the amount of spread among the scores in a group. For example, if the scores of students on a test were widely spread from low, middle to high, the scores would be said to have a large dispersion. Some common statistical measures of dispersion are VARIANCE, STANDARD DEVIATION, and RANGE.

display question *n*
> a question which is not a real question (i.e. which does not seek information unknown to the teacher) but which serves to elicit language practice. For example:
>> *It this a book?*
>> *Yes, it's a book.*
>
> It has been suggested that one way to make classes more communicative (see COMMUNICATIVE APPROACH) is for teachers to use fewer display questions and more REFERENTIAL QUESTIONs.
> see also RHETORICAL QUESTION

dissertation *n*
> a formal written paper or report describing the writer's own original research, usually as a requirement for an M.A. or Ph.D. degree.
> A THESIS is similar to a dissertation (and the two words are sometimes used interchangeably) but is not so extensive and may not necessarily report original research, e.g. it may be an extended piece of expository writing on a given topic.

distance education *n*

also **distance learning**

the linking of learners and teachers in different locations and often in real time, by telephone, telecast, satellite, computer and other technological support, or through the use of learning packages. Distance education usually has four characteristics: the physical separation of teacher and learner, the influence or control of an educational institution, the involvement of some form of media, and two-way communication in some form. Distance education is widely used both for the delivery of language courses and language teacher education courses.

see also E-LEARNING, ONLINE LEARNING

distinctive feature *n*

(in PHONOLOGY) a particular characteristic which distinguishes one distinctive sound unit of a language (see PHONEME) from another or one group of sounds from another group.

For example, in the English sound system, one distinctive feature which distinguishes the /p/ in *pin* from the /b/ in *bin* is VOICE[1]. The /b/ is a voiced STOP whereas the /p/ is a voiceless stop (see VOICE[2]).

In GENERATIVE PHONOLOGY, distinctive features play an important part in the writing of phonological rules. The features are generally shown in the form of a binary opposition, that is the feature is either present [+] or absent [–].

For example, vowels and sounds such as /l/, /n/, and /m/, where the air passes relatively freely through the mouth or nose, have the feature [+ sonorant] whereas sounds such as /p/, /k/, and /s/, where the air is stopped either completely or partially, have the feature [– sonorant].

see also BINARY FEATURE

distractor *n*

any of the incorrect options in a MULTIPLE-CHOICE ITEM. In ITEM ANALYSIS, a **distractor efficiency analysis** is conducted to investigate whether the distractors are functioning as intended (i.e. attracting test takers into choosing incorrect options when they do not know the correct answer). This analysis needs the percentage of test takers in high, mid or low ability groups who chose each correct or incorrect option to be calculated per each item. Provided together with both ITEM FACILITY and ITEM DISCRIMINATION indices, the result of the analysis helps test developers to better decide which items to keep, revise, or discard.

see also KEY, TEST ITEM, MULTIPLE-CHOICE ITEM

distractor efficiency analysis *n*

see DISTRACTOR

distribution[1] *n*

(in statistics) the pattern of scores or measures in a group. For example, the frequency distribution of scores in a test may be displayed in either tabular (e.g. a) or graphic format (e.g. b and c):

a. Table

Test scores	10	20	30	40	50	60	70	80	90	100
Frequency	1	1	3	7	10	6	5	2	2	0

b. Histogram

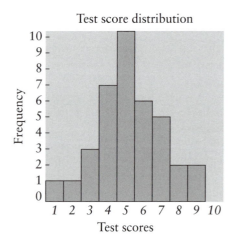

c. Frequency polygon

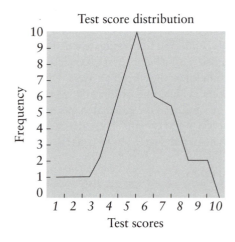

distribution² *n*

the range of positions in which a particular unit of a language, e.g. a PHONEME or a word, can occur is called its distribution.

For example, in English, the phoneme /ŋ/, usually written *ng*, cannot occur at the beginning of a word but it can occur in final position, as in *sing*. In other languages, /ŋ/ may occur word initially, as in Cantonese *ngoh* "I".

disyllabic *adj*

consisting of two SYLLABLES, e.g. the English word *garden* /ˈgɑː/ + /dən/.

see also MONOSYLLABIC

ditransitive verb *n*

see TRANSITIVE VERB

divergence¹ *n*

the process of two or more languages or language varieties becoming less like each other. For example, if speakers of a language migrate to another area, the variety of language spoken by them may become less similar to the variety spoken by those who did not migrate, i.e. there will be divergence. This has been the case with English spoken in the United Kingdom compared with the varieties of English spoken in the USA, Canada, Australia, and New Zealand.

see also CONVERGENCE¹

divergence² *n*

see ACCOMMODATION

divergent question *n*

a question that elicits student responses that vary or diverge. For example, divergent questions may be used when a teacher wishes to compare students' ideas about a topic. There are often no right or wrong answers with divergent questions.

see also CONVERGENT QUESTION, EVALUATIVE QUESTION, QUESTIONING TECHNIQUES, CLASSROOM DISCOURSE

divergent validity *n*

another term for DISCRIMINANT VALIDITY

diversity *n*

in reference to a group of learners or individuals in society, the quality of including people of many different ethnic, cultural, and linguistic backgrounds or physical abilities. The move to recognize and promote cultural diversity is known as MULTICULTURALISM. Many countries contain minority groups of many different cultural, religious, and linguistic backgrounds, but promote only the culture of the dominant group in curriculum, teaching materials, the media, etc. Proponents of the status of diversity seek acknowledgement of cultural diversity throughout society, the encouragement of tolerance, the need to redress past discrimination against minorities, and the creation of a more tolerant society.

DO *n*

an abbreviation for **direct object** or **object relative clause**
see NOUN PHRASE ACCESSIBILITY HIERARCHY

document analysis *n*

see DOCUMENTARY ANALYSIS

documentary analysis *n*

(in QUALITATIVE RESEARCH) the collection and analysis of documents at a research site as part of the process of building a GROUNDED THEORY. The documents collected may be private or public, primary documents (e.g. letters, diaries, reports) or secondary documents (e.g. transcribed and edited diaries), and both solicited and unsolicited documents.

dogme ELT *n*

a term taken from the film industry (*dogme*) and used to support the language teaching principle that the classroom should be rid of excessive materials and resources in order to focus on the inner life of the student and real communication.

domain[1] *n*

an area of human activity in which one particular speech variety or a combination of several speech varieties is regularly used. A domain can be considered as a group of related **speech situations** (see SPEECH EVENT). For instance, situations in which the persons talking to one another are members of the family, e.g. mother and children, father and mother, elder sister and younger sister, would all belong to the Family Domain. In BILINGUAL and MULTILINGUAL communities, one language may be used in some domains and another language in other domains. For example, Puerto Ricans in the USA may use Spanish in the Family Domain and English in the Employment Domain.

see also DIGLOSSIA, SPEECH EVENT

domain² *n*

see PROJECTION (PRINCIPLE)

domain³ *n*

in planning goals and OBJECTIVEs for an educational programme, the particular area or aspect of learning an objective or set of objectives is designed to address. Three general domains of objectives are often distinguished.

1 **cognitive domain:** objectives which have as their purpose the development of students' intellectual abilities and skills

2 **affective domain:** objectives which have as their purpose the development of students' attitudes, feelings and values

3 **psychomotor domain:** objectives which have as their purpose the development of students' motor and co-ordination abilities and skills.

see also BLOOM'S TAXONOMY

domain⁴ *n*

see DOMAIN-REFERENCED TEST(ING)

domain-referenced test(ing) *n*

a specific type of CRITERION-REFERENCED TEST where a test taker's performance is measured against a **domain** or a well-defined set of instructional objectives to assess how much of the domain a test taker has learned.

dominant discourse *n*

see DISCOURSE

dominant language *n*

the language that one uses most often and is most competent in. In TRANSLATION and INTERPRETATION, this is often considered more appropriate as an indication of a translator's or interpreter's ability than terms such as FIRST LANGUAGE or MOTHER TONGUE.

see LANGUAGE DOMINANCE

dominate *v*

see NODE

dorsal *n, adj*

see VELAR

dorsum *n*

see PLACE OF ARTICULATION

do-support *n*

in English, use of the "dummy" auxiliary *do* to form questions or negatives in sentences such as *Do you want some tea?* and *He doesn't want any tea*, respectively. Most of the world's languages do not have a comparable construction.

DOTE *n*

an abbreviation for **Diploma for Overseas Teachers of English** (UCLES). Now replaced by DELTA.

doubled consonants *n*

see GEMINATES

double negative *n*

a construction in which two negative words are used.
For example, in NONSTANDARD English
I never seen nothing.
instead of
I haven't seen anything.
A double-negative does not become a positive. It is used for emphasis.

double-object construction *n*

see DATIVE ALTERNATION

downtoner *n*

a group of intensifiers that indicate a lessening of an aspect of meaning, such as *hardly*, *partially*, *slightly*.
I am *slightly deaf* in one ear.

drafting *n*

see COMPOSING PROCESSES

drill *n*

a technique commonly used in older methods of language teaching particularly the **audiolingual method** and used for practising sounds or sentence patterns in a language, based on guided repetition or practice. A drill which practises some aspect of grammar or sentence formation is often known as **pattern practice**.
There are usually two parts to a drill.
a The teacher provides a word or sentence as a stimulus (the **call-word** or CUE).
b Students make various types of responses based on repetition, substitution, or transformation. For example:

type of drill	teacher's cue student	student
substitution drill	We bought a book. pencil	We bought a pencil.
repetition drill	We bought a book. We bought a pencil.	We bought a book. We bought a pencil.
transformation drill	I bought a book.	Did you buy a book? What did you buy?

Drills are less commonly used in communicative methodologies since it is argued that they practise pseudo-communication and do not involve meaningful interaction.

D-structure *n*

(in Government/Binding Theory) an abstract level of sentence representation where semantic roles such as agent (the doer of an action) and patient (the entity affected by an action) are assigned to the sentence. *Agent* is sometimes also referred to as the **logical subject** and *patient* as the **theme** of the sentence. For example (in simplified form):

Vera   shoot   intruder
agent or logical   patient or theme
subject

The next level of sentence representation is the S-STRUCTURE where syntactic/ grammatical cases such as nominative/grammatical subject and accusative/ grammatical object are assigned. For example (in simplified form):

Vera (agent)   shoot   intruder (patient/theme)
grammatical subject   grammatical object

The **phonetic form** (PF) component and the **logical form** (LF) component are then needed to turn the S-structure into a surface sentence. The phonetic form (PF) component presents the S-structure as sound, and the logical form (LF) component gives the syntactic meaning of the sentence.

The concepts of semantic roles and grammatical cases and their inter-relation have been used in first and second language acquisition research (see θ-THEORY)

DTEFLA *n*

an abbreviation for **Diploma in Teaching English as a Foreign Language to Adults** (UCLES). Now replaced by DELTA.

dual *adj n*

see LANGUAGE UNIVERSAL

dual immersion *n*
see TWO-WAY IMMERSION EDUCATION

duality of structure *n*
a distinctive characteristic of language which refers to the fact that languages are organized in terms of two levels. At one level, language consists of sequences of segments or units which do not themselves carry meaning (such as the letters "g", "d" and "o"). However, when these units are combined in certain sequences, they form larger units and carry meaning (such as *dog, god*).

durative *n*
see ASPECT

dyad *n*
two people in communication with each other. A dyad can be considered as the smallest part of a larger communication network. For example, in describing language use within a family, some dyads would be mother-child, grandmother-child, elder sister-younger sister.

dynamic verb *n*
see STATIC-DYNAMIC DISTINCTION

dynamic systems theory *n*
also **dynamical systems theory**
a theory that seeks to explain complex systems in which variables interact with each other and the system continually changes. Weather and traffic patterns are examples of dynamic systems. Such models have begun to be applied to SLA, in recognition of the fact that language learning shows some of the core characteristics of dynamic systems, including inter-connectedness of subsystems (e.g. both social and cognitive), development over time, and variation.

dysfluency *n* **dysfluent** *adj*
see FLUENCY

dysgraphia *adj*
a learning disability that causes difficulty in the ability to write at a level typical of one's age, intelligence or education. It may result is difficulty in spelling, letter formation and other difficulties and lead to both mental and physical discomfort when trying to write.

dyslexia *n* **dyslexic** *adj*
> also **word blindness**
>
> a general term sometimes used to describe any continuing problem in learning to read, such as difficulty in distinguishing letter shapes and words. Reading specialists do not agree on the nature or causes of such reading problems, however, and both medical and psychological explanations have been made. Because of the very general way in which the term is often used, many reading specialists prefer not to use the term, and describe reading problems in terms of specific reading difficulties.

dysphasia *n*
> another term for APHASIA

E

EAP *n*

an abbreviation for English for Academic Purposes

see ENGLISH FOR SPECIAL PURPOSES

early-exit/late-exit bilingual education programmes *n*

a term to distinguish two kinds of Transitional Bilingual Education programmes.

Early-exit programmes move children from bilingual classes in the first or second year of schooling. Late-exit programmes provide bilingual classes for three or more years of elementary schooling.

Ebonics *n*

another term for AFRICAN AMERICAN ENGLISH, the term derived from "ebony" + "phonics" or "black sounds". Ebonics has also been used as a superordinate term to refer generally to West-African–European language mixtures, with USEB (United States Ebonics) referring specifically to US language varieties.

echo-correction *n*

an error correction technique in which the teacher repeats a student's error with rising intonation, drawing the student's attention to the error so that he or she can self-correct it. For example:

Student: She **wear** contact lenses.

Teacher: **wear**?

Student: She **wears** contact lenses.

echoism *n*

another term for ONOMATOPOEIA

echolalia *n*

a type of speech disorder or APHASIA in which all or most of a speaker's utterances consist of the simple repetition or echoing of words or phrases which the speaker hears.

echo question *n*

see QUESTION

eclectic method *n*

a term sometimes used for the practice of using features of several different METHODS in language teaching, for example, by using both audiolingual and communicative language teaching techniques.

188

In order to have a sound eclectic method a core set of principles is needed to guide the teacher's selection of techniques, strategies, and teaching procedures.

see also AUDIOLINGUAL METHOD, COMMUNICATIVE APPROACH

ecology of language *n*
another term for LINGUISTIC ECOLOGY

economy principle *n*
in MINIMALISM, the principle that syntactic representations should contain as few constituents as possible and derivations should posit as few grammatical operations as possible.

ED-form *n*
a term used to refer to the simple past tense of a verb in English, e.g. "talked".

editing[1] *n*
the practices in second language writing classes of engaging students in activities that require correction of discrete language errors in their writing, such as errors in grammar, vocabulary, sentence structure, spelling, etc.
see also REVISION

editing[2] *n*
see COMPOSING PROCESSES

education *n*
in a general sense, the formal and informal processes of teaching and learning used to develop a person's knowledge, skills, attitudes, understanding, etc., in a certain area or domain. A distinction is sometimes made between the broader goals of education, described above, and TRAINING, which refers to the processes used to teach specific practical skills.

educational linguistics *n*
a term sometimes used to refer to a branch of APPLIED LINGUISTICS which deals with the relationship between language and education.

educational psychology *n*
a branch of psychology which studies theories and problems in education, including the application of learning theory to classroom teaching and learning, curriculum development, testing and evaluation, and teacher education.

educational technology *n*

    1 the use of machines and educational equipment of different sorts (e.g. language laboratories, tape recorders, video, etc.) to assist teachers and learners

    2 a system of instruction which contains (a) an analysis of what learners need to know and be able to do (b) a description of these needs as BEHAVIOURAL OBJECTIVES and (c) (1) above.

effect size *n*

a measure of the strength of one variable's effect on another or the relationship between two or more variables. When a researcher rejects the null hypothesis and concludes that an independent variable had an effect, an effect size is calculated to determine how strong the independent variable's effect (e.g. presence or absence of a bilingual programme) was on the dependent variable (e.g. academic performance). Effect size is often used as a common metric to make research results comparable across studies as it puts studies on the same scale.

see also META-ANALYSIS

EFL *n*

an abbreviation for ENGLISH AS A FOREIGN LANGUAGE

egocentric speech *n*

speech which is not addressed to other people. This is one of two types of speech which the psychologist Piaget observed in the speech of children learning a first language. Egocentric speech serves the purpose of giving pleasure to the child and of expressing the child's thoughts, and provides an opportunity for the child to experiment or play with speech. It may be contrasted with **socialized speech,** or speech which is addressed to other people and which is used for communication.

egocentric writing *n*

see READER-BASED PROSE

EGP *n*

an abbreviation for English for General Purposes

see ENGLISH FOR SPECIAL PURPOSES

elaborated code *n*

see CODE²

elaborative rehearsal *n*

see REHEARSAL

e-language *n*
also **externalized language**
see I-LANGUAGE

e-learning *n*
also **electronic learning**
forms of learning in which the teacher and the student are separated in space or time and connected through the use of online technologies. E-learning includes web-based learning, virtual classrooms, digital collaboration and delivery of content through the internet. It can be combined with face-to-face learning with a teacher, in BLENDED LEARNING.

electronic discussion *n*
online forums, such as bulletin boards, lists, or real-time conversation, that provide a written record of all correspondents' contributions.

electronic literacy *n*
the ability to read and write electronic texts. Electronic texts differ from written texts in numerous ways. They are often interactive, typically use nonlinear structures, and can incorporate symbolic elements not typically used with printed texts such as animation.

electronic portfolio *n*
in teacher education, a purposeful collection of a teacher's work assembled by electronic means and used to represent and display the teacher's efforts, growth and achievements in different areas. As with other kinds of PORT-FOLIO, the contents of an electronic portfolio are carefully planned and chosen in relation to its purpose and goals. The portfolio may be used as an aspect of professional development and also serve as the basis for assessment.

elementary school *n*
see SCHOOL SYSTEM

elicitation *n*
also **elicitation technique, elicitation procedure**
any technique or procedure that is designed to get a person to actively pro-duce speech or writing, for example asking someone to describe a picture, tell a story, or finish an incomplete sentence. In linguistics, these techniques are used to prompt native speakers to produce linguistic data for analysis. In teaching and second language research, the same and similar techniques are used to get a better picture of learner abilities or a fuller understanding

of INTERLANGUAGE than the study of naturally occurring speech or writing can provide.

elicited imitation *n*

an ELICITATION PROCEDURE in which a person has to repeat a sentence which he or she sees or hears. When people are asked to repeat a sentence which uses linguistic rules which they themselves cannot or do not use, they often make changes in the sentence so that it is more like their own speech. Elicited imitation can be used to study a person's knowledge of a language. For example:

stimulus sentence	elicited imitation
Why <u>can't the man</u> climb over the fence?	Why <u>the man can't</u> climb over the fence?

elision *n* **elide** *v*

the leaving out of a sound or sounds in speech. For example, in rapid speech in English, *suppose is* often pronounced as [spəʊz], *factory* as ['fæktri] and *mostly* as ['məʊsli].

see also ELLIPSIS, EPENTHESIS

ELL *n*

an abbreviation for English Language Learner

ellipsis *n* **elliptical** *adj*

the leaving out of words or phrases from sentences where they are unnecessary because they have already been referred to or mentioned. For example, when the subject of the verb in two co-ordinated clauses is the same, it may be omitted to avoid repetition:

The man went to the door and (he) opened it. (subject ellipsis)
Mary ate an apple and Jane (ate) a pear. (verb ellipsis)

see also ELISION

ELT *n*

an abbreviation for English Language Teaching. It is used especially in Britain to refer to the teaching of ENGLISH AS A SECOND LANGUAGE or ENGLISH AS A FOREIGN LANGUAGE. In north American usage this is often referred to as TESOL.

embedded sentence *n*

see EMBEDDING

embedding *n* **embed** *v*

(in GENERATIVE GRAMMAR) the occurrence of a sentence within another sentence.

For example, in:
The news that he had got married surprised his friends.

> (1) *The news*   ↑   *surprised his friends.*
> (2) (that) he had got married

sentence (2) is embedded in sentence (1) and is therefore an **embedded sentence.**

embodiment *n*

in COGNITIVE LINGUISTICS, the idea that aspects of cognition including language structure and language processing cannot be fully understood without referring to aspects of the systems they are embedded in, both the biology of the organism, including its brain, and the physical and social context.

emergentism *n*

the view that higher forms of cognition emerge from the interaction between simpler forms of cognition and the architecture of the human brain. For example, in LANGUAGE ACQUISITION, it has been proposed that categories such as the PARTS OF SPEECH are not innate but emerge as a result of the processing of INPUT by the perceptual systems.
see also CONNECTIONISM

emic approach *n*

related to the linguistic term PHONEMIC, an emic approach is one that attempts to describe phenomena from an insider's perspective, for example, in terms of categories that are meaningful to speakers of a particular language or members of a particular culture. This can be contrasted with an **etic approach** (related to the linguistic term PHONETICS), which takes an outsider's approach, attempting to describe the behavior in objective and culturally neutral terms.

emotive meaning *n*

another term for CONNOTATION

empathy *n* **empathize** *v*

the quality of being able to imagine and share the thoughts, feelings, and point of view of other people. Empathy is thought to contribute to the attitudes we have towards a person or group with a different language and culture from our own, and it may contribute to the degree of success with which a person learns another language.

emphatic pronoun *n*

a pronoun which gives additional emphasis to a noun phrase or which draws attention to it. In English these are formed in the same way as REFLEXIVE PRONOUNS, by adding -*self*, -*selves* to the pronouns. For example:

I *myself* cooked the dinner.

We spoke to the President *herself*.

emphatic stress *n*

see STRESS

empirical investigation *n*

see FIELDWORK

empirical validity *n*

a measure of the VALIDITY of a test arrived at by comparing the test with one or more CRITERION MEASURES. Such comparisons could be with:

a other valid tests or other independent measures obtained at the same time (e.g. an assessment made by the teacher) (CONCURRENT VALIDITY)

b other valid tests or other performance criteria obtained at a later time (PREDICTIVE VALIDITY)

This approach to validity can be contrasted with **judgemental validity**, such as CONTENT or FACE VALIDITY, that relies on theory rather than observation as in empirical validity.

empiricism *n*

the philosophical doctrine that all knowledge comes from experience. This can be contrasted with **rationalism**, which holds that knowledge comes from basic concepts known intuitively through reason, such as innate ideas (see INNATIST HYPOTHESIS).

empowerment *n*

the provision or development of skills, abilities, knowledge and information that could help someone improve his or her conditions. Empowerment is often viewed as a goal to assist people with low status, influence and power increase their chances of prosperity, power, and prestige. In some contexts second language courses seek not merely to teach language skills but to empower students to seek action to redress injustices they experience. Literacy and biliteracy are major means of empowering individuals and groups.

empty category *n*

(in GENERATIVE GRAMMAR) a category that has no surface realization.

see also TRACE

**empty "it " ** *n*

The function of "it" when there is no specific reference but "it" refers forward to something.

It is very cold outside today ("It" refers to the weather).

It is getting late ("It" refers to the time).

empty word *n*

see CONTENT WORD

enabling skills *n*

another term for MICRO-SKILLS

encoding *n* **encode** *v*

the process of turning a message into a set of symbols, as part of the act of communication.

In encoding speech, the speaker must:

a select a meaning to be communicated

b turn it into linguistic form using semantic systems (e.g. concepts, PRO-POSITIONS, grammatical systems (e.g. words, phrases, clauses), and phonological systems (e.g. PHONEMES, SYLLABLES).

Different systems of communication make use of different types of symbols to encode messages (e.g. pictorial representation, Morse code, drum beats).

see also DECODING

encoding specificity principle *n*

a principle of MEMORY that states that memory is improved when the information available at the time of encoding is also available at retrieval. For example, if one has learned a language in natural settings, it can be quite difficult to recall specific vocabulary words when removed from the environment in which they were learned.

endangered language *n*

a language that is in danger of falling out of use to such a degree that it ceases to have any native speakers and becomes extinct. UNESCO's Atlas of the World's Languages in Danger currently divides languages into "unsafe," "definitely endangered," and "severely endangered" languages. It is estimated that more than half of the world's languages are endangered to some degree.

En-form *n*

a term referring to the past participle form of a verb in English, e.g. *fallen*.

English as a foreign language *n*
    also **EFL**
    see ENGLISH AS A SECOND LANGUAGE

English as a Lingua Franca (ELF) *n*
    a term used to describe the status of English when it is used as a language of communication between two or more people who do not have English as a first language. As such it often reflects some characteristics of the speakers' first language or languages.
    see also ENGLISH AS AN INTERNATIONAL LANGUAGE, ENGLISH AS A WORLD LANGUAGE

English as an international language *n*
    also **EIL**
    a term used to characterize the status of English as the world's major second language and the commonest language used for international business, trade, travel, communication, etc. Like the term **World Englishes**, the notion of International Language recognizes that different norms exist for the use of English around the world. British, American, Australian or other mother-tongue varieties of English are not necessarily considered appropriate targets either for learning or for communication in countries where English is used for cross-cultural or cross-linguistic communication, for example, when a Brazilian and a Japanese businessperson use English to negotiate a business contract. The type of English used on such occasions need not necessarily be based on native speaker varieties of English but will vary according to the mother tongue of the people speaking it and the purposes for which it is being used.

English as a second dialect *n*
    also **ESD**
    the role of standard English (see STANDARD VARIETY) for those who speak other dialects of English.
    see also BIDIALECTAI, BILINGUAL EDUCATION

English as a second language *n*
    also **ESL**
    a basic term with several somewhat different definitions. In a loose sense, English is the second language of anyone who learns it after learning their FIRST LANGUAGE in infancy in the home. Using the term this way, no distinction is made between second language, third language, etc. However, English as a SECOND LANGUAGE is often contrasted with **English as a foreign language**. Someone who learns English in a formal classroom setting, with limited or no opportunities for use outside the classroom, in a country in

which English does not play an important role in internal communication (China, Japan, and Korea, for example), is said to be learning English as a foreign language. Someone who learns English in a setting in which the language is necessary for everyday life (for example, an immigrant learning English in the US) or in a country in which English plays an important role in education, business, and government (for example in Singapore, the Philippines, India, and Nigeria) is learning English as a second language.

English as a second language programme *n*
   also **ESL/ESOL programme**
   a programme for teaching English to speakers of other languages in English-speaking countries. ESL programmes are generally based on particular language teaching methods and teach language skills (speaking, understanding, reading, and writing). They may be school programmes for immigrant and other non-English-speaking children, used together with BILINGUAL EDUCATION or with regular school programmes, or community programmes for adults.

Englishes *n*
   a term used to reflect the fact that many different varieties of English exist today, including those spoken in countries where English is a mother tongue (e.g. the US, Canada), and those where it is spoken as a second language (e.g. India, Philippines).
   Thus there are said to be many different Englishes spoken today.
   see ENGLISH AS AN INTERNATIONAL LANGUAGE

English for Academic Purposes *n*
   also **EAP**
   English language courses designed to help learners study, conduct research, or teach in English, usually in universities or other post-secondary settings. Such courses may prepare students to take tests such as TOEFL or IELTS, they may prepare students to be able to deal with listening, speaking, reading and writing demands in academic courses, and may also address **study skills**. EAP is a branch of ENGLISH FOR SPECIAL OR SPECIFIC PURPOSES and based on the study of how language is used for academic purposes.

English for general purposes *n*
   also **EGP**
   see ENGLISH FOR SPECIAL PURPOSES

English for science and technology *n*
   also **EST**
   see ENGLISH FOR SPECIAL PURPOSES

English for Speakers of Other Languages *n*
     also **ESOL**
     see ENGLISH AS A SECOND LANGUAGE (1)

English for special purposes *n*
     also **English for specific purposes, ESP**
     the role of English in a language course or programme of instruction in
     which the content and aims of the course are fixed by the specific needs of a
     particular group of learners. For example courses in **English for academic
     purposes, English for science and technology,** and English for Nursing.
     These courses may be compared with those which aim to teach general
     language proficiency, **English for general purposes.**
     see also LANGUAGES FOR SPECIAL PURPOSES

English medium school *n*
     a school in which English is used as the major medium of instruction. This
     term is usually used in countries where English is a SECOND LANGUAGE.

English only *n*
     a term for a movement and philosophy in the US that seeks to make English the
     official language of the US and to discourage the use of bilingual education.

English plus *n*
     a term for a movement and philosophy in the US that advocates the belief
     that all US residents should have the opportunity to become proficient in a
     language other than English.

enhanced input *n*
     a type of spoken or written input provided to language learners in which
     some target language features are made more salient, such as by increasing
     their frequency or in speech by using stress or intonation to highlight them.

entailment *n*
     a relationship between two or more sentences (strictly speaking PROPOSI-
     TIONS). If knowing that one sentence is true gives us certain knowledge of
     the truth of the second sentence, then the first sentence entails the second.
     Entailment is concerned with the meaning of the sentence itself (see UTTER-
     ANCE MEANING). It does not depend on the context in which a sentence is used.
     see also IMPLICATION, UTTERANCE MEANING, PRESUPPOSTION

entry *n*
     (in teaching) that part of a lesson which begins it. An effective lesson is said
     to focus learners' attention on the lesson, inform them of the goals of the

lesson and what they are expected to learn, and serve as an "organizer", preparing them for an upcoming activity.
see also CLOSURE

entry test *n*
another term for PLACEMENT TEST

epenthesis *n* **epenthetic** *adj*
the addition of a vowel or consonant at the beginning of a word or between sounds. This often happens in language learning when the language which is being learned has different combinations of vowels or consonants from the learner's first language. For example, Spanish learners of English often say [espiːk] *espeak* for *speak*, as Spanish does not have words starting with the CONSONANT CLUSTER /sp/. Many speakers of other languages do not use combinations like the /lm/ or /lp/ of English and add an epenthetic vowel, for example [fɪləm] *filem* for *film*, and [heləp] *helep* for *help*.
see also ELISION, INTRUSION

epiphenomenalism *n*
the theory that events in the nervous system give rise to consciousness, but consciousness cannot effect events in the nervous system. That is, thoughts have no effect on behaviour.

episodic memory *n*
that part of the MEMORY which is organized in terms of personal experiences and episodes.
For example, if a subject was asked the question "What were you doing on Friday night at 7 pm?" he or she may think of all the things that happened from 5 pm up to 7 pm. The person builds up a sequence of events or episodes to help find the wanted information. Episodic memory may be contrasted with **semantic memory**. Semantic memory is that part of the memory in which words are organized according to semantic groups or classes. Words are believed to be stored in long term memory according to their semantic properties. Thus *canary is* linked in memory to *bird*, and *rose* is linked to *flower*. These links are a part of semantic memory.

equated forms *n*
two or more forms of a test whose test scores have been transformed onto the same scale so that a comparison across different forms of a test is made possible. For example, if both X and Y are equated forms of test Z, the test takers' scores will not be affected by which form of the test they take (i.e. X or Y).

equating *n*
> also **test equating**
> a process of establishing the scores that are equivalent on multiple forms of a test that measure the same TRAIT. Equating enables the scores of the equated forms of a test to be used interchangeably.

equative *adj*
> also **equational**
> a sentence in which the SUBJECT and COMPLEMENT refer to the same person or thing is called an equative sentence.
> For example, the English sentence:
> > *Susan   is the girl I was talking about.*
> > subject   complement

equilibration *n*
> another term for ADAPTATION[2]

equivalent form reliability *n*
> another term for ALTERNATE FORM RELIABILITY

equivalent forms *n*
> another term for PARALLEL FORMS

ERB *n*
> an abbreviation for ETHICAL REVIEW BOARD

ergative *adj*
> a term originally referring to languages in which the complement of a transitive verb and the subject of an intransitive verb are assigned the same CASE[1]. By extension, sometimes used to refer to English verbs such as *break*, which can occur in sentences such as *He broke the window* and *The window broke*, where *the window* seems to have the same THEMATIC ROLE in the two sentences even though on the surface it is object in one sentence and subject in the other.

ergative verb *n*
> a verb that can be either TRANSITIVE or INTRANSITIVE and whose subject when intransitive corresponds to the direct object when transitive. For example, *boil* in:
> > *He boiled a kettle of water.*
> > *The kettle boiled.*

error *n*

1 (in the speech or writing of a second or foreign language learner), the use of a linguistic item (e.g. a word, a grammatical item, a SPEECH ACT, etc.) in a way which a fluent or native speaker of the language regards as showing faulty or incomplete learning. A distinction is sometimes made between an error, which results from incomplete knowledge, and a **mistake** made by a learner when writing or speaking and which is caused by lack of attention, fatigue, carelessness, or some other aspect of PERFORMANCE. Errors are sometimes classified according to vocabulary (**lexical error**), pronunciation (**phonological error**), grammar (**syntactic error**), misunderstanding of a speaker's intention or meaning (**interpretive error**), production of the wrong communicative effect, e.g. through the faulty use of a speech act or one of the RULES OF SPEAKING (**pragmatic error**). In the study of second and foreign language learning, errors have been studied to discover the processes learners make use of in learning and using a language (see ERROR ANALYSIS).

2 see under SPEECH ERROR

see also DEVELOPMENTAL ERROR, GLOBAL ERROR

error analysis *n*

the study and analysis of the ERRORs made by second language learners. Error analysis may be carried out in order to:

a identify strategies which learners use in language learning

b try to identify the causes of learner errors

c obtain information on common difficulties in language learning, as an aid to teaching or in the preparation of teaching materials.

Error analysis developed as a branch of APPLIED LINGUISTICS in the 1960s, and set out to demonstrate that many learner errors were not due to the learner's mother tongue but reflected universal learning strategies. Error analysis was therefore offered as an alternative to CONTRASTIVE ANALYSIS. Attempts were made to develop classifications for different types of errors on the basis of the different processes that were assumed to account for them. A basic distinction was drawn between intralingual and interlingual errors (see INTERLINGUAL ERROR). Intralingual errors were classified as **overgeneralizations** (errors caused by extension of target language rules to inappropriate contexts), **simplifications** (errors resulting from learners producing simpler linguistic rules than those found in the target language), **developmental errors** (those reflecting natural stages of development), **communication-based errors** (errors resulting from strategies of communication), **induced errors** (those resulting from **transfer of training**), **errors of avoidance** (resulting from failure to use certain target language structures because they were thought to be too difficult), or **errors of overproduction** (structures being used too frequently). Attempts to apply such categories have been problematic however, due to the difficulty of determining the cause of errors. By the late 1970s, error analysis had largely been superseded by studies of INTERLANGUAGE and SECOND LANGUAGE ACQUISITION.

error correction *n*

strategies used by a teacher or more advanced learner to correct errors in a learner's speech. Error correction may be direct (teacher supplies the correct form) or indirect (the teacher points out the problem and asks the learner to correct it if possible).
see also FEEDBACK, RECAST

error gravity *n*

a measure of the effect that errors made by people speaking a second or foreign language have on communication or on other speakers of the language. The degree of error gravity of different kinds of errors (e.g. errors of pronunciation, grammar, vocabulary, etc.) varies; some errors have little effect, some cause irritation, while others may cause communication difficulties.
For example, in the sentences below, *a* causes greater interference with communication than *b* and shows a greater degree of error gravity.
*a   *Since the harvest was good, was rain a lot last year.*
*b   *The harvest was good last year, because plenty of rain.*

error of measurement *n*

also **measurement error, error score**
an estimate of the discrepancy between test takers' TRUE SCORES and their OBSERVED SCORES. Error can be classified as either random or systematic. **Random** or **unsystematic errors** are those that affect a test taker's score because of purely random happenings (e.g. guessing, problems with test administration or scoring errors), whereas **systematic errors** are those that consistently affect a test taker's score because of factors associated with a test taker or a test that are not related to the TRAIT being measured (e.g. a cultural bias in a test of reading comprehension).
see also CLASSICAL TEST THEORY, STANDARD ERROR OF MEASUREMENT

error score *n*

another term for ERROR OF MEASUREMENT

ESD *n*

an abbreviation for ENGLISH AS A SECOND DIALECT

ESL *n*

an abbreviation for ENGLISH AS A SECOND LANGUAGE

ESOL *n*

an abbreviation for English for Speakers of Other Languages (see ENGLISH AS A SECOND LANGUAGE (1))

ESP *n*

an abbreviation for ENGLISH FOR SPECIAL PURPOSES

essay *n*

(in composition) a longer piece of writing, particularly one that is written by a student as part of a course of study or by a writer writing for publication which expresses the writer's viewpoint on a topic.

see also METHODS OF DEVELOPMENT

essay test *n*

a SUBJECTIVE TEST in which a person is required to write an extended piece of text on a set topic.

essentialism *n*

the belief or assumption that certain group characteristics such as GENDER, sexuality, race, or ETHNICITY are universal to all members of the group, for example, the assumption that (all) humans are competitive, or that men are competitive while women are cooperative, or that there are essentially American or Russian or Japanese ways of speaking. **Anti-essentialism**, challenging such notions, is especially characteristic of FEMINIST LINGUISTICS and POSTMODERNISM.

EST *n*

an abbreviation for English for Science and Technology

see ENGLISH FOR SPECIAL PURPOSES

E-Tandem learning *n*

see TANDEM LEARNING

ethical review board *n*

also **ERB**

another term for INSTITUTIONAL REVIEW BOARD

ethnicity *n*

a term sometimes preferred to the term *race*, and used in research as a category to distinguish groups based on sociocultural characteristics, such as ancestry, language, religion, customs, and lifestyle.

ethnocentrism *n*

the belief that the values, beliefs and behaviours of one's own group are superior to those of others.

ethnographic interview *n*

a teaching technique designed to develop cultural understanding in second/ foreign language learning and that seeks to explore a culture from the point of view of an insider. An American student learning Mexican Spanish for example, might interview a speaker of Mexican Spanish by first asking him or her an open ended question such as "What are the most important values in Mexican culture?" Subsequent questions are then framed around the interviewee's responses. Unlike a *structured interview* the questions are not framed in advance.

ethnographic research *n*

see ETHNOGRAPHY

ethnography *n*

a branch of anthropology concerned with the detailed descriptive study of living cultures. The related field of **ethnology** compares the cultures of different societies or ethnic groups. As a research methodology, **ethnographic research** requires avoidance of theoretical preconceptions and hypothesis testing in favour of prolonged direct observation, especially PARTICIPANT OBSERVATION, attempting to see social action and the activities of daily life from the participants' point of view, resulting in a long detailed description of what has been observed. In studies of language learning and use, the term ethnographic research is sometimes used to refer to the observation and description of naturally occurring language (e.g. between mother and child or between teacher and students), particularly when there is a strong cultural element to the research or the analysis. However, much of this research is **quasi-ethnographic** at best, since the requirements of prolonged observation and THICK DESCRIPTION are frequently not met.

ethnography of communication *n*

the study of the place of language in culture and society. Language is not studied in isolation but within a social and/or cultural setting.
Ethnography of communication studies, for example, how people in a particular group or community communicate with each other and how the social relationships between these people affect the type of language they use.

The concept of an ethnography of communication was advocated by the American social anthropologist and linguist Hymes and this approach is important in SOCIOLINGUISTICS and APPLIED LINGUISTICS.

see also COMMUNICATIVE COMPETENCE, ETHNOMETHODOLOGY, ROLE RELATIONSHIP, SPEECH EVENT

ethnolinguistic *adj*

a set of cultural, ethnic and linguistic features shared by members of a cultural, ethnic, or linguistic sub-group.

ethnolinguistic identity *n*

an IDENTITY associated with belonging to a particular language community, including both ethnic and linguistic features.

ethnology *n*

see ETHNOGRAPHY

ethnomethodology *n* **ethnomethodologist** *n*

a branch of sociology that studies how people organize and understand the activities of ordinary life. It studies people's relations with each other and how social interaction takes place between people. Ethnomethodologists have studied such things as relationships between children and adults, interviews, telephone conversation, and TURN TAKING in conversation. Language is not the main interest of ethnomethodologists, but their observations on how language is used in everyday activities such as conversation are of interest to linguists and sociolinguists.

see also CONVERSATION ANALYSIS

etic approach *n*

see EMIC APPROACH

etymology *n* **etymological** *adj*

the study of the origin of words, and of their history and changes in their meaning.

For example, the etymology of the modern English noun *fish* can be traced back to Old English *fisc*.

In some cases there is a change in meaning. For example the word *meat*, which now normally means "animal flesh used as food", is from the Old English word *mete* which meant "food in general".

euphemism *n*

the use of a word which is thought to be less offensive or unpleasant than another word. For example, *indisposed* instead of *sick*, or *to pass away*, instead of *to die*.

evaluation *n*

in general, the systematic gathering of information for purposes of decision making. Evaluation may use quantitative methods (e.g. tests), qualitative methods (e.g. observations, ratings (see RATING SCALE)), and value judgements. In LANGUAGE PLANNING, evaluation frequently involves gathering information on patterns of language use, language ability, and attitudes towards language. In **language programme evaluation**, evaluation is related to decisions about the quality of the programme itself and decisions about individuals in the programmes. The evaluation of programmes may involve the study of CURRICULUM, OBJECTIVES, materials, and tests or grading systems. The evaluation of individuals involves decisions about entrance to programmes, placement, progress, and achievement. In evaluating both programmes and individuals, tests and other measures are frequently used.

see also FORMATIVE EVALUATION, SUMMATIVE EVALUATION

evaluative comprehension *n*

see READING

evaluative question *n*

a DIVERGENT QUESTION which requires students to make an evaluation, such as a question which asks students to say why they think a certain kind of behaviour is good or bad.

see also QUESTIONING TECHNIQUES

evidence *n*

in LANGUAGE ACQUISITION, two types of evidence are important for the learner. **Positive evidence** is evidence that something is possible in the language being learned. For example, if a learner of Spanish encounters sentences that have no subject, this serves as positive evidence that subjects do not (always) have to be overtly expressed in Spanish. **Negative evidence** is evidence that something is not possible. For example, in English, one can say *He sometimes goes there*, *Sometimes he goes there*, or *He goes there sometimes*, but it is ungrammatical to say **He goes sometimes there*, an order that is possible in some other languages (French, for example). **Direct negative evidence** in this case would consist of an explicit correction made by a teacher or conversational partner. The non-occurrence of such sentences in input may also constitute **indirect negative evidence** to the learner, but a learner could think that even though he or she has not heard such sentences they are possible. Some SLA theorists believe that neither direct nor indirect negative evidence plays a role in language learning and that only positive evidence contributes to acquisition.

exact replication *n*
see REPLICATION

exact word method *n*
see CLOZE TEST

examination *n*
any procedure for measuring ability, knowledge, or performance. An examination is normally a formally administered summative or proficiency test usually administered by an institution or examination board. The terms "examination" and "test" can be used interchangeably as there seems to be no generally accepted agreement regarding the distinction between the two.
see TEST

examinee *n*
another term for TEST TAKER

exchange *n*
a pattern of interaction among two or more people in discourse, especially in classrooms and small-group discussions. One very common such pattern is the sequence of three functional moves of teacher initiation (or opening), for example, "What's your answer to question 6, Peter?" followed by a student response, for example, "Taipei," followed by teacher feedback (or evaluation), for example, "Correct." This exchange pattern, which may account for as much as 70% of classroom discourse, is often referred to as **initiation-response-feedback (IRF)** or **initiation-response-evaluation (IRE)**.

exclamation[1] *n*
an utterance, which may not have the structure of a full sentence, and which shows strong emotion. For example: *Good God!* or *Damn!*
see also INTERJECTION

exclamation[2] *n*
also **exclamatory sentence**
an utterance which shows the speaker's or writer's feelings. Exclamations begin with a phrase using *what* or *how* but they do not reverse the order of the subject and the auxiliary verb:
How clever she is!
What a good dog!
see also STATEMENT, QUESTION

exclamation mark *n*

the form of punctuation used after an **exclamation**, such as
Well done!

exclusive (first person) pronoun *n*

a first person pronoun which does not include the person being spoken or
written to. In some languages there is a distinction between first person
plural pronouns which include the persons who are addressed (**inclusive
pronouns**) and those which do not (exclusive pronouns). For example, in
Malay:

exclusive	inclusive
kami	*kita*
"we"	"we"

see also PERSONAL PRONOUNS

exercise *n*

in teaching, an activity that is designed to practise a learning item.
see also ACTIVITY, DRILL, TASK

existential *adj*

(in linguistics) describes a particular type of sentence structure which often
expresses the existence or location of persons, animals, things, or ideas.
In English, a common existential sentence structure is:
There + a form of the verb *be*
For example:
There are four bedrooms in this house.
Another frequently used existential structure uses the verb to *have.*
For example:
English
This house has four bedrooms.
Malay
Ada dua teksi di sini. ("Have two taxis here")

exit test *n*

a type of ACHIEVEMENT TEST that is given at the end of a course.

expanded pidgin *n*

see PIDGIN

expansion *n*

see MODELLING

208

expectancy grammar *n*

see PRAGMATIC EXPECTANCY GRAMMAR

expectancy theory *n*

the theory that knowledge of a language includes knowing whether a word or utterance is likely to occur in a particular context or situation.

For example, in the sentence below, "expected" words in (1) and (2) are *dress* and *change*:

When the girl fell into the water she wet the pretty (1) she was wearing and had to go home and (2) it.

Knowledge of the expectancies of occurrence of language items is made use of in the comprehension of language.

see also PRAGMATICS

expectancy-value theory *n*

refers to a variety of theories of MOTIVATION that assume that people are motivated to do things that they perceive to have value and at which they expect to succeed.

experiencer case *n*

see DATIVE CASE

experiential learning *n*

in language learning, approaches to learning based on practical experience in using the language in real-life situations. Experiential learning can be contrasted with academic learning, which involves the study of a subject without necessarily any experience of it. For example in order to learn the language of the workplace, a learner may be asked to take part in "work-shadowing" – an opportunity to observe a work-shadow host and colleagues in a workplace, and to experience the kind of language and interaction the work-host is engaged with. Experiential learning is said to enhance motivation and awareness of required language skills and at the same time provide collaborative support to develop necessary language skills.

experiential verb *n*

a verb, such as the English verb *feel*, that has an EXPERIENCER CASE noun as its subject.

experimental design *n*

see EXPERIMENTAL METHOD

experimental group *n*

see CONTROL GROUP

experimental method *n*

an approach to educational research in which an idea or HYPOTHESIS is tested or verified by setting up situations in which the relationship between different participants or variables can be determined (see DEPENDENT VARIABLE). The plan for conducting an experimental study, specifically the plan(s) for selecting participants, manipulating dependent variables, treatment, and collecting data is called the **experimental design**.

expertise *n*

the special status someone obtains in performance of a task or occupation through experience of a special kind resulting in

1 developing a better level of performance at doing something
2 an increased level of knowledge of particular domains
3 the development of automaticity in the carrying out of operations that are needed to achieve a goal
4 an increased sensitivity to task demands and social situations when solving problems
5 greater flexibility in performance
6 understand problems at a deeper level than novices
7 greater speed and accuracy in resolving problems.

Work on expertise in teaching suggests that experienced teachers process information about classrooms differently than do novices as a result of a move from a teacher-centred to a more student-centred approach to teaching. The role of experience in developing expertise is problematic, since the two are not identical. Experience may develop fluency in carrying out tasks but not necessarily expertise. In comparing two teachers with a similar amount of teaching experience, one may be characterized as a fluent non-expert, and the other as an expert.

explanation text *n*

see TEXT TYPES

explanatory adequacy *n*

see GENERATIVE THEORY

explicit knowledge *n*

see IMPLICIT KNOWLEDGE

explicit learning *n*

learning language items (e.g. vocabulary) by means of overt strategies, such as techniques of memorization. This may be contrasted with IMPLICIT

LEARNING which refers to learning primarily by means of unconscious exposure to input.

see IMPLICIT LEARNING

explicit performative *n*

see PERFORMATIVE

explicit teaching *n*

an approach in which information about a language is given to the learners directly by the teacher or textbook.

exploitation *n*

in language teaching, the way a teacher uses teaching resources or materials in order to achieve a specific teaching or learning aim. For example magazine articles may be exploited to practise reading skills or to develop vocabulary.

exploratory factor analysis *n*

see FACTOR ANALYSIS

exponent *n*

see FUNCTIONAL SYLLABUS

exposition *n*

see TEXT TYPES

expository writing *n*

see MODES OF WRITING

expression *n*

in common usage, a phrase or group of words that has a fixed meaning, such as "*Goodness gracious me!*"

expressive *n*

see SPEECH ACT CLASSIFICATION

expressive approach *n*

an approach to the teaching of second language writing in which students focus on personal writing and development.

expressive function *n*

see FUNCTIONS OF LANGUAGE

expressive writing *n*

writing in which the writer expresses personal feelings, emotions, experiences, in personal letters, diaries, or autobiographies.

expressivist approach *n*

in the teaching of writing, the belief that the free expression of ideas leads to self discovery and that teachers should help students develop their own ideas, voice, and stance in order to produce fresh and spontaneous prose.

extension task *n*

in language teaching, an activity that gives learners further and sometimes more demanding practice of a new teaching item.

extensive reading *n*

in language teaching, reading activities are sometimes classified as extensive and intensive.

Extensive reading means reading in quantity and in order to gain a general understanding of what is read. It is intended to develop good reading habits, to build up knowledge of vocabulary and structure, and to encourage a liking for reading.

Intensive reading is generally at a slower speed, and requires a higher degree of understanding than extensive reading.

external speech *n*

see INNER SPEECH

external validity *n*

(in research design) the extent to which the results of an experimental study can be generalized to the larger population from which participants were drawn. Examples of threats to external validity include **selection bias** where a group of participants in the study is sampled with BIAS or **pre-test sensitization** where how participants respond to the TREATMENT may be affected by the pre-test they took.

see also INTERNAL VALIDITY, GENERALIZABILITY

extinction *n*

see STIMULUS-RESPONSE THEORY

extinct language *n*

another term for DEAD LANGUAGE

extraction *n*

a grammatical operation by which one CONSTITUENT is moved out of another. For example, in the sentence *Who did you say that you saw?*, the pronoun *who* has been extracted from an embedded clause (*you saw __*) and moved to the front of the sentence.

extralinguistic *adj*

describes those features in communication which are not directly a part of verbal language but which either contribute in conveying a MESSAGE, e.g. hand movements, facial expressions, etc., or have an influence on language use, e.g. signalling a speaker's age, sex, or social class.
see also PARALINGUISTICS, SIGN LANGUAGE

extraposition *n*

the movement of an element from its normal place to the end or near to the end of a sentence.
For example, the subject of some sentences can be moved to the end of the sentence:
a <u>Trying to get tickets</u> *was difficult.*
b *It was difficult <u>trying to get tickets</u>.*
In sentence *b It* is called the anticipatory subject, and *trying to get tickets* is called the **postponed subject.**
"Heavy" constituents are more likely to be placed near the end of a sentence than "light" ones. Compare *He picked the book up* with *He picked up the first book he saw.*

extrinsic motivation *n*

see MOTIVATION

extrovert (also extravert) *n* **extroversion (also extraversion)** *n*

a person whose conscious interests and energies are more often directed outwards towards other people and events than towards the person themself and their own inner experience. Such a personality type is contrasted with an introvert, a person who tends to avoid social contact with others and is often preoccupied with his or her inner feelings, thoughts and experiences. Psychologists no longer believe that these are two distinct personality types, since many people show aspects of both. Extroversion and introversion have been discussed as PERSONALITY factors in second language learning, though the contribution of either factor to learning is not clear.

eye span *n*

see READING SPAN

eye tracking *n*

a technique using special equipment to observe and record a subject's eye movements as they perform a task such as reading.

F

face *n*

in communication between two or more persons, the positive image or impression of oneself that one shows or intends to show to the other PARTICIPANTS is called face. In any social meeting between people, the participants attempt to communicate a positive image of themselves which reflects the values and beliefs of the participants. For example Ms Smith's "face" during a particular meeting might be that of "a sophisticated, intelligent, witty, and educated person". If this image is not accepted by the other participants, feelings may be hurt and there is a consequent "loss of face". Social contacts between people thus involve what the sociologist of language, Goffman, called **face-work**, that is, efforts by the participants to communicate a positive face and to prevent loss of face. The study of face and face-work is important in considering how languages express POLITENESS.

see also POSITIVE FACE, NEGATIVE FACE

face-saving *adj*

strategies used by speakers in interaction to avoid loss of FACE or to reduce the potential for loss of face, e.g. by asking questions indirectly (e.g. by asking "Are you free tonight?" instead of a more direct invitation "Would you like to go out tonight?") or by minimizing the weight of a request (e.g. "Can I talk to you *for a minute?*" instead of "Can I have half an hour of your time?").

face threatening act *n*

also **FTA**

a SPEECH ACT that is potentially threatening to the FACE of a speaker or hearer or threatening to the speaker or hearer's freedom of action. For example, apologies are potentially threatening to the good image of the speaker, while complaints are threatening to the good image of the hearer; requests potentially threaten the freedom of action of the hearer, while promises threaten the freedom of action of the speaker. In Brown and Levinson's theory of POLITENESS, potential threat to face is also influenced by SOCIAL DISTANCE and power relationships between speaker and hearer.

face to face interaction *n*

also **face to face communication**

communication between people in which the PARTICIPANTS are physically present. In contrast there are some situations where speaker and hearer may be in different locations, such as a telephone conversation.

face-to-face test *n*
see DIRECT TEST

face validity *n*
(in testing) the degree to which a test appears to measure the knowledge or abilities it claims to measure, based on the subjective judgement of an observer. For example, if a test of reading comprehension contains many dialect words that might be unknown to the test takers, the test may be said to lack face validity.
see also VALIDITY

face-work *n*
see FACE

facility *n*
see ITEM FACILITY

facility index *n*
see ITEM FACILITY

facility value *n*
see ITEM FACILITY

factitive case *n*
(in CASE GRAMMAR) the noun or noun phrase which refers to something which is made or created by the action of the verb is in the factitive case. For example, in the sentence:
Tony built the shed.
the shed is in the factitive case.
However, in the sentence:
Tony repaired the shed.
the shed is not in the factitive case as it already existed when the repair work was done. In this sentence, *the shed* is in the OBJECTIVE CASE.
The factitive case is sometimes called the **result** (or **resultative**) case.

factive verb *n*
a verb followed by a clause which the speaker or writer considers to express a fact.
For example, in:
I remember that he was always late.
remember is a factive verb.
Other factive verbs in English include *regret, deplore, know, agree.*

factor analysis *n*

a statistical procedure that is used to determine which unobserved latent VARIABLES[2], called factors, account for the CORRELATIONs among different observed variables. For example, if we give a group of students tests in geometry, algebra, arithmetic, reading and writing, we can find out what underlying factors are common to results on all these tests by using factor analysis. A factor analysis might show that there are two factors in the tests, one related to mathematics and the other related to language proficiency. These factors may be interpreted as abilities or traits that these tests measure to differing degrees. There are basically two types of factor analysis: exploratory and confirmatory. **Exploratory factor analysis**, as its name indicates, is used to explore a group of observed variables and identify any underlying variables that might explain the relationships among the observed variables, whereas **confirmatory factor analysis**, again as its name indicates, is used to test or confirm a hypothesized factor structure of a group of observed variables, specified a priori on the basis of some underlying theory or previous research, to see if the proposed factor structure is adequate to explain the relationships among the observed variables.

factual recount *n*

see TEXT TYPES

false beginner *n*

(in language teaching) a learner who has had a limited amount of previous instruction in a language, but who because of extremely limited language proficiency is classified as at the beginning level of language instruction. A false beginner is sometimes contrasted with a **true beginner**, i.e. someone who has no knowledge of the language.

false cognate *n*

also FAUX AMIS, **false friend**

a word which has the same or very similar form in two languages, but which has a different meaning in each. The similarity may cause a second language learner to use the word wrongly. For example, the French word *expérience* means "experiment", and not "experience". French learners of English might thus write or say: *Yesterday we performed an interesting experience in the laboratory.*

False cognates may be identified by CONTRASTIVE ANALYSIS.

familiarity *n*

a measure of how frequently a linguistic item is thought to be used, or the degree to which it is known. This may be measured by asking people to show on a RATING SCALE whether they think they use a given word or structure *never*, *sometimes*, or *often*. Word familiarity has been used as a way of selecting vocabulary for language teaching.

faux amis *n*

another term for FALSE COGNATE

FCE

abbreviation for Cambridge ESOL First Certificate in English
see CAMBRIDGE EXAMS

feature *n*

a property of a linguistic item which helps to mark it in certain ways, either singling it out from similar items or classifying it into a group with others.
For example, the English phoneme /b/ has the feature *voice*, it is a voiced stop. By this feature it can be distinguished from /p/, an unvoiced stop, or classified together with /d/ and /g/, other voiced stops.
Features can be used in all levels of linguistic analysis, e.g. phonetics, morphology, syntax. They can even form the basis of linguistic theories.
see DISTINCTIVE FEATURE, COMPONENTIAL ANALYSIS

feedback *n*

any information that provides information on the result of behaviour.
For example, in PHONETICS, feedback is both air- and bone-conducted. This is why we do not sound to ourselves as we sound to others and find tape-recordings of our own voices to be odd and often embarrassing.
In DISCOURSE ANALYSIS, feedback given while someone is speaking is sometimes called **back channelling**, for example comments such as *uh*, *yeah*, *really*, smiles, headshakes, and grunts that indicate success or failure in communication.
In teaching, feedback refers to comments or other information that learners receive concerning their success on learning tasks or tests, either from the teacher or other persons.
see also AUDITORY FEEDBACK, EVIDENCE, ERROR CORRECTION, KINESTHETIC FEEDBACK, PROPRIOCEPTIVE FEEDBACK, RECAST

feeding order *n*

see BLEEDING ORDER

felicity conditions *n*

(in SPEECH ACT THEORY) the conditions which must be fulfilled for a speech act to be satisfactorily performed or realized. For example, the sentence

I promise the sun will set today cannot be considered as a true promise, because we can only make promises about future acts which are under our control. The felicity conditions necessary for promises are:

a A sentence is used which states a future act of the speaker.
b The speaker has the ability to do the act.
c The hearer prefers the speaker to do the act rather than not to do it.
d The speaker would not otherwise usually do the act.
e The speaker intends to do the act.

feminine *adj*
see GENDER²

feminist linguistics *n*
the application of several aspects of linguistic theory (for example, SEMANTICS, PRAGMATICS, and DISCOURSE ANALYSIS) to the study of topics such as differences between men's and women's language, language and social oppression, and the ways in which gendered identity varies from context to context.

FFE *n*
an abbreviation for FORM-FOCUSED EPISODE

field *n*
see LEXICAL FIELD

field dependence *n* **field dependent** *adj*
a learning style in which a learner tends to look at the whole of a learning task which contains many items. The learner has difficulty in studying a particular item when it occurs within a "field" of other items.
A **field independent** learning style is one in which a learner is able to identify or focus on particular items and is not distracted by other items in the background or context.
Field dependence and independence have been studied as a difference of COGNITIVE STYLE in language learning.

field experiences *n*
(in teacher education) opportunities which are provided for student teachers to participate in real teaching situations, i.e. which involve student teachers teaching students in a school or classroom and which enable him or her to assume the role of a teacher, to gain teaching experience, and to experience teaching as a profession.

field independence *n*
  see FIELD DEPENDENCE

field methods *n*
  see FIELDWORK

field of discourse *n*
  see SOCIAL CONTEXT

field research *n*
  see FIELDWORK

field testing *n*
  also **field trial, pilot testing**
  in the production of instructional materials, the try-out of materials before
  publication or further development in order to determine their suitability or
  effectiveness and to determine the reactions of teachers and learners to the
  materials.

fieldwork *n*
  also **field research**
  the collection of data by observation or recording in as natural a setting as
  possible. Different procedures (called **field methods**) are used to obtain
  data. For example:
  a the recording of speakers to obtain speech samples for analysis of
      sounds, sentence structures, lexical use, etc. The people recorded may
      be native speakers of a particular language or speakers using a SECOND
      LANGUAGE.
  b interviews, e.g. in bilingual or multilingual communities, to obtain infor-
      mation on language choice and/or attitudes to language.
  c observation and/or video recording of verbal or non-verbal behaviour in
      a particular situation (see PARTICIPANT OBSERVATION).
  The collection and the use of data (**empirical investigation**) plays an important
  part in the research work of many applied linguists and sociolinguists.

figure of speech *n*
  a word or phrase that is used for special effect and that does not have its
  usual or literal meaning. Some examples include EUPHEMISM, **hyperbole**
  (an exaggerated statement, such as *I'm so hungry, I could eat a horse*),
  sarcasm (when a speaker means the opposite of what is said, e.g. *Great idea!*
  in response to a poor idea), **synecdoche** (using a component of something

to stand for the thing itself, e.g. saying *I got some new wheels* to refer to purchasing an automobile), **metonymy** (using an associated word to refer to something, for example, referring to the British monarchy as *the Crown*), and **simile** (an expression in which something is compared to something else by the use of a FUNCTION WORD such as *like* or *as* (for example, *Tom eats like a horse*)).

see also METAPHOR

filled pause *n*

see PAUSING

fillers *n*

expressions speakers use to create a delay or hesitation during conversation, enabling them to carry on the conversation during times of difficulty, e.g. "well", "I mean", "Actually", "You know", "Let me think". The use of fillers in second language communication is an aspect of STRATEGIC COMPETENCE.

see PAUSING

final *adj*

occurring at the end of a linguistic unit, e.g. word final, clause final. For example, a group of consonants at the end of a word such as *st* in the English word *list* is called a final CONSONANT CLUSTER.

see also INITIAL, MEDIAL, SYLLABLE

final e *n*

also **silent e**

the spelling pattern in English in which when e is the last letter in a word it is not pronounced, as in *bite*, *late*. Final e often signals a long vowel sound for the preceding vowel letter.

final intake *n*

see INTAKE

finger spelling *n*

a kind of signing behaviour (see SIGN LANGUAGE) which has been developed to help hearing-impaired persons communicate. Finger spelling provides a manual alphabet which is used to spell out words using the fingers.

finite verb *n*

a form of a verb which is marked to show that it is related to a subject in PERSON and/or NUMBER, and which shows TENSE[1]. A **non-finite verb** form is not marked according to differences in the person or number of the subject, and has no tense. The INFINITIVE and the PARTICIPLES are non-finite forms of verbs in English. For example:

We	want	
She	wants	
I	wanted	to leave.
	finite verb	*non-finite*
	forms	*form*

first conditional *n*
see CONDITIONAL FORMS

first language *n*
(generally) a person's mother tongue or the language acquired first. In multilingual communities, however, where a child may gradually shift from the main use of one language to the main use of another (e.g. because of the influence of a school language), first language may refer to the language the child feels most comfortable using. Often this term is used synonymously with NATIVE LANGUAGE. First language is also known as L1.

first language acquisition *n*
the process of learning a native language. First language acquisition has been studied primarily by linguists, developmental psychologists, and psycholinguists. Most explanations of how children learn to speak and understand language involve the influence of both the linguistic input to which children are exposed in social interaction with their parents and other caregivers and a natural aptitude for grammar that is unique to humans. However, proponents of UNIVERSAL GRAMMAR and the INNATIST POSITION, proponents of COGNITIVE PSYCHOLOGY and EMERGENTISM, and those who view language acquisition in terms of LANGUAGE SOCIALIZATION disagree strongly on the relative importance of these factors.

first language attrition *n*
see LANGUAGE ATTRITION

fixation pause *n*
(in reading) the brief periods when the eyeball is resting and during which the visual input required for reading takes place. The jump from one fixation point to another is known as a **saccade**.
see also READING SPAN

fixed expression *n*
see ROUTINE

fixed ratio deletion *n*
also n[th] word deletion
see CLOZE TEST

fixed response item *n*
see TEST ITEM

fixed stress *n*
STRESS which occurs regularly on the same syllable in a word in a particular language.
Languages which rigidly follow a fixed stress pattern are rare. There are always exceptions to the rule but Hungarian, for instance, usually stresses the first syllable of a word, and Polish usually stresses the second syllable from the end of a word (the penultimate syllable).
see also FREE STRESS

flap *n*
also **tap**
an articulation in which the tongue briefly touches a firm surface of the mouth once. An ALVEOLAR flap ALLOPHONE of /t/ is heard in many American pronunciations of words such as *little*, *city*, *dirty*, while in British English the /r/ in *very* is such a flap or tap.
see also FRICTIONLESS CONTINUANT, MANNER OF ARTICULATION, PLACE OF ARTICULATION, ROLL

flashcard *n*
(in language teaching) a card with words, sentences, or pictures on it, used as an aid or CUE in a language lesson.

FLES *n*
an abbreviation for FOREIGN LANGUAGES IN THE ELEMENTARY SCHOOL

floor effect *n*
see BOUNDARY EFFECT

fluency *n* **fluent** *adj*
the features which give speech the qualities of being natural and normal, including native-like use of PAUSING, rhythm, INTONATION, STRESS, rate of speaking, and use of interjections and interruptions. If speech disorders

cause a breakdown in normal speech (e.g. as with APHASIA or stuttering), the resulting speech may be referred to as **dysfluent**, or as an example of **dysfluency**.

In second and foreign language teaching, fluency describes a level of proficiency in communication, which includes:

a the ability to produce written and/or spoken language with ease
b the ability to speak with a good but not necessarily perfect command of intonation, vocabulary, and grammar
c the ability to communicate ideas effectively
d the ability to produce continuous speech without causing comprehension difficulties or a breakdown of communication.

It is sometimes contrasted with **accuracy**, which refers to the ability to produce grammatically correct sentences but may not include the ability to speak or write fluently.

fluent reader *n*
a person who reads without effort, with few hesitations, and with a good level of comprehension.

focus *n*
an element or phrase that contains new information can be put "into focus" in various ways. For example, to signal that *John* is the new information in the sentence *I saw John at the market*, one can use emphatic or contrastive STRESS (*I saw JOHN at the market*) or a CLEFT SENTENCE (*It was John who I saw at the market*).
see also FUNCTIONAL SENTENCE PERSPECTIVE, GROUNDING

focused interview *n*
an interview that explores a particular aspect of an event or situation, particularly with a group of individuals who have had similar experience of the event. For example, in language programme evaluation a focused interview may be held with teachers to find out how well students are reacting to a new set of teaching materials.
See also DEPTH INTERVIEW, GUIDED INTERVIEW

focus on form *n*
in general terms, any focusing of attention on the formal linguistic characteristics of language, as opposed to a pure focus on meaning in communication. In a more technical sense, focus on form has been defined as a brief allocation of attention to linguistic form as the need for this arises incidentally, in the context of communication. This may be contrasted with a **focus on forms** (plural), referring to the kind of focus on one form (or rule)

at a time that one finds in a language course where there is a "structure of the day", usually pre-specified by the teacher or the textbook.
see also CONSCIOUSNESS RAISING

focus on forms *n*
see FOCUS ON FORM

folk linguistics *n*
popular beliefs about language and languages.

foreground(ed) information *n*
see GROUNDING

foreigner talk *n*
the type of speech often used by native speakers of a language when speaking to foreigners who are not proficient in the language. Some of the characteristics of foreigner talk are:

a It is slower and louder than normal speech, often with exaggerated pronunciation.
b It uses simpler vocabulary and grammar. For example, articles, function words, and INFLECTIONS may be omitted, and complex verb forms are replaced by simpler ones.
c Topics are sometimes repeated or moved to the front of sentences, for example: *Your bag? Where you leave your bag?*

Native speakers often feel that this type of speech is easier for foreigners to understand.
see also ACCOMMODATION, CARETAKER SPEECH, PIDGIN, INTERLANGUAGE

foreignism *n*
a person's use of a word or expression from another language when speaking one's native language in order to create a special effect or to indicate special knowledge. (This should not be confused with the use of a LOAN word.) For example, when a speaker of Indonesian uses words from Dutch or English to indicate their familiarity with those languages or when a speaker of English uses a word from French or German (with a French or German pronunciation), as in "I think he lacks a certain *panache*."

foreign language *n*
also **non-native language**
a language which is not the NATIVE LANGUAGE of large numbers of people in a particular country or region, is not used as a medium of instruction in schools, and is not widely used as a medium of communication in government, media, etc. Foreign languages are typically taught as school

subjects for the purpose of communicating with foreigners or for reading printed materials in the language.
see also INDIGENOUS LANGUAGE, SECOND LANGUAGE, TARGET LANGUAGE

foreign language anxiety *n*
see LANGUAGE ANXIETY

foreign language experience (FLEX) *n*
an approach to foreign language teaching in the elementary school in the US which seeks to provide a general exposure to the foreign language and culture and to teach students to use a limited set of words, phrases and conversational expressions. Such a programme is generally less intensive than a FLES programme.
see FOREIGN LANGUAGES IN THE ELEMENTARY SCHOOL

foreign languages in the elementary school *n*
also **FLES**
1 the teaching of foreign languages in elementary schools
2 the name of a movement which aims to increase the amount of foreign language teaching in elementary schools in the USA.

Foreign Service Institute *n*
also **FSI**
a US Government agency responsible for language teaching and the accreditation of foreign service personnel, widely known in the foreign language teaching and testing community for its language proficiency scale with six levels, ranging from Level 0 (i.e. no functional proficiency) to Level 5 (i.e. native-like proficiency).
see also INTERAGENCY LANGUAGE ROUND TABLE, ACTFL PROFICIENCY GUIDELINES, AUSTRALIAN SECOND LANGUAGE PROFICIENCY RATINGS

Foreign Service Institute Oral Interview *n*
also **FSI**
a technique for testing the spoken language proficiency of adult foreign language learners. The technique was developed by the United States Foreign Service Institute. It consists of a set of RATING SCALES which are used to judge pronunciation, grammar, vocabulary, and fluency during a 30 minute interview between the learner and, usually, two interviewers.

forensic identification *n*
see FORENSIC LINGUISTICS

forensic linguistics *n*
also **language and the law**

a branch of applied linguistics that investigates issues of language in relation to the law, drawing on resources from SEMANTICS, ACOUSTIC PHONETICS, DISCOURSE ANALYSIS, PRAGMATICS, SOCIOLINGUISTICS, and other fields. Issues of concern include **forensic identification** (speaker identification in legal cases through handwriting analysis or speech analysis); INTERPRETATION for the police and courts; the semantics of legal terminology (e.g. the legal meanings of *murder*, *manslaughter*, *homicide*); the discourse of police interrogations and legal proceedings; ACCENT DISCRIMINATION; and the problems faced by non-native speakers and members of minority speech communities when dealing with the judicial system.

form *n*

the means by which an element of language is expressed in speech or writing. Forms can be shown by the standard writing system for a language or by phonetic or phonemic symbols. For example, in English:

written form	spoken form
house	/haʊs/

Often a distinction is made between the spoken or written form of a linguistic unit and its meaning or function.

For example, in English the written form -*s* and the spoken forms /s/ and /z/ have a common function. They show the plural of nouns:

/kæts/	*cats*	/dɒgz//dɔːgz/	*dogs*

formal assessment *n*

tests given under conditions that ensure the assessment of individual performance in any given area

see also INFORMAL ASSESSMENT

formal competence *n*

see COMPETENCE, COMMUNICATIVE COMPETENCE

formal grammar *n*

an approach to grammatical analysis and description in which the aim is to investigate grammatical structures as primitives to be explained in terms of their contribution to the systematic nature of language.

formal operational stage *n*

see COGNITIVE DEVELOPMENT

formal schema *n*

see CONTENT SCHEMA

formal speech *n*

a careful, impersonal and often public mode of speaking used to express a polite distance between participants, and which may influence pronunciation, choice of words, and sentence structure. For example, compare:
Ladies and gentlemen, it gives me great pleasure to be here tonight (said on a formal public occasion)
Nice to be here (said on an informal occasion between friends)
see also COLLOQUIAL SPEECH, STYLE, STYLISTIC VARIATION

formal universal *n*

see LANGUAGE UNIVERSAL

formant *n*

in ACOUSTIC PHONETICS, a group of overtones corresponding to a resonating frequency of the air in the vocal tract, used to classify vowel sounds.

format *n*

in a language test, the tasks and activities that test takers are required to do (e.g. TRUE/FALSE ITEM or MULTIPLE-CHOICE ITEM format)

formative *n*

(in GENERATIVE GRAMMAR) the minimum grammatical unit in a language. For example, in:
The drivers started the engines.
the formatives would be:
the + drive + er + s + start + ed + the + engine + s
see also MORPHEME

formative evaluation *n*

the process of providing information to curriculum developers during the development of a curriculum or programme, in order to improve it. Formative evaluation is also used in syllabus design and the development of language teaching programmes and materials.
Summative evaluation is the process of providing information to decision makers, after the programme is completed, about whether or not the programme was effective and successful.
see also EVALUATION

formative test *n*

a test that is given during a course of instruction and that informs both the student and the teacher how well the student is doing. A formative test includes only topics that have been taught, and shows whether the student needs extra work or attention. It is usually a pass or fail test. If a student fails, he/she is able to do more study and take the test again.

see also TEST, SUMMATIVE TEST

form class *n*

(in linguistics) a group of items which can be used in similar positions in a structure.

For example, in the sentence:

The . . . is here.

the words *dog*, *book*, *evidence*, etc. could be used. They all belong to the same form class of nouns.

see also WORD CLASS, OPEN CLASS

form-focused episode *n*

also **FFE**

an episode within learner-learner or learner-teacher interaction in which language form becomes the focus of attention.

form-focused instruction *n*

teaching which focuses on control of formal aspects of language such as the grammatical features of a specific type of discourse or text, e.g. narrative.

form-function relation *n*

the relationship between the physical characteristics of a thing (i.e. its form) and its role or function. This distinction is often referred to in studying language use, because a linguistic form (e.g. the imperative) can perform a variety of different functions, as the following examples illustrate.

Imperative forms	Communicative functions
Come round for a drink.	invitation
Watch out.	warning
Turn left at the corner.	direction
Pass the sugar.	request

form of address *n*

another term for ADDRESS FORM

formula *n* (plural **formulae or formulas**)

another term for FORMULAIC LANGUAGE

formulaic expression *n*
another term for FORMULAIC LANGUAGE

formulaic language *n*
also **formulae** (or **formulas**), **formulaic expression**, **formulaic sequence**
sequences of words that are stored and retrieved as a unit from memory
at the time of use, rather than generated online using the full resources of
the grammar of the language. Researchers have used many different terms
for this phenomenon, including **prefabricated routines**, **routine formulae**,
stock utterances, **lexical phrases** or **lexicalized phrases**, **institutionalized
utterances**, and **unanalyzed chunks**. Formulaic sequences may be semantically
transparent and grammatically regular (e.g. "I'll see you tomorrow," "with
best wishes," "thank you very much") or irregular in their form and meaning,
as is the case with IDIOMS. Formulaic sequences may be learned initially as a
unit, without an understanding of their internal structure, and later analyzed
so that internal elements can be used productively; formulaic sequences can
also be constructed from smaller units but stored as a unit for future use, a
process called **fusion**. Some formulae have open slots and are called **lexicalized
sentence stems**, e.g. "Who the [expletive] does [pronoun] think [pronoun]
is?" Formulaic language is believed to have several functions, including
conserving processing resources, enhancing both FLUENCY and IDIOMATIC-
ITY, and realizing specific interactional functions. Formulaic sequences that
primarily function to organize discourse (e.g. "In the first place," "So what
you are saying is X") are often referred to as **conversational routines** or
gambits. Formulaic sequences associated with a specific SPEECH ACT (e.g.
"I really like your [noun]," "If it's not too much trouble, could you X?")
are sometimes called **politeness formulas**.

formulaic sequence *n*
another term for FORMULAIC LANGUAGE

formulaic speech *n*
another term for FORMULAIC LANGUAGE

form word *n*
see CONTENT WORD

fortis *adj*
describes a CONSONANT which is produced with a relatively greater amount
of muscular force and breath, e.g. in English /p/, /t/, and /k/. The opposite
to fortis is **lenis**, which describes consonants which are produced with

less muscular effort and little or no ASPIRATION, e.g. in English /b/, /d/, and /g/.

see MANNER OF ARTICULATION, VOICE[2]

fossilization *n* **fossilized** *adj*

(in second or foreign language learning) a process which sometimes occurs in which incorrect linguistic features become a permanent part of the way a person speaks or writes a language. Aspects of pronunciation, vocabulary usage, and grammar may become fixed or fossilized in second or foreign language learning. Fossilized features of pronunciation contribute to a person's foreign accent. Some researchers are sceptical of the existence of true fossilization, which implies the impossibility of future change, and prefer the term **stabilization** instead.

see also INTERLANGUAGE

fragment *n*

see SENTENCE FRAGMENT

frame *n*

another term for SCRIPT

frame semantics *n*

a theory that relates linguistic semantics to encyclopedic or real-world knowledge, generally considered to be a form of COGNITIVE LINGUISTICS.

framing *n*

(in teaching) a QUESTIONING TECHNIQUE in which the teacher provides a **frame** for a question by asking a question, pausing, and then calling on a student response. This is said to increase students' attention to the question and thus improve the effectiveness of the question.

see also QUESTIONING TECHNIQUES, WAIT TIME

free composition *n*

see COMPOSITION

free form *n*

also **free morpheme**

see BOUND FORM

free practice *n*

see PRACTICE ACTIVITIES

free reading *n*

pleasurable, meaning-oriented reading.

see also EXTENSIVE READING

free recall *n*

see RECALL

free response item *n*

see TEST ITEM

free stress *n*

STRESS which does not occur regularly on the same syllable in words in a particular language.

For example, English has free stress. The main stress may occur:

on the first syllable: e.g. *'interval*
on the second syllable: e.g. *in'terrogate*
on the third syllable: e.g. *inter'ference*

see also FIXED STRESS

free translation *n*

see TRANSLATION

free variation *n*

when two or more linguistic items occur in the same position without any apparent change of meaning they are said to be in free variation.

For example, *who* and *whom* in the English sentence:

The man who   we saw.
          whom

Such variations are now often considered as social variations or stylistic variations.

see also VARIABLE, VARIATION

freewriting *n*

also **timed freewriting, quickwriting, quickwrite**

(in teaching composition) a pre-writing activity (see COMPOSING PROCESSES) in which students write as much as possible about a topic within a given time period (for example, 3 minutes) without stopping. The goal is to produce as much writing as possible without worrying about grammar or accuracy, in order to develop fluency in writing and to produce ideas which might be used in a subsequent writing task.

Frege's principle *n*

another term for the COMPOSITIONALITY PRINCIPLE

frequency¹ *n*

> see SOUND WAVE

frequency² *n*

> the number of occurrences of a linguistic item in a text or CORPUS. Different linguistic items have different frequencies of occurrence in speech and writing. In English, FUNCTION WORDs (e.g. *a*, *the*, *to*, etc.) occur more frequently than verbs, nouns, adjectives, or adverbs. **Word frequency counts** are used to select vocabulary for language teaching, in lexicography, in the study of literary style in STYLISTICS, and in TEXT LINGUISTICS.
> The twenty most frequently occurring words in a corpus of over one million words in a study of written American English by Kucera and Francis were:
> *the, of, and, to, a, in, that, is, was, he, for, it, with, as, his, on, be, at, by, I.*

frequency count *n*

> a count of the total number of occurrences of linguistic items (e.g. syllables, phonemes, words, etc.) in a corpus of language, such as a written text or a sample of spoken language. The study of the frequency of occurrence of linguistic items is known as language statistics and is a part of COMPUTATIONAL and MATHEMATICAL LINGUISTICS. A frequency count of the vocabulary occurring in a text or opus is known as a **word frequency count** or **word frequency list**.

frequency hypothesis *n*

> the hypothesis that the order of acquisition of linguistic items is determined by their frequency in input.

frequency polygon *n*

> see DISTRIBUTION

fricative *n*

> also **spirant**
> a speech sound produced by narrowing the distance between two articulators so that the airstream is not completely closed but obstructed enough that a turbulent airflow is produced, as in the English /f/, /v/, /s/ and /z/ sounds in *enough, valve, sister*, and *zoo*.

frictionless continuant *n*

> a speech sound (a CONSONANT) which is produced by allowing the airstream from the lungs to move through the mouth and/or nose without friction. For example, for some speakers of English the /r/ in /rəʊz/ *rose* is a frictionless continuant.

In terms of their articulation, frictionless continuants are very like vowels, but they function as consonants.

see also FRICATIVE, LATERAL, NASAL, STOP

fronting *v*

the placing of a word or phrase at the front of a clause or sentence to give it extra prominence.

I would really love to try that (object after the verb).

That I would really love to try (object fronted for greater prominence).

front vowel *n*

see VOWEL

FSI[1] *n*

see FOREIGN SERVICE INSTITUTE

FSI[2] *n*

an abbreviation for FOREIGN SERVICE INSTITUTE ORAL INTERVIEW

FSP *n*

an abbreviation for FUNCTIONAL SENTENCE PERSPECTIVE

FTA *n*

an abbreviation for FACE THREATENING ACT

full transfer/full access hypothesis *n*

in SLA, the hypothesis that, with respect to SYNTAX, there are no inherent restrictions on what can be transferred from the first language and no inherent restrictions on access to UNIVERSAL GRAMMAR by second language learners.

full verb *n*

see AUXILIARY VERB

full word *n*

see CONTENT WORD

function *n*

the purpose for which an utterance or unit of language is used. In language teaching, language functions are often described as categories of behaviour;

e.g. requests, apologies, complaints, offers, compliments. The functional uses of language cannot be determined simply by studying the grammatical structure of sentences. For example, sentences in the imperative form (see MOOD) may perform a variety of different functions:

Give me that book. (Order)
Pass the jam. (Request)
Turn right at the corner. (Instruction)
Try the smoked salmon. (Suggestion)
Come round on Sunday. (Invitation)

In linguistics, the functional uses of language are studied in SPEECH ACT theory, SOCIOLINGUISTICS, and PRAGMATICS. In the COMMUNICATIVE APPROACH to language teaching, a SYLLABUS is often organized in terms of the different language functions the learner needs to express or understand.
see also FUNCTIONS OF LANGUAGE, FUNCTIONAL SYLLABUS, NOTIONAL SYLLABUS, SPEECH ACT, SPEECH ACT CLASSIFICATION

functional grammar *n*

a term with several meanings.

In general, any approach to grammatical description that attempts to describe the ways in which meanings and FUNCTIONs are realized in language. For example, instead of describing "tense", a grammatical notion, one can investigate the ways in which "time reference", a semantic notion, is realized in language. The linguistic means for indicating time reference in English include not only TENSE and ASPECT, but also MODALS, ADVERBS, ADVERBIAL PHRASES, and ADVERBIAL CLAUSES.

More specifically, the term is used to refer to a formal model of grammar developed in the 1970s by the Dutch Scholar Simon Dik, which consists of a series of **predicate frames**, hierarchically layered templates into which lexical items are inserted.
see also LEXICAL FUNCTIONAL GRAMMAR

functional illiteracy *n*

see LITERACY

functional linguistics *n*

an approach to linguistics which is concerned with language as an instrument of social interaction rather than as a system of formal rules that is viewed in isolation from their uses in communication. It considers the individual as a social being and investigates the way in which he or she acquires language and uses it in order to communicate with others in his or her social environment.
see also PRAGMATICS, SOCIAL CONTEXT, SPEECH EVENT

functional literacy *n*
see LITERACY

functional load *n*
the relative importance of linguistic contrasts in a language. Not all the distinctions or contrasts within the structure of a language are of the same importance. For example the contrast between /p/ and /b/ at the beginning of words in English serves to distinguish many words, such as *pig – big*; *pack – back*; *pad – bad*, etc. The distinction /p/ – /b/ is thus said to have high functional load. But other contrasts such as the contrast between /u/ and /θ/ in words like *wreathe – wreath* are not used to distinguish many words in English and are said to have low functional load.

functional sentence perspective *n*
also **FSP**
a type of linguistic analysis associated with the Prague School which describes how information is distributed in sentences. FSP deals particularly with the effect of the distribution of known (or given) information and new information in DISCOURSE. The known information (known as **theme**, in FSP), refers to information that is not new to the reader or listener. The **rheme** refers to information that is new. FSP differs from the traditional grammatical analysis of sentences because the distinction between subject – predicate is not always the same as the theme – rheme contrast. For example we may compare the two sentences below:

1 *John*	*sat in the front seat.*	2 *In the front seat sat John.*	
Subject	Predicate	Predicate	Subject
Theme	Rheme	Theme	Rheme

John is the grammatical subject in both sentences, but theme in 1 and rheme in 2.
Other terms used to refer to the theme–rheme distinction are topic-comment (see TOPIC[2]), **background–focus, given–new information**.

functional syllabus *n*
(in language teaching) a SYLLABUS in which the language content is arranged in terms of functions or SPEECH ACTS together with the language items needed for them. For example, the functions might be identifying, describing, inviting, offering, etc., in different types of DISCOURSE (i.e. speech or writing). The language skills involved might be listening, speaking, reading, or writing. The language items needed for these functions are called **exponents** or realizations.

For example:

Type of discourse	Skill	Function	Exponents	
			Vocabulary	Structures
spoken	speaking listening	asking for directions	bank harbour museum	Can you tell me where X is? Where is X?

Often this term is used to refer to a certain type of NOTIONAL SYLLABUS.
see also COMMUNICATIVE APPROACH

functional-systemic linguistics *n*
another term for SYSTEMIC-FUNCTIONAL LINGUISTICS

functions of language *n*
also **language functions**
although most linguists focus primarily on the formal characteristics of language, there is also a long tradition originally deriving from work in anthropology which is equally concerned with the functions of language. Language is often described as having the following major functions:
a **descriptive function** (or **ideational function**, in Halliday's framework), organizing a speaker's or writer's experience of the world and conveying information which can be stated or denied and in some cases tested.
a **social function** (**interpersonal function** in Halliday's terms), used to establish, maintain and signal relationships between people.
an **expressive function**, through which speakers signal information about their opinions, prejudices, past experiences, and so forth; and
a **textual function**, creating written and spoken TEXTS.
These functions frequently overlap, and most utterances accomplish more than one function at the same time. For example, an utterance such as *I'm not inviting the Sandersons again*, with appropriate intonation, signals an intended future action (ideational or descriptive function), may show that the speaker does not like the Sandersons (expressive function), and is presumably part of a conversation (textual function) in which the interlocutors share a relationship that permits such expressions of dislike (social function).

function word *n*
see CONTENT WORD

functor *n*
see CONTENT WORD

236

fundamental difference hypothesis *n*

in SLA, the hypothesis that first and second language acquisition are fundamentally different processes: first language acquisition is the result of UNIVERSAL GRAMMAR and principles of acquisition associated with it; while second language acquisition is the result of general (non-language specific) cognitive processes such as PROBLEM SOLVING and HYPOTHESIS TESTING.

fundamental frequency *n*

see SOUND WAVE

further education *n*

a term used particularly in the UK to refer to education that is additional to that offered at secondary school and which is different from education offered at universities (known as **higher education**). It may refer to learning that is at the same, lower or higher level than courses at secondary education, such as vocational, certificate or diploma courses.

fused sentence *n*

another term for RUN-ON SENTENCE

fusion *n*

see CHUNKING

fusional language *n*

another term for INFLECTING LANGUAGE

future forms *n*

grammatical forms that can express future meaning, such as:
going to: *It's going to rain.*
present continuous: *I'm leaving tonight.*
simple present: *The show starts at 6 pm.*
will or shall: *It will be fine tomorrow.*

future perfect *n*

see PERFECT

future tense *n*

a tense form used to indicate that the event described by a verb will take place at a future time. For example in the French sentence:
Je partirai   demain.
I   leave + future   tomorrow.

the future tense ending -*ai* has been added to the verb infinitive *partir* (=leave). English has no future tense but uses a variety of different verb forms to express future time (e.g. *I leave tomorrow*; *I am leaving tomorrow*; *I will leave tomorrow*; *I am going to leave tomorrow*). *Will* in English is sometimes used to indicate future time (e.g. *Tomorrow will be Thursday*) but has many other functions, and is usually described as a MODAL verb.

fuzzy *adj*

a term used by some linguists to describe a linguistic unit which has no clearly defined boundary. These units have "fuzzy borders", e.g. the English words *hill* and *mountain*. Another term used for a gradual transition from one linguistic unit to another is **gradience**.

G

gain score *n*

the difference between the score obtained in a pre-test and the score obtained in a post-test, where both tests are identical or equivalent. Gain scores are interpreted as an indication of learning.

gambit *n*

(in CONVERSATIONAL ANALYSIS) sometimes used to describe a word or phrase in conversation which signals the function of the speaker's next turn in the conversation (see TURN-TAKING). Gambits may be used to show whether the speaker's contribution adds new information, develops something said by a previous speaker, expresses an opinion, agreement, etc. For example, gambits which signal that the speaker is going to express an opinion include:

The way I look at it . . .
To my mind . . .
In my opinion . . .

These examples can also be considered conversational ROUTINES.

game[1] *n*

(in language teaching) an organized activity that usually has the following properties:

a a particular task or objective
b a set of rules
c competition between players
d communication between players by spoken or written language.

Games are often used as a fluency activity in communicative language teaching and humanistic methods.

game[2] *n*

(in COMPUTER ASSISTED LANGUAGE LEARNING) rule-based competitive activities usually involving a time limit and/or visual display features in which the player must acquire and/or manipulate knowledge in order to succeed.

gap-filling *n*

also **gap-fills**

a practice exercise in language teaching in which learners have to replace words missing from a text. The removed words are chosen to practice a specific language point (e.g. past tense, conjunctions). Gap-fills contrast with **cloze** texts, where words are normally removed at regular intervals.

gatekeeper *n* **gatekeeping** *n*

in describing power relations within a society, anything that controls or limits access to something for a segment of the population. The ability to speak standard English or a prestige variety of English may have a gate-keeping role since those who do not speak this variety of English may find their access to certain professions or services restricted.

gating *n*

a research paradigm in which subjects hear fragments of a word and attempt to identify the whole word, used to determine the amount of phonetic information needed for word identification.

GB theory or **G/B theory** *n*

another term for GOVERNMENT/BINDING THEORY

geminate *adj*

in phonology, adjacent segments that are the same, such as the two con-sonants in the middle of Italian *folla* [folla] ("crowd") or Japanese [nippon] ("Japan"). Geminate consonants are sometimes called **long** or **doubled consonants**.

GEN *n*

an abbreviation for **genitive relative clause**
see NOUN PHRASE ACCESSIBILITY HIERARCHY

gender[1] *n*

refers to sex as either a biological or socially constructed category. For example, the term **genderlect** can refer to the speech of men and women and by extension to such varieties as a homosexual REGISTER in communities where such varieties exist or are recognized. In POSTMODERNISM and FEMINIST LINGUISTICS, gender is viewed more as a process (something that someone does or performs in interaction), rather than an attribute that one possesses.

gender[2] *n*

a grammatical distinction in some languages that allows words to be divided into categories such as **masculine, feminine,** or **neuter** on the basis of inflectional and agreement properties, not limited to nouns with inherent gender (see GENDER[1]). For example, in Spanish, most nouns and ending in *−a* are feminine and most nouns ending in *−o* are masculine, and both articles and adjectives agree in gender with the nouns they modify. In English, grammatical gender is limited to the distinction between *he, she,* and *it* in pronouns, and a small set of nouns that reflect the gender of the person referred to, for example *actor:actress*, *waiter:waitress*, *chairman:chairwoman* or the gender stereotypically associated with the noun, for example *mailman*. At the end of the twentieth century, many such terms were replaced by gender-neutral forms (e.g. *actor* for both men and women, *server* instead of *waiter* or *waitress*, *chairperson* or *chair* instead of *chairman*, *mail carrier* instead of *mailman*) in a number of English-speaking speech communities.

gendered domain *n*

a set of linguistic routines or contexts that is or appears to be gender-specific or more typical of one gender. For example, mathematics can be stereotyped as a male domain, while the family can be viewed as a more female gendered domain.

genderlect *n*

see GENDER

General American English *n*

also **standard American English**

an accent of American English that is perceived by most Americans to be both standard and neutral (free of regional characteristics). As represented in textbooks for learners of American English and the pronunciations most often given in American English dictionaries, "General American" was originally modeled after Midwestern dialects, but the concept is not rigidly defined, and speakers from many other parts of the US also claim to speak general or standard American English.

generalization *n* generalize *v*

1 (in linguistics) a rule or principle which explains observed linguistic data.
2 (in learning theory) a process common to all types of learning, which consists of the formation of a general rule or principle from the observation of particular examples. For example a child who sees the English words *book – books*, and *dog – dogs* may generalize that the concept of plural in English is formed by adding *s* to words.

see also OVERGENERALIZATION

general nativism *n*

see NATIVISM

generate *v*

if the application of a set of rules results in a given structure or string as output, then those rules are said to "generate" the structure or string.

see GENERATIVE GRAMMAR, GENERATIVE THEORY

generative grammar *n*

a type of grammar that attempts to define and describe by a set of rules or principles all the GRAMMATICAL sentences of a language and no ungrammatical ones. This type of grammar is said to **generate**, or produce, grammatical sentences.

generative phonology *n*

an approach to phonology which aims to describe the knowledge (COMPETENCE) which a native speaker must have to be able to produce and understand the sound system of his or her language. In generative phonology, the distinctive sounds of a language (the PHONEMES) are shown as groups of sound features (see DISTINCTIVE FEATURES). Each sound is shown as a different set of features. For example, the phoneme /e/ could be shown by the features

$$\begin{bmatrix} -\text{high} \\ -\text{low} \\ +\text{tense} \end{bmatrix}$$

Phonological rules explain how these abstract units combine and vary when they are used in speech.

see also GENERATIVE GRAMMAR, SYSTEMATIC PHONEMICS

generative semantics *n*

an approach to linguistic theory which grew as a reaction to Chomsky's syntactic-based TRANSFORMATIONAL GENERATIVE GRAMMAR. It considers that all sentences are generated from a semantic structure. This semantic structure is often expressed in the form of a proposition which is similar to logical propositions in philosophy. Linguists working within this theory have, for instance, suggested that there is a semantic relationship between such sentences as

This dog strikes me as being like her master.

and

This dog reminds me of her master.

because they both have the semantic structure of

X perceives that Y is similar to Z.

see also INTERPRETIVE SEMANTICS

generative theory *n*

a cover term for a variety of linguistic theories that have the common goals of (a) providing an account of the formal properties of language, positing rules that specify how to form all the grammatical sentences of a language and no ungrammatical ones (the principle of **descriptive adequacy**), while

(b) explaining why grammars have the properties they do and how children come to acquire them in such a short period of time (the principle of **explanatory adequacy**).

The major versions of generative theory (all associated with the pioneering work of the linguist Noam Chomsky) that have influenced the fields of first and second language acquisition have been:

transformational grammar (also **transformational-generative grammar, TG, generative-transformational grammar**), an early version of the theory that emphasized the relationships among sentences that can be seen as **transforms** or transformations of each other, for example the relationships among simple active declarative sentences (e.g. *He went to the store*), negative sentences (*He didn't go to the store*), and questions (*Did he go to the store?*). Such relationships can be accounted for by **transformational rules**. The **Standard Theory** (also **Aspects Model**) proposed in the mid-1960s, which specified a **base component** that produces or generates basic syntactic structures called **deep structures**; a **transformational component** that changes or transforms those basic structures into sentences called **surface structures**; a **phonological component**, which gives sentences a phonetic representation (see GENERATIVE PHONOLOGY) so that they can be pronounced; and a **semantic component**, which deals with the meaning of sentences (see INTERPRETIVE SEMANTICS).

GOVERNMENT/BINDING THEORY, which dominated formally orientated work in first and second language acquisition during the 1980s and 1990s.

MINIMALISM, a version of generative theory developed in the late 1990s.

generative-transformational grammar *n*
    see GENERATIVE GRAMMAR, GENERATIVE THEORY

generic *adj*
    in grammar, a reference to sentences, such as (in English) *Elephants like peanuts* or *The elephant likes peanuts* or *An elephant likes peanuts*, that have a generic meaning, that is, they are meant to apply to all elephants or elephants in general.

generic reference *n*
    a type of reference which is used to refer to a class of objects or things, rather than to a specific member of a class. For example in English:

specific reference	generic reference
The bird is sick.	*A tiger is a dangerous animal.*
The birds are sick.	*Tigers are dangerous animals.*
There is a bird in the cage.	*The tiger is a dangerous animal.*

genetic epistemology *n*

a term used to describe the theories of DEVELOPMENTAL PSYCHOLOGY of the Swiss psychologist Jean Piaget (1896–1980). Piaget listed several different stages which children pass through in mental development. The first stage is the **sensorimotor stage**, from birth to about 24 months, when children understand their environment mainly by acting on it. Through touch and sight children begin to understand basic relationships which affect them and objects in their experience. These include space, location of objects, and the relationships of cause and effect. But children cannot yet make use of abstract concepts. The next three stages are a movement towards more abstract processes. During the **pre-operational stage**, from around two to seven years, children develop the symbolic function, which includes such skills as language, mental imagery, and drawing. Children also begin to develop the mental ability to use CONCEPTS dealing with number, classification, order, and time, but use these concepts in a simple way. The **concrete operational stage** from about seven to eleven years is the period when children begin to use mental operations and acquire a number of concepts of conservation. During the formal operational stage (from around eleven onwards) children are able to deal with abstract concepts and PROPOSITIONS, and to make hypotheses, inferences, and deductions. Since the mental processes Piaget studied are important for language development, linguists and psycholinguists have made use of Piaget's ideas in studying how mental development and linguistic development are related.

genitive case *n*

the form of a noun or noun phrase which usually shows that the noun or noun phrase is in a POSSESSIVE relation with another noun or noun phrase in a sentence.

For example, in the German sentence:

Dort drüben ist das Haus des Bürgermeisters

Over there is   the house of the mayor

               the mayor's house

in the noun phrase *des Bürgermeisters*, the article has the inflectional ending -*es* and the noun has the inflectional ending -*s* to show that they are in the genitive case because they refer to the owner of *das Haus*.

In the English sentence:

She took my father's car

some linguists regard *my father's* as an example of the genitive case.

see also CASE[1]

genitive relative clause *n*

also **GEN**

see NOUN PHRASE ACCESSIBILITY HIERARCHY

genre¹ *n*

a type of discourse that occurs in a particular setting, that has distinctive and recognizable patterns and norms of organization and structure, and that has particular and distinctive communicative functions. For example: business reports, news broadcasts, speeches, letters, advertisements, etc. In constructing texts, the writer must employ certain features conventionally associated with texts from the genre in which he or she is writing. In reading a text the reader similarly anticipates certain features of the text based on genre expectations.

genre² *n*

a category of literary writing, such as tragedy, fiction, comedy, etc.

genre analysis *n*

the study of how language is used in a particular context, such as business correspondence, legal writing, staff meetings, etc. Genres differ in that each has a different goal and employs different patterns of structure and organization to achieve its goals. In the study of written texts genre analysis studies how writers conventionally sequence material to achieve particular purposes. This includes the identification of particular types of schema and how they are realized linguistically.

genre approach *n*

also **genre-based approach**

an approach to the teaching of writing, particularly L1 writing, which bases a writing curriculum on the different types of text structures or genres children encounter in school and which are crucial to school success. Genre-based approaches are particularly strong in Australia as a result of the work of functional linguists such as Halliday and Martin. Examples of genres encountered in school work are Observation and Comment, Recount, Narrative, and Report. A report, for example, has the structure of a general classificatory statement, a description, and a final comment. Proponents of a genre approach argue that control over specific types of writing are necessary for full participation in social processes.

In adult second language teaching a genre-based approach starts from a recognition of the discourse community in which the learners will be functioning, e.g. a hotel, factory or hospital. Discourses from the target speech community are studied in terms of the text types and text roles that characterize them.

see also TEXT-BASED SYLLABUS DESIGN

genre-scheme *n*

another term for SCHEME

245

gerund *n*

also **gerundive**

a verb form which ends in *-ing*, but which is used in a sentence like a noun. For example, in the English sentences:

Swimming is good for you.

I don't like smoking.

see also PARTICIPLE

gesture *n*

a movement of the face or body which communicates meaning, such as nodding the head to mean agreement. Many spoken utterances are accompanied by gestures which support or add to their meaning. SIGN LANGUAGE is a system of communication based entirely on gestures. The study of the role of gestures in communication is part of the study of non-verbal communication.

see also PARALINGUISTICS

gist *n*

the general meaning of a text. *Gist listening* means listening in order to get the main ideas of a listening passage. Reading a text for gist is known as skimming.

gisting *n*

in TRANSLATION, producing a rough or outline translation of a text, often done in order to decide whether a complete translation would be useful or desirable.

gist listening *v*

see GIST

given – new information *n*

see FUNCTIONAL SENTENCE PERSPECTIVE

glide *n*

in British linguistics, another term for DIPHTHONG.

In American linguistics, sounds produced with little or no obstruction of the airstream that do not function as syllabic nuclei, i.e. are always preceded or followed by a VOWEL. For example, the glides /j/ and /w/ occur before a vowel in the words *you* and *we*, but following the vowel (as the second element of a diphthong) in the words *bite* and *out*.

see also SEMI-VOWEL

global education *n*

also **multicultural education**

an educational philosophy or IDEOLOGY that seeks to develop students who recognize and appreciate diverse cultures and not merely the values of the dominant culture or cultures in a society. Learners are encouraged to appreciate differences between cultures and recognize common links with people from different cultures, particularly minority cultures. This approach is designed to teach tolerance and to curb racism and bigotry.

Global English *n*

also **English as an International Language, EIL**

a term used to describe the use of English as a world language rather than simply the language of native-speakers of English. Global English emphasizes that English is spoken as a first, second or foreign language both within and across national borders around the world, and that in many situations "native-speaker" accents are not considered necessary or even desirable.

global error *n*

(in ERROR ANALYSIS) an error in the use of a major element of sentence structure, which makes a sentence or utterance difficult or impossible to understand. For example:

*I like take taxi but my friend said so not that we should be late for school.

This may be contrasted with a **local error**, which is an error in the use of an element of sentence structure, but which does not cause problems of comprehension. For example:

*If I heard from him I will let you know.

global issues *n*

in language teaching, the focus on topics that have global importance, such as global warming, conflict resolution, and human rights. The goals of language teaching are seen as not simply to teach language skills but to provide learners with an awareness of global issues and the means to address them. see also CURRICULUM IDEOLOGIES

globalization *n*

the phenomenon in which people in different locations worldwide are increasingly linked in such a way that events in one part of the world have an impact on local communities around the world. The spread of English is often linked to globalization since it provides for high levels of interconnectedness among nation states and local economies and cultures.

global learning *n*

a COGNITIVE STYLE in which the learner tries to remember something as a whole. For example, a learner may try to memorize complete sentences in a foreign language.

When a learner remembers something by separating it into parts, this is called an **analytic style**, or **part learning**. For example, a learner may divide a sentence into words, memorize the words, and then combine them again to make sentences.

global question *n*

(in language teaching) a question used in a reading comprehension exercise. To answer a global question, a student needs a general understanding of the text or passage. A student's understanding of the details of a text can be tested with **specific questions**.

gloss *n*

a summary of the meaning of words in a text, usually found as notes in the margin or between the lines of a text and provided to assist the reader with an understanding of difficult or words likely to be unknown in the text. Glosses can be interpretations, explanations, or translations.

glossary *n*

a subject-specific listing of terms and definitions.

glottal *n*

an articulation involving the **glottis**, the space between the vocal chords.
see PLACE OF ARTICULATION

glottal stop *n*

a speech sound (a CONSONANT) that is produced by the momentary closing of the glottis (the space between the VOCAL CORDS), trapping the airstream from the lungs behind it, followed by a sudden release of the air as the glottis is opened.
In some varieties of British English, a glottal stop is used instead of a /t/ in words like *bottle* and *matter*.
In some varieties of American English, a glottal stop (with NASAL RELEASE) is used instead of a /t/ in words like *kitten* and *button*.

goal[1] *n*

(in TRADITIONAL GRAMMAR) a term used by some linguists to refer to the person or thing which is affected by the action expressed by the verb. For example, in the English sentence:
Elizabeth smashed the vase.
vase is the goal.

goal² *n*

(in CASE GRAMMAR) the noun or noun phrase which refers to the place to which someone or something moves or is moved. For example in the sentences:

He loaded bricks on the truck.
He loaded the truck with bricks.
the truck is the goal.

goal setting *n*

the theory that people are more motivated to accomplish a task when they have clear, specific, and difficult but achievable goals than they are when they have no clear goals or goals that are too easy.

see also MOTIVATION

goal θ-role *n*

see θ THEORY

government *n* **govern** *v*

a type of grammatical relationship between two or more elements in a sentence, in which the choice of one element causes the selection of a particular form of another element. In traditional grammar, the term government has typically been used to refer to the relationship between verbs and nouns or between prepositions and nouns. In German, for example, the preposition *mit* "with" governs, that is requires, the DATIVE CASE¹ of the noun that follows it:

Peter kam mit seiner Schwester.
Peter came with his sister.

where *sein* "his" has the dative feminine case marker *er*.

In GOVERNMENT/BINDING THEORY the concept of government is based on Traditional Grammar but it has been more strictly defined and structured into a complex system to show the relationship of one element in a sentence to another element.

For example, the verb *give* in the sentence

She will give them to me.

governs *them* because:

1 *give* is a LEXICAL CATEGORY and therefore it can be a GOVERNOR
2 they are both within a maximal projection, e.g. a verb phrase (see PROJECTION (PRINCIPLE)) and
3 they are in certain structural relationships to each other.

Government/Binding Theory *n*

a theory of language developed by Chomsky and based on his concept of a UNIVERSAL GRAMMAR. It can be seen as a network of different subtheories which consist of certain principles and conditions (PARAMETERS) Some of the subtheories are:

1 BINDING THEORY: shows the reference relationship between noun phrases
2 BOUNDING THEORY: places restrictions on movement within a sentence
3 CASE THEORY: assigns cases to the noun phrases in the sentence
4 θ-THEORY: assigns semantic roles to the elements in the sentence
5 X-BAR THEORY: describes the structure of phrases

Some aspects of the Government/Binding Theory and its subtheories have been used in research into first and second language acquisition (see, for example, ADJACENCY PARAMETER, PRO-DROP PARAMETER).

see also PROJECTION (PRINCIPLE)

governor *n*

(in GOVERNMENT/BINDING THEORY) an element in a sentence which **governs**, that is has an influence on, another element. Everything that can be the HEAD of a phrase can function as a governor, e.g. nouns, verbs, adjectives and prepositions.

gradable *adj* **gradability** *n*

(of objects, people, ideas, etc.) having a certain property to a greater or lesser degree. In English, this property is usually expressed by an adjective, e.g. *hot*, *cold*, *rich*, *poor*.

For example:

Was it really as cold last night as Thursday night?
Your plate is hotter than mine.

Usually, a comparison is implied, even if it is not expressed. *It's hot in here*, means "compared with outside" or "compared with the room temperature which suits me".

Adjectives which refer to something which can be described in degrees are known as **gradable adjectives**. The negation of a gradable adjective does not necessarily imply the opposite. For example, not hot does not necessarily mean cold, nor does not rich necessarily mean poor.

see also ANTONYM

gradable adjective *n*

see GRADABLE

gradable pair *n*

see ANTONYM

gradation *n*

also **grading, sequencing**

the arrangement of the content of a language course or a textbook so that it is presented in a helpful way. Gradation would affect the order in which words, word meanings, tenses, structures, topics, functions, skills, etc. are presented. Gradation may be based on different criteria such as the complexity of an item, its frequency in written or spoken language, or its importance for the learner.

see also SELECTION

grade *n*

a way of expressing overall results in a test using a number or letter.

graded objectives *n*

(in language teaching) objectives which describe levels of attainment at different stages within a language programme. These are intended to provide statements of practical short-term goals for learners and to provide practical levels of mastery which they could attain after relatively short periods of study. Graded objectives have been used particularly in programmes for foreign language teaching in the United Kingdom.

graded reader *n*

also **simplified reader**

a text written for children learning their mother tongue, or for second or foreign language learners, in which the language content is based on a language grading scheme (see GRADATION). A graded reader may use a restricted vocabulary or set of grammatical structures.

grade point average *n*

also **GPA**

a measure of scholastic performance used in the US and elsewhere based on the average of numerical values assigned to letter grades (e.g. A = 4, B = 3, etc.).

gradience *n*

see FUZZY

grading *n*

another term for GRADATION

grammar[1] *n*

a description of the structure of a language and the way in which linguistic units such as words and phrases are combined to produce sentences in the language. It usually takes into account the meanings and functions these sentences have in the overall system of the language. It may or may not include the description of the sounds of a language (see PHONOLOGY, PHONEMICS).

see also MORPHOLOGY, SEMANTICS, SYNTAX

grammar[2]

(in GENERATIVE GRAMMAR) a grammar which describes the speaker's knowledge of the language. It looks at language in relation to how it may be structured in the speaker's mind, and which principles (see UNIVERSAL GRAMMAR) and PARAMETERS are available to the speaker when producing the language.

see also CORE GRAMMAR, I-LANGUAGE, UNIVERSAL GRAMMAR

grammar checker *n*

a program which checks certain grammatical and mechanical aspects of writing (see MECHANICS) such as the use of passive forms, CONCORD, and punctuation. Though useful for native speakers, these programs are often less beneficial for second language users, due to the bewildering array of options they provide.

grammar clusters *n*

in writing, the co-occurrence of certain grammatical forms within a specific genre (type) of writing: for example, chronological transitions, the use of personal pronouns, and specific uses of present, past, and past-progressive forms often occur in narrative writing.

grammaring *v*

sometimes used to refer to the process by which language learners use grammar to create messages through grammaticalizing or adding grammar to a sequence of words to create finer meaning distinctions. The linguist Diane Larsen-Freeman proposed grammaring as an important process in second language acquisition. Grammaring emphasizes grammar as a dynamic process rather than a system of rules.

Grammar Translation Method *n*

a method of foreign or second language teaching which makes use of translation and grammar study as the main teaching and learning activities. The Grammar Translation Method was the traditional way Latin and Greek were taught in Europe. In the nineteenth century it began to be used to teach "modern" languages such as French, German, and English, and it is still used in some countries today. A typical lesson consists of the presentation of a grammatical rule, a study of lists of vocabulary, and a translation exercise. Because the Grammar Translation Method emphasizes reading rather than the ability to communicate in a language there was a reaction to it in the nineteenth century (see NATURAL APPROACH, DIRECT METHOD), and there was later a greater emphasis on the teaching of spoken language.

grammatical[1] *adj* **grammaticality** *n*
a phrase, clause, or sentence which is ACCEPTABLE because it follows the rules of a grammar (see GRAMMAR[1]), is described as grammatical. For example, the English sentence:
They walk to school.
would be a grammatical sentence according to a grammar of Standard English, but the sentence:
They walks to school.
would be considered **ungrammatical** according to such a grammar.

grammatical[2] *adj* **grammaticality** *n*
in GENERATIVE GRAMMAR, a sentence is grammatical if it follows the rules of a native speaker's COMPETENCE. For example:
The teacher who the man who the children saw pointed out is a cousin of Joan's.
would be a grammatical sentence because it can be generated by the rules of the grammar. However, it could be regarded as **unacceptable** because of its involved structure which makes it difficult for a listener to understand easily.
see also ACCEPTABLE

grammatical ambiguity *n*
see AMBIGUOUS

grammatical aspect *n*
see ASPECT

grammatical category[1] *n*
a class or group of items which fulfil the same or similar functions in a particular language. For example, CASE[1], PERSON, TENSE[1], and ASPECT are grammatical categories. Some linguists also refer to related groups of words such as nouns, verbs, and adjectives as grammatical categories but these groups are usually referred to in TRADITIONAL GRAMMAR as PARTS OF SPEECH.

grammatical category[2] *n*

(in GENERATIVE GRAMMAR) a concept such as a SENTENCE, a NOUN PHRASE, a VERB. Grammatical categories are shown by **category symbols** such as S, NP, and V.

grammatical competence *n*

see COMMUNICATIVE COMPETENCE

grammatical function *n*

the relationship that a CONSTITUENT in a sentence has with the other constituents. For example, in the English sentence:

Peter threw the ball.

Peter has the function of being the SUBJECT of the verb *throw*, and *the ball* has the function of being the OBJECT of the verb.

grammaticality judgment task *n*

a task in which speakers of a language are presented with linguistic stimuli (typically sentences) and asked to judge whether or not they are correct in the language. Such tasks are widely used in linguistic theory to formulate and refine claims about a speaker-hearer's internal grammar or COMPETENCE.

see also ACCEPTABILITY JUDGEMENT TASK

grammatical meaning *n*

see CONTENT WORD

grammatical metaphor *n*

see METAPHOR

grammatical morpheme *n*

see MORPHEME

grammatical sensitivity *n*

see LANGUAGE APTITUDE

grammatical syllabus *n*

another term for STRUCTURAL SYLLABUS

grammatical word *n*

see CONTENT WORD

grave accent *n*

the accent, e.g. on French *près* "near".

see also ACCENT[2]

grounded theory *n*

a general methodology of analysis in QUALITATIVE RESEARCH, in which the first level of analysis is systematically collected data, the second is the conceptualization of the data into categories and their properties (see CONSTANT COMPARISON METHOD), and the third is an inductive theory (see ANALYTIC INDUCTION), usually illustrated by characteristic examples of data.

grounding *n*

an aspect of the INFORMATION STRUCTURE of a sentence in which in an act of communication, speakers assume that some information is more important than other information. Information which is needed for the listener to understand new information is **background information**, and information which is new or considered more important is **foregrounded** or **foreground information**. For example, in the sentence *As I was coming to school this morning, I saw an accident*, *I saw an accident, this morning* is foregrounded information and *As I was coming to school* is background information. The foregrounded information is contained in the main clause of the sentence, which comes after the clause containing background information.

group discussion *n*

a teaching activity which has the following characteristics:
1   A small number of students (four to twelve) meet together.
2   They choose, or are given, a common topic or problem and a goal or objective.
3   They exchange and evaluate information or ideas about the topic.
see also CO-OPERATIVE LEARNING

group dynamics *n*

the interactions which take place within a group and the study of how such factors as leadership, interaction and decision-making affect the structure of a group. Group dynamics is an important consideration in forming classroom groups (see CO-OPERATIVE LEARNING) and in designing learning tasks and classroom materials.
see also SMALL-GROUP INTERACTION

grouping *n*

(in teaching) arranging students into groups to help them learn better. Choosing suitable grouping arrangements which match different kinds of learning tasks is an important dimension of teaching. Different group arrangements for teaching include:

1 **whole-group instruction:** the class is taught as a whole
2 **small-group discussion:** a group of between six and eight students working on a discussion topic
3 **tutorial discussion group:** a small group of usually less than five students focusing on a narrow range of materials, often to help remedy a learning difficulty.

Important issues in grouping are group size (a factor which influences learner participation in group work) and whether students learn better in mixed-ability groups or in groups of about the same proficiency level. Use of small groups is a characteristic of **Communicative Language Teaching** and **Collaborative Language Learning** since group work is said to facilitate real communication and naturalistic language use.

see also CO-OPERATIVE LEARNING, SMALL-GROUP INTERACTION

group work *n*

(in language teaching) a learning activity which involves a small group of learners working together. The group may work on a single task, or on different parts of a larger task. Tasks for group members are often selected by the members of the group.

see also PAIR WORK

guessing parameter *n*

see ITEM RESPONSE THEORY

guided discovery *n*

an inductive teaching technique in which the teacher provides examples of a target language item and then guides the students to work out the meaning or underlying rules for themselves. For example the teacher may provide a text containing several examples of the past perfect, a set of questions to prompt the students to think about time references, and ask students to try to work out the meaning of the past perfect.

see also DEDUCTIVE LEARNING

guided discussion *n*

see DISCUSSION MIETHOD

guided interview *n*

an interview in which the interviewer makes use of a set of questions that has been prepared in advance and that is used to guide and structure the interview. The list of questions used by the interviewer is known as an **interview schedule** or **protocol**. Usually the interviewer records answers to the questions into the schedule during the interview.

see also FOCUSED INTERVIEW, DEPTH INTERVIEW, STRUCTURED INTERVIEW, UNSTRUCTURED INTERVIEW

guided practice *n*
see PRACTICE ACTIVITIES

guided reading *n*
a teacher-directed mode of reading instruction in which the teacher directs the purpose, structure, and response to a reading activity, leading the readers through the reading of a text. This approach can be used to model reading behaviours and strategies.

guided writing *n*
a technique for teaching writing where the teacher provides detailed guidance in the form of questions, an outline, a model, or some other way of focusing and directing the students' writing. Guided writing seeks to reduce the number of student errors and to provide a specific focus on some aspect of either the form or content of a piece of writing or both.

H

habit *n*

a pattern of behaviour that is regular and which has become almost automatic as a result of repetition. The view of language learning as habit formation found in behaviourism has been rejected by virtually all linguists and specialists in language acquisition, but research continues into issues such as the mechanisms through which automaticity develops in language learning.

half-close vowel *n*

see VOWEL

half-open vowel *n*

see VOWEL

halo effect *n*

(in research) the effect of a feature that is not being tested, but that changes or influences the results. For example, a teacher who is rating a child according to "interest in learning English" may give the child a higher rating because he or she is well behaved in class.

handout *n*

also **worksheet**

a page or pages containing exercises, activities, tasks or explanations, given out to students to supplement activities or practice given by the teacher or in a textbook.

hard palate *n*

see PLACE OF ARTICULATION

hardware *n*

the physical equipment which may be used in an educational system, such as a computer, video-cassette player, film projector, tape-recorder, cassette or record player.

The materials used in such equipment such as programs, tapes, and films are called **software**.

Hawthorn effect *n*

(in research) the effect produced by the introduction of a new element into a learning situation, including changes in the normal behaviour of research subjects when they know that they are being observed. For example, if a new teaching method is used, there may be an improvement in learning that is due not to the method, but to the fact that it is new. Later on, the improvement may disappear.

head *n*

the central part of a phrase. Other elements in the phrase are in some grammatical or semantic relationship to the head. For example, in the English noun phrase:

the fat lady in the floral dress

the noun *lady* is the head of the phrase.

see also MODIFIER, CLASSIFIER[2]

head-first language *n*

see PARAMETER

head-last language *n*

see PARAMETER

head parameter *n*

see PARAMETER

hearing impaired *adj*

a term used to describe hearing loss, which recognizes that nearly all people with severe hearing difficulties have some degree of hearing, known as residual hearing. The degree of hearing impairment may vary across speech frequencies (see sound wave), at different levels of intensity. With the use of hearing aids, people with hearing impairment often learn to use residual hearing to maintain or improve their communication skills.

hedging *n* **hedges** *n*

also **weakeners, downtoners, detensifiers, understatements**

in speech and writing, linguistic devices that writers use either to indicate the writer's lack of commitment to the truth of a statement or a desire not to express that commitment categorically. Hedges are linguistic items such as *perhaps, somewhat, sort of, might, to a certain degree, it is possible that*. Such items may occur as often as once in every 15 seconds of conversation, depending on context of communication.

hegemony *n*

the predominant organizational and institutional form of power and domination within the economic, social, political, cultural and ideological domains of a society, or across societies.

A culture is a hegemony if it is so dominant that its beliefs, values and practices are viewed as natural or common sense. For example, deviations from culturally valued rhetorical norms in writing by people from a different cultural background may be viewed as a failure to think clearly.

heritage language *n*

sometimes used to refer to the language a person regards as their native, home, or ancestral language. This may be an indigenous language (e.g. Welsh in Wales) or immigrant languages (e.g. Spanish in the US).
see also LANGUAGE MAINTENANCE

heritage language learner *n*
also **heritage learner**

a term that is sometimes used to refer to learners who acquired a particular language as their first language at home and subsequently study that language. Special courses are sometimes designed for such learners, for example, Spanish for Spanish speakers in the US, whose verbal fluency in Spanish is often more advanced than their literacy-related skills (because their education has been in English). Other writers use the term more generally to refer to any learner of a language who considers that language to be part of his or her cultural heritage.

hesitation phenomena *n*

another term for PAUSING

heterogeneous class *n*

a class consisting of learners who are very different from each other, either by age, language proficiency level or some other characteristic. A class with learners who are very similar to each other is known as a HOMOGENEOUS CLASS.

heteroglossia *n*

the idea, proposed by Bakhtin, that humans constantly assimilate the discourses of others and make them their own, so that even a single linguistic code (such as an IDIOLECT) contains many distinct varieties within it.

heuristic *adj* heuristics *n*

1 (in education) teaching procedures which encourage learners to learn through experience or by their own personal discoveries.
2 (in learning) processes of conscious or unconscious inquiry or discovery. For example, in trying to discover the meanings of words in a foreign language, a learner may repeat aloud a sentence containing the word,

several times, in an attempt to work out its meaning. In first-language learning these heuristic processes are sometimes known as **operating principles**, i.e. ways in which learners work out the meaning of utterances based on what they understand about the structure of the TARGET LANGUAGE[1]. For example, among the operating principles a child may use are:

a word which ends in *ing* is a verb.

in a sequence of two nouns (e.g. Jane's doll) the first noun is the possessor and the second noun is the thing possessed.

heuristic function *n*
see DEVELOPMENTAL FUNCTIONS OF LANGUAGE

hidden curriculum *n*
sometimes used to refer to implicit values or goals in a curriculum or educational system such as to impart the values and ideology of a particular society or to socialize students into the dominant political and economic system and the values of that system.

hierarchical chunks *n*
see CHUNKING

higher education *n*
also **tertiary education**
education beyond the level of secondary school, such as at college, polytechnic or university.
see also FURTHER EDUCATION

high frequency word *n*
a word occurring frequently in a corpus of spoken or written texts. Such words are listed in a word frequency list.

high-inference category *n*
also **high-inference behaviour**
(in research on teaching or other aspects of classroom behaviour) a category of behaviour which cannot be observed directly but which has to be inferred. For example, the fact that students are "interested in a lesson", or "making use of higher level thinking during a lesson" cannot be observed directly and hence is a high-inference category of classroom behaviour. On the other hand a category such as "asking questions during a lesson" is easily observed and can be readily quantified (i.e. counted or measured). It is an example of a **low-inference category** of classroom behaviour. The distinction between high-inference and low-inference categories is an

important one in research on classroom behaviour, particularly when the researcher wishes to quantify such behaviour.

highlighting *n* **highlight** *v*
(in reading) marking key words or sections in a passage with the use of a coloured pen, making them easier to identify or remember when studying or reviewing.

high stakes language test *n*
a language test that has important consequences for the test taker, for example being admitted to or denied admission to a prestigious university or receiving a promotion in salary or rank by demonstrating language proficiency.

High variety *n*
see DIGLOSSIA

high vowel *n*
see VOWEL

histogram *n*
see DISTRIBUTION

historical linguistics *n*
another term for COMPARATIVE HISTORICAL LINGUISTICS

historic present *n*
a present tense used in a context where a past tense would normally be used, to create a more vivid effect, to show informality, or to show a sense of "friendliness" between speaker and hearer.
For example:
Do you know what happened to me last night? I'm sitting in a restaurant when this guy comes up and pours water over me.

history *n*
see INTERNAL VALIDITY

holistic approach *n*
an approach to language teaching which seeks to focus on language in its entirety rather than breaking it down into separate components, such as reading, listening, writing, grammar, etc. This is one of the principles of whole language as well as of some approaches to teaching language arts.

holistic evaluation *n*

> (in teaching composition) a method of evaluating writing in which the composition is viewed as a whole rather than as distinct parts.

holistic rating scale *n*

> in testing, a scale in which different activities are included over several bands to produce a multiple activity scale.

holistic scoring *n*

> a method of scoring where a single score is assigned to writing or speaking samples on the basis of an overall impressionistic assessment of the test taker's performance on a writing or speaking task as a whole.
>
> see also ANALYTIC SCORING

holophrase *n* **holophrastic** *adj*

> a single word which functions as a complex idea or sentence. Holophrastic speech is one of the first stages in children's acquisition of speech.
>
> For example:

Holophrases	intended meaning
Water!	*I want some water.*
More.	*Give me some more.*

home–school language switch *n*

> used in referring to the language used in a school setting to describe the need to change ("switch") from one language spoken at home to another used as the medium of instruction at school.
>
> see also BILINGUAL EDUCATION, IMMERSION PROGRAMME

homogeneous class *n*

> see HETEROGENEOUS CLASS

homographs *n*

> words which are written in the same way but which are pronounced differently and have different meanings.
>
> For example, the English words *lead* /liːd/ in *Does this road lead to town?* and lead /led/ in *Lead is a heavy metal*, are homographs. Homographs are sometimes called **homonyms**.
>
> see also HOMOPHONES

homonyms[1] *n*

> see HOMOGRAPHS

homonyms[2] *n*

see HOMOPHONES

homonyms[3] *n* **homonymy** *n*

words which are written in the same way and sound alike but which have different meanings.

For example, the English verbs *lie* in *You have to lie down* and *lie* in *Don't lie, tell the truth!*

It is a well-known problem in SEMANTICS to tell the difference between homonymy (several words with the same form but different meanings) and POLYSEMY (a single word with more than one meaning).

homophones *n*

words which sound alike but are written differently and often have different meanings.

For example, the English words *no* and *know* are both pronounced /nəʊ/ in some varieties of British English.

Homophones are sometimes called **homonyms**.

see also HOMOGRAPHS

homorganic *adj*

made with the same PLACE OF ARTICULATION. The sounds /n/, /d/, and /s/ as in English *hands* are homorganic, because they all share the feature ALVEOLAR.

For example, the sounds /p/ and /m/ are both produced with the two lips (i.e. are BILABIAL), although one is a STOP and the other a NASAL.

see also ASSIMILATION, MANNER OF ARTICULATION

honorifics *n*

politeness formulas in a particular language which may be specific affixes, words, or sentence structures. Languages which have a complex system of honorifics are, for instance, Japanese, Madurese (a language of Eastern Java), and Hindi. Although English has no complex system of honorifics, expressions such as *would you . . . , may I . . .* , and polite ADDRESS FORMS fulfil similar functions.

horizontal construction *n*

see VERTICAL CONSTRUCTIONS

HTML *n*

an acronym for Hypertext Markup Language, the authoring language used to create web pages. Once necessary for language teachers to know in order to produce web pages, it is now frequently built in to web-page-making software programs.

humanistic approach *n*

(in language teaching) a term sometimes used for what underlies METHODS in which the following principles are considered important:

a the development of human values

b growth in self-awareness and in the understanding of others

c sensitivity to human feelings and emotions

d active student involvement in learning and in the way learning takes place (for this last reason such methods are also said to be student centred).

COMMUNITY LANGUAGE LEARNING is an example of a humanistic approach.

see also APPROACH

human subjects committee *n*

another term for INSTITUTIONAL REVIEW BOARD

H-variety *n*

see DIGLOSSIA

hybrid course *n*

a language course that includes both face-to-face and online (Internet) interaction.

hybridity *n*

mixture, for example cultural mixing as an effect of globalization. The notion of hybridity has been applied to sociological theories of identity, multiculturalism, and racism.

hyperbole *n*

see FIGURE OF SPEECH

hypercorrection[1] *n*

overgeneralization of a rule in language use. For example, the rule that an adverb modifies a verb may be overextended and used in cases where an adjective would normally be used, as in *This meat smells freshly* instead of *This meat smells fresh*.

see also COPULA

hypercorrection[2] *n*

the incorrect use of a word, pronunciation or other linguistic feature in speaking as a result of the attempt to speak in an educated manner and in the process replacing a form that is itself correct.

For example the use of "whom" instead of "who" in *Whom do you think painted that picture?* Hypercorrections are sometimes used by a second language learner who is attempting to speak correctly or by a speaker of a non-standard variety of a language, when speaking formally. This may result in the speaker using more self-correction and using more formal vocabulary than speakers of a standard variety of the language.

hyponymy *n* **hyponym** *n*

a relationship between two words, in which the meaning of one of the words includes the meaning of the other word.

For example, in English the words *animal* and *dog* are related in such a way that *dog* refers to a type of *animal*, and *animal* is a general term that includes dog and other types of animal.

The specific term, *dog*, is called a hyponym, and the general term, *animal*, is called a **superordinate**.

A superordinate term can have many hyponyms. For example:

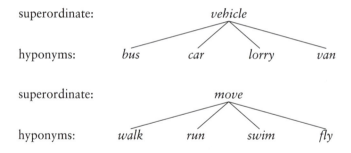

see also SYNONYM

hypothesis *n* (plural **hypotheses**)

a speculation concerning either observed or expected relationships among phenomena. Hypotheses are made and evaluated in both QUANTITATIVE RESEARCH and QUALITATIVE RESEARCH. However, in quantitative research hypotheses are formulated in advance of the research, based on theory and previous research, while in qualitative research hypotheses emerge gradually in the course of the research itself (see also GROUNDED THEORY, ANALYTIC INDUCTION). If for research purposes the speculation is translated into a statement that can be tested by quantitative methods in research, the statement is known as a **statistical hypothesis**, stated with reference to population PARAMETERS (e.g. population mean) and takes the form of two opposing but related hypotheses: a **null hypothesis**, symbolized by H_0, and an alternative hypothesis, symbolized by H_a or H_1, that are mutually exclusive and exhaustive. A null hypothesis is a statement that "No difference exists between groups A and B" or "There is no correlation between variables A and B", whereas the alternative hypothesis is an opposite statement that "The mean for group A is higher than that for group B" or "There is a positive correlation between variables A and B". The statistical analysis of research results is frequently designed to determine whether or not a null hypothesis should be rejected, thus providing support for an alternative hypothesis.

see also HYPOTHESIS TESTING

hypothesis formation *n*

(in language learning) the formation of ideas ("hypotheses") by a learner about the language he or she is learning. These hypotheses may be conscious or unconscious. Most people would agree that at least some of these ideas come from the language we see and hear around us, but scholars holding the INNATIST HYPOTHESIS claim that our most important and basic ideas about language in general are present at birth.

hypothesis testing *n*

a procedure to test a statistical hypothesis. A five-step version of hypothesis testing proceeds as follows:

1 State a null hypothesis (H_0) and an alternative hypothesis (H_a).
2 Set a level of statistical significance (α) (see ALPHA).
3 Select and calculate an appropriate **test statistic**, a numerical value calculated from the data sampled from a population and used to determine whether or not H_0 should be rejected, which results in a calculated value.
4 Compare the sample evidence from Step 3 against a criterion (i.e. a calculated value against a critical value or a *p*-value against α).
5 Make a decision regarding the null hypothesis (i.e. either to reject H_0 in favour of H_a or fail to reject H_0).

see also STATISTICAL SIGNIFICANCE

I

i + 1 *n*

in Krashen's theory of SLA, "i" represents a learner's current level of competence, and "i + 1" the stage just beyond it.

IATEFL *n*

The International Association of Teachers of English as a Foreign Language, a professional association for language teaching professionals based in the UK.

ice-breaker *n*

in teaching, an activity in a new class that gives learners an opportunity, to meet each other and exchange information and that seeks to build a positive class **climate**.

iconicity *n*

see COGNITIVE LINGUISTICS

ideal speaker/hearer *n*

see COMPETENCE

ideational function *n*

see FUNCTIONS OF LANGUAGE[2]

ideational meaning *n*

that meaning in a text which relates to the ideas, concepts, propositions, etc. contained in the text, in contrast to the *interpersonal meaning*, which relates to the attitudes and feelings of the speaker or writer towards the topic of the text.

ideational semantics *n*

see SYSTEMIC-FUNCTIONAL LINGUISTICS

identity *n*

a person's sense of themselves as a discrete separate individual, including their self-image and their awareness of self, and an important concept in SOCIOCULTURAL THEORY. People's sense of identity influences how they view themselves both as an individual and in relation to other people. Becoming a language teacher, for example, involves developing the identity of a teacher and the teacher's sense of identity may reflect his or her age, gender, ethnicity, experience, and language proficiency. In POSTMODERNISM and FEMINIST LINGUISTICS, identity is not seen as a constant but is viewed as unstable, fragmented, self-conscious, and constructed in interaction. In CRITICAL APPLIED LINGUISTICS the role of identity has been explored in relation to the role language and discourse can play in marginalizing or empowering speakers.

ideogram *n*

see IDEOGRAPHIC WRITING

ideographic writing *n*

a WRITING SYSTEM using symbols (ideograms) to represent whole words or concepts ("ideas"). The Chinese writing system is often considered to be ideographic.
For example, in Chinese the ideogram 水 represents "water".
Chinese can create new LEXEMES by combining existing ideograms to form COMPOUND WORDS. It can also combine existing ideograms into a sequence whose pronunciation is like that of a foreign word the Chinese wish to borrow, thus "transliterating" the foreign word into Chinese characters.

ideology *n*

a set of concepts, doctrines and beliefs that forms the basis of a political, educational or economic system.
The relationships between ideology, language, and discourse are a central focus of critical theory and critical linguistics.
see CURRICULUM IDEOLOGIES

ideophones *n*

a type of SOUND SYMBOLISM used to provide a vivid representation of an object or image that has no inherent acoustic qualities, such as (in English) *zig-zag*, *shilly-shally*, or *topsy-turvy*.
see also ONOMATOPOEIA

idiolect *n* idiolectal *adj*

the language system of an individual as expressed by the way he or she speaks or writes within the overall system of a particular language. In its widest sense, someone's idiolect includes their way of communicating; for example, their choice of utterances and the way they interpret the utterances made by others. In a narrower sense, an idiolect may include those features, either in speech or writing, which distinguish one individual from others, such as VOICE QUALITY, PITCH, and SPEECH RHYTHM.
see also DIALECT, SOCIOLECT

idiom *n* **idiomatic** *adj*

an expression which functions as a single unit and whose meaning cannot be worked out from its separate parts.

For example:

She washed her hands of the matter.

means

"She refused to have anything more to do with the matter".

idiomatic *adj*, **idiomaticity** *n*

the degree to which speech is not simply grammatical but also native-like in use. For example, "It pleases me that Harry was able to be brought by you" (said by a host/hostess to a guest at a party) is grammatical but not native-like or idiomatic, whereas "I'm so glad you could bring Harry" is both grammatical and idiomatic.

IDLTM *n*

an abbreviation for International Diploma in English Language Teaching Management (UCLES).

IELTS *n*

see INTERNATIONAL ENGLISH LANGUAGE TESTING SYSTEM

IEP *n*

an abbreviation for INTENSIVE ENGLISH PROGRAMME

I-language *n*

also **internalized language**

language viewed as an internal property of the human mind or a computational system in the human brain. Linguists who subscribe to this view attempt to construct grammars showing how the mind structures language and what universal principles are involved (see UNIVERSAL GRAMMAR, GENERATIVE THEORY).

I-language can be contrasted with **E-language (externalized language)**, language viewed as a collection of texts or a social phenomenon.

illiteracy *n*

see LITERACY

illocutionary act *n*

see LOCUTIONARY ACT

illocutionary force *n*

see SPEECH ACT, LOCUTIONARY ACT, PERFORMATIVE

illuminative evaluation *n*
also **process evaluation**
an approach to evaluation that seeks to find out how different aspects of a course work or how a course is being implemented and the teaching, learning and processes that it creates. It seeks to provide a deeper understanding of the processes of teaching and learning that occur in a programme without necessarily seeking to change the course in any way as a result.
see EVALUATION

ILR *n*
an abbreviation for the INTERAGENCY LANGUAGE ROUND TABLE

ILTA *n*
an abbreviation for INTERNATIONAL LANGUAGE TESTING ASSOCIATION

imagery *n*
mental pictures or impressions ("images") created by, or accompanying, words or sentences.
Words or sentences that produce strong picture-like images may be easier to remember than those without visual imagery. For example, in the following pair of sentences, (a) may be easier to remember than (b) because it creates a stronger mental image.
a The gloves were made by a tailor.
b The gloves were made by a machine.
In second language learning, imagery may be used as a learning strategy. For example, when reading a passage about agricultural machinery, a student may think of a farm scene in which people are using different kinds of machines. Later when trying to recall the passage he or she read, the student may think of the image or picture and use this to trigger recollection of the information in the text.

imaginative function *n*
see DEVELOPMENTAL FUNCTIONS OF LANGUAGE

imaginative recount *n*
see TEXT TYPES

imitation *n*
(in language learning) the copying of the speech of another person. Traditional views of language learning placed a high emphasis on the role of imitation and it has been considered basic to some methods of teaching foreign languages (see AUDIOLINGUAL METHOD, SITUATIONAL LANGUAGE

271

TEACHING). However, the basic assumption of research on first and second language acquisition is that learners use language productively and creatively and do not simply imitate the utterances of others.

see also MODELLING, CREATIVE CONSTRUCTION HYPOTHESIS

immediate recall *n*

the remembering of something shortly after studying it. The ability to remember something some time after it has been studied is known as DELAYED RECALL

immersion programme *n*

a form of bilingual education and used to describe programmes which serve **language majority students** and which use a second or foreign language to teach at least 50% of the curriculum during the elementary or secondary grades. For example, there are schools in Canada for English-speaking children, where French is the language of instruction. If these children are taught in French for the whole day it is called a total **immersion programme,** but if they are taught in French for only part of the day it is called a **partial immersion programme.**

see also SUBMERSION PROGRAMME

impact *n*

the effect of a test on individual test takers, other STAKEHOLDERS (e.g. teachers, parents, school administrators, or test developers), educational systems, or society.

see also BACKWASH, WASHBACK

impact evaluation *n*

the measurement of the effects of a course, training programme or curriculum innovation, after the innovation has been implemented. Impact evaluation seeks to assess the benefits of the programme to its stakeholders, is a measure of accountability, is summative in nature, is carried out towards the end of the lifetime of the project, and makes use of both qualitative and quantitative data.

imperative *n*

see MOOD

imperative sentence *n*

a sentence which is in the form of a command. For example:

Pick up the book!

Imperative sentences do not, however, always have the function of an order. For example:

272

Look what you've done now!
often functions as an expression of annoyance.
see also DECLARATIVE SENTENCE, INTERROGATIVE SENTENCE

impersonal construction *n*

a type of sentence in which there is no mention of who or what does or experiences something. Examples include English *It's cold*, *It's raining*, and French *Ici on parle anglais* (literally, "Here one speaks English") "English is spoken here".

implication *n*

in everyday communication, a great deal of information is implied by the speaker rather than asserted. For example, if somebody said:
Rita was on time this morning.
it could imply that Rita was usually late.
Often the hearer would understand the implication of the utterance in the way that the speaker intends (see utterance meaning) and give a suitable response but, of course, there may be misunderstandings and misinterpretations:
A: *I'm rather short of cash at the moment.*
   (meaning: I'd like you to pay for the lunch)
B: *Oh, I'm sure they accept credit cards here.*

implicational scaling *n*

a method of showing relationships by means of an implicational table or **scalogram**. For example, a group of students learning English may acquire the rule for using the DEFINITE ARTICLE before the rule for the INDEFINITE ARTICLE and they may acquire those two rules before the rule for marking the PLURAL of nouns. This can be shown by investigating their spoken or written language and presenting the results in a table. The symbol [+] means 100% correct use of the rule and the symbol × means that the rule is applied sometimes but not at other times (variable use).

student	noun plural	indefinite article	definite article
C	×	×	×
A	×	×	+
D	×	×	+
B	×	+	+
F	×	+	+
E	+	+	+

The symbol [+] in any row in the table implies a + symbol in any column to the right of it in the same row or in any row below it. In this way the students are ranked from student C through student E, who is the best student, because he or she has 100% correct use of all the rules. Implicational scaling has been used to show the order of acquisition of rules by FOREIGN LANGUAGE and SECOND LANGUAGE learners, and by people who are moving from a CREOLE towards a STANDARD VARIETY.

see also VARIABLE[1]

implicational universal *n*

    see LANGUAGE UNIVERSAL

implicature *n*

    see CONVERSATIONAL MAXIM

implicit knowledge *n*

    also **tacit knowledge, intuitive knowledge**

    knowledge that people can be shown (by their behaviour, their judgements about grammaticality, and so forth) to possess intuitively, but which they are unable to articulate. Implicit knowledge is contrasted with **explicit knowledge**, which is verbalizable.

    For example, native speakers of English intuitively know the regularities of article use (when to use the definite, indefinite, or zero article), but they are usually unable to say what any of those principles are. Foreign language learners of English, on the other hand, may have quite a lot of explicit knowledge about the rules for using English articles, while their unmonitored production may reveal that this explicit knowledge has not been internalized.

implicit learning *n*

    in general, non-conscious learning, contrasted with **explicit learning**, which is more conscious. Various writers define the difference between implicit and explicit learning in slightly different ways, for example:

    1 Explicit learning involves such conscious operations as hypothesis formation and testing, while implicit learning does not.

    2 Implicit learning is learning without awareness of what has been learned, while in explicit learning the learner is aware of what has been learned.

    3 Explicit learning is accompanied by awareness that one is learning, while implicit learning is not.

    Differing definitions and difficulties involved in operationalizing terms like "awareness" have given rise to many long-standing controversies.

implicit memory *n*

sometimes also referred to as **unintentional unconscious memory,** a type of MEMORY that is revealed when previous experiences facilitate performance even when not accompanied by conscious recollection. For example, both first and second language readers process recently encountered words faster than words that they have not encountered recently, but this speeded processing (see PRIMING) does not depend on readers remembering that they have seen the word before.

implicit negative feedback *n*

see RECAST

implicit performative *n*

see PERFORMATIVE

implosive *n*

a stop made with an ingressive airstream mechanism in which air is sucked into (instead of expelled from) the airstream during part of the articulation.

impressionistic transcription *n*

see TRANSCRIPTION

inalienable possession *n*

in many languages, there is a distinction between those objects which can change ownership, such as houses, or animals, and those which typically cannot, such as body parts, one's shadow, and one's footprints.

The first type of possession is called **alienable possession** and the latter type is called inalienable.

For example, in English, the verb *own* is typically not used with inalienable possessions: *George owns a car* but not ** George owns a big nose* (if it is his own nose). On the other hand the verb have can be used with both types of possession: *George has a car* and *George has a big nose.*

inanimate noun *n*

see ANIMATE NOUN

inchoative verb *n*

a verb which expresses a change of state. For example:

> *yellowed* in *The leaves yellowed.*

and

> *matured* in *The cheese matured.*

as the leaves "became yellow" and the cheese "became mature".
see also CAUSATIVE VERB

incidental learning *n*

learning something without the intention to learn it or learning one thing while intending to learn another, for example, unintentionally picking up vocabulary, patterns, or spelling through interaction, communicative activities, or reading for content or pleasure. This can be contrasted with **intentional learning**, for example learning by following a deliberate programme of study to enhance vocabulary or grammar.

In controlled experiments, incidental learning is usually used in a more restricted sense, operationalized as a condition in which subjects are not told in advance that they will be tested after treatment, sometimes contrasted with an intentional condition in which subjects are told what they will be tested on.

incipient bilingualism *n*

the early stages of bilingualism or second language acquisition where a language is not yet strongly developed.

inclusion *n*

in education, placing all students together for teaching rather than removing some students for separate teaching, e.g. second language students or students with learning disabilities.

inclusive (first person) pronoun *n*

see EXCLUSIVE (FIRST PERSON) PRONOUN

indefinite article *n*

see ARTICLE

indefinite pronoun *n*

a pronoun that refers to something which is not thought of as definite or particular, such as *somebody, something, anybody, anyone, one, anything, everybody, everything.*

independent clause *n*

see DEPENDENT CLAUSE

independent variable *n*

see DEPENDENT VARIABLE

indexical information *n*

(in communication) information which is communicated, usually indirectly, about the speaker or writer's social class, age, sex, nationality, ethnic group, etc., or his or her emotional state (e.g. whether excited, angry, surprised, bored, etc.).

indicative *n*

see MOOD

indicator *n*

also **performance indicator**

in standards-based education, descriptions of the specific, observable and assessable behaviours and activities that may be performed to show that a standard is being met.

For example:

standard: the teacher uses a variety of instructional strategies and resources appropriately

indicator: the teacher successfully uses whole class, group, and pair work activities together with the textbook in conducting a lesson

see also STANDARDS

indigenization *n*

another term for NATIVIZATION

indigenous language *n*

a language spoken by the indigenous (original) inhabitants of a country, for example, Hawaiian and American Indian languages in the US and aboriginal languages in Australia.

indirect negative evidence *n*

see EVIDENCE

indirect object *n*

see OBJECT[1]

indirect object relative clause *n*

also **IO**

see ACCESSIBILITY, NOUN PHRASE, HIERARCHY

indirect question *n*

see DIRECT SPEECH

indirect speech *n*
> see DIRECT SPEECH

indirect speech act *n*
> a speech act in which the communicative intention is not reflected in the linguistic form of the utterance. For example, "It is very hot in here" may be used to express a request to turn on the air conditioner.
> see SPEECH ACT

indirect test *n*
> a test that measures ability indirectly by requiring test takers to perform tasks not reflective of an authentic target language use situation, from which an inference is drawn about the abilities underlying their performance on the test. An example of an indirect test of writing includes a test that asks test takers to locate errors in a composition; an example of an indirect test of pronunciation is a test where test takers are asked to select a word that has the same pronunciation as the one in the STEM.
> see also DIRECT TEST, SEMI-DIRECT

individual bilingualism *n*
> see BILINGUALISM

individual differences *n*
> also **individual learner differences**
> factors specific to individual learners which may account for differences in the rate at which learners learn and their level of attainment. While much research in second language learning has the goal of discovering processes and stages of development that are common to all learners, this has always been accompanied by a complementary concern for differences among learners. Given the same learning environment, it is often observed that some learners are highly successful and others are not. Individual learner factors that have been frequently identified as possible causes for differential success include age (see CRITICAL PERIOD), aptitude, motivation, cognitive style, the use of learning strategies, and personality.

individualization *n*
> also **individualized instruction, individualized learning**
> a learner-centred approach to teaching in which
> *a* goals and objectives are based on the needs of individual learners
> *b* allowances are made in the design of a curriculum for individual differences in what students wish to learn, how they learn, and the rate at which they learn.

Individualized approaches to language teaching are based on these assumptions:

1 people learn in different ways
2 they can learn from a variety of different sources
3 learners have different goals and objectives in language learning
4 direct teaching by a teacher is not always essential for learning.

Individualization includes such things as one-to-one teaching, home study, self-access facilities, self-directed learning and the development of learner autonomy, since they all focus on the learner as an individual.

Indo-European languages *n*

languages which are related and which are supposed to have had a common ancestor language, called "Proto Indo-European". Languages in this group include most European languages, e.g. English, French, German, and the Celtic and Slavonic languages. They also include the ancient Indian languages Sanskrit and Pali and such languages as Hindi, Urdu, Bengali, Sinhala, and Farsi.

induced error *n*

also **transfer of training**

(in language learning) an error which has been caused by the way in which a language item has been presented or practised.

For example, in teaching *at* the teacher may hold up a box and say *I'm looking at the box*. However, the learner may infer that *at* means *under*. If later the learner uses *at* for *under* (thus producing *The cat is at the table* instead of *The cat is under the table*) this would be an induced error.

see also ERROR ANALYSIS, INFERENCING, INTERLANGUAGE

induction *n*

see DEDUCTION

inductive learning *n*

also **learning by induction**

see DEDUCTIVE LEARNING

inductive statistics *n*

see INFERENTIAL STATISTICS

inferencing *n*

(in learning and comprehension) the process of arriving at a hypothesis, idea, or judgement on the basis of other knowledge, ideas, or judgements (that is, making inferences or inferring). In language learning, inferencing has been discussed as a LEARNING STRATEGY used by learners to work out grammatical and other kinds of rules. In comprehension of both written and spoken texts, several different kinds of inferencing are thought to play a role:

1 **Propositional inferences** are those that follow on logically and necessarily from a given statement.

2 **Enabling inferences** are related to causal relationships between events or concepts.

3 **Pragmatic inferences** provide extra information which is not essential to the understanding of a text, but which expands on it.

4 **Bridging inferences** are those that are needed if a text is to be understood coherently.

5 Elaborative inferences are not actually necessary to understand a text.

inferential comprehension *n*
    see READING

inferential statistics *n*
    also **inductive statistics**
    statistical procedures that are used to make inferences or generalizations about a population from a set of data. Statistical inference is based on probability theory. A variety of different statistical techniques are used to determine the probable degree of accuracy of generalizations about the population from which a sample or set of data was selected.
    see also DESCRIPTIVE STATISTICS, STATISTICS, T-TEST, ANALYSIS OF VARIANCE

infinitive *n*
    the BASE FORM of a verb (e.g. go, come).
    In English the infinitive usually occurs with the infinitive marker to
    (e.g. *I want to go*) but can occur without to as with auxiliary verbs
    (e.g. *Do come! You may go*). The infinitive without to is known as the **bare infinitive** or **simple form**. The infinitive with to is sometimes called the "to-infinitive".
    The infinitive is a non-finite form of the verb (see FINITE VERB).

infinitive of purpose *n*
    the use of the infinitive to express reason or purpose. For example:
    I went to France *to study French*.

infix *n*

a letter or sound or group of letters or sounds which are added within a word, and which change the meaning or function of the word.

see also AFFIX

INFL *n*

a category in GENERATIVE GRAMMAR which includes finite auxiliaries (which are inflected for tense and agreement) and the infinitival particle *to*.

inflecting language *n*

also **fusional language** *n*

a language in which the form of a word changes to show a change in meaning or grammatical function. Often there is no clear distinction between the basic part of the word and the part which shows a grammatical function such as number or tense.

For example:

mice (= mouse + plural)

came (= come + past tense)

Greek and Latin are inflecting languages, although there is no clear-cut distinction between inflecting languages, AGGLUTINATING LANGUAGES, and ISOLATING LANGUAGES.

Sometimes inflecting languages and agglutinating languages are called **synthetic languages.**

see also INFLECTION

inflection/inflexion *n* **inflect** *v*

(in MORPHOLOGY) the process of adding an affix to a word or changing it in some other way according to the rules of the grammar of a language.

For example, in English, verbs are inflected for 3rd-person singular: *I work*, *he/she works* and for past tense: *I worked*. Most nouns may be inflected for plural: *horse – horses, flower – flowers, man – men*.

see also DERIVATION, CONJUGATION[2]

informal assessment *n*

procedures used for systematic observation and collection of data about students' performance under normal classroom conditions rather than through the use of standardized tests or other controlled methods of appraisal.

see FORMAL ASSESSMENT

informal speech *n*

another term for COLLOQUIAL SPEECH

informant *n*

(in research) a person who provides the researcher with data for analysis. The data may be obtained, for instance, by recording the person's speech or by asking him or her questions about language use.

see also FIELD WORK

information content *n*

see INFORMATION THEORY

information gap *n*

(in communication between two or more people) a situation where information is known by only some of those present. In COMMUNICATIVE LANGUAGE TEACHING it is said that in order to promote real communication between students, there must be an information gap between them, or between them and their teacher. Without such a gap the classroom activities and exercises will be mechanical and artificial.

In an **information gap task** or activity, such as SPOT THE DIFFERENCE, each learner has some information that that the other student(s) don't have. By sharing the information, they can solve the problem or accomplish the prescribed task cooperatively.

information processing *n*

(in psychology and PSYCHOLINGUISTICS) a general term for the processes by which meanings are identified and understood in communication, the processes by which information and meaning are stored, organized, and retrieved from MEMORY and the different kinds of decoding which take place during reading or listening. The study of information processing includes the study of memory, decoding, and HYPOTHESIS TESTING, and the study of the processes and strategies (see STRATEGY) which learners use in working out meanings in the TARGET LANGUAGE[1].

see also HEURISTIC, HYPOTHESIS TESTING, INFORMATION THEORY, INPUT, COGNITIVE PSYCHOLOGY

information report *n*

see TEXT TYPES

information retrieval *n*

1 the process of retrieving information from memory or that is stored in another source, such as a computer
2 the study of how such processes occur

information science *n*

the study of the generation, organization, communication and use of information. Information science is interdisciplinary and draws on work in linguistics, engineering, computer science, physics, communications, etc.

information structure *n*

the use of WORD ORDER, INTONATION, STRESS and other devices to indicate how the message expressed by a sentence is to be understood.

Information structure is communicated by devices which indicate such things as:

a which parts of the message the speaker assumes the hearer already knows and which parts of the message are new information (see FUNCTIONAL SENTENCE PERSPECTIVE)

b contrasts, which may be indicated by stressing one word and not another (e.g. *I broke MY pen*; *I broke my PEN*; *I BROKE my pen*).

see also GROUNDING

information technology *n*

also **IT**

a broad term referring to any aspect of computers or technology.

information theory *n*

also **communication theory**

any theory that explains how communication systems carry information and which measures the amount of information according to how much choice is involved when we send information. One well-known model (that of Shannon and Weaver) describes communication as a process consisting of the following elements. The information **source** (e.g. a speaker) selects a desired message out of a possible set of messages. The "transmitter" changes the messages into a **signal** which is sent over the communication channel (e.g. a telephone wire) where it is received by the receiver (e.g. a telephone or earphones) and changed back into a message which is sent to the "destination" (e.g. a listener). In the process of transmission certain unwanted additions to the signal may occur which are not part of the message (e.g. interference from a poor telephone line) and these are referred to as NOISE[2]. The **information content** of a unit (e.g. of a word or a sentence) is measured according to how likely it is to occur in a particular communication. The more predictable a unit is, the less information it is said to carry. The unit of information used in information theory is the "binary digit", or "bit". The related concept of REDUNDANCY refers to the degree to which a message contains more information than is needed for it to be understood.

information transfer *n*

a type of activity often associated with COMMUNICATIVE LANGUAGE TEACH-ING in which students transfer meaning from one form to another, such as when students select meaning from a reading or listening text and then reproduce it in a different form, e.g. as a diagram or table or the reverse.

informative function *n*

see DEVELOPMENTAL FUNCTIONS OF LANGUAGE

informed consent *n*

a basic ethical requirement of all research, including research into LAN-GUAGE LEARNING and the efficacy of various teaching methods, that all research subjects must give their consent to be included in the subject pool and such consent must be based on an understanding of what the research is about and how the results will be used. Obtaining informed consent requires informing subjects of any risks that may be involved in their participation, including risks that may seem minor to the researcher but may matter to subjects such as feelings of discomfort or embarrassment. Most institutions that sponsor research provide detailed guidelines for ethical research and require that **consent forms** be kept on file.

inherent lexical aspect hypothesis *n*

see LEXICAL ASPECT HYPOTHESIS

inhibition *n*

see ATTENTION, PROACTIVE INHIBITION

initial *adj*

occurring at the beginning of a linguistic unit, e.g. as word-initial, clause-initial.

For example, a group of consonants at the beginning of a word, such as /spr/ in the English word *spray*, is an initial CONSONANT CLUSTER.

see also MEDIAL, FINAL

initial state *n*

in LANGUAGE ACQUISITION, the starting point from which acquisition proceeds. In behaviourism, the starting point for first language acquisition was sometimes assumed to be zero (a **blank slate**), but GENERATIVE THEORY assumes that children are equipped with UNIVERSAL GRAMMAR as the initial state. In SLA, the initial state includes at least those resources transferred from the first language; whether universal grammar remains available to second and foreign language learners is one of the main questions investigated in formally orientated SECOND LANGUAGE ACQUISITION.

initiation-response-evaluation *n*
  see EXCHANGE

initiation-response-feedback *n*
  see EXCHANGE

innateness position *n*
  another term for INNATIST HYPOTHESIS

innatist hypothesis *n*
  also **innatist position, nativist position, innateness position, rationalist position**
  a theory held by some philosophers and linguists which says that human knowledge develops from structures, processes, and "ideas" which are in the mind at birth (i.e. are innate), rather than from the environment, and that these are responsible for the basic structure of language and how it is learned. This hypothesis has been used to explain how children are able to learn language (see LANGUAGE ACQUISITION DEVICE). The innatist hypothesis contrasts with the belief that all human knowledge comes from experience (see EMPIRICISM).
  see also MENTALISM

inner circle *n*
  a term coined by Kachru to characterize the status of English in different parts of the world. The *inner circle* refers to countries where English is spoken as a first language, such as the UK, the USA, Canada and Australia. This may be compared with the status of English in countries where it is regarded as a second language (e.g. Singapore, India, Nigeria), where it is used in such domains as education, administration, and business, where there is a high degree of individual bilingualism. This is referred to as the *outer circle*. Both contexts are compared with contexts known as the *expanding circle*, i.e. nations in which English has not had a central role in the past but where it is currently largely used for purposes of business and technology (e.g. China, Russia).
  See also WORLD ENGLISHES

inner speech *n*
  a type of "speech" discussed by the Russian psychologist Vygotsky, who distinguished between **external speech** and inner speech.

External speech is spoken or written speech, and is expressed in words and sentences. Inner speech is speech for oneself. It takes place inside one's own mind and often takes place in "pure word meanings" rather than in words or sentences, according to Vygotsky.

innovation *n*

an idea, practice, or object that is perceived as new by an individual or individuals and that is a) the result of deliberate planning, b) seeks to improve the achievement of goals. For example recent innovations in language teaching include the use of whiteboards and the introduction of E-LEARNING.

input *n*

(in language learning) language which a learner hears or receives and from which he or she can learn. The language a learner produces is by analogy sometimes called output.

see also COMPREHENSIBLE INPUT, INTAKE

input enhancement *n*

see ENHANCED INPUT

input hypothesis *n*

the idea that exposure to comprehensible input which contains structures that are slightly in advance of a learner's current level of COMPETENCE is the necessary and sufficient cause of SECOND LANGUAGE ACQUISITION.

see also COMPREHENSIBLE INPUT, INTAKE, MONITOR HYPOTHESIS

inquiry learning *n*

see DISCOVERY LEARNING

insertion sequence *n*

in conversation, speakers may interrupt themselves and insert an utterance which is not related to the main conversation. This utterance is often referred to as an insertion sequence. There may be numerous reasons for the sequence. Often it may be caused by an external event, e.g. a ring/knock at the door, a ringing telephone:

A: . . . and I actually told her that . . . (doorbell rings)
Excuse me, that must be Al. He's probably forgotten his key.
A: (returns) *Now, what was I saying before? Ah, yes. She said . . .*

In many cases, the original conversation is continued after the insertion sequence. Sometimes it is referred to briefly with utterances such as:

Sorry for the interruption. Now where were we? what was I saying? etc.

see also SEQUENCING[1], SIDE SEQUENCE

inservice education *n*
see PRESERVICE EDUCATION

Institute of Translation and Interpreting *n*
also **ITI**
see TRANSLATION, INTERPRETATION

institutional discourse *n*
also **institutional language**
patterns of discourse used in institutional contexts that reflect how inter-actions and language use are shaped by the conventions of institutional settings as well as by the need for participants to create face, agency, power, roles and institutional identities.

institutional review board *n*
also **IRB, human subjects committee, ethical review board (ERB)**
a board or committee that reviews research proposals to make sure that ethical and legal guidelines are being followed to protect the rights and welfare of research subjects or participants.

instructed second language learning *n*
also **instructed SLA**
learning a second or foreign language partly or completely in a classroom setting. This can be contrasted with NATURALISTIC SECOND LANGUAGE LEARNING, which takes place through interaction with native speakers without the benefit of instruction.

instructional framework *n*
the overall conceptual plan and organization used to design a lesson or a unit of instructional materials or to analyze teaching.

instructional objective *n*
another term for BEHAVIOURAL OBJECTIVE

instruction text *n*
see TEXT TYPES

instrumental case *n*
(in CASE GRAMMAR) the noun or noun phrase that refers to the means by which the action of the verb is performed is in the instrumental case.
For example, in the sentences:
He dug the hole with a spade.
The hammer hit the nail.
a spade and *the hammer* are in the instrumental case.

instrumental function *n*
see DEVELOPMENTAL FUNCTIONS OF LANGUAGE

instrumental motivation *n*
see MOTIVATION

intake *n*
a term referring to that part of the language to which learners are exposed (see INPUT) that actually "goes in" and plays a role in language learning. Some theorists believe that intake is that part of the input that has been attended to and noticed by second language learners while processing the input (see NOTICING HYPOTHESIS). It is also possible to distinguish between **preliminary intake,** brief notice of some feature of the input, and **final intake,** integration of knowledge of that item in one's INTERLANGUAGE.

integrated approach *n*
(in language teaching) the teaching of the language skills of reading, writing, listening, and speaking, in conjunction with each other, as when a lesson involves activities that relate listening and speaking to reading and writing.
see also LANGUAGE ARTS

integrated skills *n*
a language lesson which combines work on reading, writing, listening and speaking and that seeks to make links among different skills.

integrated syllabus *n*
also **integrated skills approach, multi-skilled syllabus**
in language teaching, a syllabus that is based upon a close relationship between different units of language (e.g. grammar, functions, skills) and which seeks to provide for mutual reinforcement between the different components of the syllabus.

integrated whole language approach *n*
see WHOLE LANGUAGE APPROACH

integrative motivation *n*
see MOTIVATION

integrative orientation *n*
see MOTIVATION

integrative test *n*

an integrative test is one that requires a test taker to use several language skills at the same time, such as a dictation test, which requires the learner to use knowledge of grammar, vocabulary, and listening comprehension.
see DISCRETE-POINT TEST

intelligibility *n*

the degree to which a message can be understood. Studies of speech PERCEPTION have found that the intelligibility of speech is due to various factors including ACCENT[3] and INTONATION, the listener's ability to predict parts of the message, the location of PAUSES in the utterance, the grammatical complexity of sentences, and the speed with which utterances are produced.

intensifier *n*

a class of words, generally adverbs, which are used to modify gradable adjectives, adverbs, verbs, or -ed. participles, as in:

It is <u>very</u> good.
It was <u>completely</u> destroyed.
I <u>absolutely</u> detest it.

see also GRADABLE

intensive course *n*

a language course that takes place over a short period of time but which consists of a high number of hours of instruction.

intensive language programme *n*

also **intensive English programme, service English programme**

a language programme designed to prepare international students or other students needing language instruction to take regular academic courses at a university.

intensive reading *n*

see EXTENSIVE READING

intentional learning *n*

see INCIDENTAL LEARNING

interaction *n*

the way in which a language is used by interlocutors.

interactional and transactional functions of language *n*

a distinction that is sometimes made between uses of language where the primary focus is on social interaction between the speakers and the need to communicate such things as rapport, empathy, interest and social harmony (interactional function), and those where the primary focus is on communicating information and completing different kinds of real world transactions (transactional function). Interactional communication is primarily person-orientated, whereas transactional communication is primarily message-focused. Interactional and transactional language may differ in terms of such things as conventions for turn-taking, topics, and discourse management.

interactional function *n*
see DEVELOPMENTAL FUNCTIONS OF LANGUAGE

interaction analysis *n*
also **interaction process analysis**
any of several procedures for measuring and describing the behaviour of students and teachers in classrooms, (a) in order to describe what happens during a lesson (b) to evaluate teaching (c) to study the relationship between teaching and learning (d) to help teacher-trainees learn about the process of teaching. In interaction analysis, classroom behaviour is observed and the different types of student and teacher activity are classified, using a classification scheme. Several such schemes have been proposed.

interaction hypothesis *n*
the hypothesis that language acquisition requires or greatly benefits from interaction, communication and especially **negotiation of meaning**, which happens when interlocutors attempt to overcome problems in conveying their meaning, resulting in both additional input and useful feedback on the learner's own production.

interactionism *n*
also **interactionist position**
(in psychology, linguistics, and research on language acquisition) the view that language development and social development are associated and that one cannot be understood without the other. Researchers who take an interactionist position focus on the social context of language development and how the relationship between the language learner and the persons with whom he or she interacts influences language acquisition. This perspective is sometimes contrasted with a linguistic approach, which holds that language acquisition can be understood through analysis of the learner's utterances, independently of his or her cognitive development or social life.

interaction patterns *n*

in teaching, the ways in which students work together in class, such as whole class, pair work, group work, and individual work.

interactive *adj*

(in COMPUTER ASSISTED INSTRUCTION) describes the ability of a user to "communicate" (or "interact") with a computer. Lessons in CAI materials may involve a question on the computer, a response from the student, and feedback from the computer telling the student if the answer is correct. In CAI such activities are said to be "interactive".

interactive listening *n*

in teaching listening, an emphasis on listening as involving an active interplay between a listener and a text or between a listener and a speaker.

interactive model of reading *n*

a model of reading that views reading as a combination of both bottom-up and top-down processes. Reading is seen as an active process involving the reader in ongoing interaction with a text as he or she reads. Both top-down and bottom-up processing occur, in an order that depends upon the topic and the reader's background knowledge.

interactive processing *n*

a theory of reading comprehension that sees reading as involving both the accurate and sequential understanding of text based on identification of the meanings of words and sentences in the text (i.e. bottom-up-processing) as well as the experiences, background information, and predictions that the reader brings to the text (i.e. top-down processing). Both kinds of processing are involved and they modify and act on each other.
see also TOP-DOWN PROCESSING

interactive reading *n*

in teaching reading, an emphasis on reading as involving an interplay between the reader and the text.

interactive whiteboard *n*

a large interactive display that resembles a traditional whiteboard but which is connected to a computer and projector, and can also be connected to a video recorder and DVD player. They are used in a variety of classroom settings and can serve to complement or even replace textbook-based teaching. Software loaded into the connected personal computer allows the user to write on the interactive whiteboard in digital ink or use a computer to control applications by pointing, clicking or dragging, as with a desk-top mouse. Many language courses now come with interactive whiteboard software.

Interagency Language Round Table *n*
also **ILR**
a collective name for a group of United States Government agencies, such as the Foreign Service Institute, the Federal Bureau of Investigation and the Defense Language Institute, involved in teaching and using languages. The ILR Language Skill Level Descriptions provide assessment in all four language skills.

intercultural communication *n*
also **interdiscourse communication/intercultural discourse**
an interdisciplinary field of research that studies how people communicate and understand each other across group boundaries or discourse systems of various sorts including national, geographical, linguistic, ethnic, occupation, class or gender-related boundaries and how such boundaries affect language use. This could include the study of a corporate culture, a professional group, a gender discourse system, or a generational discourse system.

interdental *adj*
describes a speech sound (a CONSONANT) produced with the tip of the tongue between the upper and lower teeth, e.g. /θ/ and /ð/ in the English words /θɪk/ *thick* and /ðɪs/ this.
see also MANNER OF ARTICULATION, PLACE OF ARTICULATION

interface *n*
in SLA, the relationship between implicit and explicit learning and knowledge. The **strong interface** position holds that explicit knowledge can be transformed into implicit knowledge through the process of automatization, which is a consequence of practice. The **no-interface** position holds that explicit and implicit knowledge develop independently and are encapsulated systems, i.e. changes in one do not produce changes in the other. In this view, the fact that a learner of English may have both intuitive and explicit knowledge about a particular phenomenon (such as the use of tense and aspect) would be no more than a coincidence. Various **weak-interface** positions have also been articulated. For example, explicit knowledge may be successfully incorporated into the implicit knowledge system if it becomes available at just the right time in the development of the implicit system, or explicit knowledge about the regularities of a language may help learners to notice these regularities when processing input, which leads to the development of implicit knowledge.

interference *n*

see LANGUAGE TRANSFER

intergroup communication *n*

communication between different groups, especially those which are socially, ethnically, or linguistically different. Intergroup communication is often by means of a LINGUA FRANCA, a language known by speakers of both groups.

For example, in Indonesia, where many different languages are spoken, Bahasa Indonesia, the national language, is the language most frequently used for intergroup communication.

see also INTRAGROUP COMMUNICATION

interim grammar *n*

a temporary grammatical system used by children learning their first language at a particular stage in their language development. Children's grammatical systems change as they develop new grammatical rules; hence they may be said to pass through a series of interim grammars.

see also INTERLANGUAGE

interjection *n*

a word such as *ugh!*, *gosh!*, *wow!*, which indicates an emotional state or attitude such as delight, surprise, shock, and disgust, but which has no referential meaning (see REFERENCE).

Interjections are often regarded as one of the PARTS OF SPEECH.

see also EXCLAMATION[1]

interlanguage *n*

the type of language produced by second- and foreign-language learners who are in the process of learning a language.

In language learning, learner language is influenced by several different processes. These include:

a borrowing patterns from the mother tongue (see LANGUAGE TRANSFER)

b extending patterns from the target language, e.g. by analogy (see OVER-GENERALIZATION)

c expressing meanings using the words and grammar which are already known (see COMMUNICATION STRATEGY).

Since the language which the learner produces using these processes differs from both the mother tongue and the TARGET LANGUAGE[1], it is sometimes called an interlanguage, or is said to result from the learner's interlanguage system or **approximative system**.

see also INTERIM GRAMMAR

interlanguage hypothesis *n*

the hypothesis that language learners possess a grammatical system that is different from both the first language and the target language but is nevertheless a natural language. That is, interlanguages are believed to be constrained by the same principles as all languages.

interlingual error *n*

(in ERROR ANALYSIS) an error which results from LANGUAGE TRANSFER, that is, which is caused by the learner's native language. For example, the incorrect French sentence *Elle regarde les* ("She sees them"), produced according to the word order of English, instead of the correct French sentence *Elle les regarde* (literally, "She them sees").

An **intralingual error** is one which results from faulty or partial learning of the TARGET LANGUAGE[1], rather than from language transfer. Intralingual errors may be caused by the influence of one target language item upon another. For example a learner may produce *He is comes*, based on a blend of the English structures *He is coming*, *He comes*.

interlingual identification *n*

(in second or foreign language learning) a judgement made by learners about the identity or similarity of structures in two languages. For example, in learning the sound system of a new language, a learner may have to decide whether the '*d*' sound in the new language is the same or different from the '*d*' sound in his or her native language. Learners often categorize sounds in terms of the phonemic systems of their first language, making acquisition of new target language sounds difficult.

see also PHONEME, LANGUAGE TRANSFER

interlocutor *n*

a neutral term referring to any person with whom someone is speaking. A conversation requires at least two interlocutors. In language testing, the term is sometimes used to refer to a teacher or other trained person who acts during a test as the person with whom the student or candidate interacts in order to complete a speaking task.

internal consistency reliability *n*

(in testing) a measure of the degree to which the items or parts of a test are homogeneous, equivalent or consistent with each other. It is based on a single test administration and obviates the need for PARALLEL forms of a test, which are often expensive and difficult to develop. Internal consistency reliability is often estimated by the following approaches: CRONBACH ALPHA, KUDER-RICHARDSON FORMULAS or SPLIT-HALF RELIABILITY.

internalization *n*

in psychology, the process of acceptance of external norms as one's own. An individual may start with learning what the societal norms are, go through a process of understanding why they are of value, and finally accepting the norm as their own viewpoint. In sociocultural theory, internalisation is the process by which a person's activity is initially mediated by other people or cultural artifacts but later comes to be controlled by the person as he or she appropriates resources to regulate his or her own activities. see also SELF DETERMINATION THEORY

internalized language *n*

another term for I-LANGUAGE

internal validity *n*

(in research design) the extent to which the treatment delivered to subjects in an experimental study is responsible for the observed change(s) in participants' behaviour. Examples of the threats to internal validity (i.e. possible explanations for the changes other than the treatment) include **history** where there are environmental influences on the participants, or **maturation** where participants matured, during the period between the pre-test and the post-test, which suggests that the change could have resulted from something other than the treatment itself. see also EXTERNAL VALIDITY

International Corpus of English *n*

a set of corpora representing varieties of English from over twenty countries where English is the first language or an official second language. Research teams in each country are preparing electronic corpora of their own national or regional variety of English.

International English Language Testing System *n*

also **IELTS**

a test of English for academic purposes, used widely to measure the English language proficiency of international students whose native languages are not English and who intend to enter universities in Australia, Canada, New Zealand, the United Kingdom and elsewhere.

international language *n*

a language in widespread use as a foreign language or second language, i.e. as a language of international communication. English is the most widely used international language.

International Phonetic Alphabet *n*
also **IPA**
a system of symbols designed by the International Phonetic Association to be used to represent the sounds of all human languages in accordance with a set of common principles. The symbols consist of letters and DIACRITICS. Some letters are taken from the Roman alphabet, while others are special symbols, e.g. /ʃ/, /ə/, and /ʊ/ as in the English word /ʃəʊ/ show.

International Second Language Proficiency Ratings *n*
also **ISLPR**
formerly known as the **Australian Second Language Proficiency Ratings** (**ASLPR**), the ISLPR is a proficiency scale that assesses the four language skills, ranging from "0" (no proficiency) to "5" (native-like proficiency) with 12 levels, each of which describes how a test taker at each level can perform using which language forms.
see also FOREIGN SERVICE ORAL INTERVIEW

international teaching assistant *n*
also **ITA**
in the US, many university courses are taught by teaching assistants from other countries who often speak English as a second or foreign language or have accents that students are unfamiliar with. Some universities have established special training programmes to help these instructors to deal with linguistic, communicative, and sociocultural issues.

Internet Relay Chat *n*
see **IRC**

interpersonal function *n*
see FUNCTIONS OF LANGUAGE[2]

interpersonal semantics *n*
see SYSTEMIC-FUNCTIONAL LINGUISTICS

interpretation *n*
also **interpreting**
the act of rendering oral language that is spoken in one language (SOURCE LANGUAGE[2]) into another language (TARGET LANGUAGE[2]) for the benefit of listeners who do not understand (or who understand imperfectly) the source language. Oral translation after a speaker has finished speaking or pauses for interpretation is known as **consecutive interpretation**. If the interpretation takes place as the speaker is talking, providing a continuous translation that parallels the speaker's speech, it is called **simultaneous**

interpretation. Interpretation is often required in a variety of situations, such as conferences, community settings, and the courts.

see also TRANSLATION

interpreter *n*

in general, someone who provides an oral translation of a speaker's words from one language to another. An **accredited interpreter** (or **certified interpreter**) is one who has received accreditation (or certification) from a professional organization such as the Institute of Translation and Interpreting (ITI), issued on the basis of training, experience, and examinations. Some interpreters have highly specialized skills and are accredited as CONFERENCE INTERPRETERS or COURT INTERPRETERS.

interpreting *n*

see INTERPRETATION

interpretive error *n*

see ERROR

interpretive semantics *n*

a theory about the place of meaning in a model of GENERATIVE GRAMMAR. It considers a meaning component, called the **semantic component**, as part of the grammar. This component contains rules which interpret the meaning of sentences. This theory differs from GENERATIVE SEMANTICS, which insists that the semantic component is the most basic part of a grammar from which all sentences of a language can be "generated" (see GENERATIVE GRAMMAR, RULE[2]).

In generative semantics, syntactic rules operate on the meaning of a sentence to produce its form. In interpretive semantics, semantic rules operate on the words and syntactic structure of a sentence to reveal its meaning.

inter-rater reliability *n*

(in testing) the degree to which different examiners or judges making different subjective ratings of ability (e.g. of L2 writing proficiency) agree in their evaluations of that ability. If different judges rank test takers in approximately the same order, using a RATING SCALE that measures different aspects of proficiency, the rating scale is said to have high inter-rater reliability.

see also INTRA-RATER RELIABILITY

interrogative pronoun *n*

wh-pronouns (*who, which, what, whose, who(m)*, etc.), which are used to form questions, e.g.:

> <u>*Which*</u> *is your book?*
> <u>*What*</u> *is your name?*
> see also WH-QUESTION

interrogative sentence *n*

a sentence which is in the form of a question. For example:
> *Did you open the window?*

Interrogative sentences do not, however, always have the function of a question. For example:
> *Could you shut the window?*

may be a request for someone to shut the window and not a question about whether or not the person is able to do so.

see also DECLARATIVE SENTENCE, IMPERATIVE SENTENCE

intertextuality *n*

the factors that make the use of one text depend on knowledge of other texts. In interpreting a text a reader is said to make connections between the text and other texts he or she has encountered. Thus for example, in reading a story a reader can only make sense of it by reference to other stories previously encountered. The meaning a person derives from a text is thus said to result from the interaction between the readers' knowledge of the social and literary conventions associated with the text and the genre to which it belongs, the content of the text itself, and its relationship with other texts.

interval scale *n*

see SCALE

interview *n*

a conversation between an investigator and an individual or a group of individuals in order to gather information. Interviews are used to gather data for linguistic analysis (see FIELDWORK) and may be used in NEEDS ANALYSIS.

see DEPTH INTERVIEW, FOCUSED INTERVIEW, GUIDED INTERVIEW, INTERVIEW GUIDE, STRUCTURED INTERVIEW, UNSTRUCTURED INTERVIEW

interview guide *n*

a list of topics used by an interviewer during an interview. An interview guide helps the interviewer make sure that the important topics have been covered during the interview, but it differs from an interview schedule (see GUIDED INTERVIEW) in that it contains only the topics to be asked about and not the actual questions that will be asked.

interview schedule *n*

see GUIDED INTERVIEW

intervocalic *adj*

(of CONSONANTS) occurring between two vowels. For example, English /d/ in *lady* is intervocalic.

intimate speech/intimate speech style *n*

a form of speech used by people who are in a close and personal relation, such as family members and close friends. Intimate speech is characterized by:
1 the communication of much meaning indirectly or by implication because there is a great deal of shared knowledge
2 the absence of elaborate linguistic forms.

intonation *n*

when speaking, people generally raise and lower the PITCH of their voice, forming pitch patterns. They also give some syllables in their utterances a greater degree of loudness and change their SPEECH RHYTHM. These phenomena are called intonation. Intonation does not happen at random but has definite patterns (see INTONATION CONTOUR). Intonation is used to carry information over and above that which is expressed by the words in the sentence.
see also KEY[2], PITCH LEVEL, TONE UNIT

intonation contour *n*

also **intonation pattern, pitch contour, pitch pattern**

the pattern of pitch changes that occur across an UTTERANCE, often accompanied by differences in loudness and SPEECH RHYTHM.

Intonation contours may have grammatical functions. For example, the word *ready?* – said with rising intonation – is a question, while the same word with falling intonation is a statement. Intonation may also signal the speaker's attitude towards the matter discussed. For example, the utterance *I TOLD you so* – with stress and a noticeable pitch rise on the word *told*, followed by falling pitch over the end of the sentence – expresses annoyance. Some intonation contours are associated with specific sentence types. Generally speaking, falling intonation can be associated with certainty and rising intonation with uncertainty. For example:

Declarative sentences in English typically have an abrupt pitch rise on the last stressed word of the sentence followed by a fall. For example, the sentence *Language is a social phenomenon* typically has an intonation contour consisting of a rise on the first syllable of *social*, followed by a gradual fall over the remaining syllables of the sentence.

Yes–no questions, for example, *Is language a social phenomenon?*, typically have a long gradual rise in pitch from the beginning to the end of the sentence.

Wh-questions usually have the same intonation contour as declarative sentences. For example in the question *What kind of phenomenon is language?*, the abrupt pitch rise is usually on the first syllable of the word language. Closed-choice questions, for example, *Is language a social, psychological, or biological phenomenon?*, typically exhibit **list intonation**, with a short pitch rise on each option presented by the speaker (*social, psychological*) except the last (*biological*), which has the rise-fall associated with finality. Tag-questions, for example, *Language is a social phenomenon, isn't it?*, typically have declarative intonation on the main clause, followed by rising intonation on the tag (*isn't it?*) if the speaker is requesting confirmation and falling intonation on the tag if the speaker is requesting agreement.

Intonation patterns differ between languages and may differ as well between varieties of the same language. For example, the practice of using yes–no question intonation with declarative sentences in contemporary English is widely considered to be a feature associated with younger speakers.

see also TONE UNIT

intonation pattern *n*

another term for INTONATION CONTOUR

intragroup communication *n*

communication among members of a group. In some multi-ethnic countries or communities, a language may be used for communication within a particular ethnic group although it is not known or used by the majority of the population; for example, Spanish in parts of the USA among some Mexican-Americans.

see also COMMUNITY LANGUAGE, INTERGROUP COMMUNICATION

intralingual error *n*

see INTERLINGUAL ERROR

intransitive verb *n*

see TRANSITIVE VERB

intra-rater reliability *n*

(in testing) the degree to which an examiner or judge making subjective ratings of ability (e.g. of L2 speaking proficiency) gives the same evaluation of that ability when he or she makes an evaluation on two or more different occasions.

see also INTER-RATER RELIABILITY

intrinsic motivation *n*

see MOTIVATION

introduction *n*
see ESSAY

introspection *n*
see VERBAL REPORTING

introvert *n*
see EXTROVERT

intrusion *n* **intrusive** *adj*
when an extra consonant is added at the end of a word to link it to a following word starting with a vowel, this is known as intrusion. In English, an intrusive /r/ is often added, especially before *and*. For example:
China and Japan /ˈtʃaɪnər ən dʒəˈpæn/
Lena and Sue /ˈliːnər ən ˈsuː/
see also LINKING

intuitive knowledge *n*
see IMPLICIT KNOWLEDGE

inversion *n*
a movement operation by which the order of two expressions is reversed. For example, in English the auxiliary comes after the subject noun in declarative sentences (e.g. *He will come by at 8 o'clock*) but before the subject in questions (*Will he come by at 8?*). This specific operation is called **subject–verb inversion**.

investment *n*
see SOCIAL CAPITAL

IO *n*
an abbreviation for indirect object relative clause
see NOUN PHRASE ACCESSIBILITY HIERARCHY

IPA *n*
an abbreviation for
1 INTERNATIONAL PHONETIC ASSOCIATION
2 INTERNATIONAL PHONETIC ALPHABET

IRB *n*
an abbreviation for INSTITUTIONAL REVIEW BOARD

IRC *n*

an acronym for Internet Relay Chat, a worldwide synchronous multi-user chat protocol that allows one to converse with others in real time. IRC is a free downloadable program used in language classrooms for establishing KEYPALS interested in SYNCHRONOUS communication.

IRE *n*

an abbreviation for INITIATION-RESPONSE-EVALUATION
see EXCHANGE

IRF *n*

an abbreviation for INITIATION-RESPONSE-FEEDBACK
see EXCHANGE

irregular verb *n*

see REGULAR VERB

IRT *n*

an abbreviation for ITEM RESPONSE THEORY.

ISLPR *n*

an abbreviation for the INTERNATIONAL SECOND LANGUAGE PROFICIENCY RATINGS.

isogloss *n*

a line on a map indicating the boundary of a particular linguistic theory. A bundle of such isoglosses is often taken to indicate a DIALECT boundary.

isolating language *n*

also **analytic language**

a language in which word forms do not change, and in which grammatical functions are shown by word order and the use of function words.
For example, in Mandarin Chinese:

júzi   wǒ chī le
orange I   eat (function word
                    showing completion)
"I   ate the   orange"
wǒ chī le   júzi   le
I   eat (function orange (function
        word)   word)
"I have eaten an orange"

Languages which are highly isolating include Chinese and Vietnamese, although there is no clear-cut distinction between isolating languages, INFLECTING LANGUAGES, and AGGLUTINATING LANGUAGES. English is more isolating than many other European languages, such as French, German, and Russian, but is also an inflecting language.

IT *n*

see INFORMATION TECHNOLOGY

ITA *n*

an abbreviation for INTERNATIONAL TEACHING ASSISTANT

item *n*

an individual question in a test which requires the student to produce an answer.

item analysis *n*

(in testing) the analysis of the responses to the items in a test in order to find out how effective the test items are and to find out if they indicate differences between high and low ability test takers.

see also DISTRACTOR EFFICIENCY ANALYSIS, ITEM FACILITY, ITEM DISCRIMINATION

item difficulty *n*

see ITEM FACILITY

item discrimination *n*

also **d-index**

(in testing) a measure of the extent to which a test item is sensitive to differences in ability among test takers. If a particular item in a test is answered in the same way by both the test takers who do well on the test as a whole and by those who do poorly, the item is said to have poor discrimination. In ITEM ANALYSIS, the item-total POINT-BISERIAL CORRELATION between the answers to an individual item (hence "item") and the scores on the whole test (hence "total") is often used as an estimate of discrimination. Or alternatively, an item discrimination index can be calculated using the following formula:

$$ID = IF_{upper} - IF_{lower}$$

where ID = item discrimination for an individual item, IF_{upper} = item facility for the upper third (or 33%) group on the whole test, IF_{lower} = item facility for the lower third (or 33%) group on the whole test.

The ID index ranges from +1.00 to –1.00. In a NORM-REFERENCED TEST, test items with low and negative ID indices need to be revised.

item facility *n*

also **difficulty index, facility, facility index, facility value, item difficulty, p-value** (in testing) a measure of the ease of a test item. It is the proportion of the test takers who answered the item correctly, and is determined by the following formula:

$$ItemFacility(IF) = \frac{R}{N}$$

where R = number of correct answers

              N = the number of test takers

The higher the ratio of R to N, the easier the item.

item pool *n*

    see ITEM BANK

item response theory *n*

    also **IRT**

a modern measurement theory, as opposed to classical test theory, based on the probability of a test taker with a certain underlying ability getting a particular item right or wrong. The difference among the three main IRT models is in the number of parameters estimated in each model. The **one-parameter model**, also called the **Rasch model**, estimates only item difficulty (**b-parameter**); the **two-parameter model** takes into account item difficulty and item discrimination (**a-parameter**); and the **three-parameter model** estimates a guessing factor (**c-parameter**) in addition to item discrimination and item difficulty parameters. The more parameters an IRT model has, the more complex it becomes and the larger sample size it requires. IRT is used to detect test bias (e.g., DIFFRENTIAL ITEM FUNCTIONING) and develop a COMPUTER-ADAPTIVE TEST, among other applications.

see also CLASSICAL TEST THEORY

item specifications *n*

a set of item-writing guidelines consisting of the following elements: (a) a brief general description of the skills to be measured by the item, (b) a description of the material that test takers will encounter and respond to in the item, (i.e., a **prompt**), (c) a description of what test takers are expected to do in response to the prompt (e.g., select an answer from four options in a MULTIPLE-CHOICE ITEM format) and how their responses will be evaluated (e.g., a set of RATING CRITERIA for essays), and (d) an example item, written according to specifications.

see also TEST ITEM, TEST SPECIFICATIONS.

ITI *n*

an abbreviation for the INSTITUTE OF TRANSLATION AND INTERPRETING.

J

jargon *n*

speech or writing used by a group of people who belong to a particular trade, profession, or any other group bound together by mutual interest, e.g. *the jargon of law, medical jargon.*

A jargon has its own set of words and expressions, which may be incomprehensible to an outsider. The term jargon is typically not used by the group itself but by those unfamiliar with that particular type of language, and/or by those who dislike it.

Jargon is sometimes also used for the first (developmental) stage of a pidgin language, where there is a great deal of individual variation, a simple sound system, very short sentences and a restricted number of words.

jigsaw activity *n*

in language teaching a type of INFORMATION GAP activity in which groups of learners have different information that is needed to put together the solution to a task. In jigsaw listening or reading activities, different groups in the class may process separate but related parts of a text and then later combine their information to reconstruct the whole through class discussion or group interaction.

see also CO-OPERATIVE LEARNING

journal *n*

see LEARNING LOG

juncture *n*

the boundary between two phonemes accounting for the flow and pauses between sounds in speech. Three types of juncture are commonly recognized.

1 *close juncture* is characterized by a rapid transition between two sounds, as between /s/ and /p/ in *speak*

2 *open juncture* is characterized by a slight pause between sounds, as in pronouncing I *scream* versus *ice cream*

3 *terminal juncture* is characterized by a pause after a sound, as before and after "*Mrs Brown*" in "*My employer, Mrs Brown, is from Canada*".

K

Kendall rank-order correlation *n*
  or **Kendall's tau** (τ)
  see CORRELATION

Kendall's coefficient of concordance *n*
  also **Kendall's W**
  a measure of the degree of AGREEMENT between two or more raters when
  asked to rank-order a set of data (e.g. a set of 10 essays written by ESL
  students), thus called a coefficient of CONCORDANCE. It ranges in value from
  0.00 (i.e. no agreement between the raters) to +1.00 (i.e. perfect agreement
  between them) with no negative values. Kendall's W can examine the relationship between two or more ordinal or rank-ordered variables, whereas the
  SPEARMAN'S RANK-ORDER CORRELATION is a measure of association *only*
  between two ordinal variables.

Kendall's tau (τ) *n*
  another term for KENDALL RANK-ORDER CORRELATION

Kendall's W *n*
  another term for KENDALL'S COEFFICIENT OF CONCORDANCE

KET (Key English Test) *n*
  see CAMBRIDGE EXAMS

key[1] *n*
  the tone, manner, or spirit in which a SPEECH ACT is carried out, for example
  whether mockingly or seriously. The key chosen would depend on the
  situation and the relationship of the speakers to each other. For example,
  the statement *If you do that I'll never speak to you again* may be either a
  real threat or a mock threat. The signalling of key may be verbal (e.g. by
  INTONATION) or non-verbal (e.g. by a wink, a gesture, or a certain posture).

key[2] *n*
  (in INTONATION) a level of PITCH chosen by the speaker together with an
  intonation contour (see TONE UNIT) in order to convey a particular kind of
  meaning to the listener.
  In English, a difference can be made between high key, mid key, and
  low key.
  For example, the choice of a high key often signals a contrast as in:

But she's Peter's WIFE (where *wife* also has a fall in pitch)
This could be a reply to someone who had just stated that the person concerned was Peter's sister.
see also PITCH LEVEL.

key³ *n*

(in testing) a correct option or answer in a MULTIPLE-CHOICE ITEM.
see also DISTRACTOR

keypals *n*

electronic mail correspondents (from *keyboard*, by analogy to *penpal*). Keypals are a popular, easy-to-establish feature of many second language courses.

keyword *n*

a word that occurs with high frequency in a text, and which usually reflects the topic of the text.

keyword technique *n*

(in second language learning) a learning strategy in which the learner thinks of a homophone (HOMOPHONEs) (the "key word") in the native language for the word he or she is trying to remember in the target language. The learner then imagines a situation in which the homophone and the target language word are interacting in some way. In remembering the target word, the learner recalls the homophone and the situation in which it was used. For example in learning the French word for "door" – *porte* – a learner might think of a near homophone in English, such as "a porter". Then the learner thinks of a situation involving a porter – such as a porter opening a door to carry in a bag. When the learner wants to remember the French word for door, he or she thinks of the situation and the key word – *porter*. This helps recall the French word – *porte*.

kinesics *n* **kinesic** *adj*

see PARALINGUISTICS

kinesthetic experience *n*

the sensation of bodily movement combined with perception and/or production of sound.

kinesthetic feedback *n*

(in speaking or writing) feedback we receive which comes from the movement and positions of the muscles, organs, etc., which are used to produce speech or writing. The ability to feel where our tongues are in the mouth, for example, is an important factor in being able to speak clearly. If this kinesthetic feedback is interfered with (e.g. as a result of a dental injection which causes the tongue to lose sensation), our speech may become slurred. The other kind of feedback which is used to monitor our communication is AUDITORY FEEDBACK.

Kinesthetic learner *n*

a learning style that favors learning through carrying out a physical activity rather than learning by listening or watching.
see LEARNING STYLE

koinéization *n*

see DIALECT LEVELLING

Knowledge About Language *n*

also **KAL**

in teacher education and TEACHER COGNITION theory, any kind of knowledge about language that teachers make use of in their teaching, such as knowledge of grammar, language use, and second language learning. An important issue in teacher education is the kind of KAL that should form part of the knowledge base of language teacher education as well as the extent to which teachers access and use such knowledge in their teaching.

KR20 *n*

an abbreviation for KUDER-RICHARDSON FORMULA 20

KR21 *n*

an abbreviation for KUDER-RICHARDSON FORMULA 21

K through 12 *n*

also **K-12**

in the US, the period of schooling from kindergarten through to grade 12 – the final year of high school.

Kuder-Richardson formulas *n*

measures of internal consistency used in estimating the RELIABILITY of a test with items that are dichotomously scored (i.e. scored 1 for correct responses or 0 for incorrect responses). There are two types of the Kuder-Richardson formulas: **Kuder-Richardson formula 20 (KR20)** and **Kuder-Richardson formula 21 (KR21)**. KR20 is based on information about (a) the number of items on the test (b) the difficulty of the individual items, and (c) the

VARIANCE of the total test scores. A formula that is easier to use (not requiring calculation of ITEM FACILITY) but less accurate than KR20 is KR21, which is based on information about (a) the number of items on the test, (b) the MEAN of the test, and (c) the VARIANCE of the total test scores, all of which are readily available, but requires an assumption that all items are equal in item difficulty.

see also CRONBACH ALPHA, INTERNAL CONSISTENCY RELIABILITY

kurtosis *n*

a measure of the extent to which the peak of a distribution departs from the shape of the peak of a NORMAL DISTRIBUTION. When the peak of a distribution is more pointed than a NORMAL DISTRIBUTION, the shape of the peak is described as **leptokurtic**, whereas when the peak is flatter, the shape is called **platykurtic**.

L

L1 *n*

see FIRST LANGUAGE

L2 *n*

another term for a TARGET LANGUAGE[1] or a SECOND LANGUAGE

labelled bracketing *n*

a technique for representing the phrase structure (also constituent structure) of a phrase or sentence.
For example, the structure of the English noun phrase
an experienced journalist
can be represented as: [D an] [A experienced] [N journalist]
where D is a determiner, A an adjective, and N a noun.
see also TREE DIAGRAM

labial *n*

a speech sound produced using the lips.
see also BILABIAL, LABIO-DENTAL

labialization *n*

a secondary articulation in which lip rounding is added to a sound, as in English /w/ and /ʃ/. In some varieties of English, /l/ and /r/ may be strongly **labialized** as well.

labio-dental *adj*

describes a speech sound (a CONSONANT) which is produced by the lower lip touching or nearly touching the upper teeth.
For example, in English the /f/ in /fæt/ *fat*, and the /v/ in /væt/ *vat* are labio-dental FRICATIVES.
see also PLACE OF ARTICULATION, MANNER OF ARTICULATION

laboratory experiences *n*

in teacher education, a direct or simulated teaching or learning activity that allows for the observation, application, study, and analysis of aspects of classroom teaching and learning in a controlled, usually simplified setting. They can be of varying degrees of control, reality and complexity. Among those used in teacher education are audio or video recordings, case studies, micro-teaching, role plays and simulations. Laboratory experiences allow for control over different aspects of teaching and are hence sometimes preferred to the use of real teaching experiences.

laboratory research *n*

research that takes places under controlled conditions as in a laboratory. The complexity of school-based or formal second language learning and teaching cannot always be investigated in real classrooms. In order to test hypotheses or theories about teaching and learning, experiments are sometimes conducted in which the INDEPENDENT VARIABLES are carefully defined, precise measurements are undertaken and other influences are excluded as far as possible.

LAD *n*

an abbreviation for LANGUAGE ACQUISITION DEVICE.

laminal *adj*

describes a speech sound (a CONSONANT) which is produced by the front upper surface of the tongue (the blade or **lamina**) touching the upper teeth or the gum ridge behind the upper teeth (the **alveolar ridge**).
In English, the /ʃ/ in /ʃuː/ shoe is a laminal FRICATIVE.
see also PLACE OF ARTICULATION, MANNER OF ARTICULATION

LAN *n*

abbreviation for a local area network, which connects computers locally, usually in one room or on one campus, without the need to access the Internet.

language[1] *n*

the system of human communication which consists of the structured arrangement of sounds (or their written representation) into larger units, e.g. MORPHEMES, WORDS, SENTENCES, UTTERANCES.
In common usage it can also refer to non-human systems of communication such as the "language" of bees, the "language" of dolphins.

language[2] *n*

any particular system of human communication (see LANGUAGE[1]), for example, the French language, the Hindi language. Sometimes a language is spoken by most people in a particular country, for example, Japanese in Japan, but sometimes a language is spoken by only part of the population of a country, for example Tamil in India, French in Canada.
Languages are usually not spoken in exactly the same way from one part of a country to the other. Differences in the way a language is spoken by different people are described in terms of regional and social variation

(see DIALECT, SOCIOLECT). In some cases, there is a continuum from one language to another. Dialect A of Language X on one side of the border may be very similar to Dialect B of Language Y on the other side of the border if language X and language Y are related. This is the case between Sweden and Norway and between Germany and the Netherlands.

see also REGISTER

language achievement *n*

a learner's mastery, in a SECOND LANGUAGE and FOREIGN LANGUAGE, of what has been taught or learned after a period of instruction. Language achievement may be contrasted with LANGUAGE APTITUDE, which is measured before a course of instruction begins.

language acquisition *n*

also **language learning**

the learning and development of a person's language. The learning of a native first language is called FIRST LANGUAGE ACQUISITION, and of a second or foreign language, SECOND LANGUAGE ACQUISITION. Some theorists use "learning" and "acquisition" synonymously. Others maintain a contrast between the two terms, using "learning" to mean a conscious process involving the study of explicit rules of language and MONITORING one's performance, as is often typical of classroom learning in a FOREIGN LANGUAGE context, and using "acquisition" to refer to a nonconscious process of rule internalization resulting from exposure to comprehensible input when the learner's attention is on meaning rather than form, as is more common in a SECOND LANGUAGE context. Still others use "acquisition" only with reference to the learning of one's first language.

language acquisition device *n*

also **LAD**

another term for LANGUAGE FACULTY. The term is seldom used nowadays, having been replaced by the concept of UNIVERSAL GRAMMAR.

language across the curriculum *n*

(in the teaching of English and in LANGUAGE ARTS) an approach that emphasizes the teaching of language skills in relation to their uses in the total school curriculum, particularly in the CONTENT AREAS rather than in isolation from the school curriculum. This approach reflects a functional view of language and one which seeks to teach language through activities which are linked to the teaching of other school subjects. A similar approach to the teaching of reading and writing is known as **writing across the curriculum** and **reading across the curriculum**.

language and the law *n*

another term for FORENSIC LINGUISTICS

language anxiety *n*

subjective feelings of apprehension and fear associated with language learning and use. Foreign language anxiety may be a situation-specific anxiety, similar in that respect to public speaking anxiety. Issues in the study of language anxiety include whether anxiety is a cause or an effect of poor achievement, anxiety under specific instructional conditions, and the relationship of general language anxiety to more specific kinds of anxiety associated with speaking, reading, or examinations.

language aptitude *n*

the natural ability to learn a language, not including intelligence, MOTIVA-TION, interest, etc. Language aptitude is thought to be a combination of various abilities, such as **oral mimicry ability** (the ability to imitate sounds not heard before), **phonemic coding ability** (the ability to identify sound patterns in a new language), **grammatical sensitivity** (the ability to recognize the different grammatical functions of words in sentences, ROTE-LEARNING ABILITY, and the ability to infer language rules (see INFERENCING, DEDUCTIVE LEARNING). A person with high language aptitude can learn more quickly and easily than a person with low language aptitude, all other factors being equal. see also LANGUAGE APTITUDE TEST

language aptitude test *n*

a test that measures a person's aptitude for SECOND LANGUAGE or FOREIGN LANGUAGE learning and that can be used to identify those learners who are most likely to succeed (see LANGUAGE APTITUDE). Language aptitude tests usually consist of several different tests that measure such abilities as:

a sound coding ability – the ability to identify and remember new sounds in a foreign or second language

b grammatical coding ability – the ability to identify the grammatical functions of different parts of sentences

c inductive learning ability – the ability to work out meanings without explanation in a new language (see INDUCTIVE LEARNING)

d memorization – the ability to remember words, rules, etc., in a new language

Two well-known language aptitude tests are *The Modern Language Aptitude Test* and *The Pimsleur Language Aptitude Battery*.

language arts *n*

those parts of an educational CURRICULUM which involve the development of skills related to the use of language, such as reading, writing, spelling, listening, and speaking. The term is used principally to describe approaches used in FIRST LANGUAGE teaching which try to develop LANGUAGE SKILLS together rather than separately.

language attitudes *n*

the attitudes which speakers of different languages or language varieties have towards each other's languages or to their own language. Expressions of positive or negative feelings towards a language may reflect impressions of linguistic difficulty or simplicity, ease or difficulty of learning, degree of importance, elegance, social STATUS, etc. Attitudes towards a language may also show what people feel about the speakers of that language. Language attitudes may have an effect on SECOND LANGUAGE or FOREIGN LANGUAGE learning. The measurement of language attitudes provides information which is useful in language teaching and language planning.

see also LANGUAGE EGO, MATCHED GUISE TECHNIQUE, MOTIVATION, SEMANTIC DIFFERENTIAL

language attrition *n*

language loss that is gradual rather than sudden. This may refer to the loss of a second or foreign language after instruction (**second language attrition** or **L2 attrition**), such as often occurs in settings where the language is not used in the community, or to **first language attrition** (**L1 attrition**) in situations where the community speaks a different language, as in language loss among immigrants. In these cases, the language that is lost or being lost is called the **attriting language**, while the individuals who experience attrition are called **attriters**. Language attrition may also refer to the loss of a first or second language due to ageing. Research on second language attrition has been similar to research on language acquisition, including such topics as the role of age, individual differences, social-psychological factors, individual differences, and language setting.

language audit *n*

an investigation of the language needs of a particular organization in order to determine the actions the organization needs to take in order to increase the language competence of its employees, and thereby improve contacts with foreign clients.

language awareness *n*

a movement that developed in Britain in the 1980s which sought to stimulate curiosity about language and to provide links among the different kinds of language experiences children typically encountered in school, e.g. in science, in literature, and in foreign language classes. Language awareness courses seek to develop knowledge about language and languages as an important element in the education of all children.

language change *n*

change in a language which takes place over time. All living languages have changed and continue to change.

For example, in English, changes that have recently been occurring include the following:

a Distinctions in pronunciation in words such as *which:witch* and *pour:pore:poor* have disappeared or are disappearing in many varieties of English.

b The distinction between *who* (as in *the person who bought the painting*) and *whom* (as in *the person whom I like best*) is being lost, with many speakers using *who* in both cases and a tendency among younger speakers to use *that* for both.

c New words and expressions are constantly entering the language, e.g. *subprime* (a risky loan, mortgage, or investment), *bailout* (rescue by a government of a company on the brink of failure), *blogosphere* (all the world's BLOGs and their interconnections).

Language change should not be confused with LANGUAGE SHIFT.

see also COMPARATIVE HISTORICAL LINGUISTICS, DIACHRONIC LINGUISTICS, NEOLOGISM, SOUND CHANGE

language classroom research *n*

see CLASSROOM-CENTRED RESEARCH

language comprehension *n*

the processes involved in understanding the meaning of written or spoken language. Theories of language comprehension are an important aspect of psycholinguistics, cognitive psychology, and second language acquisition. Among the different processes involved are:

a **Perceptual processing**: attention is focused on the oral or written text and parts of it are retained in SHORT TERM MEMORY. Some initial analysis of the text may begin and attention is focused on CUES which will help identify constituents or meaningful sections of the text. These cues may be pauses and acoustic emphasis in spoken text or punctuation or paragraph separation in written text.

b **Parsing**: words are identified and matched with representations in long term memory (see MEMORY) creating basic units of meaning called PROPOSITIONS. Knowledge of the grammatical structure of the target language is used to help identify constituents and arrive at propositions.

c **Utilization or elaboration**: propositions are related to other information and concepts in long term memory and connections are formed with existing concepts and schema (see SCHEME).

see also LANGUAGE PRODUCTION, INFORMATION PROCESSING, LISTENING COMPREHENSION

language conflict *n*

disagreement among groups within a nation, state, or other political entity about what languages should be officially recognized, protected, or developed. Typically, one language (or a variety of it) is supported by some and rejected by others and, since the adoption of a particular language is closely related to issues of national and regional identity, language conflict often carries the potential for political instability. Well known twentieth-century examples include many disputes over the ways that political boundaries have been drawn and redrawn in India since independence from England and policies concerning the role of French and English in public life in Canada.

language contact *n*

contact between different languages, especially when at least one of the languages is influenced by the contact. This influence takes place typically when the languages are spoken in the same or adjoining regions and when there is a high degree of communication between the people speaking them. The influence may affect PHONETICS, SYNTAX, SEMANTICS, or communicative strategies such as ADDRESS FORMS and greetings. Language contact occurs or has occurred in areas of considerable immigration such as the USA, Latin America, Australia and parts of Africa, as well as in language border areas such as parts of India.

see also **contact language** under PIDGIN

language corpus *n*

see CORPUS

language death *n*

also **language decline**

the disappearance of a "living" language as its speakers switch to using other languages and children cease to learn it.

see also LANGUAGE LOSS, LANGUAGE MAINTENANCE, LANGUAGE REVITALIZATION

language decline *n*

see LANGUAGE DEATH

language distance *n*

the relative degree of similarity between two languages. Some languages have similar linguistic features and are said to be "close". Others have very different linguistic features and are said to be "distant". For example, two languages may have similar word order rules and similar rules for certain syntactic or phonological structures. There is said to be a greater degree of linguistic distance between English and French, for example, than between French and Spanish. Language distance is thought to be one factor which influences the ease or difficulty with which learners acquire new languages.

language dominance *n*

greater ability in, or greater importance of, one language than another.

1 For an individual, this means that a person who speaks more than one language or dialect considers that he or she knows one of the languages better than the other(s) and/or uses it more frequently and with greater ease. The **dominant language** may be his or her NATIVE LANGUAGE or may have been acquired later in life at school or a place of employment.

2 For a country or region where more than one language or dialect is used, this means that one of them is more important than the other(s). A language may become the dominant language because it has more prestige (higher STATUS) in the country, is favoured by the government, and/or has the largest number of speakers.

language education policy *n*

decisions about the teaching and use of languages in educational settings. For example, some languages may be authorized for use as medium of instruction (e.g. learning math in Mandarin Chinese in a Chinese immersion school in California), while other languages may be taught as subjects (e.g. taking an introductory Chinese course in an English-medium university).

language ego *n*

(in SECOND LANGUAGE or FOREIGN LANGUAGE learning) the relation between people's feelings of personal identity, individual uniqueness, and value (i.e. their ego) and aspects of their FIRST LANGUAGE.

language enrichment *n*

a term sometimes used to describe language teaching as part of a programme of COMPENSATORY INSTRUCTION.

language experience approach *n*

an approach used in the teaching of reading to young children which draws on the experiences children have in their personal lives as well as on the language skills and vocabulary they have developed outside the classroom. In this approach, children may recount stories and experiences orally to the teacher, who writes words on charts or other visual devices and uses them as a basis for teaching reading.

language faculty *n*
also **language acquisition device, LAD**
in GENERATIVE THEORY, the view is widely held that humans are innately endowed with a specific faculty or mental module which provides them with a set of procedures for developing the grammar of their native language.

language family *n*
a group of languages that are believed to have developed from a common source, such as the Romance language family (French, Italian, Spanish, Portuguese and Romanian) which are all derived from Latin in the Middle Ages.

language for academic purposes *n*
see ACADEMIC DISCOURSE, ENGLISH FOR ACADEMIC PURPOSES

language functions *n*
another term for FUNCTIONS OF LANGUAGE[1,2]

language laboratory *n*
also **language lab**
a room that contains desks or individual booths with tape or cassette recorders and a control booth for teacher or observer and which is used for language teaching. The recorders usually have recording, listening, and play-back facilities; students can practise recorded exercises and follow language programmes either individually or in groups, and the teacher can listen to each student's performance through earphones. Language laboratories are associated particularly with the AUDIOLINGUAL METHOD and have been replaced in many institutions by a MULTI-MEDIA LABORATORY.

language learning *n*
see FIRST LANGUAGE ACQUISITION, LANGUAGE ACQUISITION, SECOND LANGUAGE ACQUISITION

language loss *n*
a general term referring to the loss or decline of linguistic skills, as may happen when immigrants have limited opportunity to use their first language in an environment where it is not spoken or valued or when second language

learners forget their second language through lack of opportunities for use. When the focus is on individuals, the more specific term language attrition is often used; when the focus is on groups of speakers, the more common term is language shift. Language loss may also be pathological, as a result of accident, disease or old age (see APHASIA).
see also LANGUAGE MAINTENANCE

language loyalty *n*

retention of a language by its speakers, who are usually in a minority in a country where another language is the dominant language (see LANGUAGE DOMINANCE).

language maintenance *n*

the degree to which an individual or group continues to use their language, particularly in a BILINGUAL or MULTILINGUAL area or among immigrant groups. Many factors affect language maintenance, for example:

a whether or not the language is an official language (see NATIONAL LANGUAGE)

b whether or not it is used in the media, for religious purposes, in education

c how many speakers of the language live in the same area. In some places where the use of certain languages has greatly decreased there have been efforts to revive languages in declining use, e.g. of Maori in New Zealand and Hawaian in Hawaii.

see also DIGLOSSIA, LANGUAGE SHIFT, LANGUAGE REVITALIZATION PROGRAMME

language majority student *n*

a term used in the US to refer to students who come from homes in which English is the primary language used. They are contrasted with **language minority students**, who come from a minority group and who speak a language other than English at home.

language minority group *n*

also **minority language group**

a group of people in a country or community who have a language other than the major or dominant language of the country or community.
see also COMMUNITY LANGUAGE, MAJORITY LANGUAGE

language mixing *n*

see CODE MIXING

language norm *n*

see NORM

language of wider communication *n*

a language used for communication within a region or country by different language groups. English is a language of wider communication for many speakers in India, as is Tok Pisin in Papua New Guinea, where many regional languages and language varieties are spoken.

language pathology *n*

see SPEECH PATHOLOGY

language pedagogy *n*

also **language didactics**

a general term sometimes used to describe the teaching of a language as a FIRST LANGUAGE, a SECOND LANGUAGE or a FOREIGN LANGUAGE.

language planning *n*

planning, often by a government or government agency, concerning choice of national or official language(s), support for minority and community languages, ways of spreading the use of one or more languages, spelling reforms, the addition of new words to the language, and other language problems. Through language planning, an official language policy is established and/or implemented. For example, in Indonesia, Malay was chosen as the national language and was given the name Bahasa Indonesia (Indonesian language). It became the main language of education. There were several spelling reforms and a national planning agency was established to deal with problems such as the development of scientific terms. In pluralistic countries or in federal states, language planning may not be monolithic and several "plans" may coexist. Teachers' implementation of programmes such as BILINGUAL EDUCATION or resistance to such plans may also have an effect on language planning at the local or micro-level.

see also LANGUAGE TREATMENT, SOCIOLINGUISTICS, SOCIOLOGY OF LANGUAGE

language policy *n*

decisions made about languages and their uses in society. Sometimes the term is used only in the narrow sense of what governments do – through laws, regulations, court decisions, or other means – to encourage or discourage the use of particular languages or to establish the rights of individuals or groups to use and maintain languages. Other times the term is used more broadly to refer to decisions about language made by individuals or groups on many different social levels. OVERT LANGUAGE POLICIES, which are explicit and formalized, can also be contrasted with COVERT POLICIES that are implicit, informal and unstated. For example, the US State

of Hawaii has two official languages, Hawaiian and English, according to its constitution. However, covert policy favours English in all domains.
see also LANGUAGE PLANNING

language production *n*
the processes involved in creating and expressing meaning through language. Numerous theories in psycholinguistics and cognitive psychology attempt to account for the different processes involved in language production. Among the different stages involved are:
Construction: the speaker or writer selects communicative goals, and creates propositions which express intended meanings.
Transformation or articulation: meanings are encoded in linguistic form according to the grammar of the target language.
Execution: the message is expressed in audible or visible form through speech or writing.
An important issue in theories of language production is whether the processes involved are analogous to those involved in language comprehension (though in reverse order).
see also LANGUAGE COMPREHENSION

language proficiency *n*
the degree of skill with which a person can use a language, such as how well a person can read, write, speak, or understand language. This can be contrasted with LANGUAGE ACHIEVEMENT, which describes language ability as a result of learning. Proficiency may be measured through the use of a PROFICIENCY TEST.

language programme design *n*
another term for COURSE DESIGN

language programme evaluation *n*
see EVALUATION

language revitalization programme *n*
a programme intended to help to revive or strengthen a language which is in danger of dying out, such as programmes for the teaching of Irish in Ireland or several American Indian languages.

languages for special purposes *n*
also **languages for specific purposes, LSP**
second or foreign languages used for particular and restricted types of communication (e.g. for medical reports, scientific writing, air-traffic control)

and which contain lexical, grammatical, and other linguistic features which are different from ordinary language (see REGISTER). In language teaching, decisions must be made as to whether a learner or group of learners requires a language for general purposes or for special purposes.

see also ENGLISH FOR SPECIAL PURPOSES

language shift *n*

the process by which a new language is acquired by a community usually resulting with the loss of the community's first language. Many minority communities (e.g. the native Maori in New Zealand and the Hawaians in Hawaii) have experienced language shift as their first language has been gradually replaced by English. Attempts to prevent language shift are known as LANGUAGE MAINTENANCE.

language skills *n*

also **skills**

(in language teaching) the mode or manner in which language is used. Listening, speaking, reading, and writing are generally called the four language skills. Sometimes speaking and writing are called the active/**productive skills** and reading and listening, the passive/**receptive skills**. Often the skills are divided into subskills, such as discriminating sounds in connected speech, or understanding relations within a sentence.

see also MICRO-SKILLS

language socialization *n*

the process by which children and other newcomers to a social group become socialized into the group's culture through exposure to and participation in language-mediated social activities. Language socialization is thought to be a key to the acquisition of both linguistic and sociocultural knowledge. Thus acquisition of specific skills in a language is shaped by the culturally specific activities within which these skills are used.

language survey *n*

investigation of language use in a country or region. Such a survey may be carried out to determine, for example:

a which languages are spoken in a particular region
b for what purposes these languages are used
c what proficiency people of different age-groups have in these languages.

see also LANGUAGE PLANNING

language transfer *n*

the effect of one language on the learning of another. Two types of language transfer may occur. **Positive transfer** is transfer which makes learning easier, and may occur when both the native language and the target language have the same form. For example, both French and English have the word *table*, which can have the same meaning in both languages. Negative transfer, also known as **interference**, is the use of a native-language pattern or rule which leads to an ERROR or inappropriate form in the TARGET LANGUAGE[1]. For example, a French learner of English may produce the incorrect sentence *I am here since Monday* instead of *I have been here since Monday*, because of the transfer of the French pattern *Je suis ici depuis lundi* ("I am here since Monday").

Although L1 to L2 transfer has been investigated most widely, it is also generally recognized that there can also be transfer from an L2 to one's native language, as well as L2 to L3 transfer from one second or foreign language to another.

see also COMMUNICATIVE INTERFERENCE, CROSS-LINGUISTIC INFLUENCE, ERROR ANALYSIS, INTERLANGUAGE

language treatment *n*

any kind of action which people take about language problems. This includes LANGUAGE PLANNING by governments and government appointed agencies, but also includes such things as: language requirements for employment in a private company, company policy on style in business letters, trade-name spelling, publishers' style sheets, and the treatment of language in dictionaries and usage guides (see USAGE[2]).

language typology *n*

see TYPOLOGY

language universal *n*

(in general linguistic use) a language pattern or phenomenon which occurs in all known languages. For example, it has been suggested that:

a if a language has **dual** number for referring to just two of something, it also has plural number (for referring to more than two). This type of universal is sometimes called an **implicational universal**.

b there is a high probability that the word referring to the female parent will start with a NASAL consonant, e.g. /m/ in English *mother*, in German *Mutter*, in Swahili *mama*, in Chinese (Mandarin) *muqin*.

see also BIOPROGRAM, UNIVERSAL GRAMMAR

language usage *n*

see USAGE

language use *n*

see USAGE

language use survey *n*

an investigation which seeks to determine which languages are spoken in different areas in a community or country, the function and uses of languages in different domains of language use, and sometimes an assessment of the proficiency of different language groups in terms of their minority and majority language. For example in a multilingual country such as Singapore with four official languages (English, Chinese, Malay and Tamil) a language use survey would seek to determine who uses which languages, for what purposes, and to what degree of proficiency.

language variation *n*

see VARIATION

langue *n*

the French word for "language". The term was used by the linguist Saussure to mean the system of a language, that is the arrangement of sounds and words which speakers of a language have a shared knowledge of or, as Saussure said, "agree to use". Langue is the "ideal" form of a language. Saussure called the actual use of language by people in speech or writing "parole". Saussure's distinction between "langue" and "parole" is similar to Chomsky's distinction between COMPETENCE and PERFORMANCE. But whereas for Saussure the repository of "langue" is the SPEECH COMMUNITY, for Chomsky the repository of "competence" is the "ideal speaker/hearer". So Saussure's distinction is basically sociolinguistic (see SOCIOLINGUISTICS) whereas Chomsky's is basically psycholinguistic (see PSYCHOLINGUISTICS). see also USAGE[1]

larynx *n* **laryngeal** *adj*

a casing of cartilage and muscles in the upper part of the windpipe (in the throat) which contains the vocal cords.

see also PLACE OF ARTICULATION

latent trait theory *n*

see ITEM RESPONSE THEORY

lateral *n*

a speech sound (a CONSONANT) which is produced by partially blocking the airstream from the lungs, usually by the tongue, but letting it escape at one or both sides of the blockage. For example, in English the /l/ in /laɪt/ light is a lateral.

see also MANNER OF ARTICULATION, PLACE OF ARTICULATION

lateralization *n*
 see CEREBRAL DOMINANCE

lateral plosion *n*
 another term for LATERAL RELEASE

lateral release *n*
 the release of a plosive by lowering the sides of the tongue, as at the end of
 the word saddle.

latin alphabet *n*
 another term for ROMAN ALPHABET

lax vowel *n*
 see TENSE/LAX

L-colouring *n*
 a type of ASSIMILATION that occurs when a front vowel preceding the consonant /l/ is pulled further back in the mouth and has a more centralized
 quality than the counterpart front vowel not preceding /l/. For example, the
 vowel of *feel* glides to a noticeably more centralized position than the vowel
 of *fee*.

LCTL *n*
 an abbreviation for LESS COMMONLY-TAUGHT LANGUAGE

lead-in activity *n*
 an activity or activities that prepares learners to work on a topic, text or
 task. It often includes an introduction to the topic of the text or task, and
 activities that activate background knowledge or pre-teach key words or
 other language that might be needed to complete the task.

learnability *n*
 a criterion for linguistic theory. An adequate theory must explain how
 children are able to learn the grammar of their native language and must
 therefore provide for grammars of languages that are easily learnable.

learnability hypothesis *n*
 the idea, attributed to Manfred Pienemann, that a second or foreign language
 learner's acquisition of linguistic structures depends on how complex these

structures are from a psychological processing point of view, defined as the extent to which linguistic material must be re-ordered and re-arranged when mapping semantics and surface form. The psycholinguistic processing devices acquired at one stage are a necessary building block for the following stage. This implies a **teachability hypothesis** as well, since structures cannot be taught successfully if the learner has not learned to produce structures belonging to the previous stage.

learnability theory *n*

any of a class of theories that attempt to explain how children can learn the language that they are exposed to, under the assumption that children do not receive systematic information about sentences that are ungrammatical (see EVIDENCE). One proposal that has been advanced within **generative grammar** is the subset principle, which posits that language learners choose options that allow the smallest number of grammatical sentences. In GENERAL NATIVISM, the same effect is achieved by the **conservatism thesis**, the idea that children make use of available concepts to formulate the most conservative hypothesis consistent with experience, and the **trigger requirement**, the principle that no change is made in the grammar without a triggering stimulus in the environment.

learner autonomy *n*

in language teaching, the principle that learners should be encouraged to assume a maximum amount of responsibility for what they learn and how they learn it. This will be reflected in approaches to needs analysis, content selection, and choice of teaching materials and learning methods.

learner beliefs *n*

also **learner belief systems**

ideas learners have concerning different aspects of language, language learning and language teaching, that may influence their attitudes and motivations in learning and have an effect on their learning strategies and learning outcomes. Learners' belief systems are relatively stable sets of ideas and attitudes about such things as how to learn language, effective teaching strategies, appropriate classroom behaviour, their own abilities, and their goals in language learning. Identification of learner beliefs (e.g. through interviews or administration of questionnaires) sometimes constitutes part of a NEEDS ANALYSIS.

see also TEACHER BELIEF SYSTEMS

learner-centred approach *n*

in language teaching, a belief that attention to the nature of learners should be central to all aspects of language teaching, including planning teaching, and evaluation. Learning is dependent upon the nature and will of the learners. Learner centredness may be reflected by:

1 recognizing learners' prior knowledge
2 recognizing learners' needs, goals and wishes
3 recognizing learners' learning styles and learning preferences
4 recognizing learners' views of teaching and of the nature of classroom tasks.

In learner-centred approaches, course design and teaching often become negotiated processes, since needs, expectations, and student resources vary with each group.

Learner-centred teaching is contrasted with teacher-centred teaching, i.e. teaching in which primary decisions are carried out by the teacher based on his/her priorities.

see TEACHER-DIRECTED INSTRUCTION

learner characteristics *n*

those characteristics specific to an individual learner and which influence his or her learning, such as their age, past learning experience, learning style, motivation.

learner corpora *n*

collections of texts produced by writers or speakers while they are learning a language and which can be used in the study of interlanguage development, language transfer, and learner errors. An example is the International Corpus of Learner English.

learner diary *n*

also LEARNER JOURNAL

in language teaching, a record prepared by a learner of a student's learning experiences and describing what activities they have done in class, the progress they have made, and any problems they may have.

learner dictionary *n*

a dictionary intended for second language learners and in which the words selected for inclusion are those likely to be most difficult or most often encountered by learners and in which the definitions are written in an accessible style, often using words found in a DEFINING VOCABULARY.

learner profile *n*

a description of a student, including his or her abilities, needs, knowledge in order to help determine what the learner's needs are and to help plan the most appropriate course or learning experience for him or her.

learner training *n*

in language teaching, procedures or activities that seek to:

1 raise learners' awareness of what is involved in the processes of second language learning

2 help learners become more involved in and responsible for their own learning

3 help learners develop and strengthen their language learning strategies.

learning *n*

the process by which change in behaviour, knowledge, skills, etc., comes about through practice, instruction or experience and the result of such a process.

see LANGUAGE LEARNING, FIRST LANGUAGE ACQUISITION, LANGUAGE ACQUISITION, SECOND LANGUAGE ACQUISITION

learning by deduction *n*

another term for DEDUCTIVE LEARNING

learning by induction *n*

another term for **inductive learning**

see DEDUCTIVE LEARNING

learning centre *n*

a location within a classroom or school which contains a variety of different learning resources for independent learning. The materials normally:

1 have clearly specified goals

2 contain specific directions for their use

3 are graded according to difficulty level

4 contain means for self-checking.

learning contract *n*

a written agreement between a learner and a teacher which usually contains:

1 a description for a plan of work to be completed

2 a time frame for the work.

Learning contracts seek to develop independent learning, self-directed learning, and to encourage self-motivation and discipline.

learning curve *n*

also **acquisition curve**

a graphic representation of a learner's progress in learning new material over time. The following graph shows the development of negation in a

Spanish-speaking learner of English. It shows the proportion of the negating devices *no + v* (e.g. *I no want*) and *don't + v* (e.g. *I don't want*) over time as found in taped samples taken over 20 different time periods.

A *learning or acquisition curve*

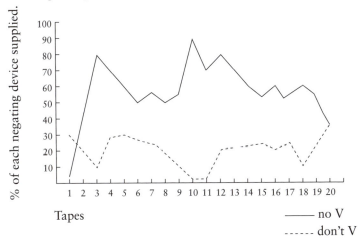

learning disability *n*

a learning difficulty which affects a particular aspect of learning on the part of a learner whose other learning abilities are considered normal. For example, specific difficulties in learning to read (DYSLEXIA) or to write (DYSGRAPHIA).

learning log *n*

also **journal, learning journal**

the use of a notebook or book in which students write about experiences both in and out of school or record responses and reactions to learning and to learning activities. Learning logs provide students with an opportunity to reflect on learning, and are usually shared with the teacher on a regular basis but not graded. In this way, the teacher may be able to find out how the student is progressing and the students gain additional opportunities to practise writing. In writing classes learning logs may be used as a prewriting activity (see COMPOSING PROCESSES) and also as a way of encouraging students to develop fluency in writing through writing regularly on topics of their own choice. When learning logs are used as a way of establishing a dialogue between teacher and student (through comments, questions and reactions), they are sometimes referred to as dialogue journals or diaries.

learning management system *n*

also **LMS, course management system (CMS)** or **virtual learning environment** software that facilitates learner-instructor and learner-learner communication through such features as chat rooms and discussion boards, permits the tracking of user behavior, and allows both instructors and students to monitor their progress. Blackboard, WebCT and Moodle are among the better known LMSs.

learning module *n*

in teaching and instructional materials, a series of linked activities and materials related to a certain objective, usually larger than a single lesson or unit.

learning outcome *n*

also **student learning outcome, SLO**

a statement of what is expected that a student will be able to do as a result of a learning activity. Learning outcomes help instructors and course designers to tell students what they are expected to do and what they can hope to gain from following a particular course or programme.

learning plateau *n*

a temporary period that sometimes occurs in learning, when after making initial progress a learner makes little or no further progress (as seen by a flat part on a LEARNING CURVE). After a period of time the learning plateau is followed by further learning. Learning plateaus are often observed in second and foreign language learning.

learning resources *n*

those materials and other sources of learning that are used in a language programme, such as books, computers, DVDs and CDs.

learning rule *n*

in CONNECTIONISM, changes in weights of the connections in a network are governed by learning rules, equations that specify how and by how much connections are strengthened or weakened based on experience. Whenever a particular pathway through the network results in a successful outcome, the relevant connections are strengthened. When a particular pathway does not result in success, some network architectures implement a procedure called **back propagation**, which weakens connections. As these learning rules are applied repeatedly over a large number of training sessions, the system is increasingly fine-tuned and errors are reduced.

learning strategy *n*

in general, the ways in which learners attempt to work out the meanings and uses of words, grammatical rules, and other aspects of the language they are learning. In FIRST LANGUAGE learning, the word "strategy" is sometimes used to refer to the ways that children process language, without implying either intentionality or awareness. For example, in trying to understand a sentence, a child may "use" the learning strategy that the first mentioned noun in a sentence refers to the person or thing performing an action. The child may then think that the sentence *The boy was chased by the dog* means the same thing as *The boy chased the dog*. In second language learning, a strategy is usually an intentional or potentially intentional behaviour carried out with the goal of learning. A number of broad categories of learning strategies have been identified, including **cognitive strategies** such as analyzing the target language, comparing what is newly encountered with what is already known in either the L1 or the L2, and organizing information; **metacognitive strategies**, which include being aware of one's own learning, making an organized plan, and monitoring one's progress; **social strategies** such as seeking out friends who are native speakers of the target language or working with peers in a classroom setting; and **resource management strategies** such as setting aside a regular time and place for language study. Learning strategies may be applied to simple tasks such as learning a list of new words, or more complex tasks involving language comprehension and production.

see also COMMUNICATION STRATEGY, COGNITIVE STYLE, HEURISTIC, INFERENCING, STRATEGY TRAINING

learning style *n*

also **cognitive style, cognitive strategy**

a particular way of learning preferred by a learner. Learners approach learning in different ways, and an activity that works with a learner whose learning style favours a visual mode of learning, may not be as successful with a learner who prefers auditory or kinesthetic modes of learning. Teachers are hence encouraged to try to recognize different learning styles among their learners. Several different learning styles are often referred to:

1 *Analytic* versus *global* refers to whether the learner focuses on the details or concentrates on the main idea or big picture.

2 *Visual* versus *auditory* versus *hands-on* or *tactile* refers to different sensory preferences in learning.

3 *Intuitive/random* versus *concrete/sequential* learning refers to a difference between thinking in an abstract or nonsequential way versus a focus on concrete facts or a preference to approach learning in a step by step, organized fashion.

Differences in learning style are thought to affect how learners approach learning tasks and may affect success on those tasks.

see also FIELD DEPENDENCE, GLOBAL LEARNING

learning to learn *n*

the acquisition of attitudes, learning strategies and learning skills that will be applied in future learning situations and make future learning more effective. Study skills and learning strategies are examples of the domain of *learning to learn*.

left brain *n*

another term for LEFT HEMISPHERE

left branching direction *n*

see BRANCHING DIRECTION

left dislocation *n*

the occurrence of a linguistic form to the left of its normal position in a sentence. For example in the sentence:

Madge made the pizza.

pizza is in its normal object position in the sentence. But in the less common sentence:

The pizza, Madge made it.

the pizza is now a left dislocation. Left dislocation is a WORD ORDER device which is often used to signal a new topic (TOPIC[2]) or to give special emphasis. With **right dislocation**, a linguistic form appears to the right of its normal position. For example:

She made the pizza, Madge did.

left-ear advantage *n*

see DICHOTIC LISTENING

left hemisphere *n*

the brain can be described as divided into the left and right cerebral hemispheres. The left hemisphere has been shown to be especially important for language processing, and it is where both BROCA'S AREA and WERNICKE'S AREA are located.

see also CEREBRAL DOMINANCE

lenis *adj*

see FORTIS

LEP *n*
an abbreviation for LIMITED ENGLISH PROFICIENCY

leptokurtic distribution *n*
see KURTOSIS

LES *n*
an abbreviation for LIMITED ENGLISH SPEAKER

less commonly-taught language *n*
also **LCTL**
of the approximately 7,000 languages spoken on earth, only a handful are widely taught, and many are hardly ever taught. As a result, the less commonly-taught languages do not have nearly the same level of resources (textbooks, trained teachers, opportunities for secure employment, scholars who specialize in the language) as languages that have a long history of support by the educational establishment.

lesson plan *n* **lesson planning** *n*
a description or outline of (a) the goals or OBJECTIVES a teacher has set for a lesson (b) the activities and procedures the teacher will use to achieve them, the time to be allocated to each activity, and the order to be followed, and (c) the materials and resources which will be used during the lesson.

lesson structure *n*
see STRUCTURING

level[1] *n*
a layer in a linguistic system, e.g. word level, phrase level. Often, these levels are considered to form a scale or hierarchy from lower levels containing the smaller linguistic units to higher levels containing larger linguistic units, e.g. MORPHEME level – word level – PHRASE level – CLAUSE level, etc.
It is also sometimes said that the items on each level consist of items on the next lower level: clauses consist of phrases, phrases of words, words of morphemes, etc.
see also RANK, TAGMENICS

level[2] *n*
see PITCH LEVEL

level[3] *n*

(in testing) a description of the degree of proficiency expected for a test taker to be placed in a certain position on a scale, such as "beginning", "intermediate", or "advanced".
see also BAND

level of comprehension *n*

1 in reading, a degree of understanding of a text, such as "literal comprehension", "inferential comprehension", "evaluative comprehension"
2 in testing, the degree of understanding of a text as measured by performance on a test.

levels of processing *n*

see REHEARSAL

levels of significance *n*

see STATISTICAL SIGNIFICANCE

level tone *n*

also **register tone**
in tone languages, tones that are relatively stable, with nongliding pitch.
see TONE[1], CONTOUR TONE

lexeme *n*

also **lexical item**
the smallest unit in the meaning system of a language that can be distinguished from other similar units. A lexeme is an abstract unit. It can occur in many different forms in actual spoken or written sentences, and is regarded as the same lexeme even when inflected (see INFLECTION).
For example, in English, all inflected forms such as *give, gives, given, giving, gave* would belong to the one lexeme *give*.
Similarly, such expressions as *bury the hatchet, hammer and tongs, give up*, and *white paper* (in the sense of a government document) would each be considered a single lexeme. In a dictionary, each lexeme merits a separate entry or sub-entry.

lexical access *n*

(in speech production) the retrieval of words from the speaker's lexicon (LEXICON[4]). According to psycholinguistic models of speech production, vocabulary is stored in some form in the speaker's lexicon and must be accessed in order to be used during the process of communication.

Researchers in BILINGUALISM have investigated whether the bilingual person stores words in different lexicons for each language. Speed of access to the lexicon may be faster in one language than the other.

lexical ambiguity *n*

see AMBIGUOUS

lexical approach *n*

an approach to language teaching that is based on the view that the basic building blocks of teaching and learning are words and lexical phrases, rather than grammar, functions or other units of organization. The lexicon is seen as playing a much more central role in language organization, language learning, and language teaching than, for example, grammar, and occupies a more central role in syllabus design, course content, and teaching activities.

lexical aspect hypothesis *n*

also **aspect hypothesis, inherent lexical aspect hypothesis**

(in LANGUAGE ACQUISITION) the hypothesis that the acquisition of TENSE and grammatical aspect is affected by lexical aspect (see ASPECT). For example, the hypothesis holds that language learners first acquire the English progressive affix *-ing* in conjunction with specific verbs like *play* or *read*, which refer to actions that are inherently durative, rather than in connection with verbs like *fall*, which refers to an action that is inherently abrupt or non-durative (although it is possible to say *I was falling*, viewing the action as durative). Also according to this view, what appears to be the acquisition of TENSE in the early stages of language learning is more likely to reflect the encoding of aspect.

lexical bundle *n*

a type of fixed phrase consisting of a sequence of three or more words that co-occur frequently in a particular type of writing or register such as academic writing. For example, *a wide variety of, one of the most, the relative importance of*.

lexical category *n*

the four main lexical categories are *n* (noun), *v* (verb), *a* (adjective) and *p* (preposition). Entries in a lexicon (see LEXICON^2) or dictionary usually show, among other information, the lexical category of a particular word, e.g. **lexical** *a*.

lexical corpus *n*

a collection of words for purposes of language analysis. Many lexical corpora contain millions of words that can be analyzed by a computer.

see also CORPUS

lexical decision task *n*

a psycholinguistic task that involves measuring how quickly people can classify stimuli as words or nonwords, which has been used in thousands of studies investigating semantic memory and lexical access.

see also PRIMING

lexical density *n*

also **Type-Token Ratio, concept load**

a measure of the ratio of different words to the total number of words in a text, sometimes used as a measure of the difficulty of a passage or text. Lexical density is normally expressed as a percentage and is calculated by the formula:

$$\text{Lexical density} = \frac{\text{number of separate words}}{\text{total number of words in the text}} \times 100$$

For example, the lexical density of this definition is:

$$\frac{29 \text{ separate words}}{57 \text{ total words}} \times 100 = 50.88$$

see also TYPE

lexical entry *n*

a term used in TRANSFORMATIONAL GENERATIVE GRAMMAR for a word or phrase listed in the lexicon (see LEXICON[3]) of the grammar.

The information given in a lexical entry usually includes:

a its pronunciation (see DISTINCTIVE FEATURE)

b its meaning, which may be given in a formalized way, e.g. (+human) (+male) (see SEMANTIC FEATURES)

c its LEXICAL CATEGORY, e.g. *n*(oun), *v*(erb), *a*(djective)

d other linguistic items it may co-occur with in a sentence, e.g. whether or not a verb can be followed by an object (see OBJECT[1])

In later models of TG Grammar, a lexical entry would also contain semantic roles such as agent, patient and goal which can be assigned to noun phrases in the sentence (see θ-THEORY).

see also PROJECTION PRINCIPLE

lexical field *n*

also **semantic field**

the organization of related words and expressions (see LEXEME) into a system which shows their relationship to one another. For example, kinship terms such as *father, mother, brother, sister, uncle, aunt* belong to a lexical field whose relevant features include generation, sex, membership of the father's or mother's side of the family, etc.

The absence of a word in a particular place in a lexical field of a language is called a **lexical gap**.

For example, in English there is no singular noun that covers both cow and bull as *horse* covers *stallion* and *mare*.

lexical functional grammar *n*

also **LFG**

a theory of grammar that holds that there are two parallel levels of syntactic representation: CONSTITUENT STRUCTURE (c-structure), consisting of context-free phrase structure trees, and **functional structure** (f-structure), consisting of attributes such as tense and gender and functions such as subject and object. An important difference between LFG and the Chomskyan tradition from which it developed is that many phenomena that were treated as transformations in the Chomskyan tradition (for example, passive vs. active sentences) are treated in the LEXICON[3] in LFG.

lexical gap *n*

see LEXICAL FIELD

lexical item *n*

another term for LEXEME

lexical meaning *n*

see CONTENT WORD

lexical phonology *n*

a model of morphology and phonology and the lexicon in which the lexicon is divided into levels or **strata**. Phonological rules are divided into **lexical rules**, which are carried out in the lexicon and include morphological conditioning, and **postlexical rules**, which apply across word boundaries in a separate component order after the rules of syntax.

lexical phrases *n*

recurrent phrases and patterns of language use which have become institutionalized through frequent use, such as "Have we met?" and "You must be joking".

lexical priming *n*
>   see PRIMING

lexical semantics *n*
>   the subfield of SEMANTICS concerned with the meaning of words.

lexical set *n*
>   a group of words or phrases that are related to the same content, topic or subject, such as *storm, rain, wind, snow, ice* in relation to the topic of *weather*.

lexical syllabus *n*
>   a vocabulary syllabus that is organized in terms of the most important, frequent, or useful vocabulary items in a language. Lexical syallabuses are often organized according to levels (e.g. the first 1000 words, the second 1000 words, etc.).

lexical verb *n*
>   see AUXILIARY VERB

lexical word *n*
>   see CONTENT WORD

lexicogrammar *n* **lexico-grammar**
>   1 the linguistic resources (both grammatical and lexical) which learners draw on in expressing meaning and communicating in a second language.
>   2 the relationship between vocabulary and grammar. These forms of language organization are normally studied separately but increasingly lexico-grammatical patterns are being seen as central to language description and language learning.
>   see SYSTEMIC-FUNCTIONAL LINGUISTICS

lexico-grammatical associations *n*
>   see CORPUS LINGUISTICS

lexicography *n* **lexicographic(al)** *adj* **lexicographer** *n* **lexicology** *n* **lexicological** – *adj*
>   the art of dictionary making. Foreign language lexicography involves the development of dictionaries for language learners.

lexicologist *n*
>   a student of the vocabulary items (LEXEMES) of a language, including their meanings and relations (see LEXICAL FIELD), and changes in their form and meaning through time. The discoveries of lexicologists may be of use to lexicographers.
>   see also ETYMOLOGY, LEXICOGRAPHY

lexicon¹ *n*

the set of all the words and idioms of any language (see lexeme).
see also LEXICOGRAPHY, LEXICOLOGY

lexicon² *n*

a dictionary, usually of an ancient language such as Latin or Greek.

lexicon³ *n*

the words and phrases listed in the BASE COMPONENT of a GENERATIVE GRAMMAR and information about them.
see also LEXICAL ENTRY

lexicon⁴ *n*

a mental system which contains all the information a person knows about words. According to psycholinguists, people's knowledge of a word includes
a knowing how a word is pronounced
b the grammatical patterns with which a word is used
c the meaning or meanings of the word.
The total set of words a speaker knows forms his or her mental lexicon. The content of the mental lexicon and how a mental lexicon is developed are studied in psycholinguistics and language acquisition.
see also LEXICAL ACCESS

lexis *n* **lexical** *adj*

the vocabulary of a language in contrast to its grammar (syntax).
see also LEXEME

LF *n*

another term for LOGICAL FORM

LF component *n*

see D-STRUCTURE

liaison *n*

another term for LINKING

Likert scale *n*

see ATTITUDE SCALE

limited English proficiency *n*

see LIMITED ENGLISH SPEAKER

limited English proficient *n*
> also **LEP**
>
> sometimes used to describe a MINORITY STUDENT in an English speaking country, whose English language proficiency is not at the level of native speakers of English. Special instruction in English is therefore needed to prepare the student to enter a regular school programme. This term is considered offensive by some and a more neutral term such as Second Language Student is preferred.
>
> see also MAINSTREAMING, SHELTERED ENGLISH, SUBMERSION EDUCATION

limited English speaker *n*
> also **LES**
>
> (in BILINGUAL EDUCATION or an ENGLISH AS A SECOND LANGUAGE PRO-GRAMME) a person who has some proficiency in English but not enough to enable him or her to take part fully and successfully in a class where English is the only MEDIUM OF INSTRUCTION. Such a person is sometimes said to have limited English proficiency. However, since these students actually speak two languages, the term "limited English speaker" has been criticized in recent years for focusing only on their linguistic weaknesses while ignoring their linguistic strengths. For this reason, in many places the term has been abandoned in favour of terms such as "ESL learner" or "bilingual student."

linear programme *n*
> see PROGRAMMED LEARNING

linear syllabus *n*
> see SPIRAL APPROACH

lingua franca *n*
> a language that is used for communication between different groups of people, each speaking a different language. The lingua franca could be an internationally used language of communication (e.g. English), it could be the NATIVE LANGUAGE of one of the groups, or it could be a language which is not spoken natively by any of the groups but has a simplified sentence structure and vocabulary and is often a mixture of two or more languages (see PIDGIN). The term *lingua franca* (Italian for "Frankish tongue") originated in the Mediterranean region in the Middle Ages among crusaders and traders of different language backgrounds. The term **auxiliary language** is sometimes used as a synonym for lingua franca.

linguicism *n*
> by analogy with "racism" and "sexism" a term proposed by Phillipson to describe practices, beliefs, policies, etc., that are designed to promote and

maintain unequal divisions of power, prestige, resources, etc., between groups on the basis of language.

see LINGUISTIC IMPERIALISM

linguist *n*

1 a person who specializes in the study of language. Different areas of specialization are indicated by the field of study, as in *applied linguist*, *psycholinguist*, *sociolinguist*, etc.

2 in popular usage, a person who speaks several languages fluently and shows a propensity for language learning.

linguistically disadvantaged *adj*

a term sometimes used to refer to a person who has an insufficient command of the dominant language in a country. This term is not favoured by linguists since it suggests the person's home language is not useful or is unimportant.

see also DEFICIT HYPOTHESIS

linguistic analysis *n*

investigation into the structure and functions of a particular language or language variety (see LANGUAGE²) or of language in general as a system of human communication (see LANGUAGE¹).

linguistic capital *n*

see CULTURAL CAPITAL

linguistic ecology *n*

also **ecology of language**

a branch of linguistics that uses the metaphor of an ecosystem to describe relationships and interaction among the languages of the world and the groups of people who speak them.

linguistic enviroment *n*

the spoken language that a learner encounters in both educational and social settings, and which serves as potential listening input to the language learning process.

linguistic imperialism *n*

the theory that languages may be seen as occupying a dominant or dominated role in a society. It is argued that English plays a dominant role internationally and plays a role in maintaining the economic and political dominance of some societies over others. Because of the role of English as the dominant international language, many other languages have been prevented from going through processes of development and expansion. The spread of English is viewed as imposing aspects of Anglo-Saxon Judaeo-Christian culture and causing a threat to the cultures and languages of non-English speaking countries.

see also CULTURAL IMPERIALISM

linguistic insecurity *n*

a feeling of insecurity experienced by speakers or writers about some aspect of their language use or about the variety of language they speak. This may result, for instance, in modified speech, when speakers attempt to alter their way of speaking in order to sound more like the speakers of a prestige variety.

see also SOCIOLECT

linguisticism *n*

a term sometimes used to refer to the use of ideologies, structures and practices to legitimize and reproduce unequal divisions of power and resources between language groups.

linguistic method *n*

a term used to refer to several methods of teaching first-language reading which claim to be based on principles of linguistics, and in particular to methods which reflect the views of two prominent American linguists of the 1940s and 1950s, Leonard Bloomfield and Charles Fries. They argued that since the written language is based on the spoken language, the relationship between speech and written language should be emphasized in the teaching of reading. This led to reading materials which made use of words which had a regular sound-spelling correspondence and in which there was a systematic introduction to regular and irregular spelling patterns. In recent years, applied linguists have continued to propose and advocate different approaches to the teaching of reading and language in general, but there is no longer any widely recognized "linguistic method."

linguistic prescriptivism *n*

the prescribing of rules for the language and its use.

see also PRESCRIPTIVE GRAMMAR, DESCRIPTIVE GRAMMAR

linguistic relativity *n*

a belief which was held by some scholars that the way people view the world is determined wholly or partly by the structure of their NATIVE LANGUAGE. As this hypothesis was strongly put forward by the American anthropological linguists Sapir and Whorf, it has often been called the **Sapir-Whorf hypothesis** or **Whorfian hypothesis**. In recent years, study of the relationships between cognition and linguistic expression has been revived in a more subtle form within COGNITIVE LINGUISTICS.

see also ANTHROPOLOGICAL LINGUISTICS

linguistic rights *n*

as a category of human rights, i.e. universal rights that belong to all persons, linguistic rights are based on the idea of human dignity and worth as well as cultural tolerance. Examples of a linguistic right are the rights of a minority language community to receive education in their language and of people to receive governmental services in languages other than the socially dominant language. Although various proposals have been put forth to define such linguistic rights, there is so far no general agreement on them comparable to the principles of human rights codified by the United Nations.

linguistics *n* linguist *n* linguistic *adj*

the study of language as a system of human communication. Linguistics includes many different approaches to the study of language and many different areas of investigation, for example sound systems (PHONETICS, PHONOLOGY), sentence structure (SYNTAX), relationships between language and cognition (COGNITIVE LINGUISTICS), meaning systems (SEMANTICS, PRAGMATICS, FUNCTIONS OF LANGUAGE), as well as language and social factors (SOCIOLINGUISTICS).

Several specialized branches of linguistics have also developed in combination with other disciplines, e.g. APPLIED LINGUISTICS, ANTHROPOLOGICAL LINGUISTICS, PSYCHOLINGUISTICS, FORENSIC LINGUISTICS.

linguistic units *n*

parts of a language system. Linguistic units can be the distinctive sounds of a language (PHONEMES), words, phrases, or sentences, or they can be larger units such as the UTTERANCES in a conversation.

see also CHUNKING, DISCOURSE, DISCOURSE ANALYSIS

linking *n*

also **liaison**

a process in continuous speech which connects the final sound of one word or syllable to the initial sound of the next. In English, words ending in a tense vowel and a following word or syllable beginning with a vowel are usually linked with a GLIDE, so that a phrase like *be able* sounds as though there is a /y/ between *be* and *able* and *blue ink* sounds as though there is a /w/ between the words *blue* and *ink*. In some varieties of English, a linking /r/ is inserted between words ending and beginning with a vowel, as in *saw Ann* or *media event*. When a word or syllable ending in a consonant cluster is followed by a syllable beginning with a vowel, the final consonant of the cluster is often pronounced as part of the following syllable, a process referred to as resyllabification. For example, *left arm* is usually pronounced as if it were *lef tarm*.

linking adjunct *n*

a word or phrase that indicates the relationship between two clauses, sentences, or paragraphs, such as additive (*also*), resultative (*so*), contrastive (*however*), inference (*in that case*), time (*eventually*), concessive (*anyway*), summative (*overall*).

linking verb *n*

another term for COPULA

lipreading *n* **lipread** *v*

also **speech reading**

a method used by hearing impaired people and others to identify what a speaker is saying by studying the movements of the lips and face muscles.

liquid *n*

a cover term for LATERALS and frictionless r-sounds. Like glides, liquids are a subclass of CONTINUANTS.

listening comprehension *n*

the process of understanding speech in a first or second language. The study of listening comprehension processes in second language learning focuses on the role of individual linguistic units (e.g. PHONEMES, WORDS, grammatical structures) as well as the role of the listener's expectations, the situation and context, background knowledge and the topic. It therefore includes both TOP-DOWN PROCESSING and **bottom-up processing**. While traditional approaches to language teaching tended to underemphasize the importance of teaching listening comprehension, more recent approaches emphasize the role of listening in building up language competence and suggest that more attention should be paid to teaching listening in the initial stages of second or foreign language learning. Listening comprehension activities typically address a number of listening functions, including **recognition** (focusing on some aspect of the code itself), **orientation** (ascertaining essential facts about the text, such as participants, the situation or context, the general topic, the emotional tone, and the genre), comprehension of main ideas, and understanding and recall of details.

see also COMPREHENSION APPROACH, NATURAL APPROACH, PERCEPTION, PSYCHOLINGUISTICS, SPEECH RECOGNITION

listening for details *v*

listening in order to understand the specific information contained in a text.

listening for gist *n*

also **listening for global understanding**

listening in order to understand the general meaning of a text without paying attention to specific details.

listening strategy *n*

in listening comprehension, a conscious plan to deal with incoming speech, particularly when the listener experiences problems due to incomplete understanding, such as by using a clarification strategy.

list intonation *n*

see INTONATION CONTOUR

literacy *n* **literate** *adj*

the ability to read and write in a language. The inability to read or write is known as **illiteracy**.

Functional literacy refers to the ability to use reading and writing skills sufficiently well for the purposes and activities which normally require literacy in adult life. An inability to meet a certain minimum criterion of reading and writing skill is known as **functional illiteracy**. A person who is able to read and write in two languages is sometimes called **biliterate**.

In recent years, several different approaches to the study of literacy have developed in education and applied linguistics, including a linguistic approach which focuses on oral–written language relationships, language variation, and genres; a cognitive approach which focuses on PERCEPTION and reading, writing and comprehension processes; and a sociocultural perspective which treats literacy as social practice and deals with issues such as socialization into literacy, the sociocultural context of literacy, and the authority of written discourse.

literacy practices *n*

culture-specific ways of utilizing literacy in everyday life, related to people's social roles and identities.

literal comprehension *n*

see READING

literal translation *n*

see TRANSLATION

literary culture *n*

see ORAL CULTURE

LMS *n*

an abbreviation for LEARNING MANAGEMENT SYSTEM

loan blend *n*

a type of BORROWING in which one part of a word is borrowed from a second language and the other part belongs to the speaker's native language. For example, in the German spoken by some people in Australia, *gumbaum* means gumtree.

loan translation *n*

also **calque**

a type of BORROWING, in which each morpheme or word is translated into the equivalent morpheme or word in another language.

For example, the English word *almighty* is a loan translation from the Latin *omnipotens*:

Omni + potens

all mighty = *almighty*

A loan translation may be a word, a phrase, or even a short sentence, e.g. the English *beer garden* and *academic freedom* are loan translations of the German *Biergarten* and *akademische Freiheit*.

loan word *n*

see BORROWING

local error *n*

see GLOBAL ERROR

locative case *n*

the noun or noun phrase which refers to the location of the action of the verb is in the locative case.

For example, in the sentence:

Irene put the magazines on the table.

the table is in the locative case.

lock-step *n*

in teaching, a situation in which all students in a class are engaged in the same activity at the same time, all progressing through tasks at the same rate.

lock-step teaching/syllabus *n*

the organization of teaching material in a sequence and where the order of teaching items is determined strictly by what has already been taught. Each item forms a necessary stage in the teaching of what comes later and items must be taught in that sequence. Grammatical syllabuses in language teaching are typically organized in this way.

see also LINEAR SYLLABUS, SPIRAL SYLLABUS

locus of control *n*

see ATTRIBUTION THEORY

locutionary act *n*

a distinction is made by Austin in the theory of SPEECH ACTS between three different types of act involved in or caused by the utterance of a sentence.

A locutionary act is the saying of something which is meaningful and can be understood.

For example, saying the sentence *Shoot the snake* is a locutionary act if hearers understand the words *shoot, the, snake* and can identify the particular snake referred to. An **illocutionary act** is using a sentence to perform a function. For example *Shoot the snake* may be intended as an order or a piece of advice.

A **perlocutionary act** is the results or effects that are produced by means of saying something. For example, shooting the snake would be a perlocutionary act.

Austin's three-part distinction is less frequently used than a two-part distinction between the propositional content of a sentence (THE PROPOSITION(s) which a sentence expresses or implies) and the **illocutionary force** or intended effects of speech acts (their function as requests, commands, orders, etc.).

locutionary meaning *n*

see SPEECH ACT

log *n*

see LEARNING LOG

logic *n*

in general, the study of reasoning, especially the formulation of deductive rules that prove statements true from given premises and axioms. In order to formalize rules for deduction, logical languages have been developed, of which the best known are **propositional logic** and **predicate logic**. More recently developed types of logical language include type logic, second-order logic, and many-valued logic.

logical form *n*
>also **LF**
>see D-STRUCTURE

logical positivism *n*
>see POSITIVISM

logical problem of language acquisition *n*
>see also PLATO'S PROBLEM

logical subject *n*
>a NOUN PHRASE¹ which describes, typically, the performer of the action. Some linguists make a distinction between the grammatical subject (see SUBJECT) and the logical subject. For example, in the passive sentence:
>>*The cake was eaten by Vera.*
>
>*the cake* is the grammatical subject but *Vera* is the logical subject as she is the performer of the action. In:
>>*Vera ate the cake.*
>
>Vera would be both the grammatical and the logical subject.
>see also VOICE¹

long consonants *n*
>see GEMINATE

longitudinal method *n*
>also **longitudinal study**
>see CROSS-SECTION(AL) METHOD

long term memory *n*
>see MEMORY

long vowel *n*
>see VOWEL

look-and-say method *n*
>a method for teaching children to read, especially in the first language, which is similar to the whole-word method except that words are always taught in association with a picture or object and the pronunciation of the word is always required.

loop input *n*
>a type of experiential teacher training process proposed by Tessa Woodwood that seeks to align both the content and processes of learning.

It involves trainees experiencing the content which is the focus of learning. For example if the trainees were learning about the nature of listening skills they would take part in activities that made use of the same skills (e.g. predicting, gist listening, etc.), and later reflect on their listening experiences.

low-inference category *n*
    see HIGH-INFERENCE CATEGORY

low variety *n*
    see DIGLOSSIA

low vowel *n*
    another term for **open vowel**
    see VOWEL

Lozanov method *n*
    another term for SUGGESTOPAEDIA

LSP *n*
    an abbreviation for LANGUAGES FOR SPECIAL PURPOSES

LTRC *n*
    an abbreviation for Language Testing Research Colloquium

L-variety *n*
    see DIGLOSSIA

M

machine translation *n*

the use of a translation program to translate text without human input in the translation process. Although great progress has been made in this field in recent decades, machine translated text still varies greatly in quality, mostly depending on the complexity of the SOURCE TEXT, and is seldom adequate for publication without human intervention to correct errors of grammar, meaning, and style.

macroskills *n*

see MICROSKILLS

macrosociolinguistics *n*

sociolinguistic research that deals with sociological or social psychological phenomena, and which studies language use in society as a whole, including the study of language maintenance and language loss.

see also MICROSOCIOLINGUISTICS

macro-structure *n*

in writing, the topic and overall organization of a text as compared with the details or MICROSTRUCTURE of a passage.

main clause *n*

see DEPENDENT CLAUSE

main idea *n*

in a composition, the central thought or topic, often identical with the TOPIC SENTENCE of the composition.

mainstreaming *n* **mainstream** *v*

the entry into a regular school programme (i.e. mainstream programme) of students for whom the language spoken in that school is a second language. In many countries where there are significant numbers of immigrant students for whom English is a second language, school ESL programmes seek to prepare students to enter mainstream classes, that is classes where English is the medium of instruction in the CONTENT AREAS.

maintenance bilingual education *n*

see BILINGUAL EDUCATION

maintenance rehearsal *n*
> see REHEARSAL

majority language *n*
> the language spoken by the majority of the population in a country, such as English in the USA. A language spoken by a group of people who form a minority within a country is known as a **minority language**, such as Italian and Spanish in the USA.
> see also COMMUNITY LANGUAGE, NATIONAL LANGUAGE

Mancova *n*
> an abbreviation for MULTIVARIATE ANALYSIS OF COVARIANCE

manner of articulation *n*
> the way in which a speech sound is produced by the speech organs. There are different ways of producing a speech sound. With CONSONANTS the airstream may be:
> a stopped and released suddenly (a stop), e.g. /t/
> b allowed to escape with friction (a fricative), e.g. /f/
> c stopped and then released slowly with friction (an affricate), e.g. /dʒ/ as in /dʒem/ *gem.*
> The vocal cords may be vibrating (a voiced speech sound) or not (a voiceless speech sound) (see VOICE[2]).
> With vowels, in addition to the position of the tongue in the mouth, the lips may be:
> a rounded, e.g. for /uː/ in /ʃuː/ *shoe*; or
> b spread, e.g. for /iː/ in /miːn/ *mean.*
> see also FRICTIONLESS CONTINUANT, LATERAL, NASAL, PLACE OF ARTICULATION

Manova *n*
> an abbreviation for MULTIVARIATE ANALYSIS OF VARIANCE

manualist *n*
> see SIGN LANGUAGE

manual method *n*
> a method for teaching the hearing impaired, based on the use of sign-language. There are many different manual communication systems; some, such as American Sign Language (A.S.L.) have their own linguistic rules which do not resemble the grammar of English. Those who are entirely dependent on A.S.L. or similar manual codes may therefore have difficulty

reading, writing, or lip-reading English. Some manual codes such as Signed English or the Pagett-Gorman system are based on English, and learning to read and write English is easier for those who have learned these codes. Those who have learned a manual method of communication normally cannot speak, and therefore have difficulty communicating with those who cannot use their particular sign language.

A third group of manual codes, e.g. Amerind, are based on universal gestural codes.

mapping *n*
see BRAINSTORMING

marginalized voices *n*
the voices of those who are left out of the DOMINANT DISCOURSE. These may include women, immigrants, and minority language speakers.

markedness theory *n*
the theory that within and across languages, certain linguistic elements can be seen as **unmarked**, i.e. simple, core, or prototypical, while others are seen as **marked**, i.e. complex, peripheral, or exceptional. Some markedness relations are binary. For example, vowels can be either voiced or voiceless. Voiced vowels are considered unmarked, while voiceless vowels (which occur in fewer languages of the world) are marked. Other markedness relations are hierarchical. For example, the NOUN PHRASE ACCESSIBILITY HIERARCHY refers to a range of relative clause structures that can be ordered from least to most marked. Markedness has sometimes been invoked as a predictor of acquisition order or direction of difficulty in second and foreign language learning. In this view, if the target language contains structures that are marked, these will be difficult to learn. However, if the target language structures are unmarked they will cause little or no difficulty, even if they do not exist in the learner's native language. This has been called the **markedness differential hypothesis**.

marker *n*
see SPEECH MARKER

masculine *adj*
see GENDER[2]

mash-up *n*
a combination of data from multiple web services, for example, a combination of an audio or video clip with an exercise and additional text.

mass noun *n*

see COUNTABLE NOUN

mastery learning *n*

an individualized and diagnostic approach to teaching in which students proceed with studying and testing at their own rate in order to achieve a prescribed level of success. Mastery learning is based on the idea that all students can master a subject given sufficient time. For example in an ESL reading programme, students might be assigned graded reading passages to read in their own time. Test questions after each passage allow the learner to discover what level of comprehension they reached, and re-read the passage if necessary. They must reach a specific comprehension level before they move on to the next passage.

matched guise technique *n*

(in studies of LANGUAGE ATTITUDES) the use of recorded voices of people speaking first in one dialect or language and then in another; that is, in two "guises". For example, BILINGUAL French Canadians may first speak in French and then in English. The recordings are played to listeners who do not know that the two samples of speech are from the same person and who judge the two guises of the same speaker as though they were judging two separate speakers each belonging to a different ethnic or national group. The reactions of the listeners to the speakers in one guise are compared to reactions to the other guise to reveal attitudes towards different language or dialect groups, whose members may be considered more or less intelligent, friendly, co-operative, reliable, etc.

matched-subjects design *n*

an experimental design where participants with similar characteristics are first matched into blocks and then participants within each block are randomly assigned to the experimental conditions. For example, when comparing two methods of teaching L2 vocabulary, a researcher wants to make sure that the participants in the study are homogeneous, so that any difference in a vocabulary test between the groups taught with different methods can be attributed to the difference in teaching methods. If one group happened to consist predominantly of L2 learners whose L1 shares many cognates with their L2, it would not be clear whether the difference in the test is due to the treatment (i.e. use of different teaching methods) or not. This problem could have been avoided by first matching participants by their L1 background and then randomly assigning participants within each L1 background block into the two classes using different teaching methods.

matching item *n*

a type of test item or test task that requires test takers to indicate which entries (e.g. words or phrases) on one list are the correct matches for entries on another list.

see also SELECTED-RESPONSE ITEM

materials *n*

in language teaching, anything which can be used by teachers or learners to facilitate the learning of a language. Materials may be linguistic, visual, auditory, or kinesthetic, and they may be presented in print, audio or video form, on CD-ROMS, on the Internet or through live performance or display.

materials adaptation *n*

see ADAPTATION

materials evaluation *n*

in language teaching, the process of measuring the value and effectiveness of learning materials.

mathematical linguistics *n*

a branch of linguistics which makes use of statistical and mathematical methods to study the linguistic structure of written or spoken texts. This includes the study of the frequency of occurrence of linguistic items (see FREQUENCY COUNT) and the study of literary style.

see also COMPUTATIONAL LINGUISTICS

matrix (plural matrices) *n*

a table consisting of rows and columns to display data or results of an analysis. For an example, see the matrix used in this dictionary under the entry for IMPLICATIONAL SCALING.

maturation *n*

see INTERNAL VALIDITY

maximal projection *n*

see PROJECTION (PRINCIPLE)

mean *n*

the arithmetic average of a set of scores. The mean is the sum of all the scores divided by the total number of items. The mean is the most commonly used and most widely applicable measure of the CENTRAL TENDENCY of a distribution.

see also MEDIAN, MODE

meaning *n*

(in linguistics) what a language expresses about the world we live in or any possible or imaginary world.

The study of meaning is called SEMANTICS. Semantics is usually concerned with the analysis of the meaning of words, phrases, or sentences (see CONNOTATION, DENOTATION, LEXICAL FIELD, SEMANTIC FEATURE) and sometimes with the meaning of utterances in discourse (see DISCOURSE ANALYSIS) or the meaning of a whole text.

see also FUNCTIONS OF LANGUAGE[1,2] PRAGMATICS

meaningful drill *n*

in language teaching and in particular AUDIOLINGUALISM, a distinction between different types of DRILLS is sometimes made according to the degree of control the drill makes over the response produced by the student. A **mechanical drill** is one where there is complete control over the student's response, and where comprehension is not required in order to produce a correct response. For example:

Teacher	Student
book	*Give me the book.*
ladle	*Give me the ladle.*

A meaningful drill is one in which there is still control over the response, but understanding is required so that the student produces a correct response. For example:

Teacher reads a sentence	Student chooses a response
I'm hot.	*I'll get you something to eat.*
I'm cold.	*I'll turn on the air conditioning.*
I'm thirsty.	*I'll get you something to drink.*
I'm hungry.	*I'll turn on the heater.*

A **communicative drill** is one in which the type of response is controlled but the student provides his or her own content or information. For example in practising the past tense, the teacher may ask a series of questions:

Teacher	Student completes cue
What time did you get up on Sunday?	*I got up _____*
What did you have for breakfast?	*I had _____*
What did you do after breakfast?	*I _____*

Drills, however, are less commonly used in language teaching today and have been replaced by more communicative teaching strategies.

meaningful learning *n*
(in COGNITIVE PSYCHOLOGY) learning in which learned items become part of a person's mental system of concepts and thought processes. The psychologist Ausubel contrasted meaningful learning with ROTE LEARNING and other types of learning in which learned items are not integrated into existing mental structures.

meaning units *n*
segments or chunks of spoken discourse which serve listeners as signals of organization and are characterized by pitch change on the most important syllable. These are also referred to as **sense groups, tone units,** or **intonation groups.**

mean length of utterance *n*
also **MLU**
(in LANGUAGE ACQUISITION research) a measure of the linguistic complexity of children's utterances, especially during the early stages of first language learning. It is measured by counting the average length of the utterances a child produces, using the MORPHEME rather than the word as the unit of measurement. As a simple countable measure of grammatical development the MLU has been found to be a more reliable basis for comparing children's language development than the age of the children. MLU is generally not considered to be a good index of development in SECOND LANGUAGE LEARNING.

meanscore *n*
another term for MEAN

means–ends model *n*
an approach to CURRICULUM DEVELOPMENT or to teaching in which a distinction is made between ends (e.g. objectives and content) and means (i.e. the process of instruction) and which generally employs a cycle of planning activities involving:
a identification of learners' need
b specification of goals
c formulation of objectives
d selection of content
e organization of content

    f selection of learning experiences
    g evaluation of learning.

mean utterance length *n*
    another term for MEAN LENGTH OF UTTERANCE

measurement error *n*
    another term for ERROR OF MEASUREMENT

mechanical drill *n*
    see MEANINGFUL DRILL

mechanical translation *n*
    another term for MACHINE TRANSLATION

mechanics *n*
    (in composition) those aspects of writing such as spelling, use of apostrophes, hyphens, capitals, abbreviations and numbers, which are often dealt with in the revision or editing stages of writing (see COMPOSING PROCESSES). These may be compared with more global or higher level dimensions of writing, such as organization, COHERENCE, or rhetorical structure.
    see SCHEME

media *n*
    a general term for television, radio and newspapers considered as a whole and as ways of entertaining or spreading news or information to a large number of people. In language teaching, teaching materials which involve the use of different kinds of media such as visual and printed media, are sometimes known as **multi media** or **mixed media**.

medial *adj*
    occurring in the middle of a linguistic unit.
    For example, in English the /ɪ/ in /pɪt/ pit is in a medial position in the word.
    see also INITIAL, FINAL

median *n*
    the value of the middle item or score when the scores in a sample are arranged in order from lowest to highest. The median is therefore the score that divides the sample into two equal parts. It is the most appropriate measure of the CENTRAL TENDENCY for data arranged in an "ordinal scale" or a "rank scale" (see SCALE).
    see also MEAN, MODE

media resources *n*

in teaching, all resources involved in teaching and learning including technology, audio and video resources, computers, multi-media language labs, projectors, films, and video.

medium *n*

the means by which a message is conveyed from one person to another. For example, an invitation to a party can be made in writing or in speech. The plural of *medium* is *media* or *mediums*.
see also MESSAGE, DECODING, ENCODING

medium of instruction *n*

the language used in education. In many countries, the medium of instruction is the STANDARD VARIETY of the main or NATIONAL LANGUAGE of the country, e.g. French in France. In some countries, the medium of instruction may be different in various parts of the country, as in Belgium where both French and Dutch are used. In MULTILINGUAL countries or regions there may be a choice, or there may be schools in which some subjects are taught in one language and other subjects in another. The plural of *medium of instruction* is *media of instruction* or *mediums of instruction*.
see also BILINGUAL EDUCATION

melting pot *n*

used mainly in the US to describe how a variety of immigrant ethnic groups have blended together and gradually assimilated into mainstream American culture. The melting pot view of immigration is sometimes used as an argument against BILINGUAL EDUCATION and in favour of the ENGLISH ONLY movement.

membershipping *n* **membership** *v*

classifying a person as a member of a group or category, e.g. shop assistant, student, or residents of a particular town. Once a category has been assigned to a person, conversation with that person may be affected.
For example, a visitor to a town may ask a passer-by whom he or she, correctly or incorrectly, memberships as a local resident: *Could you please tell me how to get to the station?* Wrong membershipping may result in misunderstanding or may cause annoyance, e.g. if a customer in a department store is wrongly membershipped as a shop assistant.
In speaking, membershipping involves the ability to display credibility and competence through familiarity or exploitation of discourse conventions typically used in a group or speech community, e.g. such as the ability to use the technical terms and concepts used by linguists or language teachers.

memorizing *n* **memorize** *v* **memorization** *n*

the process of establishing information, etc., in memory. The term "memorizing" usually refers to conscious processes. Memorizing may involve ROTE LEARNING, practice, ASSOCIATIVE LEARNING, etc.

memory *n*

the mental capacity to store information, either for short or long periods. Two different types of memory are often distinguished:

a **Short-term memory** refers to that part of the memory where information which is received is stored for short periods of time while it is being analyzed and interpreted. **Working memory** is a more contemporary term for short-term memory which conceptualizes memory not as a passive system for temporary storage but an active system for temporarily storing and manipulating information needed in the execution of complex cognitive tasks (e.g. learning, reasoning, and comprehension). In the influential model of Baddeley, working memory consists of two storage systems, the **articulatory loop** for the storage of verbal information and the **visuospatial sketchpad** for the storage of visual information, plus a **central executive**, a very active system responsible for the selection, initiation, and termination of processing routines (e.g. encoding, storing, and retrieving).

b **Long-term memory** is that part of the memory system where information is stored more permanently. Information in long-term memory may not be stored in the same form in which it is received. For example, a listener may hear sentence A below, and be able to repeat it accurately immediately after hearing it. The listener uses short-term memory to do this. On trying to remember the sentence a few days later the listener may produce sentence B, using information in long-term memory which is in a different form from the original message.

a *The car the doctor parked by the side of the road was struck by a passing bus.*

b *The doctor's car was hit by a bus.*

see also EPISODIC MEMORY, IMPLICIT MEMORY, RELEARNING

mentalism *n* **mentalist** *adj*

the theory that a human being possesses a mind which has consciousness, ideas, etc., and that the mind can influence the behaviour of the body.
see also BEHAVIOURISM, EPIPHENOMENALISM, INNATIST HYPOTHESIS

mental lexicon *n*

a person's mental store of words, their meanings and associations.
see LEXICON

mentoring *v*

in teacher development, a process by which a MENTOR TEACHER provides one-to-one support for a teacher during his or her initial teaching experience. The role of the mentor teacher usually involves modelling good teaching practice, assisting the novice teacher's integration and acceptance into a specific teaching context and community, supporting the teacher through times of difficulty, and facilitating the teacher's understanding and learning of the processes of teaching.

mentor teacher *n*

an experienced teacher in a school who works with a student teacher during teaching practice and gives guidance and feedback to the student teacher.

also **co-operating teacher**

mesolect *n*

see POST CREOLE CONTINUUM, SPEECH CONTINUUM

message *n*

what is conveyed in speech or writing from one person to one or more other people. The message may not always be stated in verbal form but can be conveyed by other means, e.g. wink, gestures. A distinction can be made between message form and message content. In a spoken request, for example, the message form is how the request is made (e.g. type of sentence structure, use or non-use of courtesy words, type of intonation) and the message content is what is actually requested (e.g. the loan of some money).

see also DECODING, ENCODING, KEY[1]

meta-analysis *n*

also **quantitative research synthesis**

a collection of statistical procedures for a quantitative review and summary of the results of statistical analyses from a group of related studies that investigate the same question in a research domain to discern overall patterns and draw general conclusions. Generally, a meta-analyst, once having identified a set of research questions to investigate in a research domain (e.g. effectiveness of Spanish-English bilingual programmes on Spanish L1 children's academic performance in L2 English), (a) searches for relevant studies, whether published or unpublished; (b) decides which studies to include in a meta-analysis, using a set of selection criteria; (c) codes each study for study characteristics; (d) calculates and then averages effect sizes from the studies; and (e) investigates relationships between study characteristics and effect sizes statistically. Meta-analysis can be contrasted with traditional narrative literature reviews in that the latter combine results from different studies qualitatively.

see also EFFECT SIZE

metacognitive instruction *n*

teaching that seeks to help learners take a more active part in their own learning by drawing attention to the cognitive processes learners employ in learning tasks and actively monitoring and regulating these processes in order to better facilitate learning. Metacognitive instruction seeks to train learners directly to employ relevant strategies in carrying out learning tasks as well as help them increase their metacognitive knowledge.

metacognitive knowledge *n*

also **metacognition** *n*

(in cognition and learning) knowledge of the mental processes which are involved in different kinds of learning. Learners are said to be capable of becoming aware of their own mental processes. This includes recognizing which kinds of learning tasks cause difficulty, which approaches to remembering information work better than others, and how to solve different kinds of problems. Metacognitive knowledge is thought to influence the kinds of learning strategies learners choose.

see also LEARNING STRATEGY, METACOGNITIVE STRATEGY

metacognitive strategy *n*

a category of LEARNING STRATEGY which involves thinking about the mental processes used in the learning process, monitoring learning while it is taking place, and evaluating learning after it has occurred. For example, metacognitive strategies a learner may use when he or she is beginning to learn a new language include:

1 planning ways of remembering new words encountered in conversations with native speakers
2 deciding which approaches to working out grammatical rules are more effective
3 evaluating his or her own progress and making decisions about what to concentrate on in the future.

meta-language *n*

the language used to analyze or describe a language. For example, the sentence: *In English, the phoneme /b/ is a voiced bilabial stop* is in meta-language. It explains that the b-sound in English is made with vibration of the vocal cords and with the two lips stopping the airstream from the lungs.

metalinguistic knowledge *n*

(in language learning) knowledge of the forms, structure and other aspects of a language, which a learner arrives at through reflecting on and analyzing the language. In linguistic analysis, researchers sometimes make use of a native speaker's metalinguistic knowledge as one source of information about the language.

metaphor *n*

in traditional literary criticism, a metaphor is distinguished from a **simile**. While a simile expresses that two things are similar (*The man is as strong as a lion*), a metaphor implies that the two are equivalent (*The man is a lion*). Metaphors are important means by which words carry both semantic and cultural meanings, and each language has its own metaphors that have accumulated over time and that must be learned by second and foreign language learners.

In COGNITIVE LINGUISTICS, metaphors are not mere poetic or rhetorical embellishments, but are considered an important part of everyday speech. The notion of **conceptual metaphor** refers to the understanding of one range of concepts (the target domain) in terms of another (the source domain), for example, understanding time in terms of space (*in the days ahead of us, the coming month, as we approach the end of the year*), the life-is-a-journey metaphor (with a destination, paths chosen and not chosen, obstacles to be overcome), or the argument-is-war metaphor (arguments can be attacked, defended, won, or lost). The question of whether such metaphors actually affect the ways in which we perceive, think, and act, a version of the LINGUISTIC RELATIVITY hypothesis, is the topic of much controversy.

In SYSTEMIC-FUNCTIONAL LINGUISTICS, **grammatical metaphor**, refers to the encoding of meanings in grammatically incongruous ways. For example, while events and processes are naturally expressed by verbs (e.g. *develop*, *decide*) and attributes by adjectives (e.g. *effective*), all of these can be remapped as nouns (*development*, *decision*, *effectiveness*) Such grammatical metaphors are usually created through the process of DERIVATION. Grammatical metaphors occur in all varieties of English (and other languages), but are especially common in scientific and technical writing and are recognized as a distinctive marker of academic discourse.

see also FIGURE OF SPEECH

metaphor analysis *n*

the study of metaphors used by teachers, learners and others as a way of identifying the subconscious beliefs and attitudes that underlie consciously held opinions. Metaphors that are used to describe textbooks, teachers and learners, for example, provide a way of making sense of experience for the individual and for others. For example:

A textbook is like oil in cooking – a useful basic ingredient. (textbook metaphor)

A teacher is like the conductor of an orchestra – he or she has to make sure that all the players in the class are in harmony. (teacher metaphor)

metathesis *n* **metathesize** *v*

change in the order of two sounds in a word, e.g. /flɪm/ for /fɪlm/ film. Metathesis sometimes occurs in the speech of language learners but it may also occur with native speakers. When a metathesized form becomes commonly and regularly used by most native speakers of a language, it may lead to a change in the word. For example, Modern English *bird* developed by metathesis from Old English *brid* "young bird".

method *n*

(in language teaching) a way of teaching a language which is based on systematic principles and procedures, i.e. which is an application of views on how a language is best taught and learned and a particular theory of language and of language learning.

Different methods of language teaching such as the DIRECT METHOD, the AUDIOLINGUAL METHOD, TOTAL PHYSICAL RESPONSE result from different views of:

a the nature of language

b the nature of second language learning

c goals and OBJECTIVES in teaching

d the type of SYLLABUS to use

e the role of teachers, learners, and instructional materials

f the activities, techniques and procedures to use.

see also APPROACH

methodology *n*

1 (in language teaching) the study of the practices and procedures used in teaching, and the principles and beliefs that underlie them.

Methodology includes:

a study of the nature of LANGUAGE SKILLS (e.g. reading, writing, speaking, listening) and procedures for teaching them

b study of the preparation of LESSON PLANS, materials, and textbooks for teaching language skills

c the evaluation and comparison of language teaching METHOD (e.g. the audiolingual method).

2 such practices, procedures, beliefs themselves. One can for example criticize or praise the methodology of a particular language course.

see also CURRICULUM, SYLLABUS

3 (in research) the procedures used in carrying out an investigation, including the methods used to collect and analyze data.

see also EXPERIMENTAL METHOD, SCIENTIFIC METHOD

methods of development *n*

(in composition) the ways in which a paragraph or extended piece of writing is developed. A number of methods of development are often used in composing in English, either individually, or sometimes within other methods of development. These are:

1 **Process Method**: the writer describes something by breaking a complex whole down into its different parts and describing them in order.

2 **Definition Method**: the writer defines a term or object by identifying it within a general class and then distinguishing it from all other members of the class.

3 **Classification Method**: the writer groups people, things or ideas according to some principle order, in this way both classifying and explaining them.

4 **Comparison and Contrast Method**: the writer describes the similarities or differences between two sets of items.

5 **Cause–Effect Method**: the writer describes why things are the way they are or why something happened, by describing causes and effects. A cause–effect paragraph is usually developed by inductive reasoning.

metonymy *n*

see FIGURE OF SPEECH

metrical phonology *n*

a cover term for several non-linear theories of STRESS. Instead of seeing stress as a property of individual segments (vowels), metrical phonology views stress as a relational property between constituents expressed in metrical trees.

micro-skills *n*

also **enabling skills, part skills**

(in language teaching) a term sometimes used to refer to the individual processes and abilities which are used in carrying out a complex activity.

For example, among the micro-skills used in listening to a lecture are: identifying the purpose and scope of the lecture; identifying the role of conjunctions, etc., in signalling relationships between different parts of the lecture; recognizing the functions of PITCH and INTONATION. For the purposes of SYLLABUS DESIGN, the four **macroskills** of reading, writing, speaking, and listening may be further analyzed into different microskills.

see also LANGUAGE SKILLS

micro-sociolinguistics *n*

see SOCIOLINGUISTICS

microteaching *n*

a technique used in the training of teachers, in which different teaching skills are practised under carefully controlled conditions. It is based on the idea that teaching is a complex set of activities which can be broken down into different skills. These skills can be practised individually, and later combined with others. Usually in microteaching, one trainee teacher teaches a part of a lesson to a small group of his or her classmates. The lesson may be recorded on tape or videotape and later discussed in individual or group tutorials. Each session generally focuses on a specific teaching task. Microteaching thus involves a scaling-down of teaching because class size, lesson length, and teaching complexity are all reduced.

mid vowel *n*

see VOWEL

migrant education *n*

education programmes for either newly arrived immigrants or for agricultural workers and their families and other shifting populations, depending on how the term "migrant" is defined in a particular context.

mim-mem method *n*

a term for the AUDIOLINGUAL METHOD, because the method uses exercises such as pattern practice (see DRILL) and dialogues which make use of the *mim*icry (imitation) and *mem*orization of material presented as a model.

mind map *n*

also **word maps, spidergrams**

a technique for organizing new vocabulary or other learning content, that involves organizing learning items in a way that shows groupings or relationships between words. A key word may serve as a link between related words and concepts, expressed diagrammatically. Mind maps are sometimes used as part of the planning stage in composition classes.

mingle *n, v*

a classroom activity in which learners walk around the classroom and talk to other learners to complete a task.

minimal-distance principle *n*

the principle that in English, a COMPLEMENT or a NON-FINITE VERB refers to the noun phrase which is closest to it (i.e. which is minimally distant from it). For example in the following sentences:

John wants Mary to study.

Penny made the children happy.

the non-finite verb to study refers to *Mary* (not *John*) and the complement *happy* to *the children* (not *Penny*).

Some sentences do not follow the principle, however. For example, in:

John promised Mary to wash the clothes.

the non-finite verb phrase to *wash the clothes* refers to *John* (not *Mary*). Such sentences are believed to cause comprehension problems for children learning English.

minimalism *n*

also **minimalist approach, minimalist programme**

a theory of grammar introduced by Chomsky in 1995 as an advance on GOVERNMENT/BINDING THEORY while remaining within the general paradigm of the principle and parameters model of UNIVERSAL GRAMMAR. The cornerstone of the theory is that grammars should make use of the minimal theoretical apparatus necessary to provide a characterization of linguistic phenomena that meets the criterion of DESCRIPTIVE ADEQUACY. This goal is motivated in part by the desire to minimize the acquisition burden faced by children and account for the fact that children will acquire any language they are exposed to.

minimalist approach *n*

see MINIMALISM

minimalist programme *n*

see MINIMALISM

minimal pair *n*

two words in a language which differ from each other by only one distinctive sound (one PHONEME) and which also differ in meaning. For example, the English words *bear* and *pear* are a minimal pair as they differ in meaning and in their initial phonemes /b/ and /p/.

The term "minimal pair" is also sometimes used of any two pieces of language that are identical except for a specific feature or group of related features.

For example, the sentences:

The boy is here.
The boys are here.

may be called a minimal pair because they are the same except for the contrast between singular and plural expressed in both noun and verb.

minimal pair drill *n*

a DRILL in which MINIMAL PAIRS are practised together, especially in order to help students to learn to distinguish a sound contrast. For example if a teacher wanted to practise the contrast between /b/ and /p/, the teacher could (a) explain how the sounds differ; (b) present pairs of words containing the contrast, for listening practice; e.g. *bore – pour*, *big – pig*, *buy – pie*; (c) get the students to show that they know which member of the pair they have heard; (d) get them to pronounce such pairs themselves.

Minimal Terminable Unit *n*

another term for T-UNIT

minority language *n*

see MAJORITY LANGUAGE

minority language group *n*

another term for LANGUAGE MINORITY GROUP

minority students *n*

in countries where English is a first language, often used to refer to students whose first language is a language other than English, for whom special instruction in English may be needed.

miscue *n*

see MISCUE ANALYSIS

miscue analysis *n*

the analysis of errors or unexpected responses which readers make in reading, as part of the study of the nature of the reading process in children learning to read their mother tongue.

Among the different types of miscue which occur are:

a insertion miscue: the adding of a word which is not present in the text (e.g. the child may read *Mr Barnaby was a busy old man* instead of *Mr Barnaby was a busy man*).

   b reversal miscue: the reader reverses the order of words (e.g. the child reads *Mrs Barnaby was a rich kind old lady* instead of *Mrs Barnaby was a kind rich old lady*).

mistake *n*

see ERROR

mitigating devices *n*

a term used for expressions that are used to soften a request or other kind of imposition or make it more indirect, such as "please" in "Please close the door" and "would you" in "Would you close the door."

mixed-ability class *n*

a class containing learners of different ability levels as reflected in differences in LANGUAGE APTITUDE, motivation, or learning styles. While most classes contain learners of mixed abilities, large differences in abilities may affect classroom dynamics and classroom management. A mixed-ability class is different from a *mixed-level class* – one which contains learners with different levels of language proficiency.

mixed level class *n*

see MIXED-ABILITY CLASS

MLA *n*

an abbreviation for Modern Language Association. A professional organization for foreign language teachers in the USA.

MLAT *n*

an abbreviation for the Modern Language Aptitude Test, a test of language aptitude.

M-learning *n*

also **mobile learning**

learning that takes place across locations or that makes use of learning opportunities made available by portable technologies. M-learning includes the use of handheld dictionaries and other portable devices for language learning, handheld computers, and the use of mobile devices in the classroom to facilitate group collaboration among students.

MLU[1] *n*

an abbreviation for MEAN LENGTH OF UTTERANCE

MLU²

an abbreviation for Multi-Word Lexical Unit, a lexeme consisting of more than one word. For example, compound nouns and phrasal verbs are MLUs.

mobile language learning *n*

language learning via mobile telephones and other means of wireless communication.

modal *n*

also **modal verb, modal auxiliary**

any of the AUXILIARY VERBS which indicate attitudes of the speaker/writer towards the state or event expressed by another verb, i.e. which indicate different types of **modality**. The following are modal verbs in English:

may, might, can, could, must, have (got) to, will, would, shall, should

Modal meanings are shown in the following examples; all are in contrast to simple assertion:

I may be wrong. (*may* = possibility)
That will be Tom at the door. (*will* = prediction)
You can smoke here. (*can* = permission)
I can play the piano. (*can* = ability)

Modality can be expressed in other ways, too:

I may be wrong. = Perhaps I'm wrong.

modality *n*

see MODAL

mode *n*

the most frequently occurring score or scores in a sample. It is a measure of the central tendency of a distribution. For example, in the following test scores, the mode is equal to 20.

score	number of students with the score
10	2
20	10
30	3
40	4
50	3

A frequency distribution with two modes is known as a **bimodal distribution,** as when the two most frequently occurring scores are 60 and 40. The

model

mode(s) of a distribution can be pictured graphically as the "peaks" in the distribution. A NORMAL DISTRIBUTION has only one peak. The following shows a bimodal distribution:

see also MEAN, MEDIAN

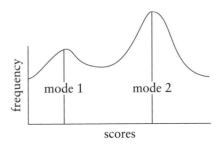

model *n*

(in language teaching) someone or something which is used as a standard or goal for the learner, e.g. the pronunciation of an educated native speaker.

see also MODELLING

modelling[1] *n*

providing a model (e.g. a sentence, a question) as an example for someone learning a language.

In SECOND LANGUAGE and FOREIGN LANGUAGE learning, some teaching methods emphasize the need for teachers to provide accurate models for learners to imitate, for example the AUDIO-LINGUAL METHOD. In first language learning, parents sometimes provide correct sentences for children to repeat, and this may be referred to as modelling. The effect of modelling on children's language development has been compared with that of **expansion** and **prompting**.

In expansion the parent repeats part of what the child has said, but expands it. The expansion usually contains grammatical words which the child did not use. This is thought to be one of the ways children develop their knowledge of the rules of a language. For example:

Child: *Doggy sleeping.*

Parent: *Yes, the doggy is sleeping.*

Prompting refers to stating a sentence in a different way. For example:

Parent: *What do you want?*

Child: (no answer)

Parent: *You want what?*

By presenting the question in two different forms the parent may assist the child in understanding the structure of questions and other language items.

modelling[2]

a learning process in which a person observes someone's behaviour and then consciously or unconsciously attempts to imitate that behaviour. For example, many of the teaching practices a new teacher uses may have been modelled from teachers he or she has observed. Students may also model behaviours from their teachers. For example, if a student sees that the teacher is not punctual and is poorly organized, he or she may decide that punctuality and organization are not important and thus not attempt to develop these qualities.

mode of discourse *n*

the medium in which language is used between two or more people in a particular situation, such as written, spoken, face to face, telephone, or via the Internet.

modernism *n*

the rejection of tradition and authority in favour of reason, science, and objectivity, closely associated with "Western" thought and the scientific method.

From the point of view of POSTMODERNISM, modernism is not "contemporary", but "out of date".

see POSITIVISM

modern language *n*

in foreign language teaching this term is sometimes used to refer to a foreign language which is an important language today such as French or Italian, as compared to an ancient language such as Latin or ancient Greek.

Modern Language Aptitude Test *n*

also **MLAT**

see LANGUAGE APTITUDE TEST

modes of writing *n*

non-creative forms of writing, particularly essay writing, have traditionally been classified into four types:

1 **Descriptive writing** provides a verbal picture or account of a person, place or thing.

2 **Narrative writing** reports an event or tells the story of something that happened.

3 **Expository writing** provides information about and explains a particular subject. Patterns of development within expository writing include giving *examples*, describing a *process* of doing or making something, analyzing

causes and effects, *comparing and/or contrasting*, *defining* a term or concept, and *dividing* something into parts or *classifying* it into categories.

4 **Argumentative writing** attempts to support a controversial point or defend a position on which there is a difference of opinion. ESL writing programmes have often been based on the assumption that novice writers should begin with the simplest mode – the descriptive essay – and gradually move to learning the most difficult – the argumentative one.

modification *n*

a type of COMMUNICATION STRATEGY in which a speaker simplifies or elaborates a normal discourse pattern in order to make a message more accessible to a listener.

modified input *n*

discourse addressed to second language learners and young children that has been adapted or "simplified" to make comprehension easier, such as by using comprehension checks, clarification requests and self-repetitions.

modified speech *n*

a term used by linguists to describe speech which is deliberately changed in an attempt to make it sound more educated or refined. The change is usually temporary and the speaker lapses back to his or her normal speech pattern.

modifier *n* modification *n* modify *v*

a word or group of words which gives further information about ("modifies") another word or group of words (the HEAD).
Modification may occur in a NOUN PHRASE[1], a VERB PHRASE, an ADJECTIVAL PHRASE, etc.

a Modifiers before the head are called **premodifiers**, for example *expensive* in *this expensive camera*.

b Modifiers after the head are called **postmodifiers**, for example *with a stumpy tail* in *The cat with a stumpy tail*.

Halliday restricts the term "modifier" to premodifiers and calls postmodifiers QUALIFIERS.

In earlier grammars, the term "modifier" referred only to words, phrases, or clauses which modified verbs, adjectives, or other adverbials, but not to those which modified nouns.

modularity hypothesis *n*

see MODULE[2]

modularity principle *n*
    see MODULE²

module¹ *n*
    an instructional unit in a course that is planned as a self-contained and inde-
    pendent learning sequence with its own objectives. For example a 120 hour
    language course might be divided into four modules of 30 hours each.
    Assessment is carried out at the end of each module. The use of modules is
    said to allow for flexible organization of a course and can give learners a
    sense of achievement because objectives are more immediate and specific.
    see UNIT

module² *n*
    an autonomous component of a larger system.
    For example, a language contains a phonological module.
    Language itself can also be seen as a module. In this view, sometimes
    referred to as the **modularity principle** or **modularity hypothesis**, the lan-
    guage faculty is considered to be autonomous with respect to such other
    human systems as the perceptual system and general cognition. In this view,
    neither the form of language nor the process through which it is acquired is
    influenced by these systems.

monitor hypothesis *n*
    also **monitor model of second language development**
    a theory proposed by Krashen which distinguishes two distinct processes in
    second and foreign language development and use. One, called "acquisi-
    tion", is said to be a subconscious process which leads to the development
    of "competence" and is not dependent on the teaching of grammatical
    rules. The second process, called "learning" refers to the conscious study
    and knowledge of grammatical rules. In producing utterances, learners
    initially use their acquired system of rules. Learning and learned rules have
    only one function: to serve as a monitor or editor of utterances initiated by
    the acquired system, and learning cannot lead to acquisition.
    see also INPUT HYPOTHESIS

monitoring¹ *n* **monitor** *v*
    listening to one's own UTTERANCES to compare what was said with what
    was intended, and to make corrections if necessary. People generally try to
    speak fluently (see FLUENCY) and appropriately (see APPROPRIATENESS), and
    try to make themselves understood. The interjections and self-corrections
    that speakers make while talking show that monitoring is taking place, and
    are usually for the purposes of making meaning clearer. For example:

He is, <u>well</u>, rather difficult.
Can I have, <u>say</u>, a glass of beer.
They own, <u>I mean rent</u>, a lovely house.
see also AUDITORY FEEDBACK, PAUSING

monitoring[2] *n*

in teaching, the observing and making assessments of what is happening in the classroom during learning activities.

monolingual *n, adj* monolingualism *n*

1 a person who knows and uses only one language.
2 a person who has an active knowledge of only one language, though perhaps a passive knowledge of others.
see also ACTIVE/PASSIVE LANGUAGE KNOWLEDGE, BILINGUAL, MULTI-LINGUAL

monolingual dictionary *n*

a dictionary in which head words, definitions and examples are given in the target language.
see BILINGUAL DICTIONARY

monophthong *n*

a vowel in which there is no appreciable change in quality during a syllable, as in English /a/ in *father*. The "long" tense vowels of some languages, such as French, are monophthongs (e.g. French *beau* /boː/, "beautiful") in comparison to the comparable English vowel, which exhibits noticeable diphthongization in its articulation (e.g. *boat* /bowt/). This is what is meant by the statement that French has **pure vowels**.
see DIPHTHONG

monosyllabic *adj* monosyllable *n*

consisting of one SYLLABLE, e.g. the English word *cow*.
see also DISYLLABIC

Montague grammar *n*

a cover term for the kind of syntactic and semantic work associated with the philosopher Richard Montague, who argued that theories of meaning for natural languages and for formal languages (such as LOGIC) should be based on the same principles, especially the COMPOSITIONALITY PRINCIPLE. For example, the sentences of English are not interpreted directly but are translated into a **categorial grammar**, a syntactic counterpart to the expressions of a logical language.

MOO *n*

in COMPUTER ASSISTED LANGUAGE LEARNING, an acronym for multi-user domain, object-orientated, a graphic- or text-based multi-user environment where language learners can chat in real time and perform a variety of simulations via the Internet.

mood *n*

a set of contrasts which are often shown by the form of the verb and which express the speaker's or writer's attitude to what is said or written.

Three moods have often been distinguished:

1 **Indicative** mood: the form of the verb used in DECLARATIVE SENTENCES or QUESTIONS. For example:

She sat down.

Are you coming?

2 **Imperative** mood: the form of the verb in imperative sentences. For example:

Be quiet!

Put it on the table!

In English, imperatives do not have tense or perfect aspect (see aspect) but they may be used in the progressive aspect. For example:

Be waiting for me at five.

3 **Subjunctive** mood: the form of the verb often used to express uncertainty, wishes, desires, etc. In contrast to the indicative mood, the subjunctive usually refers to non-factual or hypothetical situations. In English, little use of the subjunctive forms remains. The only remaining forms are:

a *be* (present subjunctive), were (past subjunctive) of *be*

b the stem form, e.g. *have*, *come*, *sing* of other verbs (present subjunctive only).

The use of the subjunctive form is still sometimes found in:

a *that* clauses after certain verbs. For example:

It is required that she be present.

I demand that he come at once.

b past subjunctive of *be* in *if* clauses. For example:

If I were you, I'd go there.

c in some fixed expressions. For example:

So be it.

Moodle *n*

see LEARNING MANAGEMENT SYSTEM

morpheme *n* **morphemic** *adj*

the smallest meaningful unit in a language. A morpheme cannot be divided without altering or destroying its meaning. For example, the English word *kind* is a morpheme. If the *d* is removed, it changes to kin, which has a different meaning. Some words consist of one morpheme, e.g. *kind*, others of more than one. For example, the English word *unkindness* consists of three morphemes: the STEM[1] kind, the negative prefix *un-*, and the noun-forming suffix *-ness*. Morphemes can have grammatical functions. For example, in English the -s in *she talks* is a **grammatical morpheme** which shows that the verb is the third-person singular present-tense form.

see also AFFIX, ALLOMORPH, BOUND FORM, COMBINING FORM

morpheme boundary *n*

the boundary between two MORPHEMES.

For example, in *kindness* there is a clear morpheme boundary between the STEM[1] kind and the suffix *-ness*. On the other hand, in the adverb *doubly* (from *double* + -ly) it is hard to establish the boundary. Does the l go with *double*, with *-ly*, or with both?

see also AFFIX, COMBINING FORM

morphology *n* morphological *adj*

1 the study of morphemes and their different forms (allomorphs), and the way they combine in word formation. For example, the English word unfriendly is formed from friend, the adjective-forming suffix -ly and the negative prefix un-.

2 a morphemic system: in this sense, one can speak of "comparing the morphology of English with the morphology of German".

see also AFFIX, COMBINING FORM

morphophonemic orthography *n*

an ALPHABETIC WRITING SYSTEM in which knowledge of how different forms of a word are pronounced is needed to read perfectly. For example, one has to know English to know that the "ea" of the present tense form *read* is pronounced with a high front tense vowel (the same as in *reed*) while the past tense form *read* is pronounced with a mid front lax vowel (the same as in *red*).

morphophonemic rules *n*

rules that specify the pronunciation of morphemes. A morpheme may have more than one pronunciation determined by such rules. For example, the plural and possessive morphemes of English are regularly pronounced /Iz/, /s/, or /z/, depending on whether the stem to which it is attached ends in a SIBILANT, VOICELESS STOP, or other sound. Similarly, the regular past tense ending "-ed" is pronounced /ɪd/, /t/, or /d/, depending on whether the stem to which it is attached ends in an ALVEOLAR STOP, voiceless consonant, or other sound.

morphophonemics *n*

variation in the form of MORPHEMES because of PHONETIC factors, or the study of this variation.

morphosyntax *n* **morphosyntactic** *adj*

an analysis of language which uses criteria from both morphology, the combining of morphemes to form words, and syntax (see SYNTAX[1]), the structuring and functioning of words in sentences.

For example, in English, the plural morpheme /s/ is added to nouns to show that more than one item is being discussed:

Those pears are pretty expensive, aren't they?

The <u>s</u>, <u>ed</u>, and <u>ing</u> of *lives*, *lived*, and *living*, are all morphemes but, at the same time, they have meanings beyond the word they are attached to.

We can really say that their meaning only becomes apparent when they are used in a sentence, e.g.

Peter lives in Paris.

Anita lived in Paris a couple of years ago.

Is she still living in Paris?

All these morphemes can be referred to as inflectional morphemes (see INFLECTION) and in order to discuss them, criteria both from morphology and syntax (**morphosyntactic** criteria) have to be used.

Other inflectional morphemes would be the case markers in some languages (see CASE[1]) which show whether a noun phrase is used as the subject or the object of a sentence, and morpheme endings on adjectives to show comparison, e.g.

These vegetables are fresh<u>er</u> than those at the other stall.

motherese *n*

another term for CARETAKER SPEECH

mother talk *n*

another term for CARETAKER SPEECH

mother tongue *n*

(usually) a FIRST LANGUAGE which is acquired at home.

motivation *n*

in general, the driving force in any situation that leads to action. In the field of language learning a distinction is sometimes made between an **orientation**, a class of reasons for learning a language, and motivation itself, which refers to a combination of the learner's attitudes, desires, and willingness to expend effort in order to learn the second language. Orientations include an

integrative orientation, characterized by a willingness to be like valued members of the language community, and an instrumental orientation towards more practical concerns such as getting a job or passing an examination. The construct of **integrative motivation** (most prominently associated with R. C. Gardner) therefore includes the integrative orientation, positive attitudes towards both the target language community and the language classroom and a commitment to learn the language (see SOCIO-EDUCATIONAL MODEL). Another widely cited distinction is between **intrinsic motivation**, enjoyment of language learning itself, and **extrinsic motivation**, driven by external factors such as parental pressure, societal expectations, academic requirements, or other sources of rewards and punishments. Other theories of motivation emphasize the balance between the value attached to some activity and one's expectation of success in doing it (see EXPECTANCY-VALUE THEORY), GOAL SETTING, the learner's attributions of success and failure (see ATTRIBUTION THEORY), the role of self-determination and learner autonomy, and the characteristics of effective motivational thinking. Motivation is generally considered to be one of the primary causes of success and failure in second language learning.

motor theory *n*

a theory of SPEECH PERCEPTION that posits that listeners rely on their knowledge of the articulatory movements they make when producing a particular sound in order to decode the acoustic signal produced by that sound.

move *n*

a basic unit in conversation and other kinds of interactive talk and which refers to the function of each UTTERANCE in a conversation. For example;

Moves:

Statement:	*I'm hungry*
Response:	*Me too.*
Offer:	*Shall I order pizza?*
Agree:	*Good idea.*

Different types of moves account for the patterns of conversational structure and the way participants negotiate the exchange of meanings in dialogue. Two-part moves in conversation are described as **adjacency pairs**.

see also SPEECH ACT

move alpha *n*

in SYNTAX, the most general formulation of possible MOVEMENT permitted by a rule. More specific rules include **move NP** and **move wh**, which in turn are more general than specific transformations such as those involved in passivization.

movement rule *n*

in SYNTAX, a rule that plays a role in deriving a surface structure by the reordering of constituents. For example, in the question *What did you see?*, *what* is assumed to be generated initially in the direct object position and then moved to initial position.

see also D-STRUCTURE, LF, S-STRUCTURE

MTMM method *n*

an abbreviation for MULTI-TRAIT MULTI-METHOD METHOD

MUD *n*

in COMPUTER ASSISTED LANGUAGE LEARNING, an acronym for **multi-user domain**. A text-based computer environment where language learners can communicate in real time and perform a variety of simulations via the Internet. In many instances, replaced by the advent of MOOs.

multicultural education *n*

see CULTURAL PLURALISM

multidimensional model *n*

in general, any model of development or learning in which development proceeds along two or more dimensions rather than a single one. Manfred Pienemann has proposed a multidimensional model of SECOND LANGUAGE ACQUISITION in which some linguistic features are acquired according to a natural order defined by psycholinguistic processing constraints, while others depend more on whether a learner orientates more towards correctness and prescriptive norms or towards fluency.

multilingual *n, adj*

a person who knows and uses three or more languages. Usually, a multilingual does not know all the languages equally well. For example, he or she may:

a speak and understand one language best

b be able to write in only one

c use each language in different types of situation (DOMAINS), e.g. one language at home, one at work, and one for shopping

d use each language for different communicative purposes, e.g. one language for talking about science, one for religious purposes, and one for talking about personal feelings.

see also BILINGUAL, MULTILINGUALISM

multilingualism *n*

the use of three or more languages by an individual (see MULTILINGUAL) or by a group of speakers such as the inhabitants of a particular region or a nation. Multilingualism is common in, for example, some countries of West Africa (e.g. Nigeria, Ghana), Malaysia, Singapore, and Israel.

see BILINGUALISM, NATIONAL LANGUAGE

multimedia *n*

1 the use of several different types of media for a single purpose, e.g. as in a video that uses film, audio, sound effects, and graphic images.
2 a collection of computer controlled or computer mediated technologies that enable people to access and use data in a variety of forms: text, sound, and still and moving images.

multi-media laboratory *n*

a room containing computers, video players and other equipment designed to help students learn a foreign language, with or without a teacher. In many institutions the multi-media lab has replaced the traditional LANGUAGE LABORATORY.

multiple-choice item *n*

a TEST ITEM in which the test taker is presented with a question along with four or five possible answers from which one must be selected. Usually the first part of a multiple-choice item will be a question or incomplete statement. This is known as the **stem**. The different possible answers are known as **alternatives**. The alternatives contain (usually) one correct answer and several wrong answers or **distractors**.

For example:

Yesterday I _____ several interesting magazines.
(a) have bought (b) buying (c) was buying (d) bought

(d) is the correct response, while (a), (b) and (c) are **distractors**.

see also SELECTED-RESPONSE ITEM

multiple correlation *n*

a coefficient of CORRELATION among three or more VARIABLES[2]. For example, if we wish to study the correlation between a DEPENDENT VARIABLE (e.g. the level of students' language proficiency) and several other variables (i.e. the independent variables, e.g. the amount of homework the students do each week, their knowledge of grammar, and their motivation), the multiple correlation is the correlation between the dependent variable and all the predictors (the independent variables).

multiple intelligences *n*

also **MI**

a theory of intelligence that characterizes human intelligence as having multiple dimensions that must be acknowledged and developed in education. Conceptions of intelligence that dominated earlier in the twentieth century, particularly through the influence of the Stanford–Binet IQ test, were based on the idea that intelligence is a single, unchanged, inborn capacity. Advocates of MI argue that there are other equally important intelligences, found in all people in different strengths and combinations. MI thus belongs to the group of instructional philosophies that focus on the differences between learners and the need to recognize learner differences in teaching. The theory of MI is based on the work of the psychologist Gardner who posits 8 intelligences:

1 **Linguistic**: the ability to use language in special and creative ways, which is something lawyers, writers, editors and interpreters are strong in.
2 **Logical/mathematical**: this involves rational thinking and is often found with doctors, engineers, programmers and scientists.
3 **Spatial**: this is the ability to form mental models of the world and is something architects, decorators, sculptors and painters are good at.
4 **Musical**: a good ear for music, as is strong in singers and composers.
5 **Bodily/kinesthetic**: having a well co-ordinated body is something found in athletes and craftspersons.
6 **Interpersonal**: this refers to the ability to be able to work well with people and is strong in salespeople, politicians and teachers.
7 **Intrapersonal**: the ability to understand oneself and apply one's talent successfully, which leads to happy and well adjusted people in all areas of life.
8 **Naturalist**: refers to those who understand and organize the patterns of nature.

The theory of multiple intelligences has been applied both in general education as well as in langage teaching, where an attempt is made to provide learning activities that build on learners' inherent intelligences.

multiple question *n*

a question with more than one wh-phrase, for example "Who hit who(m) first?" or "Where and when did you meet?"

multiple regression *n*

see REGRESSION ANALYSIS

multiplier effect *n*

in teaching and teacher training, a procedure in which a group that have received training in a particular technique or skill, in turn, teach additional learners. For example a group of teachers who have been trained in the use of a new item of instructional software return to their schools and teach others teachers how to use it, thus multiplying the effects of the original training.

see also CASCADE MODEL

multi-skilled syllabus *n*

see INTEGRATED SYLLABUS

multi-trait multi-method method *n*
also **MTMM method**

a statistical procedure to test CONSTRUCT VALIDITY of a test by means of examining a correlation of two or more TRAITS (e.g. L2 listening ability and L2 reading ability) using two or more methods (e.g. MULTIPLE-CHOICE ITEM and SELF-ASSESSMENT). For example, a positive high correlation between two different tests that are claimed to measure the same trait is evidence of CONVERGENT VALIDITY, whereas a low correlation between two tests that are claimed to measure different traits using the same method is evidence of DISCRIMINANT VALIDITY.

multivariate analysis *n*

a general term for various statistical techniques that are used to analyze MULTIVARIATE DATA, such as FACTOR ANALYSIS and REGRESSION ANALYSIS.

multivariate analysis of covariance *n*
also MANCOVA

a multivariate extension of univariate ANCOVA to experimental situations where there are multiple dependent variables.

see also ANCOVA

multivariate analysis of variance *n*
also MANOVA

a multivariate extension of univariate ANOVA to experimental situations where there are multiple dependent variables.

see also ANOVA

multivariate data *n*

(in statistics) data that contain measurements based on more than one VARIABLE^2. For example, if we were measuring a student's language proficiency and tests were given for reading, writing, and grammar, the resulting information would be multivariate data because it is based on three separate scores (three variables).

multi-word lexical unit *n*

a sequence of word forms which functions as a single grammatical unit. For example "look into" which is used in the same way as "investigate". Multi-word units tend to acquire meanings which are not predictable from the individual parts, in which case they are often described as **idioms**.

mutation *n*

a change in a sound, as in the formation of some irregular noun plurals in English by a change in an internal vowel, e.g. foot – *feet*, man – *men*, mouse – *mice*.

The term "mutation" is used when the sound change is due to the phonetic environment of the sound that changes. In the examples, mutation was due to other vowels that were present in earlier forms of the words but have since disappeared.

mutual intelligibility *n*

a situation where speakers of two closely related or similar language varieties understand one another such as speakers of Spanish and Portuguese. The degree of mutual intelligibility depends on the amount of shared vocabulary, similarity in pronunciation, grammar, etc., as well as non-linguistic factors such as relative status of the languages, attitudes towards the languages and the amount of exposure that speakers have had to each other's language.

N

N *n*

    (in testing and statistics) a symbol for the number of students, subjects, scores, or observations involved in a study (as in, e.g., N = 15).

N' *n*

    also **N-bar**
    see BAR NOTATION

N" *n*

    also **N-double bar**
    see BAR NOTATION

narrative *n*

    1 the written or oral account of a real or fictional story.
    2 the genre structure underlying stories.
    see STORY GRAMMAR

narrative inquiry *n*

    also **narrative research**
    a procedure used in research on teacher cognition and teacher education as well as other disciplines, in which teachers' stories and personal narratives are used both as a way for teachers to articulate their knowledge and practices and as a way of formulating their practical knowledge (PRACTITIONER KNOWLEDGE). Teachers' stories about their development as teachers, about critical incidents in teaching as well as other aspects of their professional experience are used as processes for teacher reflection and development, as techniques for collecting data on teaching, and as a way of legitimizing teachers' knowledge.

narrative text *n*

    see TEXT TYPES

narrative writing *n*

    see MODES OF WRITING

narrow transcription *n*

    see TRANSCRIPTION

nasal *n*

    a sound (CONSONANT or VOWEL) produced by lowering the soft palate so that there is no velic closure and air may go out through the nose. For example, the final sounds of *rum*, *run*, and *rung* are bilabial, alveolar, and velar nasals, respectively, formed by stopping the airstream at some place in the mouth, while letting air continue to flow through the nose. Some languages, such as French, have nasal vowels as well as consonants. For example, the vowel of French *bon* /bõ/ ("good") is a nasal vowel that contrasts with the nonnasal vowel /o/ of *beau* ("beautiful").

nasal cavity *n*
see VOCAL TRACT, PLACE OF ARTICULATION

nasalization *n*
a SECONDARY ARTICULATION caused by lowering of the soft palate during a sound in which air is going out through the mouth. For example, the vowels in words like *beam*, *bean*, and *king* are nasalized due to the influence of the following nasal consonants.
see also ASSIMILATION

nasal plosion *n*
another term for NASAL RELEASE

nasal release *n*
the release of a PLOSIVE by lowering the soft palate so that air escapes through the nose, as at the end of the words *hidden*, *kitten*, *Clinton*.

national curriculum in English *n*
a curriculum for the teaching of English in England and Wales, which specifies the knowledge, skills and understanding that pupils should have acquired by the end of four key stages in the period of compulsory education (5–16), roughly at the ages of 7, 11, 14, and 16. The curriculum is divided into three "profile components": speaking and listening, reading, and writing. Each profile component consists of one or more "attainment targets" within which the content of the curriculum is presented as "statements of attainment" at 10 developmental levels.

national language *n*
a language that has a connection with a country, state, or other territory, typically the language that is most widely used throughout that territory, has the most speakers, and is closely associated with national identity. For example, English is the national language of the US; German is the national language of Germany; and Bahasa Indonesia is the national language of Indonesia.
A national language is often also the **official language** of a state, a language given special legal status in its constitution or through specific laws and

used for government, law, and official business. In France, for example, French is both the national and official language. This is not always the case, however, and usage of these terms may vary considerably, especially in multilingual nations. In Southeast Asia, for example, East Timor recognizes Portuguese (a former colonial language) as its official language and Tetum (a local LINGUA FRANCA) as its national language. The Philippine constitution specifies Filipino (a standardized variety of Tagalog) as the national language, both Filipino and English as official languages, and a number of regional languages as auxiliary official languages within their regions. The official languages of Singapore are Chinese (Mandarin), English, Malay, and Tamil, while English is the major administrative language.

see also COMMUNITY LANGUAGE, INDIGENOUS LANGUAGE, MAJORITY LANGUAGE, MINORITY LANGUAGE, REGIONAL LANGUAGE

native language *n*

(usually) the language which a person acquires in early childhood because it is spoken in the family and/or it is the language of the country where he or she is living. The native language is often the first language a child acquires but there are exceptions. Children may, for instance, first acquire some knowledge of another language from a nurse or an older relative and only later on acquire a second one which they consider their native language. Sometimes, this term is used synonymously with FIRST LANGUAGE.

native speaker *n*

a person who learns a language as a child and continues to use it fluently as a dominant language. Native speakers are said to use a language grammatically, fluently and appropriately, to identify with a community where it is spoken, and to have clear intuitions about what is considered grammatical or ungrammatical in the language. One of the goals of linguistics is to account for the intuitions the native speaker has about his/her language. Dictionaries, reference grammars and grammatical descriptions are usually based on the language use of the native speaker of a dominant or standard variety. In some contexts (the teaching of some languages in some countries) it is taken as a basic assumption that the goal of learning a second or foreign language is to approximate as closely as possible to the standards set by native speakers; in other teaching and learning contexts, this assumption is increasingly being questioned and native speakers no longer have the privileged status they used to have.

native-speakerism *n*

a term coined by Adrian Holliday to describe the unjustified belief that native-speaker teachers of English are superior to English teachers whose mother tongue is not English, because native speakers are believed to be best able to represent and reflect the beliefs, values and practices of western English-speaking cultures, and that such cultures best manifest the ideals both of the English language and of English language teaching methodology.

nativism *n*

the view that the ability of humans to learn language builds upon an innate faculty of language (see INNATENESS HYPOTHESIS) which includes innate ideas. Two types of nativism can be identified: **special nativism** (also **specific nativism**), which posits that linguistic concepts (such as the notions of sentence, noun phrase, verb) are part of innate knowledge, and **general nativism**, the view that linguistic categories and principles of language are constructed from biologically determined structures and principles that are not specifically linguistic in character.

nativist position *n*

another term for INNATIST HYPOTHESIS

nativization *n* **nativize** *v*

also **indigenization**

1 the adaptation a language may undergo when it is used in a different cultural and social situation. English in India, for example, is said to have undergone nativization because changes have occurred in aspects of its phonology, vocabulary, grammar, etc., so that it is now recognized as a distinct variety of English – Indian English.

2 the process by which a borrowed word loses pronunciation features of the source language and assimilates to the pronunciation patterns of the borrowing language.

natural approach *n*

also **natural method**

1 a term for a number of language-teaching METHODS which were developed in the nineteenth century as a reaction to the GRAMMAR TRANSLATION METHOD.

These methods emphasized:

a the use of the spoken language

b the use of objects and actions in teaching the meanings of words and structures

c the need to make language teaching follow the natural principles of first language learning.

These methods lead to the DIRECT METHOD.

2 a term for an APPROACH proposed by Terrell, to develop teaching principles which:
  a emphasize natural communication rather than formal grammar study
  b are tolerant of learners' errors
  c emphasize the informal ACQUISITION of language rules.

naturalistic data *n*
also **naturally occurring data**
data that was not elicited for the purposes of research.

naturalistic second language learning
see INSTRUCTED SECOND LANGUAGE LEARNING

natural language *n*
a language which has NATIVE SPEAKERS, in contrast with an ARTIFICIAL LANGUAGE.

natural language processing *n*
the analysis of human language by a computer, for example, the automatic analysis of a text in order to determine the kinds of grammatical structures used, or the processing of spoken input for acoustic analysis.

natural method *n*
another term for NATURAL APPROACH

natural morphology *n*
a theory of morphology that describes a "natural" or "unmarked" system and the laws that govern deviations from it. The most natural type of morphology would be one in which every morpheme corresponds to one and only one meaning and every meaning has one and only one form, a relation called **bi-uniqueness**. The –*s* morpheme on the verb *goes* in the sentence "John goes to work early" does not meet this condition, because it encodes information concerning tense (present), person (3rd), and number (singular).
see also MARKEDNESS

naturalness *n* **natural** *adj*
(in GENERATIVE PHONOLOGY) the probability that particular sounds, classes of sounds, or phonological rules occur in any language. For example, the VOWELS [i] and [u] are considered to be more frequent and therefore more "natural" than the vowels [y] (an [i] pronounced with rounded lips) and [ɯ] (an [u] pronounced with spread lips). In general, a language will

have a [y], as in German /'ry:mən/ *rühmen* "to praise", only if it has an [i], as in German /'ry:mən/ *Riemen* "strap".

natural order hypothesis *n*

the hypothesis that children acquiring their first language acquire linguistic forms, rules, and items in a similar order. For example, in English children acquire progressive *-ing*, plural *-s*, and active sentences before they acquire third person *-s* on verbs, or passive sentences. This is said to show a natural order of development. In SECOND LANGUAGE and FOREIGN LANGUAGE learning grammatical forms may also appear in a natural order, though this is not identical with the ORDER OF ACQUISITION in FIRST LANGUAGE learning.

natural phonology *n*

a theory of phonology that stresses universal processes of phonology that are motivated by the physiology of the speech organs and the acoustic characteristics of speech sounds. Some examples of natural processes are the neutralization of unstressed vowels (which occurs in English) and the devoicing of final voiced stops (which occurs in German). These are contrasted with "learned" conventional phonological rules of particular languages, such as the alternation between /k/ and /s/ in the English words *electric* and *electricity*, which have no phonetic motivation. The theory suggests that learning to suppress a natural process when learning a new language will be difficult (for example, in the case of a German learner of English who must learn that final voiced stops are not devoiced), but when the phonological rules of a new language are natural ones, there will be little difficulty in learning them.

needs analysis *n*

also **needs assessment**

(in language teaching and language programme design) the process of determining the needs for which a learner or group of learners requires a language and arranging the needs according to priorities. Needs assessment makes use of both subjective and objective information (e.g. data from questionnaires, tests, interviews, observation) and seeks to obtain information on:

a the situations in which a language will be used (including *who* it will be used *with*)

b the OBJECTIVES and purposes for which the language is needed

c the types of communication that will be used (e.g. written, spoken, formal, informal)

d the level of proficiency that will be required.

Needs assessment is a part of CURRICULUM DEVELOPMENT and is normally required before a SYLLABUS can be developed for language teaching.
see SITUATION ANALYSIS

needs hierarchy *n*

the theory that individuals instigate, direct, and sustain activity to satisfy certain needs that are hierarchical in nature, beginning with biological needs and progressing upwards to psychological ones. The psychologist Maslow proposed a hierarchy of needs containing five levels of needs:

1 physiological
2 safety and security
3 belongingness and love
4 esteem
5 self-actualization.

Needs hierarchies have sometimes been referred to in research in motivation and language learning, since learners may have different motivations for learning a language associated with their varying needs.

negation *n*

contradicting the meaning or part of the meaning of a sentence. The main NEGATOR in English is *not*, often in its contracted form *n't* and combined with an auxiliary, for example:

She isn't going/hasn't gone / didn't go/doesn't want to go.

but there are other negators, e.g. *never*.

Although he lived quite close, he never visited us.

Negation can be expressed by NEGATIVE PRONOUNS, e.g.:

There was nobody there.

or by negative affixes, e.g.:

That was really unkind!

Some varieties of English may use a DOUBLE NEGATIVE, such as:

I haven't done nothing.

This does not mean that the two negators cancel themselves out and make the sentence again a positive statement. Double negation is merely used for emphasis. Often double negation is frowned on as being non-standard. However, it is typically used in a number of English DIALECTS and it follows a definite pattern, e.g. the use of *no* instead of *any-*:

We didn't hurt nobody!

In recent grammatical theory, interest has been shown in the scope of the negator, that is, how much of the sentence is actually negated and in what way the meaning of the sentence can change if the negator is put in a different place, for instance, do the two sentences:

She didn't think he could do it
and
She thought he couldn't do it
really mean the same?

negative evidence *n*
see EVIDENCE

negative face *n*
the desire of persons that their desires and freedom of action not be impeded.
see also POLITENESS

negative feedback *n*
see FEEDBACK, RECAST

negatively skewed distribution *n*
see SKEWNESS

negative politeness strategies *n*
see POLITENESS

negative pronoun *n*
a PRONOUN which stands for a negative NOUN PHRASE[1]. The following words in English are negative pronouns:
nobody, no one, none, neither, nothing
For example:
<u>*Nobody*</u> *has passed the test.*
That's <u>*none*</u> *of your business.*
Negative pronouns can function as NEGATORS.

negative question *n*
a question which includes a negative word or PARTICLE. For example,
Ca<u>n't</u> you drive?
Is<u>n't</u> it awful?
In English, negative questions are answered in the same way as positive questions:

	If you can drive	If you can't drive
Can you drive?	*Yes, I can.*	*No, I can't.*
Can't you drive?		

negative reinforcement *n*
see OPERANT CONDITIONING, STIMULUS-RESPONSE THEORY

negative transfer *n*

see LANGUAGE TRANSFER

negator *n*

a word which makes a sentence a negative sentence. For example, English negators include *not*, *hardly ever*, *never*, *seldom*, *neither*, *nothing*.

see also NEGATIVE PRONOUN

negotiated syllabus *n*

an approach to the development of a language course in which students' needs and learning preferences are taken into account during the course; these needs are discussed by students and teachers together during the course and serve to generate ideas about the content of the course. The negotiated syllabus reflects a **learner-centred** approach to teaching.

negotiation *n*

(in conversation) what speakers do in order to achieve successful communication. For conversation to progress naturally and for speakers to be able to understand each other it may be necessary for them to:

a indicate that they understand or do not understand, or that they want the conversation to continue (see FEEDBACK)

b help each other to express ideas (see FOREIGNER TALK)

c make corrections when necessary to what is said or how it is said (see REPAIR).

These aspects of the work which speakers do in order to make successful conversation is known as negotiation, in CONVERSATIONAL ANALYSIS.

see also ACCOMMODATION, CONVERSATIONAL MAXIM, ETHNOMETHODOLOGY

negotiation of meaning *n*

see INTERACTION HYPOTHESIS

neologism *n*

a new word or expression which has come into a language. It is often difficult to pinpoint the exact year when a neologism appears in a language but it has been suggested that, in English, the word *non-standard* has been used regularly since about 1923 and the word *null-hypothesis* since about 1935.

Often neologisms are the result of the opening up of new areas of art, science or technology. For example, the field of computer science brought about a large range of neologisms such as *user-friendly*, *software*, *floppy disk*.

NESB *n*

Non-English Speaking Background.

a term sometimes used to refer to a non-native speaker of English, particularly overseas students studying in colleges or universities. In the US such students are sometimes referred to as **ESL**, **ELL**, or **LES** students.

network *n*

a group of people within a larger community who are in a relatively fixed relationship to one another and who communicate among themselves in certain more or less predictable ways, e.g. a family group, a tutorial group at a university, the staff in an office. Recognition of networks and their structures is of importance for studies of language variation, language use, and language learning. There are two differences between a network and a PEER GROUP:

a In a peer group all members have equal STATUS, but in a network members may be of unequal status (e.g. parents and children in a family).

b In a network all members know one another, but in a peer group this need not be so. For example, a lexicographer may consider all lexicographers to be his or her peer group without knowing them all personally.

Nevertheless, most peer groups are networks and many networks are peer groups.

neural networks *n*

see CONNECTIONISM

Neuro-linguistic Programming *n*

also **NLP**

a training philosophy and set of training techniques first developed by John Grindler and Richard Bandler in the mid-1970s as an alternative form of therapy. Grindler (a psychologist) and Bandler (a student of linguistics) were interested in how people influence each other and in how the behaviours of very effective people could be duplicated. Grindler and Bandler developed NLP as a system of techniques therapists could use in building rapport with clients, gathering information about their internal and external views of the world, and in helping them achieve goals and bring about personal change. The principles of NLP have been applied in a variety of fields, including management training, sports training, communications, sales and marketing, and language teaching and have had some appeal within language teaching to those interested in humanistic approaches, i.e. those which focus on developing one's sense of self-actualization and self-awareness, as well as to those drawn to New Age Humanism.

neurolinguistics *n* **neurolinguistic** *adj*

the study of the function the brain performs in language learning and language use. Neurolinguistics includes research into how the structure of the brain influences language learning, how and in which parts of the brain language is stored (see MEMORY), and how damage to the brain affects the ability to use language (see APHASIA).

neuter *adj*

see GENDER²

neutralization *n*

when a contrast that is normally made in a language is not marked, this is called neutralization. For example, in PHONOLOGY, the high tense vowel of *bean* (/biːn/) and the lax vowel of *bin* (/bɪn/) are normally in contrast (they are PHONEMES), but there is no contrast between these vowels before a velar nasal, as in the suffix *–ing*. In MORPHOLOGY, English normally contrasts singular and plural forms of nouns (e.g. *cat*, *cats*), but in a few cases (e.g. *fish*, *sheep*) this contrast is neutralized.

New Rhetoric *n*

in the teaching of composition, an approach advocated by a group of genre theorists and researchers particularly in the US that argue for a redefinition of traditional notions of rhetoric to focus on the social, cultural, political and ideological assumptions and underpinnings that underlie the formal features of texts. In the analysis of texts a new rhetoric approach focuses on the social and ideological realities that underlie the regularities of texts, and employs ethnographic methods to identify the relations between texts and contexts.

node *n*

(in GENERATIVE GRAMMAR) each position in a **tree diagram** where lines ("branches") meet. At each node is a symbol for a GRAMMATICAL CATEGORY².
For example, in the tree diagram for a noun phrase, *the child*:

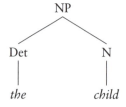

the category symbols NP (NOUN PHRASE[1]), Det (DETERMINER), N (NOUN) are all at nodes in the diagram.

The NP node is said to **dominate** the Det node and the N node.

see also BASE COMPONENT

no-interface position *n*

see INTERFACE

noise[1] *n*

when speech sounds are produced, the moving particles of air from the lungs may form regular patterns (see SOUND WAVE) or irregular patterns. These irregular patterns are called noise and occur in the production of certain consonants such as /s/.

noise[2] *n*

(in INFORMATION THEORY) any disturbance or defect which interferes with the transmission of the message from one person to another. In speech, this interference could be caused by other sounds, e.g. a pneumatic drill, a voice on the radio. Because of the presence of noise, a certain degree of REDUNDANCY is necessary in any communication.

nominal *n*

1 a term used instead of NOUN.
2 a term for a linguistic unit which has some but not all characteristics of a noun, e.g. *wounded* in *The wounded were taken by helicopter to the hospital.*

Although *wounded is* the HEAD of the noun phrase *the wounded* and is preceded by an article, it would not be modified by an adjective but by an adverb, e.g. *the seriously wounded.*

nominal clause *n*

also **noun clause**

a clause which functions like a noun or noun phrase; that is, which may occur as subject, object COMPLEMENT, in APPOSITION, or as prepositional COMPLEMENT. For example:

nominal clause as subject: *What she said is awful.*

nominal clause as object: *I don't know what she said.*

nominalization *n* nominalize *v*

the grammatical process of forming nouns from other parts of speech, usually verbs or adjectives. For example, in English: nominalized forms from the verb *to write: writing, writer* as in: *His writing is illegible. Her mother is a writer.*

nominal scale *n*

see SCALE

nominative case *n*

the form of a NOUN or noun phrase (see NOUN PHRASE[1]) which usually shows that the noun or noun phrase can function as the subject of the sentence. For example, in the German sentence:

Der Tisch ist sehr groß.

The table is very big.

the article has the ending -*er* to show that the noun phrase is in the nominative case because it is the subject of the sentence.

see also CASE[1]

non-count noun *n*

see COUNTABLE NOUN

non-defining relative clause *n*

also **non-restrictive relative clause**

see DEFINING RELATIVE CLAUSE

non-directional hypothesis *n*

see TWO-TAILED TEST

nondirective interview *n*

an INTERVIEW which is not directed or structured and in which the interviewer allows the person being interviewed to speak freely about a range of topics of his or her own choice. The difference between a nondirective interview and an UNSTRUCTURED INTERVIEW is that in the nondirective interview there is a minimum amount of questioning by the interviewer, while in the unstructured interview topic control remains largely with the interviewer.

see also DEPTH INTERVIEW, FOCUSED INTERVIEW, GUIDED INTERVIEW, INTERVIEW GUIDE

non-English proficient *n*

(in a BILINGUAL EDUCATION or ENGLISH AS A SECOND LANGUAGE PROGRAMME) a learner who has no previous experience learning English and who speaks only his or her home language on entering school.

non-finite verb *n*

see FINITE VERB

non-linear morphology *n*

in MORPHOLOGY, a theoretical framework in which the morphemes that make up a derived word are each represented at an autonomous level of representation called a tier. This framework has been shown to be especially useful in accounting for the intricate, non-linear morphology of Arabic.
see also AUTOSEGMENTAL PHONOLOGY, METRICAL PHONOLOGY

non-literate *n*

a culture or group which has no written language, i.e. which possesses an ORAL CULTURE.

non-native speaker *n*
also **NNS**

a language user for whom a language is not their first language. The language use of non-native speakers has been a focus of attention to determine such things as the effects of non-native accents on intelligibility, attitudes towards NNS accents, and the role of NNS accents as a marker of the speaker's *identity*.

non-parametric tests *n*

a group of statistical procedures that do not make the strong distributional assumptions associated with PARAMETRIC TESTS (e.g. that the data are normally distributed) and are used to analyze data measured on a NOMINAL or ORDINAL SCALE. Examples of non-parametric tests include CHI-SQUARE and SPEARMAN RANK-ORDER CORRELATION.

non-past *n, adj*

a term sometimes used for the PRESENT TENSE form of a verb in languages such as English. It emphasizes that this verb form is generally used to describe time periods other than the past, but not necessarily the present. For example:

I *leave* tomorrow. (future reference)
The sun *rises* in the east. (general truth)

non-pro-drop language *n*
see PRO-DROP PARAMETER

non-punctual *adj*
see PUNCTUAL-NON-PUNCTUAL DISTINCTION

non-restrictive relative clause *n*
another term for **non-defining relative clause**
see DEFINING RELATIVE CLAUSE

nonrhotic *adj*

see RHOTIC

non-specific nativism *n*

the view that the ability to acquire language depends on innate (biologically specified) mechanisms, but that these mechanisms are general to all cognition, not specific to language.

see also INNATIST HYPOTHESIS

nonstandard *adj*

used of speech or writing which differs in pronunciation, GRAMMAR, or vocabulary from the STANDARD VARIETY of the language. Sometimes the expression SUBSTANDARD is used but linguists prefer the term nonstandard as it is a more neutral term.

see also NORM, STANDARD VARIETY

non-verbal communication *n*

communication without the use of words. This could be done, for instance, by gestures (see PARALINGUISTICS) or signs (see SIGN LANGUAGE).

non-verbal teacher behaviour *n*

the use of silence, paralinguistic behaviour, gestures, body movement and other aspects of non-linguistic behaviour used by teachers in teaching. The study of non-verbal teacher behaviour seeks to determine the effects of such behaviour on the affective as well as other aspects of classroom life. In language teaching, teachers from one cultural background may use non-verbal behaviours that are different from those in the learners' home culture, and this may at times lead to misunderstanding.

nonword *n*

see PSEUDOWORD

norm[1] *n* **normative** *adj*

that which is considered appropriate in speech or writing for a particular situation or purpose within a particular group or community.

The norm for an informal situation may be very different from the norm for a formal one.

For example, in English, a first name (*Joe*) may be the norm for addressing people in an informal situation but title and surname (*Mr Smith*) for a formal one.

see also STANDARD VARIETY, STYLE

norm² *n*

> (in testing and statistics) the scores or typical performance of a particular group (the "norm" group) as measured in some way. Norms may be used to compare the performance of an individual or group with the norm group. Norms may be expressed by reference to such factors as age, length of previous instruction, or PERCENTILE rank on a test.

normal distribution *n*

> (in statistics) a commonly occurring DISTRIBUTION of scores, in which scores rise and fall gradually from a single peak. It forms a symmetrical bell-shaped curve. In a normal distribution, the MEAN, MEDIAN, and MODE all coincide, and the information necessary for describing the distribution is given in the mean and the STANDARD DEVIATION (SD).

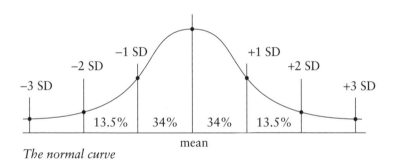

The normal curve

> The graph above shows the percentage of people who fall in various portions of the normal distribution. For example, approximately 68% of the people fall in the range between one SD below and one SD above the mean. Thus if a test has a mean of 100 and an SD of 10 and its scores are normally distributed, then approximately 68% of the people who took this test have test scores between 90 and 100 (i.e. 100 – 10 (= one SD below the mean) and 100 + 10 (= one SD above the mean)).

normalized standard score *n*

> (in statistics) a STANDARD SCORE which has been converted to a NORMAL DISTRIBUTION through a statistical procedure. For example a PERCENTILE ranking is a normalized standard score.

normative grammar *n*

> a grammar which contains rules for what is considered to be correct or appropriate usage. The rules may be based on classical literary works or the

speech of those people who are considered as models for others to copy. In a nation in which many different DIALECTs are spoken, a NATIONAL LANGUAGE may be developed and a normative grammar and dictionary produced.

see also PRESCRIPTIVE GRAMMAR, STANDARD VARIETY

norm-referenced test(ing) *n*

a test that measures how the performance of a particular test taker or group of test takers compares with the performance of another test taker or group of test takers whose scores are given as the norm. A test taker's score is therefore interpreted with reference to the scores of other test takers or groups of test takers, rather than to an agreed criterion score, which is the case with a CRITERION-REFERENCED TEST.

notation *n* **notate** *v*

also **transcription**

the use of symbols (see PHONETIC SYMBOLS) to show sounds or sound sequences in written form. There are different systems of phonetic symbols. One of the most commonly used is that of the International Phonetic Association.

A distinction is made between two types of notation:

1 Phonemic notation uses only the distinctive sounds of a language (PHONEMES). It does not show the finer points of pronunciation.
Phonemic notation is written within slanting brackets.
For example, the English word *foot* may appear in phonemic notation as /fʊt/. /f/, /ʊ/, and /t/ are phonemes of English. Phonemic notation may be used, for example:
  a for languages which have no writing system of their own
  b for teaching purposes, to show differences in pronunciation, e.g. /hed/ *head* and /hæt/ *hat*.

2 Phonetic notation (also phonetic script) uses phonetic symbols for various sounds, including symbols to show in detail how a particular sound is pronounced. It is used to show finer points of pronunciation.
Phonetic notation is written in square brackets. For example, the English word *pin* may appear in phonetic notation as [pʰɪn] with the raised *h* showing the ASPIRATION of the [p].
In phonemic notation, *pin* would be rendered as /pɪn/.
Phonetic notation may be used, for example:
  a to show the different pronunciation of closely related dialects
  b to show the pronunciation of individual speakers or groups of speakers.
  For example, students learning English may use a DENTAL
t-sound, shown by [t̪], instead of the ALVEOLAR [t] commonly used in English.

Phonemic notation is sometimes referred to as broad notation and phonetic notation as narrow notation.

see also INTERNATIONAL PHONETIC ALPHABET

notetaking *n*

also **notemaking**

while reading or listening, the writing down of main points, reactions, questions, or other responses. Such notes may be used for discussion or to help organize and retain information.

noticing hypothesis *n*

the hypothesis that INPUT does not become INTAKE for language learning unless it is noticed, that is, consciously registered.

notion *n*

see NOTIONAL SYLLABUS

notional-functional syllabus *n*

also **functional-notional syllabus**

another term for NOTIONAL SYLLABUS

notional grammar[1] *n*

a grammar which is based on the belief that there are categories such as TENSE, MOOD, GENDER, NUMBER, and CASE which are available to all languages although not all languages make full use of them. For example, a case system (see CASE[1]) is found in German, Latin, and Russian, but not in modern English.

TRADITIONAL GRAMMAR was often notional in its approach and sometimes attempted to apply some categories to a language without first investigating whether they were useful and appropriate for describing that language.

notional grammar[2] *n*

a grammar based on the meanings or concepts that people need to express through language (e.g. time, quantity, duration, location) and the linguistic items and structures needed to express them.

notional syllabus *n*

also **notional-functional syllabus**

(in language teaching) an approach to developing a communicative syllabus widely discussed in the 1970s, a SYLLABUS in which the language content is arranged according to the meanings a learner needs to express through language and the functions the learner will use the language for.

noun

The term NOTIONAL is taken from NOTIONAL GRAMMAR[2]. A notional syllabus is contrasted with a grammatical syllabus or STRUCTURAL SYLLABUS (one which consists of a sequence of graded language items) or a situational syllabus (one which consists of situations and the relevant language items (see SITUATIONAL METHOD)).

A notional syllabus contains:

a the meanings and concepts the learner needs in order to communicate (e.g. time, quantity, duration, location) and the language needed to express them. These concepts and meanings are called notions

b the language needed to express different functions or SPEECH ACTS (e.g. requesting, suggesting, promising, describing).

These notions and functions are then used to develop learning teaching units in a language course.

see also COMMUNICATIVE APPROACH

noun *n*

a word which (a) can occur as the subject or object of a verb or the object (COMPLEMENT) of a preposition (b) can be modified by an adjective (c) can be used with DETERMINERS.

Nouns typically refer to people, animals, places, things, or abstractions.

see also ADJECTIVAL NOUN, ANIMATE NOUN, COLLECTIVE NOUN, CONCRETE NOUN, COUNTABLE NOUN, PROPER NOUN, PARTS OF SPEECH

noun clause *n*

another term for NOMINAL CLAUSE

noun phrase[1] *n*

also NP

(in STRUCTURALIST LINGUISTICS, GENERATIVE GRAMMAR and related grammatical theories) a group of words with a noun or pronoun as the main part (the HEAD).

The noun phrase may consist of only one word (for example *Gina* in *Gina arrived yesterday*) or it may be long and complex (for example, all the words before *must* in: *The students who enrolled late and who have not yet filled in their cards must do so by Friday*).

noun phrase[2] *n*

(in some TRADITIONAL GRAMMARS) a participial (see PARTICIPLES) or INFINITIVE phrase which could be replaced by a noun or pronoun.

For example, the participial phrase *mowing the lawn* in:

George just hates mowing the lawn.

could be replaced by *it*:

George just hates it.

noun phrase accessibility hierarchy *n*
also **NAPH**

a way of describing the relation among different relative clause types across languages. The claims made by those who posit a hierarchy include the following:

1 All languages have some types of relative clauses.

2 The range of relative clause types includes:

subject relative clause (SU), for example, *He thanked the mechanic who fixed his car* (*who* refers to the subject of the relative clause)

object relative clause (DO), for example, *He took his car to the mechanic (who) he liked best* (*who* refers to the object of the relative clause)

indirect object relative clause (IO), for example, *I know who you told the story* (*who* refers to the indirect object of the relative clause)

object of preposition relative clause (OPREP), for example, *I moved the rock (that) you hid the money under* (*that* refers to the complement of *under*)

genitive relative clause (GEN), for example, *I know the man whose car the mechanic fixed* (*whose* refers to the owner of the car)

comparative relative clause (OCOMP), for example, *I know someone (who) you are smarter than* (*who* refers to the complement of smarter).

3 Not all languages permit all relative clause types. They form a hierarchy: SU > DO > IO > OPREP > GEN > OCOMP. The relative clause types to the left are higher in the hierarchy. If a language has any of one of these relative clause types, it will also have all types higher in the hierarchy. For example, if a language has IO, it will also have DO and SU. If it has OCOMP, it will have all other types as well.

4 The claim has also been made that second language learners will find it easiest to learn relative clause types higher in the hierarchy (such as SU and DO) and more difficult to learn those that are lower down.

see also MARKEDNESS

novice teacher *n*

a teacher who has completed his or her teacher education programme, who has little practical experience of teaching and who has just begun his or her teaching career.

see EXPERTISE

NP *n*

an abbreviation for NOUN PHRASE[1]

NPAH *n*

an abbreviation for NOUN PHRASE ACCESSIBILITY HIERARCHY

NRT *n*

an abbreviation for NORM-REFERENCED TEST(ING)

nth word deletion

see CLOZE TEST

nucleus *n*

see SYLLABLE

null hypothesis *n*

see HYPOTHESIS

null morpheme *n*

also **zero morpheme**

in MORPHOLOGY, a morpheme involved in null affixation. For example, the plural of *fish* is *fish*, which can be analyzed as the noun *fish* plus the null variant of the plural morpheme.

null subject parameter *n*

another term for PRO-DROP PARAMETER

number^1 *n*

a grammatical distinction which determines whether nouns, verbs, adjectives, etc. in a language are singular or plural. In English this is seen particularly in NOUNS and DEMONSTRATIVES.

For example:

	singular	plural
count noun	*book*	*books*
demonstrative	*this*	*these*

number^2 *n*

numbers are used either as **cardinal numbers** (or **cardinals**) or **ordinal numbers** (or **ordinals**).

Cardinal numbers are used when counting; e.g. <u>6</u> *boys*, <u>200</u> *dollars*, <u>a million</u> *years*, and they may be used as nouns (e.g. *count up to <u>ten</u>*).

Ordinal numbers are used when we put things in a numerical order; e.g. *first, second, third, fourth, fifth*, etc.

Both cardinal numbers and ordinal numbers can be written with figures (e.g. *6, 6th*) or with words (*six, sixth*).

number concord *n*

see CONCORD

O

object¹ *n*

the noun, noun phrase or clause, or pronoun in sentences with TRANSITIVE VERBS, which is traditionally described as being affected by the action of the verb. The object of a verb can be affected by the verb either directly or indirectly.

If it is affected directly, it may be called the **direct object**. In English, the direct object of a verb may be:

a created by the action of the verb, as in:
 Terry baked a cake.

b changed in some way by the action of the verb as in:
 Terry baked a potato.

c perceived by the SUBJECT of the verb, as in:
 Terry saw the cake.

d evaluated by the subject of the verb, as in:
 Terry liked the cake.

e obtained or possessed by the subject of the verb, as in:
 Terry bought the cake.

If the object of a verb is affected by the verb indirectly, it is usually called the **indirect object**. In English, the indirect object may be:

a the receiver of the direct object, as in:
 Terry gave me the cake. (= "Terry gave the cake *to* me")

b the beneficiary of the action of the verb, as in:
 Terry baked me the cake. (= "Terry baked the cake *for* me")

In English, direct objects and many indirect objects can become subjects when sentences in the active voice are changed to the passive voice (see VOICE¹):

 The cake was given (to) me.
 I was given the cake.

see also GOAL¹, OBJECT OF RESULT

object² (**of a preposition**) *n*

another term for PREPOSITIONAL COMPLEMENT
see COMPLEMENT

object case *n*

another term for OBJECTIVE CASE

object complement *n*

see COMPLEMENT

objective *n*

> a goal of a course of instruction. Two different types of objectives may be distinguished.
>
> General objectives, or **aims,** are the underlying reasons for or purposes of a course of instruction. For example, the aims of the teaching of a foreign language in a particular country might be: to teach students to read and write a foreign language, to improve students' knowledge of a foreign culture, to teach conversation in a foreign language, etc. Aims are long-term goals, described in very general terms.
>
> Specific objectives (or simply objectives) are descriptions of what is to be achieved in a course. They are more detailed descriptions of exactly what a learner is expected to be able to do at the end of a period of instruction. This might be a single lesson, a chapter of a book, a term's work, etc. For instance, specific objectives of a classroom lesson might be: Use of the linking words *and, but, however, although*. These specific objectives contribute to the general objective of paragraph writing. A description of specific objectives in terms which can be observed and measured is known as a BEHAVIOURAL OBJECTIVE.

objective case *n*

> also **object case**
>
> the noun or noun PHRASE[1] that refers to whoever or whatever has the most neutral relationship to the action of the verb is in the objective case.
>
> The noun or noun phrase in the objective case neither performs the action, nor is the instrument of the action.
>
> For example, in the sentences:
>
> > They sliced <u>the sausage</u> with a knife.
> > <u>The sausage</u> sliced easily.
> > <u>The sausage</u> was thick.
>
> *the sausage* is neither agent (like *they*) nor instrument (like a *knife*). It is in the objective case.
>
> The notion of the objective case is related to the traditional notion of OBJECT[1]. But not everything in the objective case would be an object, nor would all objects be considered to be in the objective case.
>
> see also CASE GRAMMAR

objective marking *n*

> see OBJECTIVE SCORING

objective test *n*

> a test that can be scored objectively (i.e. scored without the use of the examiner's personal judgement), which may be contrasted with a SUBJECTIVE

TEST. Tests that consist of TRUE–FALSE and MULTIPLE-CHOICE ITEMS are examples of objective tests.

objective test item *n*
a test item that requires the choice of a single correct answer, such as a MULTIPLE-CHOICE ITEM or a TRUE–FALSE ITEM.

object of comparative relative clause *n*
another term for COMPARATIVE RELATIVE CLAUSE

object of preposition relative clause *n*
also **OPREP**
see NOUN PHRASE ACCESSIBILITY HIERARCHY

object of result *n*
also **affected object**
an object of a verb which refers to something that is produced through the action indicated by the verb, e.g. *a cake* in:
Terry baked a cake.
as the cake is the result of the baking. However, in:
Terry baked a potato.
a potato is not an object of result as it is not produced by baking. It is, however, affected by baking, and so may be called an **affected object**.
see also FACTITIVE CASE

object relative clause *n*
also **direct object relative clause, DO**
see NOUN PHRASE ACCESSIBILITY HIERARCHY

observation *n*
in language classrooms, the purposeful examination of teaching and/or learning events through systematic processes of data collection and analysis. Observation of teaching is a widely used activity in teacher education programmes.

observational methods *n*
(in research) procedures and techniques that are based on systematic observation of events, e.g. using audio and video recorders, check lists, etc. Observational methods are often used in studying language use and classroom events.
see also ETHNOGRAPHY OF COMMUNICATION

observation schedules *n*

in classroom observation, analytic instruments (documents) used to record observable behaviours in classrooms, either as events occur ("real-time coding") or with electronically recorded data.

observed score *n*

see CLASSICAL TEST THEORY

observer's paradox *n*

an issue that occurs when carrying out observation in order to study language behaviour, and which refers to the fact that when we observe people's behaviour we may alter the very behavioural patterns we wish to observe. Hence an observer in a teacher's classroom may affect both the behaviour of the teacher and the students, making the data that was collected unrepresentative of real classroom behaviour. The observer's paradox is equally relevant in QUANTITATIVE RESEARCH (see HALO EFFECT, HAWTHORN EFFECT).

obstruent *n*

a speech sound (CONSONANTs) produced when the passage of the air from the lungs is obstructed in some way. Obstruents include FRICATIVES, STOPS, and AFFRICATES. NASALS such as /n/ and /m/ are not usually considered obstruents because, although the air is stopped in the mouth, it is allowed free passage through the nose.

In GENERATIVE PHONOLOGY, obstruents are often marked [-sonorant] to distinguish them from sounds such as VOWELS, NASALS, GLIDES, and LIQUIDS.

see also SONORANT

OCOMP *n*

an abbreviation for **object of comparative relative clause**

official language *n*

see NATIONAL LANGUAGE

off-task behaviour *n*

see ON-TASK BEHAVIOUR

one parameter model *n*

see ITEM RESPONSE THEORY

one-tailed test *n*

also **directional hypothesis**

a type of statistical hypothesis test that is appropriately chosen where the direction of an effect, such as a difference or correlation, is specified in advance (e.g. the experimental group will score significantly higher than the control group on a vocabulary recognition test).

one-to-one *n*

a teaching situation involving one teacher and one student.

one-way task *n*

an INFORMATION GAP task in which one participant holds all the information and the information flows in only one direction during the task.

onomatopoeia *n*

also **sound symbolism, echoism**

refers to words that are considered by convention to be imitative of nature, acoustically similar to the thing to which they refer (e.g. the *bow-wow* of a dog or the *tick-tock* of a clock) or the sound made by the thing to which they refer (e.g. a *buzz saw*). There are other words that are examples of **semi-onomatopoeia**, such as the English words *splash* or *growl*. Languages differ in the range, choice, and phonetic realizations of onomatopoeic words. An English dog goes *bow-wow* or *ruff-ruff* or *woof-woof*; a Japanese one goes *wan-wan*.

see also IDEOPHONE

onset *n*

see SYLLABLE, TONE UNIT

on-task behaviour *n*

(in a lesson or learning activity) learner behaviour which is directed towards the lesson or activity. For example, during a class in which students have been asked to read a passage and answer questions about it, students may not give their full attention to the task during the lesson. Behaviour not related to the task (i.e. **off-task behaviour**) may include getting up and talking to a classmate or doodling. The goal of an effective teacher is said to be to increase the amount of time students are engaged in on-task behaviour in order to provide them with maximum opportunities for learning.

see also TIME ON TASK, EFFECTIVE TEACHING

ontogeny *n* **ontogenetic** *adj*

also **ontogenesis**

in studies of child LANGUAGE ACQUISITION, the development of language in an individual is sometimes referred to as ontogeny, and the historical development of language in a speech community as phylogeny. Linguists are interested in whether the ontogeny of language in the child shows similar stages to those which a language has gone through in its historical development. In other words, they are interested in the famous question whether ontogeny recapitulates phylogeny.

open class *n*

also **open set**

a group of words (a WORD CLASS), which contains an unlimited number of items.

Nouns, verbs, adjectives, and adverbs are open-class words. New words can be added to these classes, e.g. *laser, e-commerce, chatroom.*

The word classes conjunctions, prepositions, and pronouns consist of relatively few words, and new words are not usually added to them.

These are called closed classes, or closed sets.

open-ended question *n*

a TEST ITEM which allows the person taking the test to answer in his or her own way, in contrast to questions with limited multiple-choice possibilities.

open-ended response *n*

see TEST ITEM

openings *n*

strategies speakers use to begin a conversation such as the use of greetings and small talk.

see also CLOSINGS, CONVERSATIONAL OPENINGS

open learning *n*

also **open education**

a system for educating adults where normal restrictions on entry to adult education are removed and where learners receive recognition for previous experience. Courses are organized flexibly according to the students' needs.

A number of features distinguish open learning:

a greater accessibility to education than with traditional courses, including accessibility in terms of academic background, age, time required, physical location and time constraints

b flexibility in terms of course structure and delivery with a considerable degree of learner control over pacing, contents, structure and means of assessment

c a variety of means of support and of study.
In open learning individuals are encouraged to take responsibility for the direction, content, and process of their own learning.

open pairs

see CLOSED PAIRS

open set *n*

another term for OPEN CLASS

open syllable *n*

see SYLLABLE

open vowel *n*

also **low vowel**
see VOWEL

operant *n*

see OPERANT CONDITIONING

operant conditioning *n*

a learning theory proposed by Skinner within the context of behaviourist psychology (see BEHAVIOURISM). It is a type of conditioning (see CONDITIONED RESPONSE) in which a child learning its first language produces an action (e.g. an UTTERANCE) that achieves some outcome (e.g. to get food). This action is called the **operant**. The outcome is positively reinforced (**positive reinforcement**) if the operant is followed by something pleasant, and negatively reinforced (**negative reinforcement**) if it is followed by the removal of something unpleasant. This concept was influential during the heyday of the AUDIOLINGUAL METHOD.

operating principle *n*

see HEURISTIC

operational definition *n* operationalize *v*

a definition of a concept in terms which can be observed and measured. In language teaching and language testing, many linguistic concepts need to be operationalized. For example, terms such as "competence" and "proficiency" need to be operationalized in preparing programme goals, OBJECTIVES, and test items.

operator *n*

(in English) the first AUXILIARY VERB to occur in a verb phrase, so called because it is the verb which "operates" as the question-forming word, by moving to the initial position in the sentence in questions. For example:

a He will   be   coming.
       aux 1 aux 2
       (operator)

b She couldn't have been   there.
       aux 1   aux 2 aux 3
       (operator)

a becomes <u>Will</u> he be coming?

b becomes <u>Couldn't</u> she have been there?

OPI *n*

an abbreviation for ORAL PROFICIENCY INTERVIEW

opposition *n*

the relationship between pairs of elements in a language, such as the distinctive sounds (PHONEMES).

For example, the opposition between /k/ and /g/ in English distinguishes between the MINIMAL PAIR *cut* /kʌt/ and *gut* /gʌt/.

In general, the term "opposition" is used when two elements differ in only one feature. So English /k/ and /g/ are said to be in opposition because they differ only in that /g/ is **voiced** and /k/ is **voiceless** (see VOICE^2). One is less likely to speak of the opposition between /k/ and /b/ (as in *cut* /kʌt/ and *but* /bʌt/), because they differ in several ways involving both PLACE OF ARTICULATION and VOICING.

see MARKEDNESS

OPREP *n*

an abbreviation for **object of preposition relative clause**

optimality theory *n*

a linguistic theory which considers **constraints** rather than rules as central to grammar. An example of a (universal) constraint is that a nasal (optimally) has the same place as a following consonant. According to optimality theory, the surface forms of language reflect the resolution of conflicts between competing constraints. The theory has been applied primarily to problems in phonology.

optimum age hypothesis *n*

see CRITICAL PERIOD HYPOTHESIS

oral[1] *adj*

a term used to stress that a spoken form of language is used as opposed to a written form, as in *an oral test, an oral examination.*

oral[2] *adj, n*

(of) a speech sound which is produced while the soft palate (the **velum**) at the back of the mouth is raised so that the airstream from the lungs cannot escape through the nose.

In English, all vowels, and all consonants except /m/, /n/, and /ŋ/ as in /sɪŋ/ *sing*, are oral.

In GENERATIVE PHONOLOGY, oral sounds are marked [-nasal] to distinguish them from NASAL sounds.

see also MANNER OF ARTICULATION, PLACE OF ARTICULATION

oral approach *n*

another term for SITUATIONAL LANGUAGE TEACHING

oral cavity *n*

see VOCAL TRACT, PLACE OF ARTICULATION

oral culture *n*

the culture of a society in which culture and cultural values are communicated through spoken language rather than through writing. A society in which written language plays an important part in culture and cultural values is said to have a **literary culture.**

see also NON-LITERATE

oralist *n*

see SIGN LANGUAGE

oral language *n*

see AURAL LANGUAGE

oral method *n*

a method for teaching the deaf, based on lip-reading and carefully articulated speech. This method is now less commonly used than the AUDITORY/ORAL METHOD.

oral mimicry ability *n*

see LANGUAGE APTITUDE

oral proficiency interview *n*

also **OPI**

a type of speaking test that elicits and assesses a ratable sample of a test taker's oral language proficiency in a structured interview format where the tester and test taker are engaged interactively in oral communication tasks. The test taker's spoken language production is often tape-recorded and later rated by one or multiple raters on the basis of a predetermined rating scale. The most widely known and influential OPI is the ACTFL OPI that is a criterion-referenced, direct, face-to-face (or telephone), integrative interview where an ACTFL certified tester takes a test taker through the four phases such as a warm-up, repeated level checks and probes, and a wind-down until the tester can identify the test taker's upper limitation or ceiling.

oral reading *n*
>see READING

order of acquisition *n*
>also **acquisition order**
>the order in which linguistic forms, rules, and items are acquired in first- or second-language learning.
>see also LANGUAGE ACQUISITION, NATURAL ORDER HYPOTHESIS

ordinal scale *n*
>see SCALE

orientation[1] *n*
>see ATTENTION

orientation[2] *n*
>see MOTIVATION

orientation[3]
>see LISTENING COMPREHENSION

orthography *n* **orthographic** *adj*
>The term "orthography" is used:
>1 for spelling in general.
>2 for correct or standard spelling.
>For some languages, the orthography is based on generally accepted usage and is not prescribed by an official body. For other languages, e.g. Swedish, it is laid down by official or semi-official organizations. Like the term "spelling" itself, the term "orthography" is more likely to be used of alphabetic writing than of syllabic writing, and is unlikely to be used of character-based writing systems (see WRITING SYSTEMS).

othering *n*

the idea that individuals and societies often define themselves in opposition to others. Othering of another group typically involves maintaining social distance and making often negative value judgements about the other group. In feminist studies, it has been pointed out that male-dominated cultures treat women as others in contrast to a male norm, and writer Edward Said applied the concept to views of colonized peoples as excluded others. Some suggest the term NON-NATIVE SPEAKER is an example of othering in TESOL.

other repair *n*

see REPAIR

outcomes-based teaching/education *n*
also **standards-based education**

an approach to education and curriculum development which involves (a) describing the learning outcomes that students should know at the end of a course of instruction (b) devising a curriculum to help them achieve the outcomes (c) using the outcomes achieved as a measure of effectiveness. In some parts of the world, particularly in the US, this approach is thought necessary to ensure that students graduate from high school with the knowledge and skills they will need in the real world.
see also COMPETENCY-BASED EDUCATION STANDARDS

outcome variable *n*

another term for DEPENDENT VARIABLE

outlier *n*

an extreme score. Typically any scores that fall beyond + or − 3 STANDARD DEVIATIONS from the mean are considered outliers.

outline *n* **outlining** *v*

(in composition) a plan for an essay or piece of writing which presents the main points the essay will cover and the order in which they will be mentioned. In an outline, main points are distinguished from supporting details, sometimes using systems of numerals and letters.
Several kinds of outlines are often used.

1 **Topic Outline:** each entry is a word or group of words.
2 **Sentence Outline:** similar to a topic outline except that the words are replaced by sentences.
3 **Paragraph Outline:** this contains only a list of TOPIC SENTENCES for each paragraph.

output *n*

    language produced by a language learner, either in speech or writing.

    see INPUT

output hypothesis *n*

    also **comprehensible output hypothesis**

    the hypothesis that successful second language acquisition requires not only COMPREHENSIBLE INPUT, but also comprehensible output, language produced by the learner that can be understood by other speakers of the language. It has been argued that when learners have to make efforts to ensure that their messages are communicated (**pushed output**) this puts them in a better position to notice the gap between their productions and those of proficient speakers, fostering acquisition.

over-extension *n*

    another term for OVERGENERALIZATION

overgeneralization *n* **overgeneralize** *v*

    also **over-extension, over-regularization, analogy**

    a process common in both first- and second-language learning, in which a learner extends the use of a grammatical rule of a linguistic item beyond its accepted uses, generally by making words or structures follow a more regular pattern. For example, a child may use *ball* to refer to all round objects, or use *mans* instead of *men* for the plural of *man*.

overhead projector *n*

    also **OHP**

    a piece of classroom equipment that projects images from an *overhead transparency* onto a wall or screen. It can be used in a classroom instead of a whiteboard or blackboard.

overhead transparency *n*

    also **OHT**

    the plastic sheet that can be written on and used with an *overhead projector*.

overt language policy *n*

    see LANGUAGE POLICY

P

paced reading *v*

  1 a reading activity designed to develop students' reading speed, in which students read at a fixed rate determined by the teacher (e.g. 100 wpm), the reading rate gradually being increased over time.

  2 in developing reading skills, the use of software in which the computer scrolls text down the screen at a rate predetermined by the reader in order to encourage faster reading.

pacing *n*

  in teaching, the speed at which material is covered during a lesson including the rhythm of a class and the degree to which class time is used well. Teachers use different strategies to ensure that pacing is appropriate. Determination of pace for some activities may be determined by learners: this is known as **learner-paced instruction**. When teachers make pacing decisions it is known as **teacher-paced instruction**. For example teachers may provide a public summary of progress or announce a time frame for activities.

paired-associate learning *n*

  a learning task in which pairs of words or other items are presented and the learner is required to make associations between them. For example:

  horse – brown
  bird – blue
  table – white

  The learner is tested with the first member of the pair to see if the second item can be remembered.

  see also ASSOCIATIVE LEARNING

pair work *n*

  also **pair practice**

  (in language teaching) a learning activity which involves learners working together in pairs.

  see also GROUP WORK

palatal *n*

  an articulation involving the front of the tongue and the hard palate, for example the initial sound in English *you*.

  see PLACE OF ARTICULATION

palatalization *n*

  see ASSIMILATION

palate *n*
    see PLACE OF ARTICULATION

paradigm[1] *n* **paradigmatic** *adj*
    a list or pattern showing the forms which a word can have in a grammatical system. For example, in English:

singular	plural
boy	*boys*
boy's	*boys'*
(of the boy)	(of the boys)

Paradigms may be used to show the different forms of a verb. For example, in French:

singular	plural
je parle "I speak"	*nous parlons* "we speak"
tu parles "you speak"	*vous parlez* "you speak"
il parle "he speaks"	*ils parlent* "they speak"
elle parle "she speaks"	*elles parlent* "they speak"

Paradigms typically show a word's INFLECTIONS rather than its derivatives (see DERIVATION).

paradigm[2] *n*
    a term used very widely and loosely to refer to a conceptual framework of beliefs, theoretical assumptions, accepted research methods, and standards that define legitimate work in a particular science or discipline. The scientist Kuhn described the process of change in the sciences as a paradigm shift. He argued that change in a scientific field does not occur as a step-by-step cumulative process. Instead, new paradigms emerge as the result of revolutions in the thinking of a particular professional community. These shifts involve the adoption of a new outlook or paradigm on the part of members of that community. A paradigm shift in the physical sciences was the shift from Newtonian to quantum physics. Paradigm shifts also occur in the social sciences such as the shift from grammar-based to communicative approaches in language teaching. THEORIES are representative of particular paradigms.

paradigmatic relations *n*
    also **paradigmatic relationships**
    see SYNTAGMATIC RELATIONS

paragraph *n*
    a unit of organization of written language in many languages, which serves to indicate how the main ideas in a written text are grouped. In TEXT

LINGUISTICS, paragraphs are treated as indicators of the macro-structure of a text (see SCHEME). They group sentences which belong together, generally those which deal with the same topic. A new paragraph thus indicates a change in topic or sub-topic.

see also DISCOURSE ANALYSIS

paragraph outline *n*
see OUTLINE

paralinguistic features *n*
see PARALINGUISTICS

paralinguistics *n* **paralinguistic** *adj*
the study or use of non-vocal phenomena such as facial expressions, head or eye movements, and gestures, which may add support, emphasis, or particular shades of meaning to what people are saying. These phenomena are known as **paralinguistic features.**

For example, in English turning the head from side to side can be used to show disagreement (equivalent to "no"), whereas in Lebanese Arabic the same meaning can be signalled by raising the chin and producing an ingressive dental affricate. The use of paralinguistic features in this sense is also called **kinesics.**

For some linguists, paralinguistic features would also include those vocal characteristics such as TONE OF VOICE which may express the speaker's attitude to what he or she is saying.

see also PROXEMICS

parallel construction *n*
a sentence containing words, phrases, clauses or structures which are repeated.
For example:
Michael *smiled* at the baby, *touched* her arm, then *winked* at her.

parallel distributed processing (PDP) *n*
see CONNECTIONISM

parallel-form reliability *n*
see ALTERNATE FORM RELIABILITY

parallel forms *n*
see ALTERNATE FORMS

parallel processing *n*

information processing in which two or more processing operations are carried out at the same time or in parallel, such as when people try to remember a word and search for its meaning, spelling and pronunciation at the same time. This may be compared with sequential processing, where the two pieces of information are processed in sequence, such as when one tries to listen to two simultaneous conversations by attending to both but going back and forth rapidly from one to the other.

parameter[1] *n*

(in GENERATIVE THEORY) an abstract grammatical category that controls several superficially unrelated surface syntactic properties. For example, the **head parameter** determines whether a language positions the HEAD of a phrase before or after its COMPLEMENT[2]. A **head-first language** (English is one) is one in which heads normally precede their complements. A **head-last language** (Japanese is one) is one in which heads normally follow their complements.
see also PRO-DROP PARAMETER

parameter[2] *n*

a numerical value that summarizes a POPULATION, such as population mean (μ), population variance (σ) and population standard deviation (σ^2). The Greek alphabet letters are used to denote parameters.
see also STATISTIC

parameter-resetting *n*

see PARAMETER-SETTING

parameter-setting *n*

the process by which children determine what setting of a PARAMETER is appropriate for the one they are learning. In SECOND LANGUAGE ACQUISITION, parameter-setting is more appropriately considered to be **parameter-resetting** (since learners already have parameter-settings initially established for their first language).

parametric tests *n*

a group of statistical procedures based on the assumptions that the data are normally distributed and are measured on an INTERVAL or RATIO SCALE. Examples of parametric tests include T-TEST, ANALYSIS OF VARIANCE, and PEARSON PRODUCT-MOMENT CORRELATION.

paraphrase *n, v*

an expression of the meaning of a word or phrase using other words or phrases, often in an attempt to make the meaning easier to understand. For example, *to make (someone or something) appear or feel younger* is a paraphrase of the English verb *rejuvenate.* Dictionary definitions often take the form of paraphrases of the words they are trying to define.

paraprofessional *n*
also **teacher's aid**
a non-certified adult who helps teachers in the classroom. In some ESL classrooms such persons may be adults from the students' home language community.

parser *n*
any apparatus that parses. For example, in CORPUS LINGUISTICS, a parser is a computer program that adds syntactic analysis to a CORPUS, identifying subjects, verbs, objects, etc., as well as more complex syntactic information. In PSYCHOLINGUISTICS, the parser is viewed as a psychological process that operates on input and produces a structural description as part of the process of comprehension.

parsing *n*
the operation of assigning linguistic structure to a sentence or phrase. Parsing is a well-established technique of TRADITIONAL GRAMMAR. For example, the sentence *The noisy frogs disturbed us* can be parsed as follows:

	subject		verb	object
The	*noisy*	*frogs*	*disturbed*	*us*
definite article	adjective	noun (plural)	verb ((past tense) plural)	pronoun (1st-person)

partial replication *n*
see REPLICATION

participant *n*
a person who is present in a SPEECH EVENT and whose presence may have an influence on what is said and how it is said. He or she may actually take part in the exchange of speech or be merely a silent participant; for example, as part of an audience to whom a political speech is made.
see also INTERLOCUTORS

participant observation *n*
(in QUALITATIVE RESEARCH) a procedure in which the researcher or observer takes part in the situation he or she is studying (hence the term

participant observer) as a way of collecting data. It is claimed that an observer who is also a participant can understand a situation more fully than someone who is totally disengaged from it and may not actually have first-hand knowledge of it, but participant observation also raises ethical issues concerning overt and covert observation and INFORMED CONSENT on the part of those observed.

participant observer *n*
    see PARTICIPANT OBSERVATION

participation structure *n*
    in using language for communicative purposes, the rights and obligations of participants with respect to who can say what, when, and to whom and an important focus of research on classroom communication and classroom discourse.

participle *n* **participial** *adj*
    a non-finite verb form (see FINITE VERB) which functions as an adjective, and is used in passive sentences (see VOICE) and to form PERFECT and PROGRESSIVE ASPECT. There are two participles in English, the **present participle** and the **past participle**.
    The present participle is formed by adding *-ing* to a verb base. It functions as an adjective (e.g. a *smiling* girl, a *self-winding* watch); it is used with *BE* to form the PROGRESSIVE (e.g. *It is raining*); it occurs in constructions such as *Let's go shopping*.
    The past participle is usually formed by adding *-ed* to a verb base; exceptions are the *-en*-suffix (*break – broken*; *fall – fallen*) and some irregular verbs (e.g. *build – built*). It is used as an adjective (e.g. *a broken window*); it is used with *BE* to form the passive (e.g. I *was amused* by her); it is used to form the PERFECT ASPECT (e.g. *She has finished*).

particle *n*
    a term sometimes used for a word which cannot readily be identified with any of the main PARTS OF SPEECH (i.e. as a noun, verb, adverb, etc.). The word *not* and the *to* used with INFINITIVES are sometimes called particles for this reason, as well as *up*, *down* and similar adverbs when they function as ADVERB PARTICLES.

partitive *n*
    also **partitive construction**
    a phrase used to express quantity and used with an uncountable noun (see COUNTABLE NOUN). There are three types of partitive in English:

a measure partitives, e.g. a <u>*yard*</u> of cloth, an <u>*acre*</u> of land, two <u>*pints*</u> of milk

b typical partitives (i.e. where a particular partitive collocates with a particular noun), e.g. a <u>*slice*</u> of cake, a<u>*stick*</u> of chalk, a <u>*lump*</u> of coal

c general partitives (i.e. those which are not restricted to specific nouns), e.g. a <u>*piece*</u> of paper/cake, a <u>*bit*</u> of cheese/cloth.

see also COLLOCATION

part learning *n*

see GLOBAL LEARNING

part skills *n*

another term for MICRO-SKILLS

parts of speech *n*

a traditional term to describe the different types of word which are used to form sentences, such as noun, pronoun, verb, adjective, adverb, preposition, conjunction, interjection. From time to time other parts of speech have been proposed, such as DETERMINER.

Parts of speech may be identified by:

a their meaning (e.g. a verb is the name of a state or event: *go*)

b their form (e.g. a verb has an *-ing*-form, a past tense, and a past participle: *going, went, gone*)

c their function (e.g. a verb may form or be part of the PREDICATE of a sentence: *They went away*).

These criteria will identify the most typical representatives of each part of speech. However, many problems still remain. For example, in the sentence:

Their <u>going</u> away surprised me.

is *going* a verb or a noun?

see also GERUND, PARTICIPLE, PARTICLE

passive language knowledge *n*

see ACTIVE/PASSIVE LANGUAGE KNOWLEDGE

passive vocabulary *n*

see ACTIVE/PASSIVE LANGUAGE KNOWLEDGE

passive voice *n*

see VOICE[1]

past continuous *n*

see PROGRESSIVE

past participle *n*
    see PARTICIPLE

past perfect *n*
    see PERFECT

past tense *n*
    the form of a verb which is usually used to show that the act or state described by the verb occurred at a time before the present. For example, in English:

present tense	past tense
is	*was*
walk	*walked*
try	*tried*

The form of the past which is used without an AUXILIARY VERB (e.g. I *left*, he *wept*) is sometimes known as the **simple past** or **preterite**.

path analysis *n*
    a statistical procedure to test a researcher's theory of the causal relationships among a set of observed (or manifest) variables by analyzing hypothesized causal effects among variables.

patient θ-role *n*
    see θ-THEORY/THETA THEORY

pattern practice *n*
    see DRILL

pausing *n*
    also **hesitation phenomena**
    a commonly occurring feature of natural speech in which gaps or hesitations appear during the production of utterances. The commonest types of pauses are:
    a **silent pauses**: silent breaks between words
    b **filled pauses**: gaps which are filled by such expressions as *um*, *er*, *mm*.
    People who speak slowly often use more pauses than people who speak quickly. When people speak, up to 50% of their speaking time may be made up of pauses.
    see also FLUENCY

PDP *n*
    an abbreviation for PARALLEL DISTRIBUTED PROCESSING

peak (of a syllable) *n*
   see SYLLABLE

Pearson product-moment correlation (r)
   see CORRELATION

pedagogical content knowledge *n*
   in teaching, a teacher's knowledge of subject matter and the ability to represent it in a way that will facilitate teaching and learning. Whereas **content knowledge** refers to knowledge of subject matter, **pedagogical content knowledge** refers to knowing how to turn that subject matter into plans for teaching and learning. It is a key component of teaching skill.

pedagogic grammar *n*
   also PEDAGOGICAL GRAMMAR
   a grammatical description of a language which is intended for pedagogical purposes, such as language teaching, syllabus design, or the preparation of teaching materials. A pedagogic grammar may be based on:
   a grammatical analysis and description of a language
   b a particular grammatical theory, such as GENERATIVE GRAMMAR
   c the study of the grammatical problems of learners (see ERROR ANALYSIS) or on a combination of approaches.

pedagogy *n*
   in general terms, pedagogy refers to theories of teaching, curriculum and instruction as well as the ways in which formal teaching and learning in institutional settings such as schools is planned and delivered. In educational theory, pedagogy is usually divided into *curriculum*, *instruction*, and *evaluation*. Since language is the essential medium of pedagogy, the role of language in pedagogy is a focus of theorizing and research by linguists, applied linguists, educators, and critical pedagogues. CRITICAL PEDAGOGY seeks to address issues related to the distribution and exercises of power and knowledge in educational settings.

peer assessment *n*
   activities in which learners assess each other's performance.

peer correction *n*
   another term for PEER REVIEW

peer editing *n*
   another term for PEER REVIEW

peer feedback *n*
> another term for PEER REVIEW

peer group *n*
> a group of people with whom a person associates or identifies, e.g. neigh-
> bourhood children of the same age, or members of the same class at school
> or of the same sports team.
> see also NETWORK

peer monitoring *n*
> in teaching, the use of observation and assessment of what is happening in
> the classroom during learning activities that is carried out for students by
> other students in the class.

peer review *n*
> also **peer feedback, peer editing**
> (in the teaching of composition, particularly according to the PROCESS
> APPROACH) an activity in the revising stage of writing (see COMPOSING
> PROCESSES) in which students receive FEEDBACK about their writing from
> other students – their peers. Typically students work in pairs or small
> groups, read each other's compositions and ask questions or give comments
> or suggestions.

peer teaching *n*
> also **peer mediated instruction**
> classroom teaching in which one student teaches another, particularly
> within a learner-centred approach to teaching. For example, when students
> have learnt something, they may teach it to other students, or test other
> students on it.

peer tutoring *n*
> see CO-OPERATIVE LEARNING

pejorative *adj*
> a word or expression that suggest disapproval or that something is not good
> or of no importance. For example to call someone a "twit" or "dickhead".

percentile *n*
> a term describing the position of a test taker within a distribution divided
> equally into 100 ranks. A test taker's percentile has a corresponding RAW
> SCORE below which a particular percentage of scores fall (see PERCENTILE
> SCORE for this interpretation). For example, the 95th percentile of a test

taker on a test has a certain raw score, which varies depending on which NORM GROUP this test taker's raw score is compared to.
see also DISTRIBUTION, PERCENTILE SCORE

percentile rank *n*
another term for PERCENTILE SCORE

percentile score *n*
also **percentile rank**
a term indicating the percentage of all the test takers in the NORM GROUP who scored below the RAW SCORE one test taker has received. It is used to describe a test taker's relative position with respect to all other test takers in a distribution. For example, if a test taker is said to have an 95th-percentile score on a test (or to be at the 95th percentile), it means that this person scored higher than 95% of the test takers in the norm group or is among the top 5% of all test takers. On most tests, the higher one's percentile score, the better. Percentile scores are used in the NORM REFERENCED TESTING context, whereas **percentage scores** (i.e. the percentage of items answered correctly) are used in the CRITERION-REFERENCED TESTING context.
see also PERCENTILE

perception *n*
the recognition and understanding of events, objects, and stimuli through the use of senses (sight, hearing, touch, etc.). Several different types of perception are distinguished:
a **Visual perception:** the perception of visual information and stimuli.
b **Auditory perception:** the perception of information and stimuli received through the ears. Auditory perception requires a listener to detect different kinds of acoustic signals, and to judge differences between them according to differences in such acoustic characteristics as their frequency, amplitude, duration, order of occurrence, and rate of presentation.
c **Speech perception:** the understanding or comprehension of speech (see CHUNKING, HEURISTIC (2)).

perceptual salience *n*
another term for SALIENCE

perfect *n*
also **perfective**
(in grammar) an ASPECT which shows a relationship between one state or event and a later state, event, or time. In English the perfect is formed from the AUXILIARY VERB *have* and the past PARTICIPLE. For example:

I have finished. She has always loved animals.

If the auxiliary is in the present tense, the verb group is described as the **present perfect** (e.g. *They have eaten*) and if the auxiliary is in the past tense, the verb group is described as the **past perfect** (e.g. *They had finished*).

English also has a fairly rare **future perfect** (*They will have finished before noon tomorrow*).

In English the perfect generally refers

a to a state or event that extends up to a point in time (e.g. *I have lived here for six years* – up to now)

b to an event that occurred within a time period (e.g. *Have you ever been to Paris?* – in your life up to now)

c to an event that has results which continue up to a point in time (e.g. *I have broken my watch* – and it's still broken now).

performance *n*

(in GENERATIVE GRAMMAR) a person's actual use of language. A difference is made between a person's knowledge of a language (COMPETENCE) and how a person uses this knowledge in producing and understanding sentences (performance). For example, people may have the competence to produce an infinitely long sentence but when they actually attempt to use this knowledge (to "perform") there are many reasons why they restrict the number of adjectives, adverbs, and clauses in any one sentence. They may run out of breath, or their listeners may get bored or forget what has been said if the sentence is too long. In second and foreign language learning, a learner's performance in a language is often taken as an indirect indication of his or her competence (see PERFORMANCE ANALYSIS), although other indexes such as GRAMMATICALITY JUDGEMENTS are sometimes considered a more direct measure of competence.

There is also a somewhat different way of using the term "performance". In using language, people often make errors (see SPEECH ERRORS). These may be due to **performance factors** such as fatigue, lack of attention, excitement, nervousness. Their actual use of language on a particular occasion may not reflect their competence. The errors they make are described as examples of performance.

see also USAGE[1]

performance-based assessment *n*

an approach to assessment that seeks to measure student learning based on how well the learner can perform on a practical real-world task such as the ability to write an essay or carry out a short conversation. This approach is thought to be a better measure of learning than performance on traditional tests such as multiple-choice tests.

performance factors *n*
see PERFORMANCE

performance grammar *n*
a description of the rules or strategies which people use when they produce and understand sentences. A performance grammar may be contrasted with a competence grammar (see COMPETENCE), which is a description of the linguistic knowledge of speakers and hearers, but not an explanation of how they use that knowledge in speaking and listening.

performance indicator *n*
in educational evaluation, a measurement that is used to measure progress toward goals and objectives. For example, a school may focus on graduation rates, standardized test scores, or other outcomes. Performance indicators must reflect an organization's goals; they must be key to its success; and they must be quantifiable (measurable).

performance objective *n*
another term for BEHAVIOURAL OBJECTIVE

performance standard *n*
the level which is set for the attainment of an OBJECTIVE, i.e. the CRITERION.
see BEHAVIOURAL OBJECTIVE

performance standards *n*
in testing and programme development, statements that specify how students will demonstrate their knowledge and skills in language as well as the level at which they must perform in order to be considered to have met the standard.

performance test *n*
a test that is based on a sample of the actual skill, behaviour or activity being measured such as testing students' composition skills by requiring them to write a composition.
see PERFORMANCE-BASED ASSESSMENT

performative *n*
(in SPEECH ACT theory) an utterance which performs an act, such as *Watch out* (= a warning), *I promise not to be late* (= a promise). The philosopher Austin distinguished between performatives and **constatives**. A constative is an utterance which asserts something that is either true or false; for example, *Chicago is in the United States*. Austin further distinguished between

explicit performatives (those containing a "performative verb", such as *promise, warn, deny*, which names the speech act or **illocutionary force** of the sentence) and **implicit performatives**, which do not contain a performative verb, e.g. *There is a vicious dog behind you* (= an implied warning).

It has even been suggested that there is no real difference between constatives and implicit performatives, because the sentence *Chicago is in the United States* can be understood to mean (*I state that*) *Chicago is in the United States*, with the implicit performative verb *state*.

performative hypothesis *n*

the hypothesis that every sentence can theoretically be derived from a deep structure containing an EXPLICIT PERFORMATIVE associated with a particular SPEECH ACT. For example, under this proposal, a sentence like *I'll be there early* would be derived from a deep structure something like *I promise to you that I will be there early*, or (under a different reading) *I predict that I will be there early*.

periphery *n*

also **peripheral grammar**

see CORE GRAMMAR

perlocutionary act *n*

see LOCUTIONARY ACT

perseveration error *n*

see SPEECH ERRORS

perseverative assimilation *n*

see ASSIMILATION

person *n*

a grammatical category which determines the choice of pronouns in a sentence according to such principles as:

a whether the pronoun represents or includes the person or persons actually speaking or writing ("first person", e.g. *I, we*)

b whether the pronoun represents the person or persons being addressed ("second person", e.g. *you*)

c whether the pronoun represents someone or something other than the speaker/writer or the listener/reader ("third person", e.g. *he, she, it, they*).

personal function *n*
see DEVELOPMENTAL FUNCTIONS OF LANGUAGE

personality *n*
those aspects of an individual's behaviour, attitudes, beliefs, thought, actions and feelings which are seen as typical and distinctive of that person and recognized as such by that person and others. Personality factors such as self-esteem, inhibition, anxiety, RISK-TAKING and extroversion (see EXTROVERT), are thought to influence second language learning because they can contribute to MOTIVATION and the choice of learner strategies.

personalization *n*
in language teaching, an activity which allows students to apply something they have learned to their own lives and to express their own ideas, feelings, preferences and opinions. For example, after reading a passage about the sport of boxing, students may work in pairs to share their ideas and feelings about boxing as a sport.

personal pronouns *n*
the set of pronouns which represent the grammatical category of PERSON, and which in English is made up of *I*, *you*, *he*, *she*, *it*, *we*, *they*, and their derived forms (e.g. *me*, *mine*, *yours*, *him*, *his*, *hers*, etc.).

personal recount
see TEXT TYPES

PF component *n*
also **phonetic component**
see D-STRUCTURE

pharyngeal *n*
a speech sound (a CONSONANT) involving the root of the tongue and the back of the throat (the PHARYNX). Several such speech sounds occur in Arabic.

pharyngealization *n*
a secondary articulation in which the root of the tongue is drawn back so that the pharynx is narrowed, as in some so-called "emphatic" consonants in Arabic.

pharynx *n*

>that part of the throat which extends from above the VOCAL CORDS up to the soft palate (**velum**) at the back of the mouth. The pharynx is like a large chamber and in the production of speech sounds its shape and volume can be changed in various ways:
>*a* by tightening the muscles which enclose it
>*b* by movement of the back of the tongue
>*c* by either raising or lowering the soft palate.
>Changes in the shape of the pharynx affect the quality of the sounds produced.
>see also PLACE OF ARTICULATION

phatic communion *n*

>a term used by the British-Polish anthropologist Malinowski to refer to communication between people which is not intended to seek or convey information but has the social function of establishing or maintaining social contact. Examples of phatic communion in English include such expressions as *How are you?* and *Nice day, isn't it?*

phi correlation (Φ)

>see CORRELATION

philology *n* **philological** *adj*

>another term for COMPARATIVE HISTORICAL LINGUISTICS

phone *n* **phonic** *adj*

>individual sounds as they occur in speech. Phones are grouped by PHONEMIC ANALYSIS into the distinctive sound units (PHONEMES) of a language.
>For example, in English, the different ways of pronouncing the vowel in the word *can*, e.g. long [æː], shorter [æ], with nasalization [æ̃], are all phones of the phoneme /æ/.
>see also ALLOPHONE, PHONEMICS, PHONOLOGY

phoneme *n* **phonemic** *adj*

>the smallest unit of sound in a language which can distinguish two words. For example:
>*a* in English, the words *pan* and *ban* differ only in their initial sound:
> *pan* begins with /p/ and *ban* with /b/
>b *ban* and *bin* differ only in their vowels: /æ/ and /ɪ/.
>Therefore, /p/, /b/, /æ/, and /ɪ/ are phonemes of English. The number of phonemes varies from one language to another. English is often considered to have 44 phonemes: 24 CONSONANTs and 20 VOWELs.
>see also ALLOPHONE, MINIMAL PAIR, PHONEMICS, PHONOLOGY

phoneme synthesis *n*

the conversion of a digital representation of phonemes into sounds by a speech synthesizer (see SPEECH SYNTHESIS)

phonemic analysis *n*

the grouping of words and sounds (PHONES) in a particular language in order to decide which are the distinctive sound units (PHONEMES) of that language and which are only variants of these.

For example, the two English words *nip* and *nib* differ only because *nip* ends with /p/ and *nib* with /b/. So /p/ and /b/ are two separate English phonemes. On the other hand, pronouncing *nip* with an aspirated /p/, [ph], does not make it into another word. So [ph] is a variant (an ALLOPHONE) of /p/ and not a separate phoneme.

There are different approaches to phonemic analysis (see DISTINCTIVE FEATURES, MINIMAL PAIRS).

see also ALLOPHONE, ASPIRATION, PHONEMICS, PHONOLOGY

phonemic coding ability *n*

see LANGUAGE APTITUDE

phonemic notation *n*

see NOTATION

phonemics *n* **phonemic** *adj*

1 the study or description of the distinctive sound units (PHONEMES) of a language and their relationship to one another.

2 procedures for finding the phonemes of a language (see PHONEMIC ANALYSIS).

The term "phonemics" has been used by American linguists, particularly in STRUCTURAL LINGUISTICS. Lately, the term PHONOLOGY has been preferred.

3 the phonemic system of a language, as in a phrase like "the phonemics of English".

see also MORPHOPHONEMICS

phonetic component *n*

another term for PF COMPONENT

see D-STRUCTURE

phonetic method *n*

another term for PHONICS

phonetic notation *n*
also **phonetic script**
see NOTATION, PHONETIC SYMBOLS

phonetics *n* **phonetic** *adj*
the study of speech sounds. There are three main areas of phonetics:
1 **Articulatory phonetics** deals with the way in which speech sounds are produced. Sounds are usually classified according to the position of the lips and the tongue, how far open the mouth is, whether or not the VOCAL CORDS are vibrating, etc.
2 **Acoustic phonetics** deals with the transmission of speech sounds through the air. When a speech sound is produced it causes minor air disturbances (SOUND WAVES). Various instruments are used to measure the characteristics of these sound waves.
3 **Auditory phonetics** deals with how speech sounds are perceived by the listener.
For example, a listener may perceive:
a differences in ASPIRATION e.g. between the aspirated /p/ of [pʰɪt] *pit* and the unaspirated /p/ of [tɪp] *tip*.
b other differences in sound quality, e.g. between the "clear" /l/ of [laɪt] *light* and the "dark" /l/ of [hɪɫ] *hill*.
see also PHONEMICS, PHONOLOGY

phonetic script *n*
another term for PHONETIC NOTATION
see NOTATION, PHONETIC SYMBOLS

phonetic symbols *n*
special alphabetic or other typographical characters which express the sounds of an actual spoken utterance in writing. A transcription of such an utterance in phonetic symbols is said to be in **phonetic notation** or **script**. For example, the sound which is written *sh* in English, *sch* in German and *ch* in French can be expressed by symbols [ʃ] or [š], e.g. English [ʃɪp] *ship*, German [ʃɪf] *Schiff* "ship", French [ʃik] *chic* "smart, stylish".
see also INTERNATIONAL PHONETIC ALPHABET, NOTATION, PHONETICS

phonics *n*
also **phonetic method**
a method of teaching children to read. It is commonly used in teaching reading in the mother tongue.
Children are taught to recognize the relationship between letters and sounds. They are taught the sounds which the letters of the alphabet represent, and

then try to build up the sound of a new or unfamiliar word by saying it one sound at a time.

see also ALPHABETIC METHOD

phonological component *n*

see GENERATIVE THEORY

phonological rule *n*

see GENERATIVE PHONOLOGY

phonology *n* phonological *adj*

1 another term for PHONEMICS.
2 (for some linguists) a cover term for both PHONETICS and PHONEMICS.
3 the establishment and description of the distinctive sound units of a language (PHONEMES) by means of DISTINCTIVE FEATURES.

Each phoneme is considered as consisting of a group of these features and differing in at least one feature from the other phonemes, e.g.

/iː/	/uː/
+ high	++ high
– low	– low
– back	+ back
– round	+ round

where the features + or – *high*, + or – *low*, + or – *back* refer to the position of the tongue in the mouth and + or – *round* to whether the lips are rounded or not.

Phonology is also concerned with:

a the study of word-to-word relations in sentences; that is, how sound patterns are affected by the combination of words. For example, /gɪv/ *give* and /hɪm/ *him* may combine to /gɪvɪm/ *give him*.
b the investigation of INTONATION PATTERNS.

see also BOUNDARIES, GENERATIVE PHONOLOGY, SUPRASEGMENTAL

phonotactics *n* phonotactic *adj*

(in PHONOLOGY) the arrangements of the distinctive sound units (PHONEMES) in a language.

For example, in English, the consonant groups (CONSONANT CLUSTERS) /spr/ and /str/ can occur at the beginning of a word, as in *sprout*, *strain*, but they cannot occur at the end of a word. A description of the phonotactics of English consonant clusters would include this information.

phrasal-prepositional verb *n*

see PHRASAL VERB

phrasal verb *n*

a verbal construction consisting of a verb plus an ADVERB PARTICLE. A distinction may be made between phrasal verbs, **prepositional verbs,** and **phrasal-prepositional verbs,** according to the different grammatical patterns in which they occur. For example:

	phrasal verb		*prepositional verb*
Particle may be stressed	*Turn OFF the light.*	Verb may be stressed	*I'll APPLY for the job.*
Particle can occur after the object	*Turn the light off.*	Particle cannot occur after the object	(*I'll *apply* the job *for*)
Short pronouns occur between the verb and the particle	*Turn it off* (*Turn off it*)	Pronouns occur after the verb+ particle	*I'll apply for it.* (*I'll *apply* it *for*)

A phrasal-prepositional verb consists of a verb, an adverb particle, and a PREPOSITION:

We must cut down on expenses.

They put their failure down to bad advice.

The meaning of some of these verbal constructions can be guessed from the meanings of their parts (e.g. *cut down on*). But the meaning of others is idiomatic (e.g. *put down to*).

Nowadays the term "phrasal verb" is often used to include phrasal verbs, prepositional verbs, and phrasal-prepositional verbs.

see also IDIOM

phrase *n*

see CLAUSE

phrase-marker *n*

also **P-marker**

a representation of the structure of a phrase or sentence.

see also TREE DIAGRAM

phrase structure *n*

also **constituent structure, syntactic structure**

a representation of the set of constituents that an expression contains. For example, the constituents of the English noun phrase *this big house* are the demonstrative *this* + the adjective *big* + the noun *house*. Phrase structure is usually represented in terms of a labelled bracketing or a tree-diagram.

phrase-structure grammar *n*

a grammar which analyzes the structure of different sentence types in a language. It consists of **phrase-structure rules** which specify the constituency of syntactic categories. For example, one phrase-structure rule specifies that a noun phrase (NP) can be expanded or "rewritten as" (Art) (Adj) N (PP), that is, an optional article plus an optional adjective plus a noun plus an optional prepositional phrase. The structure of sentences generated by such rules is often illustrated by a TREE DIAGRAM.

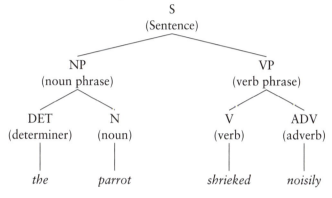

phrase-structure rule *n*

see PHRASE-STRUCTURE GRAMMAR

phylogeny *n*

also **phylogenesis**

see ONTOGENY

picture dictionary *n*

a dictionary in which meanings are shown entirely through illustrations such as pictures or photographs. Picture dictionaries usually seek to explain the words in a BASIC VOCABULARY and words are normally grouped by topic or situation.

pidgin *n*

a language which develops as a **contact language** when groups of people who speak different languages try to communicate with one another on a regular basis. For example, this has occurred many times in the past when foreign traders had to communicate with the local population or groups of workers from different language backgrounds on plantations or in factories. A pidgin usually has a limited vocabulary and a reduced grammatical structure which may expand when a pidgin is used over a long period and for many purposes. For example, Tok Pisin (New Guinea Pidgin):

yu	ken	kisim	long	olgeta	bik pela		stua
you	can	get(it)	at	all	big	(noun marker)	stores

Usually pidgins have no native speakers but there are **expanded pidgins**, e.g. Tok Pisin in Papua New Guinea and Nigerian Pidgin English in West Africa, which are spoken by some people in their community as first or PRIMARY LANGUAGE. Often expanded pidgins will develop into CREOLE languages.

Research has shown that there are some similarities between the structures of pidgin and creole languages and the INTERLANGUAGES of second language learners (see PIDGINIZATION[2])

see also PIDGINIZATION[1], SUBSTRATUM INTERFERENCE/INFLUENCE, SUPER-STRATUM/SUBSTRATE LANGUAGE

pidginization[1] *n*

the process by which a PIDGIN develops.

pidginization[2] *n*

(in second and foreign language learning) the development of a grammatically reduced form of a TARGET LANGUAGE[1]. This is usually a temporary stage in language learning. The learner's INTERLANGUAGE may have a limited system of auxiliary verbs, simplified question and negative forms, and reduced rules for TENSE[1], NUMBER[1], and other grammatical categories.

If learners do not advance beyond this stage, the result may be a PIDGINIZED FORM of the target language.

see also PIDGINIZATION HYPOTHESIS

pidginization hypothesis *n*

(in SECOND LANGUAGE ACQUISITION theory) the hypothesis that a PIDGINIZED FORM of a language may develop (a) when learners regard themselves as socially separate from speakers of the TARGET LANGUAGE[1] (b) when a language is used for a very limited range of functions.

see also PIDGINIZATION[2]

pidginized form (of a language) *n*

a variety of a language in which the sentence structure and the vocabulary of the original language have been greatly reduced.

Generally, elements from another language have been absorbed, either in the form of vocabulary items or in the way sentences are structured (see PIDGIN).

An example is Bahasa Pasar (Bazaar Malay), a pidginized form of Malay, which was spoken extensively by Chinese and other non Malays in Malaysia and Singapore and used as a lingua franca.

pied piping *n*
  see PREPOSITION STRANDING

pilot testing *n*
  see PRETESTING

pitch *n*
  when we listen to people speaking, we can hear some sounds or groups of sounds in their speech to be relatively higher or lower than others. This relative height of speech sounds as perceived by a listener is called "pitch". For example, in the Spanish question *listo?* ("ready") meaning "Are you ready?" the second syllable *-to* will be heard as having a higher pitch than the first syllable. What we can hear as pitch is produced by the VOCAL CORDS vibrating. The faster the vocal cords vibrate, the higher the pitch.
  see also SOUND WAVES, FUNDAMENTAL FREQUENCY

pitch contour *n*
  another term for INTONATION CONTOUR

pitch level *n*
  the relative height of the PITCH of a speaker's voice, as this is perceived by the listener.
  For English, three pitch levels have often been recognized: normal pitch level, higher than normal level, lower than normal level.
  These three levels cannot be identified in absolute terms. One person's high pitch will not be the same as another person's high pitch. Differences in pitch level are therefore relative (see KEY[2]).
  see also TONE UNIT

pitch movement *n*
  another term for TONE[2]

pitch pattern *n*
  another term for INTONATION CONTOUR

pitch range[1] *n*
  variations in PITCH height that an individual speaker is able to produce. Differences in the pitch of individual speakers are related to

differences in the size of their VOCAL CORDS and the structure of their VOCAL TRACT.

pitch range² *n*

variations in height which are used by a speaker or group of speakers in communication. Whether the pitch range used by individuals in a speech community is wide or narrow often depends on social or cultural conventions and may be a convention of a whole speech community.

For example, the pitch range of the average Australian when speaking English is narrower than that of many British English speakers. When speakers are in certain emotional states, they may either extend their normal pitch range, e.g. to express anger or excitement, or narrow it, e.g. to express boredom or misery.

pivot grammar *n*

a term for a now-discarded theory of grammatical development in first-language learning. Children were said to develop two major grammatical classes of words: a pivot class (a small group of words which were attached to other words, e.g. *on, allgone, more*) and an "open class" (e.g. *shoe, milk*) to which pivot words were attached. The child's early grammar was thought to be a set of rules which determined how the two classes of words could be combined to produce utterances such as *allgone milk, shoe on*.

PLAB *n*

an abbreviation for the Pimsleur Language Aptitude Battery, a test of LANGUAGE APTITUDE.

placement test *n*

a test that is designed to place test takers at an appropriate level in a programme or course. The term "placement test" does not refer to what a test contains or how it is constructed, but to the purpose for which it is used. Various types of test or testing procedure (e.g. dictation, an interview, a grammar test) can be used for placement purposes.

place of articulation *n*

there are many parts of the mouth and throat (the **oral cavity**) that are used in the production of speech sounds. The main ones for the articulation of English CONSONANTs are:

a the two lips (BILABIAL), e.g. /p/

b the lower lip touching the upper teeth (LABIODENTAL), e.g. /f/

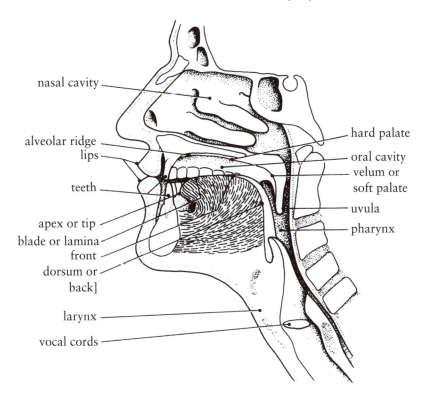

nasal cavity

alveolar ridge
lips

teeth

apex or tip
blade or lamina
front
dorsum or
back]

larynx

vocal cords

hard palate

oral cavity
velum or
soft palate

uvula

pharynx

c the tongue touching the upper teeth (INTERDENTAL), e.g. /θ/ th in thick
d the tongue touching the **alveolar ridge (alveolum)** (ALVEOLAR), e.g. /t/
e the back of the tongue touching the soft palate (**velum**) (VELAR), e.g. /k/
The production of VOWELs is conditioned by the position of the tongue
in the mouth, e.g. front vowels, back vowels, high vowels, low vowels (see
VOWEL).

see also CARDINAL VOWELS, MANNER OF ARTICULATION

planning *n*
   see COMPOSING PROCESSES

platform *n*
   in **e-learning**, a learning management system used to administer student
   courses and to provide learning content.

platykurtic distribution *n*
   see KURTOSIS

plosive *n*

another term for STOP

plural *n*

(with English COUNTABLE NOUNS, and PRONOUNS,) the form referring to more than one. For example, *books*, *geese*, *they* are the plurals of *book*, *goose*, and *he/she/it*.

plurilingualism *n*

sometimes used to mean the knowledge of several languages by an individual. **Multilingualism** is then used to refer to the societal use of several languages.

P-marker *n*

an abbreviation for PHRASE MARKER

podcast *n*

an audio BLOG that users create and upload to a server or website so it can be downloaded to computers or portable audio devices.

point-biserial correlation (r_{pbi}) *n*

see CORRELATION

point of view *n*

(in composition) the position from which the writer presents an idea or topic. In English composition, good writing is said to be written from a consistent point of view, that is, without any unnecessary shifts of point of view. In the following example, an inconsistent point of view is used because the writer shifts from referring to teachers impersonally (using "teachers" and "they") to referring to them personally (using "you").

Teachers should always prepare carefully for lessons. They should never walk into class without knowing what they are going to teach, and you should never arrive late for class.

politeness *n*

(in language study) (a) how languages express the SOCIAL DISTANCE between speakers and their different ROLE RELATIONSHIPS; (b) how face-work (see FACE), that is, the attempt to establish, maintain, and save face during conversation, is carried out in a speech community. Languages differ in how they express politeness. In English, phrases like *I wonder if I could . . .* can be used to make a request more polite. Many other languages (Japanese and Javanese are examples) devote far more linguistic resources and require more complex work on the part of a speaker to encode levels of politeness.

Politeness markers include differences between FORMAL SPEECH and COL-LOQUIAL SPEECH, and the use of ADDRESS FORMS. In expressing politeness, the anthropologists Brown and Levinson distinguished between **positive politeness strategies** (those which signal the closeness, intimacy, and rapport between speaker and hearer) and **negative politeness strategies** (those which address the social distance between speaker and hearer and minimize the imposition that a face-threatening action unavoidably effects).

politeness formula *n*
 see ROUTINE

polysemy *n* **polysemous** *adj*
 (of a word) having two or more closely related meanings, e.g. *foot* in:
  He hurt his foot.
  She stood at the foot of the stairs.
 The foot is the lowest part of the stairs just as the foot is the lowest part of the human body.
 A well known problem in SEMANTICS is how to decide whether we are dealing with a single polysemous word (like *foot*) or with two or more HOMONYMS[3].

polysyllabic *adj*
 (of a word) consisting of more than one SYLLABLE. For example, in English:
  telephone
 and in Hawaiian:
  humuhumunukunukuapua'a (the name of the Hawaii state fish) are polysyllabic words.

population *n*
 (in statistics) any set of items, individuals, etc. that share some common and observable characteristics and from which a SAMPLE can be taken. Thus, one can speak of comparing test scores across a sample of a population of students.

portfolio *n*
 a purposeful collection of work that provides information about someone's efforts, progress or achievement in a given area. It is a learning as well as assessment tool. As applied to language learners, its characteristics are:
 a the learner is involved in deciding what to include in the portfolio
 b the learner may revise material in the portfolio after feedback from the teacher or others
 c the learner is required to assess or reflect on the work in the portfolio, thus becoming aware of personal development

    d there is evidence of mastery of knowledge
    e it may include various forms of work, such as written work, audio recording, video recording, etc.
When used in teacher education the portfolio is known as a TEACHING PORTFOLIO.

portfolio assessment *n*
an approach that makes use of portfolios as a basis of assessment.

portmanteau word *n*
see BLENDING

positional variant *n*
an ALLOPHONE of a particular PHONEME that appears in a specific position. For example, the aspirated stops at the beginnings of the English words *pot*, *top*, and *cop* are positional variants of the phonemes /p/, /t/, and /k/, respectively.

positive evidence *n*
see EVIDENCE

positive face *n*
the good image that people have of others and themselves and wish others to have of them as well.
see FACE, POLITENESS

positively skewed distribution *n*
see SKEWNESS

positive politeness strategies *n*
see POLITENESS

positive reinforcement *n*
see OPERANT CONDITIONING, STIMULUS-RESPONSE THEORY

positive transfer *n*
see LANGUAGE TRANSFER

positivism *n*
a philosophical movement that began in the early twentieth century, characterized by an emphasis on the scientific method as the only source of knowledge and a desire to rebuild society on the basis of "positive" knowledge. As a version of EMPIRICISM, among the basic ideas of positivism are the idea

that the world is orderly, that all natural phenomena have natural causes, and that nothing is self-evident, but the laws of nature can be discovered through experimentation. Although few people nowadays subscribe to all of these beliefs, some degree of positivism characterizes most "scientific" approaches to understanding all phenomena, including language learning. **Logical positivism** is a specific type of positivism that rejects as meaningless all statements that cannot be empirically verified.

see also MODERNISM, POSTMODERNISM

possessive *n*

a word or part of a word which is used to show ownership or possession. In English, there are many kinds of possessives, for example:

a possessive pronouns, such as *my, her, your, mine, hers, yours*, etc.

b *'s*, as in *Helen's shoes*, and *s'*, as in *the three boys' books*

c the *of* construction, as in *the home of the doctor*

The possessive pronouns that are used before a noun (e.g. *my, her, your*) are often called "possesive adjectives" to distinguish them from those that are used after a verb (e.g. *mine, hers, yours*). The distinction can be seen in a pair of sentences like:

<u>*My*</u> book is here. *This book is* <u>*mine*</u>.

see also DETERMINER

postcolonial theory *n*

a set of theories that deal with the cultural legacy of colonial rule, including issues of national identity, gender, race, ethnicity, and literature in the former colonial language.

post-creole continuum *n*

when people in a CREOLE-SPEAKING community are taught in the standard language to which the creole is related, they form a post-creole continuum. For example, in Jamaica and Guyana, an English-based creole is spoken and Standard English is taught in schools. Those with higher levels of education speak something close to Standard English, the **acrolect**. Those with little or no education speak the creole or something close to it, the **basilect**, and the rest speak a range of varieties in between, the **mesolects**.

speech varieties	speakers
acrolect	higher education and social status
mesolects	
basilect	little or no education, low social status

see also DECREOLIZATION, SPEECH CONTINUUM

postmodernism *n*

also **postpositivism**

a term that has significantly different meanings in architecture, literary criticism, anthropology, and other disciplines. In education, the term generally refers to a rejection of POSITIVISM and MODERNISM, which are criticized for failing to recognize the cultural relativity of all forms of knowledge, for emphasizing the importance of the autonomous individual, and for failing to take a moral stand against oppression. In this view, "science" is usually interested (not disinterested) and never objective. With respect to approaches to research and theory, postmodernists are sceptical of general theories and attempts to generalize research findings.

postmodifier *n*

see MODIFIER

post-observation conference

in teacher training, an informal meeting between a teacher-supervisor and a teacher or trainee teacher following observation of a teacher's lesson. During the conference the strengths and weakness of the lesson are normally discussed and the supervisor uses a variety of strategies to help the teacher develop a reflective stance towards his or her teaching.

postponed subject *n*

see EXTRAPOSITION

postposition *n*

a word or MORPHEME which follows a noun or NOUN PHRASE[1] and indicates location, direction, possession, etc. For example, in Japanese:

Tokyo – kara

"Tokyo" "from"

"from Tokyo"

English prefers PREPOSITIONS to postpositions, but a word like *notwithstanding* can be used in either way:

The plan went ahead, <u>notwithstanding</u> my protests.

(prepositional use)

The plan went ahead, my protests <u>notwithstanding</u>.

(postpositional use)

postpositivism *n*

see POSTMODERNISM

post-test *n*

a test given after learning has occurred or is supposed to have occurred. A test given before learning has occurred is a **pre-test**. In teaching, the comparison of pre-test and post-test results measures the amount of progress a learner has made.

postverbal negation *n*

the use of a NEGATOR following a verb, as in German *Ingrid kommt nicht* (Ingrid comes not = Ingrid isn't coming), where *nicht is* the negator. Compare **preverbal negation**, the use of a negator preceding the verb, as in Spanish *Juan no va* (Juan not goes = Juan isn't going), where *no* is the negator.

postwriting *n*

see COMPOSING PROCESSES

poverty of the stimulus *n*

a term referring to the notion that UNIVERSAL GRAMMAR is needed to explain language learning because the input to learners is so impoverished that it is insufficient to explain learning. In particular, the input does not provide learners with NEGATIVE EVIDENCE necessary to avoid or retreat from incorrect hypotheses.

power *n*

the probability of correctly rejecting a NULL HYPOTHESIS when it is false, denoted by $1-\beta$, where β is the probability of a TYPE II ERROR. It is also the probability of detecting a real effect, such as a difference or correlation, in a study. Power studies, in which a preliminary effort to investigate the actual needed power of a statistical test if an effect is to be detected are not very commonly carried out in applied linguistics but would be beneficial to the field.

see also TYPE I ERROR, TYPE II ERROR

power test *n*

a type of test where every test taker is given sufficient time to complete the test. The difficulty level of some items on the test is beyond the ability of test takers so that no test taker is expected to get every item right.

see also SPEEDED TEST

PPP

an abbreviation for **Presentation Practice Production**.

a procedure used in traditional British-based language teaching methodology which refers to three stages in a language lesson, particularly one that is grammar-based.

   a **Presentation stage**: the introduction of new items, when their meanings are explained, demonstrated, etc., and other necessary information is given.

   b **Practice stage** (also **repetition stage**): new items are practised, either individually or in groups. Practice activities usually move from controlled to less controlled practice.

   c **Production stage** (also **transfer stage, free practice**): students use the new items more freely, with less or little control by the teacher.

see also STRUCTURING

practice *n*

in general, the building up of a skill through repetition or repeated exposure. In language learning, each skill requires practice in order to establish FLUENCY in the sense of the smooth operation of psycholinguistic processes.

practice activities *n*

in language teaching, practice activities are sometimes classified into three categories: **controlled practice** (activities in which learner output is managed and controlled by the teacher or the materials to avoid the possibility of student errors); **guided practice** (activities in which some guidance and support is provided but some unplanned student production is also encouraged); **free practice** (those in which control or guidance is not provided and students are free to try out their language resources in completing an activity).

practice effect *n*

the effect of previous practice on later performance. For example, in testing how much grammar improvement had occurred in students after a grammar course, if the same items appeared on a pre-test and a post-test (see POST-TEST), students might perform better on the post-test simply because they had already had practice on the items during the pre-test, rather than because of what they had learned from the course.

practice stage *n*

also **repetition stage**

see PPP

practice teaching *n*

see TEACHING PRACTICE

practitioner knowledge *n*

also **practical knowledge, personal practical knowledge**

knowledge which practitioners in a discipline (e.g. language teachers) know about the activity of teaching and which is developed from their experience of teaching, their knowledge of their teaching subject (e.g. English), and their personal beliefs about teaching and learning.

see TEACHER COGNITION, PEDAGOGICAL CONTENT KNOWLEDGE

pragmalinguistics *n*

the interface between LINGUISTICS and PRAGMATICS, focusing on the linguistic means used to accomplish pragmatic ends. For example, when a learner asks "How do I make a compliment (or a request, or a warning) in this language?", this is a question of pragmalinguistics knowledge. This can be contrasted with **sociopragmatics** and sociopragmatic knowledge, which concern the relationship between social factors and pragmatics. For example, a learner might need to know in what circumstances it is appropriate to make a compliment in the target language and which form would be most appropriate given the social relationship between speaker and hearer.

pragmatic competence *n*

being able to use language appropriately according to context (taking into account such complexities as social distance and indirectness) in order to accomplish one's communicative goals.

see also COMMUNICATIVE COMPETENCE, PRAGMALINGUISTICS, SOCIOPRAGMATICS

pragmatic error *n*

see ERROR

pragmatic failure *n*

a communicative failure that occurs when the pragmatic force of a message is misunderstood, for example, if an intended apology is interpreted as an excuse.

pragmatics *n* pragmatic *adj*

the study of the use of language in communication, particularly the relationships between sentences and the contexts and situations in which they are used. Pragmatics includes the study of:

a how the interpretation and use of UTTERANCEs depends on knowledge of the real world

b how speakers use and understand SPEECH ACTS

c how the structure of sentences is influenced by the relationship between the speaker and the hearer.

Pragmatics is sometimes contrasted with SEMANTICS, which deals with meaning without reference to the users and communicative functions of sentences.

see also USAGE

pragmatic transfer *n*

transfer of L1 norms and forms of performing SPEECH ACTS. Pragmatic transfer may result in the inappropriate transfer of forms or expressions from the L1 to the L2 as well as level or range of politeness or indirectness in the L2.

praxis *n*

the process by which a theory, belief or skill is enacted or practised. In **critical applied linguistics** praxis also refers to the process by which individuals become aware of the beliefs and values underlying their attitudes and behaviours in an attempt to find ways of resisting oppressive social practices.

predeterminer *n*

a word which occurs before DETERMINERS in a NOUN PHRASE[1]. For example, in English the QUANTIFIERS *all, both, half, double, twice,* etc., can be predeterminers.

all the bread

determiner
predeterminer

predicate *n* **predicate** *v*

that part of a sentence which states or asserts something about the SUBJECT and usually consists of a verb either with or without an OBJECT[1], COMPLEMENT, or ADVERB. For example:

Joan is tired.
The children saw the play.
The sun rose.

Adjectives, nouns, etc., which occur in the predicate are said to be used "predicatively". For example:

Her behaviour was friendly. (PREDICATIVE ADJECTIVE)
These books are dictionaries. (predicative noun)

see also ATTRIBUTIVE ADJECTIVE

predicate frames *n*

see FUNCTIONAL GRAMMAR

predicate logic *n*

see LOGIC

predication *n*
see PROPOSITION

predicative adjective *n*
an adjective that is used after a verb.
see also ATTRIBUTIVE ADJECTIVE

predictive validity *n*
a type of VALIDITY based on the degree to which a test accurately predicts future performance. A LANGUAGE APTITUDE TEST, for example, should have predictive validity, because the results of the test should predict the ability to learn a second or foreign language.

predictor *n*
see CRITERION MEASURE, DEPENDENT VARIABLE

prefabricated language *n*
also **prefabricated routine, prefabricated speech**
see FORMULAIC LANGUAGE

preferred language *n*
see PRIMARY LANGUAGE

preferred strategies *n*
the most efficient strategies for speech processing of a particular language, utilizing the phonological and metrical rules of the language.

prefix *n*
a letter or sound or group of letters or sounds which are added to the beginning of a word, and which change the meaning or function of the word.
Some COMBINING FORMS can be used like prefixes. For example, the word *pro-French* uses the prefix *pro-* "in favour of", and the word *Anglo-French* uses the combining form *Anglo-* "English".
see also AFFIX

preliminary intake *n*
see INTAKE

pre-listening *v*
activities that students carry out before listening to a listening text, in order to prepare them for listening. Pre-listening activities may pre-teach vocabulary, activate background knowledge, predict content, generate interest in a topic or check ideas and understanding of a topic.

premodifier *n*
>   see MODIFIER

preoperational stage *n*
>   see COGNITIVE DEVELOPMENT

preposition *n*
>   a word used with NOUNS, PRONOUNS and GERUNDS to link them grammatically
>   to other words. The phrase so formed, consisting of a preposition and its
>   COMPLEMENT, is a **prepositional phrase**. In English, a prepositional phrase
>   may be "discontinuous", as in:
>
>   *who(m) did you speak to?*
>
>   Prepositions may express such meanings as possession (e.g. *the leg of the
>   table*), direction (e.g. *to the bank*), place (e.g. *at the corner*), time (e.g.
>   *before now*). They can also mark the cases discussed in CASE GRAMMAR. For
>   example, in the sentence:
>
>   *Smith killed the policeman with a revolver.*
>
>   the preposition *with* shows that a revolver is in the INSTRUMENTAL CASE.
>   In English, too, there are groups of words (e.g. *in front of, owing to*) that
>   can function like single-word prepositions.
>   see also POSTPOSITION

prepositional adverb *n*
>   another term for ADVERB PARTICLE

prepositional complement *n*
>   also **prepositional object, object (of a preposition)**
>   see COMPLEMENT

prepositional dative construction *n*
>   see DATIVE ALTERNATION

prepositional phrase *n*
>   see PREPOSITION

prepositional verb *n*
>   see PHRASAL VERB

preposition stranding *n*
>   a preposition is stranded if it doesn't move along with its complement. For
>   example, *with*, *to*, *from* and *about* have been stranded in the following
>   WH-QUESTIONS:

452

Who did you speak <u>to</u>?
Who did you go <u>with</u>?
Who is that present <u>from</u>?
Who was the story <u>about</u>?
Where are you <u>from</u>?

Preposition stranding is not possible in some languages, for example Italian and French. In English, preposition stranding is disapproved of in some versions of PRESCRIPTIVE GRAMMAR, but is more common in speech than **pied piping**, the process through which the wh-word and the preposition move together, as in the following:

To who(m) did you speak?
With who(m) did you go?

Sentences exhibiting pied piping are felt by many speakers of English nowadays to be quite unnatural and in some cases unacceptable (for example, **From where are you?*).

pre-reading *v*

activities that students carry out before reading a text, in order to prepare them for reading. Pre-reading activities may pre-teach vocabulary, activate background knowledge, activate reading strategies, predict content, generate interest in a topic or check ideas and understanding of a topic.

prescriptive grammar *n*

a grammar which states rules for what is considered the best or most correct usage. Prescriptive grammars are often based not on descriptions of actual usage but rather on the grammarian's views of what is best. Many TRADITIONAL GRAMMARS are of this kind.

see also DESCRIPTIVE GRAMMAR, NORMATIVE GRAMMAR

presentation stage *n*

see PPP

present continuous *n*

see PROGRESSIVE

present participle *n*

see PARTICIPLE

present perfect *n*

see PERFECT

present perfect continuous *n*

see PROGRESSIVE

present tense *n*

a tense which typically relates the time of an action or state to the present moment in time. In English the present tense can also be used to refer to future time (e.g. *We leave tomorrow*) or to timeless expressions (e.g. *Cats have tails*), and for this reason it is sometimes called the NON-PAST tense.

see also ASPECT

preservice education *n*

also **preservice training**

(in teacher education) a course or programme of study which student teachers complete before they begin teaching. This may be compared with INSERVICE EDUCATION, which refers to experiences which are provided for teachers who are already teaching and which form part of their continued professional development. Preservice education often sets out to show future teachers basic teaching techniques and give them a broad general background in teaching and in their subject matter. Inservice education or training usually takes place for a specific purpose and often involves the following cycle of activities:

1 assess participants' needs
2 determine objectives for inservice programme
3 plan content
4 choose methods of presentation and learning experiences
5 implement
6 evaluate effectiveness
7 provide follow-up assistance.

Inservice programmes for language teachers are sometimes referred to as Continuing Education for Language Teachers (CELT).

presupposition *n* **presuppose** *v*

what a speaker or writer assumes that the receiver of the message already knows. For example:

speaker A: *What about inviting Simon tonight?*

speaker B: *What a good idea; then he can give Monica a lift.*

Here, the presuppositions are, among others, that speakers A and B know who Simon and Monica are, that Simon has a vehicle, most probably a car, and that Monica has no vehicle at the moment. Children often presuppose too much. They may say:

. . . and he said "let's go" and we went there.

even if their hearers do not know who *he is* and where *there* is.

see also COHERENCE, COHESION

pre-teaching *n*

selecting new or difficult items that students will meet in a future classroom activity, and teaching such items before the activity. For example, difficult words in a listening-comprehension exercise may be taught before students do the exercise.

preterite *n*

see PAST TENSE

pre-test *n*

see POST-TEST

pretesting *n*

also **pilot testing, trialling**

the try-out phase of a newly written but not yet fully developed test. Tests under development may be revised on the basis of the ITEM ANALYSIS obtained from the results of pretesting.

pre-test sensitization *n*

see EXTERNAL VALIDITY

pretonic *n*, *adj*

see TONE UNIT

preverbal negation *n*

see POSTVERBAL NEGATION

pre-writing *n*

see COMPOSING PROCESSES

primary cardinal vowel *n*

see CARDINAL VOWEL

primary data *n*

in LANGUAGE ACQUISITION, refers to the language that children hear.
see also EVIDENCE

primary language *n*

also **preferred language**

people speaking more than one language (see BILINGUAL, MULTILINGUAL) may not necessarily be most fluent in the first language they acquired as a child (the mother tongue). The terms primary language or preferred language are used to refer to the language which bilingual or multilingual speakers are most fluent in or which they prefer using for most everyday communicative functions. A child may have more than one primary language if he or she acquires more than one language during the period of primary language development.

primary language acquisition *n*

a term referring to the acquisition of any language from infancy, sometimes preferred over the term FIRST LANGUAGE ACQUISITION because of the difficulty in establishing which language should be considered "first" in some cases, such as in childhood BILINGUALISM.

primary language instruction *n*

an approach to the teaching of second language students in which instruction in the students' primary language – i.e. the native language of the students – is used for subjects which are the most cognitively demanding.

primary stress *n*

see STRESS

priming *n*

processing a word that has been recently encountered and activated is faster and easier than processing one that has not. This phenomenon is called priming. For example, in a LEXICAL DECISION TASK, the decision of whether a stimulus is an English word or not will be made faster for words that have recently been presented than for words that have not been activated. Concepts that are related to one another in some way are also assumed to be connected in mental networks and when one member of the network is activated, the others are as well. This phenomenon is called **spreading activation**. For this reason, when the word doctor is presented, related words such as *hospital*, *nurse*, and *medication* are also primed.

see also IMPLICIT MEMORY

principal clause *n*

see DEPENDENT CLAUSE

principle of subjacency *n*

see BOUNDING THEORY

principles[1] *n*

in teaching, beliefs and theories that teachers hold concerning effective approaches to teaching and learning and which serve as the basis for some of their decision-making. For example,

Make the lesson learner-centred.
Every learner is a genius.
Provide opportunities for active learner participation.

Teachers' principles are an important aspect of their BELIEF SYSTEMS, and may be a result of teaching experience, training, or their own experiences as learners.

principles² *n*
see UNIVERSAL GRAMMAR

Principles and Parameters framework *n*
the concept of grammar introduced by Chomsky in 1981 which views human language as a complex set of principles, each with one or more parameters of variation. The grammars of particular languages are determined by fixing those parameters.
see UNIVERSAL GRAMMAR

prior knowledge *n*
what a learner already knows and which is available before a certain learning task, such as knowledge of vocabulary, syntax, the first language, or background knowledge about a topic or event. Prior knowledge is thought to be the most important single factor influencing learning and is particularly important for students with diverse cultural backgrounds since their experience may be different from mainstream students. Many language teaching techniques are designed to activate students' prior knowledge, such as brainstorming and pre-reading discussion questions.
see also MAINSTREAMING

private speech *n*
speech which is intended for oneself. The Russian psychologist Vygotsky believed that in acquiring language, children use private speech to overcome cognitive difficulties they encounter, e.g. when playing a game or completing a puzzle. Private speech represents thinking aloud and helps clarify thought. Second language learners may also use private speech (e.g. whispering to themselves) to help them overcome difficulties they encounter when trying to communicate in a second language or to use a second language to complete a classroom task. Private speech can thus serve an important strategic function serving to mediate or redirect a learner's own activity.

PRO *n*
also **BIG PRO**

pro

This term is used in GOVERNMENT/BINDING THEORY when discussing embedded sentences with infinitives, e.g.

a *I wanted to leave*
b *I wanted Anita to leave*
c *It is time to leave*

The proposed D-STRUCTURE for these sentences would be

d *I wanted* [PRO *to leave*]
e *I wanted Anita* [PRO *to leave*]
f *It is time* [PRO *to leave*]

In *d* and *e* the element PRO behaves like an anaphor. In *d* it refers to *I* and in *e* it refers to *Anita*. In *f* PRO does not behave like an anaphor but more like a pronoun referring to someone or some people outside the sentence (see BINDING PRINCIPLE).

pro *n*

also **little pro**

this term is used in GOVERNMENT/BINDING THEORY when discussing declarative sentences which do not have an overt subject (see PRO-DROP PARAMETER).

proactive inhibition *n*

also **proactive interference**

the interfering effect of earlier learning on later learning. For example, if a learner first learns how to produce questions which require AUXILIARY VERB inversion (e.g. *I can go. Can I go?*) this may interfere with the learning of patterns where auxiliary inversion is not required. The learner may write *Don't I know where can I find it* instead of *I don't know where I can find it*. By contrast, **retroactive inhibition/interference** is the effect of later learning on earlier learning. For example, children learning English may learn irregular past-tense forms such as *went, saw*. Later, when they begin to learn the regular *-ed* past-tense inflection, they may stop using *went* and *saw* and produce *goed* and *seed*.

problematize *v*

see DECONSTRUCT

problem-based learning *n*

a teaching approach sometimes used in language teaching (e.g. business English) in which students work through problem-solving tasks that are similar to real world problems they are likely to encounter. It involves collaborative group work and may take different forms but always makes use of a focus on a problem or problems to drive the teaching-learning process. Resolving the problem typically involves research, reading, writing, group discussions, and oral presentations, activities that are used as the basis for language development.

problem-posing *n*

a teaching strategy first developed by the Brazilian educator, Paolo Friere and sometimes used in second language teaching and having the following characteristics:

1 A topic of concern or interest to students is identified. It should pose a problem for which there are several possible solutions.
2 Students discuss the problem (or problems) and relate it to their own experience.
3 Students analyze the cause of the problem and seek solutions.
4 Through the question and answer exchanges that occur students generate vocabulary and other language that the teacher later draws on to develop a series of exercises, practice opportunities and application activities that form the basis of the rest of the lesson or unit.

problem–solution pattern *n*

a rhetorical pattern that appears frequently in technical reports and other academic writings in which the writer presents an issue as a problem and presents the main point of the paper as a solution. The problem-solution pattern consist of four basic elements – **situation, problem, solution, evaluation.**

problem-solving strategy *n*

a learning STRATEGY which involves selecting from several alternatives in order to reach a desired goal. In second and foreign language learning, problem-solving strategies are often used, for example, in choosing whether to use *a* or *the* before a noun.

problem–solving tasks *n*

simple tasks, often involving word puzzles or simple drawings, used to stimulate pair work and oral discussion among small groups of second language learners. The use of such tasks is characteristic of some phases of lessons in the communicative approach.

proceduralization *n*

see ADAPTIVE CONTROL OF THOUGHT

procedural knowledge *n*

knowledge of how to perform an activity, i.e. the "how to" level of knowledge involved in employing a skill such as using a computer or operating a video camera.

see DECLARATIVE KNOWLEDGE

procedural syllabus *n*

a term sometimes used for a type of task-based syllabus in which classroom activities are organized around tasks and the procedures needed to accomplish them, such as using maps to find the quickest route to a destination or following instructions to prepare or make something. The use of sets of procedures of this kind is an attempt to replace a conventional grammar-based syllabus with a meaning-based one in which negotiation of meaning and communicative accomplishment of tasks are used to drive the second language acquisition process, rather than explicit teaching and practice of grammatical form.

process approach *n*

also **process writing**

(in teaching composition) an approach which emphasizes the composing processes writers make use of in writing (such as planning, drafting and revising) and which seeks to improve students' writing skills through developing their use of effective COMPOSING PROCESSES. This approach is sometimes compared with a **product approach** or a **prose model approach**, that is, one which focuses on producing different kinds of written products and which emphasizes imitation of different kinds of model paragraphs or essays.

processibility *n*

see MULTIDIMENSIONAL MODEL

process method *n*

see METHODS OF DEVELOPMENT

process objective *n*

an objective that is described in terms of how it will be achieved, such as "to improve discussion skills by taking part in group discussions and class debates".

process–product research *n*

an approach to educational research (particularly research on the effects of classroom teaching or teaching methods) which attempts to measure the relationship between teacher behaviour or processes (i.e. what the teacher does in class, such as presenting and practising grammar points, setting up problem-solving tasks, or asking questions) and pupil learning or products (e.g. as demonstrated by performance on a test). The assumption behind process–product research is that the process of teaching can be characterized by recurring patterns of teacher behaviour, which can be linked to particular learning outcomes.

process syllabus *n*

1 in teaching, a syllabus that specifies the learning experiences and processes students will encounter during a course, rather than the learning outcomes. Objectives developed for such a course are known as PROCESS OBJECTIVES. For example:

a to conduct classroom discussions in which learners learn to listen to others as well as express their own views

b to provide opportunities for learners to reflect on their own learning strategies.

2 a framework for classroom decision-making based upon negotiation among teachers and students applied to any chosen aspect of the curriculum.

process writing *n*

see PROCESS APPROACH

proclaiming tone *n*

see REFERRING TONE

pro-drop language *n*

see PRO-DROP PARAMETER

pro-drop parameter *n*

also **null subject parameter**

(in UNIVERSAL GRAMMAR) a parameter which determines whether the subject in declarative sentences may be deleted.

Parameters vary in different languages within certain defined limits. Languages such as Italian and Arabic can have subject-less declarative sentences, e.g. Italian *parla* 'he/she speaks/talks', and are referred to as **pro-drop languages**. However, languages such as English, French and German do not typically omit the subject in declarative sentences. They are referred to as **non-pro-drop languages**, e.g.:

	Subject	*Verb*	
Italian	(*lui*)	*parla*	pro-drop
Arabic	(*huwa*)	*yatakalamu*	pro-drop
English	*he*	*speaks*	non-pro-drop
French	*il*	*parle*	non-pro-drop
German	*er*	*spricht*	non-pro-drop

The term *pro-drop* is used because in the D-STRUCTURE of the grammar, the empty subject position is filled by the element *pro*, e.g.

   pro parla

The pro-drop parameter and other parameters of Universal Grammar have attracted the interest of researchers working in the fields of child language acquisition and language teaching. For example, the question has been raised: How do children 'set' a UG parameter to fit their particular language? Researchers in second language acquisition have investigated what happens if a parameter in the speaker's native language is different from that of their target language, making it necessary to 'reset' the parameter. This would happen, for example, in the acquisition of Spanish (a pro-drop language) by speakers of non-pro-drop languages such as English and French.

see also PARAMETER

product approach *n*

   see PROCESS APPROACH

production stage *n*

   also **transfer stage, free practice**
   see PPP

production system *n*

   a programme made up on a set of conditional statements of the form "if X, then Y". For example, part of a production system for a language (English) might have statements such as "If 'go' + past, then 'went.'" Production systems were predominant in early attempts to model cognition and are the basis of models such as ADAPTIVE CONTROL OF THOUGHT (ACT*).

productive/receptive language knowledge *n*

   also **active/passive language knowledge**
   the ability of a person to actively produce their own speech and writing is called their **productive language knowledge**. This is compared to their ability to understand the speech and writing of other people, their **receptive language knowledge**.

productive/receptive vocabulary *n*

   also **active/ passive vocabulary**
   the number of words that a person can actively use, compared with the number of words that they recognize and understand but do not use productively. Native speakers of a language can understand many more words than they actively use. Some people have a **receptive vocabulary**

(i.e. words they understand) of up to 100,000 words, but a **productive vocabulary** (i.e. words they use) of between 10,000 and 20,000 words. In language learning, an active vocabulary of about 3000 to 5000 words, and a passive vocabulary of about 5000 to 10,000 words is regarded as the intermediate to upper intermediate level of proficiency.

productive skills *n*
see LANGUAGE SKILLS

productivity *n*
in MORPHOLOGY, if a process is fully regular and actively used in the creation of new words, this process is considered productive. For example, the English suffix *-ness* can be attached to any adjective to make a noun (e.g. *happiness*, *niceness*, *gloriousness*). This can be contrasted to unproductive suffixes, such as *–th*, which only applies to a handful of words (*health*, *wealth*, *stealth*).
see also ACCIDENTAL GAP, BLOCKING

product-process distinction *n*
(in language teaching and SECOND LANGUAGE ACQUISITION research) a distinction is sometimes made between completed acts of communication or language output (products) and the underlying abilities and skills used in producing them (processes).
For example: in writing, letters, compositions, and long essays are examples of the products of writing. But in order to write a long essay, a number of processes are involved, such as collecting information, note-taking, outlining, drafting, and revising. These are among the processes of writing the essay (the product). Language teaching and the study of language learning are concerned both with products, and with underlying processes.

professionalism *n*
in teaching, the status of teaching viewed in relation to its functions, their status and the quality and skill of teachers' work. While characterizations of a profession differ, common among them are:
1 Professionalism refers to an occupation that performs an important social function.
2 It is based upon a high degree of skill.
3 The work and practice involved is not dependent upon routine behaviours.
4 It is based on a systematic body of theory and knowledge.
5 It is learned through education and training.

6 It is backed by organizational support and has its own principles and
values.

Professional organizations in teaching and language teaching have sought
to obtain greater recognition for teachers and language teachers as professionals and for improvements in the status and rewards due to them as a
consequence.

proficiency *n*
see LANGUAGE PROFICIENCY

proficiency level *n*
a description of a language learner's level of performance in a target language,
often described in terms of *beginner level*, *intermediate level* or *advanced
level*. Proficiency levels are often used to describe difficulty levels of language
courses and language teaching materials.
see COMMON EUROPEAN FRAMEWORK

proficiency scale *n*
a description in the form of band levels on a scale and which describe what a
student is able to do in the different skill areas at different stages in a language
programme. Proficiency scales have been widely used as a framework for
organizing language programme and courses and as a basis for the assessment of language ability in a second or foreign language.
see COMMON EUROPEAN FRAMEWORK, FOREIGN SERVICE INSTITUTE, FOREIGN
SERVICE INSTITUTE ORAL INTERVIEW

proficiency test *n*
a test that measures how much of a language someone has learned. The
difference between a proficiency test and an ACHIEVEMENT TEST is that the
latter is usually designed to measure how much a student has learned from
a particular course or SYLLABUS. A proficiency test is not linked to a particular
course of instruction, but measures the learner's general level of language
mastery. Although this may be a result of previous instruction and learning,
these factors are not the focus of attention. Some proficiency tests have been
standardized for worldwide use, such as the American TOEFL that is used to
measure the English language proficiency of international students who
wish to study in the USA.
see also ACHIEVEMENT TEST

profile[1] *n*
also **profiling**

(in assessment) a written or graphic description of someone's performance or progress (e.g. of a learner or a student teacher in a teacher training programme) based on a number of different tests or other information sets that can be used to provide a broadly based view of someone's abilities. For example, a profile of a student teacher may be based on:

a his/her curriculum vitae

b a personal statement of teaching philosophy

c statements by colleagues and supervisors

d a portfolio of assignments

e student evaluations.

profile² *n*

(in testing and statistics) a graphic representation of scores or VARIABLES² of an individual or group on a number of tests or measures for the purposes of comparison. For example, the profile below is based on PERCENTILE scores of a student in English, French, and Mathematics.

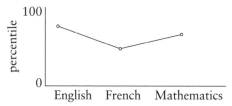

profiling *n*

see PROFILE

pro-forms *n*

forms which can serve as replacements for different elements in a sentence. For example:

a A: *I hope you can come.*
B: *I hope so.* (*so* replaces *that I can come*)

b A: *Mary is in London.*
B: *John is there too.* (*there* replaces *in London*)

c *We invited Mary and John to eat with us because we liked them.* (*them* replaces *Mary and John*)

d A: *I like coffee.*
B: *We do too.* (*do* replaces *like coffee*)

see also PRONOUN, PRO-VERB

program *n*

the sequence of instructions and routines designed to make a computer carry out a given task. The task of writing a computer program involves:

1 defining a problem or task in as much detail as possible
2 devising a procedure for carrying out the task
3 checking that the procedure will work under all circumstances
4 writing the instructions that form the actual program. These are written in a **programming language** consisting of a set of characters and rules with specific meanings and functions.

programme design *n*

another term for COURSE DESIGN

programmed learning *n*

also **programmed instruction**

an APPROACH to the design of teaching/learning in which the subject matter to be learned is presented as an ordered sequence of items, each of which requires a response from the learner. The student then compares his or her response with the correct response which is provided.

In a **linear programme** students work through learning material which is presented in graded units, at their own pace.

In a **branching programme** a student who has difficulty with a particular item is directed to supplementary or revision material in a separate part (a "branch") of the programme. Then the student is returned to the main programme. Linear programmes and branching programmes may be combined.

programme evaluation *n*

the determination of how successful an educational programme or curriculum is in achieving its goals.

see also EVALUATION, FORMATIVE EVALUATION, SUMMATIVE EVALUATION

programming language *n*

see PROGRAM

progressive *n, adj*

also **continuous**

a grammatical ASPECT in some languages which indicates that an action is incomplete, in progress, or developing. The progressive in English is formed with the AUXILIARY VERB *be* and the *-ing* form of the verb (e.g. *She is wearing contact lenses. They were crossing the road when the accident occurred*).

progressive assimilation *n*

see ASSIMILATION

progressivism *n*

see RECONSTRUCTIONISM

progress questionnaire *n*

in teaching, a learner questionnaire in which students reflect on their own progress over a given period of study.

progress test *n*

an ACHIEVEMENT TEST linked to a particular set of teaching materials or a particular course of instruction. Tests prepared by a teacher and given at the end of a chapter, course, or term are progress tests. Progress tests may be regarded as similar to achievement tests but narrower and much more specific in scope. They help the teacher to judge the degree of success of his or her teaching and to identify the weakness of the learners.

projection (principle) *n*

in some models of Generative Grammar, e.g. Chomsky's UNIVERSAL GRAMMAR, a lexical item in the lexicon (see LEXICON[3]) of a grammar, e.g. a verb, has specific information about syntactic categories (complements) which it 'projects' onto the structure of the sentence. For example, the English verb *give* has two complement noun phrases:

give [-NP_1, NP_2]

which it can project, e.g.:

She gave the accountant the file.

The influence of the properties of lexical entries only goes up to a certain structure in the sentence, e.g. a *verb* would have influence on the whole verb phrase (VP) but not beyond it. This is often called maximal projection. Points of maximal projection are often shown by " (two bars) (see BAR NOTATION), e.g. V" (VP), N" (NP), P" (PP = prepositional phrase).

The DOMAIN of an element in a sentence is considered to be the area within its particular maximal projection. For example, in the sentence:

Bill took her to an expensive restaurant.

the domain of the verb take *(took)* would be the whole verb phrase (V"), including *her to an expensive restaurant*, the domain of the preposition *to* would be the whole prepositional phrase (P"), including *an expensive restaurant*.

The concepts of maximal projection and domain are important when discussing GOVERNMENT.

project work *n*

(in teaching) an activity which centres around the completion of a task, and which usually requires an extended amount of independent work either by an individual student or by a group of students. Much of this work takes place outside the classroom. Project work often involves three stages:

1 Classroom planning. The students and teacher discuss the content and scope of the project, and their needs.

2 Carrying out the project. The students move out of the classroom to complete their planned tasks (e.g. conducting interviews, collecting information).

3 Reviewing and monitoring. This includes discussions and feedback sessions by the teacher and participants, both during and after the project.

In language teaching, project work is thought to be an activity which promotes CO-OPERATIVE LEARNING, reflects the principles of STUDENT-CENTRED TEACHING, and promotes language learning through using the language for authentic communicative purposes.

prominence *n* **prominent** *adj*

(in DISCOURSE), greater STRESS on the words or syllables which the speaker wishes to emphasize. Prominence may be given to different words according to what has been said before by another speaker, e.g.:

He may come to MORRow.

(as a reply to *"When is Mr Jones coming?"*)

He MAY come tomorrow.

(as a reply to *"Is Mr Jones likely to come tomorrow?"*)

Prominence may be accompanied by pitch movement (see TONE^2) on the **prominent syllable**.

prominent syllable *n*

see PROMINENCE

prompt *n*

see ITEM SPECIFICATIONS

prompting *n*

see MODELLING

pronoun *n*

a word which may replace a noun or noun phrase (e.g. English *it*, *them*, *she*).

see also PERSONAL PRONOUNS, POSSESSIVE, DEMONSTRATIVE, INTERROGATIVE PRONOUN, REFLEXIVE PRONOUN, INDEFINITE PRONOUN, RELATIVE CLAUSE

pronouncing dictionary *n*

a dictionary particularly for second language learners which presents information on the pronunciation of words, rather than their meanings.

pronunciation *n* **pronounce** *v*

the way a certain sound or sounds are produced. Unlike ARTICULATION, which refers to the actual production of speech sounds in the mouth, pronunciation stresses more the way sounds are perceived by the hearer, e.g.:

You haven't <u>pronounced</u> this word correctly.

and often relates the spoken word to its written form, e.g.:

In the word <u>knife</u>, the <u>k</u> is not pronounced.

proper noun *n*

a noun which is the name of a particular person, place, or thing. Proper nouns in English are spelt with a capital letter. For example: *London, Richard.*

A noun which is not the name of a particular person, place or thing is called a **common noun**. For example, book, woman, sugar. In English, common nouns are spelt with a lower-case (small) letter.

see also NOUN, ABSTRACT NOUN, ADJECTIVAL NOUN, ANIMATE NOUN, COLLECTIVE NOUN, CONCRETE NOUN, COUNTABLE NOUN

proposition *n* **propositional** *adj*

(in philosophy, LINGUISTICS and SEMANTICS) the basic meaning which a sentence expresses. Propositions consist of (a) something which is named or talked about (known as the **argument,** or entity) (b) an assertion or **predication** which is made about the argument. A sentence may express or imply (see PRESUPPOSITION) more than one proposition. For example:

sentence	underlying propositions
Maria's friend, Tony, who is a dentist, likes apples.	*Maria has a friend.*
	The friend's name is Tony.
	Tony is a dentist.
	Tony likes apples.

In SPEECH ACT theory a distinction is made between the propositional meaning of a sentence, and its **illocutionary force** (i.e. the use made of the sentence in communication, e.g. as a request, a warning, a promise).

propositional logic *n*

see LOGIC

propositional network *n*

the simpler PROPOSITIONS on which the truth of a main proposition rests. For example, the proposition:

The woman gave the man an expensive ring, which contained a large ruby.

contains the following propositional network:
> *There was a woman.*
> *There was a man.*
> *There was a ring.*
> *The ring was expensive.*
> *The ring contained a ruby.*
> *The ruby was large.*
> *The woman gave the ring to the man.*

The process of identifying the propositional networks underlying sentences or texts is thought to be a basic part of LANGUAGE COMPREHENSION.

proprioceptive feedback *n*

FEEDBACK involving muscular movements which are used in the production of speech and which can be used in MONITORING speech.

Hearing-impaired people make use of this form of feedback rather than AUDITORY FEEDBACK.

prose-model approach *n*

see PROCESS APPROACH

prosodic features *n*

sound characteristics which affect whole sequences of syllables. They may involve, for instance, the relative loudness or duration of syllables, changes in the pitch of a speaker's voice (see TONE^2) and the choice of pitch level (see KEY^2).

see also INTONATION PATTERNS, PROMINENCE, SUPRASEGMENTALS

prosody *n* **prosodic** *adj*

(in PHONETICS) a collective term for variations in loudness, PITCH and SPEECH RHYTHM.

prospective sample *n*

see SAMPLE

protocol *n*

a sample containing observation(s) of a phenomenon which is being described, observed, or measured. For example, if a researcher were studying the use of a grammatical feature, and recorded a person's speech for purposes of analysis, a transcription of the recording could be called a protocol. A completed test script and responses of subjects to an experiment are also sometimes called protocols. The term "protocol" is often also used for a person's own account of his or her thoughts and ideas while doing a task. Such a protocol can give information of value in the study of PSYCHOLINGUISTICS and COGNITIVE PROCESSES.

see also GUIDED INTERVIEW

protocol materials *n*

(in teacher development) a recorded or filmed segment of a lesson or classroom event. In teacher education programmes, video protocols of teachers in classrooms carrying out normal classroom activities are sometimes used to illustrate different aspects of teaching. It is often more convenient to use protocol materials than to observe actual classes.

protocol research *n*

in research on composition, the use of **protocols** containing the verbalized thoughts of writers as they create a piece of writing.

prototype *n*

a person or object which is considered (by many people) to be typical of its class or group.

The **prototype theory** suggests that many mental concepts we have are really prototypes. People often define a concept by reference to typical instances. For example, a prototype of a bird would be more like a small bird which flies than, for instance, a large flightless bird like an emu or a New Zealand kiwi. Prototype theory has been useful in investigations into how concepts are formed, e.g. what is considered a typical item of furniture, a typical vegetable, a typical house, and to what extent certain concepts can be considered universal or specific to certain cultures/languages.

It has also been suggested that prototype theory may account for our ability to communicate appropriately in social situations. That would mean, for example, that we learn to associate certain words, phrases, or general

communicative behaviour with people who typically use them or situations where they are typically used.

prototype theory *n*
> see PROTOTYPE

pro-verb *n*
> a verb form that may be used instead of a full verb phrase. For example, in English, various forms of *do* can be pro-verbs, as in:
>
> A: *I like coffee.*   A: *She broke the window.*
> B: *I <u>do</u> too.*   B: *So she <u>did</u>.*
>   So <u>do</u> I.
>   Alan <u>does</u> too.
>
> see also PRO-FORMS

provider *n*
> in language teaching, an institution, organization or school that is responsible for developing and teaching a course. Sometimes responsibility for planning and delivering a course may be divided between two different organizations (e.g. such as a funding body or company that requests a course and a language school that develops and teaches the course, i.e. which is the *provider* of the course).

proxemics *n* **proxemic** *adj*
> the study of the physical distance between people when they are talking to each other, as well as their postures and whether or not there is physical contact during their conversation. These factors can be looked at in relation to the sex, age, and social and cultural background of the people involved, and also their attitudes to each other and their state of mind.
> see also PARALINGUISTICS, SOCIAL DISTANCE

pseudo-cleft sentence *n*
> see CLEFT SENTENCE

pseudoword *n*
> a word that is not an actual word of a language but could be, because it follows the PHONOTACTICS of the language. For example, *vonk* and *foz* are English pseudowords, because they would be reasonable words, while *shvopls* is a **nonword**, one that is not and could not be an English word.

472

psycholinguistics *n* **psycholinguistic** *adj*

the study of (a) the mental processes that a person uses in producing and understanding language, and (b) how humans learn language. Psycholinguistics includes the study of speech PERCEPTION, the role of MEMORY, CONCEPTs and other processes in language use, and how social and psychological factors affect the use of language.

psychometrics *n*

1 A branch of psychology concerned with measurement.

2 The application of the principles of mathematics and statistics to the analysis of data.

psychomotor domain *n*

see DOMAIN[3]

pull out programme *n*

in English-speaking countries, a programme for LIMITED ENGLISH PROFICIENT students in which students are placed in a regular classroom but are "pulled out" for instruction in English for part of the day. Usually no native language instruction is provided and the goal is for the student to learn English through ESL instruction and submersion (see SUBMERSION EDUCATION).

punctual–non-punctual distinction *n*

a distinction is sometimes made between verbs which refer to actions that occur briefly and only once (punctual), for example:

She kicked the burglar down the stairs.

and verbs which refer to repeated actions or actions/states which take place or exist over a period of time (non-punctual), for example:

She sold flowers at the market.

Verbs referring to a state, such as *seem, like, know* (see STATIC-DYNAMIC) are, by nature, non-punctual but many other verbs can be used either punctually or non-punctually, for example:

Look! He waved to me just now. (punctual use)

The branches of the trees were waving in the breeze. (non-punctual use)

It has been claimed (see BIOPROGRAM HYPOTHESIS) that in situations where a CREOLE changes to the standard language (see POST-CREOLE CONTINUUM), verbs used punctually are more likely to be marked for past tense than verbs used non-punctually. Similar patterns have been found in investigations of second language acquisition, such as a large-scale investigation into English language acquisition which was carried out in Singapore. When the speech of speakers of Singapore English was analyzed in detail, it was found that of all the past tense verbs used, on average only 23% were marked for past tense when the verbs were used non-punctually, but 56% were marked for past tense when used punctually.

Marking verbs for past tense

	when used punctually	when used non-punctually
Guyana Creole	38%	12%
Hawaiian Creole English	53%	7%
Singapore	56%	23%

punctuation *n*

the use of graphic marks such as commas, semicolons, dashes and periods to clarify meaning in written sentences or to represent spoken sentences in writing.

pure vowel *n*

another term for MONOPHTHONG

pushed output *n*

see OUTPUT HYPOTHESIS

p-value *n*

see STATISTICAL SIGNIFICANCE

pyramid discussion *n*

a speaking activity in language teaching in which learners form progressively larger groups as they carry out a speaking task, which normally requires each group to reach agreement before joining another group.

Q

qualifier¹ *n* qualify *v*

(in TRADITIONAL GRAMMAR) any linguistic unit (e.g. an adjective, a phrase, or a clause) that is part of a NOUN PHRASE¹ and gives added information about the noun.

For example, *her*, *expensive*, and *from Paris* are qualifiers in the noun phrase:
her expensive blouse from Paris
see also MODIFIER¹

qualifier² *n* qualify *v*

(in Halliday's FUNCTIONAL GRAMMAR) any linguistic unit that is part of a group, gives added information about the HEAD of the group, and follows the head.

For example, *from Paris* is a qualifier in the noun group
her expensive blouse from Paris.
see also MODIFIER²

qualitative data *n*

data, such as a written account of what happened during a lesson or an interview, but not in numerical form. Data collected in qualitative form can often be converted into quantitative form.

see also QUANTITATIVE DATA

qualitative research *n*

narrowly, any research that uses procedures that make use of non-numerical data, such as INTERVIEWS, CASE STUDIES, or PARTICIPANT OBSERVATION. However, the term "qualitative research" frequently has a broader meaning as well, implying a holistic approach to social research in which experimental intervention in a research site, attempts to isolate phenomena of interest in experiments, and attempts to identify causal relationships among isolated variables are eschewed in favour of the naturalistic observation of complex settings. Qualitative researchers are also concerned with such ethical issues as entry into the research site, GATE-KEEPING, flexibility in research design, and TRIANGULATION.

see also ANALYTIC INDUCTION, CONSTANT COMPARISON METHOD, DOCU-MENTARY ANALYSIS, ETHNOGRAPHY, GROUNDED THEORY

quality assurance *n*

systems an organization has in place to ensure the quality of its practices. In language teaching organizations and institutions quality assurance is identified with:

1 the formulation of a quality assurance policy
2 the description of standards for aspects of quality, such as teachers, employment conditions, publicity materials, curriculum materials, and assessment
3 the setting up of procedures to ensure that quality is regularly assessed
4 the recognition of quality when it is attained
5 provision of support and resources to enable quality to be improved if necessary.

quantifier *n*

in English, a word or phrase which is used with a noun, and which shows quantity. Some quantifiers in English are: *many, few, little, several, much, a lot of, plenty of, a piece of, a loaf of, three kilograms of*, etc.
see also NUMERAL, DETERMINER

quantitative research *n*

narrowly, any research that uses procedures that gather data in numerical form. More broadly, the term often implies an approach to research that aims at causal explanation of phenomena through the identification of VARIABLES which can be made the basis of experimental investigation.
see also EXPERIMENTAL METHOD

quantitative research synthesis *n*

another term for META-ANALYSIS

quasi-ethnographic *adj*

see ETHNOGRAPHY

quasi-experimental design *n*

a research design that does not meet the most stringent criteria of EXTERNAL or INTERNAL VALIDITY, for example, one that has limited generalizability or one in which the design does not control for all but a single variable. Because of the complexities of teaching and learning in classrooms, much quantitative educational research is based on quasi-experimental designs.

question *n*

an utterance that is addressed to a listener/reader and asks for an expression of fact, opinion, belief, etc.
In English, questions may be formed:
a by the use of a **question word**, such as *who, what, where, when, why, how, which*
b by the use of an OPERATOR, as in <u>*Can*</u> *she come?*, <u>*Do*</u> *you want to leave?*

c through the use of intonation, as in *Ready?* (with rising intonation)

d by the use of a **question tag** such as *isn't it, is it, can he, won't she, do you,* etc. For example:

Patricia is a student isn't she?

Different types of questions have characteristic INTONATION CONTOURS and request different types of responses from a listener:

1 A **yes–no question** is formed using a MODAL verb or an AUXILIARY VERB, exhibits rising intonation and requests that an interlocutor respond "yes" or "no," for example, *Did you go to the movies last night?*

2 A **wh-question** begins with a question word, exhibits SUBJECT-VERB INVERSION, has a rise-fall intonation contour (similar to declarative sentences), and requests specific information in the response, for example, *When did you go to the movies last?*

3 A **closed-choice question** has list intonation and requires the interlocutor to respond with one of a closed series of choices, for example, *Would you rather see* Star Wars *again or a new film?*

4 A **tag question** consists of a declarative sentence followed by a question tag. When there is rising intonation on the tag, this question type requests confirmation (e.g. *He's happy, isn't he?*) but when the tag has rise–fall intonation this indicates that the speaker believes the proposition to be true and is merely requesting agreement (*He's happy, isn't he?*).

5 An **echo question** has the same structure as a declarative sentence, has rising intonation, and may request confirmation or repetition from the interlocutor or simply express disbelief in what the previous speaker has said, for example:

a They went out together last week

b They went out together? (echo-question)

c Yes, they did.

see also INTONATION, DISPLAY QUESTION, REFERENTIAL QUESTION, RHETORICAL QUESTION

questioning techniques *n*

(in teaching) the different procedures teachers use in asking questions and the different kinds of questions they ask. Since questioning is one of the most frequently used teaching techniques, the study of teachers' questions and questioning behaviours has been an important issue in classroom research in both first and second language classrooms. Among the factors which have been examined are:

a the frequency of low-level versus high-level questions

b the degree to which students are encouraged to ask questions

c the amount of WAIT-TIME teachers allow after a question

d the choice of CONVERGENT or DIVERGENT QUESTIONS
e how often teachers answer their own questions.
see also DISPLAY QUESTION, EVALUATIVE QUESTION, REFERENTIAL QUESTION

questionnaire *n*

a set of questions on a topic or group of topics designed to be answered by a respondent. Other forms for questionnaires include check lists and rating scales. Designing questionnaires that are valid, reliable and unambiguous is a very important issue. Questionnaires are used in many branches of applied linguistics, such as LANGUAGE SURVEYS, the study of attitudes and motivation, and in NEEDS ANALYSIS.

question tag *n*

see QUESTION

question word *n*

see QUESTION

R

r²
     an abbreviation for COEFFICIENT OF DETERMINATION

racialization *n*
     A process by which people are defined according to differences of skin color or other attributes and positioned as different from the majority.

raising *n*
     a syntactic operation by which some word or phrase is moved from a lower to a higher position in a structure. For example, in the sentence *It seems that David and Gloria are happily married*, *David and Gloria* is the subject of an embedded clause. However, such subjects can be raised to a higher position, producing the sentence *David and Gloria seem happily married*.

random access *n*
     see ACCESS

random error *n*
     see ERROR OF MEASUREMENT

random sample *n*
     see SAMPLE

range *n*
     1 (in statistics) the DISPERSION of a DISTRIBUTION. The range of a sample is the distance between the smallest and the largest values in a set of measurements or observations. For example, if the top score in a test is 80 and the bottom score is 32, the range is 48. Since the range does not take the distribution of scores into account, it is usually supplemented in statistical reports by the STANDARD DEVIATION.
     2 (in a frequency count) a measure of the distribution of linguistic items throughout a sample, which are generally expressed as a measure of the number of texts or samples in which a linguistic item occurs.

rank *n*
     a term used in a type of linguistic analysis in which linguistic units (e.g. sentences, clauses, words) are arranged in a certain order (**rank scale**) to show that higher units include lower ones.
     For example, on the rank scale below, each unit consists of one or more units of the next lower rank.

higher rank

clause
group (verbal, nominal, etc.)
word (verb, noun, etc.)
morpheme

lower rank

The term was first used by Halliday (see SYSTEMIC GRAMMAR, SYSTEMIC LINGUISTICS).

rank correlation *n*

a type of coefficient of CORRELATION in which the two VARIABLES[1] are measured in ranks, or on ordinal scales (see SCALE). For example, a rank correlation could be determined between the frequency of occurrence of words in two different texts based on their ranks in each text.

TEXT A		TEXT B	
rank frequency	*word*	*rank frequency*	*word*
1st	*a*	1st	*the*
2nd	*the*	2nd	*and*
3rd	*and*	3rd	*a*

In this data set, there is a negative correlation between the "rank order" of the words in Text A and Text B.

rank scale *n*

see RANK

rapid reading *n*

another term for SPEED READING

rate of articulation *n*

see RATE OF SPEECH

rate of reading *n*

another term for READING SPEED

rate of speech *n*

also **rate of utterance, speech rate**

the speed at which a person speaks. This may depend on a number of factors, such as the speaker's personality, the type of topic, the number of people present, and the speaker's reactions to them. Another factor is the speaker's familiarity with the language or dialect he or she is using.

A distinction is often made between the rate of speech, measured by the number of syllables per minute, and **the rate of articulation**, measured by the number of syllables per minute minus the time taken up by PAUSING. Usually, the longer and more frequent the pauses, the slower the speech rate.

rate of utterance *n*

another term for RATE OF SPEECH

rater *n*

a person who assigns a score or rating to a test taker's oral or written performance on the basis of a set of rating criteria.

see also INTER-RATER RELIABILITY, INTRA-RATER RELIABILITY

rater agreement *n*

see RATER RELIABILITY

rating *n*

assessing learner performance using pre-established scales, particularly when assessing spoken language performance.

rating criteria *n*

in language assessment, the aspects of a learner's second language performance on which teachers will assess their students.

rating scale *n*

(in testing) a technique for measuring language proficiency in which aspects of a person's language use are judged using scales that go from worst to best performance in a number of steps. For example, the components of FLUENCY in a foreign language could be rated on the following scales:

naturalness of language	unnatural	1	2	3	4	5 natural
style of expression	foreign	1	2	3	4	5 native-speaker-like
clarity of expression	unclear	1	2	3	4	5 clear

For each component skill, the listener rates the speaker on a scale of 1 to 5. Overall fluency can then be measured by taking account of the three scores for each speaker.

see also SCALE

rational cloze *n*

see CLOZE TEST

rational deletion *n*

see CLOZE TEST

rationalism *n*

see EMPIRICISM

rationalist position *n*
> another term for INNATIST HYPOTHESIS

ratio scale *n*
> see SCALE

raw score *n*
> (in testing and statistics) a score that is presented in terms of its original numerical value, not converted into some other value. For example, raw scores may be the number of correct answers in a test, or, in some cases, the number of errors. Usually it is necessary to convert such values into percentages, PERCENTILES, ranks, or some other form (e.g. STANDARD SCORES), in order to make the scores easier to interpret.

r-colouring *n*
> a phenomenon that occurs when a vowel preceding the consonant /r/, as in the English word *hurt*, anticipates and glides towards the central /r/ position and takes on some of the retroflex quality of /r/.
> see also RHOTICIZATION, ASSIMILATION

reaction time *n*
> the time between the presentation of a stimulus (for example, a word or pseudo-word) and a subject's response (for example, deciding whether the stimulus is a real word or not, in a LEXICAL DECISION TASK).

readability *n*
> how easily written materials can be read and understood. Readability depends on many factors, including (a) the average length of sentences in a passage (b) the number of new words a passage contains (c) the grammatical complexity of the language used. Procedures used for measuring readability are known as "readability formulae".
> see also LEXICAL DENSITY

reader-based prose *n*
> writing in which the audience is another person rather than the writer himself or herself. Inexperienced writers are often said to choose themselves as audience for their writing, producing **writer-based prose** or **egocentric writing**, rather than providing the background knowledge, information and organization that other readers may need. In the composing process, writers often begin with writer-based prose and then revise it to make it easier for another reader to read, that is, to make it reader-based. There are

said to be cultural differences concerning the degree to which standard or literary prose can be writer-based or should be reader-based.

reading *n*

1 the processes by which the meaning of a written text is understood. When this is done silently it is known as **silent reading**. The understanding that results is called **reading comprehension**. Reading employs many different cognitive skills, including letter and word recognition, knowledge of syntax, and recognition of **text types** and text structure. Comprehension that is based on clues in the text is referred to as bottom-up-processing, and comprehension that makes use of information outside of the text is known as **top-down processing**.

2 **oral reading:** saying a written text aloud (also known as **reading aloud**). In teaching reading this is often done to establish graphemic-phonemic correspondences or to learn to distinguish sense groups in a text.

Different types of reading comprehension are often distinguished, according to the reader's purposes in reading and the type of reading used. The following are commonly referred to:

a **Literal comprehension:** reading in order to understand, remember, or recall the information explicitly contained in a passage.

b **Inferential comprehension:** reading in order to find information which is not explicitly stated in a passage, using the reader's experience and intuition, and by inferring (INFERENCING).

c **Critical or evaluative comprehension:** reading in order to compare information in a passage with the reader's own knowledge and values.

d **Appreciative comprehension:** reading in order to gain an emotional or other kind of valued response from a passage.

see also SCANNING, SKIMMING, READING SPEED, EXTENSIVE READING

reading across the curriculum *n*

see LANGUAGE ACROSS THE CURRICULUM

reading age *n*

the usual age at which a child is expected to begin learning to read or to benefit from instruction in reading.

reading for details *n*

a level of reading comprehension in which the reader reads to note specific information in a passage including the sequence of information, and a common goal in teaching reading comprehension. A good reader is able to select details relevant to main ideas and also to generate implied main ideas from detailed information.

reading for gist *n*

also **reading for global understanding**

reading in order to understand the general meaning of a text without paying attention to specific details.

reading log *n*

see LEARNING LOG

reading method *n*

also **reading approach**

in foreign language teaching, a programme or method in which reading comprehension is the main objective. In a reading approach (a) the foreign language is generally introduced through short passages written with simple vocabulary and structures (b) comprehension is taught through translation and grammatical analysis (c) if the spoken language is taught, it is generally used to reinforce reading and limited to the oral reading of texts.

reading skills *n*

also **reading microskills**

text processing abilities employed in reading and that are relatively automatic in their use. For example:

1 recognizing words
2 recognizing grammatical functions of words
3 noticing specific details
4 making inferences
5 making comparisons
6 making predictions.

In second and foreign language instruction these skills are sometimes taught and practised separately.

see READING STRATEGIES

reading span *n*

also **eye span, visual span**

the amount of printed text that a person can perceive within a single FIXATION PAUSE, usually described as being between seven and ten letter spaces.

reading speed *n*

also **rate of reading**

the speed which a person reads depends on

a the type of reading material (e.g. fiction or non-fiction)
b the reader's purpose (e.g. to gain information, to find the main ideas in a passage)
c the level of comprehension required (e.g. to extract the main ideas or to gain complete understanding)
d the reader's individual reading skills.
The following are typical reading speeds:

speed	purpose	good reader
slow	study reading, used when material is difficult and/or high comprehension is required	200–300 words per minute (wpm) 80–90% comprehension
average	used for everyday reading of magazines, newspapers, etc.	250–500 wpm 70% comprehension
fast	skimming, used when highest speed is required and comprehension is intentionally lower	800 + wpm 50% comprehension

reading strategies *n*

ways of accessing the meanings of texts, which are employed flexibly and selectively in the course of reading and which are often under the conscious control of the reader. Strategies serve to make the reading process more effective. Such strategies include:
1 identifying a purpose for reading
2 planning what steps to take
3 previewing the text
4 predicting the contents of the text or text section.
However due to the nature of reading, reading specialists suggest that there is not a clear distinction between skills and strategies. The teaching of reading strategies and helping learners understand and manage the use of strategies is thought to be an important aspect of the teaching of second or foreign language reading skills.
see READING SKILLS

reading vocabulary *n*

see ACTIVE/PASSIVE LANGUAGE KNOWLEDGE

realia *n plural*

(in language teaching) actual objects and items which are brought into a classroom as examples or as aids to be talked or written about and used in teaching. Realia may include such things as photographs, articles of clothing, and kitchen objects.

reality principle *n*

(in SPEECH ACT theory) the principle that in conversation, people are expected to talk about things that are real and possible if there is no evidence to the contrary.
For example, in the following exchange:
A: *How are you going to New York?*
B: *I'm flying.*
A understands B to mean that B is travelling by plane and not literally flying through the air.

see also CONVERSATIONAL MAXIM

realization *n* **realize** *v*

the actual occurrence in speech or writing of an abstract linguistic unit. For example, the PHONEME /ɪ/ as in /bɪg/ *big* can be realized with more or less length, e.g. as [ɪ], [ɪː] or [ɪːː], where N means "with some length" and NN means "particularly long". The last example may be used when someone wants to put special emphasis on the word *big*, or to suggest by the duration of the vowel the size of the "big" thing:
It's really bíg!

real time *n*

in classroom observation and classroom research, the actual time during which an event occurs when the perception or recording of the event occurs at nearly the same time. It is often difficult to study classroom processes in real time since multiple events happen at the same time and occur rapidly. Hence the use of video and other means of observation.

real-time coding *n*

in classroom observation and classroom research, assigning events to analytic categories as the events actually happen, as opposed to analyzing them using audio or video-recorded data.

recall *n*

the ability to bring an event, idea, word, etc. that is stored in memory into conscious awareness. In certain memory tests, subjects are asked to recall (remember) items that were previously encountered, for example in a training session. **Cued recall** is when subjects are given hints, for example, *Can you remember words on the list that were related to language?* **Stimulated recall** is a technique in which learners are asked to recall their thought processes while viewing or hearing a stimulus such as a video of a language lesson to prompt their memory.

see also RECOGNITION

recast *n*

also **corrective recast, implicit negative feedback**

in second language acquisition, a type of negative feedback in which a more competent interlocutor (parent, teacher, native-speaking interlocutor) rephrases an incorrect or incomplete learner utterance by changing one or more sentence components (e.g. subject, verb, or object) while still referring to its central meaning. Recasts have the following characteristics:

a They are a reformulation of the ill-formed utterance.

b They expand the utterance in some way.

c The central meaning of the utterance is retained.

d The recast follows the ill-formed utterance.

For example when two students are comparing two pictures:

Learner 1: *What are they . . . what do they do in your picture?*

Learner 2: *What are they doing in my picture?*

Recasts are thought to be one way in which learners acquire new linguistic structures or come to notice that the ones they are using are not correct.

see also EVIDENCE, FEEDBACK

received pronunciation *n*

also **RP**

the type of British STANDARD ENGLISH pronunciation which has been traditionally considered the prestige variety and which shows little or no REGIONAL VARIATION. It has often been popularly referred to as "BBC English" because it was until recently the standard pronunciation used by most British Broadcasting Corporation newsreaders. Like all other varieties of language it has been subject to change over time.

RP differs from Standard American English pronunciation in various ways. For example, it uses the PHONEME /ɒ/ where most Americans would use another phoneme, as in *hot* /hɒt‖hɑːt/. Speakers of RP do not have an *r* sound before a CONSONANT, though most Americans do, as in *farm* /fɑːm‖fɑːrm/.

receiver *n*

see COMMUNICATION

receptive language knowledge *n*

see ACTIVE/PASSIVE LANGUAGE KNOWLEDGE

receptive skills *n*

see LANGUAGE SKILLS

receptive vocabulary *n*

> also **recognition vocabulary, passive vocabulary**
> the total number of words a person understands, either in reading or listening.
> see ACTIVE/PASSIVE LANGUAGE KNOWLEDGE

reciprocal pronoun *n*

> a PRONOUN which refers to an exchange or mutual interaction between people or groups.
> English uses the phrases *each other* and *one another* like reciprocal pronouns. For example, the sentence *X and Y smiled at each other* implies that X smiled at Y and that Y smiled at X.

reciprocal verb *n*

> a verb is called reciprocal when it suggests that the people or things represented by the SUBJECT of the sentence are doing something to one another.
> For example, the sentence, *Jeremy and Basil were fighting* may imply that Jeremy and Basil were fighting each other. In that case, the sentence uses *fight* as a reciprocal verb.

recitation *n*

> see DISCUSSION METHOD

recognition *n*

> the ability to say whether or not a word (or other linguistic unit) has been encountered before or has a particular suggested meaning. Recognition is somewhat easier than RECALL (being able to remember a word on one's own). Teachers sometimes draw on this principle to facilitate comprehension and communication with learners.
> In psychology, recognition is typically operationalized by presenting subjects with a list of words to study (for example, a list of Spanish verbs) and later asking them to identify which items were on the original list. Answers fall into four categories:
> 1 hits: responses that correctly identify items originally presented
> 2 correct negatives: responses that correctly identify items not previously presented
> 3 misses: responses that fail to identify items originally presented
> 4 false positives: responses that incorrectly identify items as having been presented previously.
> see also LISTENING COMPREHENSION

reconstruction activity *n*

an activity in which students read or listen to a text and then reconstruct it. DICTATION and DICTOGLOSS are examples of reconstruction activities.

reconstructionism *n*

this term is sometimes used to describe an approach to curriculum development which emphasizes the importance of planning, efficiency, and rationality and which stresses the practical aspects of education. In foreign language teaching this approach emphasizes the promotion of practical skills, makes use of objectives or mastery learning, and advocates a systematic approach to needs analysis, programme development, and syllabus design. Reconstructionism is contrasted with **progressivism**, which emphasizes that education is a means of providing people with learning experiences which enable them to learn from their own efforts. It advocates a learner-centred approach to education, sees the learner as a "whole person", promotes the learner's individual development, and leads to a focus on the process of learning rather than mastery of discrete learning items.

see CURRICULUM IDEOLOGIES

record keeping *n*

(in a language programme) the maintenance of a file of data on student performance.

recount *n*

see TEXT TYPES

recursiveness *n*

according to some linguistic theories, the capacity that enables the grammar of a language to produce an infinite number of sentences. This view of grammar was emphasized in Chomsky's early grammatical theories. Many linguists today argue that language use is in fact characterized by the repeated use of fixed expressions and collocations.

recursive rule *n*

a rule which can be applied repeatedly without any definite limit. For example, a recursive rule for the addition of relative clauses could produce: *The man saw the dog which bit the girl who was stroking the cat which had caught the mouse which had eaten the cheese which . . .*

recycling *n*

see SPIRAL APPROACH

reduced speech form *n*

another term for WEAK FORM

reduced vowel *n*

an unstressed vowel that is pronounced with a noncontrasting, centralized, lax quality. In many varieties of English, all unstressed nonfinal vowels are reduced to [ə] schwa, for example, the middle vowels in the words *appetite*, *avarice*, *telegraph*. In addition, a word that has a full vowel in its CITATION FORM may have a reduced vowel in connected speech. For example, the vowel /ʊ/ in the word *could* is often reduced to schwa in a phrase like *we could go*.

redundancy *n* **redundant** *adj*

the degree to which a message contains more information than is needed for it to be understood. Languages have built-in redundancy, which means that utterances contain more information than is necessary for comprehension. For example, in English, PLURAL may be shown on the demonstrative, the noun, and the verb, as in:

These books are expensive.

However, if the *s* on *books* is omitted, the message would still be understood. Therefore, the *s* is redundant in this context. 50% of normal language is said to be redundant.

reduplication *n*

repetition of a syllable, a MORPHEME, or a word. For example:
a in Tagalog (a Philippine language) *tatlo* "three", *tatatlo* "only three"
b in Malay *anak* "child", *anak anak* "children".

reference *n* **referent** *n* **refer** *v* **referential** *adj*

(in SEMANTICS) the relationship between words and the things, actions, events, and qualities they stand for.

Reference in its wider sense would be the relationship between a word or phrase and an entity in the external world (see DENOTATION). For example, the word *tree* refers to the object 'tree' (the referent). Reference in its narrower sense is the relationship between a word or phrase and a specific object, e.g. a particular tree or a particular animal. For example, *Peter's horse* would refer to a horse which is owned, ridden by, or in some way associated with Peter.

referential question *n*

a question which asks for information which is not known to the teacher, such as *What do you think about animal rights?*
see also DISPLAY QUESTION, QUESTIONING TECHNIQUES

referring expression *n*

see BINDING PRINCIPLE

referring tone *n*

an intonation pattern which indicates that something that is said is part of the knowledge shared between the speaker and the listener. In Standard British English, the referring tone (r) is often a fall and then a rise in PITCH ⤴ or a rise in pitch ➚ whereas the **proclaiming tone** (p), often shown by a fall in pitch ➘, suggests that the speaker is introducing information which is new to the listener:

a (r) He'll be twenty (p) in August.
b (p) He'll be twenty (r) in August.

In example (a) the new information is August. In example (b) the new information is the age of the person discussed.

see also KEY², TONE², TONE UNIT

reflection *n*

the process of thinking back on and considering experiences, in order better to understand the significance of such experiences. Reflection is thought to be an important component of learning in teacher development and is often a focus of teacher development activities.

see REFLECTIVE TEACHING

reflective discussion *n*

see DISCUSSION METHOD

reflective teaching *n*

an approach to teaching and to teacher education which is based on the assumption that teachers can improve their understanding of teaching and the quality of their own teaching by reflecting critically on their teaching experiences.

In teacher education programmes, activities which seek to develop a reflective approach to teaching aim to develop the skills of considering the teaching process thoughtfully, analytically and objectively, as a way of improving classroom practices. This may involve the use of

1 journals in which student teachers or practising teachers write about and describe classroom experiences and use their descriptions as a basis for review and reflection

2 audio and video taping of a teacher's lesson by the teacher, for purposes of later review and reflection

3 group discussion with peers or a supervisor in order to explore issues that come out of classroom experience.

reflexive pronoun *n*

a form of a PRONOUN which is used when the direct or indirect OBJECT in a sentence refers to the same person or thing as the subject of the sentence. In English these are formed in the same way as EMPHATIC PRONOUNS, i.e. by adding, *-self*, *-selves* to the pronoun, as in:

I hurt myself:

reflexive verb *n*

a verb used so as to imply that the subject is doing something to himself or herself.

In English, this is typically expressed by means of a REFLEXIVE PRONOUN added to the verb, e.g. *They hurt themselves*. But the same meaning may be expressed by the verb on its own, as in *I was shaving*.

reformulation *n*

an error correction technique in which a teacher reformulates a learner's written or spoken language, keeping the same content but re-encoding it to approximate target language norms more closely. A reformulation of speech in interaction is also referred to as a RECAST.

regional dialect *n*

also **geographic dialect**

a dialect associated with speakers living in a particular location. These may include national varieties of English (e.g. American versus British), as well as dialects within a country such as New England, Midland and Southern dialects in the US and the northern and southern English dialects in Britain.

regional language *n*

a language that is spoken in part of a country. For example, Cantonese is a regional language of Guangdong and nearby areas in China, and Catalan is a regional language in parts of both Spain and France.

see also COMMUNITY LANGUAGE, MINORITY LANGUAGE, MAJORITY LAN-GUAGE, NATIONAL LANGUAGE, OFFICIAL LANGUAGE

regional variation *n*

variation in speech according to the particular area where a speaker comes from (see DIALECT). Variation may occur with respect to pronunciation, vocabulary, or syntax.

For example, in the southwest of England and in the American Midwest, many speakers use an /r/ sound in words such as *her*, *four*, *part*, whereas speakers from some other places, such as the London region and New England, do not.

register *n*

    1 see STYLE

    2 a SPEECH VARIETY used by a particular group of people, usually sharing the same occupation (e.g. doctors, lawyers) or the same interests (e.g. stamp collectors, baseball fans). A particular register often distinguishes itself from other registers by having a number of distinctive words, by using words or phrases in a particular way (e.g. in tennis: *deuce, love, tramlines*), and sometimes by special grammatical constructions (e.g. legal language).

register tone *n*

another term for LEVEL TONE

regression *n*

a backward movement of the eye along a line of print when reading. Poor readers tend to make more regressions than good readers. In reading aloud, a regression is the repetition of a syllable, word, or phrase that has already been read.

regression analysis *n*

a statistical technique for estimating or predicting a value for a DEPENDENT VARIABLE from a set of INDEPENDENT VARIABLES. For example, if a student scored 60% on a test of reading comprehension and 70% in a grammar test (the independent variables), regression analysis could be used to predict his or her likely score on a test of language proficiency (the dependent variable). When two or more independent variables are present, as in this example, the statistical technique is called **multiple regression.**

regression hypothesis *n*

the idea that the order in which elements are lost in LANGUAGE LOSS is the reverse of the order in which they were learned.

see also LANGUAGE ATTRITION

regressive assimilation *n*

see ASSIMILATION

regular verb *n*

a verb which has the most typical forms in its language for grammatical categories such as TENSE or PERSON. In written English regular verbs form the past tense (a) by adding -*ed* to the verb base; *walk → walked*; (b) by adding -*d* to the base; *smile → smiled*; (c) by changing -*y → -ied*; *cry → cried*. A verb which does not have regular forms for tense, person, etc. is known as an

irregular verb. Irregular verbs in English may form the past tense (a) by using the same form as the present tense; *upset → upset*; *put → put* (b) by having an irregular past tense form which is also used as past participle; *keep → kept*; *catch → caught* (c) by having an irregular past tense form which is different from the past participle; *drive → drove → driven*.

regulatory function *n*

see DEVELOPMENTAL FUNCTIONS OF LANGUAGE

rehearsal *n*

a LEARNING STRATEGY that involves saying a new word or sentence to one-self (usually silently) in order to memorize it. In **levels of processing** models of memory, a contrast is made between **maintenance rehearsal,** which involves simple rote repetition, and **elaborative rehearsal,** which involves deep semantic processing, resulting in more elaborate associations and more durable memories. For example, if you need to remember a sequence of numbers for later recall, it is useful to transform the sequence into something that is meaningful.

rehearsing *n*

see COMPOSING PROCESSES

reinforcement *n*

(in BEHAVIOURISM) the strengthening of a response as a result of repetition followed by a positive reward. Reinforcement played an important role in some theories of learning (see STIMULUS-RESPONSE THEORY) and is still used loosely by many who do not subscribe to behaviouristic learning theories, although usually not in well-defined ways.

relatedness *n*

see SELF DETERMINATION THEORY

relative clause *n*

a CLAUSE which modifies a noun or noun phrase. For example in English:
> People *who smoke* annoy me.
> The book *which I am reading* is interesting.

The pronoun which introduces a relative clause is known as a **relative pronoun,** e.g. *who, which, that*.
see also DEFINING RELATIVE CLAUSE

relative pronoun *n*

see RELATIVE CLAUSE

relativity *n*
see LINGUISTIC RELATIVITY

relativization *n*
in SYNTAX, the process by which a relative clause is derived from an underlying non-relative clause.

relearning *n*
the regaining of lost language when individuals encounter a language they once knew but appeared to have forgotten. Among psychologists there is general agreement that information once learned is never truly lost but rather becomes increasingly inaccessible with disuse. The **savings paradigm** investigates differences in the rate of learning previously known information compared to completely new information.
see also LANGUAGE ATTRITION

reliability *n*
(in testing) a measure of the degree to which a test gives consistent results. A test is said to be reliable if it gives the same results when it is given on different occasions or when it is used by different people.
see also ALTERNATE-FORM RELIABILITY, SPLIT-HALF RELIABILITY, INTERNAL CONSISTENCY RELIABILITY, SPEARMAN-BROWN (PROPHECY) FORMULA

reliability coefficient *n*
a numerical index of test reliability that can be obtained by correlating two sets of scores on parallel tests, repeated test administrations, or the two halves of a test. Theoretically its values range between 0.0 and +1.0.

reliability index *n*
an estimate of the correlation between the actual OBSERVED SCORES and the theoretical TRUE SCORES that can be obtained by taking the square root of a test's reliability coefficient.

remedial work *n*
also **remedial teaching**
in teaching, teaching that is specially devised to address problems students are having with previously taught material.

repair *n, v*
(in CONVERSATIONAL ANALYSIS) a term for ways in which errors, unintended forms, or misunderstandings are corrected by speakers or others during conversation. A repair which is made by the speaker (i.e. which is self-initiated) is known as a **self repair**. For example:

> *I bought a, uhm . . . what do you call it . . . a floor polisher.*

A repair made by another person (i.e. which is other-initiated) is known as **other repair**. For example:

> A: *How long you spend?*
> B: *Hmm?*
> A: *How long did you spend there?*

B's response serves to indicate that a repair is needed to A's original utterance.

repeated measures design *n*
> another term for WITHIN-SUBJECTS DESIGN

repertoire *n*
> see SPEECH REPERTOIRE

repetition drill *n*
> see DRILL

repetition stage *n*
> another term for PRACTICE STAGE
> see PPP

replicability *n*
> see DEPENDABILITY

replication *n*
> conducting a research study a second time in order to test or extend the original findings. An **exact replication** is one in which the original research design is followed, while a **partial replication** is one in which certain aspects of the design are modified, for example, repeating the study with different types of participants.

reported speech *n*
> see DIRECT SPEECH

reporting *n*
> the process of communicating assessment results to students, their parents and the institution, usually through written reports.

reporting verb *n*
> a verb such as *advise, suggest, tell* used in indirect speech to report what someone has said.
> *I told her to be here at 7 pm.*

representation *n*

a notational device (such as a TREE DIAGRAM) used to represent syntactic structure. By extension, an assumed counterpart of such devices in the brain.

representative *n*

see SPEECH ACT CLASSIFICATION

representative sample *n*

see SAMPLE

research *n*

the study of an event, problem or phenomenon using systematic methods, in order to understand it better and to develop principles and theories about it. see also ACTION RESEARCH, DATA, EXPERIMENTAL METHOD, HYPOTHESIS, THEORY

residual hearing *n*

see HEARING IMPAIRED, AUDITORY/ORAL METHOD

resource management strategies *n*

see LEARNING STRATEGY

response *n*

1 see STIMULUS-RESPONSE THEORY, BEHAVIOURISM
2 see CUE

restricted code *n*

see CODE[2]

restrictive relative clause *n*

another term for DEFINING RELATIVE CLAUSE

restructuring *n*

1 in language acquisition, the integration of new forms into the learner's language system in a way which triggers reorganization of the learner's language system. Either DECLARATIVE KNOWLEDGE or PROCEDURAL KNOWLEDGE can be restructured. From an information-processing perspective, when acquiring complex skills learners create new mental structures to accommodate the new knowledge they acquire. As learning proceeds this requires the reorganization of already acquired knowledge in order to be able to use it more efficiently. Complex skills such as those

497

involved in language learning require not only the automatization of knowledge and procedures but also the restructuring of information as a central process in language learning.

2 in writing in a second or foreign language, a process that occurs during the composing process in which the writer searches for an alternative syntactic plan once he or she realizes, predicts or anticipates that the original plan is not going to work. During the process of composing, a writer may be constrained both by lack of linguistic resources but also by a series of semantic, textual, or pragmatic concerns, necessitating restructuring.

result(ative) case *n*
see FACTITIVE CASE

resultative construction *n*
see CONSTRUCTION GRAMMAR

resumptive pronoun *n*
a pronoun that appears in the position of a TRACE left behind when forming a wh-phrase, for example "it" in the sentence "I wonder where the book is that I was reading it". Resumptive pronouns are ungrammatical in STANDARD ENGLISH, but they are acceptable or obligatory in many languages (e.g. Arabic), have been noted in first language acquisition of English, and are common in INTERLANGUAGE.

resyllabification *n*
see LINKING

retention *n*
the ability to recall or remember things after an interval of time. In language teaching, retention of what has been taught (e.g. grammar rules, vocabulary) may depend on the quality of teaching, the interest of the learners, or the meaningfulness of the materials.

retroflex *adj*
describes a speech sound (a CONSONANT) which is produced with the tip of the tongue curled back to touch or nearly touch the hard palate at the top of the mouth.

Many Indian languages use retroflex /t/ and /d/, [ʈ] and [ɖ] – and many native speakers of these languages continue to use these sounds when they speak English.

The /r/ used by some speakers in the south-west of England, and in many varieties of American English, is a retroflex sound.

see also PLACE OF ARTICULATION, MANNER OF ARTICULATION

retrospection *n*

see VERBAL REPORTING

retrospective syllabus *n*

see A PRIORI SYLLABUS

reversal error *n*

see SPEECH ERRORS

reversed subtitles *n*

see SUBTITLES

reverse stress *n*

see STRESS SHIFT

revising *n*

see COMPOSING PROCESSES

revision *n*

the practices in L2 composition classes in which students "look again" at their writing holistically in order to improve such areas as organization, focus, etc.

see CONSOLIDATION

rewrite rule *n*

see BASE COMPONENT

rheme *n*

see FUNCTIONAL SENTENCE PERSPECTIVE

rhetoric *n*

the study of how effective writing achieves its goals. The term "rhetoric" in this sense is common in North American college and university courses in rhetoric or "rhetorical communication", which typically focus on how to express oneself correctly and effectively in relation to the topic of writing or speech, the audience, and the purpose of communication.

In traditional grammar, rhetoric was the study of style through grammatical and logical analysis. Cicero, the ancient Roman orator and writer, described rhetoric as "the art or talent by which discourse is adapted to its end".

rhetorical question *n*

a forceful statement which has the form of a question but which does not expect an answer. For example, *"What difference does it make?"* which may function like the statement, *"It makes no difference"*.

rhetorical structure *n*

another term for SCHEME

rhetorical structure analysis *n*

in discourse analysis or text analysis, the study of units of meaning usually beyond the level of sentences, how they relate to one another in a hierarchy and how such functional acts as exemplification, summary, expansion, etc., are added to core propositions to construct a finished text.

rhotacization *n*

the auditory property known as R-COLOURING that results from the lowering of the third formant.

rhotic *adj*

a form of English in which /r/ can occur after a vowel and within a syllable in words such as *car*, *bird*, *early*. Most forms of American English are rhotic, whereas most forms spoken in the southern part of England are **nonrhotic**.

rhyme *adj*

the nucleus + coda of a syllable, for example, the /eyn/ of *rain*.

rhythm *n*

see SPEECH RHYTHM

right brain *n*

another term for RIGHT HEMISPHERE

right branching direction *n*

see BRANCHING DIRECTION

right dislocation *n*

see LEFT DISLOCATION

right ear advantage *n*

in DICHOTIC LISTENING tasks, most subjects more correctly identify linguistic stimuli delivered to the right ear than to the left. This is taken as evidence for left hemisphere processing of language.

right hemisphere *n*

see CEREBRAL DOMINANCE

risk-taking *n*

a PERSONALITY factor which concerns the degree to which a person is willing to undertake actions that involve a significant degree of risk. Risk-taking is said to be an important characteristic of successful second language learning, since learners have to be willing to try out hunches about the new language and take the risk of being wrong.

see also COGNITIVE VARIABLE

ritual *n*

a SPEECH EVENT which follows a more or less strictly defined pattern, e.g. part of a religious service, an initiation ceremony. Often UTTERANCES must follow each other in a particular sequence and may have to be of a particular kind.

role *n*

1 the part taken by a participant in any act of communication. Some roles are more or less permanent, e.g. that of teacher or student, while other roles are very temporary, e.g. the role of someone giving advice. The same person could have a number of different roles in his or her daily activities. For example, a man may be father, brother, son, husband in his family life but colleague, teacher, employee, treasurer, counsellor in his working life. Roles affect the way people communicate with each other (see ROLE RELATIONSHIPS).

2 people also sometimes talk of the "roles" of *speaker* or *listener* in a SPEECH EVENT.

role-play *n, v*

also **role playing** *n*

in language teaching drama-like classroom activities in which students take the ROLES of different participants in a situation and act out what might typically happen in that situation. For example, to practise how to express complaints and apologies in a foreign language, students might have to role-play a situation in which a customer in a shop returns a faulty article to a salesperson.

see also SIMULATION

role relationship *n*

the relationship which people have to each other in an act of communication and which influences the way they speak to each other. One of the speakers may have a ROLE which has a higher STATUS than that of the other speaker(s),

501

e.g. school principal ↔ teacher, teacher ↔ student(s), lieutenant ↔ sergeant. Sometimes people temporarily take on superior roles, either because of the situation, e.g. bank manager ↔ loan seeker, or because one of them has a stronger personality, e.g. student A ↔ student B.

roll *n*

another term for TRILL

Roman alphabet *n*

also **Latin alphabet**

an alphabetic writing system used for many languages, including English. It consists of letters which may represent different sounds or sound combinations in different languages. For example, the letter *w* represents /w/ in English as /ˈwɔːtəʳ/ *water* but /v/ in German /ˈvasər/ *Wasser* "water". see also ALPHABET

romance languages *n*

a group of languages which are derived from Latin. French, Italian, Spanish, Portuguese and Romanian are all romance languages. Their common ancestry can still be seen in some of their words and structures, for example:

French	Italian	Spanish	English
père	*padre*	*padre*	*father*
poisson	*pesce*	*pescado*	*fish*
champ	*campo*	*campo*	*field*

Romance languages are part of the wider INDO-EUROPEAN LANGUAGE group.

root *n*

also **base form**

a MORPHEME which is the basic part of a word and which may, in many languages, occur on its own (e.g. English *man, hold, cold, rhythm*). Roots may be joined to other roots (e.g. English *house + hold → household*) and/or take AFFIXes (e.g. *manly, coldness*) or COMBINING FORMS (e.g. *biorhythm*). see also STEM[1]

rote learning *n*

the learning of material by repeating it over and over again until it is memorized, without paying attention to its meaning.

rounded vowel *n*

see VOWEL

routine *n*

also **formula, formulaic speech/expressions/language, conventionalized speech, prefabricated language/speech, fixed expression**

(generally) a segment of language made up of several morphemes or words which are learned together and used as if they were a single item. For example *How are you? With best wishes, To Whom it May Concern, You must be kidding.* Researchers use different names for these routines. A routine or formula which is used in conversation is sometimes called a conversational routine (e.g. *that's all for now, How awful!, you don't say, the thing is. . . . Would you believe it!*) and one used to show politeness, a politeness formula (e.g. *Thank you very much*).

see also GAMBIT, IDIOM, UTTERANCE

routines *n*

in teaching, procedures used by learners for accomplishing particular classroom tasks. Routines govern physical relationships, space, materials and procedures, e.g. for establishing student groups, asking questions. Effective use of routines is essential for the successful functioning of classrooms and is considered a basic teaching skill.

routinization *n*

the process by which CONTROLLED PROCESSES become routine, in the sense that they are done without explicit deliberation and require little attention, thereby allowing attention to be focused when it is most needed. In the INFORMATION PROCESSING model of language learning, it is considered essential that many low-level processes of speech production and comprehension must become routinized so that a speaker's or hearer's attention can be focused on meaning or on aspects of language that are not yet fully established within the learner's interlanguage.

RP *n*

an abbreviation for RECEIVED PRONUNCIATION

RSA

an abbreviation for Royal Society of Arts, a British multi-disciplinary institution, best known for creating the RSA Examinations Board (now part of the Oxford, Cambridge and RSA Examinations Board). The Cambridge RSA CELTA (Certificate in English Language Teaching to Adults) is a widely recognized teaching qualification for English language teachers. It was formerly known as the CTEFLA and the RSA Certificate.

rubric *n*

in tests and instructional materials, the instructions which indicate to the student what he or she has to do to complete a task or activity.

rule[1] *n*

(in TRADITIONAL GRAMMAR) a statement
1 about the formation of a linguistic unit, e.g. how to form the PAST TENSE of VERBS, or
2 about the CORRECT usage of a linguistic unit or units, e.g. that verbs are modified by adverbs *(Come here quickly)* and not by adjectives *(*Come here quick)*.

rule[2] *n*

(in GENERATIVE GRAMMAR) a statement about the formation of a linguistic unit or about the relationship between linguistic units. Rules describe and analyze (**generate**) structures in a language and change the structures into sentences.
see also BASE COMPONENT, GENERATIVE GRAMMAR

rule-governed behaviour *n*

also **rule-governed system**

a person's knowledge of a language (COMPETENCE) can be described as a system of symbols representing linguistic units (such as MORPHEMES and words) and rules that manipulate such symbols to create sentences. Language is thus often described as a "rule-governed system". Whether such rules reflect the mental processes involved in language processing (see PERFORMANCE) and whether language use should be described as "rule-governed behaviour" has been a matter of continued debate. Although the exact notion of what constitutes a rule has changed greatly in successive versions of GENERATIVE THEORY, in general, linguists and psycholinguists who work within the generative paradigm have argued for the psychological reality of linguistic rules. Those who accept the view of language put forth by CONNECTIONISM (which models language acquisition and use in networks that do not contain rules) emphasize that "rule-like" behaviour does not logically entail the psychological reality of "rule-governed" behaviour.

rule-governed system *n*

see RULE-GOVERNED BEHAVIOUR

rule narrowing *n*

see ADAPTIVE CONTROL OF THOUGHT

rules of speaking *n*

see CONVERSATION RULES

rule strengthening *n*

see ADAPTIVE CONTROL OF THOUGHT

running words *n*

the total number of words occurring in a text.

see LEXICAL DENSITY

run-on-sentence *n*

also **fused sentence**

(in composition) an error in punctuation where one or more full stops are omitted between sentences or independent clauses (see DEPENDENT CLAUSE). For example:

Mrs Lee is a great teacher she always explains things very clearly.

This could be rewritten as two independent clauses separated by a comma followed by the co-ordinating CONJUNCTION *and*.

Mrs Lee is a great teacher, and she always explains things very clearly.

S

saccade *n*

see FIXATION PAUSE

salience *n* **salient** *adj*

also **perceptual salience**

(in language learning, speech PERCEPTION, and INFORMATION PROCESSING) the ease with which a linguistic item is perceived. In language learning, the salience of linguistic items has been studied to see if it affects the order in which the items are learned. For example, the salience of a spoken word may depend on:

a the position of a phoneme in the word

b the emphasis given to the word in speech, i.e. whether it is STRESSed or unstressed

c the position of the word in a sentence.

see also NATURAL ORDER HYPOTHESIS

sample *n*

(in statistics and testing) any group of individuals that is selected to represent a POPULATION. A sample in which every member of the population has an equal and independent chance of being selected is known as a **random sample**. A sample in which the population is grouped into several strata (e.g. of high, medium, and low scores), and a selection drawn from each level, is known as a **stratified sample**. A sample which contains a good representation of the population from which it is drawn is known as a **representative sample**.

A sample that is deliberately chosen without using randomizing techniques is known as a **prospective sample**. A sample which is chosen solely from subjects who are conveniently available is called a **convenience sample**.

sampling *n*

the procedure of selecting a SAMPLE. This selection can be done in various ways, e.g. by selecting a RANDOM SAMPLE or a STRATIFIED SAMPLE.

sampling error *n*

in testing and research, the difference between the data obtained on a specific sample selected for a test or an experimental study and the data that would have been obtained if the entire population had been tested or studied.

Sapir-Whorf hypothesis *n*

   see LINGUISTIC RELATIVITY

sarcasm *n*

   see FIGURE OF SPEECH

savings paradigm *n*

   see RELEARNING

scaffolding *n*

1 the support provided to learners to enable them to perform tasks which are beyond their capacity. Initially in language learning, learners may be unable to produce certain structures within a single utterance, but may build them through interaction with another speaker. For example, in the following exchange, the learner produces the structure *"Oh, this an ant"*, across five turns:

   Child: *Oh!*
   Mother: *What?*
   Child: *This.* (points to an ant)
   Mother: *It's an ant.*
   Child: *Ant.*

Later, the child is able to produce the structure within a single turn:

   Oh, this an ant.

Scaffolding is thought to be one way in which learners acquire new linguistic structures.

2 a teaching/learning strategy where the teacher and learners engage in a collaborative problem-solving activity with the teacher providing demonstrations, support, guidance and input and gradually withdrawing these as the learner becomes increasingly independent.

The theory of scaffolding emphasizes the role of collaborative discourse in language learning. The psychologist Bruner believed that language learning is dependent upon providing appropriate social interactional frameworks for learners. Several types of scaffolding are sometimes distinguished.

1 **Vertical scaffolding** involves the adult extending the child's language by asking further questions.

2 **Sequential scaffolding** is found in games such as those played with children at meal time.

3 **Instructional scaffolding** refers to an important aspect of formal instruction. Learning is viewed as a process involving gradual internalization of routines and procedures available to the learner from the social and cultural context in which learning occurs. The language learner is assisted in a new task by a more skilled user who models the learning task.

scale *n*

(in statistics and testing) the level or type of quantification produced by a measurement. Four different scales are often used:

a A **nominal** (or **categorical**) **scale** is used to assign values to items or individuals that belong to different groups or categories. For example, we may assign the number "1" to all male students and "2" to all female students in a school. But these numbers are arbitrary and interchangeable. Thus, instead of assigning "1" to male students and "2" to female students, we can assign "1" to female students and "2" to male students.

b An **ordinal scale** makes use of ORDINAL NUMBERS (e.g. first, second, third). It ranks items or individuals in order on the basis of some criterion. For example, based on scores on a test, test takers may be rank-ordered as first, second or third in comparison to others who took the same test. However, the difference between the values on the scale is not necessarily the same. Thus, the difference in points between being first or second on a test may not be the same as the difference between being 21st or 22nd.

c An **interval scale** is similar to an ordinal scale except that it has the additional quality that the intervals between the points on the scale are equal. For example, the difference between a temperature of 8°C and 6°C is the same as the difference between a temperature of 4°C and 2°C. However, we cannot say that a temperature of 8°C is twice as hot as a temperature of 4°C because an interval scale does not have an absolute zero.

d A **ratio scale** is similar to an interval scale except that it has an absolute zero, which enables us to compare two points on the ratio scale and make a statement such as "This point is three times as high as that point". A scale for measuring height is an example of a ratio scale. Thus, we can say that a person whose height is 220 cm is twice as tall as a person whose height is 110 cm.

Scales can be converted into other scales. However, the direction of scale conversion is only one-way (i.e. a ratio scale → an interval scale → an ordinal scale → a nominal scale), not the other way round.

scalogram *n*

see IMPLICATIONAL SCALING

scanning *n*

(in READING) a type of READING STRATEGY which is used when the reader wants to locate a particular piece of information without necessarily understanding the rest of a text or passage. For example, the reader may read through a chapter of a book as rapidly as possible in order to find out information about a particular date, such as when someone was born.

Scanning may be contrasted with **skimming** or **skim-reading**, which is a type of rapid reading which is used when the reader wants to get the main idea or ideas from a passage. For example a reader may skim-read a chapter to find out if the writer approves or disapproves of something.

see also READING SPEED

scatter diagram *n*

also **scattergram, scatterplot**

a representation on a graph of two separate variables, in such a way as to display their relationship as shown below:

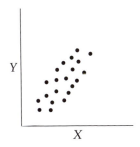

Y axis: scores on test Y
X axis: scores on test X
see also CORRELATION

scattergram *n*

see SCATTER DIAGRAM

scatterplot *n*

see SCATTER DIAGRAM

schema *n*

also **scheme, macro-structure, genre-scheme, discourse structure, frame, rhetorical structure**

1 a mental representation, plan or structure.
2 a collection of organized and interrelated ideas, concepts and prior knowledge structures that are abstract representations of objects, events and relationships in the real world.
3 (in TEXT LINGUISTICS and DISCOURSE ANALYSIS) the underlying structure which accounts for the organization of a TEXT or DISCOURSE. Different kinds of texts and discourse (e.g. stories, descriptions, letters, reports, poems) are distinguished by the ways in which the TOPIC, PROPOSITIONS,

and other information are linked together to form a unit. This underlying structure is known as the "scheme" or "macrostructure". For example the scheme underlying many stories is:

Story = Setting(= state + state + . . .) + Episodes(= Event(s) + Reaction)
i.e. stories consist of a setting in which the time, place, and characters are identified, followed by episodes leading towards a reaction. A text or discourse in which a suitable underlying scheme or macro-structure is used is said to be "coherent" (see COHERENCE).

Note that the plural of *scheme* is *schemes*, but the plural of *schema* is either *schemes* or *schemata*.

see also SCRIPT

schema theory *n*

the theory that in comprehending language people activate relevant schemata allowing them to process and interpret new experiences quickly and efficiently. Schemata serve as a reference store from which a person can retrieve relevant existing knowledge and into which new information is assimilated. When encountering a topic in reading or listening, the reader activates the schema for that topic and makes use of it to anticipate, infer, and make different kinds of judgements and decisions about it. Schema theory plays an important role in theories of second language reading and listening comprehension.

A difference is sometimes made between **content schemata** and **formal schemata**. Content schemata deal with general background knowledge related to the topic such as might be associated with the topic of *an earthquake*. Formal schemata deal with the rhetorical structure of language and a person's knowledge of the structure of a particular genre, such as *news reports* or *journal articles*.

scheme of work *n*

in some teaching contexts, a plan that indicates what will be taught for the semester or year and the order in which it will be taught. The scheme of work translates information in a curriculum concerning general objectives and course content (e.g. a syllabus) into a teaching plan for a semester or year. In language teaching, schemes of work are usually prepared by individual teachers or groups of teachers and take into consideration:

a the amount of time available per class period, week, or semester
b which items will be taught, how important each item is for learners, and how long it might require for them to reach a particular level of learning
c how the items can be graded, sequenced and combined
d how recycling and reinforcement can be incorporated into the scheme of work

e how balance and integration of different elements in the syllabus or of different skills will be achieved.

school-based curriculum development *n*
an educational movement which emerged in some countries in the 1960s and which argued that the planning, designing, implementation and evaluation of a programme of students' learning should be carried out by the educational institutions of which these students are members (i.e. schools) rather than by an external institution, such as a state department of education or a national curriculum centre. The movement towards school-based curriculum development reflects a more general philosophy of **learner-centredness** and was an attempt to develop learning programmes that were more relevant to students' interests and needs by involving schools, learners, and teachers in the planning and decision making.
see also LEARNER-CENTRED APPROACH

school-based management *n*
an approach to the management of schools advocated in some parts of the world and that shifts responsibility for curriculum planning, budgets, hiring, assessment and other aspects of schooling away from a central administration such as a ministry or department of education, to a school's principal, teachers, parents and other members of the community. In the US CHARTER SCHOOLS are an example of this approach. They operate with some public funding but with considerable freedom from state and local regulations. They are often managed by parents and teachers operating under a charter that spells out what they plan to accomplish.

school culture *n*
the patterns of communication, decision-making, interactions, role relations, administrative practice and conduct that exist within a school or educational institution. Schools, like other organizations, develop their own ethos or environment and have their own distinctive ways of doing things, which might be favourable or unfavourable to encouraging change or innovation. The process of curriculum development or change often includes changes to the school culture.

schwa *n*
also **shwa**
a short vowel usually produced with the tongue in a central position in the mouth and with the lips unrounded. The phonetic symbol for a schwa is [ə].

In English, it occurs very frequently in unaccented syllables, e.g. *-mous* in /ˈfeɪməs/ *famous*, *-ment* in /ˈmuːvmənt/ *movement* and in unstressed words in rapid speech, e.g. *to* in /təˈteɪk/ *to take*.

see also MANNER OF ARTICULATION, PLACE OF ARTICULATION

scientific English *n*
a the type of English used in scientific writing, which can be described in terms of the norms of organization and presentation, syntactic patterns, discourse features, and so on that are characteristic of this GENRE.

scientific method *n*
a methodical approach to the acquisition of knowledge that is based on evidence rather than belief. The scientific method is founded on direct observation and driven by the formulation of research questions, the collection of data, and the analysis and interpretation of data within a theoretical framework. Some but not all versions of the scientific method include prediction in the form of a research HYPOTHESIS which is put to a test through prediction and experimentation.

see also EXPERIMENTAL METHOD, QUALITATIVE RESEARCH, QUANTITATIVE RESEARCH

scope *n*
see NEGATION

scope and sequence *n*
a plan for a course, curriculum or syllabus in which the content of the course (e.g. in terms of topics, skills, functions, grammar, etc.) is organized according to the successive units or levels in which they appear in the course. It usually appears as a chart or table at the front of a course book or textbook.

see SEQUENCE

scoring *n*
procedures for giving numerical values or scores to the responses in a test.

scoring rubric *n*
a set of scoring guidelines or criteria used in scoring or judging a test taker's product, performance or response to a CONSTRUCTED-RESPONSE ITEM type of assessment task (e.g. writing an essay in L2) to make raters' subjective judgements more reliable.

see also BENCHMARK

screening test *n*

see ADMISSIONS TEST

script *n*

also **frame**

(in COGNITIVE PSYCHOLOGY) units of meaning consisting of sequences of events and actions that are related to particular situations. For example a "restaurant script" is our knowledge that a restaurant is a place where waitresses, waiters, and cooks work, where food is served to customers, and where customers sit at tables, order food, eat, pay the bill, and depart. A person's knowledge of this "script" helps in understanding the following paragraph:

Tom was hungry. He went into a restaurant. At 8 p.m. he paid the bill and left.

Although Tom was most probably shown to a table, sat down, ordered a meal, and ate it, these facts are not mentioned in the paragraph. The reader's knowledge of a restaurant script, i.e. the usual sequence of events for this situation, provides this information. Script theory has been used in studies of problem solving, reading, memory, and comprehension.

see also SCHEME

SD^1 *n*

an abbreviation for STANDARD DEVIATION

SD^2 *n*

an abbreviation for STRUCTURAL DESCRIPTION

SD^3 *n*

an abbreviation for Students with Disabilities

SE *n*

an abbreviation for STANDARD ERROR

secondary articulation *n*

an articulation made by two of the organs of speech that are not involved in the primary articulation. For example, the English alveolar lateral /l/ at the end of a syllable, as in *eel*, is often made with the back of the tongue raised, and thus has the secondary articulation of VELARIZATION.

see also ASSIMILATION

secondary cardinal vowel *n*

see CARDINAL VOWEL

secondary stress *n*
    see STRESS

second conditional *n*
    see **conditional forms**

second language *n*
    in a broad sense, any language learned after one has learnt one's native language. However, when contrasted with FOREIGN LANGUAGE, the term refers more narrowly to a language that plays a major role in a particular country or region though it may not be the first language of many people who use it. For example, the learning of English by immigrants in the US or the learning of Catalan by speakers of Spanish in Catalonia (an autonomous region of Spain) are cases of second (not foreign) language learning, because those languages are necessary for survival in those societies. English is also a second language for many people in countries like Nigeria, India, Singapore and the Philippines, because English fulfils many important functions in those countries (including the business of education and government) and learning English is necessary to be successful within that context. (Some people in these countries however may acquire English as a first language, if it is the main language used at home.)

second language acquisition *n*
    also **SLA**
    the process of acquiring a second or foreign language.
    see SECOND LANGUAGE, LANGUAGE ACQUISITION

second language attrition *n*
    see LANGUAGE ATTRITION

segment *n* **segment** *v*
    any linguistic unit in a sequence which may be isolated from the rest of the sequence, e.g. a sound in an UTTERANCE or a letter in a written text.

segmental error *n*
    (in SECOND LANGUAGE ACQUISITION) an error of pronunciation which involves individual vowels or consonants. Segmental errors often contribute to a learner's accent (see ACCENT[3]) in a second or foreign language.

segmental phonemes *n*
    sometimes a distinction is made between the segmental phonemes (i.e. the vowels and consonants of a language) and the supra-segmentals, i.e. such

sound phenomena as accent (see ACCENT[1]) and INTONATION, which may stretch over more than one segment.

selected-response item *n*

a type of test item or test task that requires test takers to choose answers from a ready-made list rather than providing an answer. The most commonly used types of selected-response items include MULTIPLE-CHOICE ITEMS, TRUE/FALSE ITEMS, and MATCHING ITEMS.

see also CONSTRUCTED-RESPONSE ITEM

selection *n*

(in language teaching) the choice of linguistic content (vocabulary, grammar, etc.) for a language course, textbook, etc. Procedures for selecting language items to include in a language course include the use of FREQUENCY COUNTS, NEEDS ANALYSIS, and PEDAGOGIC GRAMMARS.

see also SYLLABUS

selectional restrictions *n*

the semantic restrictions that a word imposes on the environment in which it occurs. For example, a verb like *hope* requires that its subject be animate.

selection bias *n*

see EXTERNAL VALIDITY

selective branching *n*

see BRANCHING

selective listening *n*

in the teaching of listening comprehension, a strategy whereby students are asked to attend to specific information that has been signalled prior to listening.

self *n*

an aspect of PERSONALITY that consists of a person's view of their own identity and characteristics. A person's sense of his or her self is formed as a result of contact and experiences with other people and how they view and treat the individual. Self has been discussed as a personality variable in second language learning.

see also COGNITIVE VARIABLE

self-access *adj*
> (of instructional materials) the capacity of materials to be used independently by learners without the guidance or direction of a teacher.
> see also SELF-ACCESS LEARNING CENTRE

self-access learning centre *n*
> also **self access centre**
> a room or area in an educational institution containing learning resources of different kinds which students can use under supervision. It may contain computers for individual student use, video and TV monitors and audio facilities, as well as print-based learning resources. Students may be directed to certain learning materials (e.g. grammar reviews) designed to complement and support regular teaching activities in a language programme.
> A number of different systems are used for the managements of self access centres:
> 1 *menu driven system* – a dedicated self-access system in which all materials are classified and information is stored electronically (or otherwise). A student refers to the menu to gain access to the system
> 2 *supermarket system* – students can look around and choose the materials they wish to use. Materials are displayed under categories
> 3 *controlled access system* – a student is directed to specific materials by a tutor, usually as a follow up to class work
> 4 *open-access system* – the centre is part of a library open for use by students studying English as well as to other students.

self-assessment *n*
> see SELF-EVALUATION

self-concept *n*
> the image a person has of himself or herself. A measure of a person's self-concept is sometimes included in the study of affective variables (see COGNITIVE VARIABLE) in language learning.

self-correction *n*
> correction by a learner of an error in his or her language use, without assistance from a teacher or other learners.

self determination theory *n*
> also **SDT**
> a theory of human motivation that emphasizes the choices that people make of their own free will, rather under coercion or to gain external rewards. SDT expands on the distinction between intrinsic and extrinsic

motivation, seeing these as a continuum rather than a dichotomy and links self-determination to the importance of three basic human needs: for **autonomy** (the need to actively participate in determining one's own behaviour), competence (the need to feel capable of controlling the environment and outcomes), and relatedness (the need to be related to others).
see also MOTIVATION

self-efficacy *n*
a person's belief in their own capabilities and their ability to attain specific goals. A learner's sense of efficacy affects their motivation to learn, the goals they set, the effort they devote to attaining these goals and their willingness to persist in the face of difficulty. Self-efficacy has been found to influence learners' achievement in language learning.

self-esteem *n*
a person's judgement of their own worth or value, based on a feeling of "efficacy", a sense of interacting effectively with one's own environment. Efficacy implies that some degree of control exists within oneself. Self-esteem is an affective variable in language learning and low self-esteem may negatively influence second language learning.

self-evaluation *n*
also **self-assessment**
checking one's own performance on a language learning task after it has been completed or checking one's own success in using a language. Self-evaluation is an example of a METACOGNITIVE STRATEGY in language learning.
see also SELF-RATING

self-instruction *n* **self-instructional** *adj*
(in education) approaches to learning in which a learner works alone or with other learners, without the control of a teacher. The use of self-instructional activities in language teaching helps to give learners a greater degree of control over their own learning. It is based on the belief that learning is sometimes more effective if learners can make choices about the kinds of things they wish to learn, the strategies they use, and the amount of time they can spend on a learning task.

self-monitoring *n*
also **self-observation**
1 observing and recording information about one's own behaviour for the purpose of achieving a better understanding of and control over one's behaviour. In TEACHER EDUCATION, teachers may be taught procedures for

self-monitoring as an aspect of their on-going professional development. Techniques used include keeping a journal of their teaching experiences, regular and systematic use of self-reports (see SELF REPORTING), or through making audio or video recordings of their own lessons.

2 checking one's performance during a learning task as a METACOGNITIVE STRATEGY during language learning.

self-rating *n*

also **self report**

(in testing) an individual's own evaluation of their language ability, generally according to how good they are at particular language skills (e.g. reading, speaking), how well they are able to use the language in different DOMAINS^1 or situations (e.g. at the office, at school) or how well they can use different styles of the language (e.g. a formal style or an informal style). Self-ratings are a way of obtaining indirect information on a person's proficiency in a language.

self-regulation *n*

also **self-regulated learning**

learning that is guided by metacognition, strategic action, and motivation to learn. Researchers in educational psychology have linked these characteristics to success in school and beyond.

see also LEARNING STRATEGY

self repair *n*

see REPAIR

self report *n*

see SELF-RATING

self-reporting *n*

(in teaching) the use of an inventory or check list of teaching behaviour used during a lesson, which is completed after the lesson has been taught. The self-report form indicates which teaching practices were used during a lesson and how often they were employed and may be completed by an individual teacher or by a group of teachers in a group session. Self-reporting is intended to assist teachers assess their own classroom practices.

self-serving bias *n*

see ATTRIBUTION THEORY

SEM^1 *n*

an abbreviation for STANDARD ERROR OF MEASUREMENT

SEM² *n*

an abbreviation for STRUCTURAL EQUATION MODELLING

semantic component *n*

see GENERATIVE THEORY

semantic components *n*

another term for SEMANTIC FEATURES

semantic differential *n*

a technique for measuring people's attitudes or feelings about words. The semantic differential makes use of a RATING SCALE which contains pairs of adjectives with opposite meanings (**bi-polar adjectives**) which are used to rate different impressions of meaning. The following scale, for example, could be used to measure the subjective meanings of words:

WORD (e.g. *democracy*)

good	–	–	–	–	bad
weak	–	–	–	–	strong
rough	–	–	–	–	smooth
active	–	–	–	–	passive

Subjects rate the word on each dimension. The ratings of different words can be compared. The semantic differential has been used in SEMANTICS, PSYCHOLINGUISTICS, and in the study of LANGUAGE ATTITUDES.

semantic feature *n*

also **semantic component, semantic properties**

the basic unit of meaning in a word. The meanings of words may be described as a combination of semantic features.

For example, the semantic feature (+ male) is part of the meaning of *father*, and so is the feature (+ adult) but other features are needed to give the whole concept or sense of *father*.

The same feature may be part of the meaning of a number of words. For example, (+ movement) is part of the meaning of a whole group of verbs and nouns, e.g. *run, jump, walk, gallop*.

Sometimes, semantic features are established by contrasts and can be stated in terms of (+) or (–), e.g.

child	(+ human)	(– adult)	
man	(+ human)	(+ adult)	(+ male)
boy	(+ human)	(– adult)	(+ male)

see also BINARY FEATURE, COMPONENTIAL ANALYSIS

semantic field *n*

another term for LEXICAL FIELD

semantic mapping *n*

a classroom technique in which a visual representation of ideas in a text or conceptual relationships within a text is used to assist with the reading of a text. The semantic map may be teacher or student generated.

semantic memory *n*

see EPISODIC MEMORY

semantic networks *n*

the associations of related words that come to mind when a certain word is thought of. Bilingual speakers may have different semantic networks for words in their lexicons. For example bilingual speakers of English and Spanish may associate "house" with "window" and "boy" with "girl" but in Spanish may associate "casa" (house) with "madre" (mother) and "muchacho" (boy) with "hombre" (man).

semantic property *n*

another term for SEMANTIC FEATURE

semantics *n* **semantic** *adj*

the study of MEANING. There are many different approaches to the way in which meaning in language is studied. Philosophers, for instance, have investigated the relation between linguistic expressions, such as the words of a language, and persons, things and events in the world to which these words refer (see REFERENCE, SIGNS). Linguists have investigated, for example, the way in which meaning in a language is structured (see COMPONENTIAL ANALYSIS, LEXICAL FIELD, SEMANTIC FEATURES) and have distinguished between different types of meanings (see CONNOTATION, DENOTATION). There have also been studies of the semantic structure of sentences (see PROPOSITIONS).

In recent years, linguists have generally agreed that meaning plays an important part in grammatical analysis but there has been disagreement on how it should be incorporated in a grammar (see BASE COMPONENT, GENERATIVE SEMANTICS, INTERPRETIVE SEMANTICS).

see also PRAGMATICS

semantic valence tendencies *n*

words in a language occur in statistical patterns that display clear semantic preferences. For example, in English, the verb *provide* typically precedes positive words (e.g. *provide work, reasons*) whereas *cause* typically precedes negative items (e.g. *cause trouble*). Online reading tasks reveal that native speakers are sensitive to such tendencies, as they read sentences containing *cause pessimism* faster than sentences containing *cause optimism*. It is an open question if non-native speakers become sensitive to such statistical shades of meaning, and whether they can learn them using simple processes of STATISTICAL LEARNING.

semi-consonant *n*
see CONSONANT

semi-direct test *n*
a test that elicits test takers' spoken language ability by asking them to respond orally on tape to a set of tape-recorded or text-based cues or stimuli, not to a set of questions delivered in real time by an interviewer present at the time of testing. A ratable sample of their oral performance is tape-recorded and later rated. An example of a semi-direct test is a tape-mediated SIMULATED ORAL PROFICIENCY INTERVIEW.
see also DIRECT TEST, INDIRECT TEST

semilingual *adj* **semilingualism** *n*
a term sometimes used for people who have acquired several languages at different periods of their lives, but who have not developed a native-speaker level of proficiency in any of them. This issue is regarded as controversial by many linguists.

semiotics *n* **semiotic** *adj*
1 the theory of SIGNS.
2 the analysis of systems using signs or signals for the purpose of communication (**semiotic systems**). The most important semiotic system is human language, but there are other systems, e.g. Morse code, SIGN LANGUAGE, traffic signals.

semiotic systems *n*
see SEMIOTICS

semi-vowel *n*
a speech sound (a CONSONANT) which is produced by allowing the airstream from the lungs to move through the mouth and/or nose with only very slight friction. For example, in English the /j/ in /jes/ *yes* is a semi-vowel. In terms of their articulation, semi-vowels are very like vowels, but they function as consonants in the sound system of a language.
see also CONSONANT

sender *n*
see COMMUNICATION

sense *n*

the place which a word or phrase (a LEXEME) holds in the system of relationships with other words in the vocabulary of a language. For example, the English words *bachelor* and *married* have the sense relationship of *bachelor = never married*.

A distinction is often made between sense and REFERENCE.

see also CONNOTATION, DENOTATION

sensitive period *n*

see CRITICAL PERIOD

sensorimotor stage *n*

see COGNITIVE DEVELOPMENT

sentence *n*

(in GRAMMAR[1,2]) the largest unit of grammatical organization within which parts of speech (e.g. nouns, verbs, adverbs) and grammatical classes (e.g. word, phrase, clause) are said to function. In English a sentence normally contains one independent clause (see DEPENDENT CLAUSE) with a FINITE VERB. Units which are larger than the sentence (e.g. paragraph) are regarded as examples of DISCOURSE.

sentence combining *n*

a technique used in the teaching of grammar and writing, in which the student combines basic sentences to produce longer and more complex sentences and paragraphs. For example:

The teacher has doubts.
The doubts are grave.
The doubts are about Jackie.
The teacher has grave doubts about Jackie.

sentence completion *n*

an exercise in which students are given part of a sentence (e.g. the first few words in a sentence) and asked to complete it. Such an activity might target specific language items or allow for a variety of responses.

sentence comprehension *n*

see TOP–DOWN PROCESSING

sentence fragment *n*

(in composition) an incomplete sentence which cannot stand on its own. For example:

Whenever I try to hold a conversation with my parents about my career is a sentence fragment because it is a DEPENDENT CLAUSE which contains a SUBORDINATING CONJUNCTION (see CONJUNCTION) and should therefore be connected to an INDEPENDENT CLAUSE (see DEPENDENT CLAUSE). For example:

Whenever I try to hold a conversation with my parents about my career, they get angry with me.

sentence meaning *n*

see UTTERANCE MEANING

sentence outline *n*

see OUTLINE

sentence pattern *n*

(in language teaching) a structure which is considered a basic grammatical pattern for sentences in the language being taught, and which can be used as a model for producing other sentences in the language. For example:

sentence pattern

Determiner	+ Noun	+ Verb	+ Article	+ Adjective	+ Noun
Our	*house*	*has*	*a*	*large*	*garden.*
My	*dog*	*has*	*a*	*big*	*tail.*

The use of sentence patterns was associated with older grammar-based approaches to language teaching.

see SITUATIONAL LANGUAGE TEACHING

sentence stress *n*

see STRESS

sentential adverb *n*

another term for **disjunct**
see ADJUNCT

sequence, sequencing *n*

also **grading, gradation**

in a curriculum plan or syllabus, the arrangement of the content over time, i.e. the order in which new items will be taught. Principles for sequencing content in language teaching courses include:

1 simple to complex (easier items occur before more difficult ones)
2 chronology (items occur according to the order in which events naturally occur, e.g. listening before speaking)
3 need (items occur according to when learners are most likely to need them outside of the classroom)

4 prerequisite learning (an item is taught because it provides a foundation for the next step in the learning process)

5 whole to part or part to whole (the overall structure of an item, such as a paragraph, may be taught before its components part, or vice versa)

6 spiral sequencing (items are recycled but with new aspects of the item appearing with subsequent appearances).

see SCOPE AND SEQUENCE

sequencing[1] *n*

(in CONVERSATIONAL ANALYSIS) the relationship between UTTERANCES, that is, which type of utterance may follow another one. Sequencing is governed by rules known as **sequencing rules**, which may be different for different languages or different varieties of the same language. In some cases, the sequence of utterances is quite strictly regulated, as in greetings and leave-takings (see ADJACENCY PAIRS) but often there is a range of possibilities depending on the situation, the topic, the speakers, and their intentions at the moment.

For example, a question is usually followed by an answer but can, in certain circumstances, be followed by another question:

A: *What are you doing tonight?*

B: *Why do you want to know?*

see also TURN-TAKING

sequencing[2] *n*

another term for GRADATION

sequencing rules *n*

see SEQUENCING[1]

sequential access *n*

see ACCESS

sequential processing *n*

see PARALLEL PROCESSING

serial learning *n*

also **serial-order learning**

the learning of items in a sequence or order, as when a list of words is memorized In PSYCHOLINGUISTICS, serial-order learning theories (also known as "linear" or "left-to-right" theories) have been compared with **top-to-bottom** or hierarchical theories of how people produce sentences.

For example in producing the sentence *The dog chased the cat*, in a serial-order model each word the speaker produces determines the word which comes after it:

The + dog + chased + the + cat.

In a top-to-bottom model, items which build the PROPOSITION are produced before other items. For example:

a *dog*, *cat*, *chase* (unordered)
b *dog + chase + cat* (ordered)
c *the + dog + chased + the + cat* (modified)

setting *n*

the time and place of a SPEECH EVENT.

For example, a conversation can take place in a classroom, a garden, a church, and it can take place at any hour of the day. The setting of a speech event may have an effect on what is being said and how it is said.

see also COMMUNICATIVE COMPETENCE

shadowing *n*

a technique sometimes used in language teaching and also in training simultaneous interpreters in which the student repeats what a speaker says. Several types of shadowing are sometimes used:

1 lecture shadowing – a listener silently shadows the speaker
2 reading shadowing – one student reads aloud and one shadows
3 conversational shadowing – a listener shadows a speaker, either by completely or partially reproducing the speaker.

Shadowing is said to train listening skills and to develop fluency.

shared knowledge *n*

knowledge which speakers and listeners have in common and which may influence the nature and form of communication between them. Such knowledge may be based on common cultural knowledge, or on more specific experiences speakers and listeners share. Shared knowledge affects many aspects of language use including definite reference, focus and topic constructions, cleft sentences, contrastive stress, and choice of pronouns.

shared reading *n*

in the teaching of reading in initial literacy programmes, activities in which the teacher leads the learners through a reading text (often using a *Big Book*) assisting the children to understand a text they might not be able to read on their own. Shared reading is said to give learners the opportunity to feel a part of a community of readers and to appreciate the enjoyment of fluent reading.

sheltered English *n*
also **sheltered instruction**
an approach to the teaching of second language students based on the Canadian model of immersion education (see IMMERSION PROGRAMME), in which content is taught in English and made comprehensible to the students by special instructional techniques. The goal of the approach is to enable the students to acquire high levels of oral English proficiency while at the same time achieving in the CONTENT AREAS, i.e. to teach academic subject matter and language simultaneously until the student is ready for MAINSTREAMING.

short circuit hypothesis *n*
(in reading research) the idea that first language reading strategies are ineffective (are short-circuited) by proficiency deficits in a second language unless a threshold level of proficiency has been reached.

short-term memory *n*
see MEMORY

shwa *n*
another spelling of SCHWA

sibilant *n*
a FRICATIVE in which there is a high-pitched turbulent noise, as in English /s/ in *sip*.

side sequence *n*
in a conversation, one of the speakers may break the main course of the conversation to check up on a particular point. Usually the other speaker(s) would supply the answer. After this exchange, the side sequence, the main conversation is often taken up again.
For example, A and B are arranging to meet:
    A: I'll be there at six.
    B: *Aren't you working late?*
    A: *Not on Thursdays.*
    B: Fine, see you at six then.
The B/A exchange in the middle of the conversation is the side sequence.
see also INSERTION SEQUENCE, REPAIR, SEQUENCING

sight method *n*
another term for WHOLE-WORD METHOD

sight vocabulary *n*

    (in teaching reading in the mother tongue) those words which a child can recognize at sight in a reading passage or text and which he or she does not need to decode using phonic or other reading skills (see PHONICS).

signal *n*

    see INFORMATION THEORY

significance level *n*

    see STATISTICAL SIGNIFICANCE

significant difference *n*

    see STATISTICAL SIGNIFICANCE

signification *n*

    see SIGNS, USAGE[2]

signify *v*

    see SIGNS

sign language *n* **sign** *v*

    a language used by many hearing impaired people and by some who communicate with hearing impaired people, which makes use of movements of the hands, arms, body, head, face, eyes, and mouth to communicate meanings. Different sign languages have developed in different parts of the world, for example American Sign Language or **Ameslan**, British Sign Language, Danish Sign Language, French Sign Language. These are true languages with their own grammars and are not simply attempts to "spell out" the language spoken in the country where they are used. The visual-gestural units of communication used in sign languages are known as "signs".

    Within the deaf community and those concerned with the education of the hearing-impaired, there is a controversy between those who are in favour of signing (people arguing this position are referred to as **manualists**) and those who oppose it (the **oralists**). Oralists argue that teaching the hearing-impaired sign language prevents them from communicating with the outside world and limits their interaction to other people who know sign language.

signs *n*

    in linguistics, the words and other expressions of a language which **signify**, that is, "stand for", other things. In English, the word *table*, for instance, stands for a particular piece of furniture in the real world. Some linguists and philosophers include a third item in the process of **signification**, that is, an abstract CONCEPT of the thing for which the sign stands, e.g.:

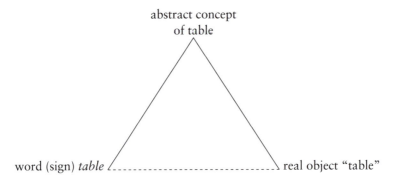

abstract concept
of table

word (sign) *table* — — — — — — — — — — real object "table"

silent pause *n*
see PAUSING

silent period *n*
just as children acquiring their first language go through a period in which they hear language but do not yet produce it, many language learners also experience a period of time in which they are unable or reluctant to speak.

silent reading *n*
see READING

silent way *n*
a METHOD of foreign-language teaching developed by Gattegno which makes use of gesture, mime, visual aids, wall charts, and in particular Cuisenaire rods (wooden sticks of different lengths and colours) that the teacher uses to help the students to talk. The method takes its name from the relative silence of the teacher using these techniques.

simile *n*
see FIGURE OF SPEECH

simple form *n*
see INFINITIVE

simple past *n*
see PAST TENSE

simple sentence *n*
see COMPLEX SENTENCE

simplification[1] *n*

(in the study of SECOND LANGUAGE ACQUISITION and ERROR ANALYSIS) a term sometimes used to describe what happens when learners make use of rules which are grammatically (or morphologically/phonologically, etc.) less complex than TARGET-LANGUAGE[1] rules, often as a result of an OVER-GENERALIZATION. For example, a learner may have a single rule for forming the past tense (by adding *-ed* to the verb base) ignoring exceptions and producing incorrect forms such as *breaked*, *standed*. In studies of the INTERLANGUAGE of second- and foreign-language learners, simplifications may be contrasted with errors which result from other processes, such as LANGUAGE TRANSFER.

simplification[2] *n*

(in language teaching) the rewriting or adaptation of original texts or materials, generally using a WORD LIST and sometimes also a structure list or grammatical SYLLABUS, to produce simplified reading or other materials suitable for second- or foreign-language learners.

see also GRADED READER

simplified reader *n*

another term for GRADED READER

simplified vocabulary *n*

the vocabulary in reading and other instructional materials in which difficult words or words outside of those on a word list have been replaced by simpler words or words from a word list.

simulated oral proficiency interview *n*

also **SOPI**

a type of performance-based speaking test developed by the Center for Applied Linguistics in Washington, DC, in the United States that approximates a face-to-face OPI as closely as possible in a tape-mediated format where a ratable sample of a test taker's spoken language production in response to a set of tape-recorded native-speaker prompts is recorded on a tape without the presence of an on-site tester and later rated by trained raters according to the ACTFL Guidelines.

simulation[1] *n*

in COMPUTER ASSISTED LANGUAGE LEARNING, software using large databases is used to present information in a simulated environment where learner input changes outcomes, e.g. controlling variables in an ecosystem.

simulation² *n*

classroom activities which reproduce or simulate real situations and which often involve dramatization and group discussion (see ROLE-PLAY, which does not include group discussion). In simulation activities, learners are given roles in a situation, TASKS, or a problem to be solved, and are given instructions to follow (for example, an employer–employee discussion over wage increases in a factory). The participants then make decisions and proposals. Consequences are "simulated" on the basis of decisions the participants take. They later discuss their actions, feelings, and what happened.

simulation-based theories of understanding *n*

theories that propose that understanding an utterance involves the activation of perceptual and motor representations. For example, comprehending a sentence such as *Give Bill the pizza* involves activation of an internal representation of moving one's arm forward.

see also EMBODIMENT

simultaneous bilingualism *n*

the acquisition of two languages at the same time both as first languages, for example, before a child is three years old.

simultaneous interpretation *n*

see INTERPRETATION

singular *adj*

the form of nouns, verbs, pronouns, etc., used to refer to only one in number. For example:

singular	plural
machine	*machines*
it	*they/them*

sister dependency *n*

in some syntactic analyses, if two constituents of a sentence are on the same level of structure, they are considered to be sisters. For example, in the English sentence:

All the children were laughing.

the noun phrase *all the children* is a "sister" to the verb phrase *were laughing*. They are mutually dependent on each other (sister-dependent). In a diagram, they would both be under the same NODE for example:

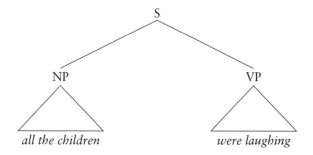

Both phrases would be DAUGHTERS of S which "immediately dominates them". That means that S is the NODE or point in the tree diagram which is immediately above them. They are daughter-dependent on S.

situated learning *n*

a term used in SOCIOCULTURAL THEORY and which views learning as not simply a cognitive process but a social one which is shaped by the situation and social context in which learning is embedded. For example language learning in a classroom is shaped by the setting, the participants, their roles, the activities undertaken, and the resources used.

Situational Language Teaching *n*
also **oral approach**

a language teaching METHOD developed by British language teaching specialists between 1940 and 1960. Situational Language Teaching is a grammar-based method in which principles of grammatical and lexical GRADATION are used and new teaching points presented and practised through situations. Although no longer in fashion, techniques derived from Situational Language Teaching are found in many widely used language teaching textbooks.

situational method *n*

(in language teaching) a term sometimes used to refer to a teaching pro-gramme or method in which the selection, organization, and presentation of language items is based on situations (e.g. *at the bank, at the super-market, at home*). A SYLLABUS for such a language course or textbook may be referred to as a **situational syllabus**. Many methods make use of simulated situations as a way of practising language items, but use other criteria for selecting and organizing the content of the course (see NOTIONAL SYLLABUS, FUNCTIONAL SYLLABUS, for example). Only if situations are used to select, organize, and practise language would the term "situational method" strictly apply.

situational syllabus *n*

see SITUATIONAL METHOD

situation analysis *n*

also **SWOT analysis, target situation analysis**

in curriculum development, the identification of key factors that might positively or negatively affect the implementation of a curriculum plan and the study of the direct and indirect effects a proposed curriculum will have on the students, on other programmes, and on other people in and outside the institution. Such factors could be political, social, economic, institutional, administrative, etc. Situation analysis is sometimes considered a dimension of NEEDS ANALYSIS. This is sometimes known as SWOT analysis because it involves examination of a language programme's internal *strengths* and *weaknesses* in addition to external *opportunities* and *threats* to the existence or successful operation of the language programme.

skewness *n*

a measure of the lack of symmetry of a DISTRIBUTION. When there are more low scores than high scores, its distribution is **positively skewed**, whereas when there are more high scores than low scores, its distribution is **negatively skewed**.

skill *n*

an acquired ability to perform an activity well, usually one that is made up of a number of co-ordinated processes and actions. Many aspects of language learning are traditionally regarded as the learning of skills, such as learning to speak, or read fluently.

see AUTOMATIC PROCESSING

skills *n*

(in language teaching) another term for LANGUAGE SKILLS

skimming *n*

a type of **reading strategy** in which the reader samples segments of a text in order to achieve a general understanding of its meaning. Skimming involves the use of strategies for guessing where important information might be in a text and then using basic reading comprehension skills on those parts of the text until a general idea of its meaning is reached.

see SCANNING

SLA *n*

an acronym for SECOND LANGUAGE ACQUISITION

slang *n*

casual, very informal speech, using expressive but informal words and expressions (**slang words/expressions**). For some people, slang is equivalent to COLLOQUIAL SPEECH but for others, it means "undesirable speech". Usually, "colloquial speech" refers to a speech variety used in informal situations with colleagues, friends or relatives, and "slang" is used for a very informal speech variety which often serves as an "in-group" language for a particular set of people such as teenagers, army recruits, pop groups, etc. Most slang is rather unstable as its words and expressions can change quite rapidly, for example:

Beat it! Scram! Rack off! (for "leave")

see also JARGON

slang words *n*

also **slang expressions**

see SLANG

SLI *n*

an abbreviation for SPECIFIC LANGUAGE IMPAIRMENT

SLO *n*

see LEARNING OUTCOME

small-group discussion *n*

see DISCUSSION METHOD

small-group interaction *n*

(in teaching) the factors which explain the interactions occurring within small groups. These include whether the interactions in the group are verbal or non-verbal, the kind of TASK involved, the roles of the group members, the leadership and the cohesion of the group.

see also GROUPING

social capital *n*

a term that refers to the monetary and social-psychological value of attributes that people have, which can be accumulated and expended. Just as education is a form of social capital, so too are prestige languages and language varieties. From this perspective, language learning can be seen as requiring **investment** (as an alternative to the concept of MOTIVATION).

social constructionism *n*
also **social construction of knowledge**
the theory that knowledge is constructed through social interaction with others and reflects the learner's culture, customs, beliefs as well as the historical, political, social and other dimensions of the learning context. This theory is sometimes used as a basis for teaching composition or rhetoric and is an important dimension of CRITICAL PEDAGOGY.

social construction of knowledge *n*
see SOCIAL CONSTRUCTIONISM

social context *n*
the environment in which meanings are exchanged. (According to the linguist Halliday) the social context of language can be analyzed in terms of three factors:
a The **field of discourse** refers to what is happening, including what is being talked about.
b The **tenor of discourse** refers to the participants who are taking part in this exchange of meaning, who they are and what kind of relationship they have to one another (see ROLE RELATIONSHIP).
c The **mode of discourse** refers to what part the language is playing in this particular situation, for example, in what way the language is organized to convey the meaning, and what CHANNEL is used – written or spoken or a combination of the two.
Example: A foreign language lesson in a secondary school.
field: language study, a defined area of information about the foreign language, e.g. the use of tenses. Teacher imparting, students acquiring knowledge about tenses and their use.
tenor: participants: teacher – students. Fixed role relationships defined by the educational institution. Teacher in higher role. Temporary role relationships between students, depending on personality.
mode: language used for instruction and discussion. Channel: spoken (e.g. questions eliciting information, answers supplying information, acted dialogues by students) and written (e.g. visual presentation on blackboard, textbooks, additional reading material).
see also FUNCTIONS OF LANGUAGE[2], SYSTEMIC LINGUISTICS

social dialect
also **sociolect** *n*
a dialect associated with a given demographic group (e.g. women versus men, older versus younger speakers, or members of different social classes).

social dialectal variation *n*
another term for **sociolectal variation**
see SOCIOLECT

social distance *n*
the feeling a person has that his or her social position is relatively similar to or relatively different from the social position of someone else. The social distance between two different groups or communities influences communication between them, and may affect the way one group learns the language of another (for example, an immigrant group, learning the language of the dominant group in a country). Social distance may depend on such factors as differences in the size, ethnic origin, political STATUS, social status of two groups, and has been studied in SECOND LANGUAGE ACQUISITION research.
see also PIDGINIZATION HYPOTHESIS, ASSIMILATION², ACCULTURATION

social function *n*
see FUNCTIONS OF LANGUAGE¹

social identity *n*
the way a person categorizes themself in relation to an identifiable social group, such as the nation state, or one's gender, ethnicity, class, or profession. Social identities are multiple, changing, and often in conflict with one another. They are constructed to a large extent through the way people use language in discourse.

socialization *n*
the process of internalization through which humans become members of particular cultures, learning how to speak the language of that culture and how to act, think and feel as a member of the culture. The term LANGUAGE SOCIALIZATION is used to refer to primary socialization that takes place during childhood within the family, but can also refer to secondary socializations throughout life, to specialized forms and uses of language in school, community, and work settings. Language socialization is a broader term than language acquisition, since it includes cultural, pragmatic and other forms of learning apart from language learning.

socialized speech *n*
see EGOCENTRIC SPEECH

social psychology of language *n*
the study of how society and its structures affect the individual's language behaviour. Investigations in this field deal, for instance, with attitudes to different languages or language varieties and to their speakers.

social strategies *n*
see LEARNING STRATEGY

societal bilingualism *n*
also **multilingualism**
the coexistence of two or more languages used by individuals and groups in society. Societal bilingualism does not imply that all members of society are bilingual: in fact a majority of members of language groups in multilingual societies may be monolingual (e.g. as with English speakers in Canada) because the different groups are separated either geographically or socially.
see BILINGUALISM

socio-cognitive approach *n*
in the teaching of second language writing, an approach in which students focus on the needs and expectations of the audience and the situation for their writing.

socio-constructivist theory *n*
see CONSTRUCTIVISM

sociocultural competence *n*
see COMMUNICATIVE COMPETENCE

sociocultural theory *n*
a learning theory derived from the work of the Russian psychologist Vygotsky which deals with the role of social context in learning. Sociocultural theory emphasizes the central role that social relationships and participation in culturally organized practices play in learning. In second language learning research sociocultural theory emphasizes the role that social interaction plays in learning and the nature of language as a communicative activity rather than as a formal linguistic system. Second language learning is viewed as resulting from the sociocultural activities in which the learner participates.
see also COMMUNITY OF PRACTICE, IDENTITY, SITUATED LEARNING, ZONE OF PROXIMAL DEVELOPMENT

socio-educational model *n*
a model of second and foreign language learning in school settings developed by Gardner. The theory emphasizes the role of INTEGRATIVE MOTIVATION.

sociolect *adj*
    also **social dialect**
    a variety of a language (a DIALECT) used by people belonging to a par-
    ticular social class. The speakers of a sociolect usually share a similar
    socio-economic and/or educational background. Sociolects may be classed
    as high (in STATUS) or low (in status).
    For example:
        He and I were going there. (higher sociolect)
        'Im'n me was goin' there. (lower sociolect)
    The sociolect with the highest status in a country is often the STANDARD
    VARIETY.
    The difference between one sociolect and another can be investigated by
    analyzing the recorded speech of large samples of speakers from various
    social backgrounds. The differences are referred to as **socio-lectal variation**
    or **social dialectal variation.**
    see also ACCENT[3], DIALECT, SPEECH VARIETY

sociolectal variation *n*
    also **social dialectal variation**
    see SOCIOLECT

sociolinguistic marker *n*
    a linguistic feature that marks a speaker as a member of a social group
    and to which social attitudes are attached, e.g. absence of postvocalic "r" in
    the speech of some New Yorkers (stigmatized) and some British speakers
    (RP).

sociolinguistics *n* **sociolinguistic** *adj*
    the study of language in relation to social factors, that is social class,
    educational level and type of education, age, sex, ethnic origin, etc.
    Linguists differ as to what they include under sociolinguistics. Many would
    include the detailed study of interpersonal communication, sometimes
    called **micro-sociolinguistics**, e.g. SPEECH ACTS, CONVERSATION ANALYSIS,
    SPEECH EVENTS, SEQUENCING[1] OF UTTERANCES, and also those investiga-
    tions which relate variation in the language used by a group of people to
    social factors (see SOCIOLECT). Such areas as the study of language choice
    in BILINGUAL or MULTILINGUAL communities, LANGUAGE PLANNING,
    LANGUAGE ATTITUDES, etc., may be included under sociolinguistics and
    are sometimes referred to as **macro-sociolinguistics**, or they are considered
    as being part of the SOCIOLOGY OF LANGUAGE or the SOCIAL PSYCHOLOGY
    OF LANGUAGE.
    see also ETHNOGRAPHY OF COMMUNICATION

sociolinguistic transfer *n*

using the rules of speaking associated with one's own language and speech community when speaking a second language or interacting with members of another community.

sociology of language *n*

the study of language varieties and their users within a social framework, for example the study of language choice in BILINGUAL or MULTILINGUAL nations, LANGUAGE PLANNING, LANGUAGE MAINTENANCE and LANGUAGE SHIFT. The sociology of language is considered either as including the branch of linguistics called SOCIOLINGUISTICS or as an extension of sociolinguistics.

sociopragmatic failure *n*

misunderstanding or breakdown in communication that is caused by the inappropriate transfer of a sociocultural feature from one language to another. This could include ways of opening or closing a conversation, use of forms of address, expression of apologies, compliments or complaints that are appropriate in one culture but not in another.

sociopragmatics *n*

see PRAGMALINGUISTICS

soft palate *n*

another term for VELUM

see PLACE OF ARTICULATION, VELAR

sonorant *n*

a speech sound that is produced with a relatively free passage of air from the lungs, either through the mouth or the nose. For example, /l/ in *lid*, /n/ in *nose*, and all vowels are sonorants.

see also OBSTRUENT

sonority *n*

see SYLLABLE

SOPI *n*

an abbreviation for SIMULATED ORAL PROFICIENCY INTERVIEW

sound change *n*

change in the pronunciation of words over a period of time. For example, there has been a sound change from Middle English /aː/ to Modern English /eɪ/:

Middle English /naːmə/ Modern English /neɪm/ *name*.

Such sound changes are still continuing and often differences can be observed between the pronunciation of older and younger speakers in a community.

sound symbolism *n*

refers to a range of phenomena in which there is a non-arbitrary relationship between the sound of a word and its meaning, including INTERJECTIONS, ONOMATOPOEIA, and IDEOPHONES.

sound wave *n*

wave-like movements of air which transmit sounds. In speech, sound waves are caused by the vibration of the VOCAL CORDS.

The rate at which the air in a sound wave moves backwards and forwards in a given time is called **frequency**. The faster the movement, the higher the frequency. A speech sound is a combination of simple sound waves vibrating at different frequencies and forming a complex sound wave, e.g.:

a simple sound wave

a complex sound wave

The lowest frequency in a complex sound wave is called the **fundamental frequency**. It is the same frequency as that at which the vocal cords are vibrating.

source¹ *n*

see INFORMATION THEORY

source² *n*

(in CASE GRAMMAR) the place from which someone or something moves or is moved.

For example, *the station* in:
  He came from <u>*the station*</u>.

source language[1] *n*

(in language BORROWING) a language from which words have been taken into another language. French was the source language for many words which entered English after the Norman Conquest (1066), e.g. *prince, just, saint, noble*, as well as for words which entered English at a later stage, e.g. *garage, restaurant*.
Chinese was the source language for Japanese during many long periods of history. During the twentieth century, English became the major source language for Japanese.

source language[2] *n*

the language out of which a translation is made (e.g. in a bilingual dictionary).
see also TARGET LANGUAGE[2]

source text *n*

a text that is to be translated into another language.
see also TRANSLATION, MACHINE TRANSLATION

SOV language *n*

see TYPOLOGY

Speaking Proficiency English Assessment Kit *n*
also **SPEAK**

see TEST OF SPOKEN ENGLISH

Spearman-Brown Prophecy Formula *n*

a formula frequently used to estimate the RELIABILITY of two parallel halves of a test (e.g., in the case of correcting or adjusting upward SPLIT-HALF RELIABILITY) when it is assumed that the two halves have equal means and variances. This formula can also be used to estimate the reliability of a new test that is shorter than an original test (e.g. when the test length of an original test has to be decreased from 100 items to 50 items due to, e.g., a strict time limit imposed on test administration and a test administrator wanting to estimate what the reliability of a shortened test would be).

Spearman rank-order correlation *n*
or **Spearman's rho (ρ)**

see CORRELATION

Spearman's rho (ρ)

another term for SPEARMAN RANK-ORDER CORRELATION

special education *n*

also **special ed**

in the US, provision of schooling or special support for those whose needs cannot be readily accommodated in the mainstream curriculum, e.g. for students who may have particular emotional, intellectual, physical or social needs.

special languages *n*

a term used for the varieties of language used by specialists in writing about their subject matter, such as the language used in botany, law, nuclear physics or linguistics. The study of special languages includes the study of TERMINOLOGY (the special LEXEMES used in particular disciplines) and REGISTER (2) the distinctive linguistic features which occur in special languages.

see also ENGLISH FOR SPECIAL PURPOSES

special nativism *n*

see NATIVISM

special needs students *n*

a term used in the US to refer to several types of students who have needs that are not met in ordinary classrooms, such as students with disabilities (SD), exceptional or gifted children, and English language learners (ELL) or limited English proficient (LEP) students.

specific language impairment *n*

also **SLI**

a developmental language disorder, affecting either expressive or receptive language, that is not related to or caused by other disorders such as hearing loss or brain injury. Symptoms include the use of short sentences, delay in the use of function words, difficulty learning new words, and problems producing and understanding complex sentences.

specific question *n*

see GLOBAL QUESTION

spectrogram *n*

see SPECTROGRAPH

spectrograph *n*

an instrument used in acoustic phonetics (see PHONETICS). It gives a visual representation of a sound, showing its component frequencies. The spectrograph 'prints' out a SPECTROGRAM on special paper. A time scale is shown along the horizontal axis and a scale of frequencies along the vertical axis. The greater the intensity (i.e. the louder the sound), the darker the ink.

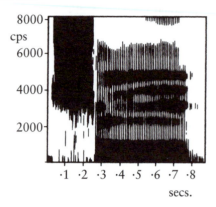

speech act *n*

an UTTERANCE as a functional unit in communication. In speech act theory, utterances have two kinds of meaning:

a propositional meaning (also known as **locutionary meaning**). This is the basic literal meaning of the utterance which is conveyed by the particular words and structures which the utterance contains (see PROPOSITION, LOCUTIONARY ACT).

b illocutionary meaning (also known as **illocutionary force**). This is the effect the utterance or written text has on the reader or listener.

For example, in *I am thirsty* the propositional meaning is what the utterance says about the speaker's physical state. The illocutionary force is the effect the speaker wants the utterance to have on the listener. It may be intended as a request for something to drink. A speech act is a sentence or utterance which has both propositional meaning and illocutionary force.

There are many different kinds of speech acts, such as requests, orders, commands, complaints, promises (see SPEECH ACT CLASSIFICATION).

A speech act which is performed indirectly is sometimes known as an **indirect speech act**, such as the speech act of requesting above.

Indirect speech acts are often felt to be more polite ways of performing certain kinds of speech act, such as requests and refusals. In language teaching, and SYLLABUS design, speech acts are often referred to as "functions" or "language functions" (see NOTIONAL SYLLABUS, FUNCTIONAL SYLLABUS).

see also PERFORMATIVE, PRAGMATICS, UPTAKE

speech act classification *n*

The philosopher Searle established a five-part classification of SPEECH ACTS:

a **commissive:** a speech act that commits the speaker to doing something in the future, such as a promise or a threat. For example:

If you don't stop fighting I'll call the police. (threat)

I'll take you to the movies tomorrow. (promise)

b **declarative:** a speech act which changes the state of affairs in the world. For example, during the wedding ceremony the act of marriage is performed when the phrase *I now pronounce you man and wife* is uttered.

c **directive:** a speech act that has the function of getting the listener to do something, such as a suggestion, a request, or a command. For example:

Please sit down.

Why don't you close the window.

d **expressive:** a speech act in which the speaker expresses feelings and attitudes about something, such as an apology, a complaint, or to thank someone, to congratulate someone. For example:

The meal was delicious.

e **representative:** a speech act which describes states or events in the world, such as an assertion, a claim, a report. For example, the assertion:

This is a German car.

speech act set *n*

the pragmalinguistic realizations of a particular speech act (see PRAGMA-LINGUISTICS). For example, the speech act of apology can be realized explicitly (e.g. *I apologize*), by assuming responsibility (*It was my fault*), by expressing concern for the hearer (*I hope I didn't keep you waiting too long*), and in various other ways.

speech community *n*

a group of people who form a community, e.g. a village, a region, a nation, and who have *at least* one SPEECH VARIETY in common.

In BILINGUAL and MULTILINGUAL communities, people would usually have more than one speech variety in common (see SPEECH REPERTOIRE).

speech continuum *n*

a range of speech varieties (see SPEECH VARIETY). Although it is common to think of a language as being divided into separate regional DIALECTS or social dialects (see SOCIOLECT), there is often no clear division between them but rather a continuum from one to another. "Speech continuum" is used particularly when referring to varieties spoken by those with varying levels of proficiency in a second language (see FOREIGN LANGUAGE), e.g. English in Singapore. The sub-variety used by those with high levels of

English medium education is frequently called the **acrolect**. The **basilect** is the sub-variety used by those with rather low levels of education and the **mesolects** are the sub-varieties in between. Naturally there are no clear-cut boundaries between these "lects".

Educated speakers of a more established ESL variety may use the acrolect or an upper mesolect in more formal situations and something close to the basilect in a more informal context.

see also POST CREOLE CONTINUUM

speech defect *n*
also **speech disorder**
any abnormality in the production of speech which interferes with communication, such as APHASIA, or stuttering.

speech errors *n*
faults made by speakers during the production of sounds, words, and sentences. Both NATIVE SPEAKERS and non-native speakers of a language make unintended mistakes when speaking. Some of the commonest speech errors include:

a **anticipation error:** when a sound or word is brought forward in a sentence and used before it is needed. For example:
I'll put your cat in the cupboard instead of *I'll put your hat in the cupboard*
b **perseveration error:** when a sound or word which has already been uttered reappears. For example:
the president of Prance instead of *the president of France*
c **reversal error**, also **spoonerism:** when the position of sounds, syllables, or words is reversed. For example:
let's have chish and fips instead *let's have fish and chips*
Speech errors have been studied by psycholinguists in order to find out how people store language items in long-term memory and how they select items from memory when speaking.

see also MEMORY

speech event *n*
a particular instance when people exchange speech, e.g. an exchange of greetings, an enquiry, a conversation. For example:
Child: *Mum, where's my red sweater?*
Mother: *Bottom drawer in your bedroom.*
Child: *Right, I'll have a look.*
Speech events are governed by rules and norms for the use of speech, which may be different in different communities. The structure of speech events varies considerably according to the GENRE they belong to.

The components of a speech event are its SETTING, the PARTICIPANTS and their ROLE RELATIONSHIPS, the MESSAGE, the key (see KEY[1]) and the CHANNEL.

The term **speech situation** is sometimes used instead of speech event, but usually it refers to any situation which is associated with speech, e.g. a classroom lesson, a party.

A speech situation may consist of just one speech event, e.g. two people meeting in the street and having a brief conversation, or it may contain a number of speech events, some going on at the same time, e.g. a large dinner party.

speech marker *n*

a linguistic feature which may give an indication of the speaker's age, sex, ethnicity or social group. A speech marker could be a particular sound, e.g. the pronunciation of /r/ in New York, or /ei/ in *today* in Australia. It could be a syntactic structure, e.g. *between my husband and I/me*, or a word or expression.

see also VARIABLE[1]

speech pathology *n*

the study of abnormalities in the development and use of language in children and adults (such as STUTTERING and APHASIA). Speech pathology includes the diagnosis of such disorders and the development of techniques (including clinical techniques) to treat them. Speech therapists (see SPEECH THERAPY) are sometimes called **speech pathologists** or **speech-language pathologists**, especially in the USA.

speech perception *n*

see PERCEPTION

speech rate *n*

another term for RATE OF SPEECH

speech reading *n*

another term for LIPREADING

speech recognition *n*

software that allows a computer to receive input through audio rather than through the keyboard or mouse. Limited in application for a long time due to cost and technical difficulties, this type of software now holds particular promise for second language teaching.

see also LISTENING COMPREHENSION

speech repertoire *n*

the languages or language varieties that a person knows and uses within his or her SPEECH COMMUNITY in everyday communication. A particular group of speakers may use not just one language or language variety to communicate with one another but several, each appropriate for certain areas of everyday activity (see DOMAIN). The speech repertoire of a French Canadian in Montreal could include Standard Canadian French, Colloquial Canadian French and English (perhaps in more than one variety).

see also DIGLOSSIA, VERBAL REPERTOIRE

speech rhythm *n*

rhythm in speech is created by the contracting and relaxing of chest muscles (pulses). This causes changes in air pressure. There are two different patterns of pulses:

a a more regular type of contraction with regular rises in air pressure (**chest pulses**)

b less frequent but stronger contractions with more sudden rises in air pressure (**stress pulses**).

The way these two systems operate together in any one language is said to cause different types of speech rhythm.

see also STRESS-TIMED RHYTHM, SYLLABLE-TIMED RHYTHM

speech segmentation *n*

the process of identifying the boundaries between words, syllables, or phonemes in spoken language.

speech situation *n*

see SPEECH EVENT

speech styles *n*

alternative ways of speaking within a community, often ranging from more colloquial to more formal. Usually, the range of styles available to a person varies according to his or her own background and the type of SPEECH COMMUNITY. The choice of a particular style has social implications. For example, choosing a formal style in a casual context may sound funny and using a very colloquial style in a formal context, such as in a sermon at a funeral service, may offend. Generally, a native speaker knows when a certain speech style is or is not appropriate (see APPROPRIATENESS).

Two types of rules which are connected with speech styles are **co-occurrence rules** and **alternation rules**. Co-occurrence rules determine which linguistic unit may follow or precede, that is, "co-occur with", another unit or units. For example:

formal style: *I should most certainly like to attend your ball, Sir Reginald.*
colloquial style: *I'd love to come to your do, Reg.*

Alternation rules determine the possible choice of "alternatives" from a number of speech styles or stylistic features which are at the speaker's disposal, e.g.

formal style: *Good morning, Mrs Smith* . . .
semi-formal style: *Hullo* . . .
colloquial style: *Hi, Penny* . . .

speech synthesis *n*

the automatic synthesis of speech-like sounds by a computer using a **speech synthesizer** or **voice synthesizer**, such as when a computer takes printed text as input and produces a spoken version of it. Many of the recorded messages heard on the telephone are not natural language but are produced by speech synthesis.

see also DIGITIZED SPEECH, COMPUTATIONAL LINGUISTICS

speech synthesizer *n*

see VOICE SYNTHESIZER

speech therapy *n*

activities and exercises which are designed to help to alleviate or cure a language or speech defect (e.g. stuttering) or to help someone to regain their use of speech after having suffered speech loss (e.g. after a stroke). A person who works in the field of speech therapy is called a **speech therapist.**

see also SPEECH PATHOLOGY

speech variety *n*

a term sometimes used instead of LANGUAGE[2], DIALECT, SOCIOLECT, PIDGIN, CREOLE, etc., because it is considered more neutral than such terms. It may also be used for different varieties of one language, e.g. American English, Australian English, Indian English.

speech vocabulary *n*

the total number of words a person uses as part of his or her spoken language repertoire.

see ACTIVE/PASSIVE LANGUAGE KNOWLEDGE

speeded test *n*

also **speed test**

a type of test where not every test taker is expected to finish the test because the time allowed to complete it is limited. The difficulty level of the items on the test is usually easy so that any test taker is expected to get every item right given sufficient time.

see also POWER TEST

speed reading *n*

also **rapid reading**

techniques used to teach people to read more quickly and to achieve a greater degree of understanding of what they read. Readers are usually trained to use more effective eye movements when reading (see REGRESSIONS), and to use better ways of understanding words and meanings in written texts.

see also READING, TACHISTOSCOPE

speed test *n*

see SPEEDED TEST

spelling pronunciation *n*

a way of pronouncing a word which is based on its spelling and which may differ from the way the word is generally pronounced. For example, a non-native speaker of British English might pronounce *yacht* as /jɒkt/ instead of /jɒt/. Native speakers also sometimes use spelling pronunciations, and some have become acceptable ways of pronouncing words, such as /ˈɒftən/ for *often* rather than /ˈɒfən/.

spiral approach *n*

also **cyclical approach**

a SYLLABUS in which items recur throughout the syllabus but are treated in greater depth or in more detail when they recur. This may be contrasted with a **linear syllabus,** in which syllabus items are dealt with once only.

spirant *n*

another term for FRICATIVE

split construction *n*

(in composition) a sentence in which the subject has been separated from the verb, making it awkward to read. For example:

Teresa, after gathering together her clothes, books, and papers, left.

A less awkward sentence would be:

After gathering together her clothes, books and papers, Teresa left.

split-half reliability *n*

a measure of internal consistency reliability based on the CORRELATION COEFFICIENT between two halves of a test (e.g. between the odd- and even-numbered items of the test or between the first and second half of the items of the test), which are assumed to be parallel. The resulting reliability estimate is a PARALLEL-FORM RELIABILITY coefficient for a test half as long as the original test. Usually the SPEARMAN-BROWN PROPHECY FORMULA is applied to the resulting split-half reliability estimate in order to estimate the reliability of the full-length test rather than its separate halves because with all other factors being equal, the longer the test the higher the reliability.

see also INTERNAL CONSISTENCY RELIABILITY

split infinitive *n*
(in composition) a sentence in which the word *to* in an infinitive has been separated from the base of the verb making the sentence awkward to read. For example:
She asked me to as quickly as possible drop over to her house.
Without the split infinitive this would be:
She asked me to drop over to her house as quickly as possible.
In some sentences, however, the split infinitive is appropriate. For example:
We expect to more than double profits this year.

spoken grammar *n*
the grammatical system underlying spoken language, as compared with the grammar of written language. Although spoken and written language share the same basic structures and grammar, some items appear much more frequently in one language mode more than the other or have different characteristics in spoken than in written language. For example co-ordination is more frequent in spoken language than written language, which makes greater use of subordination. Differences between spoken and written language reflect the fact that spoken language is processed in real time.

spoonerism *n*
see SPEECH ERROR

spot the difference task *n*
a type of INFORMATION GAP task in which two or more learners are given similar but not identical pictures and are asked to discuss their pictures together to identify the differences.

spreading activation *n*
see PRIMING

SQ3R technique *n*
an acronym for Survey – Question – Read – Recite – Review, a reading strategy often recommended for students who are reading for study purposes which makes use of the following procedures:

1 **Survey:** the student looks through the chapter or text, looks at headings, pictures, summaries, etc., to get an overall idea of what the chapter might contain.
2 **Question:** the student turns headings and subheadings into questions.
3 **Read:** the student reads to find answers to the questions, and marks any sections which are unclear.
4 **Recite:** the student covers the chapter and tries to remember the main ideas, saying them to him or herself.
5 **Review:** the student reviews the chapter and looks at the sections marked to see if they can now be understood.

S-R theory *n*
an abbreviation for STIMULUS-RESPONSE THEORY

S-structure *n*
see D-STRUCTURE

stability *n*
see ATTRIBUTION THEORY

stabilization *n*
see FOSSILIZATION

stage *n*
the different parts of a lesson.
see PPP
see also STRUCTURING

stage theory of development *n*
see COGNITIVE DEVELOPMENT

stakeholder *n*
a person or group of persons with a recognized right to comment on and have input to the curriculum of a language programme, the use of a particular test, the formation of LANGUAGE POLICY, and so forth. With respect to curriculum, different stakeholders often want different things and may have different perceptions of a programme's goals, teaching methods, and content. In other situations, linguists, teacher educators, prospective and in-service teachers, employers, and government representatives may all have different views that need to be taken into account.
see also ACCOUNTABILITY

stance *n*

in addition to communicating ideas and information, speakers and writers can also express personal feelings, attitudes, value judgements or assessments. These are known as expressions of stance. Two common means of expressing stance are adverbials, and complement clauses. For example,
Obviously, your parents don't understand you. (adverbial)
I *really doubt* that I will get the job. (complement clause)

stance words *n*

in discourse, words that indicate the speaker or writer's attitudes and **stance** towards the content of the communication, such as *actually, basically, just, really, quite, whatever*.

standard *n* **standard** *adj*

another term for STANDARD VARIETY

Standard American English *n*

see STANDARD VARIETY

Standard British English *n*

see STANDARD VARIETY

standard deviation *n*

also **SD**

(in statistics and testing) the commonest measure of the variability, or DISPERSION, of a DISTRIBUTION of scores, that is, of the degree to which scores vary from the MEAN. The more the scores spread from the mean, the larger the standard deviation or vice versa. It is defined as the square root of the VARIANCE. The formula is as follows:

$$SD = \sqrt{\frac{\Sigma(X - \bar{X})}{N}}$$

where X = a raw score
$\bar{X}$ = the mean
N = the number of participants in a study (or items on a test)
Σ = the sum of

standard dialect *n*

another term for STANDARD VARIETY

Standard English *n*

see STANDARD VARIETY

standard error *n*
also **SE**
(in statistics and testing) a statistic used for determining the degree to which the estimate of a POPULATION PARAMETER is likely to differ from the computed sample statistic. The standard error of a statistic provides an indication of how accurate an estimate it is of the population parameter. One commonly used standard error is the **standard error of the mean**, which indicates how close the mean of the observed sample is to the mean of the entire population.

standard error of measurement *n*
also **SEM**
an estimate of the range of scores wherein a test taker's TRUE SCORE lies. The standard error of measurement decreases as the reliability of a test increases which is shown by the following formula:

$$SEM = SD\sqrt{1 - r}$$

where SD = the standard deviation of test scores
r = the reliability estimate of a test
For example, a test taker obtained a score of 85 on an ESL reading test that has a standard deviation of 12 and a reliability coefficient of .91. The test's SEM is estimated as follows:

$$SEM = 12\sqrt{1 - 0.19} = 12\sqrt{0.09} = (12)(0.3) = 3.6$$

As a test taker's true scores are expected to distribute normally if this person took the same test an infinite number of times, this person's true score would be expected to lie within + or − one SEM of this person's observed score 68% of the time (i.e. between 88.6 and 81.4) and within + or − two SEM of this person's observed score 95% of the time (i.e. between 92.2 and 77.8) (see THE NORMAL CURVE).

standard error of the mean *n*
see STANDARD ERROR

standardization[1] *n* **standardize** *v*
the process of making some aspect of language USAGE[1] conform to a STANDARD VARIETY. This may take place in connection with the WRITING SYSTEM or the spelling system of a particular language and is usually implemented by a government authority. For example, a standardized system has been introduced in Malaysia and Indonesia, which provides a common standard for the spelling of Malay and Indonesian, which are both varieties of the same language.

	Indonesian	Malay	
old spelling	*tjantik*	*chantek*	"pretty, good-
new spelling	*cantik*	*cantik*	looking"
old spelling	*burung*	*burong*	"bird"
new spelling	*burung*	*burung*	

standardization[2] *n*

in testing, agreement between raters of student performance on the meaning and interpretation of criteria used for assessment.

standardized test *n*

a test

a which has been developed from tryouts and experimentation to ensure that it is reliable and valid (see RELIABILITY, VALIDITY)

b for which NORMs[2] have been established

c which provides uniform procedures for administering (time limits, response format, number of questions) and for scoring the test.

standard language *n*

another term for STANDARD VARIETY

standard nine *n*

another term for STANINE

standards *n*

also **benchmarks, bandscales, curriculum frameworks**

a type of educational aim. Standards specify high targets for learning. Identification of standards seeks to raise levels of learning by specifying expectations for success in different areas of the curriculum. Standards have been developed both for pedagogical purposes, i.e. to assist with professional development and to provide guidance in teaching, as well as for reasons related to curriculum development and accountability, i.e. for administrative purposes.

see OUTCOMES-BASED TEACHING, STANDARDS MOVEMENT

standard score *n*

(in testing and statistics) a type of DERIVED SCORE by which scores or values from different measures can be reported or compared using a common scale. For example, in order to compare a student's scores on two tests of different lengths, a standard score might be used. A standard score expresses a RAW SCORE as a function of its relative position in a DISTRIBUTION[1] of score, and is thus usually easier to interpret than the raw score. Commonly used standard scores are the T SCORE and the Z SCORE.

standards movement *n*

a movement in the US and other countries which seeks to ensure educational accountability by developing national standards for achievement in the different areas of the curriculum. Such statements are believed to lead to improvements in educational achievement by giving a clear definition of what is to be taught and what kind of performance is to be expected across the school curriculum. Statements of language standards have also been developed for foreign language teaching and for TESOL. Language standards provide a comprehensive description of what language learners know in the target language at various levels of proficiency, at various grade levels, or both. In the US the TESOL organization has developed standards for the teaching of English as a second or additional language in elementary and secondary schools which consist of nine standards grouped under three goals: using English for communication in social settings; using it for academic achievement in all school curricular areas; and using it in socially and culturally appropriate ways.

standard subtitles *n*

see SUBTITLES

standard theory *n*

see GENERATIVE THEORY

standard variety *n*

also **standard dialect, standard language, standard**

the variety of a language which has the highest STATUS in a community or nation and which is usually based on the speech and writing of educated native speakers of the language. A standard variety is generally:

a used in the news media and in literature

b described in dictionaries and grammars (see NORMATIVE GRAMMAR)

c taught in schools and taught to non-native speakers when they learn the language as a foreign language.

Sometimes it is the educated variety spoken in the political or cultural centre of a country, e.g. the standard variety of French is based on educated Parisian French. The standard variety of American English is known as **Standard American English** and the standard variety of British English is **Standard British English**.

A standard variety may show some variation in pronunciation according to the part of the country where it is spoken, e.g. Standard British English in Scotland, Wales, Southern England. **Standard English** is sometimes used as a cover term for all the national standard varieties of English. These national standard varieties have differences in spelling, vocabulary, grammar and, particularly, pronunciation, but there is a common core of the language. This makes it possible for educated native speakers of the various national standard varieties of English to communicate with one another.

see also RECEIVED PRONUNCIATION, NATIONAL LANGUAGE

stanine *n*
also **standard nine**
a NORMALIZED STANDARD SCORE sometimes used in testing, in which standardized scores are arranged on a nine-step scale. A stanine equals one ninth of the range of the standard scores of a DISTRIBUTION[1].

statement *n*
an utterance which describes a state of affairs, action, feeling or belief, e.g.
It's very cold here in winter; I don't think she looks very well.
A statement occurs in the form of a DECLARATIVE SENTENCE but not all declarative sentences make statements. For example:
I suppose you'll be there.
could be said to be more a question than a statement.

states *n*
see STATIVE VERB

static–dynamic distinction *n*
verbs are sometimes divided into two groups: **stative verbs** and **dynamic verbs**.
Stative verbs usually refer to a state (an unchanging condition). They express emotion, knowledge, belief (e.g. *love, hate, know*) and show relationships (e.g. *belong to, equal, own*). As stative verbs describe a state of affairs, they do not occur in the progressive form, for example:
Monica owns a house.
not
*Monica is owning a house.
Dynamic verbs express activity and processes (e.g. *run, come, buy, read*). When they express something that is actually in progress, the progressive form of the verb can be used, for example:
She is reading the paper.
Some English verbs such as *have* and *think*, can be used statively, describing a state, or dynamically, describing an action or activity, for example:

statively:	*I have a really bad headache.* (state)
dynamically:	*We are having a party tonight.* (activity)
statively:	*I think it's going to rain.* (opinion, mental state)

dynamically: *I'm thinking hard about how to solve this problem.*
               (mental activity)
see also PUNCTUAL-NON-PUNCTUAL DISTINCTION

statistic *n*

a numerical value that summarizes the SAMPLE, such as sample mean ($\bar{x}$), sample variance (s^2) and sample standard deviation (s). Each statistic has an equivalent numerical value that summarizes the POPULATION from which the sample was taken. The Roman alphabet letters are used to denote statistics.
see also PARAMETER

statistical hypothesis *n*

see HYPOTHESIS

statistical learning *n*

the detection of statistical regularities and patterns in the environment, typically without direct awareness of what has been learned. This type of IMPLICIT LEARNING has been demonstrated for many language-like learning situations, including SPEECH SEGMENTATION, detecting the orthographic and PHONOTACTIC regularities of words, acquiring morphological systems, and detecting long distance relationships between words.

statistical significance *n*

a term used when testing a STATISTICAL HYPOTHESIS, which refers to the likelihood that an obtained effect, such as a difference or correlation, could have occurred by chance alone (through SAMPLING ERROR). An observed **significance level**, or *p*-**value**, symbolized as *p* (for probability), is the probability of obtaining an observed effect as extreme as or more extreme than you observed if the NULL HYPOTHESIS were true. The *p*-value is compared to a predetermined **significance level**, or **alpha** (α), specified in advance before conducting a study. If the *p*-value is less than or equal to α, this means that either the observed effect is an extremely rare occurrence or the null hypothesis is wrong so that we reject the null hypothesis and the result is said to be *statistically significant*. If the *p*-value is greater than α, we fail to reject the null hypothesis and the result is said to be *not statistically significant*. The most common significance levels are $p < 0.05$ and $p < 0.01$, where the symbol < means "less than". If the difference between two means, for instance, is given as significant at the $p < 0.05$ or at the 0.05 level, this indicates that such a difference could be expected to occur by chance in only 5 out of every 100 times that a sample is randomly drawn from the population when the null hypothesis is true. A significance level of 0.01 means that the difference could be expected to occur by chance only 1 out of 100 times. Thus, the *lower* the probability of chance occurrence (*p*), the *higher* the significance level, and the *greater* the probability that the observed effect is a true one and not due to chance.

stative verb *n*

a verb which usually refers to a state (i.e. an unchanging condition), for example *believe, have, belong, contain, cost, differ, own,* as in:

This *contains* calcium.

She *believes* in God.

Stative verbs are not usually used in the PROGRESSIVE ASPECT.

A verb which can be used in the progressive aspect is known as a **dynamic verb**, for example *read, wear.*

I *am reading* a good book.

She *is wearing* dark glasses.

status *n*

higher, lower, or equal position, particularly in regard to prestige, power, and social class. Speech varieties (see SPEECH VARIETY) may have different statuses in a SPEECH COMMUNITY. For example, a variety which is limited to use in markets and for very informal situations would have a low status whereas another variety which is used in government, education, administration, etc., would have a high status (see DIGLOSSIA).

The status of people, when they are communicating in speech or writing, is also important, as it may affect the SPEECH STYLE they use to each other, e.g. ADDRESS FORMS, courtesy formulae.

see also ROLE RELATIONSHIP

stem[1] *n*

also **base form**

that part of a word to which an inflectional AFFIX is or can be added. For example, in English the inflectional affix -s can be added to the stem *work* to form the plural *works* in *the works of Shakespeare.*

The stem of a word may be:

a a simple stem consisting of only one morpheme (ROOT), e.g. *work*

b a root plus a derivational affix, e.g. *work* + -*er* = *worker*

c two or more roots, e.g. *work* + *shop* = *workshop.*

Thus we can have *work* + -*s* = *works*, *(work* + -*er)* + -*s* = *workers*, or *(work* + *shop)* + -*s* = *workshops.*

see also DERIVATION, INFLECTION

stem[2] *n*

see MULTIPLE-CHOICE ITEM

stereotype *n*

a popular concept of the speech of a particular group of people, e.g. Irish, New Yorkers, Australians. For example:

New Yorkers: /boid/ for *bird*

/toititoid/ for *thirtythird*

Australians: /woin/ for *wine*

/dai/ for day

Stereotypes are usually highly exaggerated and concentrate on only a few features of the speech patterns of a particular group.

stimulated recall *n*

see RECALL

stimulus *n*

see STIMULUS-RESPONSE THEORY, BEHAVIOURISM

stimulus-response theory *n*

also **S-R theory**

a learning theory associated particularly with the American psychologist B.F. Skinner (1904–90) (see BEHAVIOURISM), which describes learning as the formation of associations between responses. A **stimulus** is that which produces a change or reaction in an individual or organism. A **response** is the behaviour which is produced as a reaction to a stimulus. **Reinforcement** is a stimulus which follows the occurrence of a response and affects the probability of that response occurring or not occurring again. Reinforcement which increases the likelihood of a response is known as **positive reinforcement**. Reinforcement which decreases the likelihood of a response is known as **negative reinforcement**. If no reinforcement is associated with a response the response may eventually disappear. This is known as **extinction**. If a response is produced to similar stimuli with which it was not originally associated this is known as "stimulus generalization". Learning to distinguish between different kinds of stimuli is known as **discrimination**.

There are several S-R theories which contain these general principles or variations of them, and they have been used in studies of VERBAL LEARNING and language learning.

see also OPERANT CONDITIONING

stop *n*

also **plosive**

a speech sound (a CONSONANT) which is produced by stopping the airstream from the lungs and then suddenly releasing it.

For example, /p/ is a BILABIAL stop, formed by stopping the air with the lips and then releasing it.

see also CONSONANT, MANNER OF ARTICULATION, PLACE OF ARTICULATION

story completion task *n*
a task in which learners are given part of a story and told to complete it.

story grammar *n*
a theory of the cognitive representation of narrative texts, including simple stories, folk tales, fables and narratives. Some or all of the characteristics of the structure of stories is said to be incorporated into people's knowledge systems as a SCHEMA for stories. This describes the elements common to most stories, the kinds of situations, events, actors, actions and goals that occur in stories and the interrelationships among the elements of a story. People access story grammars consciously or unconsciously when encountering different types of stories. This serves as a source of prediction, inferencing, comparison, evaluation in understanding and following stories and narratives.

story preview *n*
in preparing learners to read narratives or RECOUNTS, a technique that involves giving background information about the story (e.g. the setting, characters, situation, key episodes) before they read in order to highlight key vocabulary and ideas needed to understand the text.

strategic competence *n*
an aspect of COMMUNICATIVE COMPETENCE which describes the ability of speakers to use verbal and non-verbal communication strategies (see COMMUNICATION STRATEGY) to compensate for breakdowns in communication or to improve the effectiveness of communication. For example, a learner may lack a particular word or structure and have to use a PARAPHRASE or circumlocution to compensate, or a speaker may use a deliberately slow and soft manner of speaking to create a particular effect on a listener.
see also DISCOURSE COMPETENCE

strategic plan *n*
in an organization, a description of the long-term vision and goals of an organization and the means it will undertake for fulfilling them. In language teaching, strategic planning is viewed as a crucial aspect of institutional development, particularly in the private sector.

strategy *n*
procedures used in learning, thinking, etc., which serve as a way of reaching a goal. In language learning, learning strategies (see LEARNING

STRATEGY) and communication strategies (see COMMUNICATION STRATEGY) are those conscious or unconscious processes which language learners make use of in learning and using a language.

see also HEURISTIC, HYPOTHESIS TESTING, OVERGENERALIZATION, SIMPLIFICATION[1]

strategy training *n*
also **learner training**
training in the use of LEARNING STRATEGIES in order to improve a learner's effectiveness. A number of approaches to strategy training are used, including:
Explicit or direct training: learners are given information about the value and purpose of particular strategies, taught how to use them, and how to monitor their own use of the strategies.
Embedded strategy training: the strategies to be taught are not taught explicitly but are embedded in the regular content of an academic subject area, such as reading, maths or science.
Combination strategy training: explicit strategy training is followed by embedded training.

stratified sample *n*
see SAMPLE

streaming *n*
also **banding, tracking, ability grouping**
the use of homogeneous groups in teaching.

stress *n*
the pronunciation of a syllable or word with more respiratory energy or muscular force than other syllables or words in the same utterance. A listener often hears a stressed word or syllable as being louder, higher in PITCH, and longer than the surrounding words or syllables. Different types of stress can be distinguished:
Word stress refers to the pattern of stressed and unstressed syllables in a word. A distinction used to be made in long words between stressed syllables of varying degree, i.e. it was said that the syllable with the greatest prominence had the **primary stress** and the next stressed syllable the **secondary stress**. Now it is felt that while such distinctions are relevant for CITATION FORMS, in an UTTERANCE the overall intonation tends to neutralize the degree of stress within the individual word. Word stress may distinguish between two words (e.g. a verb and a noun) that are otherwise alike. For example, *IMport* as a noun is stressed on the first syllable, and *imPORT* as a verb is stressed on the second (see also ACCENT).

Sentence stress refers to the pattern of stressed and unstressed words in a sentence or UTTERANCE. English sentence stress most commonly falls on CONTENT WORDS that contain NEW INFORMATION, for example, *He was going to LONdon*, where the strongest stress falls on the first syllable of the word *London*.

Emphatic stress: a speaker can emphasize any syllable or word that he or she wishes to highlight. Emphatic stress is considered to be **contrastive stress** when the highlighted word is explicitly or implicitly contrasted with another word, for example in the utterance *SHE was getting ON the plane while HE was getting OFF*.

stress pattern *n*
see STRESS

stress shift *n*
also **reverse stress**
in English, a change in the stress patterns of certain words or phrases when they are used in connected speech.
A stress shift depends on whether or not the word or phrase is followed by a noun which has a strong stress.
Usually, these words and phrases have a low (**secondary**) stress, shown here as /ˌ/, followed by a high (**primary**) stress, shown here as /ˈ/
For example:
    ˌindeˈpendent
    ˌplateˈglass
When, in connected speech, the word or phrase itself has the TONIC STRESS, the most important stress of the sentence (shown here by ↘), these words and phrases keep their usual stress pattern, e.g.:
    She was ˈvery ˌindepˈendent
    This window is ˌplate gˈlass
They may be followed by a noun with a low stress, e.g.:
    They are ˌplate gˈlass manuˌfacturers
However, before a noun that has either a high stress or the tonic stress, the strong (primary) stresses on the third syllable of *independent* and on the word *glass* in "plate glass" are lost and the secondary stress on the first syllable of *independent* and on *plate* in "plate glass" now becomes a primary stress, e.g.:
    He has ˈindependent mˈeans
    It's a ˌplate glass wiˈndow
    The ˌplate glass ˈwindow is brˈoken
Words or phrases which may have a stress shift are followed by the symbol /◂/ in some other dictionaries.

stress-timed language *n*

a language (such as English) with a rhythm in which stressed syllables tend to recur at regular intervals of time and the length of an utterance depends on the number of stresses rather than the number of syllables.

For example, the phrase *BILL WORKS HARD* and the phrase *BILL's been WORKing HARD* take roughly the same amount of time to say in English.

see also SYLLABLE-TIMED LANGUAGE

strong form *n*

the form in which a word is pronounced when it is stressed or spoken in isolation. This term is usually applied only to words that normally occur unstressed and with a weak form, such as *to, a, the*.

see also CITATION FORM

strong interface position *n*

see INTERFACE

strong verb *n*

(in English grammar) a term sometimes used to refer to a verb which forms the past tense and the past participle by a change in a vowel (e.g. *begin-began-begun*, *sing-sang-sung*). A regular verb which forms the past tense and participle by adding *-ed is* known as a **weak verb** (e.g. open-opened).

structural ambiguity *n*

another term for GRAMMATICAL AMBIGUITY

structural description *n*

also **SD**

(in TRANSFORMATIONAL GENERATIVE GRAMMAR) a complete grammatical analysis of a sentence typically in the form of tree-like structures (**tree diagram**) or strings of labelled constituents. The structural description shows the most abstract syntactic form of the sentence (DEEP STRUCTURE) and the changes made to it by various rules ("transformational rules").

see also BASE COMPONENT, TRANSFORMATIONAL COMPONENT

structural equation modelling *n*

a statistical procedure, combining PATH ANALYSIS and CONFIRMATORY FACTOR ANALYSIS, to test a researcher's theoretical model that involves both observed and unobserved (or latent) variables.

structural global method *n*

another term for AUDIO-VISUAL METHOD

structural(ist) linguistics *n*

an approach to linguistics which stresses the importance of language as a system and which investigates the place that linguistic units such as sounds, words, sentences have within this system. Structural linguists, for example, studied the distribution of sounds within the words of a language; that is, whether certain sounds appear only at the beginning of words or also in the middle or at the end. They defined some sounds in a language as distinctive and used in the identification of words (see PHONEME), and some as variants (see ALLOPHONE). Similar studies of distribution and classification were carried out in MORPHOLOGY and SYNTAX.

In its widest sense, the term has been used for various groups of linguists, including those of the Prague School, but most often it is used to refer to a group of American linguists such as Bloomfield and Fries, who published mainly in the 1930s to 1950s. The work of these linguists was based on the theory of BEHAVIOURISM and had a considerable influence on some language teaching methods (see AUDIOLINGUAL METHOD).

structural syllabus *n*

a SYLLABUS for the teaching of a language which is based on a selection of the grammatical items and structures (e.g. tenses, grammatical rules, sentence patterns) which occur in a language and the arrangement of them into an order suitable for teaching. The order of introducing grammatical items and structures in a structural syllabus may be based on such factors as frequency, difficulty, usefulness, or a combination of these. While most language teaching methods up to the 1970s were based on structural syllabuses, since then a number of alternative syllabus types have been adopted.

see also SYLLABUS

structural word *n*

see CONTENT WORD

structure *n*

(in linguistics) the term often refers to a sequence of linguistic units that are in a certain relationship to one another.

For example, one of the structures of a NOUN PHRASE[1] may be "article + adjective + noun" as in *the friendly ape*. One of the possible SYLLABLE structures in English is CVC (consonant + vowel + consonant) as in *concert*.

see also SYNTAGMATIC RELATIONS

structure dependency *n*

see UNIVERSAL GRAMMAR

structured interview *n*

an interview in which the organization and procedure of the interview, as well as the topics to be asked about, the questions, and the order in which they will be presented, have all been determined in advance. This may be contrasted with an **unstructured interview** that is exploratory in nature with no fixed format.

structured response item *n*

see TEST ITEM

structure word *n*

see CONTENT WORD

structuring *n*

also **structure, lesson structure**

(in describing a lesson) the degree to which a lesson has a recognizable purpose, organization, and development. A lesson which has a good degree of structure is said to be one in which:

1 both teacher and students understand what the goals of the lesson are
2 the tasks and activities employed during the lesson occur in a logical sequence
3 the directions which students are asked to follow are clear
4 students have a clear understanding of what they are supposed to accomplish during the lesson.

Students are believed to pay more attention and learn more effectively if a lesson is well structured. In language teaching, lesson structure is identified with the stages which occur during a lesson and the different components that make up a lesson. Common lesson structures are:

Presentation, Production, Practice
Warm-up, Opening, Activities, Closing

student-centred learning *n*

approaches to teaching in which:

a students take part in setting goals and OBJECTIVES
b there is a concern for the student's feelings and values (see HUMANISTIC APPROACH)
c the teacher is seen as a helper, adviser, or counsellor.

Many contemporary language-teaching approaches seek to give learners an active role in learning and are hence said to be less teacher-centred and more student centred than many traditional methods.

student-centred teaching *n*
> methods of teaching which (a) emphasize the active role of students in learning (b) try to give learners more control over what and how they learn and (c) encourage learners to take more responsibility for their own learning. This may be contrasted with more traditional teacher-centred approaches, in which control rests with the teacher.

student learning outcome *n*
> also **SLO**
> see LEARNING OUTCOME

student talking time *n*
> also **STT**
> the total amount of time students spend talking during a lesson, compared with the amount of time the teacher spends talking – **Teacher Talking Time** or **TTT**. Many classroom activities seek to increase the amount of STT in a lesson (e.g. group work). Student talking time is sometimes a focus for classroom observation or self-reflection.

study skills[1] *n*
> abilities, techniques, and strategies (see MICRO-SKILLS) which are used when reading, writing, or listening for study purposes. For example, study skills needed by university students studying from English-language textbooks include: adjusting reading speeds according to the type of material being read (see READING SPEED), using the dictionary, guessing word meanings from context, interpreting graphs, diagrams, and symbols, note-taking and summarizing.

study skills[2] *n*
> (in reading) those specific abilities that help a student understand a reading assignment, such as surveying the material, skimming for main ideas, paying attention to headings, interpreting graphs and illustrations, and identifying key vocabulary.
> see also SQ3R TECHNIQUE

stuttering *n* **stutter** *v*
> a speech disorder with one or more of the following characteristics and which leads to disfluent speech:
> 1 abnormal repetition of segments of speech (sounds, syllables, words).
> For example:
> *d-d-d-don't*
> *I've gota-gota-gota-cold.*

2 excessive pausing between words
3 abnormal lengthening of sounds. For example:
   I *fffffffeel cold.*
4 introduction of extra words or sounds at points of difficulty, such as
   oh, or *gosh.*

Stutterers vary in the precise nature of their stuttering and in the situations which cause them to stutter. Several theories have been suggested to account for stuttering but no single cause has been identified.

style *n* **stylistic** *adj*

1 variation in a person's speech or writing. Style usually varies from casual to formal according to the type of situation, the person or persons addressed, the location, the topic discussed, etc. A particular style, e.g. a formal style or a colloquial style, is sometimes referred to as a **stylistic variety.**

Some linguists use the term "register" for a stylistic variety while others differentiate between the two (see REGISTER).

2 style can also refer to a particular person's use of speech or writing at all times or to a way of speaking or writing at a particular period of time, e.g. Dickens' style, the style of Shakespeare, an eighteenth-century style of writing.

see also STYLISTIC VARIATION

style shift *n*

a change in STYLE during a verbal or written communication. Usually, a style shift takes place if the writer reassesses or redefines a particular situation. For example, a writer may add an informal note at the end of a formal invitation because he or she is on familiar terms with the person the invitation is addressed to. In a job interview, an applicant may change his or her formal style to a less formal style if the interviewer adopts a very informal manner.

see also STYLISTIC VARIATION

stylistics *n*

the study of that variation in language (STYLE) which is dependent on the situation in which the language is used and also on the effect the writer or speaker wishes to create on the reader or hearer. Although stylistics sometimes includes investigations of spoken language, it usually refers to the study of written language, including literary texts. Stylistics is concerned with the choices that are available to a writer and the reasons why particular forms and expressions are used rather than others.

see also DISCOURSE ANALYSIS

stylistic variation *n*

differences in the speech or writing of a person or group of people according to the situation, the topic, the addressee(s) and the location. Stylistic variation can be observed in the use of different speech sounds, different words or expressions, or different sentence structures.

For example, in English:

a Pronunciation: People are more likely to say /'sɪtn/ *sitt'n* /'meɪk¦n/ *mak'n* instead of /'sɪtɪŋ/ *sitting* /'meɪkɪŋ/ *making* if the style is more informal.

b Words and sentence structures:

more formal: *We were somewhat dismayed by her lack of response to our invitation.*

less formal: *We were rather fed up that she didn't answer when we invited her.*

The stylistic variation of an individual or group can be measured by analysing recorded speech and making comparisons.

see also STYLE

stylistic variety *n*

see STYLE

SU *n*

an abbreviation for subject relative clause

see NOUN PHRASE and ACCESSIBILITY HIERARCHY

subcategorization *n*

restrictions on a verb indicating which syntactic categories can or must occur with it. For example, a transitive verb must be followed by a direct object NP. This establishes transitive verbs as a subcategory of the category of verbs.

subcategory *n*

a subset of some category.

For example, COUNTABLE NOUNS are a subcategory of the category NOUN.

subjacency *n*

see BOUNDING THEORY

subject *n*

(in English grammar) generally the noun, pronoun or NOUN PHRASE[1] which:

a typically precedes the main verb in a sentence and is most closely related to it

b determines CONCORD

subject complement

c refers to something about which a statement or assertion is made in the rest of the sentence.

That part of the sentence containing the verb, or VERB GROUP (and which may include OBJECTS, COMPLEMENTS, OR ADVERBIALS) is known as the PREDICATE. The predicate is that part of the sentence which predicates something of the subject. For example:

subject	predicate
The woman	*smiled.*
Fish	*is good for you.*

see also OBJECT[1]

subject complement *n*
see COMPLEMENT

subjective marking *n*
another term for SUBJECTIVE SCORING

subjective scoring *n*
(in testing) the assignment of marks, grades or scores for a test taker's performance based on someone's opinion or judgement. Speaking tests are usually based on subjective scoring.
see also OBJECTIVE SCORING

subjective test *n*
a test that is subjectively scored (i.e. scored according to the personal judgement of the marker), such as an essay examination, which may be contrasted with an OBJECTIVE TEST.

Subject-Prominent language *n*
a language in which the grammatical units of SUBJECT and PREDICATE are basic to the structure of sentences and in which sentences usually have subject-predicate structure. English is a Subject-Prominent language, since sentences such as the following are a usual sentence type:

| *I* | *have already seen Peter.* |
| (Subject) | (Predicate) |

A language in which the grammatical units of topic and comment (see TOPIC[2]) are basic to the structure of sentences is known as a **Topic-Prominent language**. Chinese is a Topic-Prominent language, since sentences with Topic-Comment structure are a usual sentence type in Chinese. For example:

Zhangsān wǒ yǐjǐng   jiàn guo   le
Zhangsan I   already see aspect particle marker
i.e. *Zhangsan, I have already seen (him).*

| (Topic) | (Comment) |

568

subject relative clause *n*
also **SU**
see NOUN PHRASE ACCESSIBILITY HIERARCHY

subject-verb agreement *n*
the inflection of the verb to correspond or agree with the subject of the sentence, as in the third person present tense of verbs in English which is marked by adding "s". *She arrives tonight.*

subject-verb inversion *n*
see INVERSION

subjunctive *n*
see MOOD

submersion education *n*
a term which is sometimes used to describe a situation in which English second language students are placed in regular classrooms and compete with native speakers, and are given no special assistance with English – i.e. a kind of "sink or swim approach". Few adaptations are made to meet the students' special needs and the goal is to ensure that the students learn English as quickly as possible.

submersion programme *n*
a form of BILINGUAL EDUCATION in which the language of instruction is not the FIRST LANGUAGE of some of the children, but is the first language of others. This happens in many countries where immigrant children enter school and are taught in the language of the host country.
see also IMMERSION PROGRAMME

subordinate clause *n*
another term for DEPENDENT CLAUSE

subordinating conjunction *n*
see CONJUNCTION

subordination *n*
see CONJUNCTION

subordinator *n*
see CONJUNCTION

subset principle *n*
see LEARNABILITY THEORY

subskills *n*
another term for MICROSKILLS

substandard *adj*
a term which expresses a negative value judgement on any part of the speech or writing of a person or group that does not conform to the STANDARD VARIETY of a language and is therefore thought to be undesirable. For example, the double negative used in some dialects of English:
I don't know nothing.
would be considered by some people as substandard. A more neutral term used by linguists for forms which do not belong to the standard variety of a language is NONSTANDARD.

substantive *n*
a term sometimes used for a NOUN or any word which can function as a noun, such as a pronoun, an adjective (e.g. in *the old*), a GERUND, etc.

substantive universal *n*
see LANGUAGE UNIVERSAL

substitution *n*
an ERROR in which the learner substitutes a form from one language (usually the learner's first language) for a form in the TARGET LANGUAGE[1]
For example a French speaker may say *"I'll be leaving demain"* instead of *"I'll be leaving tomorrow"*.

substitution drill *n*
see DRILL

substitution table *n*
(in language teaching) a table which shows the items that may be substituted at different positions in a sentence. A substitution table can be used to produce many different sentences by making different combinations of items. For example:

The post office	is	behind	the park.
The bank		near	the hotel.
The supermarket		across from	the station.

Substitution tables were widely used in older teaching methods such as Situational Language Teaching.

substrate language *n*

see SUBSTRATUM LANGUAGE

substratum influence *n*

the influence of a speaker's original language on the acquisition of another language, whether taught formally or acquired informally (as in the case of PIDGIN languages). The influence may be on pronunciation, sentence structures, vocabulary or various aspects of COMMUNICATIVE COMPETENCE.

For example, it is common in a number of ESL varieties to use the verbs open and close for turning radios and lights on and off. This can often be seen as a substratum influence:

Philippine English	Tagalog			
"open the radio"	*buksan*	*mo*	*ang*	*radyo*
	open	*you*	*the*	*radio*
"close the light"	*isara*	*mo*	*ang*	*ilaw*
	close	*you*	*the*	*light*

substratum interference *n*

see SUBSTRATUM INFLUENCE

substratum language *n*

the original language of those who have acquired another language. The term was first used for speakers of PIDGIN and CREOLE languages.

For example, the substratum languages of West African Pidgins were the various local West African languages, e.g. Akan, Ewe, Ga, Hausa, Igbo, Yoruba. Lately, the term substratum language has been extended to include the first language of those acquiring a second/foreign language.

see also SUBSTRATUM INFLUENCE/INTERFERENCE, SUPERSTRATUM LANGUAGE

subtest *n*

a test that is given as a part of a longer test. For example, a language proficiency test may contain subtests of grammar, writing, and speaking.

subtitles *n*

also **captioning**

the practice of superimposing written text on film or video. From the perspective of a language learner, subtitled film or video may have the audio portion in the target language and the text in the native language (**standard subtitles**), the audio portion in the native language and the text in the foreign language (**reversed subtitles**), or both the audio and the video in the target language (**closed-captions**). Closed-captioning, also known as **bi-modal input**, was originally developed for the hearing impaired and required special equipment but is now a standard function on most televisions and video cassette recorders (VCRs). Digital video disks often provide all three options. There is some research evidence that all three types of captioning can be useful aids to language learning.

subtractive bilingual education *n*
also **subtractive bilingualism**
see ADDITIVE BILINGUAL EDUCATION

subvocalization *n*
see SUBVOCAL READING

subvocal reading *n*
also **subvocalization**
a type of reading said to be characteristic of all readers (by some researchers) and of poor readers (by other researchers), in which the reader pronounces words silently while reading, sometimes also making slight movements of the tongue, lips, and vocal cords.

successive bilingualism *n*
the acquisition of a second language after competence in the first language has been established to some extent, e.g. by the time when a child is three years old.

suffix *n*
a letter or sound or group of letters or sounds which are added to the end of a word, and which change the meaning or function of the word.
see also AFFIX

suggestopaedia *n*
also **desuggestopedia, suggestopedy, Lozanov method**
a METHOD of foreign-language teaching developed by the Bulgarian educator, Lozanov. It makes use of dialogues, situations, and translation to present and practise language, and in particular, makes use of music, visual images, and relaxation exercises to make learning more comfortable

and effective. Suggestopaedia is said to be a pedagogical application of "suggestology", the influence of suggestion on human behaviour.

summary *n*
brief statements of the main ideas in a text or passage, often produced while or after reading something. The ability to produce summaries is sometimes referred to as SUMMARY SKILLS and is a focus of instruction in the teaching of reading.

summative evaluation *n*
the process of providing information to decision-makers, after a course of instruction, about whether or not the programme was effective and successful.
see also FORMATIVE EVALUATION

summative test *n*
a test given at the end of a course of instruction, that measures or "sums up" how much a student has learned from the course. A summative test is usually a graded test, i.e. it is marked according to a scale or set of grades.
see also FORMATIVE TEST

superlative *n, adj*
also **superlative degree**
see COMPARATIVE

superordinate *n, adj*
see HYPONYMY

superstratum language *n*
the language from which most of the lexical items of a PIDGIN or CREOLE have been derived. Usually the superstratum language is the language of the former colonial power in the region where the pidgin or creole is spoken. For example, English is the superstratum language of Jamaican Creole and of Tok Pisin, spoken in Papua New Guinea.
see also SUBSTRATUM/SUBSTRATE LANGUAGE(S)

supervision *n*
(in teacher education) the monitoring and evaluation of a student teacher's teaching performance by a supervisor. Current approaches to supervision differ with respect to whether the supervisor's primary role is seen to be as an evaluator of teaching performance or as a facilitator or consultant. When the former is the case, the supervisor seeks to point out the differences

between actual teaching performance and ideal teaching behaviour, guiding the student teacher's development and offering suggestions for improvement. When the supervisor acts more as a consultant or facilitator, the goal is to explore aspects of teaching that have been determined through negotiation, and to encourage teacher self-development through reflection and self-observation.

see also REFLECTIVE TEACHING, CLINICAL SUPERVISION

supplementary materials *n*

in language teaching, learning materials which are used in addition to a course book. They often deal more intensively with skills that the course book does not develop or address in detail.

suppletion *n*

(in MORPHOLOGY) a type of irregularity in which there is a complete change in the shape of a word in its various inflected forms (see INFLECTION).

For example, English *good – better – best* does not follow the normal pattern as in *tall – taller – tallest* but uses different forms for the comparative and the superlative (see COMPARATIVE) of the adjective *good*.

supporting sentences *n*

(in composition) sentences in a paragraph which support, illustrate or explain the TOPIC SENTENCE.

suprasegmental *n*

(in PHONETICS and PHONOLOGY) a unit which extends over more than one sound in an utterance, e.g. STRESS and tone (see TONE,[1] TONE[2]). The term suprasegmental is used particularly by American linguists.

see also INTONATION, PROMINENCE, SEGMENTAL PHONEMES

surface structure *n*

see GENERATIVE THEORY, PHRASE STRUCTURE

surrender value *n*

(in language teaching) a term borrowed from life insurance and sometimes used to refer to the functional skills which a learner has acquired at any given point in a language course, and which the learner would be able to use even if he or she did not continue learning beyond that point. Courses where elements are organized so that items of high need are taught first have high surrender value.

sustained attention *n*

see ATTENTION

sustained silent reading (SSR) *n*

in the teaching of reading, an activity in which classroom time is devoted to silent reading, when students read materials of their own choice. Such activities usually occur regularly. The teacher does not interrupt the students during these reading periods.

SVO language *n*

see TYPOLOGY

SWOT analysis *n*

see SITUATIONAL ANALYSIS

syllabic consonant *n*

a consonant that functions in a weak syllable without the support of a vowel. In English, /n/ and /l/ have the capacity to be syllabic in words like *kitten* (syllabic /n/) and *little* (syllabic /l/).

syllabic writing *n*

a WRITING SYSTEM in which each symbol represents a SYLLABLE, e.g. the Japanese syllabic systems Katakana and Hiragana. Examples from Katakana:

イ ギ リ ス

Igirisu (Great Briain)

ト ラ ン プ

toranpu (playing cards)

see also ALPHABETIC WRITING, IDEOGRAPHIC WRITING

syllabification *n* **syllabify** *v*

dividing a word up into SYLLABLES.
For example, *locomotive* can be divided up into four syllables: *lo-co-mo-tive*. The syllabification of the spelling of a word can differ from the syllabification of its pronunciation. For example, in
styl-is-tics /staɪˈlɪstɪks/
the first syllable of the spelling is *styl*, but the first syllable of the pronunciation is /staɪ-/.

syllable *n*

a unit of speech consisting minimally of one vowel and maximally of a vowel preceded by a consonant or consonant cluster and followed by a consonant or consonant cluster. For example, the English word *introductions* consists of four syllables: *in-tro-duc-tions*.

In PHONETICS, the syllable is often related to chest pulses, contractions of chest muscles accompanied by increased air pressure, to **sonority**, the loudness of a sound relative to that of other sounds with the same length, stress, and pitch, or **prominence**, a combination of sonority, length, stress, and pitch. In PHONOLOGY, the syllable is defined by the way in which VOWELs and CONSONANTs combine to form various sequences. Vowels can form a syllable on their own (e.g. *oh!*) or they can be the "centre" of a syllable, preceded or followed by one or more consonants, e.g. *bay, ate, bait*. Syllables that end in a vowel are **open syllables**, e.g. the first syllables in English *open, highway, even*; syllables that end in one or more consonants are **closed syllables**, e.g. the first syllables in English *magpie, pantry, completion*.

A syllable can be divided into three parts:
a the beginning, called the **onset**
b the central part, called the **nucleus** or **peak**
c the end, called the **coda** or **final**.
In the English word *bite*, /bayt/, /b/ is the onset, /ay/ the nucleus, and /t/ the coda.

see also SYLLABIC CONSONANT

syllable-timed language *n*

a language (such as Spanish) with a rhythm in which syllables tend to occur at regular intervals of time and the length of an utterance depends on the number of syllables rather than the number of stresses.

see also STRESS-TIMED LANGUAGE

syllabus *n*

also **curriculum**

a description of the contents of a course of instruction and the order in which they are to be taught. Language-teaching syllabuses may be based on different criteria such as (a) grammatical items and vocabulary (see STRUCTURAL SYLLABUS) (b) the language needed for different types of situations (see SITUATIONAL METHOD) (c) the meanings and communicative functions which the learner needs to express in the TARGET LANGUAGE[1] (see NOTIONAL SYLLABUS) (d) the skills underlying different language behaviour or (e) the text types learners need to master.

see also CURRICULUM[2], GRADATION, LANGUAGES FOR SPECIAL PURPOSES, SPIRAL APPROACH, SYNTHETIC APPROACH

syllabus design *n*
a phase in curriculum development that deals with procedures for developing a syllabus.
see COURSE DESIGN, CURRICULUM DEVELOPMENT

syllogism *n*
an argument (see PROPOSITION) in the form of two premises and a conclusion drawn from them. For example:
Major premise: All boys like sports.
Minor premise: John is a boy.
Conclusion: John likes sports.

symbolic functions of language *n*
the capacity of a language to express ideas and concepts that are not based on physical perception, such as images, metaphors, etc.

symbolic processing *n*
also **symbolic architecture**
symbolic processing refers to the widely held view in psychology and linguistics that mental processes consist of representations in which symbols are manipulated by a set of rules. More recently, this approach to understanding cognition has been challenged by CONNECTIONISM, which relies upon an entirely different type of architecture.

synchronic *adj*
see DIACHRONIC LINGUISTICS

synchronic linguistics *n*
see DIACHRONIC LINGUISTICS

synchronous communication *n*
in COMPUTER ASSISTED LANGUAGE LEARNING, this refers to communication that is instantaneous, with all participants logged onto their computers and sending messages in real time. Language classes often use this type of communication in the form of Internet chat, or with specialized programs such as DAEDALUS INTERCHANGE.
see also ASYNCHRONOUS COMMUNICATION

synchronous computer-mediated communication *n*
communication via computer networks which takes place in real time, such as online chats.

synecdoche *n*

see FIGURE OF SPEECH

synonym *n* **synonymous** *adj* **synonymy** *n*

a word which has the same, or nearly the same, meaning as another word. For example, in English *hide* and *conceal* in:

He *hid* the money under the bed.

He *concealed* the money under the bed.

Often one word may be more appropriate than another in a particular situation, e.g. *conceal* is more formal than *hide*.

Sometimes two words may be synonymous in certain sentences only. For example, in the sentences:

I must *buy* some more stamps at the post office.

I must *get* some more stamps at the post office.

buy and *get* are synonyms, as it would usually be thought that *get* in the second sentence means *buy* and not *steal*.

see also ANTONYM, HYPONYMY

syntactic *adj*

see SYNTAX

syntactic structure *n*

see CONSTITUENT STRUCTURE, PHRASE STRUCTURE, SYNTAX

syntagm *n*

also **syntagma, syntagmatic**

a structurally significant combination of two or more units in a language. For example, a syntagm may consist of:

a two or more morphemes forming a word, e.g.:

re- + *write* = *rewrite*

or

b combinations of words forming PHRASES, CLAUSES, and SENTENCES, e.g.:

the + *train* + *is* + *leaving* + *now*

see also SYNTAGMATIC RELATIONS, SYNTAX

syntagmatic relations *n*

the relationship that linguistic units (e.g. words, clauses) have with other units because they may occur together in a sequence. For example, a word may be said to have syntagmatic relations with the other words which occur in the sentence in which it appears, but **paradigmatic relations** with words that could be substituted for it in the sentence.

For example:

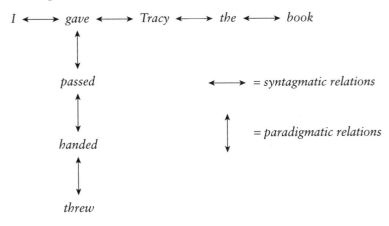

$I \longleftrightarrow gave \longleftrightarrow Tracy \longleftrightarrow the \longleftrightarrow book$

passed $\longleftrightarrow$ = *syntagmatic relations*

handed $\updownarrow$ = *paradigmatic relations*

threw

see also STRUCTURE

syntax¹ *n* **syntactic** *adj*

a major component of the GRAMMAR of a language (together with LEXICON, PHONOLOGY, and SEMANTICS), syntax concerns the ways in which words combine to form sentences and the rules which govern the formation of sentences, making some sentences possible and others not possible within a particular language. The interface between syntax and morphology (for example, the rules for modifying words to reflect their grammatical roles in sentences) is called MORPHOSYNTAX. One of the major goals of linguistics is to identify the syntactic rules of a language and to provide descriptions that group together those words in a sentence which hang closely together both formally and semantically. These groups are called CONSTITUENTS (see also CONSTITUENT STRUCTURE, PHRASE STRUCTURE). The study of syntax has been perhaps the most active branch of linguistics for the past half century and disputes concerning syntax and the ways in which it is to be represented have been the basis of many theoretical proposals and controversies. In GOVERNMENT/BINDING THEORY, a number of different modules, such as CASE THEORY, X-BAR THEORY and BINDING THEORY, define the constraints on various aspects of syntax. Other variants of GENERATIVE GRAMMAR and other types of grammars handle syntax in a variety of different ways.

see also CATEGORIAL GRAMMAR, LEXICAL FUNCTIONAL GRAMMAR, LOGICAL FORM, MINIMALISM, TRANSFORMATIONAL RULE

syntax² *n*

the rules which determine how the commands of a COMPUTER LANGUAGE are used and how they fit together.

579

synthetic approach *n*

(in language teaching) a term sometimes used to refer to procedures for developing a SYLLABUS or a language course, in which the language to be taught is first analyzed into its basic parts (e.g. the grammar is analyzed into parts of speech and grammatical constructions) and these are taught separately. The learner's task is to put the individual parts together again (i.e. to synthesize them). A syllabus which consisted of a list of grammatical items arranged in order of difficulty would be part of a synthetic approach to language teaching. In this sense, many traditional syllabuses would be called "synthetic".

This may be contrasted with an **analytic approach** in which units of language behaviour are the starting point in syllabus and course design (e.g. descriptions, requests, apologies, enquiries, and other SPEECH ACTS). At a later stage, if necessary, the vocabulary and grammar used for different functions can be analyzed. In this sense, a NOTIONAL SYLLABUS would be called "analytic".

synthetic language *n*

a cover term for AGGLUTINATING LANGUAGE or INFLECTING LANGUAGE

synthetic speech *n*

see DIGITIZED SPEECH, SPEECH SYNTHESIS

systematic error *n*

see ERROR OF MEASUREMENT

systematic phonemics *n*

a theory that a native speaker's knowledge of a language includes knowledge of the phonological relationships between different forms of words. It is claimed that the forms of words as they occur in actual speech (e.g. the English words *serene* and *serenity*) are produced from an underlying abstract level called the "systematic phonemic level". The abstract form, called the **underlying form,** for both *serene* and *serenity* is said to be //serēn//, with //ē// representing a long //e// SEGMENT. This form does not exist in actual speech.

see also GENERATIVE PHONOLOGY

systematic phonetic transcription *n*

see TRANSCRIPTION

systemic-functional grammar *n*

another term for SYSTEMIC-FUNCTIONAL LINGUISTICS

systemic-functional linguistics *n*

an approach to linguistics developed by M.A.K. Halliday that sees language as a resource used for communication in social contexts, rather than as an abstract formal system. The word "systemic" refers to the view of language as a network of interrelated systems (SEMANTICS, lexicogrammar, PHONOLOGY), and the term "functional" indicates that the approach is concerned with the choices that people make in order to exchange meanings through language. SEMANTICS includes **ideational semantics** (the propositional content of a message), **interpersonal semantics** (including speech functions such as requests and expressions of attitude), and **textual semantics** (how the text is structured as a message, for example, as given or new information). The **lexico-grammar** combines SYNTAX[1], LEXICON, and MORPHOLOGY as a single system, analyzing utterances in terms of functional roles such as AGENT, THEME, and MOOD. Systemic-functional linguistics has had a major impact on educational linguistics, especially in Australia.

see also SOCIAL CONTEXT, TRANSITIVITY[2]

systemic-functional theory *n*

another term for SYSTEMIC-FUNCTIONAL LINGUISTICS

systems approach *n*

(in education, language teaching, and COURSE DESIGN) an approach to analysis, planning and development in which (a) all the different elements involved are identified (e.g. society, parents, teachers, learners, time, materials, etc.) (b) their interactions are analyzed and studied (c) a plan or system is developed which enables OBJECTIVES to be reached.

The curriculum, plan, course, etc. is seen as composed of elements that work together as an integrated system, such that changes in one element affect other aspects of the system.

T

taboo language *n*

words or expressions, usually of a negative nature, that are considered offensive or embarrassing and that are discouraged in pubic usage. For example, swear words.

tacit knowledge *n*

also **implicit knowledge**

knowledge which people possess but which they may not be aware of and which they may not be able to describe or verbalize, such as the ability to recognize a grammatical from an un-grammatical sentence or the ability to recognize someone's face. Tacit knowledge is often learned from experience. Turning tacit knowledge into explicit knowledge is known as **codification** or **articulation**. Tacit knowledge may be embedded in a COMMUNITY OF PRACTICE, such as knowledge of a school culture.

tag *n*

a word, phrase, or clause added to a sentence in order to give emphasis or to form a question.
For example:
    They're lovely and juicy, <u>these oranges.</u>
    Jill's coming tomorrow, <u>isn't she?</u>
The latter is called a **tag question**.

tagging *n*

the process of annotating the words in a linguistic corpus (see CORPUS) by adding information such as part of speech, syntactic information, semantic information, or prosodic information for spoken corpora. Specialized programs are available to perform some of these annotations.

tagmeme *n, adj*

(in TAGMEMICS) the basic unit of grammatical analysis. A tagmeme is a unit in which there is a relationship between the GRAMMATICAL FUNCTION, for instance the function of SUBJECT, OBJECT[1] or PREDICATE, and a class of **fillers**.
For example, in the sentence:
    The baby bit Anthea.
the subject tagmeme is filled by the NOUN PHRASE[1] *the baby*, the predicate tagmeme is filled by the TRANSITIVE VERB *bite* in its past tense form *bit*, and the object tagmeme is filled by the proper noun *Anthea*.

tagmemics *n*

a theory of language originated by the American linguist, Pike. In tagmemic analysis there are three hierarchies or systems: grammatical, phonological, and lexical. In each of these systems there are a number of levels. For example, in the grammatical system there are: the morpheme level, the word level, the phrase level, the clause level, the sentence level, the paragraph level. On each level of the grammatical system there are TAGMEMES displaying relationships between grammatical functions and classes of linguistic items which can fill these functions (**fillers**).

tag question *n*

see QUESTION, TAG

talk-in-interaction *n*

see CONVERSATION ANALYSIS

tandem learning *n*

a situation in which two people who are both knowledgeable in their own language and culture and meet regularly to learn each other's language and culture as well as to socialize and exchange information. Each partner is responsible for his or her own learning and decides what, how, and when to learn. Normally it is a complement to formal instruction in a language course. When such learning takes place over the internet it is known as E-TANDEM LEARNING.

tap *n*

see FLAP

tape script *n*

see AUDIO SCRIPT

target language[1] *n*

also **L2**

(in language teaching) the language which a person is learning, in contrast to a FIRST LANGUAGE or mother tongue.

target language[2] *n*

the language into which a translation is made (e.g. in a bilingual dictionary). see also SOURCE LANGUAGE[2]

target situation *n*

in language curriculum development and LSP, the situation or setting in which the student will have to use the target language. This may be a study

task

or work situation or any context in which the learner needs to use the language. Analysis of the communicative and linguistic demands of the target situation is an essential phase in NEEDS ANALYSIS.

see SITUATION ANALYSIS

task *n*

(in teaching) an activity which is designed to help achieve a particular learning goal. A number of dimensions of tasks influence their use in language teaching. These include:

goals – the kind of goals teachers and learners identify for a task

procedures – the operations or procedures learners use to complete a task

order – the location of a task within a sequence of other tasks

pacing – the amount of time that is spent on a task

product – the outcome or outcomes students produce, such as a set of questions, an essay, or a summary as the outcome of a reading task

learning strategy – the kind of strategy a student uses when completing a task

assessment – how success on the task will be determined

participation – whether the task is completed individually, with a partner, or with a group of other learners

resources – the materials and other resources used with a task

language – the language learners use in completing a task (e.g. the mother tongue or English, or the particular vocabulary, structures or functions the task requires the learners to use).

The concept of task is central to many theories of classroom teaching and learning, and the school curriculum is sometimes described as a collection of tasks. From this viewpoint, school work is defined by a core of basic tasks that recur across different subjects in the curriculum. The teacher's choice of tasks determines learning goals, how learning is to take place, and how the results of learning will be demonstrated. In second language teaching, the use of a variety of different kinds of tasks is said to make teaching more communicative (see COMMUNICATIVE APPROACH) since it provides a purpose for a classroom activity which goes beyond the practice of language for its own sake.

see TASK-BASED LANGUAGE TEACHING

task analysis *n*

a systematic study of the individual components of a skill or activity in order to determine a focus or sequence for learning. Task analysis is an aspect of needs analysis particularly in the design of courses in ESP, EOP and EAP and in TASK-BASED TEACHING.

task-based language teaching *n*
also **TBLT, task-based instruction, task-based learning**
a teaching approach based on the use of communicative and interactive tasks as the central units for the planning and delivery of instruction. Such tasks are said to provide an effective basis for language learning since they:
a involve meaningful communication and interaction
b involve negotiation
c enable the learners to acquire grammar as a result of engaging in authentic language use.
This approach does not require a predetermined grammatical syllabus since grammar is dealt with as the need for it emerges when learners engage in interactive tasks. In using tasks in the classroom teachers often make use of a cycle of activities involving a) preparation for a task b) task performance c) follow-up activities that may involve a focus on language form. Task-based language teaching is an extension of the principles of Communicative Language Teaching and an attempt by its proponents to apply principles of second language learning to teaching.

task syllabus *n*
also **task-based syllabus, procedural syllabus**
(in language teaching) a SYLLABUS which is organized around TASKs, rather than in terms of grammar, vocabulary or functions. For example the syllabus may suggest a variety of different kinds of tasks which the learners are expected to carry out in the language, such as using the telephone to obtain information; drawing maps based on oral instructions; performing actions based on commands given in the target language; giving orders and instructions to others, etc. It has been argued that this is a more effective way of learning a language since it provides a purpose for the use and learning of a language other than simply learning language items for their own sake.

taxonomic *adj* **taxonomy** *n*
(in linguistics) classification of items into classes and sub-classes. Taxonomic approaches have been used in PHONOLOGY, SYNTAX and SEMANTICS. For example, in taxonomic PHONEMICS, the distinctive speech sounds of a language are classified as VOWELs and CONSONANTs, the consonants are classified as STOPS, FRICATIVES, NASALS, etc., the stops are classified as voiced or voiceless (see VOICE^2) and so on.
see also CLASS

TBLT *n*
an abbreviation for TASK-BASED LANGUAGE TEACHING

teachability hypothesis *n*

the idea that the teachability of language is constrained by what the learner is ready to acquire. Instruction can only promote acquisition if the interlanguage is close to the point when the structure to be taught is learnable without instruction in natural settings.

see also LEARNABILITY HYPOTHESIS

teacher aids *n*

resources that a teacher makes use of in presenting a lesson, such as CUISENAIRE RODS, white-boards, computers and educational software designed for use in classrooms. Those which make use of visual support such as video, powerpoint, posters, visuals, etc. are known as audio-visual aids.

teacher belief systems *n*

in language teaching, ideas and theories that teachers hold about themselves, teaching, language, learning and their students. Teachers' beliefs are thought to be stable constructs derived from their experience, observations, training and other sources and serve as a source of reference when teachers encounter new ideas, sometimes impeding the acceptance of new ideas or practices. Beliefs also serve as the source of teachers' classroom practices. Beliefs form a system or network that may be difficult to change. In teacher education a focus on belief systems is considered important since teacher development involves both the development of skills and knowledge as well as the development or modification of belief systems.

see LEARNER BELIEFS

teacher burnout *n*

a condition sometimes triggered by the demands of teaching or job conditions and which results in a state of physical and emotional depletion. Burnout can lead to fatigue, depression, decreased motivation, anxiety and stress. It is often a reason teachers leave the teaching profession.

teacher-centred instruction *n*

also **teacher-directed instruction, teacher-fronted instruction**
a teaching style in which instruction is closely managed and controlled by the teacher, where students often respond in unison to teacher questions, and where whole-class instruction is preferred to other methods. Many current teaching approaches try to encourage less teacher-directed interaction through the use of individualized activities or group work.

see also CO-OPERATIVE LEARNING, COMMUNICATIVE APPROACH, GROUP WORK

teacher cognition *n*
also **teacher thinking**
a field of educational research and theory which focuses on the thinking processes, beliefs, and decision-making used by teachers at various levels during the planning, delivery, and evaluation of teaching. Teacher behaviour is seen as resulting from the thoughts, judgements, beliefs, and decisions employed by teachers, and such processes need to be understood in developing approaches to teacher research. Teacher cognition plays an important role in teacher development and hence is of interest to those concerned with the planning of teacher development programmes and activities.

teacher development *n*
the professional growth a teacher achieves as a result of gaining increased experience and knowledge and examining his or her teaching systematically. A number of stages in teacher development are sometimes distinguished:
1 developing survival skills
2 becoming competent in the basic skills of teaching
3 expanding one's instructional flexibility
4 acquiring instructional expertise
5 contributing to the professional growth of colleagues
6 exercising leadership and participating in decision-making.

teacher-directed instruction *n*
see **teacher-centred instruction**

teacher education *n*
also **teacher training**
the field of study which deals with the preparation and professional development of teachers. Within the field of teacher education, a distinction is sometimes made between **teacher training** and **teacher development**.
Teacher training deals with basic teaching skills and techniques, typically for novice teachers in a PRESERVICE EDUCATION programme. These skills include such dimensions of teaching as preparing lesson plans, classroom management, teaching the four skills (i.e. reading, writing, listening, speaking), techniques for presenting and practising new teaching items, correcting errors, etc.
Teacher development looks beyond initial training and deals with the on-going professional development of teachers particularly in IN SERVICE EDUCATION programmes. This includes a focus on teacher self-evaluation, investigation of different dimensions of teaching by the teacher (see ACTION RESEARCH), and examination of the teacher's approach to teaching.

teacher evaluation *n*

procedures used to gather information about how and how well a teacher teaches. Teacher evaluation may be based on observation, learner evaluations, student results, self-evaluation, interviews, portfolios, etc., and serves a number of different purposes, including identifying strengths and weaknesses, contract renewal and promotion, and as part of the process of staff development.

see APPRAISAL SYSTEM

teacher-centred instruction *n*

another term for TEACHER-DIRECTED INSTRUCTION

teacher research *n*

a term to describe teacher-initiated investigations of their own classrooms, including action research. The notion of teacher research seeks to redefine the roles of teachers who are viewed as active investigators of learning and interaction within their own classrooms. Such a view is said to empower teachers.

teacher's edition *n*

a comprehensive guide or manual that accompanies a textbook or course book and which provides detailed information on the goals and methodology of the book, how to use the materials, answer keys and may also contain supplementary materials and tests.

teacher self-evaluation *n*

the evaluation by a teacher of his or her own teaching. Procedures used in self-evaluation include the video- or audio-recording of a teacher's lesson for the purpose of subsequent analysis or evaluation, the use of self-report forms on which a teacher records information about a lesson after it was taught, as well as the keeping of journal or diary accounts of lessons in which a teacher records information about teaching which is then used for reflection and development.

teacher talk *n*

that variety of language sometimes used by teachers when they are in the process of teaching. In trying to communicate with learners, teachers often simplify their speech, giving it many of the characteristics of FOREIGNER TALK and other simplified styles of speech addressed to language learners.

see also CARETAKER SPEECH

Teacher Talking Time *n*

see STUDENT TALKING TIME

teacher training *n*
another term for TEACHER EDUCATION

teaching portfolio *n*
see PORTFOLIOS

teaching practice *n*
also **practicum, practice teaching**
(in teacher education) opportunities provided for a student teacher to gain teaching experience, usually through working with an experienced teacher – the CO-OPERATING TEACHER – for a period of time by teaching that teacher's class. Practice teaching experiences may include MICROTEACHING, teaching an individual lesson from time to time, or regular teaching over a whole term or longer, during which the student teacher has direct and individual control over a class. Practice teaching is intended to give student teachers experience of classroom teaching, an opportunity to apply the information and skills they have studied in their teacher education programme, and a chance to acquire basic teaching skills.

teaching style *n*
a teacher's individual instructional methods and approach and the characteristic manner in which the teacher carries out instruction. Teachers differ in the way they see their role in the classroom, the type of teacher–student interaction they encourage, their preferred teaching strategies and these differences lead to differences in the teacher's teaching style.

team teaching *n*
a term used for a situation in which two teachers share a class and divide instruction between them. Team teaching is said to offer teachers a number of benefits: it allows for more creative teaching, allows teachers to learn through observing each other, and gives teachers the opportunity to work with smaller groups of learners.

technical word *n*
also **technical term**
1 a word whose occurrence is limited to a particular field or domain and which has a specialized meaning. For example *morpheme, phoneme*, in linguistics.
2 a common word that has a specialized meaning in a particular field, such as *significance* in statistics.
see also TERMINOLOGY

technical writing *n*

specialized genres of writing that occur in technical fields, such as computer science, engineering or mechanics.

see GENRE

technique *n*

in teaching, a specific procedure for carrying out a teaching activity, such as the ways a teacher corrects students' errors or sets up group activities.

see APPROACH

TEFL *n*

an acronym for Teaching English as a Foreign Language, used to describe the teaching of English in situations where it is a FOREIGN LANGUAGE. This term is becoming less frequently used than TESL, or TESOL.

telegraphic speech *n*

a term sometimes used to describe the early speech of children learning their first language, so called because children's early speech lacks the same sorts of words which adults leave out of telegrams (e.g. prepositions, AUXILIARY VERBS, articles). For example:

Baby no eat apple.

tenor of discourse *n*

see SOCIAL CONTEXT

tense¹ *n*

the relationship between the form of the verb and the time of the action or state it describes.

In English, verbs may be in the PAST or PRESENT TENSE. However, the present tense form of the verb is also used in:

a timeless expressions: *The sun rises in the east.*

b for future events: *I leave/am leaving next Monday.*

c past events for dramatic effect: *Suddenly she collapses on the floor.*

The past tense form of the verb may also occur in conditional clauses (see CONDITIONAL): *If you worked harder, you would pass the exam.*

see also MOOD

tense²/lax *adj*

features that divide vowels into two classes on phonological grounds. Tense vowels are produced with a comparatively greater degree of muscular tension and movement and are slightly longer in duration and higher in tongue position and pitch than the corresponding lax vowels. In English, the **tense**

vowels are those that can occur in stressed open syllables such as *bee, bay, bah, saw, low, boo, buy, bough, boy, cue*. The lax vowels are those that can occur in monosyllables closed by /ŋ/ such as *sing, length, sang, long, hung*.

terminology *n*

    1 the special lexical items which occur in a particular discipline or subject matter. For example CLAUSE, CONJUNCTION, and ASPECT are part of the terminology of grammar.

    2 the development or selection of lexical items for concepts in a language. Terminology is often a part of LANGUAGE PLANNING, since when languages are being adapted or developed for different purposes (e.g. when a NATIONAL LANGUAGE is being developed) new terms are often needed for scientific or technical concepts.

    see also SPECIAL LANGUAGES, STANDARDIZATION

term of address *n*

    another term for ADDRESS FORM

TESL *n*

    an acronym for Teaching English as a Second Language, used either to describe the teaching of English in situations where it is a SECOND LANGUAGE or to refer to any situation where English is taught to speakers of other languages.

TESOL *n*

    Teachers of English to Speakers of Other Languages. The acronym can be used to refer both to the US-based organization of that name and to describe the teaching of English in situations where it is either a SECOND LANGUAGE or a FOREIGN LANGUAGE. In British usage this is more commonly referred to as ELT, i.e. English Language Teaching.

test *n*

    any procedure for measuring ability, knowledge, or performance.

    see also ACHIEVEMENT TEST, CLOZE TEST, DISCRETE-POINT TEST, LANGUAGE APTITUDE TEST, PLACEMENT TEST, PROFICIENCY TEST, PROGRESS TEST, TOEFL TEST

test battery *n*

    another term for BATTERY OF TESTS

test bias *n*

    see BIAS

testee

testee *n*
another term for TEST TAKER

test equating *n*
see EQUATING

test format *n*
a description of the task type which is used to elicit any given language sample from students during a test.

testing *n*
a use of TESTS, or the study of the theory and practice of their use, development, evaluation, etc.

test item *n*
a question or element in a test that requires an answer or response. Several different types of test items are commonly used in language tests, including:
a **alternate response item**: one in which a correct response must be chosen from two alternatives, such as True/False, Yes/No, or A/B.
b **fixed response item**, also **closed-ended response**: one in which the correct answer must be chosen from among several alternatives. A MULTIPLE-CHOICE ITEM is an example of a fixed response item. For example: *Choose (a), (b), (c), or (d).*
Yesterday we _____ a movie. (a) has seen (b) saw (c) have seen (d) seen.
(b) is the correct response, while (a), (c) and (d) are called **distractors**.
c **free response item**, also **open-ended response**: one in which the test taker is free to answer a question as he or she wishes without having to choose from among alternatives provided.
d **structured response item**: one in which some control or guidance is given for the answer, but the test takers must contribute something of their own. For example, after reading a passage, a comprehension question such as the following:
What is astrology?
Astrology is the ancient _____ of telling what will _____ in the future by studying the _____ of the stars and the planets.

Test of English as a Foreign Language *n*
also **TOEFL**
a STANDARDIZED TEST of English proficiency administered by the EDUCATIONAL TESTING SERVICE, and widely used to measure the English language proficiency of international students wishing to enter American universities.

592

Test of English for International Communication *n*
also **TOEIC**
a test of overall English language proficiency in real-life day-to-day and business contexts, unlike the TOEFL test that focuses on academic English, originally developed by the EDUCATIONAL TESTING SERVICE but now administered by the Chauncey Group International, a subsidiary of ETS. The TOEIC test consists of two sections (Listening and Reading), each with 100 multiple-choice items, and takes 2 hours for test takers to complete.

Test of Spoken English *n*
also **TSE**
a SEMI-DIRECT test of oral communication in English, developed by the EDUCATIONAL TESTING SERVICE, where test takers are asked to respond orally on tape to a set of tape-recorded and text-based stimuli within approximately 20 minutes. International students whose native languages are not English and who apply for teaching assistantships may be required to take the TSE test or the **Speaking Proficiency English Assessment Kit** test, a locally administered TSE test.

Test of Written English *n*
also **TWE**
a DIRECT TEST of academic writing, developed by the EDUCATIONAL TESTING SERVICE. Test takers are given 30 minutes to write an essay on an assigned topic, which is scored by at least two raters on the basis of a six-point scale. The TWE is offered on certain test dates as part of the paper-based TOEFL test, where the TWE is scored separately from the TOEFL test, or as part of one of the four sections of the computer-based TOEFL test, where the TWE is mandatory for all test takers.

test-retest reliability *n*
an estimate of the RELIABILITY of a test determined by the extent to which a test gives the same results if it is administered at two different times. It is estimated from the coefficient of CORRELATION that is obtained from the two administrations of the test.

test specifications *n*
a set of test-writing guidelines for deciding what a test is constructed to measure and what language skills (e.g. listening, speaking, reading and writing or an integration of these skills) and language content will be measured in the test that is being developed.
see also ITEM SPECIFICATIONS

test statistic *n*
see also HYPOTHESIS TESTING

test taker *n*
also **candidate, examinee,** or **testee**
a person who takes a test or examination. The term "test taker" is used throughout this dictionary.

test-teach-test *n*
also **TTT**
an approach to teaching where students first do an activity without teacher support (the first **Test**) to see how well they know a target item. The teacher then presents the new learning item (**Teach**), then asks the students to carry out another task to assess their learning (the second **Test**). This is said to be a useful technique at intermediate levels and above, since it enables the teacher to determine the learners' needs.

test type *n*
in testing, the overall description of a test in terms of the purpose it serves and its objectivity or subjectivity.

test wiseness *n* **test wise** *adj*
a test-taking skill that enables a person to do well on certain kinds of test by using their familiarity with the characteristics and formats of tests to help them guess the correct answer. For example, in taking a reading comprehension test based on multiple choice questions, a test taker may analyze the alternatives given, eliminating unlikely choices, until only one remains, and then choose this as the correct answer. Test writers try to avoid test items that can be answered in this way.

tetrachoric correlation *n*
see CORRELATION

text *n* **textual** *adj*
a segment of spoken or written language that has the following characteristics:
1 It is normally made up of several sentences that together create a structure or unit, such as a letter, a report, or an essay (however one word texts also occur, such as *DANGER* on a warning sign).
2 It has distinctive structural and discourse characteristics.
3 It has a particular communicative function or purpose.
4 It can often only be fully understood in relation to the context in which it occurs.

Whereas linguistic description traditionally focused on the structure and function of sentences and their constituents, texts are thought of as a more appropriate unit of analysis for many purposes since learning to understand and produce appropriate texts is an important goal in language learning and teaching.

text-based syllabus design *n*
also text-based approach

an approach to the design of a language syllabus which is based on study of the oral and written texts students encounter in particular learning contexts. This approach is sometimes used when a specific context for language learning has been identified (e.g. a work-place or study context). Target situation analysis is used to identify the types of texts most frequently encountered in the context, and units of work are then developed in relation to the texts and the linguistic features they exemplify. Such a syllabus may regarded as a type of SITUATIONAL SYLLABUS.

text-based teaching *n*
also text-based approach

in language teaching, a methodology that focuses on teaching explicitly about the features of spoken and written texts and that links texts to the cultural context of their use. Units of work are built around different text-types and learners develop skills in relation to the use of whole texts. A 5 stage sequence is often used involving 1) building the context for a text 2) modeling and deconstructing a text 3) joint teacher-student construction of a text 4) independent construction of a text by the learners 5) linking texts to other texts.

textbook *n*

a book on a specific subject used as a teaching/learning guide, especially in a school or college. Textbooks for foreign language learning are often part of a graded series covering multiple skills (listening, reading, writing, speaking, grammar) or deal with a single skill (e.g. reading).

text linguistics *n*

a branch of linguistics which studies spoken or written TEXTs, e.g. a descriptive passage, a scene in a play, a conversation. It is concerned, for instance, with the way the parts of a text are organized and related to one another in order to form a meaningful whole. Some linguists prefer to include the study of all spoken texts, particularly if they are longer than one sentence, under DISCOURSE ANALYSIS.

text processing *n*
theories of how readers comprehend texts and the sequence of operations
they make use of to do so.
see INTERACTIVE PROCESSING, TOP-DOWN PROCESSING.

text structure *n*
the organizational pattern of ideas and information found in a text. Different types of texts (e.g. paragraphs, essays, letters, reports) are identified by
the way information is sequenced and organized and this structure creates
the text's COHERENCE.
For example common patterns of paragraph structure are comparison-
contrast, cause-effect, and problem-solution.

text types *n*
a classification of texts according to their purpose and features. The notion
of text types is based on the assumption that texts are structured in particular
ways in order to achieve certain communicative and socio-cultural purposes.
The different stages in the schematic structure of a text make a particular
contribution to the text achieving its communicative purpose. Recognizing
the features of different text types plays an important role in both reading
and writing. Numerous classifications of text types have been made. The
following are often recognized.

text type	*purpose*
narrative	to tell a story or entertain
recount	to tell what happened
personal recount	to relate personal experience
factual recount	to report on an event
imaginative recount	to describe an imaginary event
instruction	to describe how to make or do something
explanation	to explain how or why something works
information report	to define, classify, and give the characteristics of a thing or class of things
exposition	to express an opinion and convince the reader/ listener

see TEXT-BASED TEACHING

textual function *n*
see FUNCTIONS OF LANGUAGE

textual semantics *n*
see SYSTEMIC-FUNCTIONAL LINGUISTICS

TG *n*

another term for TRANSFORMATIONAL-GENERATIVE GRAMMAR
see GENERATIVE GRAMMAR

that-trace effect *n*

in English, a subject cannot be extracted when it follows the complementizer *that*. Thus, while the sentences *Did you think that Jennifer would win?* and *Who did you think would win?* are both grammatical, the sentence **Who did you think that would win?* is ungrammatical. This is called a that-trace effect. It does not apply in all languages.

see also TRACE

thematic roles *n*

see θ-THEORY/THETA THEORY

theme *n*

see FUNCTIONAL SENTENCE PERSPECTIVE

theory *n*

1 a statement of a general principle or set of propositions, based upon reasoned argument and supported by evidence, that is intended to explain a particular fact, event, or phenomenon. One view of the difference between a theory and a HYPOTHESIS is that a theory is more strongly supported by evidence than a hypothesis. Another view is that the distinction is related to breadth of coverage, a theory being broader than a hypothesis.

2 the part of a science or art that deals with general principles and methods as opposed to practice: a set of rules or principles of the study of a subject.

thesaurus *n*

an arrangement of the words and phrases of a language not in alphabetical order but according to the ideas they express. A thesaurus is different from a dictionary. Whereas a dictionary aims at explaining the meaning of words and expressions, a thesaurus suggests a range of words and phrases associated with an idea. For example, an excerpt from *Roget's Thesaurus of English Words and Phrases* shows under *"Amusement"* expressions such as:

fun, frolic, merriment, whoopee, jollity, joviality, laughter

thesis *n*

see DISSERTATION

thesis statement *n*

in some schools of composition, a sentence which states the central idea of an essay. A thesis statement comes at the beginning of the essay – usually in the introductory paragraph. It describes the aim or purpose of the essay, and contains the main ideas that will be developed in the *topic sentences* of the paragraphs which make up the rest of the essay. For example, the underlined sentence in the following introductory paragraph of an essay is the thesis statement.

Reading is the process of getting meaning from printed material. Reading is a complex process and depends upon learning specific skills. <u>*The purpose of teaching reading in school is both to teach children to become independent active readers and to introduce them*</u> *to* <u>*the pleasure and knowledge which effective reading makes possible.*</u>

θ-roles *n*

also **thematic roles.**

see θ-theory/theta theory

θ-theory/theta theory *n*

(in UNIVERSAL GRAMMAR) a sub-theory which deals with semantic relationships. In the lexicon of the grammar (see LEXICON[3]), each LEXICAL ENTRY for a verb shows the semantic roles (θ-ROLES or thematic roles) that go with it. For example, the English verb *smash* would have the θ-roles:

AGENT (the person or thing carrying out the action)

and

PATIENT (the person or thing affected by the action) The θ-roles are assigned to the relevant noun phrases in the sentence, e.g.:

> <u>*Rose*</u>   *smashed*   <u>*the vase*</u>
> agent   patient

The theory of Universal Grammar draws a distinction between these thematic roles, such as agent and patient, sometimes also called **themes,** and grammatical cases, such as grammatical subject and grammatical object (see CASE THEORY). In the example above, *Rose* is the grammatical subject and *the vase* is the grammatical object, but in the sentence:

> *The vase broke.*

the vase still has the patient or theme role but it is now the grammatical subject of the sentence. There is no agent role in this sentence. In second language acquisition research, theta-roles and their relationship to grammatical cases have been used, for example when distinguishing between verb groups which require an agent role (e.g. *hit, walk, work*) and those which do not (e.g. *fall, occur, suffer*).

see also D-STRUCTURE

thick description *n*

see CLOSE DESCRIPTION

think aloud procedure *n*

a technique used in investigating LEARNING STRATEGIES, in which learners think aloud as they are completing a task, in order that the researcher can discover what kinds of thinking processes or strategies they are making use of. For example, while writing a composition, a student may record his or her thoughts into a tape recorder during the planning, drafting, and revising of the composition. Later, the recording may be used to determine the planning or revision processes used by the student.

see also VERBAL REPORTING

third conditional *n*

see CONDITIONAL FORMS

three parameter model *n*

see ITEM RESPONSE THEORY

threshold hypothesis *n*

a hypothesis first proposed by Cummins which states that in learning a second language, a certain minimum "threshold" level of proficiency must be reached in that language before the learner can benefit from the use of the language as a medium of instruction in school. This hypothesis is related by Cummins to the **developmental interdependence hypothesis** which says that the development of proficiency in a second language depends upon the level of proficiency the child learner has reached in the first language at the time when extensive exposure to the second language begins.

threshold level *n*

a term used by the European regional organization, The Council of Europe, to refer to the minimal level of language proficiency which is needed to achieve functional ability in a foreign language. It serves as an OBJECTIVE for foreign language teaching. The threshold level is defined according to the situations in which the language will be used, the activities it will be used for, the topics to be referred to, the functions the language will be used for, and the language forms (e.g. vocabulary and grammar) which will be needed.

see also NOTIONAL SYLLABUS

timbre *n*

another term for VOICE QUALITY

timed freewriting *n*

another term for FREEWRITING

time expressions *n*
words or phrases that indicate time, such as *after, last weekend, in an hour.*

time lines *n*
in teaching grammar, a visual representation of time consisting of a horizontal line from left (earlier) to right (later), on or parallel to which are indicated points or periods of time, and the relationship between them. Time lines are used to teach the meanings of verb tenses.

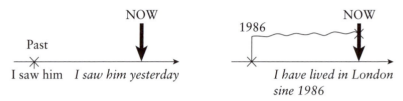

time on task *n*
also **on-task time**
(in teaching) the amount of time within a lesson in which students are actively thinking about and working with the content of a lesson. The amount of time that students spend "on task" in a lesson is one of the most basic predictors of learning. Research has distinguished several ways in which time is used within a lesson:

1 **allocated time:** the amount of time provided by the teacher for student learning within a lesson. In secondary schools with a 50 minute class period, teachers typically allocate between 30–35 minutes for instruction.

2 **time on task or engagement rate:** time during which students are working on learning tasks.

3 **academic learning time:** a category of time on task which consists of "high-quality" use of time, i.e. when students devote themselves to, and succeed in, meaningful tasks.

Time-on task rates vary greatly in lessons and may be as low as 30% in some lessons and as high as 90% in others. Effective teachers are said to be successful in maintaining high rates of time on task and academic learning time in lessons.

tip-of-the-tongue phenomenon *n*
the feeling that one is almost but not quite able to find a word that one is trying to produce. People having the tip-of-the-tongue experience are often able to recall some characteristics of the word, for example the initial phoneme or the number of syllables, suggesting that these aspects of word structure may be stored independently of others.

TKT *n*

also **Teaching Knowledge Test**

a test from Cambridge ESOL for teachers of English to speakers of other languages that may be taken by teachers at any stage of their career. It forms part of a framework that includes the CELTA and DELTA. Like these two exams, the TKT covers subject knowledge, pedagogical knowledge, and pedagogical content, but it does not attempt to assess knowledge of teaching ability or practical classroom skills.

T-list *n*

a form of notetaking in which the main ideas from a passage are noted on the left side of a page and the corresponding details are listed on the right. The "T" is derived from the fact that the learner makes a vertical line to separate the main ideas from the details and a horizontal line at the top of the page on which to write the words "main ideas" and "details".

see also OUTLINE

TOEFL test *n*

also **TOEFL**

an acronym for the Test of English as a Foreign Language, a STANDARDIZED TEST of English proficiency administered by the Educational Testing Service, and widely used to measure the English-language proficiency of foreign students wishing to enter American universities.

TOEIC *n*

an abbreviation for TEST OF ENGLISH FOR INTERNATIONAL COMMUNICATION

token *n*

see TYPE

tone[1] *n*

height of PITCH and change of pitch which is associated with the pronunciation of syllables or words and which affects the meaning of the word.

A **tone language** is a language in which the meaning of a word depends on the tone used when pronouncing it.

For example, Mandarin Chinese, a tone language, makes a distinction between four different tones:

mā (high level tone)	"mother"
má (high rising tone)	"hemp"
mǎ (fall-rise)	"horse"
mà (high falling tone)	"scold"

Other tone languages are spoken in Vietnam, Thailand, West Africa, and Central America.

tone

tone² *n*
    also **pitch movement**
    a change in PITCH which affects the meaning and function of utterances in
    discourse.
    In English, linguists have distinguished four or five different tones:
        Tone 1 fall in pitch
        Tone 2 rise in pitch
        Tone 3 a slight rise in pitch
        Tone 4 fall in pitch followed by a rise
        Tone 5 rise in pitch followed by a fall
    In a unit of intonation (see TONE UNIT) the syllable on which pitch move-
    ment begins is often called the **tonic** or the **tonic syllable**. The tonic syllable
    is often the last prominent syllable in the unit. For example, in:
        They flew to Frankfurt.
    the pitch of the speaker's voice begins to fall on the syllable *Frank*.
    see also KEY², REFERRING TONE

tone group *n*
    another term for TONE UNIT

tone language *n*
    see TONE¹

tone unit *n*
    also **tone group**
    the basic unit of INTONATION in a language. A tone unit is usually divided
    into several parts. The most important part contains the syllable on which

	unstressed syllables	*onset* first stressed syllable	*tonic syllable* where major pitch movement begins	continuation and completion of pitch movement
Crystal	(prehead)	head	nucleus	(tail)
Halliday	pretonic		tonic	
Brazil	(proclitic segment)	tonic segment		(enclitic segment)
e.g.	*That's a*	VERY TALL	STO	*ry*

a change of pitch begins: the **tonic syllable**. The ways in which linguists have divided the tone unit into its different parts and the terms they have used for these parts are not always the same. The simplified diagram above shows the main parts of a tone unit together with different divisions and terms which have been used, where the first syllable of *very* is the **onset**, the first prominent syllable in the tone unit, and the first syllable of *story* is the tonic syllable, where the pitch of the speaker's voice begins to fall. Some linguists refer to a tone unit as an **intonation contour**.

see also PROMINENCE, TONE[2]

tonic *n, adj*
see TONE[2]

tonicity *n*
the choice of the places in an utterance or part of an utterance where a movement in pitch begins (see **tonic syllable** under TONE UNIT). The choice depends on what the speaker wishes to emphasize. For example, in *She came last SATurday* the change in pitch would often be placed on the *SAT* of *Saturday* but in a dialogue such as:
A: *She never comes on Saturdays.*
B: *But she came LAST Saturday.*
a change in pitch would start on *LAST*.

tonic segment *n*
see TONE UNIT

tonic syllable *n*
see TONE[2], TONE UNIT

top-down processing *n*
in PSYCHOLINGUISTICS, COGNITIVE PSYCHOLOGY, and INFORMATION PROCESSING, a contrast is made between two different ways in which humans analyze and process language as part of comprehension and learning. One way, known as top-down processing, makes use of "higher level", non-sensory information to predict or interpret "lower level" information that is present in the data. The other way, **bottom-up processing**, makes use of the information present in the input to achieve higher level meaning. The meanings of these terms varies depending on the unit of analysis. For example, in **word recognition**, the higher level information is knowledge of permissible words as well as actual words of a language, while the lower level information is the actual phonetic input (or orthographic input in

topic

the case of written word recognition). In **sentence comprehension** or the interpretation of an UTTERANCE, the lower level information is words, while the higher level information includes knowledge of GRAMMAR, SEMANTICS, and PRAGMATICS. As applied to the full understanding of a novel, lower level information consists of words and sentences, while higher level information includes the reader's previously existing knowledge of the world, including cultural and moral values, SCRIPTS, SCHEMAS, and literary GENRES.

see also COMPREHENSION, INTERACTIVE PROCESSING

topic[1] *n*

what is talked about or written about. In different speech communities (see SPEECH COMMUNITY) there are different rules about what topics may or may not be discussed. For example, in some communities, illness, death, a person's income, and a person's age may be considered unsuitable topics for conversation.

topic[2] *n*

in describing the INFORMATION STRUCTURE of sentences, a term for that part of a sentence which names the person, thing, or idea about which something is said (the **comment**). The concept of Topic and Comment is not identical with SUBJECT and PREDICATE. Subject-Predicate refers to the grammatical structure of a sentence rather than to its information structure (see SUBJECT-PROMINENT LANGUAGE). The difference is illustrated in the following example:

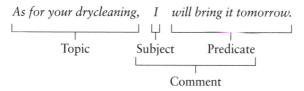

In some sentences in English, however, Topic-Comment and Subject-Predicate are identical. For example:

Hilary	*is a dancer.*
Subject	Predicate
Topic	Comment

topic[3] *n*

in composition, the general idea or theme which the whole passage is about, often expressed in a phrase or sentence.

see TOPIC SENTENCE.

604

topic-centred approach *n*
also **topic-based approach** *n*
in language teaching, a curriculum, course or syllabus in which content and teaching and learning activities are centred around topics or themes, such as "the family", "leisure", "music", etc. Other aspects of the course (skills, grammar, etc.) are all linked to the core topics of the course.
see CONTENT-BASED INSTRUCTION

topic outline *n*
see OUTLINE

Topic-Prominent language *n*
see SUBJECT-PROMINENT LANGUAGE

topic sentence *n*
according to some schools of composition theory, a sentence which describes the topic, purpose or main idea of a paragraph, i.e. which states what the paragraph is about. A topic sentence may be the first sentence in a paragraph, with the other sentences adding illustrative or supporting details (a paragraph which follows deductive reasoning – see DEDUCTION) or it may be the final sentence of a paragraph (a paragraph which follows inductive reasoning – see INDUCTION). Sometimes the topic sentence in a paragraph may be unstated but implied. In English a topic sentence often contains an opinion that will be proved or supported in the paragraph or a statement which the writer will explain in more detail in the paragraph. For example, the first sentence in the following paragraph is the topic sentence. *In order to get a summer job, there are a number of things you should do. You should first decide on the kind of job you want. You should check all relevant sources for jobs. You should also start looking early. It is also useful to prepare a short résumé. Above all, be confident and don't be discouraged by any refusals you may get.*

top-to-bottom *adj*
see SERIAL LEARNING
see also TOP-DOWN PROCESSING

total communication *n*
a method of teaching hearing impaired children which is based on the simultaneous use of both SIGN LANGUAGE and spoken language. This allows the child to use both vision and residual hearing. The results achieved may depend on the MANUAL METHOD employed and the skill of the teacher

in matching the two systems of communication. Acquisition of spoken language is said to be limited by this approach.

Total Physical Response *n*
also **TPR**
a language teaching METHOD developed by Asher in the early 1970s in which items are presented in the foreign language as orders, commands, and instructions requiring a physical response from the learner (e.g. opening a window or standing up). TPR gives greater emphasis to comprehension than many other teaching methods. Both this and the emphasis on teaching language through physical activity are to lead to more effective learning.

trace *n*
according to **trace theory**, when an element is moved in the course of a DERIVATION, it leaves behind a trace in its original position. For example, in (i) since "who" has been moved from subject position in a lower clause, a trace is left behind in that position:
(i) who did you say [t$_i$ left]
A trace can be treated as an EMPTY CATEGORY.
See also RESUMPTIVE PRONOUN, MOVEMENT

trace theory *n*
see TRACE

traditional grammar *n*
a grammar which is usually based on earlier grammars of Latin or Greek and applied to some other language, often inappropriately. For example, some traditional grammars of English stated that English had six CASES[1] because Latin had six cases. Traditional grammars were often notional and prescriptive in their approach (see NOTIONAL GRAMMAR, PRESCRIPTIVE GRAMMAR).

trainer development *n*
the formal as well as informal processes which contribute to the professional development of teacher educators. The content of professional development for language teacher educators may include advanced qualifications in applied linguistics, mentor training, management and counselling, teacher evaluation, as well as courses on the design, implementation and evaluation of training programmes and teacher education courses.

training *n*
see EDUCATION

trait *n*

a person's enduring psychological attribute or characteristic (e.g. her L2 ability) underlying and explaining her behaviour (e.g. her performance on a test) from which an inference is drawn.

transaction *n*

an event or series of actions which involves interactions between two or more people and has a particular goal. In describing language use (particularly for the purpose of developing language programmes), the term "transaction" is sometimes used to refer to the activities people carry out in specific situations, for example, the activities of a server in a restaurant. The language demands of particular transactions such as "serving a customer and taking the customer's order" may be a focus of NEEDS ANALYSIS. The term TASK is sometimes used with a similar meaning. A transaction between a worker and a client is sometimes known as a **service encounter**.

transactional functions of language *n*

see INTERACTIONAL FUNCTIONS

transcription *n*

also NOTATION

the use of symbols to represent sounds or sound sequences in written form. There are different systems of phonetic symbols. One of the most commonly used is the INTERNATIONAL PHONETIC ALPHABET.

A distinction is commonly made between two general types of transcription:

1 a **narrow transcription** (also called a **phonetic transcription**) is one that shows phonetic details (for example, aspiration, length, etc.), by using a wide variety of symbols and, in many cases, DIACRITICS. A **systematic phonetic transcription** shows all the phonetic details that can be recorded.

2 a **broad transcription** (also called an **impressionistic transcription**) is one that uses a simple set of symbols and does not show a great deal of phonetic detail. A **phonemic transcription** is a broad transcription that shows all and only those sounds that are distinctive PHONEMES in the language being transcribed.

transfer *n*

(in learning theory) the carrying over of learned behaviour from one situation to another. **Positive transfer** is learning in one situation which helps or facilitates learning in another later situation. **Negative transfer** is learning in one situation which interferes with learning in another later situation.

see also LANGUAGE TRANSFER, PROACTIVE INHIBITION

transfer of training *n*
the transfer of what has been learned in a limited setting (for example, a laboratory experiment) to a new but similar situation.
see also GENERALIZATION, INDUCED ERROR

transfer stage *n*
another term for PRODUCTION STAGE
see STAGE

transformational component *n*
see GENERATIVE THEORY

transformational-generative grammar *n*
see GENERATIVE GRAMMAR, GENERATIVE THEORY

transformational grammar *n*
also **transformational-generative grammar, TG, generative-transformational grammar**
see GENERATIVE GRAMMAR, GENERATIVE THEORY

transformational rule *n*
in SYNTAX, a rule that transforms syntactic structure, such as DELETION and MOVEMENT.
see also D-STRUCTURE

transformational rules *n*
see GENERATIVE THEORY

transformation drill *n*
see DRILL

transforms *n*
see GENERATIVE THEORY

transitional bilingual education *n*
see BILINGUAL EDUCATION

transition words *n*
also **transitions, transition devices**
(in composition) adverbs which are used to indicate relations or transitions between sentences in a paragraph or piece of writing. These may be either single words or phrases. Transition words often give COHERENCE to a composition. Different transition words are used to signal different kinds of relations between sentences. For example: transition words in English include:

Time: *after a while, afterwards, later*
Place: *nearby, there*
Addition: *also, besides, furthermore*
Result: *accordingly, hence, therefore*
Comparison: *likewise, similarly*
Contrast: *however, nevertheless, otherwise*
Concession: *naturally, of course*
Summary or conclusion: *in brief, finally, to sum up*
Illustration and example: *for example, for instance, indeed*

transitive verb *n*
a verb which takes an OBJECT[1]. For example:
They saw the accident.
A verb which takes an indirect and a direct object is known as a **ditransitive verb**. For example:
I gave the money to my mother. = *I gave my mother the money.*
        DO   IO   IO   DO
A verb which takes a direct object and an object complement (see COMPLEMENT) is known as a **complex transitive verb**. For example:
We elected Mary chairman.
        DO   object complement
A verb which does not take an object is an intransitive verb. For example:
The children danced.
see also COMPLEMENT

transitivity[1] *n*
the state of being a TRANSITIVE VERB. In this sense, one can speak of the transitivity of the verb *saw* in the sentence:
They saw the accident.

transitivity[2] *n*
(in SYSTEMIC GRAMMAR) a choice between the three main processes that can be represented in a sentence:
a a physical or "material" process as in *Fred cut the lawn.*
b a "mental" process as in *David saw Rosemary.*
c a "relational" process as in *This view is magnificent.*
Related to this choice of processes is:
a the choice of participants. A participant is someone or something involved in the process, e.g. in the above examples, *Fred* and *the lawn*, *David* and *Rosemary* and
b the choice of circumstances, e.g. David saw Rosemary *yesterday/in the garden/by accident.*

Further choices associated with transitivity would be which roles the participants had in a process and how processes, participants, and circumstances are combined.

see also SYSTEMIC LINGUISTICS

translation *n*

the process of rendering written language that was produced in one language (the SOURCE LANGUAGE[2]) into another (the TARGET LANGUAGE[2]), or the target language version that results from this process. Translation in which more emphasis is given to overall meaning than to exact wording is known as **free translation**. A translation that approximates to a word-for-word representation of the original is known as a **literal translation**. A translation that has been produced by a computer is known as a MACHINE TRANSLATION. The terms *translation* and *interpretation* are often used interchangeably. While both activities involve transferring a message between two different languages, translation refers to transfer between written texts and interpretation refers to spoken discourse and the unrehearsed transfer of a spoken message from one language to another.

see also INTERPRETATION

translation equivalence *n*

the degree to which linguistic units (e.g. words, syntactic structures) can be translated into another language without loss of meaning. Two items with the same meaning in two languages are said to be **translation equivalents**.

translator *n*

in general, someone who translates written language from one language (SOURCE LANGUAGE) into another (the TARGET LANGUAGE). An **accredited translator** (or **certified translator**) is someone who has received accreditation (or certification) from a professional organization such as the Institute of Translation and Interpreting (ITI) or the American Translators Association (ATA), issued on the basis of training, experience, and examinations. In some countries (e.g. Germany) translators may hold titles if they have graduated from programmes at degree level. Some translators have specialized skills necessary for specific types of translation, for example medical translation, legal translation, or literary translation.

transmission mode of teaching *n*

also **transmission orientated teaching**

a term used to describe teaching practices in which teaching is viewed as a one-way process in which information, skills, knowledge, etc., is transmitted from the teacher to the learners. This is generally regarded as a traditional approach to teaching that fails to acknowledge an active role for learners in the learning process. It can be contrasted with other more LEARNER-CENTRED teaching approaches such as:

1 problem-solving approach: students and the teacher collaborate in the exploration of issues and topics

2 co-operative learning approach: students work in small groups under the supervision of the teacher.

treatment *n*

in research, the independent or predictor variable that is hypothesized to have an effect on some other variable (see DEPENDENT VARIABLE).

tree diagram[1] *n*

a visual representation of the phrase structure (also CONSTITUENT STRUCTURE) of a phrase or sentence.

For example, the structure of the English sentence

The parrot shrieked noisily.

can be shown by the simplified tree diagram:

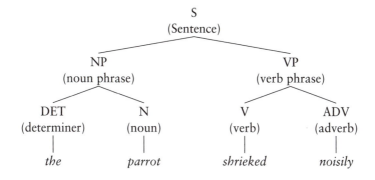

see also LABELLED BRACKETING

tree diagram[2] *n*

see BASE COMPONENT, CONSTITUENT STRUCTURE, NODE, PHRASE-STRUCTURE GRAMMAR

trialling *n*

see PRETESTING

triangulation *n*

(in QUALITATIVE RESEARCH) the process of collecting data from several different sources or in different ways in order to provide a fuller understanding of a phenomenon. Obtaining data from more than one source (e.g. interviews, observations, and documents) is the most commonly used type of triangulation. Triangulation may also involve using multiple methods (e.g. from interviews, questionnaires, observation schedules, test scores, etc.), multiple researchers (i.e. the use of more than one researcher in a study), or multiple theories for the interpretation of data. Issues concerning the use of triangulation in research include whether triangulation overcomes problems of BIAS, RELIABILITY and VALIDITY or merely produces a fuller picture of a phenomenon and whether or not it is legitimate to combine research methods based on theoretical paradigms which include different assumptions about the nature of social reality.

see also MULTI-TRAIT MULTI-METHOD METHOD

trigger requirement *n*
see LEARNABILITY THEORY

trill *n*
also **roll**
a speech sound (a CONSONANT) in which the tongue vibrates against the roof of the mouth, producing a series of rapid taps. In some forms of Scottish English, /r/ as in *rip* is a trill.

triphthong *n*
(in PHONETICS) a term sometimes used for a combination of three vowels. For example, in English:
/aɪə/ as in /faɪəʳ/ *fire*
is a triphthong.
see also DIPHTHONG, MONOPHTHONG

true beginner *n*
see FALSE BEGINNER

true/false item *n*
a type of test item or test task that requires test takers to decide whether a given statement is either "true" or "false", which is a dichotomous choice, as the answer or response.
see also SELECTED-RESPONSE ITEM

T score *n*
(in statistics) a STANDARD SCORE whose DISTRIBUTION has a MEAN of 50 and a STANDARD DEVIATION of 10.

TSE *n*

an abbreviation for TEST OF SPOKEN ENGLISH

T-test *n*

(in testing and statistics) a quantitative procedure for determining the STATISTICAL SIGNIFICANCE of the difference between the MEANS on two sets of scores.

see also CHI-SQUARE

T-Unit *n*

also **Minimal Terminable Unit**

a measure of the linguistic complexity of sentences, defined as the shortest unit (the Terminable Unit, Minimal Terminable Unit, or T-Unit) which a sentence can be reduced to, and consisting of one independent clause together with whatever DEPENDENT CLAUSES are attached to it. For example the sentence *After she had eaten, Kim went to bed* would be described as containing one T-Unit.

Compound sentences (see COMPLEX SENTENCE) contain two or more T-Units. The study of T-Units in written language has been used in the study of children's language development.

turn *n*

see TURN-TAKING

turn-taking *n*

in conversation, the roles of speaker and listener change constantly. The person who speaks first becomes a listener as soon as the person addressed takes his or her **turn** in the conversation by beginning to speak.

The rules for turn-taking may differ from one community to another as they do from one type of SPEECH EVENT (e.g. a conversation) to another (e.g. an oral test). Turn-taking and rules for turn-taking are studied in CONVERSATIONAL ANALYSIS and DISCOURSE ANALYSIS.

see also SEQUENCING[1]

TWE *n*

an abbreviation for TEST OF WRITTEN ENGLISH

two parameter model *n*

see ITEM RESPONSE THEORY

two-tailed test *n*

also **non-directional hypothesis**

a type of statistical hypothesis test that is appropriately chosen where – based on previous studies – no direction of an effect, such as a difference or correlation, is specified in advance (e.g., There will be a significant difference in vocabulary recognition scores between the experimental and control groups).

two-way immersion education *n*

a type of mainly US bilingual education in which students learn through two languages in programmes that aim to develop dual language proficiency along with academic achievement. Both minority and English-speaking students acquire a second language. Instruction is provided both through the L1 of the minority students and through English. Such programmes integrate language minority and language majority students and provide content area instruction as well as language development in two languages. Students from the 2 language backgrounds are in each class and they are integrated for most or all of their content instruction.

two-way task *n*

a type of INFORMATION GAP task in which each participant has some information not shared by the other and that information needs to be shared to complete the task.

type *n*

in linguistics, a distinction is sometimes made between classes of linguistic items (e.g. PHONEMES, WORDS, UTTERANCES) and actual occurrences in speech or writing of examples of such classes. The class of linguistic units is called a **type** and examples or individual members of the class are called **tokens**. For example, *hello, hi, good morning* are three different tokens of the type "Greeting".
In MATHEMATICAL LINGUISTICS the total number of words in a text may be referred to as the number of text tokens, and the number of different words as the number of text types. The ratio of *different* words in a text to *total* words in the text is known as the LEXICAL DENSITY or **Type-Token Ratio** for that text.
see also LEXICAL DENSITY

Type 1 error *n*

also **alpha (α) error**
rejection of a NULL HYPOTHESIS when it should be accepted.

Type 2 error *n*

also **beta (β) error**
failure to reject a NULL HYPOTHESIS when it should be rejected.

Type-Token Ratio *n*
> another term for LEXICAL DENSITY

typology *n*
> the classification of languages into types. For example, languages may be classified according to whether or not they are tone languages (see TONE[1]) or according to their most typical SYNTACTIC STRUCTURES, e.g. whether they are **SVO languages** (Subject – Verb – Object languages) like English or **SOV languages** (Subject – Object – Verb languages) like Japanese.

U

UG *n*

an abbreviation for UNIVERSAL GRAMMAR

unacceptable *adj*

see ACCEPTABLE

unaccusative verb *n*

a type of INTRANSITIVE VERB whose syntactic subject is not a semantic agent. For example, in sentences such as *The window broke* or *The ball fell to the ground*, the grammatical subject (*window*, *ball*) is not actively responsible for the action of the verb.

see also ERGATIVE

unanalyzed chunks *n*

also **unanalyzed language**

see FORMULAIC LANGUAGE

unaspirated *adj*

see ASPIRATION

uncountable noun *n*

see COUNTABLE NOUN

underachiever *n*

a learner who performs below an expected level as indicated by tests of intelligence, aptitude, ability, especially in school work.

underlying form *n*

see SYSTEMATIC PHONEMICS

underlying structure *n*

another term for DEEP STRUCTURE

underspecification *n*

in PHONOLOGY, the theory that underlying representations are not fully specified and that redundant (predictable) information is not present in underlying representations. For example, in English, voiceless stops are ASPIRATED when syllable initial and unaspirated when they follow /s/ (as in *spy*, *sty*, *sky*). According to underspecification theory, neither of these variants is taken as more basic. Aspiration is simply left unspecified in the underlying representation, with the information added post-lexically.

unergative verb *n*
an intransitive verb whose subject is an active participant, e.g. *walk, run, swim, work, sleep.*
see also UNACCUSATIVE VERB

ungrammatical *adj*
see GRAMMATICAL[1]

unintentional unconscious memory *n*
see IMPLICIT MEMORY

uninterrupted sustained silent writing *n*
a period in a writing or composition class in which a specified, relatively short period of time is set aside for students to practise their writing without interruption, usually in order to develop fluency in writing.

unit *n*
in a course or textbook, a teaching sequence that is normally longer than a single lesson but shorter than a MODULE and consists of a group of lessons planned around a single instructional focus. A unit seeks to provide a structured sequence of activities that lead towards a learning outcome.

unit-credit system *n*
a language-learning system suggested by the European regional organization The Council of Europe in connection with their THRESHOLD LEVEL. In this system the OBJECTIVES for a foreign language programme are divided into portions or units. Each of these units represents a selection of the learner's language needs and is related to all the other units in the programme.
If after successful completion of each unit the learners receive some sort of official recognition, the system is known as a unit-credit system.

universal *n*
see LANGUAGE UNIVERSAL

universal grammar *n*
also **UG**
a theory which claims to account for the grammatical competence of every adult no matter what language he or she speaks.
It claims that every speaker knows a set of **principles** which apply to all languages and also a set of PARAMETERS that can vary from one language to another, but only within certain limits.

The theory was proposed by Noam Chomsky and has been stated more specifically in his model of GOVERNMENT/BINDING THEORY.

According to UG theory, acquiring a language means applying the principles of UG grammar to a particular language, e.g. English, French or German, and learning which value is appropriate for each parameter.

For example, one of the principles of UG is structure dependency. It means that a knowledge of language relies on knowing structural relationships in a sentence rather than looking at it as a sequence of words, e.g.:

not *The/policeman/raised/his/revolver*

but

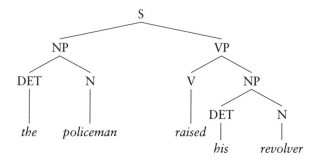

One of the parameters in Universal Grammar which may vary, within certain limits, from one language to another, is the **head parameter**. It concerns the position of HEADS (principal elements) within each phrase.

In English, the head is first in a phrase, for example:

<u>with</u> *the car* (prepositional phrase)

In Japanese, the head is last in the phrase:

Nihon   <u>ni</u>

Japan   in

The role of Universal Grammar (UG) in second language acquisition is still under discussion. Three possibilities are emerging:

1 UG operates in the same way for L2 as it does for L1 (see CORE GRAMMAR). The learner's knowledge of L1 is irrelevant.

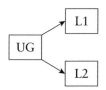

2 The learner's Core Grammar is fixed and UG is no longer available to the L2 learner, particularly not to the adult learner.

3 UG is partly available but it is only one factor in the acquisition of L2. There are other factors and they may interfere with the UG influence.

unmarked *adj*
see MARKEDNESS

unreleased *adj*
see ALLOPHONE

unrounded vowel *n*
see VOWEL

unstructured interview *n*
see STRUCTURED INTERVIEW

unsystematic error *n*
see ERROR OF MEASUREMENT

uptake[1] *n*
the illocutionary force (see SPEECH ACT) a hearer interprets from an utterance. For example in the following exchange:
Child: *I'm tired.*
Mother: *You can stop doing your homework now.*
the uptake or interpretation by the mother is as if the child had said "Can I stop doing my homework now?" But sometimes there may be a difference between the intended uptake (what the speaker wants the hearer to understand) and the actual uptake (what the hearer actually understands).
see also PRAGMATICS

uptake[2] *n*
in interactionist SLA, a learner's response to feedback that acknowledges that feedback in some way, for example, when a learner repeats a teacher's correction or incorporates it into a subsequent utterance.

usage[1] *n*
the ways people actually speak and write. In this sense, usage is closely related to PERFORMANCE, and can be studied by the analysis of specimens of AUTHENTIC language and by experiments of various kinds. The study of usage can reveal, for example, that the passive voice (see VOICE[1]) is more than ordinarily frequent in scientific writing, or that the spellings *all right* and *alright* both occur. It is also possible to study reactions to usage, and on this basis to make recommendations when usage is divided. **Usage guides**

attempt to do this. They may say, for example, that people write both *all right* and *alright*, but that there are still strong feelings against the spelling *alright*, and that therefore it is better to write *all right* as two words.

usage[2] *n*

a distinction made by Widdowson between the function of a linguistic item as an element in a linguistic system (**usage**) and its function as part of a system of communication (**use**). For example the PROGRESSIVE ASPECT may be studied as an item of grammar or usage (i.e. to consider how it compares with other ASPECTs and TENSEs in English and the constructions in which it occurs) and in terms of its use (i.e. how it is used in DISCOURSE for performing such communicative acts as descriptions, plans, commentaries, etc.).

The meaning a linguistic item has as an example of usage is called its **signification**, and the meaning it has as an example of use is called its **value**.

see also SPEECH ACT, UPTAKE

usage-based learning *n*

the idea that language knowledge, language use, and language learning are inseparable.

use *n*

see USAGE[1]

utterance *n*

a unit of analysis in speech which has been defined in various ways but most commonly as a sequence of words within a single person's turn at talk that falls under a single intonation contour. Utterances may sometimes consist of more than one sentence, but more commonly consist of stretches of speech shorter than sentences.

In POSTMODERNISM, following Bakhtin, utterances are not seen as individual creations, but are viewed as dialogic: each utterance is a response to a prior utterance and is inhabited by the voices of others.

see also MOVE, SEQUENCING[1]

utterance meaning *n*

the meaning a speaker conveys by using a particular utterance in a particular context situation. For example:

My watch has stopped again.

could convey, according to the context situation:

a I can't tell you the time.

b This is the reason for my being late.

c I really have to get it repaired.

d What about buying me another one?

see also ILLOCUTIONARY FORCE, IMPLICATION, PRAGMATICS, SENTENCE MEANING

uvula *n*

see PLACE OF ARTICULATION, UVULAR

uvular *adj*

describes a speech sound (a CONSONANT) which is produced by the back of the tongue against the very end of the soft palate (the **uvula**), or by a narrowing in the VOCAL TRACT near the uvula.

The /r/ used by some speakers in the northeast of England, and by some speakers of Scottish English, is a uvular ROLL [R].

see also PLACE OF ARTICULATION, MANNER OF ARTICULATION

V

V', V'' n
>see BAR NOTATION

vague language n
>words or phrases that have a very general or imprecise meaning, and that are common in spoken language. For example, *thing, stuff, anything, sort of.*
>Do you want a coffee *or something*?
>He's *kind of* cute.

valency n
>see DEPENDENCY GRAMMAR

validation n
>(in testing) the process of accumulating evidence to support the inferences drawn from the scores of a test, using a combination of methods (e.g. MTMM METHOD and VERBAL PROTOCOL ANALYSIS)
>see also CONSTRUCT VALIDATION

validity n
>(in testing) the degree to which a test measures what it is supposed to measure, or can be used successfully for the purposes for which it is intended. A number of different statistical procedures can be applied to a test to estimate its validity. Such procedures generally seek to determine what the test measures, and how well it does so.
>see also CONCURRENT VALIDITY, CONSEQUENTIAL VALIDITY, CONSTRUCT VALIDITY, CONTENT VALIDITY, CONVERGENT VALIDITY, CRITERION MEASURE, CRITERION-RELATED VALIDITY, DISCRIMINANT VALIDITY, DIVERGENT VALIDITY, EMPERICAL VALIDITY, FACE VALIDITY, PREDICTIVE VALIDITY

validity coefficient n
>a numerical index of test validity that can be obtained by correlating scores on a predictor variable and scores on a criterion variable. Theoretically its values range between 0.0 and +1.0.

value n
>see USAGE[2]

values clarification n
>an instructional activity which requires students to explore their values and attitudes towards a topic, and in so doing discover the positive and negative

aspects of their own value systems as well as learn about the values of others. For example, questions such as the following might be posed: What would you do if you discovered a family member was shoplifting?

a inform the police
b ask the person to return the stolen property to the store
c talk to other family members about it
d nothing.

Values clarification activities are often used as a communicative activity in COLLABORATIVE LEARNING and communicative language teaching (see COMMUNICATIVE APPROACH).

variable¹ *n*

a linguistic item which has various forms (**variants**). The different forms of the variable may be related to differences in STYLE or to differences in the socio-economic background, education, age, or sex of the speakers (see SOCIOLECT). There are variables in the PHONOLOGY, MORPHOLOGY, SYNTAX, and LEXICON¹ of a language.

Examples in English include:

a the *ng* variable as in *coming, working*. In careful formal speech it often occurs as /ɪŋ/, e.g. /ˈkʌmɪŋ/ *coming*, /ˈwɜːkɪŋ/ *working*, but in informal or regional speech it often occurs as /ˈkʌmn/ *com'n*, /ˈwɜːkn/ *work'n*

b the marker on verb forms for 3rd-person singular present tense (as in *He works here*), which is a variable because in some NON-STANDARD and some new varieties of English a variant without the ending (as in *He work here*) may occur.

Linguistic rules which try to account for these variables in language are referred to as **variable rules**.

variable² *n*

(in statistics and testing) a property whereby the members of a set or group differ from one another. In comparing teaching methods, for example, different variables may be (a) the level of interest each creates (b) the amount of teaching time each method is used for and (c) how difficult each method is to use.

see also DEPENDENT VARIABLE

variable rule *n*

see VARIABLE¹

variance *n*

(in statistics and testing) a statistical measure of the DISPERSION of a SAMPLE. The variance of a set of scores on a test, for example, would be based on how much the scores obtained differ from the MEAN, and is the square of the STANDARD DEVIATION.

variant *n, adj*
see VARIABLE[1]

variation *n*
also **language variation**
differences in pronunciation, grammar, or word choice within a language. Variation in a language may be related to region (see DIALECT, REGIONAL VARIATION), to social class and/or educational background (see SOCIOLECT) or to the degree of formality of a situation in which language is used (see STYLE).
see also FREE VARIATION

variety *n*
see SPEECH VARIETY

velar *adj*
describes a speech sound (a CONSONANT) which is produced by the back of the tongue touching the soft palate (the **velum**) at the back of the mouth. For example, in English the /k/ in /kin/ *kɪn* and the /g/ in /get/ *get* are velars, or, more precisely, velar STOPS.
Because the back of the tongue is called the **dorsum**, these sounds are sometimes called **dorsal**.
see also PLACE OF ARTICULATION, MANNER OF ARTICULATION

velarization *n*
in phonology, a SECONDARY ARTICULATION in which the back of the tongue is raised towards the soft palate. In many forms of English syllable final /l/ as in *hill* is strongly velarized.

velum *n*
also **soft palate**
see PLACE OF ARTICULATION, VELAR

Venn diagram *n*
in teaching, a type of graphic organizer that is used to show how concepts are interrelated as well as how they are different. For example Venn diagrams might be used to compare two short stories and to show how they are alike and how they are different in plot, character, style, etc.

verb *n*

(in English) a word which (a) occurs as part of the PREDICATE of a sentence (b) carries markers of grammatical categories such as TENSE, ASPECT, PERSON, NUMBER[1] and MOOD, and (c) refers to an action or state.

For example:

He opened the door.

Jane loves Tom.

see also AUXILIARY VERB, FINITE VERB, INCHOATIVE VERB, MODAL, PHRASAL VERB, REGULAR VERB, STATIVE VERB, TRANSITIVE VERB, VERB GROUP, VERB PHRASE

verb group *n*

a VERB, together with an associated MODAL VERB or AUXILIARY VERB(s).

For example:

He didn't come.

She can't have been there.

verbal *n*

(in GENERATIVE GRAMMAR) a WORD CLASS including VERBs and ADJECTIVES. The reason for considering verbs and adjectives as belonging to one class is that they have many properties in common. For example, some verbs and adjectives in English can occur in IMPERATIVE SENTENCES: *Throw the ball! Be quiet!* while other verbs and adjectives normally cannot: **Resemble me!* **Be tall!*

verbal association *n*

see VERBAL LEARNING

see also WORD ASSOCIATION

verbal deficit hypothesis *n*

another term for DEFICIT HYPOTHESIS

verbal learning *n*

an alternative term for LANGUAGE LEARNING, associated with BEHAVIOURISM, and no longer current.

verbal repertoire *n*

the speech varieties (LANGUAGES[2], DIALECTs, SOCIOLECTs, STYLES, REGISTERS) which an individual knows.

Sometimes a language may be part of someone's verbal repertoire although he or she has no chance to use it.

For example, a person who knows English and Welsh and moves from Wales to New Zealand may not be able to continue using Welsh. It would *verbal reporting*

still be part of his or her verbal repertoire but it does not belong to the SPEECH REPERTOIRE of the community, in this case, New Zealand.

verbal reporting *n*
(in research) a procedure used for collecting data about the processes a person employs in carrying out a task. Verbal reporting involves the subject giving an oral description of the processes they are using while they are completing a task. Verbal reporting attempts to gather information about the cognitive and linguistic aspects involved in different kinds of tasks. For example, in order to learn how someone writes a summary of a text, a person may be asked to describe the decisions and judgements they make as they complete a summary task. Several different kinds of verbal reporting techniques have been used in studies of second language learning. They include: THINK-ALOUD PROCEDURES. These involve saying aloud every-thing that occurs while performing a task. For example; in studying how a person revises a piece of writing (such as a draft of a term paper), the learner describes everything that occurs to them as they revise the paper.
Introspection. This involves the subject reflecting on the kinds of decisions they make and the kinds of strategies they use while carrying out a task, and reporting them as they occur.
Retrospection. This involves reflecting on how a task or activity was carried out after it occurred. This requires the subject to infer his or her own mental processes or strategies from their memory of a particular mental event under observation.

verb-pattern *n*
the sequence in which a verb occurs in relation to other elements in a sentence.
Verbs occur in different relationships or sequences with other sentence elements, such as Verb + Object (*open the door*), Verb + Object + Adverbial (*put the food on the table*) Verb + that-clause (*believe that it is true*), Verb + infinitive (*need to leave*).
Learning a language involves learning the patterns in which verbs occur.

verb phrase[1] *n*
also **VP**
(in TRANSFORMATIONAL GENERATIVE GRAMMAR) the part of a SENTENCE which contains the main verb and also any OBJECT[2](s), COMPLEMENT(s) and ADVERBIAL(s).
For example, in:
Tom gave a watch to his daughter.
all the sentence except *Tom* is the verb phrase.
see also NOUN PHRASE

verb phrase² *n*

in traditional grammar, the auxiliary and main verbs in a sentence that function together as in *have been studying English* in "I have been studying English for 10 years".

vernacular *n*, *adj*

    a term used of a language or language variety:

        a when it is contrasted with a classical language, such as Latin, e.g.:

        Church services in the Roman Catholic church used to be conducted in Latin, but now they are in the vernacular. (e.g. in English, Italian, Swahili, etc.)

    b when it is contrasted with an internationally used language such as English, e.g.:

        If you want to teach English in that country, it will be useful to know the vernacular.

    c in BILINGUAL and MULTILINGUAL countries, when it is spoken by some or most of the population but when it is not the official or the NATIONAL LANGUAGE of a country, e.g.:

        In addition to schools that teach in the national language, there are also vernacular schools.

see also BLACK ENGLISH, DIGLOSSIA, DOMAIN

vertical construction *n*

in conversational interaction, the co-construction of meaning over a number of turns. Both speakers are said to create propositions that are distributed across a number of different turns in the conversation. This is contrasted with **horizontal constructions,** that is, the expression of several propositions within a single turn. The ability to use horizontal constructions is thought to represent a developmental stage in the development of a learner's grammar.

VESL *n*

see VOCATIONAL ENGLISH

videoconferencing *n*

software that allows Internet correspondents to see each other in multiple windows on screen.

video teleconferencing *n*

the linking of students and teachers in different locations via satellite and television, to provide interaction between native speakers of language and students learning the language as well as cultural exchange.

Vienna-Oxford International Corpus of English *n*

an electronic corpus compiled at the University of Vienna of spoken English as a LINGUA FRANCA, for example, a Hungarian educator discussing education issues with Danish, Finnish and Portuguese colleagues, or a Korean sales representative negotiating a contract with a German client.

virtual learning *n*

also **virtual education**

Forms of learning in which teachers and students are separated in space or time and where course content and teacher-student communication is provided through technology such as the internet or video conferencing.

virtual learning environment *n*

see LEARNING MANAGEMENT SYSTEM

virtual world *n*

an internet based interactive environment in which participants create their own identities and communicate via chat and global messages.

visual learner *n*

a learner who finds it easier to learn things when they see them written down, rather than simply hearing them (an **auditory learner**).

visual organizer *n*

in teaching, visual systems using spatial frameworks such as diagrams, maps, or charts to organize knowledge or information related to a given topic or learning theme. They display in visual form, the key conceptual framework or key elements of the subject matter in a given area. For example, spider maps, network trees, Venn diagrams, or storyboard.

visual perception *n*

see PERCEPTION

visual span *n*

see READING SPAN

visuospatial sketchpad *n*

see MEMORY

vocabulary *n*
a set of LEXEMES, including single words, COMPOUND WORDS and IDIOMS.
see also ACTIVE/PASSIVE LANGUAGE KNOWLEDGE, CONTENT WORD, FRE-
QUENCY[2], TYPE

vocabulary control *n*
(in the preparation of materials for language teaching, reading, etc.) the
practice of using a limited vocabulary based on a WORD LIST or other source.
GRADED READERS are often written using vocabulary control.

vocal cords *n*
the folds of tough, flexible tissue in the LARYNX extending from back to front.
The space between the vocal cords is the **glottis**. When the vocal cords are
pressed together, the air from the lungs is completely sealed off. During speech,
the vocal cords open and close the air passage from the lungs to the mouth.
In the production of vowels and voiced consonants (see VOICE[2]) the vocal
cords vibrate.

glottis
wide open for breathing

vocal cords
loosely together and vibrating
as for a voiced sound

see also PITCH, PLACE OF ARTICULATION

vocal tract *n*
(in phonetics) the air passages which are above the VOCAL CORDS and which
are involved in the production of speech sounds.
The vocal tract can be divided into the **nasal cavity**, which is the air passage
within and behind the nose, and the **oral cavity**, which is the air passage
within the mouth and the throat.
The shape of the vocal tract can be changed, e.g. by changing the position
of the tongue or the lips. Changes in the shape of the vocal tract cause
differences in speech sounds.

vocational English *n*
also **vocational ESL, VESL**
English taught for use in a particular job or occupation.
see also LANGUAGE FOR SPECIAL PURPOSES

vocative *n*

a NOUN PHRASE[1] which is an optional part of a sentence, and which names or indicates one being addressed.
For example:
> Really *dear*, do you think so?
> That's a pretty dress, *Mrs Johnson*.

voice[1] *n*

the ways in which a language expresses the relationship between a verb and the noun phrases which are associated with it. Two sentences can differ in voice and yet have the same basic meaning. However, there may be a change in emphasis and one type of sentence may be more appropriate (see APPROPRIATENESS).
For example, in:
> The wind damaged the fence.

the wind is the subject of the verb *damaged*, which is in the **active voice**, while in:
> The fence was damaged by the wind.

the fence is the subject of the verb *was damaged*, which is in the **passive voice**.
The first sentence would be a suitable answer to the question:
> Did the wind damage anything?

while the second sentence would be a suitable answer to the question:
> How did the fence get damaged?

The so-called "agentless" passive, e.g.:
> The fence has been damaged.

is used when the speaker or writer does not know or wish to state the cause, or when the cause is too obvious to be stated.

voice[2] *n*

speech sounds which are produced with the VOCAL CORDS vibrating are called "voiced". Such vibration can be felt when touching the neck in the region of the LARYNX.
For example, VOWELS are usually voiced, and, in English:
a the /d/ in /den/ *den is* a voiced STOP
b the /z/ in /zɪŋk/ *zinc is* a voiced FRICATIVE.
Speech sounds which are produced without vibration of the vocal cords are called "voiceless".
For example, in English:
a the /t/ in /tɪn/ *tin is* a voiceless stop
b the /s/ in /sæd/ *sad is* a voiceless fricative.

When a speech sound which is normally voiced is pronounced without vibration or only slight vibration, this is called **devoicing**. Devoicing of voiced consonants often occurs in English when they are at the end of a word, e.g. *lid* is pronounced [lɪd̥] where the mark '̥' under the /d/ means devoicing.

see also INTERNATIONAL PHONETIC ALPHABET, MANNER OF ARTICULATION, PLACE OF ARTICULATION

voice³ *n*

in writing, the self-representation or positioning that a writer presents in a text. Voice may be reflected in the writer's way of representing the world, in the writer's relative tentativeness or authority in terms of his or her relationship with the reader, and in the writer's preferred way of turning meaning into text.

see also AUDIENCE

voice onset time *n*

also **VOT**

when pronouncing STOPS, such as /p/, /b/ in *pin*, *bin*, the two articulators (i.e. the lips) are closed and then opened again. With /b/ the VOCAL CORDS are vibrating to produce a voiced stop (see VOICE²). The voice onset time is a relationship between these two factors. It is the point in time at which the voicing starts in relation to the opening of the two articulators. For example, the voice onset time for French, Spanish and Thai /b/ is generally earlier than that for English /b/.

voice-over *n*

commentary spoken by an unseen narrator, for example in films, television programmes, and commercials.

voice quality *n*

the overall impression that a listener obtains of a speaker's voice. It is also sometimes called timbre, and refers to those characteristics of a particular voice that enable the listener to distinguish one voice from another, such as when a person is able to identify a telephone caller. Voice quality is known to be influenced by many factors, including, gender, age, anatomy (e.g. height, weight, muscularity, geometry of the laryngeal structures, respiratory volume), emotional states (e.g. fear, anger, sexual arousal), and state of health (e.g. laryngitis, emphysema, Parkinson's disease, intoxication), as well as by the habitual adjustments made by individual persons of the vocal tract (resulting, for example, in "harsh", "whispery", or "creaky" voice), and also by the characteristic ARTICULATORY SETTING associated with a specific language, dialect, or social variety of a particular language.

voice synthesizer *n*
see SPEECH SYNTHESIS

VO language *n*

a language in which the verb usually precedes the object, in contrast to an OV language, where it usually follows the object. English is a VO language whereas Japanese is an OV language.

vowel *n*

a speech sound produced without significant constriction of the air flowing through the mouth.

Vowel sounds can be divided into sets in a number of different ways:

1 in terms of voicing. In English, all vowels are voiced (except when whispering), but some languages, such as Japanese, have voiceless vowels as well.

2 in terms of which part of the tongue is raised, distinguishing between **front vowels** (as in *eat*), in which the tongue is positioned forward in the mouth, **central vowels** (as in *cup*), and **back vowels** (as in *coop*), in which the tongue is positioned towards the back of the mouth.

3 in terms of how high the tongue is raised, distinguishing between **high vowels** (or close vowels) as in *beat*, **mid vowels** (or half-close vowels) as in *bait*, and **low vowels** (or open vowels) as in *bat*.

4 in terms of whether or not the vowel is **tense** or **lax** (see TENSE/LAX).

5 in terms of whether or not the lips are **rounded** (as in *shoe*) or **unrounded** (as in *she*). In English, rounding is allophonic (back vowels are rounded; front vowels are not), but some languages (such as French) contain front rounded vowels and some others (such as Turkish) contain back unrounded vowels.

6 in terms of length, distinguishing between long vowels such as in *knee* and short vowels as in *knit*. In English, length is allophonic (tense vowels are long; lax vowels are short), but some languages distinguish between vowels that are the same in quality and only different in length.

see also CARDINAL VOWEL, VOWEL LENGTH, VOWEL QUALITY

vowel harmony *n*

a modification (ASSIMILATION) of the pronunciation of vowels in a word so that one agrees or "harmonizes" with another one.

For example, in Turkish the word for the number *1* is *bir* and for the number *10* is *on*. When suffixes are added to them, the vowel of the suffix must be either a front vowel or a back vowel, depending on the vowel that precedes it, e.g.:

bir + de = birde "at one"
both /i/ and /e/ are front vowels
on + da = onda "at ten"
both /o/ and /a/ are back vowels.

vowel length *n*

the duration of a vowel sound.

In phonetic script (see NOTATION), vowel length is often shown by /ː/ after the vowel.

Many languages have pairs of similar vowels that differ in length and usually also in VOWEL QUALITY. For example, in English, /iː/ (as in /siːt/ *seat*) may be longer than /ɪ/ (as in /sɪt/ *sit*), but it is also higher and tenser, and may have the quality of a DIPHTHONG.

vowel quality *n*

features other than length which distinguish one vowel from another. Vowel quality is determined by the shape of the mouth when the particular vowel is produced. The shape of the mouth varies according to the position of the tongue and the degree of lip rounding (see VOWEL).

VP *n*

an abbreviation for VERB PHRASE

W

wait time *n*

(in questioning) the pause after a teacher has asked a question before a student is asked to respond. The effectiveness of questioning is said to be partly dependent on the use of wait time. Teachers tend to use insufficient wait time and to either answer questions themselves or call on another student to answer the question. Increasing wait time both before calling on a student to respond and after a student's initial response (i.e. before the teacher comments on the response) often increases the length of students' responses, increases the number of questions asked by students, and increases student involvement in learning.

washback *n*

also **backwash**

(in testing) the positive or negative impact of a test on classroom teaching or learning. In some countries, for example, national language examinations have a major impact on teaching and teachers often "teach to the tests". In order to bring about changes in teaching, changes may have to be made in the tests. For example, if the education department in a country wanted schools to spend more time teaching listening skills, one way to bring this about would be to introduce a listening comprehension test component into state examinations. The washback would be that more class time would then be spent on teaching listening skills. When teaching is found to exert an important effect on testing, this impact is called a reverse washback.

weak form *n*

see STRONG FORM

weak interface position *n*

see INTERFACE

weak verb *n*

see STRONG VERB

WebCT *n*

see LEARNING MANAGEMENT SYSTEM

webquest *n*

an activity that requires learners to use the Internet in order to complete the task. Webquests can extend over an entire course, several classes, or be integrated into a single lesson.

weighting[1] *n*
 in testing, the relative importance of different skills and language which is assigned in the assessment process.

weighting[2] *n*
 also **weighted scoring**
 (in testing) determining the number of points to be given to correct responses in a test, when not all of the responses in a test receive the same number of points. Such a SCORING procedure is known as **weighted scoring**.

Wernicke's area *n*
 an area in the posterior section of the left (or dominant) cerebral hemisphere of the brain that is associated primarily with the perception and language processing of spoken words.

whole-group instruction *n*
 instruction in which an entire class is taught together rather than in groups.
 see also GROUPING

whole language approach *n*
 also **integrated whole language approach**
 an approach to first language reading and writing instruction that has been extended to middle and secondary school levels and to the teaching of ESL and that views language as a "whole" entity. Whole language emphasizes learning to read and write naturally with a focus on real communication and is opposed to the idea of teaching the separate components of language (e.g. grammar, vocabulary, word recognition, phonics) in isolation. Principles of whole language include:

1 Language is presented as a whole and not as isolated pieces. The approach is thus **holistic** rather than **atomistic**, attempts to teach language in real contexts and situations, and emphasizes the purposes for which language is used.

2 Learning activities move from whole to part, rather than from part to whole. For example, students might read a whole article rather than part of it or an adapted version of it.

3 All four modes of language are used, thus lessons include all four skills of listening, speaking, reading and writing, rather than a single skill.

4 Language is learned through social interaction with others, hence students often work in pairs or groups instead of individually.

whole-word method *n*
 also word **method, sight method**

a method for teaching children to read, commonly used in teaching reading in the MOTHER TONGUE, in which children are taught to recognize whole words rather than letter-names (as in the ALPHABETIC METHOD) or SOUNDS (as in PHONICS). It usually leads to the use of a SENTENCE METHOD, where whole sentences are used.

Whorfian hypothesis *n*
    see LINGUISTIC RELATIVITY

Wh-question *n*
    see QUESTION

wiki *n*
    the Hawaiian word for "quick," used to refer to a website with pages that any user can contribute to and edit, often including text, photos and videos.

within-subjects design *n*
    also **repeated measures design**
    an experimental design where each participant serves in more than one experimental condition.

women's speech *n*
    see GENDER[1]

word *n*
    the smallest of the LINGUISTIC UNITS which can occur on its own in speech or writing.
    It is difficult to apply this criterion consistently. For example, can a FUNCTION WORD like *the* occur on its own? Is a CONTRACTION like *can't* ("can not") one word or two? Nevertheless, there is evidence that NATIVE SPEAKERS of a language tend to agree on what are the words of their language.
    In writing, word boundaries are usually recognized by spaces between the words. In speech, word boundaries may be recognized by slight pauses.
    see also BOUNDARIES, CONTENT WORD, LEXEME

word association *n*
    ways in which words come to be associated with each other and which influence the learning and remembering of words. In a word association test, a person is given a word or list of words and asked to respond with another word or words. Word associations have been studied in SEMANTICS, VERBAL LEARNING theory and PSYCHOLINGUISTICS. The following are common associations to words from American college students:

word	response
accident	*car*
airplane	*fly*
American	*flag*
baby	*child*
depression	*recession*

see also ASSOCIATIVE MEANING

word bank *n*

see BRAINSTORMING

word blindness *n*

another term for DYSLEXIA

word boundary *n*

see BOUNDARIES

word-by-word reading *n*

a type of reading characterized by:
1 in silent reading, a very slow rate of reading with undue concentration on individual words and inability to focus on broader chunks of text, sometimes also accompanied by lip movements
2 in oral reading, a slow and halting style of reading with excessive pausing on individual words and often poor comprehension.

word class *n*

a group of words which are similar in function. Words are grouped into word classes according to how they combine with other words, how they change their form, etc. The most common word classes are the PARTS OF SPEECH: NOUN, VERB, ADJECTIVE, ADVERB, PREPOSITION, PRONOUN, ARTICLE, DEMONSTRATIVE, CONJUNCTION, INTERJECTION, etc.

see also FORM CLASS, OPEN CLASS

word formation *n*

processes used in a language for the creation of new words. There are several ways of doing this, including:
a the addition of an affix in DERIVATION
b the removal of an affix: BACK FORMATION
c the addition of a COMBINING FORM
d the construction of a COMPOUND WORD
e the shortening of an old word, as when *influenza* becomes *flu*

f the repetition of a word or part of a word: REDUPLICATION
g the invention of a completely new word, such as the mathematical term *googal*

In addition, other processes are sometimes regarded as part of word formation. These include:

h the addition of an affix in INFLECTION
i the use of words as different PARTS OF SPEECH, as when the noun *cap* is used as the verb to *cap*.

word frequency *n*
the frequency with which a word is used in a text or corpus.
see also FREQUENCY[2]

word frequency count *n*
also **word frequency** list
see FREQUENCY COUNT, FREQUENCY[1]

word list *n*
a list of the basic and most important words in a language or in a REGISTER of a language, generally intended for use as a basis for language teaching or for the preparation of teaching materials. Word lists are usually based on FREQUENCY COUNTS, often supplemented by other measures of the importance of words (see COVERAGE).

word method *n*
another term for WHOLE-WORD METHOD

word order *n*
the arrangement of words in a sentence. Languages often differ in their word order.
For example, the past participle occurs in German at the end of the main clause rather than after the auxiliary as in English:
Er hat mir das Buch gegeben.
He has to me the book given
"He has given me the book."
In English, the position of a word in a sentence often signals its function. Thus, in the sentence:
Dogs eat meat.
the position of *dogs* shows that it is the SUBJECT, and the position of *meat* shows that it is the OBJECT. In some languages, including English, a change from the usual word order may often be used to emphasize or contrast, e.g.
That cheese I really don't like.

where the object of the sentence is shifted to the beginning.

see also FUNCTIONAL SENTENCE PERSPECTIVE

word recognition *n*
see TOP-DOWN PROCESSING

word stress *n*
see STRESS

workbook *n*
a book that accompanies a textbook and which contains additional supplementary exercises and activities.

working memory *n*
a more contemporary term for SHORT-TERM MEMORY. Working memory is thought of as an active system for both storing and manipulating information during the execution of cognitive tasks such as comprehension and learning. In the influential model of Baddeley, working memory consists of two storage components and a central executive function. The two storage components are the articulatory loop, which holds traces of acoustic or speech-based material for a few seconds (longer if the material is rehearsed, see REHEARSAL) and the visuospatial sketchpad for the storage of verbal and visual information. The central executive is a limited capacity, supervisory attentional system used for such purposes as planning and trouble shooting.
see also MEMORY

workplace language *n*
the specialized type of language used in work settings. Workplace language includes, the communication that takes places among workers and between workers and supervisors, the language used in particular occupations and organizations, and both verbal and nonverbal communication. The study of workplace language is an aspect of Target Situation Analysis in the design of EAP courses.

worksheet *n*
see HANDOUT

World Englishes *n*
a term proposed by Kachru to refer to the fact that there are multiple and varied models of English across cultures and that English is not limited to countries where it has traditionally been regarded as a mother tongue. World Englishes thus includes British, American, Australian as well as

other mother tongue Englishes but also newer varieties of English that have emerged in countries that were once colonies and dependencies of the United Kingdom or the USA. These new Englishes are seen to take their place as legitimate varieties of English fulfilling distinctive functions in pluralistic societies such as Singapore, India, Pakistan, the Philippines, Nigeria and Fiji.

writer-based prose *n*
  also **egocentric writing**
  see READER-BASED PROSE

writing across the curriculum *n*
  see LANGUAGE ACROSS THE CURRICULUM

writing-centre *n*
  a centre on a college or university campus where English-second language students can obtain support in their academic writing assignments. Such support may involve peer tuition and feedback by instructors.

writing conference *n*
  (in teaching composition) an activity in which the teacher and a student meet for a short period of time to discuss student writing and different aspects of the composing process (see COMPOSING PROCESSES).
  Through regular conferences with students during a writing pro-gramme either in a part of the classroom or elsewhere, the teacher tries to promote awareness of writing strategies, to personalize writing for the student, and to make learners more confident about their writing.

writing log *n*
  see LEARNING LOG

writing-modes approach *n*
  a teaching approach in which L2 composition students write paragraphs and essays whose primary purpose is to focus on such organizational modes as definition, comparison-contrast, classification, cause-effect.

writing portfolios *n*
  see PORTFOLIO

writing processes *n*
  the strategies, procedures and decision-making employed by writers as they write. Writing is viewed as the result of complex processes of planning,

drafting, reviewing and revising and some approaches to the teaching of first and second language writing teach students to use these processes.
see PROCESS APPROACH

writing system *n*

a system of written symbols which represent the sounds, syllables, or words of a language. The three main types of writing system are ALPHABETIC, based on sounds; SYLLABIC, based on syllables; and IDEOGRAPHIC, based on words.

WWW *n*

the World Wide Web, an information network of text, pictures, and sound to which people have access when they use the Internet. World Wide Web software provides interactive multimedia on the Internet.

X

X-BAR syntax *n*

see X-BAR THEORY

X-BAR theory *n*

(in UNIVERSAL GRAMMAR) an approach to syntax, X-BAR SYNTAX, which attempts to show the general principles of language rather than deal with the structures of one particular language.

The syntax is based on four main lexical categories (see LEXICAL CATEGORY): verbs, nouns, adjectives and prepositions, which become the HEADS of phrases, e.g. the noun *dog* becomes the head of the noun phrase *The dog with black ears*.

To show the structure within each phrase and within the phrase marker of the whole sentence, constituents are marked N, N', N'' etc. (see BAR NOTATION).

Y

Yes-No question *n*
    see QUESTION

young learners *n*
    in language teaching, children of pre-primary and primary school age.
    Other second language learner age groups are referred to as *adolescent*
    learners, and *adult learners*.

Z

zero anaphora *n*

a type of ANAPHORA in which a form may be omitted because its referent (see REFERENCE) is known or can be guessed. For example in:

Kim went down town and met Kenji.

the verb *met* has a "zero" subject: neither a noun nor a pronoun appears as subject, but the referent "Kim" can be inferred.

zero article *n*

see ARTICLE

zero morpheme *n*

another term for NULL MORPHEME

ZISA *n*

abbreviation for Zweitspracherwerb Italienischer und Spanischer Arbeiter, an investigation of the acquisition of German by Italian and Spanish workers.

zone of proximal development *n*

also **ZPG**

in SOCIO-CULTURAL THEORY, the distance between what a learner can do by himself or herself and what he or she can do with guidance from a teacher or a more capable peer. The theory assumes that learners use the techniques used during collaborative efforts when encountering similar problems in the future.

ZPG *n*

an abbreviation for ZONE OF PROXIMAL DEVELOPMENT

z score *n*

(in statistics) a STANDARD SCORE expressed in STANDARD DEVIATION units with a mean of zero and a standard deviation of one. As the following formula for a z score shows:

$$z = \frac{X - \bar{X}}{SD}$$

where X = a raw score
  $\bar{X}$ = the mean
  SD = the standard deviation,

a raw score is expressed in terms of the number of standard deviations it deviates from the mean. Thus, a student with a z score –1.0 is one standard deviation below the mean.